$1\frac{1}{2}$

Imperial State and Revolution

Imperial State and Revolution

The United States and Cuba, 1952–1986

Morris H. Morley
Macquarie University

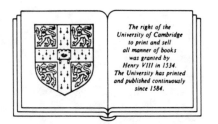

The right of the
University of Cambridge
to print and sell
all manner of books
was granted by
Henry VIII in 1534.
The University has printed
and published continuously
since 1584.

Cambridge University Press

Cambridge
London   New York   New Rochelle
Sydney   Melbourne

Published by the Press Syndicate of the University of Cambridge
The Pitt Building, Trumpington Street, Cambridge CB2 1RP
32 East 57th Street, New York, NY 10022, USA
10 Stamford Road, Oakleigh, Melbourne 3166, Australia

© Cambridge University Press 1987

First published 1987

Printed in the United States of America

Library of Congress Cataloging-in-Publication Data
Morley, Morris H.
    Imperial state and revolution.
    Bibliography: p.
    1. United States – Foreign relations – Cuba.
2. Cuba – Foreign relations – United States.
I. Title.
E183.8.C9M7 1987   327.7307291   87-11638

British Library Cataloging in Publication Data
Morley, Morris H.
    Imperial state and revolution: the
    United States and Cuba, 1959–1985.
    1. Cuba – Foreign relations – United States.
2. United States – Foreign relations – Cuba.
I. Title.
327.7291073   F1776.3.U6

ISBN 0-521-30988-3
ISBN 0-521-35762-4 pb.

To the memory of my father, Woolf Morley
For my mother, Celia Morley

Contents

vii

Acknowledgments

First and foremost, I want to thank my good friend, teacher, and collaborator, Professor James Petras, for encouraging me and supporting this project from its inception as a doctoral dissertation in the Department of Sociology at the State University of New York at Binghamton to its finished form. His commitment to rigorous, critical scholarship has helped me improve the quality of this study at each stage of its preparation. Also, Professor Terence Hopkins offered trenchant criticisms of the manuscript in its early stage and Professors William LeoGrande and Thomas Paterson made helpful suggestions on a later version. I am grateful as well to Frank Smith of Cambridge University Press for his valuable comments and suggestions, both substantive and literary. The clarity of the writing and of the argument owes a great deal to my wife, Adriane Despot. Her analytical and editing skills are equaled only by the great care and attention she gave to the manuscript. Finally, I wish to express my appreciation to Helma Neumann for typing the final draft.

I would like to thank the staffs of the following libraries: the Eisenhower Presidential Library, the Kennedy Presidential Library, the Johnson Presidential Library, the Library of Congress, The National Archives, the Princeton University Library, the Columbia University Library, the Yale University Library, and the University of North Carolina's library at Chapel Hill.

The research and fieldwork for this study were facilitated by grants from the State University of New York at Binghamton and the American Philosophical Society.

1. The U.S. imperial state: theory and historical setting*

This book interprets the events and trends constituting U.S. relations with Cuba between 1952 and 1980 with a view toward elaborating the notion of the imperial state – a state with boundaries for capital accumulation located far beyond its geographic limits. I attempt to explicate the involvement and effectiveness of the United States as an imperial state in prerevolutionary Cuba and how the United States responded to the fundamental challenge to capital accumulation embodied in the Cuban Revolution.[1]

The central focus of this enquiry is the evolution, implementation, and consequences of U.S. imperial-state policy toward Cuba since 1952. The success or failure of this policy are evaluated at different historical moments, distinguishing between particular policies as they were initially conceived and their eventual outcomes: The hopes of U.S. policymakers are measured against their actual achievements. Underlying this emphasis is the question of the capacity – the available resources and instruments – to execute each policy.

This first chapter describes the imperial state, the origins of the U.S. imperial state, the processes by which the United States promotes and sustains conditions for worldwide capital accumulation, and the nature of capitalist-class influence over the making of state policy. A discussion of the policymaking process is important for what it reveals about the complexity of the distinct, but interdependent, agencies that compose the imperial-state framework. The chapter concludes with an overview of the history of U.S.-Cuban relations that further illustrates the notion of the imperial state and enhances our comprehension of U.S. policy toward Cuba after 1952.

*Part of this chapter draws on some ideas and materials first presented in James F. Petras and Morris H. Morley, "The U.S. Imperial State," *Review*, Vol. IV, No. 2, Fall 1980, pp. 171–222. Copyright © 1980 Research Foundation of SUNY. Reprinted by permission of Sage Publications, Inc.

Chapter 2 analyzes U.S. policy toward the Batista dictatorship from 1952 to 1958 and the emergence of a broad-based antiregime movement under the leadership of rural guerrillas. Long-term economic concerns shaped a U.S. attitude of accommodation toward this nonelected military government promoting capitalist development "from above and outside." The appearance of an organized political and military challenge to Batista in the late 1950s, however, forced Washington policymakers to devise new strategies to meet the changed circumstances – strategies geared to influence the outcome of the internal social struggle in a manner favorable to American goals in Cuba. There was uniform hostility in the Eisenhower administration to the idea of a successful antidictatorial movement dominated by radical nationalists. Such an outcome, it was thought, would mean a considerable loss of U.S. political and economic power in Cuba. The White House response to the rapid disintegration of the Batista regime after mid-1958 took the form of numerous initiatives (covert, political, regional) short of direct military intervention to ensure a post-Batista government that either excluded or severely circumscribed the role of the Castro guerrilla forces. American hostility to Castro before 1959 is central to an understanding of the U.S. response to the Cuban Revolution after 1959.

Chapter 3 focuses on the period of socialist transition in Cuba from 1959 to 1961. It presents a detailed examination of U.S. policy toward a combined national and social revolution taking place under the aegis of a government with a solid class base in state power. The Castro leadership's determination to remake the Cuban state and society to serve an alternative, anticapitalist economic project dictated the relatively swift development of a confrontational approach on Washington's part. In the process the imperial state sought to direct a fragmented and vacillating U.S. capitalist class in Cuba to help destabilize the revolutionary regime. American policymakers initially attempted to work through groups in Cuban society hostile to the Castro government, with economic and political sanctions playing only a complementary role. The failure of this "insiders" strategy to overthrow the emerging anticapitalist government in Havana evidenced no less than the disintegration of those elements in Cuban society that identified with Washington's objective and their loss of social support. This state of affairs forced the Eisenhower White House to shift the bulk of its energies toward a dual "outsiders" strategy: political confrontation with Cuba on a regional scale and economic confrontation on a world scale.

Chapters 4 and 5 discuss U.S. policy toward Cuba during the period of socialist development from 1961 to 1968. This policy was rooted in several strategies – political and economic, clandestine and public – designed to terminate the island's relations with the capitalist world. At the regional level, I examine the decision to intervene militarily at the Bay of Pigs, the so-called secret or covert war, and the means by which Cuba was politically isolated within Latin America. Washington managed considerable success in this latter endeavor, partly by threatening economic sanctions or clandestinely manipulating domestic political institutions, but also by working with sympathetic state institutions in countries governed by unstable nationalist regimes. The global economic blockade strategy is the subject of a lengthy analysis, since it spans almost the entire period under discussion. The blockade also provides a unique opportunity for investigating the effectiveness of using economic sanctions for political goals.

The construction of a worldwide blockade around the Cuban state and society reached its apogee during the Johnson administration (1964–1968), which gave priority to eliminating Cuba's economic links with its major trading partners: Canada, Japan, France, Spain, and England. The exposition and analysis of the capitalist-bloc embargo – the central concern of Chapter 5 – raise important questions on the nature of the relationship between the United States and its senior capitalist allies. The rapid growth of the war-devastated economies of Western Europe and Japan during the 1950s and 1960s has been interpreted by some writers as tantamount to a decline in the dominant position of the United States. The presumed willingness of these economically revitalized countries to take positions at variance with U.S. interests provided the basis for subsequent assertions regarding the 1960s as a period of heightened rivalry and competition among capitalist countries. By focusing on one issue – the American economic blockade of Cuba and the degree of cooperation with U.S. objectives – this book shows that there was no deliberate attempt by any capitalist country to challenge Washington, even though these governments maintained moderate trade with Havana. Indeed, the divergencies coexisted with a more powerful accommodation impulse. On the whole, allied governments were more interested in cooperating with the United States than in trading with Cuba. Limiting America's global power was of minimal interest.

Chapter 6 describes and analyzes U.S. policy toward Cuba during the Nixon, Ford, and Carter presidencies. A number of distinct issues are highlighted: the disintegration of the global economic blockade and the effective collapse of Cuba's regional political isolation; the seminal importance of Cuba's foreign policy in shaping Washington's continuing hostility toward the revolutionary regime; the nature and significance of the legislative branch response to executive policymaking; and the multiplicity of attitudes within the U.S. corporate and business community regarding the profitable normalization of economic ties with Havana. Although the economic blockade began to unravel after 1968, the Nixon and Ford administrations continued to police it and link any change in the bilateral relationship to major Cuban concessions, especially in the area of foreign policy and external alignments. The Carter White House decision to jettison the Cold War policies and rhetoric of its predecessors and relax tensions with Cuba was abruptly terminated at the end of its first year in office because of the Castro government's involvement in revolutions in the Horn and parts of southern Africa. Cuban support for nationalist and socialist revolutions in the Third World ran counter to the primary expressed goal of all postwar administrations: to open, and keep open, as much of the world economy as possible in the interests of foreign capital accumulation and expansion.

This study addresses itself to three major empirical questions that revolve around the making and implementation of U.S. foreign policy. First, how adequate is the highly influential bureaucratic politics model of policymaking to an understanding of what it purports to explain? Second, what constraints, if any, does the appearance of an increasingly interdependent global economy set on the policies and objectives of a hegemonic state functioning within that economy? Third, is the state (or its executive branch) the articulator and director, rather than the servant and mediator (or opponent) of, the interests of the capitalist class?

The structure and process of U.S. policymaking are examined with a recognition of two dimensions often counterposed: the continuities and common purposes frequently evident in policymaking, and the bureaucratic conflicts and disagreements that are so much a part of the foreign-policy apparatus. This examination illuminates certain fundamental weaknesses in the bureaucratic politics model of policymaking when applied to Washington's response to the Cuban Revolution. This study reveals that during the 1960s, for instance, the interagency conflicts were entirely tactical in nature and occurred within a strategic consensus aimed at overthrowing the Castro regime.

In the process of highlighting the postwar global operations of the U.S. state in the interests of capital accumulation, I also raise the question of the obstacles to integrating Third World countries into an American-dominated world economy. These include the power of social revolutionary movements in the Third World, the existence of the Soviet Union as a potential countervailing political, economic, and military presence in these regions of the world, and the evolution of a highly differentiated capitalist world. In analyzing the interaction between the imperial state and the international system, this study pays considerable attention to the capacity of the United States to shape and influence the behavior of its allies. Considering specific policy issues such as economic boycotts, this book also examines the relationships among a leader nation and follower countries within a confrontational context where interests both diverge and converge.

A major premise is that the mechanisms of capitalist development are tightly interwoven with the activities of the state. The U.S. government, conceived of as the imperial state, is viewed as the engine of a worldwide system of capital accumulation. Its actions are deliberate and pragmatic; they reflect and rationalize the interests of the capitalist class as a whole. Hence, while this work seeks to analyze individual and institutional commitments to and roles within the larger organization of the state, it also attempts to anchor these varying commitments within the larger orientation of the state. Although specific individuals and agencies project operational idiosyncrasies – styles of procedures, organizational peculiarities, kinds of emphasis – these disparities do not constitute assorted intentions about the structure of the state or sufficient reason for interpreting operational traits of multiple agencies to be independent of the general development of overseas markets and global capitalist activity.

Instead of viewing institutions and ideas as epiphenomena or simple reflections of the process of capital accumulation, this study addresses the way in which they establish the boundaries for political action that are essential to the greater expansion of capital. Contending that there is a high degree of consensus between state and class over general policy positions, punctuated only by specific, usually limited disagreements, this book also addresses itself to the interrelated questions of how the state acts on and changes the behavior of capitalists and how capitalists themselves react to state initiatives. To define U.S. foreign policy principally in terms of economic pursuits or as the multinationals' handmaiden is to absent consideration of the state's mobilizing resources, activating policy instruments, and taking all kinds of actions to implant and sustain the conditions for worldwide capital accumulation. This study accents the primal role politics plays in instrumentalizing the capitalist class and promoting historic capitalist goals – how the state shapes agendas, timetables, tactics, and strategies, choosing among an array of policy instruments to nurture and safeguard the collective interests of the overseas capitalist class. The concept of the imperial state redefines the traditional role and nature of the state, assigning equal importance to both the political and the economic dimension of any comprehensive understanding of the theory and practice of imperialism.

Imperial state: origins and development

There is a recurring problem with contemporary writings on the state that has not been adequately critiqued: The "state" has been conceived as a national unit, and the "national state" has been the point of departure for most discussions of classes and class struggle.[2] There has been limited, if any, consideration given to external factors that shape the character of the state and influence the internal makeup of classes as well as their action orientation. This notion of the national state has also been reproduced in analyses of the colonial state – the capitalist state transplanted to the colonial setting, but retaining its linkages to the metropolis.[3] Definitions of the state have extended its function from that of simple enforcer to that of an ideological and legitimating body and to the state as the agent of economic promotion as well as coordinator of particular interests. (This last notion sometimes involves a return to traditional liberal ideas of the state as broker.)[4] Yet, what has been striking, especially since the latter half of the nineteenth century, is not the elaboration of internal functions or its role as primarily a regulator of the domestic sphere, but the extended jurisdiction of the state as an imperial state with powers reaching far beyond its territorial boundaries.

The notion of imperial states creating and sustaining the conditions for worldwide capital accumulation was implied in the

writings of a number of early twentieth-century theorists of imperialism. The non-Marxist J. A. Hobson's study of the outward
migration of capital from nineteenth-century European nation-
states is essentially a discussion of the organization of a capitalist
world economy taking shape through the aegis of competing
imperial powers acting to assure satisfactory conditions for overseas capital investment in the so-called peripheral areas.[5] With the
capitalist world economy as a departure point, the Marxist V. I.
Lenin developed an interpretation of imperialism derived from a
theory of capitalist development during its monopoly phase
(1871–1914) when the contradiction between industrial growth
and increasingly socialized production on the one hand and the
uninterrupted process of private capital accumulation on the
other resulted in the movement of large amounts of capital from
"advanced" nation-states into "a number of backward countries."[6] The global struggle between Europe's imperial powers
during 1914 and 1918 for the division of the capitalist world
economy was precisely an outgrowth of competition between late
developing (Germany) and early maturing (England, France) capitalist countries with different dynamics in their internal and international economic drives. Although economic power and corporate decisions remained prerequisites for capital movements
overseas, these strictly "economic" imperatives were, in the era
of monopoly capitalism, accompanied in importance by the political, financial, and military activities of the central imperial states.

The internationalization of economic life and the parallel emergence of aggressive competition between nation-states as imperial
states is even more clearly articulated in the writings of the Soviet
political economist Nikolai Bukharin: "The state apparatus has
always served as a tool in the hands of the ruling classes of its
country, and it has always acted as their 'defender and protector'
in the world market."[7] In his discussion of the worldwide movement of investment capital, Bukharin also attributed considerable
importance to the activities of centrally organized banking institutions or finance capitalists located in the most powerful capitalist countries, but with "their tentacles over the entire globe."[8]

The imperial state, by its global reach, in effect sets up new
rules of statehood within the interstate system. In due course,
these rules influence the behavior of all other states. As the scope
of the imperial state expands, the sovereignty of the imperialized
states is diminished.

To study such an imperial state, as opposed to a capitalist one, we must develop some new conceptions. The political, social, and economic contexts in which the capitalist state and the imperial state function are quite different. Within the geographically bounded nation-state, the capitalist state is the only source of sovereign authority. In contrast, the imperial state (an outgrowth of the capitalist state) exercises its authority in a crowded field of aspiring sovereigns – competing imperial states, regional powers, and local authorities. The primary authority is not clearly delineated either in fact or law.

Discussing the United States today, we are not dealing with the "capitalist state" or the "state in capitalist society," but with the imperial state. It is time to discard the notion that imperialism is merely an economic phenomenon that can be analyzed by looking at corporate behavior and the flow of capital. Literature on the multinationals, rich in detail as it is, tends to forget the institution that created the universe in which they function.[9] No discussion of capital accumulation on a world scale can be meaningful unless we understand the central role of the imperial state in creating the conditions for it. The imperial state does not function on the basis of its own inner logic, but responds to the interests and demands of capitalists seeking to move capital abroad and to pursue accumulation. The U.S. state, as an imperial state shaped and controlled by outward looking capital, assumes a multiplicity of tasks to facilitate the goals of its outwardly oriented capital class.[10] Initially, it moves to create and develop the conditions (state "building," infrastructural economic assistance) for long-term, large-scale multinational capital flows into targeted countries. Over time, it seeks to maintain and, if necessary, recreate (by destabilizing political regimes, by electoral intervention) the optimal environment for capital accumulation and expansion in particular Third World societies.

Since the 1890s, no movements of American (proto) multinational capital have taken place without the involvement of the U.S. imperial state, whether we are talking about the entree, the expansion, or the survival of such capital.[11] Conversely, by its dominant position in the U.S. social formation, imperial capital defines the domestic and external structures and functions of the state, as well as its policy. The roots of the state are anchored in the United States; its branches span the globe. Its origin was the national unit; its functions and operations have grown by processes into a multiplicity of societies and transnational organizations.

The postwar imperial-state framework   In the setting of world-wide accumulation, the emergence of the United States as a competitive, and subsequently the dominant, imperial power is relatively recent. Despite its subordinate and isolated position in the European-centered (specifically, British-centered) capitalist world economy during the nineteenth century, the United States emerged as a regional power by 1850, competitive with Spain, England, and France in Central America and the Caribbean and, to a lesser extent, in South America. By the late nineteenth century, in response to changes in the positions of key European imperial states, the United States not only began to assume the role of dominant hemispheric imperial power, but was also being transformed into a globally competitive imperial power.[12]

During the first three decades of the twentieth century, the U.S. imperial state sought to expand, bolster, and consolidate its position as a world economic power through the maintenance of an "open door" for trade and investment in Latin America, Europe, the Far East, Africa, and the Middle East. This goal was facilitated by congressional passage of the Federal Reserve Act in December 1913, which provided for the establishment of a worldwide system of American private banks to operate in the interests of American capital and commerce looking to expand abroad. By the 1920s, the newly formed U.S. foreign banking network was competitive with, if not dominant among, the world's major banking systems. This new financial reach, principally centered in Latin America, provided an immediate and positive stimulus to U.S. foreign trade, which increased in value from $4.3 billion in 1913 to $13.5 billion in 1920.[13]

The global military conflict from 1939 to 1945 produced irrevocable changes in world capitalism, notably the decline of some of the most formidable prewar imperial states (e.g., British, French, Dutch) and the emergence of the United States as the dominant imperial state in the capitalist world. The U.S. imperial-state structure exhibited a double character during this period: as it sought to defeat European fascism militarily, it also set about establishing the groundwork that would sustain the dynamic growth in industrial capacity and export expansion that the American economy had experienced during these years of intercapitalist hostilities.[14] Senior foreign-policy officials in the Departments of State, Commerce, and the Treasury, as well as in the White House, were convinced that there was a profound connection between long-term U.S. prosperity and the transformation and reorganization of the postwar world economy. In concert with an outward-oriented capitalist class, they reasoned that the continuation of wartime growth dictated a world economy in which capital and goods could move around with maximum freedom and minimum restraint.[15] In testimony before a special congressional Committee on Postwar Economic Policy and Planning in 1944, Dean Acheson emphasized the importance of the link between U.S. economic prosperity and expanding foreign markets: "The most important thing is markets. We have got to see that what the country produces is used and is sold under financial arrangements which make its production possible."[16]

The foundations for U.S. dominance of the postwar international economy were laid at Bretton Woods in July 1944, where agreement was reached to establish two new economic organizations: an International Monetary Fund to eliminate foreign exchange problems, particularly currency restrictions that complicated American export expansion, and an International Bank for Reconstruction and Development to make long-term loans to supplement and promote private foreign investment worldwide.[17] Bretton Woods participants also agreed to create a new capitalist-bloc monetary system by tying all other national currencies to the American dollar. Thereafter, the U.S. imperial state began to supply dollars as a means of exchange to other capitalist countries for the purchase of American manufactured goods.

In the postwar context of uncontested American global and regional hegemony within the capitalist world economy, U.S. corporations also stood poised to expand on an unprecedented scale. Former State Department international economic advisor Herbert Feis wrote of the large accumulations of capital potentially available for overseas expansion: "American business enterprise will be exploring the world for new investment opportunity in the operation of public utilities, the exploitation of natural resources, the establishment of factories, and the conduct of trade."[18] Both American investment and commercial entrepreneurs confronted powerful obstacles to expansion in the form of war-devastated economies of Western Europe and the persistence of discriminatory trade barriers that ran counter to the notion of an open-world trading system envisioned by U.S. imperial-state officials. The ultimate responsibility of assuming the costs of rebuilding the capitalist economies to reestablish profitable investment centers, for dissolving such closed trading systems as the British sterling bloc, and for promoting the emergence of collaborator regimes in the Third World devolved upon the U.S. imperial state (in association with newly created American-dominated international political, banking, and monetary organizations).[19] To a considerable degree, the imperial state became the instrument or enabling condition for promoting "a world environment in which the American system [could] survive and flourish."[20] It mobilized resources, took initiatives, and provided organizational expertise that contributed mightily to pushing American capital and commerce into the world economy. The key agent of this process of capital expansion and the accumulation and centralization of larger and larger industrial capitals was the multinational corporation. Yet, it was the imperial state that created the global political, economic, and military environment to sustain multinational investment and trade on a highly diversified scale.

Between 1945 and 1948, there existed a fundamental consensus among the highest American civilian and defense officials "that long-term American prosperity required open markets, unhindered access to raw materials, and the rehabilitation of much – if not all – of Eurasia [Europe and Asia] along liberal capitalist lines."[21] Pentagon planners agreed with cabinet secretaries on the equal importance of projecting U.S. global military power and the economic rehabilitation of the capitalist world in containing Soviet goals and aspirations. There was no dispute within the imperial state, whether we are talking about the Secretary of State or the Joint Chiefs of Staff, on the need for an immediate, massive foreign economic assistance program to deter the Soviets and local Communist parties from taking advantage of "economic dislocation, social unrest, and political instability" in wartorn Europe and Asia and, simultaneously, to provide the "building blocks" for long-term American economic hegemony in these areas of the world.[22] This new set of postwar U.S. policymakers was determined to translate America's unmatched military and economic strength within the capitalist world into a reconstructed global political-economic order presided over indefinitely by Washington.

But the policymakers determined that the available institutional structures were inadequate for the task of maximizing U.S. opportunities for worldwide economic expansion. As a result, the expansion of agencies and personnel as part of a general overhaul of the

U.S. imperial-state structure became a priority: New agencies and institutions were created and linked to the old, while the internal structures and functions of several existing agencies were redefined or expanded. In the area of foreign economic policy, the State Department underwent major organizational changes to accommodate the growing importance of diplomacy to trade, finance, agriculture, and transportation. An array of new divisions was established to deal with commercial policy, petroleum, international labor affairs, international finance and investment, overseas economic development, commodities, and strategic industrial raw materials. Other Departments, including Treasury, Agriculture, Interior, Commerce, and Labor, also assumed new responsibilities.[23] The Treasury Department's jurisdiction, for instance, was expanded to include responsibility for U.S. policy in the newly created multinational financial institutions such as the International Bank for Reconstruction and Development (World Bank) and the International Monetary Fund (IMF). The urgently needed interagency coordination dictated by these changes within the foreign policy bureaucracy took place in two ways: greater consultation between State Department officials and the staffs of other agencies, and the formation of interdepartmental committees, such as the National Advisory Council on International Monetary and Financial Problems (NAC), which was responsible for coordinating imperial-state actions in the international banking organizations.[24]

As part of the effort to institute a more rational policymaking process, a number of new agencies were established. In July 1947, the U.S. Congress passed the National Security Act, creating three executive-branch departments: a National Security Council (NSC) to advise the President about "the integration of domestic, foreign, and military policies relating to the national security";[25] a Department of Defense and Joint Chiefs of Staff committee to streamline the Pentagon's internal decisionmaking and promote more effective relations with other agencies; and a Central Intelligence Agency (CIA) to coordinate government intelligence activities, evaluate and disseminate intelligence data, and perform "other functions and duties" designated by the NSC.[26]

Before 1947, the CIA's covert activities were confined largely to psychological warfare. With the onset of the first phase of the Cold War, there was growing support among senior executive-branch officials for expanding CIA operations to include "a covert political action capability" as well – an initiative motivated by the appearance of large-scale working-class mobilizations in Western European countries under Communist and Socialist leadership. In June 1948, the NSC adopted a directive that authorized "a dramatic increase in the range of covert operations directed against the Soviet Union including political warfare, economic warfare, and paramilitary activities."[27]

The global projection of American military power, according to imperial-state policymakers, was necessary to provide a security framework for the movement of American investments and commodities into the far-flung corners of the capitalist world. The postwar concept of national security included not only "a strategic sphere of influence within the Western Hemisphere [and] domination of the Atlantic and Pacific oceans," but also an extensive network of military, naval, and airforce bases that would, among other objectives, guarantee "access to the resources and markets of most of Eurasia."[28] The formation of the North Atlantic Treaty Organization (NATO) at the end of the 1940s was regarded by U.S. officials as a way of enhancing the military capabilities of allied European regimes supportive of an open world economy.[29] This decision to expand its military presence abroad also meshed with the U.S. government's policy of active opposition to indigenous nationalist and anticapitalist movements or regimes, especially those that raised the specter of closed economic spheres. The Truman Doctrine enunciated in March 1947 to rationalize large-scale military (as well as political and economic) assistance to Greece and Turkey subsequently provided the legislative authority for military and nonmilitary forms of assistance to anticommunist and procapitalist regimes – especially in areas of the Third World (e.g., in Korea).

The shift from the predominance of imperial-state investments in the postwar decade to the dominance of private investment is evident in the changing ratio of U.S. state overseas loans and grants to new U.S. direct private investment. The ratio stood at 5.7 to 1 between 1945 and 1954, but declined to 1.44 to 1 between 1955 and 1964, and to 0.63 to 1 between 1965 and 1974.[30] State investments prior to 1954 took the forms of technical aid, long-term loans, and massive military outlays directed principally toward rebuilding the economies of Western Europe, promoting foreign capital and commercial expansion, extinguishing embryonic experiments in national capitalist development, and forestalling the possibilities of social revolution. In the Third World, economic infrastructure development loans and credits and expanded military relations were geared toward creating durable, pro-U.S. state structures and reconstructing economies to a level that would facilitate long-term, large-scale foreign capital inflows in manufacturing as well as extractive sectors. The networks fashioned by these state and public investments created the groundwork for accelerating private-capital investment.[31] From the mid-1950s to the mid-1970s, enormous flows of private investment circulated the globe, largely through the vehicle of the multinational corporation. This wave of investment, directed at all areas of society, was especially concentrated in industrial undertakings in Western Europe and the Third World. Imperial-state investments declined, relatively, and centered on financing power, communications, and transportation systems, as well as on the new facilities of advancing industrial capital.

This state-private investment sequence generated a substantial body of literature that failed to comprehend adequately the significance of, or the relationship between, the two phases of the process. Some writers who adopted a short-term view of the initial dominance of public expenditures and noneconomic activities over private investment, for example, used this phenomenon to argue against the theory of imperialism. By emphasizing military organization and spending, they have given the major coercive agency of the imperial state a false sense of autonomy, and its growth was ascribed either to strategic thinking ("national security") or to the "imperatives of bureaucratic organization."[32] The long-term global impact of voluminous military and nonmilitary expenditures and activities, however, was soon surpassed by the flow and accumulation of private capital. From this latter phenomenon, a new group of writers – conservative, liberal, and Marxists alike – asserted the autonomy of multinational capital. They discussed the global nature of the multinational corporations in isolation from the imperial state, each perceived as having separate interests, but they forgot the state's role in providing and sustaining the universe within which multinational capital operates.[33]

Imperial state: complexity and specialization

The U.S. imperial state can be defined as those governmental bodies charged with promoting and protecting the expansion of capital across state boundaries by the multinational corporate community. Some agencies, such as the Departments of Commerce and the Treasury, are more directly linked to the private corporate world than others, but the actions of all are directed toward worldwide U.S. capital accumulation and reproduction.

The imperial state can also be imagined as a web of interrelated, yet functionally specific agencies coordinated at the top levels of the executive branch. The decisionmaking and organizing body at the apex of the process since the early 1950s usually has been the National Security Council (NSC), which emerged as the principal arena for "debating alternative strategic courses of action" within agreed policy contours originating in the White House.[34] Below the NSC are several line agencies responsible for making policies operational, devising strategies, and selecting instruments to realize basic imperial-state objectives. This distinction between agencies that articulate and those that implement policy makes it possible to observe the continuities and common purposes in policymaking on the one hand, and, on the other, the differing institutional interests and bureaucratic conflicts that come up within the larger consensus.

The transformation of the NSC from an essentially policy-coordinating body under Truman to the directing agency in the formulation of global policy under Eisenhower was part of a larger reorganization of the foreign policymaking apparatus initiated by the new Republican president to meet the need for a more coherent, integrated process.[35] National Security Council official Dillon Anderson described the Council of the 1950s as the group in which "the full expression of views, divergent in many instances" produced the basis for presidential decisionmaking.[36] Eisenhower asked the NSC to consider current and long-term policy; occasionally, he held special NSC meetings to discuss particularly pressing issues. He also established NSC support committees: a Planning Board to evaluate departments' policy recommendations, mediate interagency differences, and prepare policy papers for consideration by the Council; and an Operations Coordinating Board that "translated board policies into more specific operational guidelines and sought to assure, primarily through a system of reports from action agencies, that policies were being implemented and coordinated."[37]

The NSC retained its preeminence in the transition from Eisenhower to Kennedy despite changes in its responsibilities, which were less a matter of substance than of symbolism, style, and organizational innovation. A senior White House official at the time articulated the differences: "It was very much more structured, a military-type staff system under [Robert] Cutler and Eisenhower.

Under Kennedy, there was a much more intimate, informal, physically proximate relationship between [McGeorge] Bundy and the President."[38] Kennedy erased the distinction between planning and operations, delegated responsibility for both areas to the NSC staff, met less regularly with the NSC in formal sessions and viewed the Council as "one [policy] instrument among many."[39] To deal with conflicts requiring swift and immediate action (e.g., the October 1962 Cuban Missile Crisis), he substituted NSC Executive Committees for Eisenhower's NSC special meetings.

According to McGeorge Bundy, the NSC operated as a policy-advisory body in areas of crisis decisionmaking and the evolution of long-term policy planning during his tenure as Special Assistant for National Security Affairs under both Kennedy and Johnson.[40] However, Johnson preferred to deal with important foreign-policy questions "that required prompt presidential action" in the less structured setting of informal weekly "Tuesday Lunch" meetings.[41] These gatherings, which performed as functional equivalents of the NSC, were attended by "a handful of top advisers, confidants [and] close friends" of the President.[42] Among the regular participants were the Secretaries of State and Defense and the Special Assistant for National Security Affiars, while the involvement of other officials depended on the subjects under discussion.[43]

The Nixon White House instituted major organizational changes in the imperial state to correct what it perceived as serious deficiencies in the policymaking process. The NSC, under the leadership of Henry A. Kissinger, reemerged as the primary instrument for dealing with critical foreign-policy issues and integrating them into the larger context of long-term U.S. regional and global interests.[44] The Council's membership almost tripled from eighteen during the Johnson presidency to a high of fifty-two in early 1971.[45] The broad purpose ascribed to the NSC was one of "anticipat[ing] crises and organiz[ing] options in advance of crises."[46] Its policy coordinating and policymaking responsibilities were further enhanced by a series of executive-department changes between 1969 and 1971 that assigned the Council a central role in shaping military and intelligence policies as they impinged on global issues. Kissinger was appointed chairman of the new Defense Programs Review Committee "whose purpose [was] to keep the annual defense budget in line with foreign policy objectives," and the NSC was designated by President Nixon to head a special intelligence committee established to evaluate global intelligence reports.[47] These various changes had the effect of diminishing the authority or influence of State, Defense, and the CIA in the foreign-policy area. With the appointment of Kissinger as Secretary of State in mid-1973, however, the Council's policymaking role was downgraded. Kissinger remained in this post until the end of the Ford presidency in January 1977, retaining the position as the President's senior foreign policymaker.

The Carter administration restored the NSC to a role at the center of the imperial-state structure, making it responsible for shaping and coordinating U.S. global strategic and security policies. In an effort to increase the authority of Cabinet secretaries, Carter streamlined the NSC structure, concentrating its operations in two committees: the Policy Review Committee (PRC) chaired by Secretary of State Cyrus Vance and the Special Coordination Committee (SCC) headed by NSC Advisor Zbnigniew Brzezinski. Apart from its policy-coordination functions, the SCC also had primary responsibility for "crisis management" and played a leading role in the areas of arms control and intelligence. In practice, however, the NSC Advisor and his staff provided the dominant influence on White House decisionmaking. Presidential action ensured that the NSC closely coordinated all policymaking proposals originating in the State Department and Defense Department. Brzezinski offers a concentrated description and assessment of the Council's role:

All major cables with policy implications had to be cleared with relevant NSC staff before they could be sent out. Since much of policy is made by cables, control in this area gave the NSC staff considerable leverage over both the making and implementation of policy. In addition, before any major foreign discussions, talking points used by the Secretaries of State and Defense were sent over to the NSC for Presidential clearance. This meant, in practice, that I would review them, recommend changes, and, if necessary, carry the argument to the President.[48]

Whether the PRC or the SCC reached a policy consensus on a particular issue, Brzezinski was also responsible for preparing and transmitting the results of committee deliberations to the President. These written reports were not resubmitted to the committees for their agreement before going to the White House. In his memoirs, Secretary of State Vance concedes that he "made a serious mistake in not going to the mat on insisting that the draft memoranda be sent to the principals before they went to the president."[49]

The State Department and the Secretary of State have played roles of shifting importance within the postwar imperial state. During Eisenhower's tenure in office, John Foster Dulles was the dominant foreign-policy voice in the Eisenhower administration. By contrast, William Rogers played a less than central policy-shaping role as Secretary under the Nixon White House in the late 1960s and early 1970s. Basically, the State Department has performed as the executive-branch line agency responsible primarily for operationalizing general policy positions.[50] In its concern to balance several related political, economic, and strategic issues affecting U.S. global and regional goals – leading Treasury and other executive-branch officials to speak slightly disparagingly of the State Department's "perpetual flexibility" – State has tended to embrace a longer term perspective than the other line agencies.

Under Kennedy, the State Department usually headed the Interagency Task Forces, established as devices for "the day-to-day handling of complex and critical operations."[51] The most notable of these was the Special Group on Counter-insurgency, which emerged in response to the Cuban Revolution. It also chaired a number *ad hoc* interagency committees (e.g., the Cuban Coordinating Committee and a Latin American Policy Committee) formed by the White House to help coordinate and rationalize policymaking in areas of permanent concern to the imperial state. The State Department's leadership of these ad hoc coordinating mechanisms carried over into the Johnson presidency, and the agency's operational responsibilities were further expanded as a result of a major reorganization of the foreign-policy apparatus in March 1966. The Secretary was put in charge of all overseas operations affecting two or more agencies. In effect, the Department was allocated "the decisive voice in all independent efforts abroad except military operations under area military commands."[52] Throughout the Nixon-Ford-Carter era, the State Department maintained its position as the dominant line agency and, during the period of Kissinger's stewardship, played an unusually significant role within the policymaking process.

Beyond the State Department, the other operational or line agencies within the U.S. imperial state can be divided into three categories: economic, coercive, and ideological. The economic agencies in turn divide into those serving particular forms of capital (for example, the Department of Agriculture) and those performing specific tasks that cut across different forms of capital (the Departments of Commerce and the Treasury) to promote foreign

investment and trade in general. While an agency such as Treasury develops close relations with particular forms of overseas
capital (banking and investment) and works within the imperial
state to maximize their interests, its initiatives in the areas of foreign economic, financial and monetary policy essentially seek to
benefit the whole outwardly oriented capitalist class. A similar
commitment is evidenced in the Department of Commerce, which
is primarily concerned with promoting U.S. exports amid periods
of growing intercapitalist competition. By contrast, a specific task-
oriented agency such as the Department of Agriculture develops
ties inside the United States to a particular capitalist fraction and
confines itself to promoting the fraction's interests abroad (agro-
exports) and at home (quotas on foreign agricultural imports).

The Treasury Department became the most important economic agency as a result of its role in laying the foundations of the
postwar capitalist international economic order: "The organization of all work for postwar economic planning for the world as a
whole took place in this [Treasury] building. . . . Treasury was
responsible for setting up the IMF and the World Bank."[53] The
Department's dominant position in the foreign economic policy
area subsequently was enhanced not only by the growing importance of multinational corporation earnings to the domestic economy, but also because of the dollar's declining strength and a
more or less permanent postwar balance-of-payments crisis.[54]

The Treasury Secretary's influence over international economic
policy has been exercised in part through his appointment of, and
influence over, the American representatives in the multilateral
development banks (MDBs). The 1965–1966 executive-branch
reorganization increased the Secretary's already direct power in
a significant way: while he retained power over the Treasury-
chaired and dominated National Advisory Council for International Monetary and Financial Policies (NAC) as the coordinator
of U.S. participation in the MDBs, the responsibility for instructing the American Executive Directors in these international financial institutions (who are treasury officials) about how to vote on
or respond to loan applications was transferred from the NAC to
the Secretary himself.[55] Despite these and other powers that
accrue to the Secretary in the field of foreign economic policy, it
should be pointed out that these levers have not been applied uniformly by successive officeholders. Some have sought to maximize
their authority (e.g., John B. Connally), while others (e.g., C.
Douglas Dillon) have adopted a circumspect, less aggressive pos-

ture. Such variations may be partly attributable to personality traits and the nature of the relationship between the Secretary and the President.

Among other agencies of the imperial state that operationalize policy, the second type of functional category is the coercive agency. These include the military (Department of Defense) and the intelligence institutions (Central Intelligence Agency, Defense Intelligence Agency, National Security Agency, National Reconnaissance Office), and specialized groups in each branch of the armed forces. The military has two responsiblities: to cultivate close relations with the military of target areas, and to intervene directly to forestall social revolution through invasions and occupations when their collaborator counterparts in target areas are incapable of or unwilling to act in concert with U.S. interests.[56] The intelligence agencies commonly are heavily involved in recruiting liaisons (information contacts within regimes and leaders of key state and societal institutions) and in organizing client groups in target countries to manipulate social forces for overt and covert actions.[57] The activities of all such intelligence groups usually are coordinated through agency heads, and their activities typically are complementary, though jurisdictional disputes do emerge.

Policymakers in the United States traditionally have viewed the coercive institutions of Third World states as the last-resort guarantor of capital accumulation and the social-political conditions that sustain the capitalist mode. Consequently, massive imperial-state resources have been authorized to develop close military and political relationships with a region's armed forces' hierarchies. Sometimes, as in the case of pre-1959 Cuba, the ties date back to the creation of the local military apparatus. Since World War II, the Department of Defense assiduously has sought to consolidate and deepen these relationships in myriad ways: ongoing military training programs (and accompanying ideological indoctrination); the provision of sophisticated military equipment and parts; military, naval, and air force missions as well as political-military-intelligence "liaisons"; and periodic joint warfare maneuvers.

Between 1950 and 1978, almost 500,000 Third World officers participated in the U.S. military assistance training program, which continuously reinforced the personal as well as the professional links between the armed forces of the imperial state and its Third World allies. As a senior Pentagon official told a congressional committee at the time of the Carter administration, such ties "endure long after the actual training experience is complete."[58] By the 1970s, the emphasis on expanding political relations assumed an importance second to none in Department of Defense thinking. United States Military Assistance Advisory Groups around the world now devote much of their time and effort to "dialogue" activities with host military officials to make them increasingly receptive to "suggested improvements and the American way [and] to establish or enhance working relationships."[59] The most striking political consequence of such primary external identification among Third World military leaders has been their propensity to intervene in the political arena to overthrow nationalist or anticapitalist governments promoting policies that conflict with the interests of foreign capital, in particular, and with U.S. policy objectives in general.[60]

The Central Intelligence Agency (CIA) is the most influential coercive intelligence body in the imperial state. Although this covert agency is responsible for intelligence collection and espionage, for the purpose of this book the focus is on the CIA's covert operations designed to influence internal political, economic, and social developments in target countries. These include the establishment of liaisons with local military and police forces; subsidies to political parties, labor unions, local businesses, and employer organizations; funding mass-media (newspapers, radio, television) propaganda campaigns, including the complementary activities of research and technical institutes; recruitment and training of local operatives and personnel exchange programs; planning and financing economic sabotage operations and various types of paramilitary missions; "buying" local officials (e.g., cabinet ministers) to influence regime policies in a manner favorable to American interests; intelligence deception operations (channeling bogus information to a foreign government or its intelligence service); employing American multinational corporations as conduits for purchasing intelligence information or paying off pro-U.S. politicians; funding foreign intelligence services to undertake intelligence operations to the common benefit of each; and even financing proxy penetrations of third countries by allied foreign governments.[61] The CIA also performs important economic intelligence advisory roles in such areas as export licensing and foreign debt negotiations.[62]

In addition to agencies of the imperial state with economic and coercive responsibilities are those that deal with ideological issues through institutional activities directly tied to the state through the "subcontracted" activities of unofficial groups drawn from the imperial society and collaborator groups. The U.S. Information Agency and related propaganda organizations of the state fulfill the purposes of creating favorable images of U.S. imperial activity and denigrating revolutionary action and programs of social-economic transformation.[63] Psychological warfare, including the creation of false consciousness, is a principal activity. In the postcolonial period, however, societal forces (cultural, religious, educational) have taken on special importance in the ideological task of defending U.S. goals. Their unofficial status is used to give them the aura of objectivity and independence and thus increase the credibility of the propaganda message. These auxiliaries of the imperial state usually are contracted covertly by intelligence agencies or overtly by others, ostensibly for an apolitical purpose – that is, to "promote cultural exchanges."[64] This illusory separation between state and society obscures a convergence of purposes and allows the imperial state to pursue its ideological goals through several additional instruments.

Among those executive-branch agencies that operationalize imperial-state policy, bureaucratic conflicts over priorities and procedures necessarily arise. The arguments largely have centered around the foreign-policy concerns of the Departments of State, Defense, and Treasury, recurring with greatest frequency over matters of foreign economic policy. During the Eisenhower presidency, there were numerous conflicts rooted in Treasury's preoccupation with balance-of-payments deficits and spending constraints. In 1954, for instance, over vigorous Treasury opposition, the White House sided with Secretary of State Dulles in agreeing to expand Export-Import Bank activities and create a "soft loan" World Bank affiliate, the International Finance Corporation, to accommodate pressing Latin American demands for economic assistance.[65] There were also regular disputes involving Treasury confrontations with both State and Defense officials over the annual level of military appropriations. Air Force Chief General Nathan F. Twining addressed this problem: "[Secretary of State] Dulles would always, you know, back us up on anything we wanted to do. When the military got up [before Congress] and asked . . . for foreign aid or whatever the hell it was, Dulles was our champion."[66] General Maxwell Taylor recalled that the Pentagon "fought with [Secretary of the Treasury] Humphrey far more than with the State Department."[67]

These periodic interagency conflicts over the direction of foreign economic policy persisted through most of the 1960s and 1970s precisely because of the steadily worsening U.S. trade situation. The conflict materialized as the Defense hierarchy repeatedly advocated increased levels of military assistance, while the State Department, according to a number of Treasury officials, appeared to want to just "spend, spend, spend."[68]

State and Treasury have often clashed over what measures offer the best chance of protecting U.S. multinational corporations under challenge from nationalist regimes in the Third World. When host government policies toward individual enterprises presage a fundamental rupture in ties with foreign capital (e.g., expropriation without compensation), Treasury is likely to sanction hardline confrontation in support of "vital economic interests." Often, this posture is exercised most vividly in the international financial institutions, where Treasury officials move aggressively to mobilize support for the withholding of loans and credits. However, the subordination of political considerations embodied in such efforts has often generated conflicts with State's concern to balance a number of considerations that extend beyond the immediate interests of private corporate investors. As one Treasury official with responsibilities in this area observed dryly: "The Treasury Department tries to force the issue in all these [expropriation] cases on the basis of fair, prompt and useable compensation. The State Department agrees with that concept, but if it makes life hard for the Ambassador in Lima they don't like it."[69] In the event that a concrete, antagonistic response is deemed appropriate by State, however, economic retaliation then is viewed as but one instrument among many (covert subversion, diplomatic pressures, rupturing of trade ties, indirect military intervention) in an integrated and escalating response.

In the area of foreign economic policy, there is a constant push and pull between State and Treasury for control over strategic priorities. In periods of intercapitalist economic rivalries and declining U.S. investment and trade competitiveness (e.g., the early 1970s), the White House had inclined toward the more hardline Treasury defense of American property holders abroad.[70] Treasury's influence over foreign economic policy has also tended to rise at State's expense in periods when there has been a shift away from bilateral aid programs in favor of increased U.S. funding of the multilateral development banks. At the same time,

State's role as the preeminent operational agency ensures that it continues to play an important, ongoing role in foreign economic policy deliberations – especially as they cut across White House political objectives. Furthermore, in the context of a fundamental challenge to foreign capital operations by a nationalist regime anchored in a mobilized working class, the State Department assumes a dominant tactical role to formulate effective, coherent, and "flexible" responses to such a systemic threat to imperial-state goals.

This State-Treasury rivalry over economic issues has been accompanied by bureaucratic infighting between the State and Defense Departments over political-military issues. Eisenhower's Secretary of Defense, Neil McElroy, noted the "fairly basic differences of point of view – which will always be there, because in the conduct of our foreign policy the State Department is bound to think more in terms of reconciliation than the military is."[71] From the beginning of World War II until the end of the 1950s, the agencies differed over the political and diplomatic implications of U.S. military programs in Latin America, each attempting to assert control over the programs' administration.[72] This struggle for operational supremacy carried over into the 1960s and 1970s, centering around which Department should have the greater role in shaping American military and security assistance programs in the region.[73]

On occasion, the State Department and the National Security Council also have become embroiled in tactical debates over foreign-policy questions. During the Carter presidency, the constant effort by NSC Advisor Brzezinski to assert the Council's preeminence, as well as his "tougher line" on detente with the Soviet Union, U.S. policy in the Horn and southern Africa, and even toward Cuba, generated recurring conflicts with Secretaries of State Vance and Muskie.[74] An NSC staff member explained these "tactical differences of opinion" in terms of "personalities" and as a result of "different perceptions of what would do the job."[75] He also hastened to emphasize the need to anchor such disagreements within the larger policy consensus, noting that "on questions of general policy objectives I have not seen a significant difference between State and the NSC." State Department officials agreed with Brzezinski's statement of July 1980 that there were no differences with Secretary Muskie "on any major issue."[76]

In different contexts, specific agencies play more or less prominent roles in pursuit of capitalist policy goals. Sometimes the
functions of agencies may complement each other directly; at
other moments, agencies may engage in specialized (if interrelated) actions. In part, the kind of struggle (e.g., rising political
and economic nationalism) and its implications for capital accumulation and expansion will determine the specific agencies and
institutions on which imperial-state processes will rely. In practice, agencies' perceptions of their separate missions coexist with
the understanding that their overlapping jurisdictions create permanent lines of interchange in the imperial-state structure.[77]
Thus, bureaucratic conflicts usually are resolved internally and, if
serious enough, at the apex of the decisionmaking apparatus.

There is no denying that inter- and intradepartmental rivalries
derived from unique functional priorities are common among
executive-branch foreign-policy agencies. But whether we talk of
conflicts between State and Treasury over economic and financial
issues or of interservice and branch rivalries inside the Pentagon
over budget allocations, the pursuit of idiosyncratic agency concerns, the defense of traditional bureaucratic turfs, and the proliferation of action proposals do not amount to the existence of multiple decisionmaking centers. Neither do they provide any basis
for asserting that different departments pursue "their own" policies "in open conflict with" other departments.

Although it is important to recognize the existence of interagency tensions and try to measure and compare the varied positions, these conflicts cannot be discussed independently of the
larger context. To do so would vitiate any possibility for a sustained evaluation of the cohesiveness in U.S. foreign policymaking. As this study attests, in situations where there is a perceived,
fundamental challenge to the U.S. political economy – the likelihood that a part of the world will move out of the capitalist political and economic orbit – a centralized policymaking apparatus
emerges, delineates a general position, and delegates to each individual imperial-state agency specific, but complementary, tasks in
pursuit of the overall objective. Policy is not the outcome of several decisionmaking centers with the personnel of each acting at
cross purposes with one another. On the contrary, policy manifests itself in the mobilization of resources (physical, economic,
political, military, and covert) acting in concert to achieve goals
that remain consistent.

Imperial state and capitalist class

Capitalist social forces in the United States play a pivotal role in fashioning the boundaries and goals of the U.S. imperial state. There is a fundamental cohesion between the executive-branch agencies that frame imperial policies and the capitalist class, a cohesion revealed by looking at how class processes manifest themselves within the imperial-state structure. This view provides not only a fairly complete understanding of the policymaking process, but also rather sound insight into the different U.S. responses to various species of political and economic nationalist regimes in the Third World.[78]

Senior policymaking positions in the U.S. traditionally have been monopolized by corporate executives drawn from all class segments, but predominantly recruited from the largest multinational corporations. From a study of the social origins and prior career patterns of 234 key foreign policymakers active between 1944 and 1960, Gabriel Kolko concluded that they were "a highly mobile sector of the American corporate structure, a group of men who frequently assume and define high level policy tasks in government rather than routinely administer it, and then return to business."[79] A similar investigation conducted by the Brookings Institution for 1933 to 1965 found that 63 percent of all cabinet secretaries and 86 percent of all military secretaries were in either corporate law or business before their appointments.[80] Peter Freitag's analysis of the Eisenhower (1953–1961) and Johnson (1963–1969) administration cabinet appointees reveals that, before their government appointments, an extraordinarily large number served as directors of or corporate lawyers for the largest industrial, banking, insurance, public utility, and retail corporations in the United States. Furthermore, over 85 percent of cabinet members in both administrations had business interlocks.[81]

This mobility between public and private sectors establishes a bias within the imperial state in favor of multinational capital. Yet, the importance of homogeneous social origins should not be exaggerated. As Kolko himself points out, correlation at the level of class background is not necessarily causation, and attempts by even the most prestigious individual to promote policies counter to permanent capitalist interests are likely to bring loss of position and influence. Ultimately, socioeconomic backgrounds and the external linkages of policymakers may be less important than the processes of recruitment, socialization on-the-job, promotion procedures, and other norms in establishing the orientation of imperial decisionmakers.

Although the boundaries of imperial-state policymaking are erected by the imperatives of the capitalist social system, the world of the policymakers themselves is not so easy to describe or simple to manage. The complexities of worldwide capitalist competition, internal class struggles, regional power blocs, and so forth, intervene and force policymakers to consider carefully their capacity to realize policies vis-à-vis the power configurations in each situation. In these circumstances, policymakers have *discretionary* powers to make immediate or short-term decisions affecting particular interests according to their own estimates of priorities and possibilities, though their decisions may not always coincide with the tactics favored by all segments of the capitalist class. Such disjunctions, however, do not add up to acting independently of the class.

Only in specific historical contexts is it possible to speak of a state having "limited autonomy" from the capitalist class.[82] For instance, when a fragmented class cannot subordinate the individual interests of its members to the larger class interest, the state, with policymakers drawn from all sectors of capital, may formulate a line of action on behalf of the entire class. This discretionary power of the imperial state, however, always operates in the universe of the capitalist system: The state, acting with "limited autonomy," as Ralph Miliband notes, does so within "a capitalist context which profoundly affects everything that state does."[83] The process of accumulation and reproduction, the defense of the class and state structure that facilitate this process, are the decisionmakers' ultimate strategic goals. Within this framework, differences among agencies and between the imperial state and the outward-oriented capitalist class are less a reflection of "state autonomy" than of different manners of pursuing the same end. The methods vary, but the imperatives are constant, causing decisionmakers to be rational and direct about maximizing imperial interests. To exaggerate the autonomy of the state, then, is to miss the fact that decisionmakers are immersed in the symbols and substance of capitalist power.[84]

The illusion of state autonomy is enhanced when conflicts occur between the imperial state and the capitalist class.[85] Since capitalists largely operate within the universe of their own firms, conflicts with the state come up when they make demands, suggest actions, and seek redress from the state as their interests are affected.[86]

There are perhaps three levels of consciousness among members of the imperial capitalist class, ranging from enterprise- and industry- to class-consciousness. Enterprise-centered capitalists respond to policies that directly affect their firms. For instance, threats of nationalization evoke in these entrepreneurs either demands for precipitous action by the imperial state or attempts to reach individual settlements. Industry-centered capitalists focus on coordinating activities among firms sharing a purpose (mining enterprises, for example) to develop a common policy and induce the state to act for their collective purpose. But class-conscious capitalists advocate a coordinated policy at the imperial-state level, fashioning agendas that take account not only of their immediate needs, but also of pontential threats to the whole capitalist system. A high degree of calculation in the pursuit of "rational self-interest" and the formulation of a policy encompassing an array of social forces and political circumstances is characteristic of class-conscious (imperial) capitalists.

For the most part, decisions on this scale are made by the imperial-state, and it may appear that the imperial state is "using" the capitalist class to serve its policy ends. But this is a narrow interpretation. The point is that the collective needs of the class are mediated through the state, which instrumentalizes, directs, sacrifices, or defends individual firms and sometimes whole industries in pursuit of historic goals. This overarching imperial-state function in relation to the class marks the division of labor between the task of profitmaking and the broader chore of the state's creating the conditions for profitmaking. Thus, there emerges the apparent paradox that the consciousness of outward-oriented class interests is more concentrated in the imperial state than in the capitalist class itself.

It is important to distinguish the argument presented here regarding the state-class relationship from one asserting that the pursuit of capitalist interests necessarily involves the intersection of all capitalist enterprises in the same policy at all times and in all circumstances. For, as implied above, in certain contexts imperial-state policy clearly is viewed as an obstacle to profit maximization by individual multinationals. Conversely, an American multinational corporation's agreements with a revolutionary or nationalist government sometimes conflict head-on with a White House commitment to political confrontation with that regime.

What is significant about these types of conflict, besides their tendency to recur, is the limited depth of disagreement – limited by
the multinationals' uniform support of the entire imperial framework (foreign aid programs, military alliances, multilateral development banks) that provides much of the wherewithal for their
overseas expansion and accumulation. The more important the
region or social formation to imperial expansion, the greater the
coincidence of interest between capital and state and the more
directly will state policy be an expression of class interest.

It is worthwhile asking whether every policy the imperial state
pursues is best for the capitalist system. Would capital's interests
have been better served, for example, if the U.S. government had
not exacerbated the conflict with Castro? Would American-owned
oil refineries have been seized in mid-1960 if Washington had
substituted negotiation for confrontation? This study does not
contend that state officials take the best position in every conflict.
What it does presume is that, just as business executives don't
always make investment decisions that maximize profits, likewise
capitalist governments pursuing capitalist interests may make
poor decisions. The hardline position, "conflict over accommodation," may not always gain the objective. As we will see in the
case of Cuba, given the country's profound integration into the
U.S. agro-industrial complex and its thorough vulnerability to
American economic integration, Washington policymakers plau-
sibly assumed that the initiatives taken at the behest of the state
would weaken the island economy, erode the Castro regime's
social basis of support, and substantially strengthen the position of
the United States and its social-class allies in Cuba. They were
wrong.

Imperial state and collaborator state: the historical context of U.S.-Cuban relations

Throughout the Third World, the United States as an imperial
state by necessity functions through the existence of "collaborator
states," mediating its policies through local state, class, and societal forces to whom the imperial state is linked by military or economic alliances or bilateral ties. These linkages are sustained by
exchanges that benefit the ruling classes or factions in each country. The management of imperial-state domination thus rests on
three factors: the capacity to penetrate another nation's social

structure, create durable linkages with key institutional or state forces, and sustain collaborating classes.[87]

The "collaborator state" possesses several features that facilitate its subordination to the imperial states. Its state and societal organizations or institutions (political, military, cultural) have leaders formed by and loyal to the ideas and definitions of economic reality offered in the imperial centers. This type of external penetration is matched by the organization and direction of the economy toward a complementary role within an international division of labor shaped by the imperial centers. The most crucial and strategic sectors of these economies are controlled or managed by multinational capital, and the kinds of goods produced, the terms of exchange, and the direction of exchange all maximize gains to the imperial centers and the principal classes and institutional groups in the collaborator state.

Within the collaborator state, two pivotal groups can be identified: the bureaucratic or political strata who, through control over the state, seek to maintain a disciplined and quiescent labor force, repress class conflict, negotiate labor contracts, and receive part of the surplus generated by multinational enterprise; and the socioeconomic classes such as landowners and import-exporters, joined in more recent decades by local industrialists and businesspeople, who develop joint ventures with the multinationals, rent technology and managerial skills, and the like.[88] The relationship between the latter – these "new" capitalists – and the multinationals is based on subordination and collaboration. The collaboration manifests itself in bargaining over the terms of their involvement, shifts in market demand, and questions of political influence and power. In other words, these local collaborator classes, while acknowledging their dependence on the multinationals, are busy establishing political and economic roles for themselves to prevent their displacement by more dynamic, imperial partners.[89]

From the imperial state's viewpoint, the critical concern is to sustain and, if necessary, realign with collaborator groups and classes as contexts change. The internal dynamics of any one Third World society determine what options are activated by the imperial state to facilitate capital accumulation and expansion, and also to limit both fundamental (indigenous nationalist and anticapitalist forces) and competitive (indigenous capitalist) opposition to the capital accumulation process.

The history of U.S.-Cuban relations between 1898 and 1952 is the history of the creation and maintenance of a collaborator state serving American economic, political, and strategic interests. A narrative and interpretive overview of this period will serve to illuminate the Cuban Revolution's historical setting and provide a basis for understanding the changes in imperial-state policy after 1952 and the survival of the collaborator state project.

Washington's direct and persistent interventions into republican Cuba's internal social and class struggles were dictated not only by specific conjunctural crises (the protection of particular capitalist interests, repression of insurrectionary movements, fiscal "irresponsibility") but also, and at a more profound level, by the requirements of different phases of the capital accumulation process (survival, consolidation, and expansion).

Almost a century ago, American military intervention into Cuba in 1898 aborted a national liberation struggle, replaced Spanish colonial rule with an imperial army of occupation, and eliminated the threat of large-scale support for an independent Cuba. The problem then confronting U.S. policymakers was how to transform Cuba from a European colony into an American neocolonial protectorate that would permit optimal capital accumulation, but not the emergence of a national state.[90] In an economy largely destroyed by insurrection and war, the recreation of an environment for profitable private enterprise demanded the immediate provision of large-scale infrastructural investments. Beyond that, however, the imperial state's desire to secure the conditions for development in Cuba required elaborating a set of political, administrative, military, cultural, and economic policies, structures, and programs. From the long-term viewpoint, perhaps the most critical development in the transition from direct American rule to republican status was the organization of outward-oriented "satellite" groups – the military, police, bureaucracy, political parties, educators – who would provide a relatively permeable Cuban state and society after 1902 and become the major local beneficiaries of subsequent U.S. involvement in the island's affairs.[91]

During the first quarter of the twentieth century, the effort to contain nationalist mobilizations opposing the imperial presence and the state-class structure that encouraged this presence dictated periodic U.S. military interventions (1906, 1909, 1912, 1917–1921). When necessary, Washington also engaged in diplomatic, electoral, economic, financial, and other forms of nonmilitary intervention to support its objectives on the island.[92] A highly developed state coercive apparatus was pivotal to the metropole's determination to sustain a neocolonial state tied to foreign capital interests, especially after the formation of a supposed "national" army in 1908. The ongoing development of professional and personal linkages between key imperial-state agencies and the Cuban military continually reinforced the latter's external orientation: "By 1925, officers from virtually every branch of the Cuban armed forces . . . had attended various military academies in the United States."[93]

The interaction between American economic expansion and imperial-state interventions in Cuba had a striking impact on the evolution of the Cuban class structure. At the level of the Cuban state, "institution building" meant that the peripheral state functioned not as the instrument of a local socially and economically integrated ruling class, but as the vehicle for promoting external capital movements into the Cuban economy's most dynamic sectors. The source of capital accumulation remained inside Cuba, but the locus was outside. By 1929, American investments in Cuba accounted for over one-quarter of total U.S. investments in all of Latin America and were dominant in practically every strategic sector of the peripheral economy: sugar, tobacco, railways, iron ore, copper, manganese, telephone and telegraph, banking, docks, fruit, warehouses, public utilities, and hotels. American capitalists controlled between 70 percent and 75 percent of Cuban sugar production. While U.S. capital made up perhaps 85 percent of total foreign investments on the island, the American market absorbed between 75 percent and 80 percent of Cuba's exports, and imperial traders provided approximately two-thirds of its total imports.[94] One result of these developments was the evolution of a Cuban bourgeoisie subordinated to imperial capital and lacking any degree of class consciousness that could have turned it into an ideologically hegemonic force.

The Machado government (1925–1933) presided over the consolidation of an agro-export Cuban economy based on large inflows of foreign capital. The dominant position of American capital in agriculture and the accompanying spread of capitalist social relations of production in the countryside profoundly transformed the island's rural class structure: The pattern of individual sugar mill ownership was supplanted by plantations that proletarianized the rural labor force and reorganized it into a concentrated group. This socialization of production "urbanized" the rural population, increased its national and class awareness, and made it available for radical political action.

Beginning in 1925, the Cuban sugar industry, under the sway of capitalist world market operations and the dominance of U.S. banking and corporate interests, entered a period of prolonged structural crisis that persisted for over two decades. The precipitous fall in Cuban sugar production from over 5 million tons in 1924–1925 to less than 2 million tons in 1932–1933, due to the global depression, expanding sugar industries in Europe and Asia, and U.S. tariff policy, was compounded by a significant contraction in Cuba's share of the American market and a dramatic fall in the price of Cuban sugar.[95] These developments created a profitability crisis for foreign and local sugar capitalists as production costs began to exceed market prices. Their response was to heighten existing levels of labor exploitation, principally by lowering wages for cane cutters, mill operators, and field workers.[96] In the urban centers, industrial workers experienced a similar decline in salaries and standards of living.[97]

The resurgence of nationalist and antidictatorial struggle in the late 1920s and early 1930s, which assumed a decidedly class content under largely Communist Party leadership, was principally a function of the incapacity of capitalist productive forces to meet the socioeconomic needs of the island's urban and rural working classes. Accompanying this resurgence was the appearance of a highly corrupt and repressive state structure. From the perspective of U.S. policymakers, the rising level of social struggle in Cuba was incompatible with both capital accumulation and efforts to halt the decline in American commodity purchases. Diplomatic failures to pressure Machado to eliminate the more reprehensible aspects of his rulership and his unbridled refusal to leave office voluntarily led to a sharp break with Washington. The revival of U.S. exports, renewed economic assistance, and a renegotiation of the Cuban debt to U.S. public and private agencies dictated a political settlement based on Machado's overthrow. Charles Taussig, an influential State Department economic official and advisor to President Roosevelt, put it succinctly: "the prospect of increased economic advantages is a plum which will not be granted until the Cuban Government has taken positive and satisfactory steps to conclude the present unrest."[98] The plum was wielded by U.S. policymakers in an effort to isolate Machado from his capitalist supporters, and the effort coincided with Ambassador Sumner Welles' persistent actions to undermine and disintegrate the Cuban President's political base in Cuba's Congress. Although Washington's decision to withdraw support for Machado and seek his overthrow seriously weakened the regime's position, it was not the decisive factor in his ouster.

The spreading social conflict and class polarization catalyzed a class- and status-based crisis within the Cuban military, releasing sectors of the army to become expressions of a particular class or social movement. The polarization signalled the incapacity of the Machado regime to hold together even its own repressive apparatus, and it combined with the workers' refusal to endure further privations to engineer the collapse of the Machado presidency. This development was "followed immediately [by] a country-wide wave of labor unrest such as Cuba had never seen, accompanied by aggressive agitation, the extension of labor organization, and the increasing prominence of Communist leadership."[99] During the resulting massive national uprising, rural workers established "soviets" at a number of sugar complexes; municipal governments came under the control of the organized working class; and a situation of dual power began to emerge. This revolutionary insurrection coincided with the resolution of the armed forces' internal rebellion in favor of junior officers grouped around Colonel Fulgencio Batista. The outcome of these twin upheavals was the emergence of a nationalist government in September 1933 under the heterogeneous leadership of radicalized petty-bourgeois forces.

The new regime, headed by former University of Havana professor Ramón Grau San Martín, outlined a development program that did not decisively challenge the capitalist mode of production or seek to move Cuba out of the capitalist political-economic sphere. Even so, Washington's response was hostile. Its opposition was driven both by the appearance of this type of regime at a time of severe worldwide capitalist depression and by concern over the weight and long-term impact on policymaking of class-anchored tendencies in the governing coalition. The antagonistic stance of imperial-state officials was occasioned not merely by economic nationalism, but also by the maturation of a mass movement of urban and rural workers who supported, but were not organizationally linked to, the nationalist government.

During its brief tenure, the Grau regime proposed or enacted a wide-ranging social and economic program benefiting the island's working class: the eight-hour day, a minimum daily wage for cane cutters, the establishment of a Department of Labor, a substantial reduction in electricity rates, and the initiation of an agrarian reform program. Selective confrontations with sectors of foreign capital also took place: Payments on an $86 million public-works loan contracted by Machado with the Chase National Bank were suspended; sugar mills owned by the Cuban-American Sugar Company in Oriente province were provisionally intervened; and the properties of the Cuban Electric Company were seized in a dispute over rates and labor-management hostilities. These changes were directed toward achieving a *national* capitalist, rather than an *anti-capitalist,* solution to Cuba's pressing problems, but they also led to a more restrictive ambience for capital operations and profitmaking.

The Achilles heel of the nationalist government, however, was the old state structure, which remained essentially intact and in the hands of opposition forces. Most important, for the duration of its rule, the Grau regime shared political power with an "independent" military whose established linkages to the outside made it a potential counterrevolutionary factor. United States imperial-state agencies and officals exploited this schism and other access points in the state and society, according to their strategic importance, to mobilize allied social forces, shift the internal balance of power against the government, and divert the nationalist challenge to imperial capital accumulation in Cuba. Efforts at negotiation by Grau were constantly rebuffed by Washington, which privately opposed coexistence with the regime. Exercising discretion to avoid a premature rupture in relations, the U.S. government moved to destabilize Grau's coalition and its development project on a number of fronts: diplomatic and political pressures; economic sanctions; interaction with opposition political and military leaders; the maintenance of communications channels with the nationalist leadership in order to identify pressure points and take advantage of any internal divisions; and diplomatic nonrecognition to exacerbate internal social and political conflicts. Finally, Washington strengthened its ties with the proimperial sector of the Cuban armed forces and specifically with Colonel Batista, as a conviction took hold among senior policymakers that, short of direct military intervention, only a "break in the army" could definitively terminate the Grau regime.[100]

The U.S.-backed military coup of January 1934 and the massacres that accompanied the repression of political strikes involving thousands of workers in February–March 1934 and March 1935 destroyed the organs of mass democratic control, devastated the workers' movement, and consolidated military rule in Cuba. The military-controlled regimes that governed Cuba after Grau's overthrow not only demobilized and "disciplined" the working class, but also selectively reversed nationalist policies and reconstituted the state in the image of U.S. imperial interests. Capitalist development "from above" and "the outside" gradually restored a political-economic milieu conducive to external capital accumulation and commerce. The linchpin of the renewed U.S. economic aid program was the reciprocal trade agreement of 1934 that primarily benefited imperial capitalists and exporters, served to stabilize and streamline sugar industry operations, and discouraged agricultural diversification, except in those areas that did not involve competition with U.S. economic interests on the island.[101]

Relations between Havana and Washington in the decade following Grau's demise, while notable for the absence of what U.S. policymakers viewed as the intolerable restrictions that characterized the nationalist interregnum, were, at the time, paradoxically complicated by the emergence of an institutionalized labor movement that impinged on the possibilities for maximizing profits. The workers' movement was the only viable alternative to the Batista-controlled regimes that governed Cuba between 1934 and 1940 – regimes that lacked any semblance of large-scale support or political legitimacy. To overcome this problem of regime isolation and legitimacy, the "military strongman" Batista decided to strike a compromise with the major political organization of the working class – the Communist Party.

The essence of the Batista-Communist Party relationship beginning in the late 1930s was reciprocity. In return for accepting capitalist property relations and underwriting Batista by mobilizing mass support for his successful 1940 presidential compaign, the Communist Party was legalized, and Batista proceeded to grant a number of social and economic benefits to the working class: wage increases to sugar workers; laws dealing with minimum wages, job security, the eight-hour day, maternity insurance. Trade unions were recognized and union organizing drives, collective bargaining, and strikes were legalized. Moreover, the regime frequently intervened to support the economic demands of labor or, more likely, refrained from the use of force.

The impact of organizational legality, political access, limited class struggle (strikes at the industrial level on the basis of social and economic issues), and prolabor state intervention in wage disputes contributed to incremental gains in income for the working class and a substantial expansion in labor organization. By 1945, approximately one-third of the workforce was unionized. Yet, an unforeseen consequence of labor's institutionalization was its capacity to set limits on capital's efforts to modernize production to optimize capital accumulation. The power of labor during this period, despite its lack of political radicalism, was a major factor in the withdrawal of U.S. capital from its traditional investment area – sugar.

The election of the Auténtico Party governments of Ramón Grau San Martín (1944–1948) and Carlos Prío Socarrás (1948–1952) did not lead to changes in this state of affairs. Grau was amenable to the same relationship with the Communist Party that Batista cultivated: exchange of incremental reforms and salary increases for political support of his essentially capitalist regime. Under Prío, the purge of Communist Party leadership of the Confederation of Cuban Labor in 1947–1948 did not have noticeable effects on labor-state relations. Wages and salaries increased, temporary government interventions in enterprises beset with labor disputes continued, and protective legislation was enacted. Washington's underlying hostility toward Auténtico labor policies was manifested through diplomatic entreaties to Cuban authorities to "reject more firmly the demands of labor for continuous wage and other benefits."[102]

American policy toward Cuba during the Grau-Prío era was also characterized by constant carping on the need for a more favorable investment climate and by a willingness to apply economic pressures (withholding economic and technical assistance) to achieve this goal.[103] American officials identified a quartet of irritants affecting the operations of capital: the exploitation of political office for private profitmaking; bureaucratic graft and corruption or the absence of an environment in which, to quote Max Weber, "the official business of public administration [could be] discharged precisely, unambiguously, and with as much speed as possible";[104] the failure to provide satisfactory compensation to aggrieved American investors who were owed an estimated $9 million; and the inability of the regimes to maintain debt repayments to U.S. public and private agencies. Particularly aggravating was the lack of any "regularized vechicle for collecting sundry debts or for otherwise protecting American enterprises in Cuba. Each case had to be individually contested, with the results seeming to depend on caprice."[105]

Late in Grau's tenure, the United States, in 1947–1948, sought
to negotiate a new commercial treaty with Cuba that "would
legally delimit the rights and privileges of Americans doing business in Cuba and could provide for the prompt adjudication of
claims."[106] Havana pressed for a larger sugar quota in return for
this treaty, only to be told by the State Department that no additional purchases of Cuba sugar could be contemplated until a
treaty was signed and other outstanding economic problems were
resolved.

Increasingly, the U.S. executive branch saw the sugar quota as
a diplomatic weapon to force resolution of bilateral economic disputes. It sought authority from Congress to manipulate the sugar
quota to make Cuba deal more equitably with U.S. business and
pay outstanding financial claims. American economic aggression
culminated in Section 202(e) of the Sugar Act of 1948, which
allowed the Secretary of State to change the sugar quota of any
country that "denies fair and equitable treatment to the nationals
of the United States, its commerce, navigation or industry."[107]
However, Cuba's opposition and its capacity to mobilize Latin
American nationalism ensured that the bill would never become
operational. "Within six weeks of the bill's enactment, American
diplomats recognized that it could never be used. Within a year
the [State Department] acquiesced in its repeal."[108]

Washington's concern for the stability of the Cuban state
extended beyond economic and investment opportunities to
include geopolitical questions – a desire that Cuba provide a
secure flank in the event of an outbreak of military hostilities in
the Caribbean as well as a reliable source of important foods and
strategic commodities. In this context, a 1950 secret State Department policy statement commented disapprovingly on Havana's
"impatience to eliminate U.S. air bases in Cuba promptly after the
period of active wartime cooperation."[109]

Although American policymakers and Havana Embassy officials
decried Grau's "narrow economic nationalism" and Prío's
"unpredictable legislation affecting business," the absence of conflicts of a systemic or structural nature dictated Washington's
preference for a negotiating, nonconfrontational approach in its
efforts to resolve differences – especially the recurrent problems
affecting the operations of American capitalists in Cuba. Moreover, neither government sought to elaborate a foreign policy that
clashed with American interests. In the United Nations and other
international forums, both Grau and Prío remained "fully coop-

erative with the United States" when their support was requested by Washington policymakers.[110] Still, imperial-state officials discretely welcomed the Batista military coup of March 1952 as offering the possibilities for constraints on the organized labor movement, enlarging the role for foreign capital within the national economy, developing a less corrupt and more efficient state administration to facilitate the reproduction of capital, and eliciting increased Cuban cooperation in programs designed to maintain a stable and secure Caribbean region.

For Washington, the second Batista-led regime presented the promise of Cuba's continued integration within an American-dominated capitalist world economy and international division of labor on the basis of the island's traditional agro-mining-tourist orientation, the relegation of the Communist Party to the margins of political life along with a more disciplined and docile workforce, no change in Havana's "follower" status within global and regional political organizations, and confidence that Cuba's position in the U.S. political-economic network was unlikely to change.

The growing vulnerability and ultimate collapse of the Batista regime and the American project in Cuba at the end of 1958, though not a concern of this book, must be understood in terms of two interrelated factors: the cumulative impact of U.S. policy on the Cuban polity, economy, and class structure; and the persistent failure of state and societal institutions (military, bureaucracy, political parties) since the nationalist interregnum of 1933 to respond to class-anchored socioeconomic demands – a failure that weakened the bonds of allegiance to these "outward-oriented" ruling groups and eroded their legitimacy among the population.

The Cuban Revolution of 1959 profoundly ruptured an imperialist relationship that had flourished for six decades. This book describes the origins, nature, and consequences of the break in all its manifestations and the globalization of the conflict as it became part of an international class struggle. In the process, the focus is on imperial-state efforts to mobilize Cuban and external resources to revive some form of imperialist relationship within the larger matrix of a changing, but still U.S.-dominated, capitalist world economy.

2. The United States in Cuba 1952–1958: policymaking and capitalist interests*

The regional context

United States policy in Latin America between 1945 and 1958 was based upon what David Green called the principle of "a closed hemisphere in an Open World."[1] Washington's desire for political dominance over the region led it both to oppose the intrusion of fascism and other ideologies and to respond antagonistically to governments promoting independent foreign policies and development programs that constrained foreign capital. The American objective was expressed by deepening the region's dependence in the areas of trade, finance, and investment on U.S. public agencies, multinational corporations, and export-importers,[2] and via agreements wrested from regimes for the production and transfer to the United States of certain "raw and semi-processed materials."[3] The major aim of U.S. participation in the Chapultepec conference in February 1945, which ostensibly gathered to discuss inter-American economic relationships, was to oppose Peronist nationalism. Accordingly, the American delegation resisted tariff protection, supported increased foreign capital participation in local enterprises, and denounced economic nationalism and the emergence of statist regimes.

The rationale for extending the "closed hemisphere" concept to cover military relations was outlined cogently by U.S. Secretary of War Robert Patterson in a statement supporting congressional passage of the Inter-American Military Cooperation Act in 1947:

... I feel obliged to re-emphasize the advantage to hemisphere security by standardizing the military establishments of the American Republics as to equipment, training, and organization. Of these, the provision of

---

*An earlier version of this chapter was published in the *Journal of Latin American Studies* (U.K.), Vol. 14, No. 1, May 1982, pp. 143–170.

United States equipment is the keystone since United States methods of training and organization must inevitably follow its adoption along with the far-reaching concomitant benefits of permanent United States military missions and the continued flow of Latin American officers through our service schools. Thus will our ideals and ways of life be nurtured in Latin America, to the eventual exclusion of totalitarianism and other foreign ideologies.[4]

The Truman administration's Latin American policy was highlighted by its ratification of the Inter-American Treaty of Reciprocal Assistance (the Rio Treaty) in 1947 and its support of the formation of the Organization of American States (OAS) in 1948. Both actions were motivated partly by Washington's desire to establish regional institutions that could provide the appearance of collective decisionmaking, even though the United States was the dominant power. In theory, the Rio Treaty provision against military and nonmilitary aggression made the hemisphere's defense responsibilities a common concern for all countries. In practice, however, Washington's disproportionate power gave it the ability to identify "an aggression which is not an armed attack."[5] American officials conceived of the OAS, from its inception, as a political counterweight to the United Nations and a means of limiting the U.N.'s jurisdiction in the hemisphere.[6] But the region's voting record at the United Nations was not a worry during the Truman presidency. In March 1951 congressional testimony, Edward G. Miller, Jr., Assistant Secretary of State for Inter-American Affairs, declared:

There is no doubt that since Korea they have gone down the line for us in the U.N. They have done that on virtually everything we have stood for. The 20 Latin American votes on some issues, such as the issue of not seating the Communist Chinese, were the only bloc of votes we could count on. That includes Argentina and Guatemala.[7]

In January 1952, Secretary of State Dean Acheson summed up the results of postwar American policy toward Latin America: "We are, I think, in pretty good shape in the continent. There are two places where we have vociferous anti-American people in the saddle. That is Argentina and Guatemala." He observed that Argentina "is anti-American, but it is Peronista and not Communist. I think that is one we just have to live through."[8]

The objective of American policy under Eisenhower's presidency (1952–1960) was singleminded, according to one high-ranking State Departmental official: "to keep the area quiet and keep communism out . . . [Secretary of State Dulles] was very tolerant, I think, of dictatorships so long as they took a firm stand against Communism."[9] Anticommunism was a dominant factor influencing U.S. policy in Latin America, serving as the central distinguishing element between accommodation and hostility toward regimes there. It was the natural outgrowth of antifascist measures introduced into the Western Hemisphere during World War II. An internal State Department study from March 1948 articulated this concern:

Ample precedent for common measures to combat Communism in the Americas exists in the programs and activities carried out during the last World War. . . . Specific action was taken through the work of the Emergency Advisory Committee for Political Defense with headquarters at Montevideo; through the exchange of information among the American Governments; through programs of police cooperation; and through a coordination of effort in the control of travel, communications, and the issuance of passports and visas.[10]

This ideological commitment was the rationale for indirect military responses to "external threats"; simultaneously, it allowed U.S. policymakers to define hemispheric communist parties as agents of Soviet expansion. Although the OAS charter incorporated the doctrine of nonintervention in sovereign states' internal affairs (inserted mainly at the insistence of Latin American governments), Washington managed to include a special resolution condemning international communism as incompatible with the inter-American system.

The anticommunist component of U.S. policy toward Latin America during the 1950s was linked to the larger East-West conflict. The Eisenhower administration vigorously maintained Washington's postwar opposition to the forces of national and social revolution in the Third World, its rigid anticommunism, and its profound distrust of the Soviet Union. Eisenhower, writes his biographer Stephen Ambrose, "refused to trust the Russians to even the slightest degree. He continued and expanded the economic, political, diplomatic and covert operations pressure on the Kremlin in his entire two terms."[11] A State Department OAS official during the 1950s recollected that U.S. Latin American policy could only be understood in the context of "the Cold War and Dulles' theory that we had to stop the advance of Communism anywhere."[12]

The CIA's clandestine warfare capabilities were upgraded and broadened as it became the prime White House instrument for containing the spread of Communist influence, which the President associated with the rising tide of nationalism, neutralism, and nonalignment throughout the Third World.[13] The growing activities of the CIA in the hemisphere typified this preeminent orientation of American policy makers. The "spillover" effect of the Communist victory in China in 1949 and the tendency to see revolutionary movements or governments as instruments of Soviet "destabilization" or "disruption politics" shaped CIA evaluations of political events on the southern continent: "The CIA was not narrowly concerned with protecting investments or that kind of thing. The CIA interest was much more a geopolitical concern with the ebb and flow of Soviet influence in Latin America."[14]

The Eisenhower White House viewed Central America and the Caribbean as the "soft underbelly" of American power in the hemisphere – the most likely entry point of Soviet or other external influence. Paradoxically, although officials defined the threat to regional or national security as external, the anticommunist policy focused on internal challenges to state regimes or nationalist governments, challenges that prefigured potential transformations of the political and economic status quo.

The U.S. set policy toward nationalist regimes in Latin America during the 1950s on the basis of three considerations: the relationship of nationalist measures (expropriation, land reform) to the direction of political and economic policy (whether capitalist or anticapitalist); the influence of divergent, class-anchored segments within the governing coalition; and the willingness and capacity of certain groups (especially the armed forces) to contain or reverse nationalist projects at the behest of Washington. Those considerations shaped the decision to apply diplomatic pressure to resolve conflicts with Paz Estenssoro and the Movimiento Nacionalista Revolucionario in Bolivia (1952–1956) and the decision to use military means to destabilize and overthrow the "antagonistic" nationalist regime of Jacobo Arbenz in Guatemala (1950–1954).[15] But apart from these interregnums and Perón's Argentina, the Eisenhower administration presided at a time when, in the words of one involved State Department official,

Latin American problems were considered secondary to those from other areas, such as Europe and Asia. Latin America did not receive priority attention from the [U.S. government] . . . as long as things were rocking along, and while many of the Latin American issues seemed to be between the "ins" and "outs" rather than ideological.[16]

This relatively stable and quiescent political environment provided much of the framework for Latin America's emergence as a major area of U.S. economic expansion. In the decade after 1946, the region absorbed about 30 percent of new direct U.S. foreign investments, principally in the petroleum, manufacturing, mining, and smelting sectors, and in trade and service industries.[17] In a March 1950 memorandum to the Secretary of State, Department counselor George F. Kennan argued that expanding U.S. economic commitments in the hemisphere and the accompanying growth of economic nationalist and anti-imperialist sentiments imposed a responsibility on the executive branch to devise "a more effective system of techniques and instrumentalities than we now have whereby our influence can continue to be brought to bear on the Latin American countries."[18]

The decision of the U.S. Congress to raise appropriations for the Export-Import Bank substantially and the subsequent establishment of the Point Four technical aid program, represented two significant moves to increase American private corporate activities in the hemisphere. Additional Export-Import Bank credits concentrated on infrastructure projects (heavy industry, highway construction, public utilities) designed to encourage and accelerate foreign capital flows. By limiting most credits to the purchase of American materials, equipment, and services, the Bank also fulfilled its statutory directive to "supplement and encourage [but not] compete with private capital."[19] The Point Four technical aid program for Latin America performed a similar function;

Technical assistance had begun to take hold [recalled a State Department official] following the 1949 inauguration but, by and large, under the Eisenhower government, it was essentially a sort of classical policy in which the promotion of American business and commercial interests in Latin America was probably the central theme. . . . By and large, you would call it a conservative, classical attitude, highly paternalistic, and only oriented in a limited sense toward development.[20]

Initially, however, the Eisenhower administration discouraged public economic assistance to Latin America in favor of a Treasury Department formula for sustained economic growth: free trade and inflows of private foreign capital. Export-Import Bank loans to the region declined from $147 million in 1952 to a miniscule $7.6 million in 1953.[21] The shift back to an emphasis on foreign aid was part of an overall change in American foreign economic policy toward the Third World, reflecting three developing White House concerns: the failure of the strategy propounded by Treasury Secretary George M. Humphrey for generating economic development and political stability; the growth of economic and political nationalism; and, above all, the burgeoning Soviet economic presence in these regions. The White House described the expanded Soviet technical assistance, trade ties, and financial commitments to the Third World as "a dangerous ploy whose implications for the West were almost as serious as military aggression."[22] In Latin America, recessionary trends persisted in many economies, and the value of total trade between the hemisphere and the Soviet bloc climbed from less than $80 million in 1953 to $340 million in 1955.[23]

Indications of support within the highest echelons of the executive branch for a change in aid policy came as early as 1954 when Eisenhower bowed to Secretary of State John Foster Dulles' argument that the upcoming Inter-American Conference in Caracas, Venezuela, could prove a diplomatic debacle for the United States unless the Export-Import Bank substantially increased its development financing program. Such a reversion in Bank policy, Dulles contended, would serve a dual purpose: It would undercut more radical economic proposals certain to be put forward at the conference, and it would improve U.S. efforts to isolate the nationalist Arbenz regime in Guatemala. During the second Eisenhower presidency, in the context of domestic recession and a growing U.S. balance of payments problem, the White House sought to distribute the burden of its foreign aid commitment through multilateral assistance programs based on expanding the resources of the World Bank and the International Monetary Fund, and through support for regional development schemes – particularly in Latin America.[24]

During the 1950s, new foreign subsidiaries of U.S. multinational corporations expanded at a greater rate in Latin America than in any other area of the world.[25] On the eve of the Cuban Revolution, U.S. direct investments in the hemisphere totalled almost $8.5 billion out of an overall Third World investment approaching $11 billion.[26] But the actual market worth of these regional investments far exceeded the book value. A Department of Commerce study covering 1950 to 1956 estimated that total expenditures by American corporations were double the book value of new investments during this period.[27] These neighbor economies also provided substantial export markets for U.S. commercial interests. In 1955, for instance, U.S. interests sold $2.3 billion worth of commodities in the region – excluding sales by American trade and service industries.[28] The most important recipients of American capital and commerce were Brazil, Mexico, Venezuela, and Cuba.

The growing U.S. political and economic commitments were paralleled by the establishment of protective regional and military organizations, the consummation of military assistance pacts with thirteen Latin American countries during the 1950s, and the increased funding of hemispheric military advisory and assistance programs to support client regimes in repelling "external aggressions."[29] Because the area's military forces were usually the most cohesive and organized institutions in society, Eisenhower's rationale for consolidating and extending existing linkages was primarily political. An NSC official addressed this issue directly in August 1956: "The unique political position of military groups in Latin America makes it important to the United States to maintain influence with these groups."[30] United States military aid to Latin America, virtually nonexistent under Truman, amounted to $387.4 million though the Eisenhower years.[31]

United States executive-branch agencies all operated to ensure that Latin America maintained an "open door" for foreign capital accumulation and identified with American political-military objectives during this highpoint of the Cold War. Policymakers were disposed to negotiate conflicts with nonsocialist nationalists (Argentina, Bolivia), but actively seek the disintegration of anticapitalist nationalism or regimes incorporating social forces attempting to move away from capitalism (Guatemala). A State Department Latin Americanist from the period recalled that the demise of the Arbenz government in Guatemala in 1954 shifted the major focus of White House concerns to other parts of the world, since "the right-wing dictatorships were pretty much in command of the situation [and] there did not seem to be a meaningful challenge coming from the left."[32] The hemisphere reverted to secondary importance in U.S. global strategy until mid-1958, when this huge "safe precinct" demanded reevaluation because of rising political and military conflict in Batista's Cuba.[33]

U.S. business and the Batista dictatorship

In pursuit of geopolitical and strategic goals in Latin America during the 1950s, U.S. policy found expression in support of several anticommunist governments, including the military junta that ousted an elected government and ruled Cuba from March 1952 to December 1958. The Batista regime's consistent support of U.S. Cold War objectives struck a responsive cord in Washington. A confidential memorandum from the American Embassy in Havana to the State Department in February 1958 declared:

The Cubans are basically and firmly pro-American. The Batista Government has taken a resolute stand against Communism, breaking off diplomatic relations with Soviet bloc countries, and giving constant support to the United States in its efforts to prevent the spread of Communism in the world.[34]

In regional and international political forums, Batista could be relied upon to provide active, unequivocal support for American foreign policy. An Embassy report prepared in October 1958 reflected on this point:

The present Cuban Government has a record of excellent cooperation and solidarity with the United States in the international field on all issues of major importance. Cuban representatives have on occasion taken the lead in opposing Communism, and in advocating policies and courses of action desired by the United States. Cuban officials approached in this connection by United States representatives have consistently been friendly and cooperative.[35]

The Batista government accorded foreign investment a pivotal role in Cuba's development, sustained Cuba's position as a major regional market for U.S. manufactured goods, and continued to provide the American economy "full access to Cuban materials essential to the national security."[36] American economic links extended beyond the earlier concentration on resources (e.g., sugar exploitation) into other sectors (tourism, manufacturing). The problem of labor "discipline," corruption and incompetence within the Cuban state and government, and the rising level of regime repression were not issues of major concern for American policymakers, as long as they did not affect U.S. economic activities there. With the emergence of a broadly based, nationalist opposition to Batista, under the leadership of rural insurgents, however, the United States began to interpret the excesses of the dictatorship from a different vantage point. In the final analysis, the perceived threat to foreign capital motivated the strategic confrontation between the Eisenhower administration and the nationalist, guerrilla movement. A Castro government was seen by the White House and State Department as inevitably placing in jeopardy all American investments in Cuba. Before we can discuss the policies of various American executive-branch agencies toward Cuba, therefore, it is necessary to consider the conditions and extent of U.S. economic expansion in Cuba under the Batista regime.

Betwen 1940 and 1952, the organized labor movement was a major force in Cuban society, even though it was incapable of changing that society. At the same time, economic development was stagnant. To American multinational corporations active in Cuba, the workers' organized presence was a fetter on business– the primary obstacle to efficient and expanding production. This concern was spelled out in the 1950 World Bank report on the Cuban economy that recommended the following measures to "discipline" labor if satisfactory business conditions were to be restored: greater flexibility in the job tenure system, the introduction of a merit system in the bureaucracy, and termination of extensive government participation in setting wages and other aspects of the labor contract (hours, tenure, vacation). In place of a dominant state role in setting wage levels in almost every branch of industry and agriculture, the report advocated substituting collective bargaining procedures.[37]

American and Cuban businessmen responded favorably to Batista's return to political power in 1952 through a military coup, perceiving it as the beginning of a period of stability, law and order, and the reimposition of labor discipline.[38] They hoped that Batista would incorporate many of the World Bank's proposals on labor and thereby recreate good conditions for investment and doing business. One of the regime's earliest acts was to return to their former owners four companies seized by the previous administration in response to worker demands.[39] Furthermore, the constant threat of state intervention in industrial enterprises to resolve labor disputes now virtually ceased. Whereas the Prío government intervened temporarily in forty-five enterprises beset by labor conflicts between 1949 and 1951, there are no recorded instances of this type of state intervention between November 1952 and November 1955.[40] An executive of the Cuban subsidiary of Bethlehem Steel assessed the changed climate for industrial operations as follows: "The problem during the Grau and Prío governments was labor strikes. I found economic conditions under Batista more stable."[41] In mid-1953, John M. Cabot, Assistant Secretary of State for Inter-American Affairs, commented that, despite some minor "friction," the United States had "no serious problems in Cuba."[42]

In April 1954, the Cuban government prosposed major revisions of existing labor legislation. "The idea of the project,"declared Minister of Labor Dr. Carlos Saladrigas, "is to bring about a radical change in labor-employer relations and remove obstacles for investment of national and foreign capital."[43] The envisaged law specified a number of justifications for the dismissal of workers, including employer economy drives and inefficient employee performance. Businessmen would be accorded the right to enforce worker lockouts in the events of the failure of arbitration to resolve wage or other disputes. The right to strike would be maintained, but only in limited circumstances. American corporate executives judged this proposed law "[an] excellent step in the right direction."[44]

To reinvigorate the stagnating Cuban economy, Batista also announced new measures designed to stimulate additional foreign investment in industry. These included generous, long-term multiple-tax exemptions, lightened controls on capital remittances, increased state (infrastructure) investments, and the like. Between 1949 and 1957, for instance, state investments increased from 14 percent to 40 percent of total investments in the Cuban economy.[45] Total outstanding loans from government development banks increased from 4.1 million pesos in December 1952 to 277 million in September 1957.[46] The bulk of new state expenditures financed infrastructure projects, principally in transportation (dock facilities, roads, railways), contributing significantly to the growth of a proper "ambience . . . for American business."[47] The Havana manager of the U.S. stockbroking firm of Merrill Lynch offered a pithy evaluation of the new regime's attitude toward capitalist activity: "Batista permitted business, the competitive system, the free enterprise system, to operate."[48] To a degree, the military regime attempted to substitute itself for the absence of a dynamic and entrepreneurial, class-conscious Cuban bourgeoisie, using its control of the state as the vehicle for economic development.

Between 1954 and 1956, new foreign investments quadrupled, flowing into almost every strategic sector: petroleum, public utilities, petrochemicals, mining, nonsugar manufacturing, tourism, and construction.[49] "The measure of business confidence," one U.S. businessman observed, "can be judged from the varied nature and size of the investment programs of private business."[50] This increase of foreign capital in Cuba did not, however, stimulate new productive industrial development, but was primarily absorbed by the nonproductive, tertiary sector of the economy. Probably the most important growth sector under Batista was the American-dominated tourist industry. Extensive Cuban government concessions and supports resulted in the construction of twenty-eight new hotels and motels at a cost of over $60 million.[51] Each new building received substantial tax exemptions and profits (usually 10 years for capital going into luxury hotels) and, in the case of the Havana Hilton and Havana Riviera hotels, direct state financial assistance during construction. This type of investment remained highly profitable, compared to equivalent investments in the United States, even beyond the period of tax concessions.[52] Meanwhile, overseas investors encountered relatively few obstacles to repatriating profits. In 1957, Batista made a pact with the United States that insured investors against intervention and nationalization. The lack of controls on capital remittances between 1952 and 1958 allowed American subsidiaries to channel $378 million back to their home offices or corporate headquarters.[53]

Batista's Cuba not only granted specific tax exemptions to U.S. investors but also, for all practical purposes, excluded them from any significant tax burden whatsoever. A 1956 U.S. Department of Commerce study concluded that "of the nearly 200 taxes and levies in effect many are of limited importance and there is little evidence that the burden of Cuban taxation has been a factor in discouraging the investment of foreign capital."[54] Moreover, American multinationals imaginatively exploited the island's tax laws for purposes other than profits. Texaco Oil, for instance, constructed a 20,000-barrels-per-day refinery in the provincial capital of Santiago de Cuba in Oriente province that was intended to operate at a loss – that is, as a tax deduction in the United States.[55] A company official commented that, overall, Texaco "had no problem with the Batista government."[56] American investors also followed the Commerce Department's advice to "[estimate] . . . expected profits of the year and [declare] a capital at least 10 times greater than the anticipated profits" in order to evade Cuba's excess profits tax on all profits exceeding 10 percent of annually declared capital.[57] Finally, in September 1958, Batista issued a decree that transformed Cuba into the investor's free port: "Under this decree U.S. corporations may control from a central office in Cuba all transactions originating or consummated outside of Cuba without being subject to Cuban taxes."[58]

Substantial new U.S. investments flowed into the Cuban economy almost for the duration of the Batista dictatorship. In early 1958, Reynolds Metal, Goodyear, International Telephone & Telegraph, American & Foreign Power, and Texaco Oil expanded their existing operations; Freeport Sulphur's Moa Bay Mining Company moved ahead with the development of a $75 million open nickel and cobalt mine in Oriente province; and the Firestone Tire and Rubber Company began construction of a new tire plant. In tourism, seven hotels and three motels either were projected or under construction, financed mostly by American and Canadian capital, at an estimated total cost of $90 million.[59] In October 1958, the Havana Embassy reported in a confidential memorandum to the Department of State that "Cuban legislation for the encouragement of private enterprise and foreign investment could hardly be improved."[60] By year's end, the total book value of U.S. enterprise in Cuba was, with the exception of Venezuela, the highest in Latin America.[61]

Under Batista, the island's commercial and financial dependence on exporters, private financial institutions, and the American market, which absorbed most of the Cuban sugar crop sold overseas, may even have deepened compared to earlier decades. The government's increased resort to external sources of financing offered international banking institutions, in which the U.S. played leading roles, a means for extending their participation in and influence over the economy. Between 1952 and 1958, Cuba imported 60 percent to 65 percent of its total needs from American sources at an average annual cost of approximately $428 million.[62] This sustained high level of imports, together with the large-scale profit remittances by the Cuban subsidiaries of U.S. multinational corporations, caused negative trade balances. To counter this trend, Batista resorted to short-term borrowings on the international capitalist money markets. During 1957 and 1958, the Cuban National Bank and the Cuban Monetary Stabilization Fund increasingly looked "to seasonal borrowing from the IMF and in the New York market for balance of payments purposes."[63] These initiatives, however, failed to achieve their purpose, and by 1958 the accumulated deficit in the balance of payments had grown to $373.9 million.[64]

Although Batista agreed with the World Bank recommendations that the needs of business dictated a break with the constraints that labor represented, he also recognized the need for some form of labor cooperation to pursue his goal. He resolved this dilemma by relying on the Confederation of Cuban Labor bureaucracy, signing pacts with the union leadership and attacking regional, sectional, and rank-and-file members who created obstacles to the expansion of capital. He sanctioned limited economic struggles by sectors of organized labor and allowed for selective economic gains. In return, the union bureaucracy sought to block each and every effort by rank-and-file groups to engage in "unauthorized" and independent action against the dictatorial regime in either the political or economic arena.

During the first three years of the military dictatorship, the U.S. Department of Commerce noted a general improvement in the capital-labor-government relationship, largely attributable to the union leadership's support of increased local and foreign investment in industry and their moderate wage demands.[65] Even so, individual American subsidiaries, such as the Cuban Electric Company, continued to voice opposition to the seeming ease with which unionized workers were able to gain government backing for wage demands. As one Havana-based official of the Company put it, "the unions were extremely strong in Cuba. So Batista would invariably back the wage demands of the unions. . . . We didn't see anything particularly positive about the Batista period. We had a rough time. We couldn't get rate increases to compensate for increased labor costs we were incurring."[66]

Beginning in 1955, wage levels rose markedly as the regime offered concessions to head off political problems.[67] Like his nationalist predecessors, Batista also issued government decrees or involved the state in resolving union-management stalemates over labor demands. In the latter part of 1957, for example, workers in three key economic sectors (petroleum, banking, and pharmaceuticals) all benefited from regime actions in achieving wage and salary increases.[68] According to a labor report prepared by the Havana Embassy, these wage increases "signified the insistent demand of organized workers to participate in the prosperity of the island."[69] And in April 1958, the government promulgated a new minimum-wage law.[70] The 10 to 30 percent wage gains made during the last year of the Batista regime came out of both collective-bargaining contracts and government resolution of labor and management disputes.[71] The politically necessary partial accord with the trade unions sustained the basic conflict between labor and management, which continued to revolve around such traditional issues as salary demands, job tenure, mechanization of industry, and union-directed work practices. The regime's decision to compromise with labor is a striking reflection of the extent to which an effective, institutionalized labor movement can be more of a day-to-day problem for business than a radicalized labor movement that engages in sporadic and short-term violent action.

The labor problems encountered by the American investment community, nonetheless, were still substantially outweighed by the advantages of locating in Batista's Cuba, especially when compared with most other countries in the region. "Batista," a member of the American Embassy in Havana at the time astutely observed, "represented stability, as much social peace as could be had, and the opportunity for profits."[72] American companies that encountered problems always found Cuban government agencies and officials extremely accessible and highly cooperative – conditions that a number of U.S. businessmen contrasted favorably with those encountered under the Grau and Prío regimes.[73] Some American-owned enterprises, such as the Moa Bay Mining Company, cultivated ties with high-level Batista officials, while others exploited influential Cuban bourgeoisie "who had very good government connections" by appointing them to their Boards of Directors.[74] Few American multinationals had public relations offices in Havana, according to a CIA field operative, "because all you needed was to find a way to get a phone call into Batista and he could fix it."[75] The access to regime officials was facilitated by the American Embassy that functioned, in part, as a "service organization" for the business community in Cuba. In negotiations between Batista and U.S. investors, for example, the Embassy was always prepared to interpose itself on behalf of the involved corporation and exert limited pressures to ensure the most favorable outcome. One Embassy official forthrightly declared that he "was never refused an audience for any American company which had a complaint with a ranking official of the government."[76]

Among American investors as a whole, there was a strong tendency to regard the nascent guerrilla movement as secondary when evaluating Cuba as an environment for profitable operations. During late 1957, however, a geographical division of opinion emerged over the guerrillas' capacity to lead a large-scale struggle against the Batista state. According to an American Consulate official in Santiago de Cuba, "U.S. business firms with interests in eastern Cuba were much more informed about, and realistic concerning, what was happening than those solely in Havana."[77] Pressured by guerrilla activities, some important U.S.

agricultural and mining properties in Oriente province impro-
vised responses to specific rebel demands. Ignoring Ambassador
Earl T. Smith's opposition, many paid "taxes" and provided
requested supplies to the rebels because they "would probably
have been burned out if they had not cooperated."[78] But representatives of these beseiged enterprises were relatively unsuccessful in efforts to impress on their Havana counterparts the seriousness of the situation. Until mid-1958, the majority viewpoint
in Havana was that the antidictatorial struggle was a minor concern. As an executive of the Moa Bay Mining Company described
the thinking of American businessmen in the capital city, "I would
see American business friends in Havana and they would tell me
. . . that it was a lot of nonsense."[79]

During the early months of 1958, a number of U.S. companies
– among them, Cuban Electric, Cuban Telephone, and Sinclair
Oil – suffered substantial property damage from the growing military confrontation between the guerrilla movement and the
Batista regime. But the disruptions failed to erode dramatically
overall corporate optimism regarding the island's investment
advantages. The response of Standard Oil's Cuban subsidiary was
typical: "We expect to be in business here a long time. Political
differences come and go."[80] The widespread perception of the
Cuban polity and society as a secure environment for business
operations and of the economy as structurally resistant to fundamental change was encapsulated in the comment of a New York
banker: "Anybody who gets in there rides a gravy train. No matter
how radical he might be, the way things are done will make him
turn conservative."[81]

Not until Washington's decision to impose an embargo on arms
shipments to the Batista government in March 1958 did members
of the American business community in Havana begin to reassess
the guerrilla threat, and then they became the most active supporters of political confrontation with Castro. According to a
director of the American Chamber of Commerce who was a prominent businessman in Havana, a number of local subsidiaries were
locked in conflict with their parent companies, with the disputes
growing out of differing estimates of the capacity of foreign business interests to negotiate an accommodation with a Castro-led
government. The U.S. headquarters of the large banking, petroleum and sugar corporations instructed their Washington lobby-
ists not to pressure for actions to guarantee against this political
outcome, according to a senior executive of an American multi-

national subsidiary in Havana, because although "they were aware of our opinions . . . they felt they could get along with Castro."[82]

U.S. policy and the Batista regime: the politics of accommodation

The overthrow of parliamentary rule in Cuba in March 1952 by an anticommunist military regime that promised to be "very cooperative on matters affecting American business"[83] was viewed with considerable favor in a number of U.S. government quarters. Within days of the Batista coup, the Cuban Minister of State, Dr. Miguel Angel de la Campa, informed American Ambassador Willard L. Beaulac that the new regime "would do everything reasonable and practical within the law to attract and protect private capital."[84] Similar public and private statements by other senior regime officials weighed significantly in the White House decision to offer swift formal diplomatic recognition to the Batista government.[85] Washington's response also was shaped by the new government's "intention to take steps to curtail international communist activities in Cuba,"[86] the country's status as a primary source of strategic commodities and raw materials (sugar, nickel, etc.), and its role as an important market for American exports.

In subsequent dealings with Batista, several disagreements and concerns arose, including the military government's foot-dragging on the settlement of American private claims and debts already adjudicated by the Cuban courts.[87] But perhaps foremost among the issues causing unease in Washington was the widespread and persistent corruption within the Cuban regime. Alfred Padula gives an evocative description of this aspect of the Batista state: "Every government activity was milked – the lottery, the school lunch program, drivers' licenses, parking meters, teachers' certificates. The police routinely extorted millions in protection money from Havana merchants."[88] Officials of the U.S. Treasury Department were critical of Batistia's fiscal and monetary policies, his inability to control inflation because of bureaucratic disorganization, the lack of an effective tax system, and the failure of the government to assert sufficiently its dictatorial powers to deflect the labor movement's demands. At the State Department, an internal memorandum from 1955 criticized Batista's economic decisions as detrimental to the island's financial stability.[89] The elimination of such frictions and obstacles was not, however, a major source of confrontation and conflict. In practice, the differences were overlooked in view of the larger economic interests of the United States in Cuba.

The evolving U.S. position   Eisenhower administration policy toward Cuba after 1952, according to a State Department participant, "was predominantly one of accepting Batista and doing what we could to get along with him."[90] On assuming his ambassadorial post in Havana in 1952, Arthur Gardner informed Embassy officials that his instructions were from the White House and were basically twofold: to support the existing government and promote the expansion of American economic interests.[91] In 1957, Ambassador Gardner was succeeded by Earl T. Smith, who likewise insisted that his instructions were direct from the White House: "[We] were not to do anything to overthrow Batista but to support Batista as the Government of Cuba that we recognize."[92]

And yet, executive-branch debates over relations with the Batista regime were triggered by the beginning of the guerrilla struggle in December 1956 and the growth of corruption and repression in Cuba. The impetus for a limited reevaluation came from personnel in the Havana Embassy, in the Santiago de Cuba Consulate, and from the Assistant-Secretary level (Inter-American Affairs) in the State Department. These officials sought to distance U.S. policy from the more brutal and parasitic activities of the controlling military formation. Within the Embassy, one officer noted the emergence of "continual disagreements" between those "who felt that something like the Batista regime was about all you could expect in Cuba" and others who argued that the U.S. government should not "spend our days and nights in bed [with the dictatorship]."[93] On the other hand, Ambassador Smith's close personal ties to American business representatives operating out of Havana (whose advocacy of Batista and his policies at this time was unquestioning) powerfully influenced his rigid opposition to any weakening of Washington's support for the military regime.

The sharply differing responses of the U.S. business community in eastern Cuba and that in Havana to the guerrilla threat were mirrored in the American diplomatic community on the island. Cables and other memoranda from officials in the Consulate at Santiago de Cuba discussing the guerrillas' potential and the need to consider new strategies to meet future contingencies were invariably dismissed as alarmist by the upper echelons of the Havana Embassy. To downplay this rurally based challenge to

Batista, some cables from Park Wollam, the American Consul, were doctored by high-ranking Embassy officials before their transmission to the State Department.[94]

Through most of Batista's second presidency, the U.S. executive branch showed little awareness of the need for a coherent strategy for dealing with the guerrillas. This lack of concern, though, did not preclude the appearance of discrete, tactical debates over how to respond to problems created by Batista's armed antagonists. The kidnapping of thirty-one American marines by the insurgents in July 1957, for example, provoked substantial disagreements between the State Department and the Defense Department. The immediate Pentagon request for direct military intervention to rescue the marines was resolutely, and successfully, opposed by State in a series of meetings. The latter, at least initially, favored negotiation on the rationale "that getting into the island would not be difficult but that getting out would be interminable."[95]

At no time between 1952 and March 1958 did bureaucratic antagonisms over Cuba portend a fundamental reevaluation of the relationship between the two governments. The proponents of a changing U.S. policy spoke essentially of marginal or symbolic adjustments of existing relations – that is, fixing up the appearance of ties with the dictatorship. The immediate policy choices of the relevant agencies generally remained anchored in traditional commitments. The State Department sought to maintain diplomatic and political relations and other channels of communication and influence; the Treasury endeavored to persuade Cuban authorities to apply more effective, stringent measures to control inflation and arrest the growing balance-of-payments deficit; the Defense Department continued to cultivate and expand ties with Batista's armed forces; and the Central Intelligence Agency sought a network of reliable Cuban "assets." The "safe precinct" interpretation of Cuba prevented any individual agency from asserting dominance over the application of Cuban policy until the last year of Batista's rule. It was the arms embargo debate inside the executive branch and the Congress during early 1958 that led to a major White House reassessment of support for the military dictatorship. This debate was partly precipitated by rising congressional concern over reports of widespread human rights violations perpetrated by the Cuban military and police forces. Prior to this time, the legislative branch sought little active participation in the shaping of Cuban policy. According to a Cuban Desk officer in the State Department, Congress exerted minimal pressure "on the executive branch to do something about Batista."[96]

The arms embargo debate: origins and outcome

The United States' concentration on diplomatic and political measures to contain and, if possible, mediate Cuba's internal social struggle met with limited success. Despite Batista's arrangements with the national trade union leadership, his policies were beginning to erode the social, economic, and political gains achieved by the working class over the previous twenty years. A crisis grew within the organized labor movement and among nonaffiliated wage workers. Divisions reflecting class, regional, and generational differences began to appear. In mid-1957, extensive interviewing of second-level trade union leaders in Havana, Santiago de Cuba and Pinar del Río, led the Cuban correspondent for the *New York Times* to conclude that "a majority of the rank and file [workers are] anti-Batista."[97] He described the working class in the provincial capital of Santiago as being in "open revolt" against the central government.[98]

The same year, influential segments of the Havana bourgeoisie began to defect from the strategy of civic dialogue and compromise with the repressive regime. Industrialists, whose declining economic position derived from "the intrusion of Batista and his cronies into the private business sector,"[99] and civic, religious, and professional groups opposed to the state's growing use of violence against its opponents became instrumental in organizing urban opposition to Batista and providing material support for the armed guerrillas in the countryside.[100] By early 1958, the deepening social polarization and expanding nationalist opposition to Batista forced U.S. officials to question the viability of the military regime and, principally, its capacity to safeguard foreign economic interests. The military assistance program quickly became the focal point of interagency debate.

The Cuban military had always been dependent on U.S. aid.[101] During the Batista period, the Pentagon provided sophisticated military equipment and arms valued at over $16 million to the Cuban armed forces and organized practical training for over 500 Cuban officers at service institutions in the Panama Canal Zone or at military bases in the United States.[102] The American military assistance program to Cuba in 1956, costing an estimated $6 million, was the second largest in Latin America during that twelve-month period.[103] In concert with its "Overall Plan of Operations for Latin America" in the 1950s, Washington maintained military, naval, and air-force missions and a military assistance and advisory group (MAAG) in Cuba for the supposed purpose of equipping and training the country's forces to meet hemispheric defense responsibilities.[104] Throughout Batista's tenure, American military officials worked to consolidate political and personal ties with the dictatorship and its armed forces.[105]

The bulk of U.S. military assistance grants to the Batista regime came between 1954 and 1958, coinciding with the intensification of the nationalist struggle. Although executive-branch officials regularly explained this aid on the grounds of regional defense commitments, as early as December 1957 a Senate Foreign Relations Committee report offered a more precise assessment: "We have a military mission in Cuba and the Batista government from time to time requests that we sell Cuba arms to supply the Government forces. These arms are, of course, used by the interlocking Army and police to maintain the Government's power."[106] In March 1958, the Assistant Secretary of State for Inter-American Affairs, R. Richard Rubottom, Jr., conceded that "the Cuban Government is certainly using the military equipment which it has at its disposal to beat back armed insurrection."[107] In practice, therefore, American military assistance not only bolstered anticommunist "hemispheric defense" requirements, but also provided essential support for the Bastista government in its effort to maintain political power.

Although Congress had not taken more than passing interest in the Cuban situation prior to early 1958, the deterioration of the human rights climate and the growing domestic unpopularity of the Batista regime led individual legislators to question current White House policy, particularly U.S.-Cuban military relations. Senator Wayne Morse, for instance, characterized the regime as a "fascist dictatorship" and accused the Eisenhower administration of guaranteeing Batista's hold on political power by continuing to ship weapons and Pentagon experts to the island.[108] Some representatives, such as Adam C. Powell, Jr. and Charles Porter, called for an immediate halt to all U.S. military assistance and the withdrawal of the U.S. army, naval, and air-force missions that existed only to serve the Batista coercive apparatus.[109] Porter was also troubled by American support for a regime that was quickly generating domestic opposition among all classes and groups in Cuban society, including important segments of the petty bourgeoisie: "Last month [February] more than 40 religious and professional groups, whose names sound like a roster of Who's-Who Among Respectable Organizations, signed a public statement denouncing Batista's latest farce, an attempt to hold elections on June 1." And the ongoing U.S. military commitment served no purpose beyond "identifying us with [Batista's] unpopular regime." Administration efforts, Porter argued, should be directed toward a negotiated political settlement of the Caribbean conflict.[110] In June, during Senate debate on the 1958 Mutual Security Act, William Proxmire castigated the White House for "yielding to expediency" over Cuba, for providing Batista with military assistance "so he can use [it] to crush the Cuban rebellion."[111]

Despite some evidence of a minor groundswell of legislative concern over the nature of U.S. policy toward a highly repressive political regime – one not loathe to resort to fraudulent elections to legitimate its rule – congressional opposition was confined basically to a few legislators outside the leadership circle. There was no indication of any desire on the part of Congress as a whole to pressure the executive branch for a change in Cuba policy before that branch had made up its own mind.

The major administration antagonists in the debate leading to the March 1958 Cuban arms embargo were the Departments of State and Defense. The Department of Defense argued against the embargo on both ideological and strategic grounds: "The [Cuban] Government has traditionally supported the United States . . . in the United Nations against the onslaughts of communism in the world . . . and I think that we must not overlook the hemispheric defense responsibilities which we have and which Cuba shares with us, of course, under the Rio Treaty."[112] Cuba's geopolitical position in the Caribbean, Batista's support for U.S. regional and global policy, and the vital political and military relationships between the two countries were the preeminent factors shaping Pentagon opposition. Defense officials viewed the embargo as foreshadowing a serious rupture in bilateral ties, as well as a weakened American influence over the Cuban armed forces.

The State Department countered these arguments by saying that the Pentagon lacked sufficient appreciation of how best to safeguard the aggregate U.S. political and material stake in Cuba. Its officials expressed the need to avoid "an explosion" that would endanger the totality of American military and economic interests on the island.[113] It is reasonable to assume that agency officials viewed the continued arms shipments, along with Batista's rejection of Washington's requests to reduce repression and state corruption, as fuel for a widened conflict and a possible strengthening of the Castro guerrilla forces. The scanty nature of the available evidence still shows, however, that the interagency conflict was always framed by the basic commitment to a secure environment for American business in Cuba. In any event, the arms embargo was not a clear-cut victory for the State Department, since the Pentagon maintained its various missions in Havana. This ambiguous outcome may be explained partially by the volatility of the social situation at that moment in Cuba, when key elements of society were shifting or reevaluating their allegiance to the dictatorial regime.

Nationalist struggle and the failure of U.S. strategy

Before 1958, the White House and the State Department were "not particularly interested in Cuba affairs."[114] American policymakers occasionally exerted limited pressures for discrete reforms, but mostly it was business as usual. This posture changed abruptly during the first half of 1958 as the appearance of a broad-based opposition movement incorporating such unlikely allies as conservative business executives and nationalist guerrillas revealed the growing political isolation of the Batista dictatorship. The shifting internal correlation of forces impressed upon U.S. officials the need to develop a strategy that could influence the outcome of this burgeoning social conflict and prevent any possibility of anticapitalist or radical nationalist forces gaining power in Cuba. In this crisis context, complicated by the collapse of Batista's major military offensive against the guerrillas in June and July 1958, the State Department, the executive-branch agency most directly concerned with overall U.S. political and economic interests in any given country, assumed primary operational responsibility for ensuring a resolution acceptable to the imperial state.

Confronted with the possible collapse of a longstanding client regime, the fundamental issue for Washington in the event of Batista's demise was how to conserve the institutional power of the military and preserve other U.S. strategic, as well as economic, interests during and after any political transition. Of immediate concern was the threat to the interests of the business community in Cuba and to overall U.S. influence in the state and society posed by a Batista armed forces that was fragmenting with each passing day. One State Department official recalled: "U.S. policymakers were concerned with the disintegration of the Cuban army in the sense that a breakdown of the military as an institution would present a threat to commercial interests. That is, the army was law and order."[115] Another addressed the more general U.S. concern in the event of a military collapse: the loss of "a resource for the maintenance of relative order during a [political] transition period."[116] This uneasiness over the Batista state structure was not confined to worries about the military: "Yes, we were concerned about the distegration of the Cuban army but also about the disintegration of most of the functioning institutions in Cuba which supported the regime."[117]

The abrupt deterioration of Batista's political and military position created confusion within the State Department and other agencies, forcing officials to improvise strategies hastily. Policymakers were operating in a remarkably fluid context that nearly dissolved their capacity to anticipate and influence events. The turmoil was described by a participant in the tactical debate:

The U.S. was caught in a dilemma. Nobody was all that enthusiastic about Batista. Everybody understood that he was unpopular, his government corrupt, etc. At the same time, one had great reservations about Castro. Earlier on there seemed to be other options – Castro was not the only anti-Batista movement – but by the summer of 1958 with the failure of the Batista campaign and the subsequent rise in Castro's stocks, he became the option and all other revolutionary groups had to fall in or fall out.[118]

Within the Havana Embassy, disagreements surfaced between the Ambassador, Earl T. Smith, and some of his senior officials. Daniel Braddock, Deputy Chief of Mission, interpreted the failure of Batista's summer military offensive as signalling the imminent demise of his regime. Forcing Batista's swift ouster in favor of a moderate transitional government, he believed, offered the only chance, although remote, of preventing a Castro victory.[119] But in early August 1958, the Ambassador transmitted to the State Department a confidential paper assessing the costs and benefits of various policies. Strict neutrality was viewed as "a drifting policy under which we would not use our influence to direct the course of events in Cuba." Political party fragmentation and polarized social forces presented "overwhelming" obstacles to any effort to implement the electoral option. A strategy to "encourage moderate elements within the Armed Forces and the legal opposition to overthrow Batista and establish a provisional government" offered the greatest likelihood of a regime "capable of maintaining law and order." The major drawbacks to supporting a military and civilian coup, according to the confidential policy paper, were the almost certain risks and difficulties involved in how to do so: "How far the United States can go about promoting a change of government by this means is hazardous. Such steps would mean direct intervention for the overthrow of the Government of Cuba, and the possibilities of success are problematical. Therefore, it is too risky to attempt." The final choice, favored by Ambassador Smith, was to forego any tampering with the existing government-to-government relationship and "support the Batista government to the extent of complying with our commitments and contractual agreements and not give moral support to the revolutionary opposition."[120]

The Eisenhower administration's paramount concern was to deny political power to the nationalist forces under Fidel Castro. The preferred alternative was a procapitalist government not identified with the excesses of Batista's rule, but oriented toward constructing a more efficient and less corrupt state. "Nobody in the State Department," said one official, "wanted Castro to get in."[121] Eisenhower himself stated that if intelligence reports about Castro's radicalism proved accurate, then the only option was "some kind of nondictatorial 'third force', neither Castroite nor Batistiano."[122] Batista, though, refused to capitulate to Washington's requests for his resignation in favor of a transitional, antidictatorial, anti-Castro regime. Fearing that Batista's obstinacy would let loose "a more extreme reaction, a government extremely hostile to the United States,"[123] State Department officials decided upon a multifaceted strategy combining diplomacy and coercion to, at once, forestall the guerrillas, oust Batista, and create an interim or transitional government composed of anti-Castro civilian and military individuals hostile to the Batista dictatorship but compatible with American political and economic objectives in Cuba. The CIA became the designated instrument in this last gasp at preventing a nationalist guerrilla victory *"without openly violating our non-intervention commitments."*[124] Washington's frustration over Batista's refusal to take any intiative that might undermine the Castro challenge was evident in Assistant Secretary of State R. Richard Rubottom's recollection of the period and the particular issue: "we were doing whatever we could . . . to get Batista to do some of the things that . . . would at least have presented a chance for some kind of junta government or civilian front government in which Castro would not have been the sole voice. Of course, Batista didn't pay any attention to any of this."[125] Instead, he presided over fraudulent national elections in November 1958 that further isolated the regime and divested it of its last shreds of legitimacy.

Secretary of State Herter kept in close communication with President Eisenhower on Department activities regarding Cuba during the final months of 1958. "The Department clearly does not want to see Castro succeed to the leadership of the Government," he told the White House in a December memorandum. *"We are therefore seeking, by all means short of outright intervention to bring about a political solution in Cuba which will keep the Castro movement from power."*[126]

The State Department attempted to enlist regional support for its anti-Castro policy and help find an alternative to Castro. It even entertained application of the anticommunist Caracas Resolution of the Organization of American States (OAS), which had been successfully employed in the 1954 overthrow of the Arbenz government in Guatemala. In a brief to the National Security Council, CIA Director Allen Dulles stated that "Communists and other extreme radicals appear to have penetrated the Castro movement."[127] But Secretary Herter reluctantly admitted that there was "insufficient evidence on which to base a charge that the rebels are communist-dominated." Consultations with regional governments about the possibility of calling the OAS to action made no headway: "except for Ecuador, none of them has expressed willingness to take any initiative."[128]

Although the U.S. government instituted an embargo on military materials and all forms of combat arms to the Batista regime in March 1958, the executive order did not exclude every type of military assistance. In addition, Pentagon officials maintained liaisons and other channels of influence through their army, naval, and air-force missions and shipments of "non-combat" equipment such as communications materials.[129] Although it is difficult to measure with precision the military and psychological impact of the embargo on the Cuban armed forces, the partial rupture allowed American military officials to contribute important logistical and tactical support to the Batista forces up to the very moment of the nationalist victory. The Havana Embassy, especially Ambassador Smith, also maintained communication with the military high command, partly to monitor any anti-Castro *golpista* tendency within the armed forces capable of favorably affecting the outcome of the conflict.[130]

One of the most notable, albeit unsuccessful, nonmilitary interventions involved the so-called Pawley Mission to Cuba in December 1958. William Pawley, a former American Ambassador to Peru and Brazil, initially proposed to the State Department and the CIA that a U.S. representative be sent to Cuba to convince Batista "to capitulate to a caretaker government unfriendly to him, but satisfactory to us, whom we could immediately recognize and give military assistance to in order that Fidel Castro not come to power."[131] President Eisenhower showed considerable interest in the scheme, to the point of "instructing the State Department to work out a program offering inducements to make the proposal attractive to Batista," including an immediate provision of $10 million in military equipment to an interim regime. By Pawley's own testimony, he was at first given the authority to speak in the name of the White House. At the last meeting of administration officials to coordinate the mission, however, it was decided to withdraw the envoy's authorization to act on behalf of the President.[132] This action probably reflected the State Department's concern to "hedge its bets" in a situation now fraught with intangibles. Characteristically, the decisionmaking process in this instance was highly centralized so that strategy discussions in Washington deliberately bypassed the Havana Embassy and the U.S. Ambassador.[133] Embassy official Wayne S. Smith writes that only the CIA station chief, Jim Noel, was privy to the Pawley-Batista meeting before it took place.[134]

The December 9 Pawley mission to Batista took place amid another effort (one involving the CIA more directly) to forestall a Castro victory by promoting a military coup and placing Colonel Ramon Barquín in command of the armed forces. Barquín, a former Cuban military attache to the United States was, at the time, imprisoned on the Isle of Pines for his leadership role in a mid-1956 abortive *golpe* against Batista by dissident officers. A liberal career professional, he was regarded by many of his peers as "one officer who could defeat Castro."[135]

In late 1958, Justo Carrillo, Agricultural Development Bank president under Prío and a leader of the small anti-Batista Montecristi Movement, sought State and Defense Department interest in freeing Colonel Barquín to conduct another military coup to both oust Batista and confront Castro. For reasons not known, U.S. officials decided not to act then. Later Carrillo, exiled in Miami, was invited to a November meeting with William H. Carr (president of Carr Aluminum and a close friend of CIA Director Allen Dulles), who apparently was there on behalf of the CIA. After discussing the plan to free Barquín, Carr sent two people (whom Carrillo believed were CIA operatives) to assess the quality of the weapons and explosives, together with a plane, that Carrillo's group already had purchased for use in the commando-type raid. Contacts continued, but there was still no U.S. interest in freeing Barquín to run a coup. Carr informed Carrillo that the plan was too risky, noting that Carrillo's participation, as an exile living in the United States, would be illegal under American neutrality laws.[136]

On December 26, Carrillo received another American visitor (apparently with Washington ties) who expressed interest in the Barquín scheme, but who dismissed the feasibility of a commando raid and suggested bribing the Isle of Pines warden to release Barquín[137] According to Hugh Thomas, a CIA operative with Carrillo's backing was dispatched to the Isle of Pines on December 30 with $100,000 for Barquín's release.[138] But it was not until January 1 or 2 that Barquín was freed, and then it was on orders from the new chief of the Joint General Staff, General Eulogio Cantillo, who assumed power when Batista fled on December 31. Cantillo also had expressed hope that Barquín could regroup the armed forces and prevent a Castro victory, but the hope was in vain, for the guerrilla leaders wanted the complete and unconditional surrender of Batista military forces and refused to consider negotiations with the army leadership. With the arrival of the first guerrilla columns in Havana at the beginning of January, the Barquín gambit ended, and Barquín, who had been given command of the armed forces by General Cantillo, relinquished control to the revolutionary forces.[139]

The CIA was a pervasive presence in Batista's Cuba, developing "assets," "propaganda outlets," and other liaisons throughout the political, social, coercive, and administrative fabric of Cuban society and its state structure.[140] For the duration of Batista's rule, the Agency performed as an instrument of executive-branch policymakers.[141] In discussing the activities of covert field personnel, an Havana Embassy official commented that "they did exactly what they were told to do."[142]

After December 1956, the CIA began to reassess the notion of Cuba as a "safe precinct" and advocate a long-range strategy to

counter the renewed historic guerrilla struggle for national liberation. This created "considerable dissension" between successive
CIA Chiefs of Station and Ambassadors Gardner and Smith, who
"were both absolutely convinced that Castro wasn't going to
come out of the hills."[143] During 1957 and 1958, the agency's
Havana Station sided with those Embassy "liberals," such as Richard Cushing, Daniel Braddock, and John Topping, who expressed
concern over the fragility of the military regime's social and institutional supports.[144] These Embassy and CIA officials emphasized
the seriousness of the guerrilla challenge, raising the possibility
that these rurally based nationalists eventually might threaten
Batista's hold.

In late 1958, as Washington increasingly embraced the idea of
clandestine operations, the CIA assumed an important role in the
State Department's effort to develop courses of action which
might lead to a viable solution."[145] The CIA, according to Deputy
Director of Plans Richard Bissell, was instrumental in executive-
branch efforts to apply the "intermediate solution." He put it this
way: "We were quite involved in some efforts to persuade Batista
to step down voluntarily in favor of a group that he might desig-
nate."[146] Batista's refusal then led Agency officials to lobby for a
longer term strategy that would, at a minimum, limit the impact
of a victorious antidictatorial guerrilla movement. As one covert
field officer at the time observed,

The CIA prediction was that Castro would come out of the hills but into
a vacuum in Havana. Better that he come into Havana into a coalition
government. . . . The CIA wanted Castro in a context of checks and
balances.[147]

The notion of "checks and balances" was, to some extent,
appropriated by the State Department in the waning days of Batista's presidency. "With Batista out and an interim government in,"
a then Department Cuba specialist declared, "Castro and the 26th
of July Movement would have been effectively, if not totally, isolated. Or they would have had to come into the picture with other
elements."[148] Ultimately, these and other belated attempts by the
Eisenhower administration to take charge and shape the direction
of events in Cuba were unable to derail the political revolution
fought by the nationalist guerrillas. Castro's call for a revolutionary general strike at the end of December was the *coup de grace*
to these imperial endeavors. The strike facilitated the gradual
movement of the guerrilla forces from eastern Cuba to Havana

"and their consolidation of all strategic military points," thereby
undermining the possibility of any successful military coup taking
place in the capital city.[149]

Conclusion

With the decline of the liberal parliamentary governments of the
1940s, the nonsocialist alternative in Cuba gradually lost its integrity. The Batista military coup of March 1952 forced to the margins of political life those petty bourgeois and bourgeois elements
that had controlled the Cuban state since 1944. The historical
meaning of the coup is found largely in Cuba's greater receptive-
ness to foreign capital, which generated limited industrial growth
while maintaining a monoculture economy producing for and subject to foreign markets. A repressive capitalist economy based on
the dominance of foreign companies, a state administration mired
in corruption, and inadequate state redistributive mechanisms all
contributed to the creation of social tension out of which new
political forces emerged to take up the nationalist mantle.

The July 26 Movement grew out of the failure of reform elements in Cuba to meet either the challenge of the U.S. presence
or the need for fundamental socioeconomic change. The base on
which the emerging nationalist movement built its support was
partly the tradition and subculture of political resistance and
armed popular struggle incorporating a distinct anti-imperialist,
anticapitalist perspective.[150] The Movement began as an amor-
phous and relatively undisciplined body of groups united around
a common end. Its growth into a coalition of many groups incorporating diverse social and political forces espousing several ideological perspectives required that the Movement's appeal not be
focused primarily on any particular class.

During 1957 and 1958, the Batista dictatorship also was confronted by a revolt of wage and salaried workers and local trade
union leaders in the provincial cities who were acting independently of the national trade union bureaucracy. Although the
Communist Party was not a direct contributing factor to the success of the national liberation struggle, its role as a transmitter of
anticapitalist interpretations of social change and its active leadership of the Cuban proletariat for almost three decades were crit-

ical to the emergence of the urban and rural workers as the instruments of the national and social revolution after January 1959.[151]

Between 1952 and 1958, the Batista government accorded foreign capital a central role in Cuba's development; provided the U.S. economy easy access to sugar, tobacco, minerals, and other products; cooperated in restrictions on trade in strategic materials with the socialist bloc; and consistently supported American Cold War global and regional policies. Prior to March 1958, Washington thus viewed Cuba as a relatively "safe precinct" for capital accumulation and expansion, notwithstanding the emergence of large-scale urban and rural opposition to the Bastista dictatorship. Washington also displayed minimal interest in devising a coherent policy toward the internal political struggle. The limited debates that took place in Washington were largely confined to the Departments of State and Defense and did not presume a shift in overall policy of support for Batista. The twin issues of state corruption and repression were important only as they affected foreign business operations. They did not lead directly to major changes in U.S. policy.

The first intimation of a movement toward disengagement from the Batista government coincided with the March 1958 decision to embargo arms sales to Cuba, despite the Pentagon's vigorous opposition. The resolution of the arms-embargo debate underscored a growing State Department concern over the possibility that the guerrillas would dominate the leadership of the increasingly formidable antidictatorial movement. Contrary to standard accounts, American policy toward Batista's opponents was not distinguished by "evenhandedness" or "flexibility," but by its determination to prevent the emergence of a post-Batista government under Fidel Castro. Following the collapse of Batista's military offensive against the guerrillas in mid-1958, the State Department took active charge of the debate over tactics to apply to the new situation which, from Washington's vantage point, potentially threatened the U.S. economic stake in Cuba. Within limited time and other constraints, the State Department relied heavily on CIA covert politics, exercised through a network of Cuban "assets," in an unsuccessful effort to defeat the guerrilla forces.

The changing political context in Cuba dictated a shift to tactics more flexible than probably would have been originally contemplated. The U.S. government collaborated with and supported the military dictatorship so long as it firmly controlled the population and state apparatus and promoted American economic interests. During the initial growth of relatively uncoordinated, local political opposition, the Eisenhower administration worked with the regime, but criticized its lack of tactical flexibility while simultaneously developing ties with the nonrevolutionary civilian opposition. The change in Cuba from slowly growing opposition to extensive revolt then pressed U.S. policymakers to try to strengthen the antidictatorial conservative-reformist-liberal forces and contemplate alliances with the military in order to isolate the guerrillas. But the advanced state of disarray and demoralization within the armed forces following the failure of the 1958 summer offensive against the guerrillas and Washington's lack of any significant internal political or social base of support sharply limited the U.S. government's area for maneuver.[152] The evidence suggests that it may have been precisely the massive internal support enjoyed by the rural insurgents, combined with the American failure to secure regional (Organization of American States) support for anti-Castro actions, that limited serious consideration of direct U.S. military intervention.

United States policy was not geared to maintain any one individual or political clique, but rather to preserve the Cuban state and economic system and the American position therein. The question Batista's activities posed was: Under what circumstances does a cooperative dictator become expendable? What appeared from one perspective as ambivalent policy toward Batista during 1958 in fact expressed two concerns: a perception in Washington that his effectiveness had eroded beyond repair, and a willingness by senior policymakers to recognize the need for political changes, for a changing of the guard.

The Eisenhower administration's unease over what to do about Batista and what form its intervention should take in the Cuban struggle during 1958 cannot be explained as just another instance of "bourgeois morality" acting as a brake on American policy. Although "bourgeois morality" has always been an important ideological element in U.S. policy toward Latin America (evidence Woodrow Wilson's "making the world safe for democracy," Franklin D. Roosevelt's "Good Neighbor Policy," John F. Kennedy's "Alliance for Progress," Jimmy Carter's "human rights" doctrine), its role has always coincided with perceived or actual challenges to U.S. regional dominance. In all instances, the fundamental purpose of these moral appeals has been to assert American dominance. But neither the overthrow of Eisenhower-supported dictatorial regimes in Peru and Venezuela (and eventually in Cuba) nor the hostile reception accorded Vice President Richard Nixon during his Latin American tour in the spring of 1958 led the administration to jettison its notion of the continent as a "safe precinct" or to make major changes in policy. There was no strong support within the White House or State Department for weakening ties with traditional political allies.[153] While the United States looked with dismay at the possibility of a Castro-dominated government in Cuba, there was little disposition at that time to view the events in Cuba as part of some deeper current that might threaten the American position in the hemisphere. But what made the Cuban experience different from other successful antidictatorial movements of the period, and had profound implications for future U.S.-Cuba relations, was its virtual destruction of the military and police forces of the old state.

3. The United States in Cuba 1959–1961: national-social revolution, state transformation, and the limits of imperial power*

> I do feel this: here is a country that you would believe, on the basis of our history, would be one of our real friends. The whole history . . . would seem to make it puzzling matter to figure out just exactly why the Cubans and the Cuban Government would be so unhappy when, after all, their principal market is right here, their best market. You would think they would want good relationships. I don't know exactly what the difficulty is.
>
> President Eisenhower (October 1959)[1]

> In the face of these unwarranted and unjustified attacks, the United States Government has maintained an attitude of patience and forebearance.
>
> White House Telegram to
> Latin American Missions (January 1960)[2]

United States policy toward Cuba after 1959 had a clear-cut political purpose: to destabilize and overthrow the Castro government. Faced with a working-class-based government looking to assert local control over the Cuban economy, a consensus emerged within the executive branch in support of confrontation on a bilateral and, subsequently, regional and global scale. The closure of historic "access points" (military, political parties, and so forth) in the Cuban state and society during the transition to socialism made it impossible for the United States to rely on local allies and instead to concentrate on external pressures to create economic

*This chapter contains material that appeared in an article entitled "Reinterpreting the State-Class Relationship: American Corporations and U.S. Policy Toward Cuba, 1959–1960," *Comparative Politics*, Vol. 16, No. 1, October 1983, pp. 67–83.

disruption, societal dislocation, and the disintegration of the Castro regime.

The Eisenhower administration's policymaking process exhibited much greater coherence and less disarray than is commonly assumed. During the early period of the Cuban Revolution, the United States was quite active in behalf of American economic interests on the Caribbean island. Executive-branch officials followed a strategy for dealing with the Castro regime according to their own conception and schedule of how best to achieve its demise. It sought to direct a business class that appeared disoriented, fragmented, vacillating, and particularistic in outlook, lacked a coherent political perspective and was noticeable for the absence of sufficient class consciousness to confront the immediate tasks.

The United States and the Cuban revolution: initial responses

The Eisenhower White House was distinctly worried about political developments in Cuba following Batista's overthrow.[3] Senior policymakers envisioned an erosion of relations and barely concealed their hostility toward the idea of a Cuban government dominated by the guerrilla wing of the antidictatorial movement. There was particular "concern in the administration over expropriation, or the possibility of expropriation, from the time Castro came in."[4] Washington placed the onus for a satisfactory working relationship more or less squarely on the new Cuban leadership. To the extent that a "viable relationship" was given any credence by the White House and its foreign-policy agencies, it was qualified to the effect that "one had to be very, very wary."[5] A State Department officer characterized the atmosphere within the CIA, the NSC, and the Pentagon in terms of "a fair amount of panic."[6] CIA Director Allen Dulles even predicted that "Blood will flow in the streets [of Havana]."[7]

The decision to appoint Philip W. Bonsal as the new Ambassador was both an index of U.S. mistrust of the Castro leadership and part of the attempt to order the course of events in a manner favorable to the anti-Castro forces. Bonsal previously had served as Ambassador to Bolivia, presiding between March 1957 and January 1959 when American public-aid agencies and international financial institutions joined forces to exploit the Bolivian regime's dependence on external financing and force the government of Paz Estensorro to moderate its nationalist development program:

"he had proved an effective instrument of our policy to slow down the revolution [of 1952] and to persuade Bolivians to postpone reforms in favor of budget balancing. Sending Bonsal to Cuba revealed clearly what we expected from the island."[8] A senior political officer in the Havana Embassy described Bonsal's instructions from the State Department on his departure for Cuba. They were to remain "cool and distant" until Castro showed himself willing to establish a "friendly" relationship with the United States.[9]

United States policymakers also were preoccupied with the likely ideological orientation of the new regime.[10] In February, CIA Director Dulles told Eisenhower that he was troubled by the fact that, "though Castro's government is *not* Communist-dominated, Communists have worked their way into the labor unions, the armed forces and other organizations."[11] Concerning Castro's visit to the United States in April 1959, a senior member of the Cuban delegation later wrote, "the subject of Communist infiltration arose at every opportunity."[12] An official of the CIA's clandestine division was secretly dispatched to New York to meet with Castro "and gave him a two hour briefing on the dangers of Communism in Cuba."[13] Vice-President Nixon expressed a similar concern in his celebrated meeting with the Cuban leader, whose apparent refusal to give credence to the issue led Nixon to write a memorandum to the CIA, the State Department, and the White House describing Castro as "either incredibly naive about Communism or under Communist discipline," a factor that would have to be considered in future dealings.[14] Secretary of Defense Neil McElroy discussed the subject of Castro and communism with President Eisenhower during the April visit:

I remember clearly having a discussion with President Eisenhower about the threat to our country of having a communist island so close to our shores and expressed to the President the belief that if the Castro government turned out clearly to be Communist oriented, we should have to take whatever action was necessary, to remove him and his group from their control of the Cuban Government. It's my clear recollection that President Eisenhower agreed. This of course is not to say that we agreed on any specific action at that time.[15]

Initial possibilities for a short-term *modus vivendi* with the nationalist government rested largely on two developments. First, the transfer of the remnants of Batista's armed forces to the constitutionalist Colonel Ramon Barquín created some optimism in the government about a reorganized, old military apparatus that conceivably could neutralize Castro's independent military force and "add a certain amount of stability to the situation."[16] Second, there was Castro's selection of "reasonable, liberal, reputable people whom we knew" to form a substantial portion of the governing cabinet, especially the allocation of senior economic ministries to noted procapitalist figures.[17] The key appointees included Felipe Pazos (National Bank president under Prío and Batista and former IMF official) as president of the Cuban National Bank, Rufo López-Fresquet (formally an economic consultant to Cuba's National Association of Manufacturers) as Minister of the Treasury and Finance, and Regino Boti (recalled from his position with the United Nations Economic Commission for Latin America) as Minister of the Economy. In all, of the seventeen cabinet members, only six had been actively involved in urban resistance and only three were members of the guerrilla movement.[18]

On January 15, 1959, the Havana Embassy provided its assessment of the first cabinet in a dispatch to the Department of State: "[It is] basically friendly toward the United States and oriented against communism."[19] The strategic location of antidictatorial capitalists within the new Cuban government led U.S. policymakers to the dual approach of maintenance of diplomatic relations with the nationalists to facilitate communication with forces opposed to social revolution in Cuba, and symbolic hostility toward individual actions that threatened large-scale social and economic change. One such symbolic act was the immediate dispatch of destroyers to Havana harbor in early January in response to the sporadic destruction of various foreign-owned public utility and tourist enterprises at the time of the guerrilla army's arrival in Havana.

Congressional reaction to the Castro victory was mixed, extending from those who approved of Batista's ouster, to segments hostile to the possibility of a Castro-dominated government, to others who "had some reservations about Castro but thought it might be possible to encourage or persuade him to be a sort of populist reformer instead of a revolutionary."[20] Among the more vociferous opponents were some conservative legislators who "went so far as to recommend shutting off United States' credit or barring Cuban sugar,"[21] and liberals such as Wayne Morse, the chairman of the Senate Foreign Relations Subcommittee on Latin American Affairs, who evoked the image of a "blood bath" in reacting to the

relatively limited number of executions carried out by the revolutionary courts during the early months of 1959.[22]

Economic nationalism and external dependence: a vulnerable Cuban economy

During the first twelve months of the Cuban Revolution, enormous pressures were put on the island's limited financial
resources and foreign-exchange reserves. The institution of an
ambitious social redistributive program took place amid declining
revenues from trade and tourism, large-scale capital flight, a fall
in available tax revenues, and the diversion of approximately $100
million for military purchases to guarantee the regime's survival
from hostile internal and external forces.[23] Not surprisingly, the
U.S. was in the forefront of efforts to take advantage of Cuba's
economic vulnerability, through diplomatic and other means, to
constrict the nationalist regime's access to alternative external
sources of credits, loans and markets necessary to sustain and
accelerate the process of socioeconomic change.

The new regime's most immediate political objective was to
create mass commitment to a structural transformation of the
economy, which meant the working population had to have a
material stake in the process from its inception. Redistribution of
the country's wealth became a natural priority. Despite inherited,
formidable economic problems, the need to acquire political and
social support relegated issues such as rationality in economic
planning to secondary consideration.

To consolidate and deepen its support among the island's urban
and rural workers, the nationalist government mandated a series
of wage and salary increases, allocated funds for major new public
projects, reduced mortgage and electric power rates, lowered the
costs of purchasing medical supplies, and cancelled the U.S.-
owned Cuban Telephone Company's 1957 rate increase. It also
decreased urban rents by 30 to 50 percent and announced a new
law requiring the sale of vacant urban properties if the owners
failed to begin immediate construction.[24] The Vacant Lot Law
eliminated speculative profits on unimproved land and eroded the
economic base of the local bourgeoisie, whose combined personal
income from urban and rural rents in 1956 was $173 million.[25] A
correspondent for *Fortune* magazine reported: "The real-estate
laws have adversely affected almost everyone of any degree of
wealth in Cuba."[26] But they contributed to their purpose: to

increase disposable income and hence the purchasing power of
the working class while maintaining prices at a stable level.
Between January and April, there was an income redistribution
from the propertied and entrepreneurial classes to the wage-
laboring class of at least 15 percent of the country's national
income.[27] In the countryside, the initial land reform beneficiaries
were the squatters and tenant farmers in the province of Oriente,
although not at the expense of indigenous or foreign agricultural
capitalists.

In practice, U.S. economic interests were relatively untouched
by these early measures. The extension of controls on import and
foreign exchange transactions, for example, was not accompanied
by new restrictions on profit remittances abroad. In some
instances, the government's policies were described by the business community as beneficial, if indirectly, to capitalist enterprise.
The institution of a more effective tax program was greeted with
approval by the investment community, since "it greatly
simplifie[d] the old code . . . and offer[ed] strong incentives for
investment in manufacturing enterprises."[28]

Although the initial economic measures were designed for a primarily political purpose, the depressed state of the Cuban economy remained a central, immediate problem for the new regime.
Not only had high-ranking Batista officials sacked the treasury up
to the last minute, but also the annual budget was running a $50
million deficit at the time of the Castro victory.[29] The rapid application of foreign-exchange and import controls to stem the outflow of capital and decrease the level of imports failed to produce
the desired results. "The impact of these regulations [was] largely
psychological since imports [were] licensed freely and the
exchange controls (except for the importation of banknotes)
[were] more nominal than real."[30]

Cuba's monoculture dependence also fueled the fires of economic recession. In June 1959, the world-market price of sugar
fell to its lowest level in eighteen years. A U.S. Treasury Department study estimated that this would result in a loss of foreign
exchange of $150 million compared to 1958. Since available for-
eign-exchange reserves at the time of Batista's overthrow stood at
around a mere $77 million, the severity of this projected loss is
clear. Treasury also anticipated that Cuba's balance-of-payments
deficit could reach as high as $200 million by the end of 1959.[31]
The nationalist regime's financial problems were compounded by
the fall in the value of the peso from $1 to 30 cents during Feb-

ruary, curtailed domestic private capital investment, large-scale unemployment, and a gradual decline in tourist expenditures to an estimated $10 million in 1959 (compared to $60 million in 1955).[32]

The U.S. government attempted to capitalize on these inherited serious economic problems to limit the degree of change. In early January 1959, E. M. Bernstein, economic advisor to Cuban National Bank president Felipe Pazos, held an informal discussion on the island's financial situation with the U.S. Director of the IMF, Frank Southard. He informed Southard that Pazos wanted to increase Cuba's foreign-exchange reserves while holding the peso at par with the dollar. Bernstein then detailed the government's preferred strategy, which centered around the application of heavy excise taxes to limit certain categories of imports, the introduction of foreign-exchange controls on capital and other transactions by local businessmen, and possible multimillion dollar borrowings from the International Monetary Fund (IMF), the U.S. Department of the Treasury, and private American banks "to provide confidence in [the] peso."[33] The American IMF Director responded that any Fund mission to Cuba to assess requests for financial assistance "would be particularly concerned with budget and credit prospects," rather than with foreign-exchange controls.[34] The State Department concurred in this lack of enthusiasm for making foreign exchange controls one element in the Castro government's strategy for shoring up the island's floundering economy.[35] Meanwhile, segments of the U.S. private banking community were calling for a "get tough" approach by Washington and the financial institutions. At an Export-Import Bank meeting in March, Paul Brand, an IMF official recently returned from Cuba, referred to a First National City Bank report that attributed the island's "creeping financial paralysis" exclusively to the new government's policies.[36] Brand told Export-Import Bank officials that First National City Bank executives had indicated that they "would not consider any credit to the Cubans, and hoped that the U.S. government would not get involved until it learns all the facts."[37]

In April, Castro accepted an invitation from the American Society of Newspaper Editors to visit the United States. He was accompanied by a delegation composed of the government's senior economic officials – Felipe Pazos (President of the National Bank), Rufo López-Fresquet (Minister of Finance), Regino Boti (Minister of the Economy) and Ernesto Betancourt (Managing

Director of the Foreigh Trade Bank). The unofficial nature of the visit derived from Castro's "express[ed] fears of being invited to the White House and of being photographed with the President of the United States as one more Latin American leader 'sold out' to imperialism."[38] Eisenhower greeted the news of the trip with coldness and investigated the possibility of denying Castro a visa. "Advised that under the circumstances this would be unwise," he later wrote, "I nevertheless refused to see him."[39]

Although senior officials of the Cuban government informed IMF official Paul Brand that Havana was not currently prepared to consider a Fund standby agreement "which would involve Cuban commitments regarding fiscal monetary, foreign exchange policies,"[40] they did express interest (via a memorandum to the Havana Embassy) in obtaining U.S. economic assistance for long-term development projects (e.g., agricultural and industrial credit banks, sewer and aquaduct construction) and a balance-of-payments loan to help lower unemployment. A U.S. Treasury's background briefing paper composed in preparation for Castro's visit recommended a "hardline" response to any Cuban request for aid, to the extent that it be made contingent on acceptance of an IMF stabilization loan or concrete assurances regarding the future role of foreign capital in the nationalist development program.[41] This report quite likely reflected Treasury thinking that, by applying a freeze on badly needed economic assistance, the pressure might erode Castro's political base and shift governmental power to capitalist modernizers in the cabinet.

Despite the hostile Treasury posture, all the involved U.S. government and international financial institutions were favorably impressed by the "competent orthodox professional officials" in the Cuban delegation.[42] With Castro's concurrence, these economic and fiscal specialists discussed Cuba's problems and plans with officials of State, Treasury, the IMF, the World Bank, and the Export-Import Bank. Finance Minister López-Fresquet also travelled to New York City for meetings with American businessmen interested in Cuba as an investment site.[43] Although Castro had expressly forbidden any direct request for economic assistance, these gatherings did advance the professional and personal ties among the participants.

It was apparent that some U.S. government agencies and multilateral development banks were disposed to offer large-scale aid in the hope of containing the socioeconomic changes taking place in Cuba. As Felipe Pazos recalled, "the attitude of the U.S. at this pre-preliminary stage was that of a most willing lender."[44] A State Department official who attended the meeting between the Cuban ministers and State and Treasury representatives recalled that "we were prepared to offer them a loan of $25 million then and there. . . . Boti, the spokesman for the group that included Pazos and López-Fresquet, got up and said 'We are here to talk to you' and they just wanted Mr. Rubottom to know that they were not prepared to discuss any assistance to Cuba, and at that moment they had not decided that they wanted assistance."[45]

John Parke Young, the State Department's chief of the division of international finance, played a key role in executive-branch efforts to coordinate the various funding proposals emanating from the U.S. government, the IMF, and the private New York multinational banks.[46] Ultimately, according to Young, the Cubans left "without even requesting financial aid," and projected future discussions in Washington by members of the Mission never occurred.[47]

Although the Cuban economic team held assiduously to the position that the purpose of the trip was expository and not linked to requests for aid, the explicit conditions attached to economic assistance from these public and banking institutions helped shape the Cuban and, more important, Castro's response, or nonresponse. State Department officials informed Castro's advisors that American budgetary and balance-of-payments assistance was, in the first instance, dependent on Havana's ability to negotiate an IMF stabilization loan. Argentina's recent experience with a similar loan – which was accompanied by lowered wages, price increases, social-welfare budget cuts, and a rise in the cost of living – was solid evidence of the likely political and economic consequences of Cuban acceptance of the "general performance" conditions attached to an IMF loan.[48] Beyond the U.S. pressure on Cuba to seek IMF funds, however, it became more and more evident that no assistance would be forthcoming "until the character and goals of the new government [were] clearer" and, as one Washington official put it, "the dust had settled."[49] Ultimately, all the potential aid donors desired prior "clarification" of the evolving social nature and development orientation of the nationalist regime.

Castro's visit produced a difference of opinion in the United States over whether "to sit back and await developments – 'to let the Castro government go through the wringer'" and thereby force Havana's acceptance of an IMF loan, or "to take the initiative by manifesting a willingness to give aid upon Cuba's agreement to a stabilization program."[50] With the announcement of the proposed agrarian reform law in mid-May, the bureaucratic debate essentially ended. On June 3, the "dust settled" with the enactment of the agrarian reform.

The agrarian reform law and its consequences

Although the CIA conceded that there was no evidence to prove Castro was a communist or procommunist during 1959,[51] American officials still identified with the anticommunist rhetoric of those Cuban bourgeoisie who were targets of the revolution's redistributive phase. Nor were U.S. officials reticent to apply the communist label as code language to denote their opposition to Castro's policies. With the adoption of the agrarian reform law in June 1959 – the first important class issue of the revolution – the description of the Castro leadership as communist was etched into Washington's public posture.

The law itself in fact combined reformist as well as radical nationalist measures. The major goal of the land redistribution was to create a more efficient and productive agriculture. Individual ownership was henceforth limited to a maximum of 995 acres, and a National Agrarian Reform Institute (INRA) was established to orchestrate the program's application. Compensation for expropriated property was computed as the assessed value for taxation purposes. Payments were in the form of redeemable twenty-year government bonds with interest not to exceed 4½ percent. Not surprisingly, the tax figures contrived by former owners underestimated the value of nationalized properties. Yet the landowners could not challenge the figures without exposing earlier tax evasions based on their own estimates.

Although the agrarian reform law initially led to expropriations mainly of large Cuban-owned cattle ranches in Camagüey and did not touch American properties, it was immediately perceived in Washington as a watershed in the process of revolutionary change, the precursor of state takeovers of foreign interests.[52] Before enacting the law, Cuban officials made a number of approaches to the Havana Embassy for U.S. government support and advice in preparing the necessary legislation. These requests were given scant consideration by the executive branch: "[They] fell on totally unsympathetic ears in Washington. Bonsal's instructions were to be correct and suitably distant."[53]

Despite the measure's emphasis on increased production, the bourgeoisie and its government representatives vigorously opposed the law both before and after its enactment. According to López-Fresquet, the law was drawn up primarily by noncabinet members, including Fidel Castro and Ernesto Che Guevara.[54] Ambassador Bonsal cabled the State Department that a number of cabinet officials "are known to have opposed the law but to have gone along with it rather than be counted out altogether."[55] These included the ministers of Social Welfare, Interior, Health, Agriculture, Foreign Relations, and the Treasury, all of whom were hostile to at least "some particulars" of the law. One result was a number of ministerial dismissals and resignations.[56] In a telegram to the Secretary of State on June 5, Ambassador Bonsal noted the growing polarization in Cuba: "Opposition to the government among middle and upper classes is mounting as [a] result [of the] agrarian reform law, and [the] Embassy has heard numerous reports that counterrevolutionary plots are germinating."[57]

The U.S. sugar industry received the first announcement of the proposed law "with some shock, but also with expressions of confidence that 'in the long run, a reasonable solution will be worked out.'"[58] The industry was predisposed to "wait and see." The law, however, triggered increased dialogue between American corporations with major economic interests in Cuba (especially the sugar capitalists) and the U.S. government. These discussions centered both on particular investment concerns and the direction of the whole revolutionary process.[59] There is little doubt that U.S. business confidence in Cuba was severely jolted by the proposed law; one index was the fall in the demand for Cuban securities.[60]

From Washington, the State Department telegrammed the Havana Embassy requesting that the Cuban government be informed of U.S. property holders' concern over the proposed law as well as of the importance of "prompt, adequate and effective compensation for property taken."[61] On June 1, Ambassador Bonsal told the Cuban Minister of State, Roberto Agramonte, that the Eisenhower administration was not antagonistic to "sound land reform" or the principle of expropriation itself, provided that compensation was satisfactory.[62] On June 5, Bonsal advised the Secretary of State that if Cuba refused to revise the new law, the United States should threaten the loss of its American sugar market. The designation of Cuba as an unreliable source of supply could obligate the Secretary of Agriculture "to take measures to assure [the] American market of its requirements." In any event, the Cubans were to be put on notice regarding the insistence of the United States on "prompt, adequate and effective compensation to American properties expropriated in accordance with accepted principles of international law."[63]

The official U.S. government response to the agrarian reform law was delivered to the Cuban Minister of State on June 11. The note interspersed support of an approach to agrarian reform that emphasized increasing production rather than changes in land-tenure relations with subtle threats of retaliation in the event of nationalization of U.S.-owned properties unaccompanied by appropriate compensation. It contrasted a "soundly conceived and executed program for rural betterment" with a redistribution strategy that was bound to lower productivity and limit "desirable public and private investment." It expressed concern for "the interests of the consumers in the United States of Cuban products and of private United States' investors, present and prospective in Cuba."[64] The note also was clear about possible policy options that included a reduction in the sugar quota, a formal prohibition on U.S. private investment in Cuba, and a formal embargo on economic aid.

The possibilities for limited accommodation with the nationalist regime now hinged on the way in which the law was applied to American investors "whose properties may be affected."[65] Meanwhile, individual capitalists with large agricultural investments in Cuba were in constant communication with American officials. Robert Kleberg, owner of the King Ranch in Texas, informed the Secretaries of State and the Treasury that the imminent loss of his $3 million investment in the island's rural economy and the likely impact of the law on all American-owned sugar properties were sufficient reasons for the immediate imposition of economic sanctions.[66] At this time, Assistant Secretary of State for Inter-American Affairs R. Richard Rubottom counselled a measured response on the grounds that "a demanding attitude" might have serious consequences for the entire U.S. investment stake in Cuba.[67] Eschewing the more aggressive policy options, State Department officials advocated maintaining the channels of communication and pursuing negotiations in an effort "to obtain more satisfactory terms for American investors."[68]

The seizure of 400 of the largest U.S.- and Cuban-owned cattle ranches during June and July, covering around 2.3 million acres, became the basis for intensified internal and external attacks on the new development project.[69] The ferocity of the opposition

response, Filipe Pazos noted, "did not exactly help" those bourgeois cabinet officials sympathetic to the interests of affected
property holders and endeavoring to restrain government policy.[70] Their position was undermined further by the U.S. Congress' decision to provide a forum for denunciations of the revolutionary regime by the former Cuban Air Force Chief, Pedro
Díaz Lanz. In the Senate, legislators also considered restoring a
clause deleted from the Sugar Act of 1951 authorizing the Secretary of Agriculture "to limit imports from any sugar supplier if
American nationals were being discriminated against."[71]

On October 14, the U.S. government transmitted a second
response, no less hostile than the first, on the agrarian reform law
that again raised the specter of economic reprisals. At a followup
meeting between Ambassador Bonsal, Cuban President Osvaldo
Dorticós and Foreign Minister Raúl Roa, Bonsal again linked
American approval to the nature of the compensation provided
affected U.S. investors.[72] In early November, U.S. agricultural and
mining properties (Bethlehem Steel, International Harvester, the
King Ranch, and others) in Oriente and Camagüey provinces were
expropriated. These Cuban actions fueled executive and legislative support for revising the island's preferential position in the
American sugar market in the upcoming debate on renewal of the
U.S. Sugar Act.

With the implementation of the agrarian reform law, U.S. policymakers declared that the period "of probing and testing to see
what Castro would do, what he was like, and how he'd react to
situations" was over. The fact that he selected "the most extreme
of the two versions of the agrarian reform law and pass[ed] up the
advice of the more responsible anti-Communist members of his
Cabinet" was sufficient evidence that "Castro was not going to be
a man with whom the United States could work."[73] By identifying
U.S. policy with the agrarian transformation in Cuba that threatened all foreign investments, the Eisenhower administration
hoped to mobilize more easily the capitalist class as a whole in
support of a confrontation with Castro. On the other hand, United
States antagonism toward this transformation polarized Cuban
society in a manner overwhelmingly unfavorable to American
interests. It substantially enhanced and strengthened working-
class support for the nationalist leadership.

Because the agrarian reform law raised the prospect of a profound structural rearrangement of the Cuban economy in which
all foreign property interests would be endangered, the U.S.

began to give serious consideration to various courses of action – covert, economic, political, diplomatic – that might bring down the Castro government. Sometime during the fall of 1959, officials of the Department of State and the Central Intelligence Agency initiated discussions that culminated in the President's approval in March 1960 of a covert action and economic sabotage memorandum.[74] Also that autumn, Secretary of State Herter prepared a statement on Cuba for President Eisenhower in which he recommended that U.S. policy be directed toward achieving the revolution's demise "by no later than the end of 1960." Accordingly, the State Department sought a major expansion of covert operations to "avoid giving the impression of direct pressure or intervention against Castro [and being] blamed directly for his failure or downfall." The substance of the Herter strategy was "to encourage opposition by suitable elements presently outside of the Castro regime with a view towards a step-by-step development of coherent opposition."[75] Herter interpreted the statist economic measures, the growing constraints on local and foreign capital, transformations in the Cuban state and class structure, and Castro's support for hemispheric revolutionary movements as inimical to U.S. political and economic interests throughout Latin America. The more broadly based Washington concern was not any particular nationalization or other policy initiative, but "the direction the revolution was taking."[76] A negotiated settlement was no longer given credence.

Castro's decision to pursue an independent foreign policy was, however, singled out for attention. In a dispatch to the Department of State on November 27, 1959, the supposedly accommodating Ambassador Bonsal decried Cuba's "independent position in world affairs" and its refusal to echo U.S. positions in global and regional forums. He was just as critical of Havana's new mining legislation, asserting that it seriously threatened American access to strategic raw materials.[77]

Contributing to Washington's growing enmity were the personnel changes taking place in the upper reaches of the nationalist government. One of the most important occurred in November with the replacement of the "sound moneyman" Felipe Pazos as head of the Cuban National Bank by the Argentine guerrilla, Ernesto Che Guevara.[78] By year's end, few of the "responsible" cabinet ministers ("the balancing wheels keeping the revolution from veering further to the left"[79]) retained their posts. With the notable exceptions of Treasury (López-Fresquet) and Economy

(Boti), almost all the ministries were now staffed by former guerrillas or Fidel Castro's close civilian supporters.

Meanwhile, the United States remained hopeful that Cuba's
critical economic problems would slow down the process of social
and economic transformation. In September 1959, with International Monetary Fund approval, Castro instituted an emergency
program based on increasing the tax burden on imports, mainly
from the United States, in an effort to halt the decline in foreign-
exchange reserves.[80] In mid-December, supplemental import and
exchange controls were introduced. Although these measures
brought most all commodities under licensing control, lowered
the amount of foreign exchange that Cuban citizens travelling
abroad could purchase, and reduced other types of remittances,[81]
they had no appreciable effect on the nearly exhausted reserves –
which declined from approximately $77 million in January 1959
to $49.6 million at the end of December 1959.[82] At the same time,
between $50 million and $60 million were withdrawn from private banks following Pazos' ouster as National Bank president;
more than one-quarter of the workforce was still without full-time
employment; and the balance-of-payments deficit appeared likely
to double between 1958 and 1959 to around $200 million. Amer-
ican officials declared that Castro was "in a box," because measures to reduce unemployment would worsen the balance-of-payments deficit while any decision to deal with the deficit almost
certainly would undercut the social and economic program.[83]
Any balance-of-payments assistance from U.S. public agencies
was still predicated on Cuba's acceptance of an IMF stabilization
loan.

Although U.S.-owned industrial and agricultural properties had
been nationalized on a lesser scale than had Cuban-owned land by
the end of the first year of the revolution, this did not temper U.S.
apprehension over the prospect of "permanent revolution" and a
major confrontation with American investors. Washington's
unease was advanced when it was forced, in effect, to write off
Cuban repayment of outstanding Export-Import Bank loans made
to the nationalized subsidiaries of International Telephone and
Telegraph and American & Foreign Power Company in the
1950s. In what turned out to be the last official broaching of this
issue with the Cuban government, a senior Bank official was told
by Guevara in Havana in early 1960 essentially that "We are not
going to pay."[84]

In a major policy restatement in late January 1960, a year after the revolution, President Eisenhower repeated the public position of "moderation" and strict adherence to the principle of nonintervention. He also expressed "confidence in the ability of the Cuban people to recognize and defeat the intrigues of international communism" and underlined his government's determination to support the compensation demands of expropriated U.S. investors through bilateral negotiations or "other appropriate international procedures."[85]

For American policymakers, Cuba's movement out of the capitalist orbit entered a decisive stage when the Soviet Union and Cuba signed a commercial-aid agreement in February 1960. This breach in the traditional U.S. monopoly of the island's trade was interpreted as "the opening wedge of a massive economic offensive in the Western Hemisphere" by Moscow.[86] Under the contract's terms, the Soviets agreed to purchase 425,000 tons of Cuban sugar in 1960 and 1,000,000 tons in each of the succeeding four years at the world market price of 3 cents per pound, with 80 percent of the payment in the form of Soviet manufactured goods and the remainder in U.S. dollars. The terms stabilized the Cuban sugar industry by eliminating its dependence on the U.S. Congress's yearly whims and provided the basis for a period of growth and expansion in sugar production. The Soviet Union also extended $100 million in credits to Havana for the purchase of equipment, machinery, and other materials, in addition to technical assistance, over a five-year period.[87]

This new trade agreement, in the context of rising threats to American investments and the Cuban National Bank's policies under Guevara, was the subject of several hastily organized meetings in Washington and New York between Assistant Secretary of State Rubottom and U.S. business leaders.[88] The public White House position remained one of "patience and forebearance."[89] In private, however, consideration was given to a "much stronger" response: a continental strategy to mobilize Latin American opposition to the revolutionary regime to moderate its policies or suffer regional isolation; a change in the U.S. Sugar Act to permit reduction of American subsidies for Cuban sugar; the application of a 1¼ cent-a-pound duty on Cuban sugar to be used to compensate affected American property owners; the mediation of American investor claims over nationalized or "intervened" property by hemispheric governments or some form of international arbitration; and the expansion of anti-Castro mass-media operations for transmission to Cuba.[90]

In the first quarter of 1960, the State Department began a program to "discreetly block" loans and credits from Western Europe to the Castro regime.[91] In March, while Cuba's foreign exchange reserves had risen slightly but still stood at a perilously low $67 million, a consortium of Dutch, French, and West German banks, under heavy Washington pressure, countermanded an apparent agreement to negotiate $100 million in loans to the revolutionary government. The bankers acted in concert with U.S. interests, even though Cuba "was reported to be willing to float a bond issue in Western Europe."[92]

The refusal of American and most Western European exporters to provide credit did indeed leave Castro with no alternative but the socialist bloc. During the first half of 1960, Cuba signed trade agreements not only with the Soviet Union, but also with Poland, East Germany, and Communist China, which provided both markets for primary exports and access to industrial plant equipment and raw materials (often on credit) critical to sustaining the immediate and long-term operations of the Cuban economy.[93] On March 31, the House Foreign Affairs Committee proposed the termination of all U.S. economic aid to Cuba "unless the president determined that such assistance was 'in the national and hemispheric interest.'"[94] This amendment was written into the foreign-aid legislation, overwhelmingly approved by both the House and the Senate, and signed by the President.

Remaking the Cuban state and society: "closure to the outside"

In 1917, amid the first socialist revolution of the twentieth century, Lenin observed that "the key question of every revolution is undoubtedly the question of state power [and] which class holds power decides everything."[95] The Cuban leaders were well aware of earlier attempts by Latin American nationalist regimes to rule in contexts of divided political power, specifically their incapacity to exert control over key sectors of the state structure such as the armed forces (e.g., in Cuba 1933 and in Guatemala 1954). So was Washington, as shown by its last-minute efforts to force Batista's resignation in December 1958 – that is, sacrifice a particular leader to salvage some of the old state apparatus.

One of Castro's immediate goals, therefore, was to forge a basic congruity between the new governing regime and the state sector.

The rapid disintegration of the old state and the equally swift establishment of a new apparatus closed to foreign political and economic influence helped trigger Washington's antagonistic response. Despite the initial allocation of key cabinet ministries to representatives of the procapitalist democratic forces, Castro did not transfer to this body the substance of political power. In his role as commander-in-chief of the rebel army, he set about organizing a proto-state independent of the cabinet and anchored in the working class.

In place of Batista's defeated army, new military and security forces based on armed popular militias were created as part of the leadership's intention to bring the working class to prominence. In the process, the long-established relationship between the CIA and Batista's military intelligence and security forces was terminated, creating additional problems for U.S. covert operations.[96] The role allocated the Cuban Communist Party (PSP) within a reconstituted bureaucracy was also designed to hamper future Washington efforts to reestablish an effective network of covert "assets" in the Cuban state and society — reflecting the importance of the security issue to Castro and his closest advisors. The PSP, with its discipline and organizational expertise, served as a structured substitute for the declining bourgeois and petty bourgeois support of the nationalist regime after mid-1959. During the implementation of the agrarian reform law, Communist Party cadres were visible "in every part of the state organization, especially in the new Agrarian Reform Institute."[97] An Havana Embassy official commented that "one could see how people associated with the PSP were moving into third and fourth level positions, into the key elements in the government, and this was disturbing."[98] Further, despite an increase in the number of both permanent and short-term CIA staff members in Cuba during 1959, all efforts to penetrate the highest echelons of the guerrilla leadership went unrewarded.[99]

Concurrently, efforts by procapitalist cabinet ministers to enlist U.S. business expertise in setting up an efficient state bureaucracy were rebuffed in Washington. According to a senior executive of an American multinational subsidiary in Havana, Embassy officials attempted to get the Eisenhower administration to "prevail on the head offices of American businesses opposing the idea of getting into the [Cuban] government and helping to administer and reorganize the executive departments [to change their minds]." But the decision was made in Washington "to keep at arm's length and don't get involved."[100] Confronting a disintegrated bourgeois state and the nationalists' attempt, with scarce administrative expertise, to create a new state structure, neither the U.S. government nor Havana-based representatives of American business were prepared to institute a strategy that, while favorable to investors, might inadvertently strengthen Castro's position.

The prospect of a state transformation in Cuba created a situation in which all foreign enterprises were endangered, although no particular enterprise was threatened at any one moment. Dismembering the old state initially did not involve large-scale nationalizations. Nonetheless, the state was the issue over which the class struggle in Cuba emerged through conflict between the Castro-led nationalists and the Eisenhower White House, which promoted anticommunism and opposed both Cuban nationalism and socialism. United States policymakers opposed the new direction precisely because they comprehended the breadth of the transformation. As the bourgeois state's breakup became a *fait accompli*, Washington came to interpret each conflict between the Castro forces and individual American investors as a reflection of this larger process of state transformation.

As the transformation gathered momentum, American influence dissolved. The reconstruction of the armed forces, the establishment of a new administrative apparatus, and the perennial irrelevance of the old regime's political parties together posed a serious problem for the U.S. policymakers trying to devise a response. Their options were limited further by the new government's strategy toward likely collaborator groups in Cuban society. The network of professional and employer organizations of the Cuban bourgeoisie – sugar mill owners, sugar cane growers, cattlemen, industrialists, lawyers, doctors – to varying degrees were potential strongholds of opposition. The nationalist leadership, therefore, deliberately exacerbated fissures that had already taken hold within these organizations during Batista's last year and took advantage of the large exodus of this class during the early post-1959 period. The government bolstered the positions of pro-Castro forces in the organizations and contributed to the development of competing groups.

The Association of Sugar Mill Owners had been substantially compromised by its support of Batista. Confronted with hostile sugar planters, workers, and technicians, and internal Association opposition from small landowners, the big sugar companies tried to ingratiate themselves with the new government. They paid their taxes in advance and offered measured support for initial agrarian reforms. Incapable of withstanding such government-nurtured forces, however, the Association collapsed with "each *hacendado* going his own way, some fleeing, some compromising, some waiting for the Marines."[101]

The Association of Sugar Cane Growers, which included large mill owners, disintegrated following more direct government actions. To increase the political weight of the Association's numerous small and medium-sized cane growers, the Agriculture minister forced a revision of the organization's electoral procedures in 1959, leading to gains for the small at the expense of the rich. The agrarian reform law and the new National Agrarian Reform Institute (INRA), however, forecast the end of the Association. During the latter half of 1960, INRA moved to substitute a progovernment cane growers' organization. It arranged elections, which the small cane growers dominated, voting to disband the Association and form an organization of small farmers.

The large cattle ranchers also resisted the agrarian reforms of mid-1959; their Association went so far as to fund $500,000 to bribe the Cuban press to denounce the new law.[102] Such counter-revolutionary activities reinforced the government's determination to transfer control of the Association of Cattlemen to the small and medium-sized farmers. Efforts at resistance were sharply circumscribed by the absence of the previous basis of landowner power, the traditional army, and the lack of any substitute force that could offer a serious challenge to the agrarian transformation. By January 1960, the state had extended its control over all the island's cattle acreage.

On another front, the National Association of Cuban Industrialists at first supported the nationalist economic program. Segments of its membership made advance tax payments, too, largely in the hope of guaranteeing their continued operations. Influential Association members such as Bacardi Rum President José M. "Pepín" Bosch, who became director of the Hanabanilla hydroelectric project, and the banker Julián de Zulueta, appointed president of the Social Security Institute, offered their expertise and skills to the new government. What doomed this Association was that its most prominent members were representatives of U.S. multinational corporations.[103] As a result, it lacked the legitimacy that might have allowed it to mobilize an effective response to government pressure on its interests.

Another potential source of opposition to the revolutionary regime was the Catholic Church, which had traditionally viewed its mission as "the education of the sons and daughters of the bourgeoisie."[104] Soon after assuming power, the new government revoked all degrees and credits awarded by the Catholic University of Havana after November 1956. But it was the agrarian reform program that divided the predominantly Spanish-born church hierarchy and launched the Church on a course of active hostility toward the Castro leadership. On May 16, 1960, the Archbishop of Santiago in a pastoral denounced the restoration of Cuban-Soviet diplomatic relations as evidence of "an intolerable government policy regarding communism. . . . Though the pastoral was not issued on behalf of the whole Cuban hierarchy, its influence was felt throughout the country."[105]

The issuance four months later of a collective pastoral letter by the Church leadership speaking to the communist issue had important consequences, for it prompted Castro to support the establishment of a new nationalist Church that could accommodate the revolution and its goals. Existing press outlets were closed, church properties were nationalized, cutting heavily into the Church's financial resources, and many of the hierarchy were exiled to Spain. In these circumstances, the "old" Church was for all practical purposes eliminated as an ally of counterrevolution.

The organized labor leadership also provided a potential opening for American government and trade union efforts to influence the process of change in Cuba. During the late 1940s and 1950s, the anticommunist leadership of the Confederation of Cuban Workers (CTC) consistently promoted Washington's interests in Cuba and Latin America. The CTC "played a very significant role" in establishing the Inter-American Regional Organization of Workers (ORIT) in 1949, which became the main vehicle of American labor in its drive to organize a regional anticommunist trade union movement.[106] During Batista's rule, the AFL-CIO supervised the training of Cuban colleagues in the techniques of collective bargaining and made provision for island labor officials to undergo extensive practical and ideological training in the United States. "There are few leaders of promise who have not now had some training in the United States," declared the Havana Embassy's "Outline Plan of Operations for Latin America" prepared in February 1958. "The problem is how best to utilize this training after they return to Cuba."[107] In October 1958, the Embassy submitted an updated report to the State Department on

the "Operations Plan" noting that "already over 60 trade unionists have been sent to the United States for training."[108]

In January 1959, the labor section of the July 26 Movement
appointed a provisional committee on the CTC composed of anti-
communists and noncommunists. The ORIT immediately made
contact, hoping to help create an anticommunist trade union organization in Cuba. Elections held in the spring of 1959 gave the
July 26 Movement unionists control of 29 of 33 federations.[109] The
revolution's growing radicalization and the scheduled first
national CTC convention in November led the anticommunist faction among Cuba's new union leadership to attempt to consolidate
its position through external alliances, specifically with the American AFL-CIO.[110]

Under pressure from the rank and file of organized labor and
the Castro leadership, shifts occurred within the labor leadership
after mid-1959 that gradually eroded the power of the anticommunist unionists. Although the latter played a major role in organizing a meeting of CTC, AFL-CIO, and ORIT officials in October, for example, none were included in the Cuban delegation to
this meeting which was composed of individuals who "had no
power to commit the CTC to anything."[111] The government-supported transfer of authority to communist and noncommunist
trade union officials was essentially ratified at the November 1959
CTC convention in Havana, which also advocated withdrawal
from ORIT. "Until 1960," recalled AFL-CIO official Andrew
McClellan, who was a conference participant, "we felt that if the
CTC could retain its international affiliations, then we could hope-
fully exercise some influence on it. . . . When the confederation
began to disaffiliate from ORIT, the ICFTU [International Confederation of Free Trade Unions], and internationally, the battle was
lost."[112]

There were no anticommunist officials on the new CTC Executive Board that emerged in the aftermath of the November meeting. In January 1960, the Board adopted a resolution that called
for the dismissal of counterrevolutionary trade union officials. Following the occupation of the Cuban Palace of Labor by government troops under the command of Raúl Castro in April 1960,
more and more antiregime trade unionists began to offer their
services to the antirevolutionary cause.[113]

Despite its wealth and numbers, the bourgeoisie at the time of
Batista's overthrow was in no position to hegemonize the nation-

alist movement and realize particular social and economic demands within the framework of capitalism. The struggle for power within the July 26 Movement after 1959 was resolved decisively in favor of the guerrilla leadership rooted in an organized social force (workers) and with a means of coercion (popular militias) over a politically immobilized bourgeoisie that was incapable of responding organizationally or militarily to revolutionary initiatives. By 1961, two years after the revolution, neither the bourgeoisie and its organizations, now bereft of coherent leadership or policies anchored in any significant social group, nor pre-1959 collaborator factions such as the organized labor hierarchy were able to "mediate" American political and economic interests in Cuba.

The United States shifts tracks: from "insider" to "outsider" strategy

By the end of 1959, the Cuban Revolution had become a most pressing concern at the White House. The emergence of numerically significant opposition to the Castro leadership late in the year at first buoyed the hopes of American policymakers about organizing a formidable resistance movement. Between June and December, Cuban state bureaucrats, military officials, cabinet ministers, and other bourgeois and petty bourgeois supporters of the antidictatorial struggle disaffiliated themselves from the revolutionary regime and became potentially available for enlistment in a counterrevolutionary movement. Some of these individuals, such as Treasury Minister López-Fresquet who began "conspiratorial activities" against the government in September, and the military governor of Camagüey province, Huber Matos, had translated their disaffection into action. Matos opposed the agrarian reform and proselytized anticommunism among the armed forces' leadership.[114]

Meanwhile, the CIA was busy trying to impose some sort of coherence on the opposition to channel its energies. "In meetings with Cuban officials," writes CIA covert officer David Phillips, "I found some disillusioned with the drift toward Communism and recruited them as intelligence sources for the CIA.[115] The goal of recreating a network of capable "assets" received a temporary shot in the arm with the appearance of those "pro-Castro people [who were] beginning to change their minds" and were prepared to collaborate with the CIA.[116]

In the absence of structured, bourgeois organizations, but in the face of a coherent and vigorous Cuban response, these CIA-conjured possibilities surfaced in a political vacuum. The new "assets" capacity to alter the power configurations and class alignments were limited. In his memoir of the period, Ambassador Philip Bonsal recalled Washington's dilemma: "A leadership willing to fight Castro and his policies would have had scope for its activities. But there was none."[117]

By early 1960, President Eisenhower privately decided that "something would have to be done."[118] Discussing with Secretary of State Herter on January 25 the withdrawal of the American Ambassador, he added that, "if we get to a point where we are being pushed too hard, we may have to do something drastic such as blockading the island."[119] At a conference between the President and senior State Department officials the next day, "The President said that Castro begins to look like a mad man."[120] The White House now shifted to a policy of prolonged confrontation with the Cuban Revolution in which covert politics was assigned an important role.

Throughout 1959, the U.S. government's public willingness to negotiate with Cuba was paralleled by clandestine CIA efforts "to embarrass Castro in a piecemeal and uncoordinated fashion."[121] During the winter of 1959–1960, there was a significant increase in CIA-supervised bombing and incendiary raids piloted by exiled Cubans.[122] In early 1960, however, when Agency Director Allen Dulles requested presidential authorization "for a sabotage effort directed against Cuban sugar refineries,"[123] the President already had concluded that particular actions must be integrated into an overall strategy if the United States was to bring about Castro's demise. According to a member of his White House staff, Eisenhower wanted a comprehensive program "to change the Cuban government."[124] The National Security Council meetings of March 10 and 14 were both preoccupied with the issue of how the United States swiftly and effectively could "bring another government to power in Cuba."[125]

On March 17, Dulles and Richard Bissell brought to the White House an ambitious scenario prepared by the CIA and endorsed by the Special Group, a subcommittee of the National Security Council responsible for authorizing Agency covert action operations. The plan proposed the development of a unified exile opposition; the creation of a psychological and propaganda apparatus for use against the Castro regime; the creation of a covert intelligence and action organization inside Cuba; and the establishment of a paramilitary exile force for future military operations on the island.[126] According to a National Security Council staff official who attended the meeting, Dulles also argued in favor of increased economic sanctions and sabotage operations against Cuba's oil refineries.[127] During these meetings at which the clandestine option originated, the CIA's attitude was never one of attempting "to pressure the government into this policy," in the opinion of an Agency official, but rather that of "the lawyer presenting the brief to his client."[128] Although operational responsibility ultimately rested with the CIA, regular interagency meetings involving officials of State, Defense, and the CIA were held throughout 1960 to monitor and evaluate the progress of the Cuban "assets."

The initial paramilitary approach centered on the infiltration of a trained guerrilla cadre into Cuba to provide organizational expertise and fighting capabilities needed by the anti-Castro movement. A clandestine radio station, Radio Swan, was set up on Swan Island following the March meeting, and a Cuban front organization, the Frente Revolucionario Democrático, was also established. In August, Eisenhower met with Secretary of Defense Thomas Gates and CIA officials Dulles and Bissell to discuss progress to date in the four areas of the covert-action plan. The President received favorable reports on the propaganda project and the paramilitary exile force, but highly pessimistic accounts of efforts to develop a viable armed resistance movement inside Cuba and of getting the various exile factions to cooperate with each other and select an acceptable leader. Eisenhower agreed to approve a $13 million budget to expand the counterrevolutionary program and to assign Pentagon personnel and equipment to the project. But, according to Bissell, the President made it clear that "he would not approve any action . . . without a popular, genuine government-in-exile."[129]

The failure of CIA efforts to create the basis of an antiregime resistance organization on the island was due to two interrelated factors: limited active domestic opposition to the Castro regime and an effective revolutionary security network that accounted for the virtual absence of CIA "assets" inside the country. The consequence was an Agency decision to substitute an alternative strategy that drew heavily on the combined military-psychological scenario that was so successful in ousting the Arbenz government in Guatemala in 1954. Operation Trinidad, as it was called, was based on a heavily armed strike force of 600 to 700 exiles to be deposited on Cuban soil where, under cover of air strikes and supply drops, it would establish a beachhead, create social and political chaos, and detonate a general uprising that would "tip the balance against Castro."[130] Although this plan featured basically the same inbuilt problems that undermined the original paramilitary approach, it received the go-ahead from the Special Group; a Pentagon guerrilla warfare expert was put in charge of its military aspects; and on January 11, 1961, a working committee representing State, Defense, the CIA, and the Joint Chiefs of Staff was established to coordinate Operation Trinidad activities.[131]

The question of keeping the entire covert action program a secret was of less concern to the White House and the CIA than was the need to "insulate the United States from any direct involvement."[132] At a November 29, 1960, White House meeting, State Department officials expressed concern over the fact that the exile operation was becoming public knowledge. Eisenhower responded by chiding the Department for its failure "to take more chances and be more aggressive." He emphasized that "the main thing was not to let the U.S.' hand show."[133] From the inception of the exile project, however, the CIA encountered obstacles that proved insurmountable, transforming the whole operation into "an American-directed enterprise entirely," which made it virtually impossible to hide Washington's role. These obstacles centered around the incapacity of the exiles to develop a consensus "at the political level." As a result, it was impossible to develop "a cohesive, effective Cuban manned organization" to take responsibility for the training, planning, logistical, and intelligence aspects of the program.[134] The internecine conflicts among the exile "assets," which continued unabated through the final months of the Eisenhower administration, were especially frustrating to the President, who continued to insist that the emergence of a leader and a government-in-exile that the United States could recognize were the *sine qua non* for his approval of any military operation.[135]

American covert operations against Cuba during the Eisenhower presidency extended to efforts to assassinate the revolution's leaders. In December 1959, CIA Director Dulles approved an internal agency memorandum recommending that "thorough consideration be given to the elimination of Fidel Castro."[136] On January 13, 1960, in what was probably the first Special Group discussion of a covert program to overthrow Castro, the State

Department representative cautioned against any hastily devised action against the Cuban leadership in the absence of "a solidly based opposition" that could step into the vacuum and assume political power. Dulles acknowledged the importance of timing an assassination and "emphasized that we do not have in mind a quick elimination of Castro, but rather actions designed to enable responsible opposition leaders to get a foothold."[137] During the March 1960 interagency discussions, consideration of "direct positive action" against the senior revolutionary leaders repeatedly was linked to the existence of an organized collaborator group capable of asserting control. The minutes of the March 14 Special Group meeting at the White House reveal that American officials worried "that the only organized group within Cuba today were the Communists and there was therefore the danger that they might move into control. . . . Col[onel] King said there were few leaders capable of taking over so far identified."[138] Both President Eisenhower and Secretary of State Herter were opposed to the premature assassination of Castro in the absence of a government-in-exile approved by the White House that could provide the necessary leadership to the exile invasion force. Otherwise, there was always the risk that an even more unacceptable figure, such as Raúl Castro or Che Guevara, would take Fidel Castro's place.[139]

The idea of assassination continued to receive "serious consideration" during the latter half of 1960 in the form of two abortive CIA efforts (a proposed "accident" and a plan to poison Castro's cigars)[140] and a decision by the Agency to enlist the aid of the American criminal underworld, some of whose members had suffered major losses of gambling casinos, hotels, and other assets in Cuba in the backwash of Batista's overthrow. In August, Sheffield Edwards, the CIA Director of the Office of Security, met with Robert Mahue, an ex-FBI agent with reputed entree into the world of organized crime. The outcome was an approach to John Roselli, an underworld figure, who agreed to participate in the project "using other Mafia contacts whose gambling interests in Cuba had been confiscated by Castro in 1959. By October, Roselli had recruited Sam Giancana and Santos Trafficante, who in turn began to recruit Cubans who might do the job."[141] According to Mahue, who remained in constant contact with Giancana during this period, it was Giancana's responsibility "to locate someone in Castro's entourage who could accomplish the assassination."[142] Following the change in administration, the assassination option was pursued at least as vigorously, if not more so, after January 1961 by the Kennedy White House.

The response of U.S. business

The U.S. investment community in Cuba responded to Castro's victory with mixed pragmatism, self-interest, and concern. Although some were "alarmed" or merely "cautious" and "wary" and determined to maintain a low profile, others hoped the new developments would bring an end to the unstable and disruptive ambience of the late Batista period.[143] The growing problem of "just sheer graft and corruption and oppression" under Batista had become a serious obstacle to efficient business operations and profit maximization.[144] The composition of the first Castro cabinet was favorably received not only by the U.S. government, but also by many American businessmen who pointed to individuals such as Felipe Pazos who "had a background in public service, finance, that was recognizable. . . . They were people who knew their business, who knew how to write a budget and run a government, and believed in a free enterprise system as opposed to a Marxist system."[145] American businessmen in Havana, according to U.S. intelligence dispatches to President Eisenhower, were "urging rapid recognition on the basis that this government appears far better than anything they had dared hope for."[146] The delegation of responsibility for economic policy to known, "sound," procapitalist officials intent on eliminating corruption and administrative incompetence opened up the possibility of national capitalist development in which foreign capital would be accorded an important role.

The initial hostility of particular fractions of foreign capital to the nationalist government was balanced by the response, for example, of the large agro-mining interests in Oriente province who "felt they could get along" in a new situation.[147] The U.S. banking community, according to a Havana-based American business executive, also thought that accommodation was possible.[148] Merrill Lynch officials in Cuba were optimistic that the stockbroking firm's subsidiary "could stay on indefinitely."[149] Naturally, those U.S. capitalist interests most immediately affected by government actions, such as the Cuban Electric Company (whose non-Havana rates were reduced to capital-city levels in March 1959) and the Cuban Telephone Company (which was "intervened" and had its 1957 rate increase cancelled) tended to send the most extreme proposals to executive-branch officials. A leading representative of the Cuban Electric Company told a meeting of State Department officials and U.S. sugar company heads that the only issue on the agenda should be how to overthrow Castro. Only one of the sugar company executives responded by explicitly dissociating himself from this line of argument.[150]

Whether derived from individual perceptions regarding an eventual accommodation with the Castro government or based on the nature of the particular investment, influential fractions of U.S. capital were clearly of the opinion that the changing climate in Cuba "was not going to be so bad." [151] Another measure of American business confidence was the minimal effort by the multinationals to revise projected investment plans for Cuba during 1959 or to avail themselves of the U.S. government's Investment Guarantee Program for new foreign investment. In 1959, new direct U.S. investment totalled $63 million, which represented the largest annual increase in capital flows to the island since World War II.[152]

It was the cumulative impact of wage increases, tax payment disputes, obstacles to repatriating capital, and other aspects of the Castro regime's redistribution policies and efforts to grapple with the foreign-exchange crisis during the first part of 1959 that moved some U.S. investors to oppose the nationalist development program.[153] In the second half of the year, the Labor Ministry was authorized to intervene temporarily in enterprises unable to resolve serious labor disputes or engaged in work-force retrenchment; new taxes were levied on the value of exported minerals and on mineral concessions; a National Petroleum Institute was established to regulate the refining and marketing of petroleum products; and U.S. firms were requested to provide on-the-job training for members of the rebel army. These and other new laws and decrees designed to limit foreign capital activities had the net effect of transforming what U.S. Ambassador to Cuba Philip Bonsal described as the "restrained optimism"[154] of American bankers and businessmen around mid-1959 into what the *Wall Street Journal* called a case of "the galloping jitters" at year's end.[155]

By March 1960, there was a noticeable increase in the multinationals' appeals to the State and Commerce Departments to do something about their Cuban problems, but there were "few specific suggestions" about what to do.[156] Most offered little more than slogans – "We must be tough from now on."[157] A few businessmen proposing a more activist policy did have a particular action in mind. The president of the Continental Can Company, which was in the process of abandoning its small but valuable operations in Cuba (with Washington's encouragement), wrote to the Treasury Secretary Robert B. Anderson that the time had arrived when "immediate and powerful economic sanctions should be invoked."[158] On the other hand, the attitude of a number of established U.S. enterprises, representing the dominant force within the American Chamber of Commerce in Havana, apparently clung to the belief that the Castro regime would not find alternative trade and financial sources (even in the socialist bloc) to sustain a structural transformation. Therefore, Cuba's economic dependence on the U.S. eventually would force the revolutionary leadership to seek "accommodation" with key American corporations on the island in order to achieve projected economic goals.[159]

The growing constraints on foreign capital rendered business activities less and less efficient and profitable, leading to more companies ready to, or actually, pulling up stakes. But, as a Department of Commerce official noted, those American corporations with large, fixed investments in mining and agriculture faced substantial problems in terminating their Cuban operations and, therefore, looked at other alternatives. This consideration quite likely led some U.S. businessmen to encourage the American government to pursue accommodation. "Whatever we do," declared one administration official, "a lot of businessmen want us to do it carefully. They seem to feel the need for us to reach a modus vivendi."[160] A group of executives representing the major American sugar and cattle interests in Cuba met with Secretary of State Christian Herter in January 1960 and informed him that they "would prefer to try and work out their problems individually rather than have an over-all approach made."[161] Other sectors of the U.S. business community involved in Cuba and elsewhere in Latin America also cautioned against the application of aggressive policies. Roy L. Hileman, a regional specialist for the Harris Trust & Saving Bank of Chicago, described Cuba as "too important a country politically and economically for the United States to act rashly now."[162] Into the first half of 1960, some American companies, such as Caterpillar Tractor and General Motors, were still selling farm equipment and spare parts to Havana on credit.[163] The influential U.S. financial journal *Barron's* estimated that around $100 million in credits had been extended to Havana by American merchandizing, banking and nickel and petroleum companies between August 1959 and July 1960.[164]

With the disintegration of the bourgeois state in Cuba and the establishment of an alternative state structure serving working-class needs, with the shift from redistributive policies to large-scale property nationalizations (domestic and foreign), and with the incapacity of dissolving local groups to counter these developments, it became increasingly apparent to Washington in the early months of 1960 that no accommodation with Castro was possible. The Eisenhower administration began to interpret specific conflicts between the revolutionary regime and individual capitalists as reflections of this larger process of state transformation and, in the absence of a coherent American business opposition, assumed the initiative by using the corporations in a determined effort to destabilize the Castro government. In March, as noted earlier, the White House, the National Security Council, and the State Department conjured a covert action plan as part of a comprehensive attempt "to bring another government to power in Cuba" that would reconstitute the conditions for capital accumulation and expansion.

Instrumentalizing the capitalist class: the oil conflict

Among the most important American initiatives growing out of these strategy deliberations concerned the refining of Soviet crude oil in U.S.-owned Cuban refineries.

On the eve of the Cuban Revolution, the major foreign oil companies operating on the island (Standard Oil of New Jersey, Texaco Oil Company, and Royal Dutch Shell) occupied a strategic place in the local economy, providing virtually all of Cuba's 90,000-barrel daily consumption of petroleum (local production accounting for around 5,000 barrels a day). The companies could profoundly disrupt the Cuban economy by closing refineries, but the country itself was not an important area of their global operations. In 1960, the three multinationals had approximately $132 million invested in their Cuban operations, but their total combined assets were over an estimated $122 billion.[165] Yet the oil companies' Cuban investment had an importance beyond its actual dollar value by providing a much needed outlet for the rising volume of Venezuelan oil. The Venezuelan industry, with its high-priced crude, was dominated by Standard Oil, Shell, and

Texaco, whose massive investments in crude production facilities there were partly "predicated upon an assured market for Venezuelan oil in Cuba."[166] Standard Oil derived approximately one-third of its profits from Venezuelan operations; Royal Dutch Shell obtained nearly half of its total petroleum output from its operations there; and the country was a significant source of supply for the Texaco Company.[167]

The Cuban Petroleum Law of November 1959 was designed to impose state controls on oil exploration by foreign companies. Concessions not being exploited were to revert to state ownership, and the production royalty payable to the government was increased from 10 to 60 percent.[168] The foreign oil companies' position was more immediately jeopardized by the Soviet Union-Cuba trade agreement of February 1960, which included a Cuban commitment to import one-third to one-half of its total annual petroleum imports from the Soviet Union. This arrangement benefited the Cubans by designating sugar, not hard currency, as the payment for the Soviet crude oil, while the latter was less expensive than the equivalent Venezuelan product. The barter promised an improvement in the island's dangerously low foreign-exchange reserves position.

The likelihood that the U.S.-owned refineries would be requested to process Soviet crude led the petroleum multinationals to seek advice from the State Department. The manager of Standard Oil's operations in Cuba, L. J. "Tex" Brewer, conferred with State officials in early March 1960 to report on a recent discussion with Cuba's National Bank president, Che Guevara. According to Brewer, Guevara exhibited "a definite hostility toward private enterprise" and left the petroleum executive feeling that it would be "impossible for the United States to negotiate with the present Cuban regime."[169] At a meeting attended by officials of Texaco on May 11, Assistant Secretary of State for Inter-American Affairs R. Richard Rubottom was asked how the company should respond to overall developments in Cuba, and specifically to future demands that its facility refine Soviet oil. The senior State Department official replied that the petroleum companies should feel free to exert pressure on Castro.[170] This implied administration directive that the oil companies act in concert with the evolving American policy coincided with a deliberate decision by Standard Oil and Texaco to steadily reduce the number of American personnel employed in their Cuban operations. By the end of May, only six of Texaco's thirty-two U.S. employees remained in Cuba.[171]

In late May, Castro informed the Standard Oil, Texaco, and Royal Dutch Shell subsidiaries that Soviet crude oil was available for refining.[172] Simultaneously, the government cancelled the exclusive marketing contracts between the foreign oil companies and the retail gasoline outlets and announced its intention to market and distribute Cuban oil. The Banco Nacional de Cuba notified the "big three" that they were expected to process 2,220,000 barrels of Soviet crude yearly. The oil companies' immediate public response was a mixture of pragmatism and resignation. "If we didn't take it," observed one oil company executive, "we would be taken over, so what would we gain?"[173] The American petroleum industry's authoritative *Oil and Gas Journal*, hearing the plea, discerned no other signals that the companies were opposed to processing Soviet crude oil.[174] Ambassador Bonsal was also of the opinion that the companies reluctantly would refine the Soviet crude and attempt to seek redress through local judicial procedures.[175] Another senior Embassy official commented on a divergence between executives of the parent firms and those of the Cuban subsidiaries: "the oil people in Havana, living in Havana, were saying 'we have got to get along' but the oil people in Washington were taking a broader global view."[176]

On June 1, officers of Standard Oil, Texaco, and Royal Dutch Shell conferred with State Department officials and were informed that "if a decision not to process Russian crude was made this would be consonant with U.S. Government policy."[177] The very next day, according to an Havana Embassy cable to the Secretary of State, the manager of the Cuban Texaco refinery advised the Santiago Consulate that the three affected oil companies "will not refine 'one drop' of Russian crude oil."[178] On June 3, senior executives of the two U.S. multinationals were summoned to a meeting with the Secretary of the Treasury, Robert Anderson. One of the participants subsequently relayed the gist of the meeting to a surprised Ambassador Bonsal. Secretary Anderson told the oil company officials that "a refusal to accede to the Cuban government's request would be in accord with the policy of the United States government toward Cuba," and that Royal Dutch Shell headquarters in London was being similarly advised.[179]

The foreign oil companies publicly declared their intention not to refine Soviet crude on the ostensible grounds of prior commitments to other supply sources. Ambassador Bonsal's failure to anticipate this decision echoed in both Havana and Washington. A senior American executive of Standard Oil's Cuba subsidiary told Ambassador Bonsal that the decision was "unexpected" by the Cuban Government, while an American employee of the Cuban Petroleum Institute informed State Department officials that the companies' refusal to refine the Soviet crude oil came as "a great surprise" to the Castro leadership.[180] The Cuban correspondent of the *Wall Street Journal* characterized the companies' response as "a surprise here" and described the Cuban government as the "most surprised of all."[181] *Business Week* called the rejection a "distinct change in the oil companies' attitudes."[182] None, of course, had been privy to the discussions between American officials and oil corporation executives that instigated the decision. Castro combined an aggressive response, advising the companies to reconsider their decisions or "take the consequences," with a more diplomatic expression of confidence that they would eventually "quietly start refining Russian oil as soon as we deliver it to them."[183]

The confrontational posture of the oil multinationals may not have been unrelated to their individual and industry objections to Cuban government policy. According to Royal Dutch Shell officials, the Castro regime had made no dollar payments on $17 million worth of crude oil supplied since May 1959, while the combined amount owed the "big three" totalled more than $60 million.[184] Shell, Texaco, and Standard Oil also resented the demand that they refine Soviet crude oil in refineries geared to the higher grade Venezuelan product, the precedent-setting impact of complying with such a request, and the certainty of lowered profits under the proposed conditions. At the time, companies' executives also expressed the private conviction that Havana would eventually capitulate to an industry "hardline" rather than risk chaos in a vital sector of the economy due to a lack of skilled labor to operate the refineries. In the final analysis, however, their apparent turnabout was the result of pressure from an American government determined to "get tough" with the nationalist regime.[185]

In the interim between the public announcement by the oil multinationals that their Cuban subsidiaries would not refine Soviet crude and the "intervention" of these subsidiaries by the Castro government, the State Department acted to block Havana's efforts to engage smaller American oil companies as substitute refiners. Assistant Secretary of State Rubottom, for instance, told Sinclair Oil Company officials that, "should the company, after considering its own position with respect to its operations and responsibility to its shareholders, decide to reject the Cuban proposal, such action definitely would not be counter to the present policy of the United States toward Cuba."[186] The State Department then informed Standard Oil executives that Sinclair Oil "had been told in no uncertain terms that the Department would take a very critical position toward any company which might attempt to capitalize on the difficulties of the presently established companies."[187] At this same meeting in late June, Standard Oil told State officials that Cuban approaches to Superior Oil Company had been summarily rejected, leading Deputy Assistant Secretary of State Lester Mallory to express pleasure that "the companies have maintained a united front."[188]

The takeover of the three foreign-owned oil-refining facilities began on June 29, 1960. The official State Department response for submission to the Cuban government was prepared in collaboration with senior officials of the affected U.S. petroleum multinationals.[189] It described Cuba's action as "arbitrary and inequitable, without authority under Cuban law, and contrary to commitments made to these companies." It characterized the expropriation as a further manifestation of Castro's effort "to destroy Cuba's traditional investment and trade relations with the rest of the world."[190]

The affected parent oil companies' most immediate response was to "hit back where they could" through such actions as "putting the government airline – Cuban Airlines – on a cash basis for fuel at foreign airports."[191] Soon after, they settled on a more elaborate strategy in the form of a global petroleum boycott of Cuba. The boycott had two distinct, but interrelated aims. First, it was intended to limit the worldwide distribution of Soviet crude oil and refined export products which in some cases had forced U.S. companies to lower their own crude oil prices. Second, the Cuban boycott proper was designed to render the lost refineries inoperable, or able to perform only at a low level. In fact, for some time before the June 1960 takeover, the foreign multinationals had begun to allow their crude oil inventories to decline and to repatriate key skilled American and Cuban personnel.[192] They then placed an embargo on the shipment of spare parts critical to the refineries' operations.

The oil industry also established a blacklist of independent tanker owners who chartered ships of the Soviet Union that could be used to transport oil back to Cuba. The chief advocate of the blacklist tactic and activist proponent of the global embargo was Standard Oil of New Jersey. On July 7, 1960, it issued a direct warning to ship owners and tanker brokers around the world to cease transactions with the Soviets and Cuba or risk any further association with Standard Oil and its affiliates.[193] In a crafty, complementary move to limit the Soviets' ability to charter independent tankers outside the socialist bloc, some of the largest U.S. oil companies began "to charter tonnage above and beyond normal seasonal requirements."[194]

In the short term, the global boycott had a great disruptive effect on the Cuban economy, since the tankers reaching the Caribbean island during the first half of August 1960 were estimated to be carrying only about half of Cuba's normal daily petroleum import requirements.[195] Although New York ship brokerage sources noted a slight increase in the number of independent tanker operators chartering to the Soviet Union at this time, they discerned "no evidence to support reports that the independents were ready to do any mass business with the Russians."[196] Nonetheless, these brokers remained skeptical about the longer term success of Standard Oil's anti-Castro efforts, given that the industry was in the throes of a severe recession.[197]

For its part, the United States sought to further the boycott-embargo in any way it could. The American Ambassador to Mexico arranged a meeting with the head of that country's oil industry following reports that the Cubans may have been negotiating with Mexico for the sale of crude oil. "It is considered almost certain," the New York Times reported, "that the United States is prepared to go to unusual lengths to discourage the sale of Mexican crude."[198] Meanwhile, the Eisenhower administration pursued legislative action to undercut Cuban efforts to charter tankers and cargo ships from Japan and other countries to carry oil and sugar between the Soviet Union and the Caribbean island. As a result, the Japanese Shipowners Association parried Cuban requests on the grounds that ships calling at Communist ports were forbidden to enter U.S. harbors, and might even be refused entrance to other capitalist-bloc ports.[199]

"Getting tough": the sugar conflict

The manipulation of the Cuban sugar quota was viewed by Eisenhower administration officials as a powerful weapon for use "in restraining Castro if he should develop into a menace."[200] At the

State Department there was growing support during the second half of 1959 for permitting the President to revise or eliminate the quota at his discretion.[201] In early December, Secretary of State Herter issued a "thinly veiled" threat against the Castro regime to negotiate differences or invite a major reduction in Cuban sugar's access to the American market.[202] At the end of January 1960, Assistant Secretary of State Thomas C. Mann conferred with Speaker of the House of Representatives, Sam Rayburn, and Congressman John W. McCormack, both Democrats, on the Cuban problem and sugar legislation. During the meeting, Mann floated an administration proposal that would give the executive branch some "limited power" to adjust sugar quotas in order to deal with the "menace."[203]

In February 1960, *Business Week* reported that "Administration officials are thinking of asking Congress to give President Eisenhower discretionary authority to cut sugar imports from Cuba."[204] On February 4, the White House declined a Brazilian offer to mediate, having already decided, according to the *New York Times*, to seek congressional authority to change any country's sugar quota on the grounds of "national interest" and "to use language blunt enough to make plain to Premier Castro why it was seeking this authority."[205] There was increasing business-community support for a more hardline response, but differences over the most effective strategy.[206] While the community as a whole was not adverse to executive-branch action against the Cuban sugar quota, the National Beet Growers Federation which, in theory, stood to benefit most from any change in the quota, opposed substantive alterations in the structure of the program. This industry group, which supplied the bulk of domestic sugar supplies, worried that any temporary industry boom might lead to overexpansion and overproduction that would nullify short-term benefits. Officials of the United States Beet Sugar Association (sugar processors) similarly adhered to this "let's not rock the boat" position, although they were prepared to concede limited authority to the President to lower the Cuban quota if deemed in the national interest. But as long as Cuba was willing to supply the U.S. market, existing world conditions were "too fluid" to risk a significant revision of the sugar production and marketing system.[207]

The House Agriculture Committee dominated postwar U.S. sugar legislation. When the issue of doing something about the Cuban sugar quota surfaced within the administration, Democratic Committee chairman Harold Cooley expressed the view that the existing quota system was "fair and equitable."[208] He sided with the nationally anchored groups that saw few gains to be achieved from meddling with the program. Throughout the early months of 1960, Cooley repeated his opposition to granting the executive branch the power to "revise or juggle" the quotas.[209] He appealed for "great care and caution," arguing that Castro would interpret any change in Cuba's sugar quota as "a reprisal and economic aggression."[210] Although the Agriculture Committee chairman did not realize it, this was the White House's intent.

On March 15, Secretary of State Christian Herter presented legislation to Congress requesting presidential authority

to reduce the quota to any country . . . when [the White House] found it necessary to do so in the national interest or to insure adequate supplies of sugar. . . . I need not tell you that our concern [is] with conditions in Cuba.[211]

Several meetings followed, at which administration officials pressured the House Agriculture Committee for White House discretionary authority on "national security" grounds. On June 1, the Committee rejected the executive-branch request (voting along strict party lines), but reported out a bill granting a one-year extension of the 1948 Sugar Act. In partial concession to administration lobbying, however, an amendment delegated to the Secretary of Agriculture "the additional right to declare deficits and to increase quotas for the current year in any area, where he deems it advisable."[212]

In accordance with Washington's desire to "take a good solid slap at Cuba,"[213] the White House and State Department squeezed Congress for unfettered authority to manipulate foreign sugar quotas. Before the House Agriculture Committee on June 22, Secretary Herter said "this would be an appropriate time for the United States to seek ways to diversify its sources of supply and reduce the dependence of its consumers on Cuban sugar, the supply of which may become increasingly uncertain." But Herter admitted, under questioning, that the Committee's bill already insured an adequate sugar supply.[214]

In full congressional debate, Republican spokesmen assailed the existing bill and castigated Cooley for his refusal to support the White House wholeheartedly in the global anticommunist struggle.[215] Ambassador Bonsal states that Herter informed a closed executive session of the Committee that presidential discretion was "a necessary weapon to overthrow Castro and defeat Communist penetration of the territory of America's former staunch friend and ally."[216] During prolonged Committee debate, Republican members interpreted support for the Cooley amendment as being "soft on Communism and pro-Castro."

Congressional and executive pressures finally produced the desired outcome. According to Under Secretary of Agriculture True Morse, once Cooley recognized that the White House "was going to move in spite of the lack of action in Congress, he got very busy and reported out the legislation we needed."[217] The House Agriculture Committee produced a new bill granting the President authority to determine the Cuban sugar quota for the remainder of 1960 and set the 1961 quota "at any level he finds to be in the national interest."[218]

The newly amended bill provided for most of the Cuban quota to be apportioned among other foreign producers, assuring overwhelming support in the House where the sugar-refining interests who favored increased imports from the Philippines and elsewhere had very powerful friends. Introduced into the House on June 30, the bill was swiftly approved by a vote of 359 to 0 in a debate punctuated by references to "the Communist-studded Castro government," calls for harsher sanctions, and suggestions that the White House seriously consider severing diplomatic relations. Representative Mendel Rivers even declared that the United States should "reassert the Monroe Doctrine [and] threaten Castro with blockade. We should, if necessary, and, if conditions demand it, occupy Cuba."[219]

The Senate, where supporters of the domestic sugar-beet growers predominated, refused to consider the House bill and substituted a unanimous resolution authorizing the President to determine the quota only for the remainder of 1960. Its intent was to slow down the legislation to allow sugar-beet interests time to encourage advantageous changes in the bill. The Senate's obstruction created a constitutional impasse and intensified White House lobbying efforts. William B. Macomber, Jr., Assistant Secretary of State for Congressional Liaison, and Bryce Harlow, Deputy Assistant to the President for Congressional Affairs, "wandered among the Congressmen to tell them Eisenhower would be furious if no bill were passed."[220] The Senate ultimately approved the House bill, but opposed extension of the amended Sugar Act beyond 1960. However, following a joint committee debate, the Senate compromised, accepting the House bill in return for that chamber's agreement to extend it only through March 1961. On July 3, 1960, the consensus bill was transmitted to President Eisenhower.

On July 6, immediately preceding the public announcement on the fate of Cuba's sugar quota, an extrordinary interagency meeting was convened to review this issue in terms of future American policy toward the Castro government. The participants included State Department officials Douglas Dillon, Thomas Mann, and R. Richard Rubottom, Jr., Undersecretary of Agriculture True Morse, Treasury Secretary Robert B. Anderson, White House Staff members including David Kendall, John Eisenhower, James Hagerty, and Don Paarlberg, and President Eisenhower. They discussed drafting an official statement attributing the cut in Cuba's sugar quota not to economic retaliation, but to a dual concern over a dependable supply and Cuba's threat to the U.S. "national interest"; Ambassador Bonsal's "moderate" stance over the type and timing of economic reprisals against Havana; and the importance of mobilizing regional support for current and future actions. On this latter question of the need (as Thomas Mann put it) "to carry Latin America with us," Douglas Dillon suggested asking Congress for increased funds to finance long-term development projects in the hemisphere. Meanwhile, the President emphasized to those assembled that the sugar actions to be taken later that day were "in effect economic sanctions" against Cuba.[221]

Almost alone among senior executive-branch officials, Ambassador Bonsal assumed a number of contrary tactical and strategic positions. He argued that eliminating almost 900,000 tons of Cuban sugar constituted "far too drastic action under present circumstances" and would inevitably accelerate the expropriations of American-owned properties, expand and deepen Castro's internal support, and halt a growing regional tendency to support the U.S. position – rather than produce the overthrow of the revolutionary regime. While adhering to the overall contours of the existing policy, he argued in favor of "more moderate action [that] would be readily defendable and understood here and abroad."[222] This meant holding to a policy of diplomatic pressure to seek redress for "legitimate U.S. economic interests [that] have been and are being prejudiced by arbitrary, discriminatory, and unilateral actions" of the Cuban government. Such actions included nationalization without compensation of U.S.-owned properties, the "virtually confiscatory taxes" on mineral exports by American companies, the termination of the U.S. government-owned Nicaro nickel plant's tax-exempt status, and the tax dispute initiated by the Cuban regime that had led to the closure of the U.S. Moa Bay Mining Company.[223] Both State and Treasury participants at the July 6, 1960, meeting, however, responded to Bonsal's moderate position with irritation, if not disdain.[224]

Bonsal's primary concern, outlined in a letter to Assistant Secretary Rubottom, was that the administration had no "carefully thought out program" of economic sanctions that would "bring this Government to its knees" without its demise being directly attributable to Washington's policies. His supposed moderation was not over the basic goal, but over the utility and timing of particular tactics, such as the oil and sugar initiatives and the strategy of "apparently encouraging American business interests to abandon their activities here [e.g., Continental Can Company, Cuban-American Sugar Company, United Fruit Company]." Nonetheless, the Ambassador opposed any negotiated settlement based on recognizing the revolution's permanence: "I am as convinced as anyone could be that we cannot do business with Castro and the people who currently control him."[225]

Late afternoon on July 6, President Eisenhower signed the new sugar legislation into law and immediately reduced the Cuban sugar quota by 700,000 tons in response to what he described as the Castro government's "deliberate policy of hostility toward the United States" and its commitment to sell large quantities of sugar to the Soviet Union, "thus making its future ability to fill the sugar needs of the United States ever more uncertain." He then eliminated an additional 156,000 ton share of the U.S. market that was to have been allocated to Cuba to cover deficits in the quotas of other sugar suppliers.[226] The following day, at a National Security Council meeting on Cuba, Secretary of Defense Thomas Gates briefed Eisenhower "on a full range of military and paramilitary operations" up to and including direct U.S. intervention.[227]

The Cuban response was to accelerate the pace of socialization of the economy. A new law extended the nationalization process beyond the agro-mining, public utility, and tourist sectors to include foreign industrial and financial investments. American-owned enterprises that had been "intervened" but not nationalized (the Cuban Electric Company, the Cuban Telephone Company, Standard Oil, Texaco Oil, etc.) were formally taken over by the state. During August and September, U.S. interests in manufacturing, commerce, finance, and transportation were expropriated. Washington denounced it all as "in essence discriminatory, arbitrary and confiscatory" and insisted on prompt, adequate, and effective compensation payments.[228]

On October 13, 1960, a second nationalization law was enacted. It led to the virtual demise of large-scale private capitalist enterprise in Cuba. The banking industry and almost 400 foreign and locally owned properties came under government control. Sugar lands totalling 2.7 million acres were expropriated and placed under the National Agrarian Reform Institute's (INRA) authority. On October 26, another 166 U.S.-owned properties valued at around $250 million (including the $100-million Nicaro nickel mining complex) were nationalized. Meanwhile, a second Urban Reform Law completely dissolved the economic base of the urban bourgeoisie dependent on income from rents.[229]

For most American policymakers, the structural transformation of the Cuban economy and Havana's expanding links with Moscow were sufficient to justify a confrontation. In the opinion of one State Department official, the "expropriations, nationalizations, confiscations" and the "development of a close relationship with the Soviet Union" stood out as the central factors shaping Washington's response.[230] More broadly, the hostile U.S. posture reflected the degree to which Castro had moved Cuba out of the American political and economic orbit. "The essence of it," according to one official, "was that Castro revealed himself to be increasingly radical and nationalistic."[231]

The evolving regional strategy

Throughout the early 1960s, one of Washington's primary goals was to limit Cuba's role as an exporter of revolution and its impact as an anticapitalist development model in Latin America. "What we were demonstrating," asserted one imperial-state official, "was that any regime that came to power and pursued the line Castro pursued faced the real prospect of facing the relentless disapproval of the United States."[232] American policymakers linked political developments in the region to events in Cuba, defining the Castro government as a magnet and source of support for other hemispheric movements seeking to oust existing regimes. Given persistently fragile social and economic structures in a number of countries, the Eisenhower administration began to visualize "spreading revolution and overturning of governments throughout Latin America [where] a number of countries and governments were thought to be quite vulnerable – countries of major importance such as Brazil and Argentina."[233]

These concerns were not simply a function of the size of the American economic stake in Cuba. Rather, the cluster of economic relations between the two countries was part of a larger set of forces that could infect the whole continent. Cuba embodied many economic relationships that were reproduced in other parts of Latin America and whose collective importance to the U.S. economy was substantial. A State Department Cuba specialist observed that, "if we gave in to Castro all along the line we would get kicked around in the hemisphere."[234]

In a memorandum to the President in November 1959, Secretary of State Herter proposed that "all actions and policies" should henceforth be directed toward promoting internal (Cuban) and regional opposition to the Castro leadership.[235] At the same time, Herter also advised the White House that the "prolonged continuation of the Castro regime in Cuba in its present form would have serious adverse effects on the United States position in Latin America," especially if its "'neutralist' anti-American foreign policy [was] emulated by other Latin American countries."[236]

On January 26, 1960, President Eisenhower commented to a group of senior State Department and White House staff officials that "he thought the best course of action in the hemisphere would be if the OAS went down the line for us in trying to put some restraints on Castro." Informed by Assistant Secretary Rubottom that the United States would encounter considerable difficulty in mobilizing hemispheric support for any major initiative against Cuba, Eisenhower replied that "if the OAS is not going to support us, they show themselves as fair weather friends and we may have to take other action."[237] Although the White House hoped for OAS legitimation of its Cuba objectives, Eisenhower made it clear that the United States was prepared to act unilaterally, if necessary, without recourse to the regional body.

During the first half of 1960, there was a notable absence of regional support for the hardline U.S. position toward Cuba. In late February, for instance, Eisenhower visited the politically strategic countries of Argentina, Brazil, Chile, and Uruguay where he raised the Cuban problem with each head of state. Much to his irritation, all four allied leaders "just would not reply to his question."[238] In early March, the President told the National Security Council that "every effort" should be made to get OAS members "to recognize the dangers involved in the Cuban situation and support action with respect to them."[239] The problem remained, however, to convince countries disposed to view the conflict as essentially a bilateral dispute and skeptical of supporting OAS action under the Caracas anti-Communist resolution, since even U.S. intelligence assessments did not describe Cuba as "under Communist control or domination."[240] Large-scale popular support for the Cuban Revolution throughout Latin America also constrained a number of governments from acceding to U.S. pressures. In a memorandum to the President on April 23, Secretary of State Herter acknowledged that, despite a continuing diplomatic offensive, U.S. efforts had not reached a point "where we can count on the Latin American support which would be necessary for successful action in the OAS."[241] This lack of enthusiasm displayed by some of its closest Latin American supporters forced Washington to adjust its plans for hemispheric action against Castro.

Another factor limiting U.S. efforts to organize OAS action against Cuba was the regional body's insistence that Washington also take forceful action against the Trujillo dictatorship in the Dominican Republic. Diplomatic pressures to encourage Trujillo's voluntary resignation had been to no avail, and the White House was not prepared to use other means to accelerate his removal. Administration officials wanted to be certain that whoever succeeded Trujillo would pursue policies compatible with American interests in the region. Meanwhile, the Dominican dictator could at least be counted on not to develop military ties with the Soviet Union.[242]

On June 21, 1960, the U.S. government sent a memorandum to the OAS Inter-American Peace Committee describing its "patience and forebearance [with] irresponsible efforts by the Cuban Government to portray the United States Government as planning an armed attack."[243] In mid-July, the Peruvian government requested a hemisphere foreign ministers meeting to consider the issue of regional solidarity. This initiative "coincided somewhat suspiciously with a $53.2 million loan from the United States and an increase in the Peruvian sugar quota."[244] Meanwhile, the Cubans had asked the United Nations Security Council to take up the issues of U.S. economic sanctions and Washington's "repeated threats, harassments, intrigues, reprisals and aggressive acts."[245] The Eisenhower administration continued to insist that Cuba was bound by mandate (of the August 1959 OAS foreign ministers' meeting) and tradition to bring its concerns to the

regional body.[246] On July 18, simultaneous with the Security
Council's opening debate on the Cuban request, the OAS Council
announced a conference of regional foreign ministers "for the
purpose of considering the requirements of continental solidarity
and the defense of the regional system."[247]

In the Security Council, the American position was expressed in
a draft resolution submitted by Argentina and Ecuador that contended Cuba had a legal responsibility to "try the OAS first." During the debate, U.S. Ambassador Henry Cabot Lodge insisted that
Washington had not engaged in any "aggressive acts" and had "no
aggressive purposes" against Cuba.[248] Although only two Security
Council members (England and France) supported the U.S. argument that Cuba was obliged to "try the OAS first," the draft resolution was sustained by a vote of 9 to 0 (with the Soviet Union
and Poland abstaining).

The Cuban Revolution also accelerated the Eisenhower administration's evolving commitment to a large-scale program of economic and social development assistance to Latin America. This
strategy originated with White House Special Ambassador Milton
Eisenhower's trip to the region in 1957, which produced a series
of recommendations for dealing with the recurring problem of
"ultra nationalism."[249] Advocacy of a greatly expanded foreign-aid
program for the hemisphere, however, aroused the opposition of
the Treasury Department, with its fiscally conservative outlook
and its belief in the private sector as the key to economic development in the Third World.[250] Within the executive-branch
bureaucracy, Treasury offered strong resistance to this plan and
was able to "hold the fort" until the full implications of Vice-President Nixon's hostile reception in Venezuela in 1958 began to be
assessed by the White House. The result was a bureaucratic compromise, of sorts. In mid-year, the administration announced that
it would support a moderate increase in social and economic
development assistance and agree to the establishment of a
medium-sized regional banking institution. To underscore the
proposed limited scope of this new financial commitment, dubbed
"Operation Pan America," Washington refused to consider such
important Latin American objectives as trade preferences and
export price stabilization supports.[251] Furthermore, when the
Inter-American Development Bank was formally set up in April
1959, its prime goal as seen from the White House was to act as a
"bridge" for, and not to compete with, private capital flows into
the area economies.[252]

The decision to fund a major program of social and economic development in Latin America coincided with Eisenhower's trip to the region in February 1960 and its failure to achieve a primary goal: undermine popular support for the Cuban Revolution. Castro's Cuba now "became sufficient stimulus to induce the President to overrule the opposition of the Treasury and the lending agencies to financing social development projects in Latin America."[253] A special executive-branch technical group was organized to draft proposals about social and economic reforms for discussion at an autumn Inter-American conference in Bogotá, Colombia. In August, Congress approved a presidential request for $500 million to establish a development fund. At the final meeting of the so-called Committee of Twenty-One in Bogotá in September 1960, the United States announced a new $500 million commitment to social and economic programs throughout the continent. This "Act of Bogotá" was the basis of and forerunner of the Kennedy administration's Alliance for Progress.

Prior to the Bogotá conference, a Meeting of Consultation of OAS Foreign Ministers was convened at San Jose, Costa Rica. Preparing for this meeting, President Eisenhower declared that the new aid program would only benefit those countries whose governments "show a willingness to cooperate" in advancing U.S. regional policy goals.[254] Secretary of State Herter also telegrammed each American Embassy in Latin America directing them to emphasize the multilateral nature of the Cuba problem and "discourage" any proposals for hemispheric governments "[to] offer [their] good offices to conciliate U.S.-Cuban differences."[255] Executive-branch policymakers hoped for unanimous condemnation of Communist infiltration in the hemisphere by conference participants. At a minimum, they desired strong censure of "the communist direction" in which Cuba was moving as well as the nation's expanding links with the Soviet Union.[256] Preliminary conference discussions, however, indicated that outside the right-wing dictatorships of Guatemala, Nicaragua and Paraguay, there was very little support for even a verbal rebuke of Cuba's ties with the Soviet Union. Most regional governments "wanted no part" of a conflict they viewed as essentially a bilateral dispute between Washington and Havana.[257] The conference finally adopted a "Declaration of San Jose," but only after strong hints from Secretary of State Herter that it was necessary to the projected development assistance program.[258] This document defined totalitarian governments as incompatible with the inter-

American system and opposed extracontinental intervention, but in neither instance was Cuba or communism singled out for censure. One of its Articles, which applied as much to the United States as to Cuba, also strongly reaffirmed the principle of nonintervention "by any American state" in the internal or external affairs of member countries.[259] In reference to the conference deliberations, President Eisenhower remarked that the lack of a formal commitment to collective action should not inhibit any government from acting unilaterally when the so-called national interest was at stake or, as he phrased it, "when the chips are finally down."[260]

American policymakers were not prepared to write off the possibility of future regional action. The State Department persisted in informal diplomatic efforts to mobilize area governments in support of the U.S. position. Under Secretary of State Douglas Dillon told a White House meeting in late November 1960 that Latin American ambassadors were being pressured diplomatically to support an OAS Foreign Ministers meeting in early 1961 to take action against Cuba under the Rio Treaty. Specific measures would include the formal termination of diplomatic and economic relations and some form of military action "to seal off Cuba and the export of arms." However, he conceded that apart from the right-wing dictatorships of Central America there was little, or no, enthusiasm for this line of action among most of Latin America's governments.[261] In January 1961, President Eisenhower told Department officials that "Latin America must be brought to see the necessity of action."[262] By the end of his presidency, some frustrated executive-branch officials had become convinced that "we must give more thought to working outside the OAS, which is not an effective forum for dealing with this problem."[263]

U.S. economic sanctions and the origins of the global economic blockade

The program approved by Eisenhower in March 1960 to overthrow the Castro government "touched about every front you could touch," including "economic warfare."[264] The primary assumption behind the strategy of economic sanctions was that the revolutionary regime would be unable to find suitable alternative markets, credits, and commodities to operate its economy at maximum efficiency. In theory, the export-dependent Cuban economy was highly vulnerable to a U.S.-directed embargo since "almost everything, from the large boilers in the sugar mills to ordinary electric sockets, was built and worked according to American designs and specifications."[265] Over 90 percent of the country's industrial plants and transportation systems depended on equipment, spare parts, and machinery from American sources.[266] Further, most senior managerial, administrative, and technical personnel in U.S.-owned or controlled enterprises were American citizens. And, fearing intervention or nationalization, most of these companies operating on the island during 1959 and 1960 deliberately had kept inventories of replacement parts, machinery, fuel, and other necessities at a low level.[267]

On June 16, the Treasury Department received a memorandum from the State Department listing a number of actions under consideration, such as "den[ial] to the Cubans [of] premium payments for sugar" and "encouragement of U.S. creditors to press their claims and obtain liens on Cuban assets" in the United States.[268] At a follow-up meeting, three distinct, but related, possible actions were discussed: a hold on public and private Cuban assets in the United States (totalling approximately $200 million), a prohibition on all transactions with Cuba, and a total ban on Cuban imports. The participating State and Treasury officials also decided that the imposition of blocking controls by Treasury should take place "in conjunction with the exercise by the Commerce Department of its export control authority to stop all exports from the United States to Cuba."[269]

Although the elimination of Cuba's preferential access to the American sugar market commanded strong interagency support, it also raised the problem of adequate legal justification. Withdrawal or suspension of tariff concessions under the Trading with the Enemy Act could be explained on the grounds that Cuba was communist dominated or controlled; alternately, legislation existed to abrogate most-favored-nation status to countries that discriminated against the United States. The State Department appeared to favor the latter rationale because of what it described as "documented" cases of "Cuban discrimination and violations of its GATT [General Agreement on Trade and Tariffs] obligations to the United States." Yet, both State and Treasury officials conceded that "the clearest legal justification in both cases would be to base action on Communist domination, control and subversion [even though such an assertion] is difficult to demonstrate."[270]

Other economic blockade measures under State Department consideration included possible Commerce Department action to

limit American exports to Cuba under the Export Control Act of
1949, invoking the Battle Act to prevent shipment of strategic
materials to a socialist bloc country, and encouraging "a voluntary
embargo against Cuba by private U.S. companies."[271] Treasury
Department officials identified two other areas of the Cuban economy vulnerable to U.S. economic sanctions, recommending that
consideration be given to blacklisting all capitalist-bloc tanker
operators chartering out their vessels to Cuba or the socialist bloc
and denying the Castro government access to those international
cable facilities that transit the United States. Because each individual transaction depends on large amounts of cable traffic,
action on this latter suggestion could have significantly disrupted
Cuban sugar sales, which are made largely on the spot market to
capitalist buyers outside the United States.[272]

On July 7, the National Security Council decided that any
future actions against Havana should be taken under a new proclamation specifically directed to the Cuban situation. The State
Department was given the responsibility for drafting the decree,
but it soon became clear that there was "strong opposition"
within its ranks to this course of action and a widespread preference for anchoring any initiatives under the Trading with the
Enemy Act in the ongoing state of national emergency declared in
1950 over the Korean War. State officials wary of a new proclamation made the following points: A decision of this magnitude
would contain "the unflattering implication" that Cuba's actions
constituted a "threat" to the U.S. "national security"; it would
commit American prestige to the successful prosecution of what
would, in effect, be a declaration of "all out economic warfare on
Cuba"; and it might have the unanticipated consequence of generating increased support for the Castro government in other
parts of Latin America.[273] These arguments were transmitted by
State Department legal advisor Eric Hager to one of the President's senior "national security" officials, General Andrew Goodpaster, who "felt that the Department's line [i.e., these
arguments] was sound."[274]

Through August and September 1960, State and Treasury officials continued to disagree over the breadth of any proposed economic embargo of Cuba: to maintain telephone and cable communications for the benefit of American citizens in Cuba (State),
or sever all communications that could be used in commercial
transactions between Havana and Western Europe (Treasury); to
exempt food and pharmaceuticals "for propaganda reasons"

(State), or apply any announced economic measures to the strict letter of the law (Treasury); to retain an existing license allowing individuals and religious, charitable, or educational organizations in foreign countries to receive gifts worth up to $50 from the United States "on humanitarian grounds" (State), or close every loophole that might in any way ease Cuba's precarious foreign exchange position (Treasury).[275]

In the meantime, the Cuban response to the loss of the American sugar market was, as noted previously, marked by the extensive takeovers of American-owned properties. The second nationalization law of October 13, 1960, catalyzed the White House to transform an emerging policy into fact. On October 20, the President instituted a comprehensive embargo on exports under the general authority of the 1949 Export Control Act.[276] The decision to invoke this Act, rather than the Trading with the Enemy Act, in theory allowed overseas subsidiaries of U.S. multinationals to escape compliance with the new policy. The aim of the embargo, according to Eisenhower, "was to deny Cuba items, particularly spare parts for American-made equipment, and thus cause costly shutdowns and have . . . a snowballing effect."[277] The *Wall Street Journal* reported that Washington also was planning to prevent Western European and Latin American countries from transshipping American products to Cuba.[278]

American economic sanctions against Cuba assumed major proportions with the elimination of the Cuban sugar quota in early July 1960. Notes taken by White House agricultural and trade advisor Don Paarlberg at the interagency meeting preceding the official announcement reveal quite clearly that the administration was looking beyond this bilateral sanction to an escalating regional and global economic blockade of Cuba. When the President asked the meeting for suggestions on how to proceed next, Douglas Dillon's response was brief and pointed: "Boycott. Trading with the Enemy Act." Although Treasury Secretary Robert Anderson agreed that such a move would virtually eliminate access to U.S. spare parts and other commodities critical to the day-to-day operations of the Cuban economy, he emphasized that no matter how successful it was it would not achieve Washington's ultimate objective without the collaboration of Canada, England, France, West Germany, Holland, and other Western allies. Eisenhower concurred and then turned to the problem of how to "keep the Latin Americans in line." Dillon argued for a two-pronged initiative: payment of generous above-world-market prices for regional sugar imports, and consideration of increased economic assistance to the hemisphere.[279]

A Treasury memorandum of July 12 expanded on Secretary Anderson's contention that no embargo, no matter how effective, could achieve the desired objective "unless a number of leading industrial countries joined us in extensive control measures." These included the denial or reduction of markets for Cuban exports; the blocking of Cuban assets; embargos on petroleum shipments to Cuba and the use of locally owned tankers in this trade; and a prohibition on spare-parts exports vital to Cuba's industrial, transport, and communications sectors.[280] That same day, Secretary of State Herter sent a telegram to the Paris Embassy outlining the presentation to be made in appealing for NATO countries' support in operationalizing the embargo strategy. State's appeal was based on the contention that Cuban-Soviet activities in the Western Hemisphere constituted a profound threat "to Free World security and unity." The telegram also singled out the White House desire that allied governments direct their private tanker owners not to ship Soviet oil to Cuba.[281]

Committed to Cuba's total isolation within the capitalist world economy, the United States was intent not merely on limiting Havana's trade and commercial ties with the nonsocialist bloc, but also on preventing it from finding Western sources of military assistance. The Herter telegram stated that the Castro regime had made "very substantial [arms] purchases from [the] FW [Free World]," even though the Eisenhower administration was successful in forcing a halt to a number of proposed allied weapons sales to Cuba since early 1959. Washington, for instance, played a central role in the British decision not to sell Cuba its Hunter jet fighter in late 1959. "The British did not give in," Secretary Herter told a closed session of the Senate Foreign Relations committee in early 1960, "until I had an exchange of three very personal letters with [Foreign Minister] Selwyn [Lloyd] telling him how damaging it would be if they began selling arms now to the Cubans."[282] The Italian government was also understood to have been responsive to American requests. Perhaps the most notable exception was Belgium, where the American Embassy could not stop some arms purchases by Havana early in the revolution.[283]

In early 1960, Frederick Nolting, Counsellor of the American NATO delegation, formally requested "political, economic and moral support" from member countries for U.S. policy toward Cuba."[284] Although Western European governments appeared

ready to provide "full assurances regarding sales and transportation of arms to Cuba," there was less enthusiasm for a ban on traditional commerce carried on by individual businessmen or companies.[285] Meanwhile, nations receiving U.S. Mutual Security Act
economic assistance were notified that a condition now attaching
to this aid was agreement not to purchase Cuban sugar. To the
American embassies in Paris and The Hague in mid-July, Secretary Herter had already expressed White House displeasure over
NATO purchases of Cuban sugar: "if [the] Netherlands or other
allies see fit [to] cease or suspend such purchases on economic or
any other grounds they consider justifiable, [the] U.S. would not
find this displeasing."[286] In August, the U.S. International Cooperation Administration amended a loan agreement with Morocco
to fund the purchase of $10 million worth of sugar from suppliers
other than Cuba. Because Morocco was the only country at that
time with an outstanding sugar-loan authorization, it was singled
out. But the directive was expected to have more extensive application, given an International Cooperation Administration estimate that $20 million to $25 million annually in United States
loans and grants was available for sugar purchases, usually from
Cuba.[287] In September, the Mutual Security Appropriations Act
was amended to exclude countries providing economic or military
assistance to Cuba from all U.S. foreign-aid programs. The countries most immediately affected were Italy, Belgium, Poland,
Israel, and Yugoslavia.[288]

Washington policymakers believed that the success of the economic embargo would depend, in large part, on Havana's incapacity to locate alternative capitalist trading and financial partners. In this regard, the State Department's most immediate
concern centered on Canada because of the ease with which this
country could fill the gap left by the U.S. embargo on industrial
and manufactured exports to Cuba. Nearly all of Canada's automotive product specifications, for example, were identical with
American specifications. The unease of the Americans was heightened by Ottawa's amicable relations with the Castro regime.
Major Canadian banking and insurance interests on the island had
been excluded from the sweeping nationalizations of September
and October 1960.[289]

The Canadian response to the embargo was lukewarm at best.
The conservative government of John Diefenbaker declared that
it would "not encourage Dominion companies to fill the gap left
by the U.S. embargo," but neither would it "brook pressure or

interference from Washington."[290] On December 10, Bradley Fisk, the U.S. Assistant Secretary of Commerce for International Affairs, revealed that Secretary of State Herter had actually attempted to enlist Canadian participation in the October 20 embargo decision. He declared that efforts to gain Ottawa's support would continue, despite the current impasse.[291]

In December 1960, the Canadian Minister of Trade and Commerce, George Hees, told a Cuban trade mission in Ottawa headed by Minister of the Economy Regino Boti that Canada was unlikely to find better business partners "anywhere."[292] But while the Diefenbaker government was not prepared to consider a total embargo, since Canada was both highly dependent on exports and skeptical about the American objective, it still sought to walk a fine line between practical compliance with the U.S. position and an independent trading policy. During the embargo's early months, Canada showed little disposition to antagonize Washington. On the contrary, it reasserted a refusal to sanction the sale of strategic items to Havana and revised export regulations to establish a legal basis for denying export licenses to individuals seeking to re-export third-country goods from Canada to Cuba.

The first indication of private Canadian compliance with the American concern over manufactured exports was the government's failure to approve a proposed Cuban purchase of $800,000 worth of automobile parts in November 1960.[293] Despite a temporary rise in Canadian-Cuban trade at this time, Havana's shortage of foreign-exchange and dollar reserves obstructed any significant increase in bilateral trade.[294]

On December 12, Diefenbaker reaffirmed his government's opposition to the export of strategic military goods and "the bootlegging of goods of United States origin" to Cuba while continuing to insist that practical considerations militated against a blanket embargo on nonstrategic transactions.[295]

By the end of the Eisenhower presidency, it was evident that economic sanctions against Cuba had aggravated the inevitable dislocation that accompanies any rapid process of large-scale social and economic change. Washington's measures had an initially severe impact on three key areas of the Cuban economy. First, the island's port and storage facilities could not adequately accommodate the large-socialist-bloc freighters. The port system was geared to smaller vessels from the United States; storage facilities were sufficient only for short-haul trade. Although a sudden crisis was averted by the temporary mobilization of workers from other economic sectors, the basic problem remained. Second, Cuba's dependence on imported raw materials and industrial goods-in-process from the United States meant that industrial production levels declined significantly. Third, and most important, were the day-to-day problems in operating the economy resulting from the American spare-parts embargo. The crucial transportation, petroleum, and sugar sectors were hardest hit by the parts crisis which, in turn, disrupted other areas such as food distribution.[296] By the end of 1960, trained economic managers and skilled technical workers were also in short supply because of the policies historically followed by American companies (allocating most of the senior administrative and skilled positions to their own nationals, almost all of whom were repatriated during 1959 and 1960) and the politically or economically motivated migration of large numbers of Cubans with the requisite skills. To the extent that the economy "performed surprisingly well" during the revolution's redistributive phase, it was attributable largely to expanded domestic demand for local commodities achieved by the downward redistribution of income, and to greater use of available land, labor, and capital compared to the Batista period.[297]

In mid-December 1960, President Eisenhower extended the sugar embargo until March 1961, leading to the swift formalization of the numerous Soviet-Cuba trade agreements entered into during 1960 and a Soviet commitment to purchase at least 2.7 million tons of sugar at 4 cents per pound in 1961, if the American boycott endured.[298] On January 3, 1961, the Cuban government demanded that the American Embassy in Havana reduce its staff to eleven within forty-eight hours. At a hastily convened White House meeting, President Eisenhower declared that "the U.S. should not tolerate being kicked around" in this manner and that a break in relations was inevitable and desirable. The only question now was the "timing" of the decision. Treasury Secretary Robert Anderson even raised the alternative of simply "get[ting] rid of Castro." Central Intelligence Agency Director Allen Dulles and his Deputy Director of Plans Richard Bissell injected the exile project into the discussion and broached the possibility of an actual invasion in mid-March 1961. Eisenhower agreed that this was the only "reasonable . . . course of action" short of abandoning the entire operation and hoped it would find favor with the new administration. In the absence of a suitable exile leadership, though, he was not prepared to consider activating the military option in the waning moments of his presidency, even though he supported a further expansion of the exile force.[299] When General Goodpaster expressed concern that "the operation was building a momentum of its own that would be difficult to stop," the President emphasized that the United States was under no obligation or commitment, and any decision to operationalize the Cuban "assets" would depend exclusively on "political developments."[300]

Despite opposition from some within the executive branch, senior administration officials now were convinced that there was nothing to be gained from maintaining diplomatic relations. They also believed that an immediate break in relations "might be the signal for other Latin American countries to do the same."[301] The *Washington Post* reported that, to encourage a "chain reaction" within the region, the White House probably would intensify efforts to halt the movement of arms to Cuba, institute a joint hemispheric tracking program to monitor the movement of Cuban government officials throughout Latin America, and accelerate the economic warfare program.[302] The U.S. Congress received the executive-branch decision to terminate relations with Havana "uncritically for the most part."[303] Most legislators concurred with the statement by Senate Foreign Relations Committee chairman J. William Fulbright that the United States "certainly had sufficient provocation."[304] On January 12, 1961, in his final annual message to Congress, President Eisenhower declared that "Communist penetration of Cuba is real and poses a serious threat."[305]

Conclusion

The political revolution against the Batista dictatorship and foreign economic domination, and the initial measures to control indigenous and foreign property interests, culminated in a telescoped national and social revolution in Cuba that saw the end of capitalism there. The first nationalizations of locally owned properties were not accompanied by assurances that particular sectors of the economy would be excluded from the threat of state takeover. Neither did these initial property expropriations, from the point of view of the U.S. government, set a satisfactory precedent in terms of "prompt, adequate, and effective" compensation. On the contrary, they signalled the eventual displacement of foreign capitalists in favor of locally anchored control over the economic surplus based on a transformed state and class structure. The immediate extension of the revolution's social base into the urban and rural proleteriat created a social movement whose new demands required satisfaction as a condition for cooperation with the new project.[306]

Socialist revolution appeared on the agenda in Cuba because the nationalist leadership had no binding ties to the capitalist system and was determined to substitute a locally controlled economy for decades of capitalist growth dominated by external forces. As the revolution contracted the prerogatives of the indigenous landowning and foreign investment groups, a process that began as a struggle against a dictator by nonsocialist nationalists appealing to all classes became a struggle against all capitalist interests. Any attempt at economic transformation when U.S. companies dominated Cuba was bound to engender conflict, and it was the incapacity of political revolutionaries to institute partial changes in the face of internal and external opposition that led to a major confrontation with the United States and eventual nationalization of all alien enterprises.

In all crucial respects, the U.S. state appears to have assumed the leadership in proposing, formulating, and executing strategies in response to the Cuban Revolution during 1959 and 1960. The U.S. capitalist class in Cuba, on the other hand, lacked the unity of purpose or the necessary instruments that might have allowed it to mount any effective response to the policies of the Castro regime. The vacillations of American businesses on the island toward the unfolding revolution reflected both the scale of their investments and the importance of their Cuban investments relative to their other subsidiaries around the world. Another factor was the shifting perceptions among different enterprises of the possibilities of reaching an accommodation with the Castro government. Some companies (e.g., Cuban Electric) that were the first to be affected by the regime's policies advocated the most extreme solutions, while others (e.g., sugar and cattle plantation owners) continued to operate in the hope that an acceptable arrangement could be worked out.

The decision to press the U.S. oil companies to refuse Cuban demands to refine Soviet oil and the elimination of Cuban access to the American sugar market in mid-1960 did not originate primarily from within the business community. On the contrary, these confrontations were promoted by the Eisenhower administration, and not in response to immediate economic conflicts such as nationalization of U.S.-owned properties, but as part of a larger executive-branch effort to destabilize the new Cuban government. The White House orchestrated the oil and sugar actions as it sought to gain adherence by the corporations and legislators to its strategic conception of how to reinstate the conditions for private enterprise on the island.

As the probability of irreversible change emerged in Cuba, the State Department assumed the dominant role even in the area of foreign economic policy. The State Department, not Treasury, led the interagency debates preceding the most important American initiatives (e.g., the oil, sugar and trade sanctions) directed against the revolutionary regime in Havana.

The Eisenhower administration's profound hostility toward the guerrilla leadership of the July 26 Movement before 1959 carried over into the postrevolutionary period. American policy toward the Castro forces could never be accurately described as cautious, ambiguous, or flexible, or as watchful waiting or simply muddling through. Washington first advanced a policy of selective hostility that over time blossomed into an unqualified refusal to accept the continued existence of the Castro government and its program of social and economic development. In the early months, individual policymakers encouraged the growth of a "manageable" Cuban leadership, The procapitalist orientation of senior economic officials in the first post-Batista cabinet and the continuing substantial nonnationalized U.S. economic stake led some officials, especially in the State Department, to confine initial overt hostility to the Castro faction of the new regime, rather than identify the whole government as unacceptable. Taking account of the fragile nature of the economy inherited from Batista, Treasury officials took a much harder line from the beginning, proposing the use of economic levers to limit the scope and pace of change in the hope of toppling Castro.

Between April and June 1959, the impact of Havana's redistributive policies, the institution of stringent monetary and fiscal controls, and the accelerating pace of social transformation narrowed, but did not completely eliminate the gap between negotiating and hostile tendencies in the U.S. government. Following the agrarian reform law's enactment in June, over the opposition from procapitalist cabinet ministers, it became apparent to State Department and other executive-branch policymakers that these ministers could not contest the guerrilla forces or direct the Cuban economy along "constructive" national-capitalist lines. The nationalization of agriculture was pivotal for Washington: It raised fundamental political and economic issues beyond the immediate conflicts it generated and led many senior U.S. officials to the inescapable conclusion that a thorough transformation of the economy was imminent. As a result, the limited "give and take" over tactical issues gave way to a convergence between "liberals" and "conservatives" by late 1959 in support of destabilization.

At this moment, however, the United States had no internal Cuban allies or sympathetic social forces capable of nurturing a strategy of subversion and counterrevolution. The speed with which Cuba moved out of the American political and economic orbit, in other words, limited the new regime's vulnerability to external pressures. Eisenhower's decision to make the U.S. challenge a global one, primarily through economic sanctions, was a direct outcome of this situation.

American policy toward the Cuban Revolution during the Eisenhower presidency was based on uniform executive-branch opposition to the very existence of the Castro regime, supporting its overthrow "by all means available to the United States short of the open employment of American armed force in Cuba."[307] Discrete U.S. measures that have been attributed – even if accurately – principally to prior Cuban actions (e.g., the sugar quota cut as a "counterpunching" response to the intervention of the foreign-owned petroleum refineries[308]) must still be anchored to the larger imperial-state consensus over Cuba. As early as March 1960, months in advance of the oil and sugar actions, the White House, National Security Council, and State Department originated a multilayered program of public and covert confrontation designed to "bring another government to power in Cuba."[309]

The initial diplomatic measures adopted to defend American economic interests in Cuba were not cautious or moderate: They were the result of policymakers' evaluations of the threat posed to capital accumulation, and they were based on a perception that the social revolution was reversible. But the dialectic of conflict and escalation propelled the radicalization process. In the context of unrelenting United States opposition to large-scale socioeconomic change in Cuba, the process of "permanent revolution" – from redistributive measures to the agrarian reform law to the nationalization of locally owned agricultural properties to the expropriation of all foreign investments – became necessary to the survival of the Castro regime and its development project. In Cuba between 1959 and 1961, the imperial state suffered a decisive setback, not a momentary loss, that went beyond the interests of affected multinationals. For while the multinationals bore the costs of nationalization (and Cuban workers gained the benefits), a valuable, highly productive area was catapulted out of the world of capital accumulation.

4. The United States against Cuba 1961–1968: politics of confrontation in Latin America

The Alliance for Progress

> According to us, relations between Cuba and the United States may currently be compared to an automobile and a train traveling more or less at the same speed. But the automobile has to cross over the railroad track; and as the train and the automobile approach the level crossing, the possibilities of confrontation and collision increase. If the automobile – that is, Cuba – reaches the level crossing before the train (that is, if the Latin American revolution reaches a certain state) . . . Cuba loses its importance. In fact, Cuba is not being attacked by imperialism out of spite; it is being attacked because of its significance.
>
> Ernesto Guevara (1964)[1]

The Cuban Revolution profoundly influenced U.S.-Latin American policy during the 1960s. Raising the twin issues of control over national resources and alternative, noncapitalist paths to development, it forced Washington to reformulate hemispheric strategies. Apprehensive lest the socialist experiment in Cuba heighten historic conflicts between the United States and its traditional sphere of influence, executive-branch policymakers settled on the Alliance for Progress to contain the influence of the Cuban Revolution and maintain U.S. regional hegemony. The Alliance for Progress, State Department official Chester Bowles observed, "in large measure grew out of the Cuban situation."[2]

Some policymakers envisioned the Alliance primarily as enlarging the scope of U.S. economic activity in Latin America and extending Wilsonian liberalism to the Third World. And many saw no contradiction between the Alliance's proclamation of democratic ideals and their own advocacy of intervention and counterrevolution. Any serious assessment of the Alliance must therefore distinguish between the appeals, intentions, and personal motivations of the Kennedy White House, however idealist and democratic, and the way these preferences were translated into commitments and actual "alliances." Despite the program's moralistic ideology and liberal idealism, the United States pursued a number of contradictory objectives in its name: economic development, reformist electoral politics, anticommunism, military buildups, and counterinsurgency operations. Ultimately, the policies adopted and alliances consummated proved incompatible with the principal goal of hemispheric social and economic change.[3]

The dilemma built into the Alliance was readily apparent in economic policy. The Charter signatories were existing governments, many of which were profoundly hostile to any consideration of even limited, let alone structural, economic change. Meanwhile, the United States remained committed to the notion of private capital dominating this project, and most Alliance funds were "tied loans" – essentially, disguised subsidies for American exporters offered precisely to those ruling groups that expressed the least interest in agrarian reform and social programs. Per capita agricultural and food production declined in most of the Alliance countries between 1961 and 1968. Only Venezuela achieved the annual 2.5 percent per capita growth rate goal over this time span.[4] In other words, Alliance funds, instead of generating a period of dynamic economic growth and expansion, played a more significant role in bolstering the political and military power of the most conservative regimes in the hemisphere.

The dual strategy of capitalist modernization and large-scale military assistance to existing regimes incorporated two distinct policy innovations: the introduction of counterinsurgency programs, and the effort to expand U.S. influence within state structures such as the bureaucracies and military and within the societies at large, for instance, by financing the growth of anticommunist trade unions.[5]

The demands of political stability and economic change dictated a White House shift away from traditional anticommunist economic allies, such as the large landowning elites that found favor in Washington during the 1950s and the military regimes that governed in their interests. Liberal parliamentary regimes, rising industrialists, and other capitalist forces were now deemed more likely to promote the reforms that would undermine the appeal of groups advocating social transformation. The diversification of postwar U.S. private investment in Latin America beyond the agri-

cultural and extractive minerals sectors into industry and manufacturing and tourism facilitated this substitution of political and
economic allies. But the power of the hemisphere's forces massed
against social and economic change and the forms of "resistance"
they employed (capital flight, military coups) doomed such
"showcase" Alliance governments as those in Brazil, Chile,
Argentina, Ecuador, Bolivia, and the Dominican Republic.[6]

The failure of these reformist experiments generated the very
outcome the Alliance for Progress was designed to forestall: unful-
filled expectations, widespread social discontent, and mobilized
populations supporting transformations that went beyond whatever incremental changes had already been wrought. Rather than
identify with the rising forces of popular nationalism, Washington
reverted to the politics of stabilization, which found practical
application in the growing militarization of Latin American society during the mid-1960s.

This policy shift was reflected, beginning in the latter part of
1961, in the increasing emphasis given to security issues and the
preservation of existing regimes at the expense of democratic
reform. Even earlier, in May 1961, the Kennedy administration's
response to the downfall of the Trujillo dictatorship in the Dominican Republic indicated that America was preeminently concerned with avoiding "other Cubas."[7] But the centerpiece of the
new American policy was the successful naval blockade of Cuba
in October 1962, the first major reassertion of the United States
as the dominant hemispheric power since the Castro victory in
January 1959. With this, Washington began to see force as acceptable for achieving stability and Latin American military coups as
a preferred alternative to a "second Cuba."

The expansion of U.S. military assistance under the Alliance for
Progress was accompanied by a White House determination that
the most serious threats to established rulers were internally, not
externally, based. This refocus on indigenous forces translated
into a strengthening of the military and police capabilities of
regional allies, especially those confronting formidable nationalist
movements. Here, priority was given to counterinsurgency warfare programs and police assistance and training programs.[8] Both
were directly linked to the Cuban Revolution's continental
influence.

New centers were established in the United States and the Panama Canal Zone to train Latin American officers in antiguerrilla
warfare, and the 1962 White House budget included a request for

sufficient funds to double to over 6,000 the number of U.S. Army Special Forces personnel involved in the program.[9] The Panama Canal Zone provided not only geographic proximity and suitable terrain, but also facilitated direct involvement of American counterinsurgency experts in actual military conflicts.[10] As part of this overall program, the United States provided large amounts of military equipment (small arms, communications technology) adapted to the circumstances of guerrilla warfare. In January 1962, the Special Group on Counterinsurgency was formed to coordinate regional activities and ensure "the use of all available sources with maximum effectiveness."[11] That July, Washington also established an Inter-American Police Academy to give "considerably greater emphasis to police assistance programs" in Latin America and throughout the Third World.[12] Within a year, U.S. training programs were operating in a dozen regional countries; by the end of 1963, 600 police officers from fifteen hemispheric countries had passed through the Academy's training program in crowd control, counterintelligence, and guerrilla warfare operations.[13]

The shift of support in favor of established political and economic ruling groups was reflected vividly in the allocation of Alliance for Progress funds: Whereas total U.S. military assistance to Latin America during the nine-year period ending in 1961 was $524 million (approximately $58 million annually), between 1962 and 1965 military loans and grants amounted to $516.9 million (approximately $129 million annually). For the period 1962 to 1968, allied governments received $818.7 million in military assistance – $117 million yearly, or more than double the figure for the 1950s.[14]

The Kennedy administration presided during a period of growing military or military-controlled rule in Latin America. Military coups occurred in Argentina (March 1962), Peru (July 1962), Guatemala (March 1963), Ecuador (July 1963), Dominican Republic (September 1963), and Honduras (October 1963).[15] Washington accommodated these regime changes, which furthered the regional political isolation of Cuba and lessened the guerrilla threat, pushing remaining insurgent movements outside the large urban centers. The Alliance, in effect, had come full circle. The rhetoric of democratic forms was swallowed up by policies that precluded significant social change by providing the social cement that allowed dictatorial and autocratic regimes, including or linked to the most powerful economic groups, to consolidate their hold over government and state power.

In March 1964, Thomas C. Mann, the Assistant Secretary of State for Inter-American Affairs, informed a group of senior American officials serving in Latin America that the Johnson White House would not be bound by any "good guys and bad guys" distinction in dealing with nonelected regimes.[16] Diplomatic recognition and forms of assistance would be determined by pragmatic, case-by-case assessments although, as Mann pointed out, this was, in fact, "no departure from the practice which has prevailed in the most recent years."[17] As military assistance was resumed to the dictatorships ruling Brazil, Honduras, and the Dominican Republic, U.S. policymakers began to describe such regimes as "modernizing" and "predemocratic." In April 1965, the White House strikingly exposed the administration's hemispheric priorities by ordering massive military intervention into the Dominican Republic in support of right-wing military forces locked in a then losing civil war with constitutionalist military forces and armed urban workers. Similarly, throughout 1965, the armed forces and police in Venezuela, Colombia, Bolivia, Guatemala, Peru, and Uruguay received extensive training from Pentagon antiguerrilla experts and large amounts of weaponry suitable for use against local insurgent movements.[18]

In early 1966, the White House proposed the creation of an Inter-American Military Force "to help keep internal situations from spilling over and disrupting the peace of the hemisphere."[19] The proposal was not pursued but that does not detract from the milieu that prompted it: The drift toward direct action as the goals of the Alliance for Progress became explicitly equated with "law and order" governments and the "continued development of indigenous military and paramilitary forces."[20]

Prosecuting the Cold War: Kennedy and the Bay of Pigs

The multiple tracks that U.S. policy followed toward Cuba during the Kennedy presidency aimed at thwarting the revolutionary leadership's decision to move the island from a capitalist to a socialist economy. Administration officials repeatedly justified their stance in terms of the absence of democratic politics and an open, competitive party system. The most comprehensive presentation of this rationale is to be found in the "White Paper" on Cuba written by White House advisor Arthur Schlesinger under the President's supervision, which became the ideological basis for the April 1961 Bay of Pigs invasion.[21]

Although the Cuban Revolution was fought and consummated by defensive military organizations, and "indirect representation" through varied forms of defensive organizations predominated over direct representation, the drift toward centralist government was not simply the result of authoritarian dispositions or ideological inclinations. Rather, it derived from the leadership's determination to consolidate state power and an appreciation of the unequal allocation of resources – Cuba's compared to the immense capacity and willingness of the United States to mobilize regional and global resources against the regime. The U.S. response to a variety of economic nationalist regimes in Latin America from the turn of the century to the present offered compelling evidence that the chance for a "peaceful transition to socialism" in Cuba was minimal at best.

Instead of acknowledging the legitimate security problems confronting the new Cuban government, Washington focused on the closed nature of a society that cauterized points of imperial-state or capitalist-class access and on the absence of democratic politics, pluralist values, and an open political system. To the Cubans, however, the most efficacious method of securing socioeconomic change was a mobilized civil society – an armed and organized working class and nonparliamentary forms of political representation. The necessity for the emerging one-party state *during this phase of the revolution* flowed directly out of – and cannot be viewed in isolation from – this larger, hostile setting. The failure of imperial-state policy to overthrow the Castro regime was occasioned principally by the appearance of a civil society that no longer allowed the United States a basis for intervening. Traditional imperial-state collaborator groups had fragmented or collapsed, having proved incapable of offering any structured opposition to the transformation of the social order.

During the 1960 presidential campaign, both Richard Nixon and John Kennedy advocated a vigorous effort to isolate and overthrow Castro. Rhetoric by both brandished the Monroe Doctrine and a replication of the 1954 "Guatemalan tactic." Although Nixon raised the issue of military intervention in Cuba and was a proponent of an exile invasion at the earliest opportunity, Kennedy postured that "Castro's Cuba was a clear symbol of American decline under Eisenhower" and could not be tolerated, but he did not specifically advocate the military option.[22] What was striking in the Kennedy program, granted campaign exaggerations, was the enunciation of ideas subsequently put into practice: an insistence on restoration of an open political system as a prerequisite for negotiating outstanding conflicts; support for anti-Castro exiles, including reduced U.S.-government restrictions on their freedom of action; exhortations to capitalist-bloc allies (principally in Latin America and Western Europe) to join with Washington in actions against Cuba; proposals for "more stringent economic sanctions" such as the blocking of Cuban assets in the United States; and measures to halt the transshipment of American goods to the island via a third country.[23]

The Kennedy administration presumed from the outset that the Castro government had relinquished control of Cuba to "external forces" and collaborated in the imposition of "an ideology which is alien to this hemisphere."[24] Zeroing in on communist penetration, the administration sought to bolster its position that the conflict was multilateral. Hence, the White House summarily rejected Argentine proposals in February–May 1961 to mediate a bilateral settlement.[25]

In late November 1960, CIA Director Allen Dulles and Deputy Director of Plans Richard Bissell briefed the President-elect on the "most important details" of the covert plan to overthrow Castro.[26] Eisenhower discussed the subject with Kennedy on December 6 and January 11, recommending that the CIA's military training program for the Cuban exiles be improved and accelerated and that, once the exiles were "properly organized," the new administration should begin planning a military operation.[27]

On January 28, 1961, Kennedy received his first briefing as president and decided to quicken the pace of clandestine operations in the form of increased propaganda operations, political action, sabotage missions, and continued U.S. air surveillance of the island. The Pentagon was instructed to assess the CIA's Operation Trinidad, their exile invasion proposal; the Department of State was directed to secure Cuba's regional diplomatic and political isolation.[28]

On February 3, the Joint Chiefs of Staff evaluation of Operation Trinidad was forwarded to the State Department. The administration's senior military officials gave measured support, but emphasized that the ultimate objective would only be achieved if there was "a sizeable popular uprising or substantial follow-up forces." Their report recommended that the Pentagon investigate the "combat effectiveness" of the exile force and the operation's logistics.[29]

Before an upcoming (February 8) White House meeting on Cuba, the President's Special Assistant for National Security Affairs, McGeorge Bundy, forewarned Kennedy of tactical disagreements between the CIA and the Defense Department, which "feel quite enthusiastic about the invasion," and the State Department, which "takes a much cooler view" because of its concern over negative political fallout in the United Nations and throughout Latin America. State, according to Bundy, preferred to emphasize Castro's diplomatic isolation.[30] The White House did not want to unleash a premature exile invasion, but as time elapsed the revolutionary regime was likely to become securely entrenched. "Diplomatic and public opinion are surely not ready for an invasion," a Bundy memorandum informed the President in mid-February, "but Castro's internal strength continues to grow."[31]

Meanwhile, a team of Joint Staff officers had been dispatched to take a first-hand look at the exile army in its Guatemalan training base. Their report estimated that the odds against a surprise invasion, which the Pentagon high command thought necessary, were 85 to 15. The Joint Chiefs of Staff approved the report on March 19, 1961, and told the State Department that "the military portion of the plan . . . could be expected to achieve initial success." They again cautioned, however, that further gains would be dependent "on the extent to which the initial assault serves as a catalyst for further action" by antiregime opponents inside Cuba.[32]

The other major concern was how to conceal the American role and avoid major diplomatic problems. This was the basis of State Department opposition to certain features of the CIA's Operation Trinidad. White House advisor Arthur Schlesinger also worried that, since the Cuban exiles could not remain on Guatemalan soil indefinitely, the CIA might use the "disposal" argument to precipitate a resolution: "there seems to me a slight danger of our being rushed into something because CIA has on its hands a band of people it doesn't quite know what to do with."[33] The result was a decision by the President and his closest advisors to ask the CIA for alternatives to Operation Trinidad.

On March 11, the National Security Council considered the military option and what CIA Director Dulles told the assembled officials would be a "disposal problem" if the invasion plan was aborted. In that circumstance, the U.S. government would be obliged to transfer the exiles to the American mainland where their presence and behavior could prove extremely embarrassing.[34]

Domestic political considerations, especially charges that the administration was "soft on communism," laid to rest any consideration of abandoning the overall project, but Kennedy refused to endorse the Trinidad scheme. Instead, he directed CIA planners to devise a "quiet" plan for transporting the exile force to Cuba. The State Department and the CIA were delegated a number of operational assignments, among them to prepare a "White Paper" on Cuba and a presentation to the Organization of American States (State), and to develop exile political organizations to complement the military activities and devise "the best possible plan" for repatriating "an appropriate number of patriotic Cubans" following a successful invasion (CIA).[35]

In mid-March, the President was briefed on several alternatives by the CIA paramilitary staff. He concurred with the Joint Chiefs' preference for landing the exile brigade in the eastern Zapata area of the island, but authorized the CIA to incorporate some changes before proceeding. Leading up to the invasion attempt, the question of air strikes increasingly monopolized the bureaucratic debate. The State Department opposed any "spectacular" air attack on the grounds that it would be impossible to attribute it to squadrons based in Cuba. Over Defense and CIA objections, the decision was made to stage limited air strikes only, to coincide with a diversionary landing of exiles in eastern Cuba.[36]

On April 4, Kennedy chaired the interagency meeting that decided to "unleash" the Cuban exile force. The participants were most impressed by two possibilities; the imminent completion of a program to establish an effective air defense system in Cuba which, for all practical purposes, would signal the military consolidation of the Castro regime; and the potential domestic political problems of a demobilized exile brigade.[37] Of all the officials involved in the ongoing debate, only Under Secretary of State Chester Bowles and White House advisor Arthur Schlesinger expressed any skepticism over the probability of a successful outcome. Bowles was concerned about the likelihood that a covert operation "with such heavy built-in risks," not to mention its contravention of OAS treaty obligations, would fail and seriously "jeopardize the favorable position we have steadily developed in most of the non-Communist world." Furthermore, if the venture failed it would solidify Castro's hold.[38] Schlesinger articulated his misgivings in an April memorandum to the President. While adhering to the general line that a change in government was imperative ("If we could achieve this by a swift, surgical stroke, I would be for it"), he considered the proposed operation too hazardous and fraught with likely unpalatable consequences. He believed that, despite the use of Cuban personnel and equipment, the United States would be "held accountable" for the invasion; that the plan exaggerated the possibilities of a large-scale, internal uprising coinciding with the invasion; and that any "protracted" struggle would lead to ever-increasing direct American military involvement. Last, Schlesinger doubted whether Washington could elicit much support for the operation from its allies in Western Europe or Latin America.[39]

Somewhat paradoxically, one of the strongest advocates of Cuba's regional isolation, Senate Foreign Relations Committee chairman J. William Fulbright, emerged as the most articulate critic of the invasion plan. Like Schlesinger and Bowles, Fulbright invoked America's treaty commitments and was dubious that Washington's role could be kept secret. He also feared both the larger consequences to U.S. economic interests in Latin America from an invasion of Cuba and its impact on America's political standing within the region.[40]

The crucial April 4 meeting did not produce a White House decision to invade Cuba. Neither did an April 12 conference attended by the President, the Secretary of State, the Joint Chiefs of Staff, the CIA's Richard Bissell, and NSC officials, even though the invading exile force already had boarded American ships at Puerto Cabezas in Nicaragua en route to Cuba. In this climate of external threats to the revolution's survival, immediately preceding the actual invasion, the Castro government arrested thousands of suspected exile collaborators or sympathizers. Thomas Powers writes that a number of CIA sources informed him that "virtually every CIA asset on the island was caught up in the general sweep."[41] This factor, together with the failure of an April 15 White House-authorized air strike to destroy all of Castro's air force on the ground and an aborted diversionary landing by a small number of exiles on April 14 and 15, "which was intended to draw Castro's forces to the east and confuse his command,"[42] had devastating consequences for the counterrevolutionary project.

On April 16, Kennedy, with the concurrence of all his senior advisors, approved the exile military invasion at the Bay of Pigs. The following day, however, seeking to protect the operation's covert character, he decided to cancel a second air strike that CIA planners considered crucial to the success of the Bay of Pigs landing. Secretary of State Rusk rejected CIA entreaties to get the White House to change its mind: "there were policy considerations against air strikes before the beachhead airfield was in the hands of the landing force and completely organizational, capable of supporting the raids."[43] Nonetheless, on April 17, the CIA proceeded with the invasion. Castro's forces "though tactically surprised, reacted with speed and vigor."[44] Richard Bissell told a Senate Foreign Relations Committee investigation that the Cuban military "displayed a greater will to fight . . . [and] were more expertly directed than we had expected."[45] The Cuban air force sank the main ammunition supply ship and another supply freighter, effectively terminating any possibility of the landing force establishing a beachhead, setting up a provisional government, and requesting U.S. air power to consolidate their position.

In the early hours of April 17, Kennedy agreed to a second air strike for the next morning with the limited objective of providing some "breathing space" for the exile forces on the beach. Three B-26 aircraft sent to accomplish this mission were shot down by Cuban artillery and, on April 19, the exiles, numbering about 1,400, surrendered to the revolution's armed forces. The massive defeat suffered by the United States at the Bay of Pigs dealt a fundamental setback, if not fatal blow, to the "insiders" subversion strategy.[46]

In memoirs and oral history interviews, senior Kennedy administration officials have sought to portray the President as a "prisoner of events" set in motion during the Eisenhower period over which he had no control.[47] He inherited a project that had assumed a life of its own which, according to Chester Bowles, "nobody quite knew how to stop."[48] Theodore Sorenson evoked an almost ethereal atmosphere surrounding the Bay of Pigs deliberations: "The whole project seemed to move mysteriously and inexorably toward execution without the President being able either to obtain a firm grip on it or reverse it."[49] Central Intelligence Agency Deputy Director of Plans, Richard Bissell, underlined the pivotal role of domestic factors in shaping the course of events: To have abandoned the operation would have exposed

Kennedy "to the accusation that he was dismantling the government's major effort to unseat Castro."[50]

Explanations that minimize White House responsibility complement efforts to blame the CIA for the project's failure. The Agency's monopoly over the covert program, including intelligence collection and evaluation, subject only to Pentagon "refinements," as Arthur Schlesinger put it, meant that the CIA dictated the course of events. "The same men," Schlesinger wrote, both "planned the operation and judged its chances of success."[51] They exploited their monopoly over information to gain executive-branch support for the invasion option as a domestic political imperative and a viable military operation.[52] President Kennedy thought he was approving a quiet, clandestine invasion by exile forces who would either detonate an insurrection or provide expertise and personnel to augment domestic opposition to Castro.[53] The CIA was able to play such a dominant role because the new administration was still "finding its feet" within the foreign-policy bureaucracy, could not at this early date make accurate assessments of the competence of key appointees and holdovers from the Eisenhower presidency, and was not organized to deal with crisis situations, especially one shrouded in so much secrecy and where time was of the essence.[54] Curiously, all the accounts of this period seem to ignore the conclusion reached by the authorized White House investigation of the Bay of Pigs debacle headed by General Maxwell Taylor and completed in June 1961: "Although intelligence was not perfect . . . we did not feel that any failure of intelligence contributed significantly to the defeat."[55] Allen Dulles himself has forcefully rejected assertions that the Agency ever promoted the idea of a causal link between an invasion and internal revolts. According to the CIA Director, Agency planners believed that revolts might occur if the exiles were able to establish a secure beachhead on Cuban soil. He also maintained that he told President Kennedy that the invasion force had, at best, only "a good fighting chance."[56]

The evasive and tortuous explanations of the events leading up to the Bay of Pigs invasion contained in the memoirs of senior White House and State Department officials like Theodore Sorenson (1965), Arthur Schlesinger, Jr. (1966), and Roger Hilsman (1967) served a number of interrelated purposes. Basically, they reflected the efforts of a group of former government appointees, who espoused the traditional values of political choice and responsibility and a commitment to a democratic foreign policy, to disassociate themselves and their like-minded President from involvements in actions in the public sphere that ran directly counter to these professed beliefs. The explanations attempt to rationalize this fundamental contradiction and, in the process, reaffirm liberal credentials. The actual policies these individuals defended at the time of the military invasion stood in sharp contrast to the political values they brought with them to government and which they continued to enunciate after leaving office. These accounts of the Bay of Pigs episode represent an effort to come to terms with the fact that, on this occasion, the liberals sacrificed their beliefs in defense of historic American foreign-policy goals: opposition to national and social revolution in the Third World.

Paradoxically, by shifting much of the onus for this attempt to overthrow an established government by military means onto a predetermined policy – one inherited from Eisenhower and which they had no say in making – Kennedy apologists continue to deny his administration's responsibility for the final decision to invade Cuba. Their interpretations do absolve them from the unpalatable ease with which they jettisoned lifelong values in support of an undemocratic and interventionist foreign policy. Ultimately, these memoirs fail to salvage the Kennedy White House from primary responsibility for the Bay of Pigs, but they reveal a great deal about the dilemma of intellectuals who aspire to and achieve political power and the tensions generated by exercising such power under constraints that conflict with their particular beliefs and goals.

Some Kennedy officials also criticized the exclusionary nature of the policy debate which, according to Robert Hurwitch, the State Department's Officer in Charge of Cuban Affairs, resulted in "a divorce between the people who daily, or minute by minute, had access to information, to what was going on, and to people who were making plans and policy decisions."[57] Not only was Assistant Secretary of State for Inter-American Affairs Thomas Mann the lowest ranking Department participant in the invasion debate, but Secretary Rusk actually refused to allow his own Director of the Bureau of Intelligence and Research, Roger Hilsman, to make an independent assessment of the strength of Castro's internal opposition.[58] In remarks critical of the Joint Chiefs of Staff (JCS) for "acquiescing" to the Bay of Pigs plan despite their initial belief that Operation Trinidad was a more feasible military option, the official White House investigation headed by General Taylor observed that this earlier JCS preference "apparently never reached the senior civilian officials."[59] According to another source, neither the Joint Chiefs' assessment of Trinidad nor their privately held opinion that all the landing options considered, including Trinidad and the Bay of Pigs, offered minimal chances of success were ever transmitted to the President.[60] Two persuasive arguments have been offered to account for the Joint Chiefs' refusal to become embroiled in a major bureaucratic dispute with the CIA, despite their subdued support for the Bay of Pigs option. First, the overall project did not impinge on the Pentagon's bureaucratic turf. Second, the Joint Chiefs presumed that the absence of a White House response on Trinidad meant rejection of their evaluation by the civilian policymakers.

In the area of intelligence assessments, CIA officials directing the project made almost no use of their own internal resources to gauge the liklihood of a spontaneous insurrection in the wake of a military invasion of Cuba. In fact, in early March, the chairman of the Agency's Board of National Estimates, Sherman Kent, sent a memorandum to CIA Director Dulles that cast considerable doubt on any such spontaneous outcome. But both Kent and Robert Amory, who headed the CIA's Directorate of Intelligence, were "completely cut out of Cuban invasion planning."[61] So also were Bissell's Deputy Chief of Operations Richard Helms and other CIA officials, who were less than enthusiastic about Agency involvement in this type of high-risk operation.[62]

Efforts by Kennedy administration officials to shift the burden of responsibility away from the White House by emphasizing the role of the CIA, intelligence errors, the exclusion of middle-level bureaucrats from the decision-making process, and tactical mistakes and organizational problems have been complemented by more detached assessments that attempt to explain the Bay of Pigs outcome in many of these same terms under the rubric of a modified bureaucratic model of foreign policymaking. Lucien S. Vandenbroucke, for example, has argued that the CIA was able to emerge victorious in the "push and pull" bargaining between executive-branch agencies and individuals largely because it was just this type of project that defined the covert agency's mission and responsibilities. Its control over information sources in this area gave the CIA an enormous advantage over the other departments in shaping the ultimate policy outcome.[63]

The fundamental problem with most all accounts of the Bay of Pigs invasion is their exclusion of the larger setting. American policy at the highest echelons before, during, and after the invasion premised on the notion that a permanent Castro regime was unacceptable and its overthrow was to be sought by virtually any means short of direct American military intervention. This longer time frame exposes the continuities in policy between administrations. The decision to "take Cuba away from Castro" was initiated by Eisenhower, but pursued with even greater vigor by Kennedy. A senior State Department Latin Americanist in the early 1960s recalled: "There was no change in policy between the Eisenhower and Kennedy administrations. A difference in tactics but not a difference in purpose."[64]

In his assessment of the Bay of Pigs defeat, Kennedy reaffirmed support for the invasion's premises, reasserted the unilateral nature of U.S. hemispheric policy, and warned Havana that Washington was prepared to act with or without regional support if it deemed in its interests to do so. The failure to overthrow Castro militarily did not mean that the objective of getting rid of the revolutionary regime would be abandoned. The major lesson that Kennedy drew from the episode was the need to rethink U.S. tactics with a view to pursuing "a struggle in many ways more difficult than war."[65] The National Security Council's postinvasion debate apparently included consideration of some extreme proposals. At its April 22 and 24 meetings, chaired by the President, Chester Bowles reported that "specific proposals were made that the United States should move directly against Castro." He described schemes for "all kinds of barely clandestine harassment" and even some discussion of the use of economic sanctions to punish countries, such as Mexico and Brazil, which had voted in the United Nations to condemn U.S. involvement in the invasion.[66] To provide a multilateral umbrella for future actions, the President raised the possibility of creating a Caribbean Security Agency to act as an interhemispheric force "to whom any nation attacked could appeal for help."[67] At White House behest, the Inter-American Defense Board voted to bar Cuba from its secret meetings. American ambassadors in Latin America were instructed to pressure governments to support collective action against the Castro regime. The President was also reported to be considering reviving the wartime antisubversion Committee for Political Defense of the Hemisphere. Finally, he offered Cuban exile leader José Miró Cardona public monies to travel the continent speaking against the Cuban Revolution.[68] Washington's call at this time for closer ties between regional security forces and an accelerated program of covert warfare against Cuba apparently originated with Attorney General Robert Kennedy, who "was convinced that we could upset Castro by a long campaign of meddling, infiltration and so on."[69]

With failure of the Bay of Pigs, President Kennedy concluded that there were structural flaws in the policymaking apparatus that hampered effective responses to major crises. A memorandum from White House official Richard Goodwin stressed the need for more organized and coordinated "non-military overseas operations to reflect our basic objective in Latin America" and improved lines of communication between these groups and Washington policymakers.[70] Subsequent organizational changes were intended to coordinate the multiple threads of U.S. foreign policy to more effectively carry out confrontations with Cuba and other Third World nationalist regimes. Regarding Cuba specifically, the newly appointed Coordinator of Cuban Affairs was instructed by the White House to prepare a policy memorandum outlining available options for NSC consideration. "The thrust was to isolate Cuba," he recalled, "rather than overpower the country with military force." White House advisor McGeorge Bundy gained interagency consensus for this approach "by 'leaning' on the Pentagon" to drop its advocacy of a more aggressive approach up to, and including, direct intervention.[71] Above all, the administration was determined to prevent a "second Cuba" in the hemisphere. The President made this clear when he approved the actions of a National Security Council meeting convened in early May 1961 to discuss spreading political unrest in the Caribbean, particularly in the Dominican Republic and Haiti.[72]

In June 1961, the final report by the White House Committee, chaired by General Maxwell Taylor to investigate the Bay of Pigs disaster, recommended that covert paramilitary operations remain a major policy instrument, especially in situations of limited risk, and that a special coordinating and planning interdepartmental mechanism be created (the Special Group on Counterinsurgency) for this purpose. Addressing itself to Cuba, the Committee strongly tilted in favor of escalating confrontation. Consideration of even limited accommodation was discounted: "We have been struck with the general feeling that there can be no long-term living with Castro as a neighbor."[73]

Covert politics and the shifting pattern of intervention

The role of covert politics in postwar U.S. foreign policy rivals that of public diplomacy. Between 1955 and 1967, a secret executive-branch interagency committee (the Special Group) "charged by various NSC directives with exercising political control over foreign covert operations" approved or reconfirmed 409 clandestine projects. Under Eisenhower, 104 were authorized, rising dramatically to 163 during the short Kennedy presidency, and then reverting to 102 for the period covering the bulk of Johnson's tenure.[74] By 1967, CIA paramilitary operations absorbed a greater proportion of Agency budgetary allocations than either psychological propaganda or political actions programs.[75] Field operations of the CIA were formally under the coordinating authority of U.S. Ambassadors and, on the testimony of an Agency official stationed in Latin America during the 1950s and 1960s, the failure of an Ambassador to maintain control over clandestine actions was the exception, not the rule.[76]

The expansion of covert operations against Cuba, costing as much as $100 million annually,[77] was a direct outcome of the Bay of Pigs failure. The White House became more determined than ever to "get rid of Castro and the Castro regime."[78] Secretary of Defense Robert McNamara characterized the administration as "hysterical about Cuba at the time of the Bay of Pigs and thereafter" and recalled that "no major action taken by the CIA during the time I was in the government was not properly authorized by senior officials."[79] Richard Bissell, the CIA's Deputy Director of Plans from January 1959 to February 1962, stated that "almost from the beginning of the Kennedy administration, the President himself and a number of Cabinet members and other senior officials took a very active interest in the operation[s] concerning Cuba."[80]

In July 1961, the Special Group defined the "basic objective" succinctly: "to develop opposition to Castro and to help bring about a regime acceptable to the U.S."[81] Under enormous White House pressure, the CIA first decided to refocus the bulk of its efforts away from recruiting agents inside Cuba to attempting to infiltrate agents. In this connection, the Agency sought to take advantage of Cuba's role as a hemispheric guerrilla warfare training center "to place agents in the groups sent for training."[82] Ultimately, however, the revolution's security network virtually foreclosed this option to U.S. policymakers. Evaluating U.S. intelligence failures at the time of the Bay of Pigs and thereafter, the chairman of President Kennedy's Foreign Intelligence Advisory Board, Clark M. Clifford, offered the following comment: "We sent teams at one time or another into Cuba to try to get information. They were 'all rolled up,' is the expression, and we never heard from them again."[83]

During the summer of 1961, CIA sabotage operations, such as burning sugar cane, forced Castro to divert scarce human and financial resources into bolstering the regime's defensive military capabilities. Nonetheless, the White House continued to express dissatisfaction with CIA results, which it attributed to an insufficiently aggressive approach. In the fall, the Kennedy brothers met with Deputy Director Bissell to discuss the progress of the covert program. The assistant to the chief of Task Force W (the CIA section responsible for clandestine Cuban operations) stated that Bissell was "chewed out in the Cabinet Room of the White House by both the President and the Attorney General for, as he put it, sitting on his ass and not doing anything about getting rid of Castro and the Castro regime."[84]

The Cuban Revolution and the growth of other revolutionary movements coincided with expanded CIA involvement in Latin America. Between 1960 and 1965, the personnel of the Western Hemisphere CIA Division grew in numbers by 40 percent.[85] In the mid-1960s, various estimates placed the percentage of CIA officials in American Embassy "teams" as low as 25 percent, rising occasionally to as much as 75 percent.[86] Allocations of CIA "human resources" continued to reflect disproportionate concentration on the Cuba problem for, as late as October 1966, almost one-third of all Western Hemisphere Division headquarter officers were attached to the Cuban section.[87] In the field, the Agency "was heavily engaged everywhere in Latin America in covert action, trying to influence people to work against Castro to keep him from being successful."[88]

For the duration of the Kennedy administration, open political and economic warfare against the Castro regime was complemented by an ambitious "secret war" extending from economic sabotage to assassination attempts. According to the Defense Department's Roswell Gilpatric, the sabotage activities not only had specific targets but also "the more general objective of keeping the Castro regime so off stride and unsettled that it couldn't concentrate its activities in harmful ends elsewhere."[89] Before the Bay of Pigs, the CIA tried to construct a network of liaisons inside the Cuban armed forces.[90] This effort to recruit "agents of influence" for sabotage and other clandestine operations, however, was not helped by the nonexistence of an American Embassy in Havana. In the Agency's lexicon, Cuba was a "denied area" and, without a diplomatic base, it became "infinitely tougher" to recruit dissidents there. "The people inside the country were not in a position to really change the course of the Cuban Revolution. Without an Embassy, without being able to talk to people outside," their usefulness was limited.[91]

President Kennedy decided to bring in counterinsurgency expert General Edward Lansdale to make a detailed reexamination of existing covert operations in order to accelerate Castro's demise. Lansdale recommended that CIA "harassment" be replaced by the effort to improve the quality of the Cuban exile leadership.[92] During November 1961, General Lansdale and White House assistant Richard Goodwin, with Robert Kennedy, devised a new program combining intelligence collection and paramilitary, sabotage, and political propaganda activities. Yet, a report prepared at this time by the CIA's Office of National Estimates underlined the growing pessimism over the possibilities for internal revolt, noting that "the Castro regime has sufficient popular support and repressive capabilities to cope with any internal threat likely to develop within the foreseeable future."[93]

In December 1961, as a result of White House pressure for a more vigorous secret war, CIA Director John McCone relieved Richard Bissell of control of Cuban affairs and replaced him with Richard Helms. Later that month, President Kennedy inaugurated a major covert project, "Operation Mongoose": The goal was to "use our available assets . . . to help Cuba overthrow the Communist regime."[94] At the apex of the project's chain of command was the White House itself, assisted by the Special Group Augmented (SGA), an interagency committee composed of the administration's most senior officials. Those responsible for implementation included head of operations General Lansdale, Task Force W, and the CIA operational unit. On January 16, 1962, the key participants met with Attorney General Robert Kennedy. George McManus, executive assistant to the new CIA Deputy Director for Plans, Richard Helms, wrote that the President's brother treated the assembled officials to a "very vehement" speech in which he informed them that the White House "really wanted action." McManus' meeting notes stated: "No time, money, effort – or manpower is to be spared."[95] A Task Force W official set it straight: "We are at war with Cuba."[96]

To coordinate the expanded covert war against Cuba, Task Force W set up a Miami Station (JM-WAVE) "to serve as the command post for all the CIA's worldwide anti-Castro operations."[97]

The Station was soon the largest of its kind, with an annual budget in excess of $50 million and a permanent staff of over 300 American officials who were responsible for the activities of some 2,000 Cuban agents.[98]

Meanwhile, sabotage teams were infiltrated into Cuba during 1962 to destroy strategic targets such as bridges, sugar mills, and oil refineries.[99] The Miami Station sent more than one team to blow up the cable-car system that transported ore from the large Matahambre copper mines in Pinar del Rio to the Santa Lucia port.[100] Central Intelligence Agency efforts apparently also extended to creating a state of mass starvation through sabotage of the island's food supplies. In one instance, a Canadian agricultural advisor to the Castro government was paid $5,000 by Agency officers to infect the turkey population – a vital source of food – with a fatal virus. It occurred at a time of efforts to raise production to meet the increased demand for meat occasioned by the U.S. trade embargo and the initial decline in agricultural production that accompanied the collectivization process. Approximately 800 turkeys on one state farm died, mysteriously, from neglect and other causes as claimed by the Canadian advisor or as a result of CIA actions, as believed by some Cuban and U.S. officials.[101]

In January 1962, General Lansdale, with SGA approval, assigned thirty-five planning tasks to U.S. government agencies involved in "Operation Mongoose," ranging from intelligence collection to sabotage operations to the possible "use of U.S. military force to support the Cuban popular movement." Consideration was also given to chemical warfare to "incapacitate" rural workers during the sugar harvest. Lansdale drew a scenario in which the cumulative impact of a series of escalating pressures would lead to "an open revolt and the overthrow of the Communist regime" by October.[102] Officials of the CIA Cuban Branch established by Helms were more than a little skeptical of Lansdale's blueprint: "With What?" they asked. "We haven't got any assets. We don't even know what's going on in Cuba."[103] And in fact, through most of 1962, "Operation Mongoose" performed largely as an intelligence collection body by infiltrating teams into Cuba.[104]

On August 31, the day following an unsuccessful attempt to blow up the Matahambre copper mine, General Lansdale presented a plan to the SGA targeting several strategic production areas – copper, nickel, petroleum – for future sabotage projects.

The memorandum also suggested "encouraging destruction of crops by fire, chemicals, and weeds, hampering of harvest by work slowdown, destruction of bags, cartons, and shipping containers."[105] By this time, however, the White House had become exceedingly unhappy with the disjunction between Mongoose planning and practice. At an SGA meeting on October 4, Robert Kennedy declared that the President wished to see a substantial increase in the number of sabotage missions, and he "urged that 'massive activity' be undertaken within the MONGOOSE framework."[106] While agreeing with the need for "new and imaginative approaches" that might hasten Castro's overthrow, the SGA remained "generally apprehensive of sabotage proposals."[107]

Following the SGA decision at the end of October to halt all sabotage operations, the White House overhauled the entire executive-branch covert decisionmaking apparatus. The SGA was disbanded and responsibility for generating covert action proposals was delegated to a new interagency Cuba Coordinating Committee headquartered in the State Department. The Special Group, chaired by White House Liaison for Cuban Affairs and senior foreign policy advisor McGeorge Bundy, reassumed responsiblity for evaluating and approving clandestine operations against Cuba. And, finally, the NSC's Standing Group (the successor to the Executive-Committee of the NSC formed during the October 1962 Missile Crisis) also became an active participant in discussions of Cuba policy.

In February 1963, a memorandum prepared by Sterling Cottrell, the Coordinator of Cuban Affairs, was transmitted to McGeorge Bundy; it included a tacit acknowledgment that Castro had solved the regime's security problem. U.S. intelligence reports, according to Cottrell, emphasized the combat effectiveness of the Cuban armed forces and the loyalty of its military leadership to the political regime. By contrast, these dispatches noted the absence of effective leadership, the lack of organization, and the internecine conflicts displayed by the antiregime resistance groups.[108] On April 3, Bundy stated that all authorized sabotage had been halted on the basis of a Special Group consensus "that such activity is not worth the effort expended on it."[109] Agreement over the absence of "practical measures" to overthrow the Castro regime did not, however, dissuade the Special Group from endorsing "harassment" in hope of favorable consequences.[110] On April 23 and May 28, the Special Group convened to discuss Cuba strategy, focusing on three proposals: the pursuit of "a non-Com-

munist solution in Cuba by all necessary means," sustaining a level
of hostilities that could achieve "major but limited ends," or moving toward gradual accommodation.[111] Central Intelligence
Agency Director McCone was still the forceful advocate of an
accelerated economic offensive complemented by sabotage. Such
a strategy, he argued, was the one most likely to generate a break
in the army and Castro's demise.[112] Secretary of Defense
McNamara, although sympathetic, questioned the benefits of further sabotage.

Still determined to "do something against Castro,"[113] the Kennedy administration decided to shift tracks and attempt to reestablish a clandestine network. "This effort apparently began in
May or June and consist[ed] of smuggling trusted Cuban exile
agents, cash, arms and other equipment into the country."[114]
Through the second half of 1963, the CIA steadily increased its
infiltrations to build up an organized underground. The agency
was reportedly also financing and cooperating with some internal
independent antiregime groups that had developed efficient clandestine networks of their own.[115]

During "Operation Mongoose," the United States constantly
tried to control the Cuban exile movement to maximize its effectiveness. By early 1963, officials noted an increasing tendency on
the exiles' part to take up the slack in sabotage operations resulting from the Special Group's constraints on CIA covert undertakings. Although American policy was designed to provide "support
and encouragement for their useful engagement in tasks appropriate to the future in a liberated Cuba," executive-branch policymakers did not intend the exiles to have the freedom of action
"to determine war-and-peace decisions of the U.S."[116] Unauthorized raids could have negative consequences in areas only indirectly related to Cuba. In March, this fear became reality when
exiles reportedly attacked two Soviet vessels, in separate inci-
dents, near the Cuban coast. This potential threat to developing
U.S.-Soviet detente forced Washington to divert Coast Guard,
Customs, Immigration and Naturalization, FBI and CIA personnel
to guard against any repetition of such counterproductive
actions.[117] Administration officials were not only critical of the
exiles' "quite narrow" focus, which took virtually no account of
U.S. global interests, but also dismissed their unauthorized raids
as ineffective.[118]

On June 19, 1963, President Kennedy approved yet another
new sabotage program, hoping to create socioeconomic fissures

generating internal discontent that would take appropriate political and military forms. The sabotage plans were directed once again at the most vital sectors of the Cuban economy: electric power plants, oil refineries and storage facilities, communications networks, sugar mill complexes, and other production centers.[119] To bolster the CIA's paramilitary capabilities, two "advisers" from the regular U.S. armed forces were assigned to train small commando infiltration units in skills including the use of explosives.[120] In late October, the Special Group approved thirteen sabotage operations against key communications and economic targets to be executed between November 1963 and January 1964.[121] "As late as 1964," according to one study of this so-called secret war, the CIA "was landing weapons in Cuba every week and sending up to fifty agents on missions to destroy oil refineries, railroad bridges, and sugar mills."[122]

In April 1964, the Special Group convened to discuss the effectiveness and the future of sabotage raids. Secretary of State Rusk termed them "unproductive," suspecting that the exiles were not adverse "to leav[ing] fingerprints pointing to U.S. involvement in order to increase that involvement." Central Intelligence Agency Director McCone insisted that the sabotage operations were "well planned," but the issue for senior presidential advisor McGeorge Bundy was the actual extent to which they had contributed to U.S. objectives: "[Since June 1963] policy makers . . . had turned sabotage operations on and off to such an extent that [the program] simply does not, in the nature of things, appear feasible."[123] On the same day, April 7, 1964, President Johnson announced the end of CIA-directed sabotage infiltration raids revived by Kennedy in July 1963. With this decision, CIA Director McCone contended, the White House "had abandoned the objective of Castro's overthrow."[124] Over a year later, John Hart, Deputy Chief of the Western Hemisphere Division for Cuban Affairs, acknowledged that "the Agency has practically no agent sources reporting from inside Cuba."[125]

American efforts to assassinate the Cuban Revolution's senior officials were not confined to the Eisenhower period: They were intensified during the Kennedy presidency and continued into the early Johnson years. Officials of the CIA interpreted White House and Special Group Augmented (SGA) directives to "dispose of Castro" and "knock off Castro" as including the possibility of assassination.[126] Deputy Director Helms described White House pressure on the Agency as "very intense," especially during the

"Operation Mongoose" period. "It was made abundantly clear
. . . to everybody in the operation that the desire was to get rid of
the Castro regime and to get rid of Castro. . . . The point was that
no limitations were put on this injunction."[127] In this context,
Helms also recalled," we had so few assets inside Cuba at that
time that I was willing to try almost anything."[128] In fact, one of
those assets, Rolando Cubela, a Cuban army major with access to
the inner leadership, was involved in one, possibly two, CIA
attempts to assassinate Castro as early as February to mid-April
1961.[129] For his part, President Kennedy's major concerns regarding this particular course were whether a successful assassination
"could be pinned on the United States" and the possible regional
impact.[130]

In early 1962, William Harvey, the head of Task Force W, acting at the behest of Helms, resumed contact with those elements
in the American underworld that had participated in earlier assassination attempts. This time working through underworld figure
John Roselli, the Agency provided poison pills, small arms, and
explosives for delivery to his Cuban contacts. In June, Roselli
informed Harvey that a three-man assassination team had been
dispatched; in September, he told Harvey that a second assassination team was being prepared. But by then the Task Force W
chief had become skeptical about the entire operation, telling
Roselli that "there's not much likelihood that this is going any-
place, or that it should be continued."[131] The second assassination
team never left for Cuba and, in February 1963, Harvey terminated the operation.

In early 1963, task Force W was renamed the Special Affairs
Staff, William Harvey was replaced by Desmond Fitzgerald, and
two new bizarre plans were developed to eliminate the Cuban
leader; placing an exploding device where Castro regularly went
skindiving and presenting Castro with a contaminated diving
suit.[132] That autumn, Fitzgerald met with Cubela and agreed to
provide him with an arms cache, including a high-powered rifle
with scopes. Cubela was also offered a poison pen which, according to Richard Helms, was handmade "to take care of a request
from him that he have some device for getting rid of Castro, for
killing him, murdering him, whatever the case may be."[133] In
March and June 1964, Cubela received two separate caches of
arms. In early 1965, he informed Agency officials of his desire to
assassinate Castro and requested a weapon with a silencer. The
CIA refused to supply him directly and instead put him in contact

with Manuel Artime, a leading participant in the Bay of Pigs invasion who was subsequently appointed to oversee CIA commando expeditions into Cuba from Nicaragua and Costa Rica. Artime provided Cubela with the silencer and prepared to deliver one pistol and one rifle, both with silencers.[134]

Yet in June 1965 the CIA terminated all contacts with Cubela and his associates. There were indications that the Cuban exile employed by the Agency to arrange the meeting between Artime and Cubela was a Castro agent.[135] In partial confirmation of the contention that the CIA generally acts not independently but at the direction of the White House, Thomas Powers notes that the Agency's "direct involvement in Cubela's assassination plans came to an end at a time when it was probably clear they [the CIA] did not have the President's sanction."[136]

The regional isolation strategy

The Bay of Pigs debacle forced the Kennedy administration to reassess the hemispheric quotient of its relations to the Cuban Revolution. A newly appointed Coordinator of Cuban Affairs prepared a policy memorandum for the National Security Council that raised a number of options extending from political and economic sanctions to the threat of some kind of military action to prevent the "export of revolution" or Soviet military involvement in the hemisphere. The memo emphasized that the United States should concentrate on efforts "to isolate Cuba rather than overpower the country with military force."[137]

Categorically dismissing the prospect of peaceful coexistence with Havana,[138] the administration decided to concentrate on persuading the Organization of American States (OAS) to take collective action against Cuba and on using economic and other forms of pressure to push regional governments to sever diplomatic relations with the Castro regime. Over the next three years, the U.S. government meddled with the economic, commercial, and political affairs of sovereign Latin American countries to realize these objectives.[139] Washington's most receptive hemispheric supporters were those Central American and Caribbean regimes that provided training facilities for the exile invasion (Guatemala, for one), and Costa Rica and Nicaragua, whose governments allowed the CIA to establish bases for raids by Cuban exiles into Cuba.

Enforcing the multilateral approach: Cuba's exclusion from the OAS   In June 1961, United Nations Ambassador Adlai Stevenson headed a mission to Latin America to drum up support for a regional economic embargo of Cuba. The mission's failure is captured in the Ecuadorian President Velasco's refusal to discuss any aspect of the Cuba issue.[140] Most countries rejected a multilateral interpretation of what they saw as a bilateral conflict. Secretary Rusk acknowledged the trip's minimal gains but reaffirmed the notion of Cuba as an OAS problem, declaring that the United States would not weaken its resolve to gain a regional solution consonant with its hemispheric objectives.[141]

On November 14, 1961, with U.S. prodding, the Colombian delegate asked the OAS Governing Council to convene a Meeting of Consultation of the Ministers of Foreign Affairs "to consider the threats to the peace and to the political independence of the American states that might arise from the intervention of extra-continental powers directed toward breaking inter-American solidarity."[142] The Governing Council debate on the Colombian request, which provoked great irritation and displeasure in Washington, centered around three issues: What constituted a "threat to the hemisphere"; was a "potential threat" sufficient to justify a meeting of foreign ministers; and what *was* the precise nature of the Cuban threat? Mexico and Chile argued against the proposed meeting on juridical grounds while other states such as Argentina, Brazil, Bolivia, and Ecuador noted their intention to abstain from or oppose the final vote. When the Council meeting ended in early December, the United States had barely managed to round up a two-thirds majority needed to support the Colombian conference proposal.

The Eighth Meeting of Consultation of Foreign Ministers of the OAS opened at Punte del Este, Uruguay, on January 22, 1962, amid more doubts over what purpose the conference might serve. The Kennedy White House instruction to the U.S. delegation was described concisely by Walt W. Rostow, chairman of the State Department's Policy Planning Council: "to effect the removal of Cuba from the OAS." Also, congressional members of the delegation "made it clear" to Secretary of State Rusk that continued legislative support for the Alliance for Progress rested on the outcome of the meeting.[143]

Initially, the assembled delegations were divided. Some supported the American position, others opposed mandatory sanctions. Uruguay and Haiti both voted to convene the meeting and both sent delegations. But Uruguay's was wracked by indecision and Haiti's had decided, for mercenary reasons, to redefine its position on the Cuba issue as one of "nonalignment." The divergent positions resulted from a number of factors, including U.S. pressures, domestic politics, concern over the principle of nonintervention, unease over the dubious precedent that could be established by so general an interpretation of the Rio Treaty and the OAS Charter, and widely varying evaluations of Cuba's supposed threat.[144]

The U.S. delegation, composed of both congressional and executive-branch officials, agreed that a "direct relationship" existed between the appropriation of Alliance for Progress funds and the conference outcome.[145] The executive-branch members expressed concern that the outcome be consistent with regional American policy interests. In the case of Brazil, for example, some U.S. officials speculated that a sharp cleavage over Cuba with the nationalist Goulart government might further his regime's radicalization just when there existed "no viable alternative" in Brazil that might be more receptive to Washington's support.[146] Given Brazil's politically strategic position, U.S. Ambassador Lincoln Gordon urged Secretary of State Rusk to consider a less ambitious Cuba objective to increase the possibility of a favorable Brazilian vote.[147]

Rusk addressed the OAS General Committee on the regional and global dimensions of the Cuba problem: "The Castro regime has extended the global battle to Latin America. It has supplied Communism with a bridgehead in the Americas."[148] He defined four conference "working tasks": to recognize that Cuba's link with the socialist bloc and its support of Latin revolutionary movements are "incompatible" with membership in the inter-American system; to work for the expulsion of the Castro government from the OAS; to devise means of eliminating existing trade ties between Cuba and the rest of the continent; and to establish a timetable for the rapid buildup of the military capabilities of the OAS and its member states.[149] A majority of the twenty governments supported the maximum demand for collective political and economic sanctions. But opposition by six states (Argentina, Brazil, Bolivia, Chile, Ecuador, Mexico) and wavering by two others (Uruguay, Haiti) meant that the necessary fourteen votes were lacking.

The U.S. delegation applied "a lot of arm twisting," largely using economic pressures to make stubborn states "line up on our anti-Cuban stance."[150] But the failure to wrest a meaningful consensus in support of collective sanctions against Cuba ultimately forced Washington to revise its goals and settle on a resolution that declared any regime based on Marxism-Leninism "incompatible" with the inter-American system.[151] This was acceptable to Uruguay and, in association with a multimillion dollar bribe, to Haiti as well.[152] Although the American delegation managed to garner the bare majority of votes necessary to exclude Cuba from the OAS, its satisfaction was marred by the refusal of a group of countries, including the most populous and politically powerful in the region, to endorse the U.S. objective. Mexico opposed Cuba's expulsion while Argentina, Brazil, Chile, Bolivia, and Ecuador abstained on the final vote.

The Castro government was formally expelled from the OAS in mid-February 1962, coinciding with the U.S. government decision to expand its trade embargo. New economic sanctions were justified by actions taken at the OAS Punta del Este meeting even though, with the exception of the arms embargo, the foreign ministers did not advocate the "ordering [of] a general trade embargo."[153] Cuba's political and economic isolation, according to a National Security Council document of February 28, 1962, was to be pursued without let-up in the coming months: " . . . we shall continue to tighten the noose around the Cuban economy and to increase the isolation of the Castro regime from the political life of the hemisphere until the regime becomes a complete pariah."[154]

The regional strategy sustained   In early January 1963, White House advisor McGeorge Bundy wrote to President Kennedy about improving the administration of Cuba policy, especially as it related to the OAS where the regional isolation of the Castro government "should be pursued intensively." Within days of Bundy's memorandum, the President approved a major reorganization of the foreign policy apparatus "to facilitate the coordinated management of all aspects of our current policy toward Cuba."[155] The State Department's Coordinator of Cuban Affairs, Sterling Cottrell, assumed control, with his responsibilities including reporting on covert operations directly to the Special Group. Cottrell prepared an internal memorandum on the Cuba isolation strategy which argued that attention should be focused on action that "would advance us toward our objective, would be politically feasible," and would involve minimum adverse international effects." The first move should be a submission of two resolutions to the OAS: one condemning Cuba for behavior "which continue[s] to endanger the peace" of the hemisphere; the other recommending an extension of the arms embargo to include all trade except food and medicine, as well as a more comprehensive shipping and airline blockade to limit Soviet bloc-Cuba contacts.[156]

Cuba's isolation was also on the agenda of an Alliance for Progress meeting between President Kennedy and the Central American heads of state in San Jose, Costa Rica, the following March. The United States was anxious to gain a subregional consensus over what it deemed "the real threat" posed by Cuba: internal subversion, not external aggression. A State Department Policy Planning memorandum proposed that two ways to deal with the threat be given particular attention: improving the organizational capabilities of the area's internal security forces with respect to intelligence, surveillance, "and control of clandestine movements of agents and arms"; and more regular visits by U.S. naval vessels to, and increased American Coastguard monitoring of, the entire Central American-Caribbean basin.[157] American officials apparently anticipated that the presidents of Costa Rica, El Salvador, Honduras, Guatemala, Panama, and Nicaragua would propose strategies at San Jose based on insufficient appreciation of their societies' vulnerability to internal subversion:

Their suggestion for dealing with Cuba will probably lean toward actions *outside* their countries against the Castro regime rather than being concerned with measures they can adopt *internally* with U.S. cooperation to limit and control the threat from *within*.[158]

The anticipated debate never materialized. The March conference failed to reveal any sharp disagreements at the strategic level, much to the satisfaction of President Kennedy, who singled out the agreement reached over the need "to take effective measures" to halt the flow of arms and personnel between Cuba and the rest of Latin America.[159] In April, U.S. and Central American intelligence and security officials convened in Managua, Nicaragua, to carry out the San Jose conference recommendations.[160] Washington's overall objective was to establish an ongoing and coordinated regional surveillance of Cuba.[161]

But major opposition to U.S. Cuban policy remained, surfacing at an OAS Council meeting in July 1963. On the agenda was a Special Inter-American Security Committee resolution to ban hemispheric travel to Cuba and increase cooperation between members' security forces. The refusal of Mexico, Brazil, Chile, and Venezuela – among the most politically influential regimes – to support these measures forced the Kennedy administration to set aside a planned request to the OAS to institute a regional economic embargo of Cuba.[162] Meanwhile, State Department officials continued to insist that the United States was determined to isolate Cuba "economically and politically" and to eliminate the Castro regime without resort to direct military intervention.[163]

In July 1963, Washington also tightened its Cuba embargo with a State Department directive to Treasury officials to ban all financial and currency transactions under authority of the Trading with the Enemy Act. A freeze was immediately placed on $33 million in Cuban public and private deposits in the United States. Officials asserted that Cuban agents had taken advantage of U.S. currency and banking channels to finance revolutionary activities in Latin America. It was hoped this measure would curtail Cuban access to the dollar and force the use of other currencies less common to the hemisphere and, hence, easier to detect. Washington also hoped that limiting the dollar's availability would contract Cuba's transactions with Western Europe.[164]

There was no slowdown in the pursuit of Cuba's "diplomatic, political and economic isolation" in Latin America, bilaterally or miltilaterally, in the transition from the Kennedy to the Johnson administration.[165] In December 1963, the OAS appointed a mission to investigate a Venezuelan complaint that Havana was training and arming its rural guerrilla movement. The mission's findings upheld the Venezuelan contention, and Caracas demanded the application of hemisphere-wide sanctions against Cuba. The Ninth Meeting of the OAS Foreign Ministers in late July 1964 convened principally to act on Venezuela's request. In the weeks before the conference, American and Venezuelan officials lobbied vigorously to condemn Cuba's actions and apply punitive sanctions. Early that July, several meetings were arranged at the White House between the President, senior State Department officials, and Latin American ambassadors. Ostensibly organized to exchange ideas on such issues as hemispheric defense and the Alliance for Progress, the meetings also, as the *Hispanic American Report* pointed out, "served an obvious preparatory function" for the upcoming Foreign Ministers meeting.[166]

To assembled delegates at the July 1964 OAS conference, Secretary of State Rusk called for sanctions and the application of "the full weight of the regional security system" if Cuba persisted in its active identification with continental revolutionary movements.[167] Although the United States wielded "considerable influence,"[168] the initial response to the sanctions proposal was mixed. The previous February, Mexican President Lopez Mateos dismissed President Johnson's concern over Cuba's "export of revolution" as evidenced by the Venezuelan episode, replying that "it was impossible to export revolutions."[169] During a subsequent conversation with Mexican President-Elect Diaz Ordaz in November, it became clear to Johnson that Mexico still opposed the sanctions against Cuba ratified by the July Foreign Ministers conference: "[Diaz Ordaz] implied that Cuba's complicity in the plot to overthrow the Venezuelan government had not been proven to Mexico's satisfaction."[170] Together with Chile, Bolivia, and Uruguay, Mexico oppposed any form of conference sanctions against Cuba, while Argentina expressed its preference for nonmandatory sanctions.

Although in complete agreement with the Venezuelan position, Washington agreed, for tactical reasons, to compromise on the timing of compliance with the sanctions. White House concern with this question largely pertained to the 1964 presidential election in Chile. The Johnson administration did not want to force Chile's hand over an issue that might shift the electoral balance away from the Christian Democratic Party candidate, Eduardo Frei. The recipient of massive U.S. financial and covert assistance, Frei was locked in a close contest with a coalition of left-wing political parties under the leadership of Salvador Allende. The final conference vote to obligate member nations to terminate diplomatic relations and suspend commercial and shipping ties with the Castro regime was passed by fifteen to four, with one abstention.[171]

The 1964 conference had negligible success in forcing the Cubans to adhere to a policy of "peaceful coexistence" with regional capitalist regimes. Three years later, another Foreign Ministers' meeting was held expressly to deal with Cuban-supported challenges for state power by nationalist and revolutionary movements in Venezuela, Bolivia, and elsewhere. All the delegates except Mexico's pledged to intensify efforts to curb Cuban assistance to insurgent forces around the continent. The process was facilitated by the existence of an increasing number of pro-U.S. military regimes. To the degree that only Mexico maintained formal political ties with Havana from late 1964 until 1970, American policymakers can be said to have achieved their goal of isolating and containing the Cuban Revolution within Latin America.

The "soft seven" and Cuba: imperial leverage and the limits of hemispheric resistance   During the Castro regime's first three years, all but seven Latin American countries severed diplomatic and consular relations with Havana. American officials took the credit, with one declaring "We were exercising our influence wherever we could."[172]

Economic assistance and multilateral development bank loans and credits were used as levers in the isolation policy. The Inter-American Development Bank, in which the United States exercised veto power, was, according to a Bank official, established as "an anti-Cuban instrument . . . designed to pump money into the weakest countries."[173] Between 1962 and 1965, the Bank provided $671.5 million to hemispheric governments.[174]

Throughout the Kennedy and early Johnson presidencies, the seven "holdout" countries discussed below were subjected to political, economic, and covert pressures, often through strategically placed local forces, to induce or force them to support Cuba's isolation.

Argentina   The Frondizi government in Argentina (1958–1962) succeeded a military dictatorship that had promoted an economic development strategy based on repression, a demobilized working class, and efforts to roll back Peronist gains. Frondizi supported limited economic nationalism and the reconsolidation of workers' postwar advances. His strategy, rooted in national industrialists and organized labor, envisioned the erosion of the rural oligarchy's power. But Frondizi's subsequent tilt in favor of the industrial bourgeoisie generated a hostile response from both labor and the landed oligarchy. In desperation, Frondizi turned to external financing, negotiating International Monetary Fund (IMF) assistance by agreeing to economic austerity and stabilization measures that principally affected the working class through wage controls, higher prices, and a lowered standard of living. Meanwhile, the oil multinationals took advantage of these measures and invested heavily in Argentina. This reopening of the economy to foreign capital during Frondizi's four years helped raise the cost of living by 323 percent, increased the external debt enormously, and sent inflation spiralling.[175] Amid these developments, the Argentine military apparatus confronted Frondizi over the country's diplomatic ties with Cuba.

Throughout 1961, the armed forces and intelligence services repeatedly pressured Frondizi to break with Havana. Both institutions had long-established ties with their U.S. counterparts, relationships enlivened by the Cuba problem. In late 1961, Secretary of State Rusk, to dramatize these ties and the power at his command, presented Frondizi with several letters supposedly acquired by CIA and Argentine intelligence operatives from Cuba's Embassy in Buenos Aires that included names of Argentinians allegedly working for the Castro government. Frondizi denounced the letters as forgeries and declared that the individuals named as Cuban agents had his "absolute confidence."[176]

Despite these pressures, Frondizi refused to sever ties and continued to oppose regional actions against Cuba on the principle of nonintervention. At Punta del Este in January 1962, Frondizi ignored his armed forces' urge to break with Cuba and instructed his foreign minister to abstain on conference votes about sanctions. The military retaliated: reverse positions or accept the consequences. Frondizi bowed to the threat, proposing that Argentina withdraw its Havana Ambassador as a step toward ending all diplomatic links,[177] but also made a last effort to rally working-class support for the Punta del Este actions.[178] The economically discontented workers' failure to respond to Frondizi's plea left him only compliance with the military's ultimatum.

On February 8, 1962, Argentina broke with Cuba. Later that month, the U.S. government extended the financially strapped Buenos Aires regime a $150 million loan for development purposes. Coincidentally, this was followed in July by $500 million in credits from a consortium of American public and private financial institutions, the World Bank, the IMF, and the Inter-American Development Bank.[179]

In November 1962, the "Paris Club" countries of Western Europe and Japan surprisingly agreed to postpone Argentina's repayment of half of its foreign debt due at the end of 1964 and recommended a $150 million grant for economic development during 1963 and 1964. The Club's generosity was attributed partly to Argentina's swift support of U.S. policy toward Cuba over the missile crisis. For the ruling generals, who ousted Frondizi from political power the previous March, contributed destroyers and aircraft to the blockade flotilla in October 1962 – and even offered to provide troops.[180]

Ecuador   In August 1960, José María Velasco Ibarra, campaigning as a populist reformer, was elected president. His immediate problem was how to revive a stagnant economy resulting from a slump in cacao and coffee prices and competition in banana markets from other Central American producers. Velasco proved incapable of translating his populist rhetoric into practice. He presided over a fiscal crisis: rising prices, a precipitous fall in international reserves, widespread unemployment, and declining exports. The country's trade setbacks were particularly critical because almost half the government's income normally came from import and export taxes.[181] Velasco, like Frondizi, attempted to resolve the financial squeeze through foreign capital. But, as with Frondizi, access to, in this case, American economic assistance (rather than IMF loans) was dependent on Ecuador's policy toward Cuba.

Velasco's advocacy of noninterference not only blocked the possibility of U.S. help in this area, it also became a rallying point for his political opponents. Right-wing organizations, the Church, large landowners, and fractions of the armed forces aligned themselves with CIA efforts to force a break in diplomatic relations between Quito and Havana. Despite Ecuador's pressing need for economic assistance, Washington "dragged its feet in approving loans to Ecuador." Then, shortly after Adlai Stevenson's mission in June 1961 and his chilly reception on the topic of Cuba, the Velasco government began to shift.[182]

The workers' movement, already dissatisfied with Velasco, opposed the shift. In October, the Confederation of Ecuadorian Workers struck over wages and other demands; their action helped lead to Velasco's demise. His formal ouster was made a *fait accompli* by the military's withdrawal of support in November 1961.[183]

During the Velasco period, the CIA expanded its Ecuador activities "to promote a break in diplomatic relations [with Cuba] through propaganda and political-action operations." Its Station in Quito took on three projects: intelligence collection and "technical penetration" of strategic anti-U.S. organizations, such as the Cuban Mission; inserting agents in key Ecuadoran government and state institutions, in opposition political parties, and among antigovernment armed forces leaders; and a massive propaganda and psychological warfare campaign emphasizing mass-media manipulation in support of anticommunist political, labor, and youth organization leaders.[184]

Cuban Embassy and Ecuadoran regime penetrations were successful. Treasury Minister Jorge Acosta Velasco became an "asset": "He has been keeping [James B.] Nolan [Chief of Station] informed on Velasco's obstinacy over breaking with Cuba, but now he'll be able to work on the problem from within the Cabinet."[185] The CIA also aggressively propagandized and employed local agents to pressure the Ecuadoran Church to intensify denunciations of communism and Castro's Cuba. All these activities dovetailed to become an anticommunist front financed and organized by the Agency to weaken Velasco's government.[186]

In November 1961, these pressures and a falling out with Vice-President Carlos Julio Arosemena Monroy finally undermined Velasco. Arosemena, with armed forces' backing, formed a government and immediately dispatched former President Galo Plaza to Washington to inform the Kennedy administration that Ecuador remained committed to the Alliance for Progress and the inter-American system.[187] But also, with cabinet approval, Arosemena announced his support for the OAS principle of nonintervention. In July 1962, Arosemena was invited to the White House to be encouraged to support U.S. policy toward Cuba and exert greater control over Ecuador's left. "This was the main purpose of the visit," declared Assistant Secretary of State for Inter-American Affairs Edwin M. Martin. "It didn't go too well in terms of actual results."[188]

Paralleling these pressures was a determined American effort to link up with Ecuador's armed forces and the labor movement, the former a recipient of U.S. counterinsurgency training and assistance, the latter, with American labor movement help, deeply involved in trying to undermine the left-wing leadership of the Confederation of Ecuadoran Workers and substitute anti-communist leaders "open" to Washington's suggestions. The American Institute for Free Labor Development (AIFLD) and Inter-American Regional Organization of Workers (ORIT) affiliates in Ecuador also acted as conduits for CIA funding of antigovernment labor groups during this period.[189]

Ecuador's diplomatic relations with Cuba heightened social polarization in the country in late 1961 and early 1962. After Ecuador's abstentions on Cuba votes at the January 1962 Foreign Minister's conference at Punta del Este, the CIA Station "step[ped] up its campaign of anticommunist propaganda, support for right-wing groups, and infiltration of pro-Castro forces."[190] Rising military opposition to relations with the Castro government provided fertile ground for the CIA and its local allies. As anticommunist demonstrations in late March 1962 called for an end to ties with Cuba, the military reported "strong support for a break in relations . . . from the minister of defense down to the last conscript."[191] These developments produced a crisis: conservative elements withdrew from the government; into the Cabinet came the center-left National Democratic Front which supported the military's position on Cuba. On April 2, the day after the cabinet reshuffle, diplomatic ties between Ecuador and Cuba were terminated.

The CIA spent an estimated $11 million in Ecuador between 1960 and 1963, but this relatively modest amount funded a highly successful covert action program in no small measure due to the existence of a distinctive political culture that featured a fragmented and impoverished left, and fragile state, government, and societal institutions very susceptible to penetration and manipulation by outside forces.[192]

Chile   Toward the end of the conservative Alessandri presidency (1958–1964), U.S. officials and American multinationals expressed concern over the Chilean electorate's move to the left. To forestall a left-wing presidential victory under Salvador Allende (a consistent supporter of strengthened Chile-Cuba relations), the White House and the State Department initiated massive direct political, economic, and covert intervention to "help create a climate favorable" for the Christian Democratic Party hopeful Eduardo Frei.[193] The State Department's senior Latin American policymaker, Thomas Mann, outlined the general course of action Washington would follow: "the United States should completely favor Frei's election, avoid contact with Allende and his supporters, and take no action and make no statement that would lend respectability to Allende's Chile. There should be no doubt in Chile as to where the United States stands."[194]

Frei's campaign received millions of dollars, clandestinely, but also U.S. public aid almost tripled from $97.7 million in 1963, the year before the election, to $260.4 million in 1964, including a $40 million general economic development grant to alleviate unemployment. "We did not want to have a condition of vast unemployment," an involved Agency for International Development official conceded, "as Chile was going into an election."[195] On its front, the CIA orchestrated a mass-media propaganda operation designed to portray Allende as the forerunner of a government modeled after Cuba. The campaign had a powerful, negative impact, despite Allende's declared commitment to a gradual shift to socialism in Chile. As the *Hispanic American Report* commented, this state of affairs limited Allende's ability to conduct a vigorous campaign aganst Frei without running the risk of "appearing to confirm rightist press claims that he would apply Cuban-style measures to Chile if elected."[196]

During his tenure, President Alessandri had resisted American requests to break with Cuba. But while he parried Washington's pressures and abstained on the exclusion vote at the January 1962 OAS conference, Alessandri nonetheless maintained a formal relationship with Cuba. In the midst of the 1964 election contest between Frei and Allende, he deferred action on Cuba to the new president, due to popular opposition to a break in ties and charges that he was acting on the orders of external forces.[197] Yet, as the American Embassy apparently sought to force his hand,[198] on August 11, 1964, Alessandri severed diplomatic relations with Cuba. White House official McGeorge Bundy then told President Johnson that "our friends in Santiago" wanted Washington to be quiet about the break: "If we look as if we are interfering . . . it will be bad for our friend Frei and good for the Communist-supported Allende."[199]

Brazil   Brazil occupied a crucial place in American efforts to isolate the Cuban Revolution. Aspiring to political and economic leadership of the region, its support was viewed by Washington as pivotal. But in 1961, the nationalist government of Jânio Quadros made several foreign policy moves that departed sharply "from Brazil's traditional international policy, which previously had almost always hewed docilely to United States leadership."[200] The U.S. Ambassador, John Moors Cabot, took a measured view of this by distinguishing between actions over domestic pressures, such as the need "to mollify ultra nationalists, neutralists and leftists," and no intention on Quadros' part "to abandon [the] basic western orientation of Brazilian policy."[201] Washington policymakers more harshly judged Quadros' refusal to terminate relations with Cuba on the bases of self-determination, national sovereignty, and nonintervention. Accordingly, a Quadros offer to mediate between the United States and Cuba was rejected.

In March 1961, the White House sent Adolph Berle to Brazil to make Quadros concede to the multilateral nature of the conflict, cooperate in Cuba's regional isolation, and support a projected exile "attack on Cuba." Cabot was present at the Berle-Quadros meeting and recalled the American envoy's offer of massive financial aid if Quadros agreed. Not deterred by the Brazilian's first refusal, Berle went "back again and again mentioning a hundred million dollars. . . . It was obvious that it was just a bribe. I mean that's what it amounted to. And Quadros, with increasing irritation, said no. And they finally had to leave it on that basis."[202]

Secretary of State Rusk acknowledged that, while there was "no present intention of refusing all aid to Quadros," the amount and timing of such assistance was still to be decided by the Kennedy administration: "As for the question of economic aid, [the State] Department intends to play this by ear."[203] Cabot was concerned that pressures be applied in a way that would not push the nationalist regime toward a more radical socioeconomic transformation.[204]

On March 16, the interdepartmental Task Force on Latin America under Adolph Berle met to discuss hemispheric issues, including Quadros' behavior. While describing Quadros' attitude toward Cuba as "the bad aspect of Brazilian policy," Berle rejected the view that labelled the broader contours of country's foreign policy as "neutralist." So doing, he discouraged actions that might have "forc[ed] President Quadros into the arms of Castro." Concerning aid, Berle basically agreed with Under Secretary of State Thomas Mann that it be limited to whatever would "prevent [the] collapse of the Brazilian economy." The United States could then maintain its "leverage" and "avoid the impression" that Washington "rewarded countries that follow 'exotic' foreign policies." The Task Force recommended that aid continue "to meet Brazil's actual needs" but that there be no let-up in U.S. pressures to effect changes in Quadros' foreign policy.[205] In May 1961, the White House approved $100 million in new credits to Brazil, although Ambassador Cabot argued that "we shouldn't go all out for Quadros' requirements without getting some 'muffling' of Quadros in return."[206]

Quadros' resignation and João Goulart's elevation to the presidency in August–September 1961 produced "a cautious, but perceptible shift in United States–Brazilian relationships . . . based upon the conviction of responsible United States officials in Brazil that Goulart would be hard to work with."[207] The worry was confirmed as Goulart indicated his desire to expand national control over the country's resources as part of a populist program that included income redistribution, restrictions on investment, and a modest agrarian reform. He also renewed Brazil's relations with the Soviet Union. His (and Quadros') nationalist foreign minister,

Francisco San Tiago Dantas, was among the first to declare that Brazil "would spare no effort to keep Cuba within the inter-American system."[208] At the January 1962 OAS conference at Punta del Este, San Tiago Dantas helped mobilize opposition to collective sanctions against Cuba. And overall, Goulart consistently advocated nonintervention and peaceful coexistence and repeatedly stated that negotiation was the only way to resolve the U.S.– Cuban conflict.

Kennedy administration efforts to force Goulart to break with Cuba after that OAS conference were tied to Washington's principal objectives in Brazil. Goulart's reformist political and economic policies increasingly were perceived by Washington and its Brazilian allies as anticapitalist and procommunist. They instigated social conflict and political instability as bourgeois and petty-bourgeois forces hostile to the lower classes emerged to oppose the nationalist central government. Together, external and internal pressures on Goulart led the armed forces into the political arena and to the termination of parliamentary democracy in Brazil.[209]

The United States's initial goals were to keep Goulart "in the center,"[210] undercut the influence of the Brazilian left and limit socioeconomic change. Economic pressure involved manipulating foreign aid; political pressures involved direct American intervention in Brazilian elections. Witness the October 1962 elections, when millions of dollars were channeled by the Kennedy administration and American corporations in Brazil into the campaigns of several hundred anti-Goulart candidates running for gubernatorial, congressional, state, and municipal office.[211] A U.S. Embassy official recalled that Cabot's successor as Ambassador, Lincoln Gordon, "was [very] involved."[212]

With Goulart's second year, the regime's refusal to stop its state governments from expropriating International Telephone and Telegraph (ITT) and American and Foreign Power properties distressed the White House and senior State Department officials. A U.S. mission to Brazil in early 1962 recommended that further assistance for development or balance-of-payments and debt crisis purposes be withheld "unless and until a stabilization plan satisfactory to the IMF was put in effect."[213] That kind of austerity program would most affect just those classes that constituted Goulart's major support. The new ambassador was "requested to threaten a cutoff of even emergency balance of payments assistance unless Brazil immediately began to plan a comprehensive stabilization and 'sound' development program" that would include "real encouragement to private foreign capital."[214]

In December, a National Security Council memorandum listed similar concerns: resolving the dispute over the nationalized ITT subsidiary; eliminating the "defects" in the profit remittance law; public statements supporting the Alliance for Progress; and the institution of anti-inflationary measures. It also addressed Brazil's foreign policy under Goulart, but cautioned that "unless Brazil should make a clear break with the rest . . . of this hemisphere . . . effective confrontation will be difficult." Finally, the memorandum outlined elements of a strategy to pressure Goulart to "take public postures on issues which are critical for U.S.-Brazilian cooperation," such as consolidating ties with key Brazilian groups and individuals in the government "who advocate domestic and foreign policies which we can support."[215]

In early 1963, Goulart sought to mollify American concerns by settling the ITT dispute, influencing Congress to pass a tax reform bill, and taking measures to deal with inflation. Yet, when Francisco San Tiago Dantas, now the Finance Minister, visited Washington to seek economic assistance, he confronted a President and a Secretary of State preoccupied with Communist influence in Brazil and Cuba's ties with Goulart and the country's political left.[216] Dantas and Goulart were left in no doubt that new aid and credits were contingent on further concessions to foreign capital, the IMF "seal of approval" for its economic stabilization program, and the completion of debt negotiations with Brazil's European creditors. The only short-term exception was a U.S. agreement to release $84 million outstanding from a 1961 loan to the Quadros government if Goulart was willing to negotiate the purchase of all the American and Foreign Power properties in Brazil – highly unprofitable enterprises that the utility wanted to get rid of anyway.[217]

By 1963, the policy of forcing Goulart into the "political center" essentially had been abandoned, as U.S. policymakers began to bolster anti-Goulart forces and exacerbate the country's economic problems. A cornerstone of this effort was the "island of [administrative] sanity" tactic that originated, according to Ruth Leacock, at the December 1962 meeting of the National Security Council Executive Committee.[218] The aim was to provide large-scale financial resources to selected state governments, autonomous public agencies, and private organizations hostile to the central Brazilian administration.[219] Meanwhile, Washington not only halted virtually all economic assistance to Goulart's beleaguered regime beginning in early 1963, but also influenced the multilateral development banks to do likewise. Though more than $600 million in U.S. Agency for International Development loans were approved for Brazil between 1960 and 1964, over three-quarters were not disbursed until after Goulart's overthrow.[220] The World Bank extended no loans or credits to the Goulart government; the Inter-American Development Bank provided a mere $66 million in urgently needed funds.[221] Economic pressures were intensified by Washington's refusal to consider any renegotiations of Brazil's foreign debt to the United States until Goulart had come to terms with his European creditors.[222]

The CIA and the AFL-CIO were active participants in this destabilization strategy. The covert agency conducted a large propaganda and political-action campaign, providing funds and training key regime opponents and maintaining close ties with Brazilian armed forces. Throughout the Goulart years, the Agency (together with American military attaches) retained extraordinary access to intelligence information and antiregime military developments.[223] The AFL-CIO played a less direct, though important, role through its sponsorship of the American Institute of Free Labor Development (AIFLD), which trained a number of anti-Goulart trade-union leaders who played significant counterrevolutionary roles.[224]

In the months preceding Goulart's demise, American officials began to think "in terms of Brazil as another Cuba."[225] The pragmatic Mann Doctrine regarding U.S. recognition of nonelected military regimes encouraged the *golpista* tendency within the Brazilian armed forces.[226] Washington's pressures against the nationalist regime were paralleled by an increasingly intimate relationship between the military and civilian coup conspirators and high-ranking U.S. Embassy and Consulate officials in Rio de Janeiro and São Paulo.

On March 27, 1964, Ambassador Lincoln Gordon transmitted an evaluation of recent developments and possible responses to a military coup against Goulart. The document recommended immediate support for the *golpistas* by providing them with petroleum and sending a U.S. carrier task force to the Brazilian coast.[227] Washington approved both suggestions and also discussed sending arms and ammunition to the military conspirators.[228] Within hours, the task force was en route "to establish [a] U.S. presence [in Brazilian waters] and be prepared to carry out tasks as may be assigned."[229]

Goulart's parliamentary regime was overthrown, and a military dictatorship instituted a repressive political rule and an economic model based on massive financial borrowings from American public agencies and multilateral development banks. The imposition of a drastic austerity program, an agreement to buy the American and Foreign Power properties, the weakening of restrictions on the repatriation of profits by foreign companies, and the signing of an investment guarantee agreement with the U.S. government during the first year of armed forces' rule all signalled the determination of the new regime to put private capital at the center of its economic program.[230] With Goulart's fall, the foreign assistance faucets gushed: more than $2.3 billion in credits and loans flowed from the combined coffers of the U.S. government, the World Bank, and the Inter-American Development Bank between April 1964 and December 1968.[231]

To no one's surprise, one of the military's first acts was to terminate diplomatic relations with Cuba. Brazil's new rulers also "took the lead in efforts to set up a strict economic blockade of Cuba by the Organization of American States."[232] Increased U.S. Agency for International Development funds and personnel was its "reward" for breaking with Havana.[233]

Bolivia   The second Paz Estenssoro administration (1958–1964) presided over the demise of the nationalist currents in Bolivia's 1952 revolution and the reconstruction of the country's armed forces. Provoked by the Cuban Revolution, Washington provided military assistance and training necessary to reestablish an effective coercive apparatus ready and willing to deal with the Paz government's domestic opponents – especially the class-conscious worker's militias linked to the economy's strategic tin mining centers. The regime was also a major beneficiary of the Alliance for Progress to the tune of almost $200 million between 1962 and 1964.[234] Despite its generous military and economic authorizations, U.S. government urgings to break relations with Cuba went largely unheeded.

Before the 1964 elections, right-wing pressures forced Paz Estenssoro (who was running for reelection) to choose General René Barrientos as his running mate. Their victory predated a long period of social and political unrest, developments that substantially weakened the central government and aroused right-wing opposition. During this time, U.S.–Bolivian relations deteriorated to "an open quarrel" over the issues of Cuba and continued American economic assistance.[235] In August 1964, President Johnson reportedly personally requested Paz to sever ties with Havana "in the name of political solidarity."[236] In some quarters it was believed that the Bolivians were prepared to if Mexico, Uruguay, or Chile would "take the lead."[237] According to a senior U.S. Embassy official in La Paz, a shift in the Bolivian position was indeed linked to action that might be taken by the Alessandri government in Chile.[238]

The Bolivian economy's overwhelming dependence on external sources of financing and the threat of a substantial reduction in U.S. aid eventually forced the Paz government's hand and, on August 21, 1964, diplomatic and commercial relations with Cuba ended.[239] The *New York Times* editorialized on the role of American pressures in shaping this decision:

The break in diplomatic and trade relations between Bolivia and Cuba provides evidence of the power that the United States, the 'Colossus of the North,' still wields in Latin America. President Paz Estenssoro and the key elements in the ruling MNR [Movimiento Nacionalista Revolucionario] party did not want to conform to the Organization of American States resolution calling for sanctions against Cuba. Bolivia reportedly had no choice. It was a case of conforming or facing a severe cut in United States aid – and Bolivia cannot carry on without such aid.[240]

Before year's end, Vice-President Barrientos, with Washington's tacit support, engineered a successful military coup against Paz Estenssoro and "set up the type of government," as one State Department official put it, "we thought we could deal with."[241] The Johnson administration recognized the new regime because it was compatible with American policy objectives in Bolivia and because the military leaders "uttered the right words about communism and especially Cuba."[242]

Uruguay   Before Mexico, Uruguay was the last to fall into the rank and file of Washington's isolation strategy for Cuba. During 1964, the CIA mounted a large covert action program to force Uruguay "to effect a break in diplomatic relations with Cuba."[243] For here, the Agency confronted formidable obstacles: a disciplined, organized Communist Party and a standard of living that limited workers' susceptibility to financial blandishments.[244]

Ostensibly, the Uruguayans' decision to break relations with Cuba was tied indirectly to the actions of the July OAS Foreign Ministers meeting in Washington. After almost nonstop deliberations, the Uruguayan National Executive Council voted six to three to terminate the diplomatic link in early September 1964.[245] Although evidence of a direct relationship between CIA operations and the Council vote has not surfaced, it is quite likely that the cumulative effect of the Agency's actions helped produce this decision. The *New York Times* correspondent in Montevideo observed that the Council action "was seen as a signal success for the policy promoted by the United States which seeks to isolate the Castro government politically and economically from the rest of Latin America."[246]

Mexico   The governments of Adolfo Lopez Mateos (1958–1964) and Gustavo Diaz Ordaz (1964–1970) craftily finessed American pressures to sever relations with Cuba by balancing no direct criticism of U.S. policy with limited kinds of private compliance that, in practice, contributed to Cuba's isolation in Latin America. To justify maintaining ties, Mexican officials consistently appealed to juridical arguments, while Mexico's own revolutionary tradition rendered Cuba's revolution an event of more than symbolic importance to large segments of the country's population. Moreover, Mateos and Ordaz "were not about to take an action that *would appear* to be kowtowing to our [U.S.] pressures."[247]

But even as Mexico opposed Cuba's expulsion from the OAS at Punta del Este in January 1962, it did align with the U.S. delegation to declare the Cuban Revolution "incompatible" with the inter-American system, support creation of a Special Security Committee to investigate Communist subversion in the region, and condemn the Communist offensive in Latin America.[248]

In June 1962, Lopez Mateos informed President Kennedy that, while he was "willing to take a rather limited commitment to try to do something if something could be shown that would have an important practical effect in assisting the countries of Central America or in restraining Castro . . . he was unwilling to undertake gestures in view of certain political problems at home."[249] Mexican officials were downplaying Cuba's role as a destabilizing force and arguing that the United Nations, not the OAS, could deal most effectively with any threat emanating from Havana.

They preferred to focus on containing communism inside Cuba rather than imposing pariah status on the revolutionary regime.[250]

Domestically, however, the Mateos government cooperated in the relatively successful, U.S.-orchestrated effort to tighten travel restrictions between Cuba and the rest of Latin America during 1963 and 1964.[251] Collaborating with the local CIA Station, Mexico was "strict about permitting the entry by air of anything it consider[ed] Cuban propaganda, including Cuban newspapers carried by passengers arriving here from Havana."[252] The CIA was also allowed to photograph departures, arrivals, and even individual's passports.[253] Further, Mexican officials provided the CIA with Cubana Airlines passenger lists and regularly acceded to CIA requests that specific American citizens be prevented from leaving for Havana.[254]

The Kennedy administration was prepared to accommodate bilateral differences over Cuba, especially in light of Mexico's preparedness to make a number of concessions short of breaking diplomatic ties with the Castro regime and its essentially symbolic opposition to Washington's regional policy goals.[255] Soon after Johnson assumed the Presidency, the *Washington Post* correspondent in Mexico City observed that "no outstanding question is causing great friction between the two countries."[256] In February 1964, the new American president declared that "relations between the United States and Mexico had never been better."[257]

Conclusion

The process of large-scale structural transformation in Cuba raised, from Washington's perspective, the possibility of an economic development model that might take hold in other parts of the Third World. The initial U.S. response was to seek to destabilize and overthrow the revolutionary regime. But the speed with which Castro constructed a new state structure, largely socialized the means of production, and the ease with which he disenfranchised bourgeois political institutions and neutralized non-working-class opposition created insurmountable obstacles to the internal subversion goal.

With the swift elimination in Cuba of strategic groups allied with Washington, American policymakers lacked the means to orchestrate a serious "insiders" challenge to the developing socialist society. Hence, the decision to shift tracks and concentrate resources on other forms of opposition, one of which was the strategy of regional isolation designed to limit the "multiplier" effect of the Cuban Revolution in the hemisphere. "After the Bay of Pigs," said a CIA field participant, "throughout Latin America, not only was the policy persistent, but it was uniform." He continued:

Everyone who worked in the Embassies throughout Latin America knew the U.S. government wanted that country to break relations with Cuba. Just no question about it. Never known a clearer policy as far as being understood right down to the lowest member of the Embassy.[258]

Operationally, the U.S. tolerated alignments with nonelected regimes whose domestic policies were hostile to professed Alliance for Progress goals in return for cooperation with the isolation of Cuba.

Regionally, the imperial state applied formidable diplomatic, political, economic, and covert pressures on hemispheric governments to ensure cooperation in achieving its objective. Executive-branch officials vividly recall the employment of "a hell of a lot of muscle"[259] or invoke the image of the "sledgehammer"[260] to describe the intensity of Washington's actions. Others spoke of "a lot of government-to-government persuasion"[261] and "a great deal of arm twisting."[262] At regional forums, U.S. pressures were relentless:

There wasn't a single conference held at the OAS level that was informally devoid of U.S. pressure. [There was] a certain paranoia, [an] obsession on our part. . . . Our disposition was to use the OAS where possible as an isolating instrument and as an instrument to isolate the activists.[263]

The pivotal role of covert politics in affecting the desired outcome in different countries "operational environments" in Latin America was indirectly commented on by the CIA's Richard Bissell in a 1968 address to the Council on Foreign Relations. He observed that Third World nations are generally highly susceptible to clandestine operations "simply because [such] governments are much less highly organized; there is less security consciousness, and there is apt to be more actual or potential diffusion of power among parties, localities, organizations and individuals outside of the central government."[264] The case studies discussed in this chapter lend substantial credence to Bissell's remark. The impact of the isolation strategy depended largely on the types of peripheral regimes in power prior to, during, and following the decision to break relations with Havana. Washington's successes were greatly enhanced by the fact that key centers of nationalist support for the Cuban Revolution (e.g., Argentina, Brazil, and to a lesser extent, Ecuador) were unstable regimes unable to sustain their nationalist posture due to a lack of control over state power anchored in a solid working-class base.

By late 1964, the regional impact of the Cuban Revolution had been contained, the Castro government temporarily isolated. The militarization of a large part of Latin American civil society stood as testimony to the momentary consolidation of U.S. hegemony. This environment lubricated U.S. military intervention in the Dominican Republic in 1965. But all this elaborate imperial control rested on a fragile socioeconomic foundation that invited the resurgence of nationalist struggles. Thus, Latin America's contradictions between political stability and economic insecurity boiled over in the late 1960s and early 1970s as new national and class struggles led to regime changes, the breakdown of Cuba's political pariah status, and once again threatened the dominant power's regional position.

5. The United States against Cuba 1961–1968: politics of global economic blockade*

I can't think of any instance of a policy of economic and political isolation
being followed so vigorously as we followed it toward Cuba on the basis
of no documents or justification under international law.

(State Department official)[1]

The aims of this chapter are to analyze how the United States
under successive Democratic administrations orchestrated a
global economic blockade of Cuba for political objectives, and to
investigate the responses of Washington's allies – their degree of
cooperation and cleavage – in the effort to apply multilateral economic pressures to corner the revolutionary regime.

Economic sanctions have been and continue to be employed by
the U.S. government in attempts to disintegrate nationalist and
socialist regimes in the Third World deemed inimicable to American political, economic, or strategic interests. These countries are
highly vulnerable to this form of external aggression and its consequences: economic chaos, political and social unrest, and even
the demise of regimes. Three major factors account for their
susceptibility to economic pressures: First, most Third World
countries are export-oriented, monoculture economies highly
dependent on external sources of financing and trade for their
day-to-day and long-term development needs; second, the U.S.
holds a pivotal position within the international economy as a market for Third World products, as a source of economic assistance,
and as the most powerful actor in the international lending institutions; third, there are limited alternative sources of capital and
markets to which affected countries in these regions of the world

*This chapter contains material that appeared in an article entitled "The United
States and the Global Economic Blockade of Cuba: A Study of Political Pressures
on America's Allies," *Canadian Journal of Political Science*, Vol. XVII, No. 1, March
1984, pp. 25–48.

178

can turn. But since the 1960s, the capacity of the United States to mobilize support for an economic blockade against a target country has been tempered by the emergence of an increasingly differentiated capitalist world economy. The decline in postwar U.S. economic power and the growing competitiveness of Western Europe and Japan, as the following discussion reveals, have, to varying degrees, constrained U.S. actions and objectives.

The forming of multilateral coalitions to enforce economic sanctions has received insufficient attention in international relations literature. Most studies describe economic denial programs, collective measures through regional and international institutions, and the application and effectiveness of sanctions against the target country.[2] Attention less often has centered on political pressures applied to enforce support for such sanctions. Among the factors on which coalition building depends, these are central: a common interest in a particular policy; agreement on the sanction's desirability and the measures used; and a uniform commitment among the coalition partners to enforce adherence (through regulations and penalties) by economic groups located in their countries. In addition, the coalition's sacrifices and costs must be shared: The country spearheading the coalition cannot expect allies to suffer greater economic losses than it will itself, for an imbalance will produce fissures.

Competing or complementary economic interests are another issue. Allies competing in a common market may be reluctant to collaborate in an embargo that involves their withdrawing exports of great importance. The American effort to mobilize global support for a grain embargo of the Soviet Union after its intervention into Afghanistan in late 1979, for example, foundered largely because Argentina, both an ally and a competitor, refused to go along. Such partial sanctions leave the target country less vulnerable.[3]

Generally, it is difficult to coordinate the interests of states over time. As Margaret Doxey has observed, "Any program of collective action which requires a series of national decisions, and the sustaining over time of a group will to deprive, is likely to exhibit strains. Interests soon begin to diverge."[4]

Sanctions are most effective when an overwhelmingly powerful country intent on an economic blockade can influence its allies' exports. If the American market is critical to an ally's heavy-industry exports, Washington can use considerable leverage over that government to halt its exports to the targeted area. Boycotts are most successful when the target is a small country or an insignificant market, and when the world economy is expanding and interstate competition is limited. Conversely, countries are less likely to participate in sanctions when they depend heavily on exports or are asked to hold back items whose worldwide sales they monopolize, especially when there are no alternative markets.

In sum, where the effort is to influence major industrial countries with export-dependent economies amid shrinking markets and strong competition, boycotts are virtually impossible to maintain. That was the case for capitalist-bloc trade with the Soviet Union during the 1930s depression, a time of intense economic rivalries. And a principal feature of the 1960s capitalist world economy was the resurgence of competition, when the United States attempted to erect an economic "iron curtain" around Cuba.

The 1960s brought a spectacular expansion of American capital overseas. The value of U.S. direct manufacturing investment abroad increased from $11 billion in 1960 to almost $26.5 billion in 1968.[5] Western Europe received almost half of this new investment, as subsidiaries of U.S.-controlled multinational corporations more than doubled from 667 in 1959 to 1,438 in 1967.[6] Of the 100 largest multinationals in the capitalist world, 65 were under American control, 30 under European control, and only 5 were owned by Japanese capital.[7] Paradoxically, the very factors responsible for pushing the dollar outward in search of profits during this period – balance-of-payments deficits at home, domestic economic recessions in 1957–1958 and 1960, and the pull of the European Economic Community (EEC) which converted local currencies into dollars – weakened confidence in the dollar on international money markets. This trend was enhanced by the massive United States commitment in Indochina and the seemingly endless balance-of-payments crisis, as the deficit increased by an average of $1.2 billion annually between 1964 and 1968.[8]

The 1960s also witnessed a resurgence of economic rivalries as Western Europe and Japan challenged the United States' dominance in international trade. The following table shows the extent of American export losses to Western Europe and Japan during these years. In the strategic industrial export sector, the American share of global exports of principal manufactures declined from 30.5 percent of the total in 1954–1956 to 25.3 percent in 1961 to 22.7 percent in 1966.[10]

Total world exports (in percent)[9]

	1953	1963	1970
U.S.	21.0	17.0	15.5
E.E.C.	19.3	27.8	32.0
U.K.	9.7	8.7	7.0
Japan	1.7	4.0	7.0

To some commentators, these developments signalled the erosion of the "absolute superiority" of the United States within the capitalist world economy.[11] Although the United States did remain first among equals, heightened competition dictated the development of a more consultative relationship between Washington and its senior allies.[12]

It seems reasonable that these now formidable economic rivals in Western Europe and Japan would be more willing to take paths conflicting with American foreign policy. Their extent of cooperation and cleavage with the U.S. global economic blockade of Cuba raises several questions: How much did American policy influence these countries' trading behavior? Were their policies a result of American pressures or of independent assessments? Did opposition to U.S. pressures result from a perception of the blockade as ineffective or from changes in the international picture that encouraged policies less tied to Washington's interests?

This context of a highly competitive capitalist world is basic to any understanding of individual responses to the United States' effort to terminate Cuba's economic relations with the Western world.

The Cuban missile crisis*

American efforts to arrest and roll back the process of large-scale structural change in Cuba between 1959 and 1962 – from diplomatic pressures and economic sanctions to indirect military inter-

---

*This subject is the single most written-about episode in post-1959 United States–Cuban relations. As the footnotes to this section reveal, memoirs by senior Kennedy administration officials who participated in the decisionmaking process complement an exhaustive body of secondary literature. This study also makes use of relevant materials declassified by the Kennedy Presidential Library. However, for the issues addressed here, the spectacle of the missile crisis is not particularly significant. It is accorded limited treatment because I am primarily concerned with its role in accelerating the shift in U.S. policy toward postrevolutionary Cuba from an emphasis on an "insider" to an "outsider" approach.

vention – were unsuccessful for three major reasons. First, powerful groups from the old Cuban state, government, political parties, class structure, and society at large that had long-established ties with Washington either dissolved or suffered a profound loss of influence under nationalist rule. Second, the revolutionary leadership controlled the military apparatus of the post-1959 Cuban state. Third, that leadership was able to obtain substantial military and economic assistance from noncapitalist sources.

The demise of the collaborator groups is central to explaining the Cuban Revolution's capacity to survive and consolidate. For the success of American policy during this period depended on pro-U.S. elements inside Cuba being willing and able to take advantage of Washington's destabilizing initiatives by detonating a political challenge to the Castro government. The closure of these imperialist "access points" gradually forced U.S. policymakers to concede that the "insider" strategy was not working, was unlikely to work, and probably should be abandoned.

No particular moment or event can be isolated as the most decisive in accounting for Washington's loss of confidence in the "insider" strategy. At the same time, no explanation would be complete without reference, however brief, to the momentous superpower confrontation over Cuba in October 1962 between the United States and the Soviet Union and to its consequences.[13] Ironically, the resolution of this so-called Cuban Missile Crisis effectively terminated any possibility of disintegrating the Cuban Revolution from within. It also reinforced an already observable shift within the Kennedy administration to globalize Washington's political and economic challenge to the Cuban Revolution.

On September 1, 1962, Republican Senator Kenneth Keating first publicly raised the possibility that the Soviet Union was constructing sites for medium-range missiles in Cuba. In the weeks that followed, Republican and Democratic congressional leaders were in the forefront of efforts to increase domestic political pressure on the Kennedy administration to "do something" about Cuba, and particularly about the current increase in the level of Soviet military activities on the island. In late September, the House of Representatives and the Senate passed a resolution authorizing direct military intervention, if necessary. By exposing Kennedy's "weakness" in dealing with Cuba, the Republicans also sought to make electoral gains: Mid-term congressional elections were scheduled for early November.[14]

On October 14, 1962, U-2 reconnaissance plane photos confirmed that missile sites were under construction in Cuba. Two days later, the White House was presented with what American officials described as irrefutable evidence that the Soviets had sent medium-range nuclear missiles to these new bases. Kennedy, determined to force the missiles' removal from Cuba at the risk even of nuclear confrontation, began discussions in the White House on the morning of October 16 with a group of senior officials (subsequently designated the Executive Committee of the National Security Council or EXCOM) to evaluate options ranging from secret negotiations with Khrushchev or Castro to a military invasion. The administration's initial abrupt dismissal of diplomatic pressure as a viable approach was in part shaped by domestic political considerations, particularly worries over legislative passage of its economic program in a context where almost all senior Republican and Democratic officeholders sided with the advocates of an air strike or military invasion.[15]

Most of the participants at the October 16 White House meetings supported either a combined air strike and military intervention or a quarantine based on a naval blockade. The division brought a vigorous debate. The Joint Chiefs of Staff advocated a direct invasion as the only means of forcing Moscow to get the missiles out of Cuba, and they opposed a surgical air strike against only the missiles in favor of a more comprehensive bombing of other military targets as well. Secretary of State Rusk and the President's National Security Affairs advisor McGeorge Bundy countered that there were political advantages to be gained from confining the attack to missile sites and that America's strategic nuclear superiority virtually ensured no Soviet retaliation. The chairman of the Joint Chiefs of Staff, General Maxwell Taylor, also raised the possibility of a joint air strike-naval blockade, but was cautious about any rash decision to invade the island: "that's the hardest question militarily in the whole business – one which we should look at very closely before we get our feet in that deep Cuban mud."[16]

Although Secretary of Defense Robert McNamara and Attorney General Robert Kennedy were later among the most forceful advocates of a "blockade first" approach, they initially aligned themselves with the proponents of a more aggressive interventionary response. McNamara dismissed out of hand the "political course of action," because it was unlikely to achieve the basic American objective and "it almost certainly [would stop] military action." While telling the White House meetings that some form of "direct military action" against Cuba almost assuredly would produce "a Soviet military response in another part of the world," he also slipped in that "it may well be worth the price." Robert Kennedy's statements were just as provocative. At one point he inquired whether it might be possible to create a pretext to justify direct military intervention "through, uh, Guantánamo Bay, or something, er, or whether there's some ship that, you know, sink the *Maine* again or something." Toward the end of the meeting, Defense Secretary McNamara began to shift gears, initiating the first extended discussion of the naval blockade option. Irrespective of what action was finally taken, President Kennedy told the assembled officials that one thing was certain: "We're going to take out these, uh, missiles." Undecided in Kennedy's mind was whether to undertake "a general air strike" and a "general invasion."[17]

In the course of the October 16 White House debate, McNamara challenged the Joint Chiefs' contention that the Soviet missiles affected the strategic balance, that is, America's demonstrable nuclear superiority.[18] But he missed the point, for Kennedy, according to senior White House advisor Theodore Sorenson, was much more preoccupied with the appearance of American power in Moscow and elsewhere than with strategic balances: "Regardless of strategic importance . . . the Kennedy people thought the very placement of missiles a diminution of American credibility and a direct challenge to American hegemony in Latin America."[19]

On October 17, Sorenson summarized the options:

Track A – Political action, pressure and warning, followed by a military strike if satisfaction is not received.

Track B – A military strike without prior warning, pressure or action, accompanied by messages making clear the limited nature of this action.

Track C – Political action, pressure, and warning followed by a total naval blockade, under the authority of the Rio Act and either a Congressional Declaration of War on Cuba or the Cuban Resolution of the 87th Congress.

Track D – Full-scale invasion, to "take Cuba away from Castro."[20]

Although the White House tentatively set an air strike for October 20, as the week wore on, sentiment among some of the President's most influential advisors – Robert Kennedy, Theodore Sorenson, Robert McNamara, and Rosewell Gilpatric – began to coalesce in favor of a naval blockade. McNamara offered the most persuasive argument: Unlike the irreversible nature of an air strike, a blockade provided the flexibility to shift to a riskier option, if necessary.[21] Sorenson made the same point, saying "Precisely because it was a limited, low-level action . . . the blockade had the advantage of permitting a more controlled escalation on our part, gradual or rapid as the situation required."[22] The minutes of the October 21 White House meeting attended by General Taylor, Secretary McNamara, CIA Director John A. McCone, Attorney General Kennedy, and General Walter C. Sweeny, commander of the Tactical Air Command, show that only Sweeny still endorsed the air-strike plan. The President opted for the more flexible quarantine option, but declared that the air strike would be retained as the option of last resort.[23]

On October 22, President Kennedy publicly disclosed the existence of Soviet missiles in Cuba, announced a naval quarantine of the island, and (falsely) accused Moscow of shifting the nuclear balance of power by placing long-range missiles only 90 miles from Florida. As the Strategic Air Command was placed on nuclear alert across the length and breadth of the United States, the President directed the Pentagon to prepare for possible military operations. Approximately 100,000 troops were readied in the southern United States.[24] The President's definition of the missiles as offensive weapons contradicted not only Soviet arguments that they were purely defensive, but also a CIA study that tended to support Moscow's position[25] Later, Kennedy and Sorenson both conceded the accuracy of McNamara's assessment – that the missiles, in fact, did not alter the global strategic military balance.[26]

Kennedy's October 22 decision brought the world to the edge of nuclear confrontation. Having received no commitment from Khrushchev to withdraw the missiles by October 27, while U.S. intelligence officials were reporting daily improvements in the island's air defense system and more missiles becoming operational, the President convened a White House EXCOM meeting where he endorsed plans for an invasion of Cuba on October 29, to be preceded by air strikes against missile sites, air bases, and anti-aircraft installations.[27] On October 28, the Soviet Union finally agreed to a Kennedy proposal to resolve the conflict peacefully. In return for Moscow's commitment to withdraw its missiles from Cuba, Washington would remove its nuclear-warhead missiles from Turkey. The settlement also included a verbal agreement relating to Cuba: In return for Moscow's word not reintroduce nuclear weapons, Washington pledged to jettison the direct military intervention of Cuba from its policy arsenal.

Marc Trachtenberg persuasively argues that the key to understanding not only the Soviet's ultimate decision regarding the missiles but also their failure to make any preparations for military confrontation with the United States during the Missile Crisis period is to be found in the fact of overwhelming U.S. nuclear dominance and the Kennedy administration's refusal to rule out a first-strike option to gain its objective:

> ... the Soviets seem to have been profoundly affected by their [U.S.] "strategic superiority."... The danger of provoking an American preemptive strike tended to rule out countermeasures – or even the serious threat of countermeasures, around Berlin or elsewhere – that would significantly increase the risk of war. The effect therefore was to tie their hands, to limit their freedom of maneuver, and thus to increase their incentive to settle the crisis quickly.[28]

During the crisis, the Soviets acted without consulting Havana, where the outcome was viewed as, at best, a partial victory. Moscow agreed to remove the missiles, safeguard against their reintroduction and, "in effect," as a State Department memorandum to the EXCOM put it, "eliminate Cuba's defense military potential also, once the United States has given the assurances of noninvasion."[29] Excluded from these negotiations, Castro refused to countenance United Nations inspection of the missile sites, logically proposing that the international body simultaneously investigate the missiles' withdrawal and the anti-Castro exile bases on the American mainland. Washington refused.

The decision to initiate a confrontation with the Soviet Union in the Western Hemisphere without even consulting the Organization of American States (OAS) writ large the U.S.'s hegemonic status in its part of the world. Accordingly, the OAS Council unanimously, *post facto*, supported Washington's demand for the missiles' complete withdrawal and, except for Mexico, Brazil, and Bolivia, authorized armed intervention to achieve the result.[30] Argentina, Costa Rica, Nicaragua, Panama, El Salvador, Honduras, Ecuador, and Colombia even offered military assistance to police the naval quarantine.[31] In a sense, the superpowers' actions gave these countries no choice. At the same time, though, overwhelming allied support in Latin America and Western Europe for Kennedy's stance toward the missiles did not translate automatically into increased global cooperation with overall U.S. policy toward the Cuban Revolution.

The Kennedy-Khrushchev settlement, by reasserting America's regional dominance, contributed to Cuba's political isolation within Latin America. Perhaps more important, as mentioned, it shut down, for all practical purposes, Washington's "insider" destabilization option. However, U.S. officials were quick to point out that they would not lower their confrontational posture or acknowledge the revolution's permanence. "It is not coexistence," Assistant Secretary of State for Inter-American Affairs Edwin M. Martin told a House subcommittee in May 1963. "We want to get rid of Castro and Communist influence in Cuba. It is not passive."[32] A State Department memorandum to the White House described three goals: "to increase the isolation of the Castro regime; to aggravate its serious economic difficulties; to block Cuban-based and supported subversion of Latin American governments."[33]

Henceforth, Washington shifted largely to the "outsider" strategy to isolate Cuba politically and economically from the capitalist world. Following the missile crisis, the Kennedy administration substantially expanded the trade embargo with two objectives in mind: to render the Cuban experience unattractive as an economic model for the Third World and, most important, to create the economic dislocation and social conflict in Cuba that it hoped would lead to the disintegration of the Castro government and state.

In September 1963, Assistant Secretary of State Martin conceded that military intervention in Cuba was no longer possible. The short-term benefits of a successful invasion would be more than offset by the likely costs: a prolonged guerrilla war, numerous casualties, and, as McNamara suggested, the impossibility of calculating regional and worldwide consequences. Any direct military operation "could be expected to spill over into other areas, with unpredictable results."[34]

The trade embargo and the debate over policy options

In mid-February 1961, over a year before the missile crisis, President Kennedy, reflecting his strong desire to tighten the economic noose around Cuba, inquired of Special Assistant for

National Security Affairs McGeorge Bundy whether it would "save us valuable dollars in gold reserves" and also "make things more difficult for Castro" if the United States stopped purchases of tobacco, vegetables, fruits, and other goods from Cuba.[35] A memorandum to the White House from Secretary of State Dean Rusk favoring such a course argued that import cuts could exacerbate Cuba's already precipitous foreign exchange position and were worth any adverse regional consequences.[36]

Two months later, the Department of State requested a Treasury evaluation of the legality of a far more expansive measure: "a complete economic blockade of Cuba by the United States' enforced if necessary by the naval and military forces." Treasury's reply was that, while "traditional international law and principles do not afford much support for the unilateral imposition of such a blockade," any White House determination to apply an economic quarantine could be based legally either on the 1954 OAS Caracas Resolution against the intervention of international communism in the hemisphere or on the Trading with the Enemy Act. In practice, reliance on the Act could enable Washington to "accomplish a significant proportion of all of the effects which might be desired to be obtained through the institution of an economic blockade."[37] The broad powers embodied in the Trading with the Enemy Act and their potential for inflicting major damage on the Cuban economy were also highlighted in a June 1961 memorandum authored by Secretary of the Treasury Henry Fowler for discussion by the National Security Council Planning Group. Specifically, Fowler proposed that the meeting consider imposing global aviation and shipping sanctions, preventing subsidiaries of American multinationals from trading with Cuba, terminating aid to countries sending strategic commodities to the Castro regime, and using the authority of the Act "to halt foreign transactions with Cuba."[38]

During 1961, a groundswell of congressional support emerged for an embargo on all trade with Cuba. But the introduction of a bill to this effect was strenuously opposed by the Department of State on tactical and strategic grounds. In hearings before the House Committee on Interstate and Foreign Commerce at the end of August, State, Commerce, and Justice Department officials argued that the Export Control Act of 1950, the Mutual Assistance Act of 1954, and the Trading with the Enemy Act already provided the "broad authority" to terminate the negligible volume of trade left between the United States and Cuba, and that the timing of actions of this sort was traditionally at the "discretion" of the executive branch. The proposed bill, according to Deputy Attorney General Byron R. White and Under Secretary of Commerce Edward Gudeman, would limit the President's flexibility in conducting foreign policy and constrict his ability to tailor policy to ever-changing circumstances. Assistant Secretary of State Robert F. Woodward also vigorously contended that, while the Department supported the legislation's objective, its passage would merely "lend weight to the idea of the bilateral [nature of the Cuba] problem as compared with the broader multilateral problem which we are convinced is the one which exists."[39]

In December, State and Treasury once again became embroiled in a dispute over the expanded embargo. Treasury officials suggested extensions founded on both Section 620 (a) of the Foreign Assistance Act of 1961 and Section 5 (b) of the Trading with the Enemy Act. They maintained that their Department's ability to administer an embargo on imports or financial transactions would be seriously hampered by litigation problems, the absence of "satisfactory investigative and penal provisions," and the ability of Cuban exporters to take advantage of "loopholes" in the Foreign Assistance Act if the Trading with the Enemy Act was not invoked.[40] Some Treasury officials opposed lending Department support to any embargo on financial transactions not based on the Act or on some equivalent authority.[41] The State Department's decided lack of enthusiasm for taking this route at this juncture was linked to past White House objections to the use of Section 5 (b) for the purposes of an economic embargo of Cuba:

It was apparently felt [in the White House] that for political reasons in LA [Latin America] it would be inadvisable to call Cuba an "enemy," which would be the impression created by invoking the Trading with the Enemy Act. . . . State believes that this objection was largely responsible for the fact that the White House did not approve [deleted] recommendation last May for a blocking of Cuba under the Trading with the Enemy Act.[42]

The Kennedy administration anticipated that Havana would try to circumvent the new export controls to procure needed commodities of U.S. origin. To counter this, the Department of Commerce was given additional resources to enforce its control over American trade with Cuba. As well, supplemental congressional appropriations footed the bill for an expanded export-control investigation staff and for the Bureau of Customs forces in New York, Miami, the Gulf Coast ports, and key Mexican border locations. Cargo destined for Cuba and other countries by ship and plane was subjected to special examination to prevent diversions of goods to Cuba; the baggage of departing travellers and crews was inspected; and sophisticated detection equipment was installed at appropriate airports to minimize smuggling. American intelligence personnel and trade sources cooperated with Commerce officials to halt diversions, while foreign-service officers throughout Latin America received training in how "to handle the special problems related to export control created by the Cuban embargo."[43]

The new controls had important effects. Between January and October 1961, approximately $500,000 in spare parts and heavy machinery produced in the United States was seized en route to Cuba. In addition, American-made machine bearings valued at more than $84,000 were confiscated in transit from Canada through New York to Cuba. Meanwhile, a group of U.S. exporters voluntarily withheld the transhipment of almost $150,000 worth of automobile and aircraft tires to an allied country when informed by the Department of Commerce that the tires were destined for Cuba.[44] Every vessel docking at a U.S. port that originated in Europe and was scheduled to make a stopover in Cuba was searched, whether or not Commerce officials had concrete information about their cargoes.[45] Despite the stringent measures applied, Commerce Assistant Secretary Behrman conceded that black marketeering persisted: "The trade appeared to be highly profitable, and since it was conducted under the cloak of legality, there seemed little the U.S. government could do to stop it."[46]

In an effort to halt such activities, particularly the now illegal export of industrial equipment, butter, lard, and automotive, marine, and aircraft equipment via Mexico to Cuba, the Kennedy administration barred a number of offending businesses and individuals from any U.S. export transactions for 90 days. The Commerce Department also requested American manufacturers and suppliers who traditionally engaged in trade with Cuba to question customers about the destination of goods purchased and to refer "doubtful transactions" to the agency.[47] American corporations were quite willing to report "unexpectedly large orders from third parties for goods known to be needed by Cuba."[48] In return, Washington was prepared, where possible, to subsidize losses incurred by enterprises forced to terminate their Cuban trade. The decision to include molasses in the embargo, for example, placed the Publicker Chemical Corporation in a quandary over alternative markets. To alleviate this problem, the U.S. government arranged to sell surplus corn to the Corporation "at a loss as a substitute for the molasses in the manufacture of industrial alcohol."[49]

Although a small, but lucrative illegal U.S. trade coincided with sizable increases in Canadian and Mexican exports to Cuba, the Department of Commerce was reticent to attribute more than a sliver of that growth to the re-export of U.S. goods. On at least two occasions, the Canadians informally collaborated with Washington to prevent the transshipment of American manufactured commodities to Cuba. One involved the earlier mentioned shipment of machinery bearings that was partially intercepted at New York's Idlewild (now JFK) airport. The other came about as a result of information passed to Ottawa that a Canadian intermediary had purchased auto parts worth thousands of dollars for resale to Havana. *Business Week* reported that only some of the parts reached their destination "before the Canadian government grabbed the intermediary."[50] In confidential, closed Senate Foreign Relations Committee hearings in December 1961, Secretary of State Rusk noted that "Canada has helped us very well in preventing the flow of American parts and American produce to Cuba."[51]

Making the trade embargo global

In February 1962, the State Department's Policy Planning Council Chairman, Walt W. Rostow, and Deputy Assistant Secretary of State for Inter-American Affairs, Richard Goodwin, visited Europe "to seek a crackdown by the NATO allies on trade with Cuba."[52] In a confidential briefing to the NATO Council, Rostow requested the elimination of Western European trade with Cuba in military and strategic commodities and a reduction in current levels of nonstrategic trade. He also appealed for NATO support of U.S. policy toward Cuba and the decision to expel the Castro government from the Organization of American States.[53] On another front, covertly, high-ranking policymakers involved in "Operation Mongoose" were considering "sabotaging merchandise in third countries – even those allied to the United States – prior to its delivery to Cuba."[54]

According to Robert Hurwitch, the Kennedy administration did not believe that "an economic denial program in and of itself would bring down the Castro regime." Rather, the strategy was to make Cuba's transition from a capitalist economy to a socialist economy "as difficult as possible," and to render the Soviet Union's role as an alternative commercial partner "as burdensome as possible." Policymakers hoped that the effect of the embargo on the Cuban economy "might translate itself into open active opposition to the regime."[55] To this extent, the "insider" policy persisted.

The pressures exerted on NATO countries during 1962 to cooperate in the blockade – what one American official described as "moral suasion"[56] – produced partial gains. Although Western Europe continued to sell Cuba diesel motors, chemicals, machinery, lard, sulphur, and other commodities, there was a significant decline in the export of quasistrategic goods and almost no military purchases by Havana from these sources.[57] Still, existing capitalist trade with Cuba remained a principal concern and Japan and Canada were singled out for attention.

Japan was watched as the main nonsocialist market for Cuban sugar. About 98 percent of Cuba's exports to Japan during 1962 ($35.8 million) and 1963 ($22.9 million) derived from the sale of sugar.[58] The value of Cuban imports (steel, cotton, textiles, industrial and other machine items) from Japan was a mere $13.4 million over the same period.[59] American diplomats in Japan, encouraging alternative sources of sugar and reductions in other trade with Cuba, had some initial success, in part because of the limited importance of Cuba's nonsugar purchases to Japan's economy.

In September 1962, the Cuban Embassy in Tokyo was advised to "suspend" the arrival of an official economic mission, ostensibly because Japanese officials were to be tied up in discussions with an American machinery mission and an Australian sugar delegation. Japanese diplomatic and business circles, however, interpreted the suspension as "a desire to be pleasant to the United States."[60] Under Secretary of State George Ball told a Senate Select Committee that, "as a result of discussions with the Japanese government, the Japanese are shifting their purchases of sugar to other free world sources."[61] Tokyo's pressure on the country's sugar-importing companies to comply with "requests" from Japan's leading trade partner were responsible for a decline in Cuban sugar imports from 423,000 tons in 1961 to 161,000 in 1963.[62]

Washington pestered the Japanese about Cuban sugar imports throughout the Kennedy presidency. Japan's compliance was complicated by the global scarcity of sugar and the higher costs of non-Cuban sugar, while the Japanese also feared that a complete shift would increase the already high domestic price. As an exporter, though, Japan confined itself to minimal sales of non-strategic manufactured goods to Cuba; it banned the sale of strategic and military items; and, with some exceptions, diverted nationally owned or registered vessels away from Cuban ports.

On May 17–18, 1961, President Kennedy visited Canada's Prime Minister, John Diefenbaker. In a memorandum prepared by the State Department's Walt W. Rostow entitled "What We Want from the Ottawa Trip," a reduction in Canadian trade with Cuba was high on the agenda.[63] Although the trade pattern overwhelmingly favored Canada, U.S. policymakers insisted that Canadian dollars were contributions to Havana's "export of revolution." Washington particularly opposed the potentially strategic character of some of Canada's exports and its credit guarantees to companies engaged in the sale to Cuba of locally produced goods. During 1960 alone, Canada's Export Credits Insurance Corporation (ECIC) handled Cuban transactions valued at around $2 million, or approximately 16 percent of Canada's total trade with the Caribbean island.[64] The Prime Minister restated his country's formal opposition to economic sanctions, according to a State Department official with the Presidential party, and refused to make substantive concessions to the American position.[65]

The dissonance was further aggravated by Diefenbaker's refusal to denounce the Castro regime as a "communist dictatorship."[66] Nonetheless, while he believed the trade embargo to be a strategic mistake, Diefenbaker remained steadfast in his decision not to provoke a major confrontation with Washington over military equipment exports and Canada's use as "a backdoor for the evasion of controls which the United States Government has seen fit to impose on its nationals."[67]

The value of Canadian exports to Cuba increased from $13.9 million in 1960 to $31.1 million in 1961, but declined in 1962 to $10.9 million, leading Ottawa to withdraw its trade commissioner from Havana.[68] This decline, wrote one authority, "tended to confirm the government's claim that it was preventing the shipment of strategic goods; had it been otherwise, in spite of his dollar difficulties, Premier Castro would probably have found the means to make extensive purchases in Canada."[69]

Cuba's scarce dollar reserves conveniently defused the U.S.-Canadian conflict. By late 1960, most Canadian exporters had begun to demand cash from their Cuban buyers, despite the available export-credit guarantees, and the trend grew in the wake of a mid-1961 Canadian Senate debate over amending the Export Credits Insurance Act. Testimony revealed that Cuban purchasers were in default on almost $500,000 worth of government-guaranteed credits,[70] and the ECIC eventually paid $275,000 in claims. The program virtually ended since exporters were required to carry 15 percent of the liability for any future government-underwritten sales. Almost all bilateral trade between Cuba and Canada during 1962 was on a strictly cash basis.[71] On January 31, 1962, however, Prime Minister Diefenbaker restated the basic Canadian position: "So long as our trade with Cuba was in non-strategic materials there was no reason whatever to interfere with it. . . . No consideration was being given to a change in policy."[72]

When Walt W. Rostow briefed the NATO Council in February 1962 on the issue of allies' trade with Cuba, it was generally assumed that his hostile remarks were directed toward a small group of countries, including Canada.[73] By April, though, it was evident that both Washington and Ottawa had begun to soften their positions in the interest of preventing any rupture in the larger relationship, for Secretary of State Rusk acknowledged that Canada was in full compliance with the prohibition on the export of strategic materials to Cuba. "Anything we say from here," observed one American official who supported a less abrasive approach, "will just get their backs up and do more harm than good."[74]

Some American policymakers also noted potential advantages in Canada's diplomatic and commercial ties with the Castro regime, especially in the field of intelligence collection. While the evidence is scanty on this point, the Canadian Ambassador to Cuba from 1964 to 1967, M. Leon Layrand, has acknowledged that at least one of his Havana Embassy officials was on the payroll of the U.S. Central Intelligence Agency.[75]

During 1962, the Canadians were thoroughly cooperative in preventing the transshipment of American-origin goods to Cuba. Their customs officials impounded U.S.-manufactured automobile pistons discovered in the cargo of a ship bound for Havana and siezed 1,685 bags of chemicals that had "Made in Canada" superimposed on "Made in USA" from a Cuban freighter, the Bahia de Siguanea, docked in Montreal.[76] Although Ottawa failed to heed U.S. entreaties to ban national shipping engaged in the Cuba trade, arguing that most of the ships were under British registry and, therefore, beyond its jurisdiction,[77] it toed the line with domestically registered vessels. After October 1962, none participated in the Cuba trade, whether private or government-owned or operated, principally because of increased costs and the certainty of U.S. sanctions.[78] The Liberal government of Lester Pearson that took office in April 1963 upheld its conservative predecessors' basic policy toward Cuba, maintaining diplomatic relations but preventing Canada from being a conduit for American goods to Cuba.[79]

The United States, meanwhile, sought to strengthen its global embargo on capitalist trade with Cuba. The Cuban Import Regulations of February 1962 had banned goods of Cuban origin from entering the American market, but did not apply to the subsidiaries of U.S.-owned or controlled multinationals. To close this loophole to Canadian-based U.S. subsidiaries, "Ottawa was informally asked to deny export licenses to these firms, which it did quietly, though not without apparent reluctance."[80]

In July 1963, the Kennedy administration promulgated the Cuban Assets Control Regulations (CACR), which supplanted the February 1962 law and "removed any uncertainties arising from possible failure to secure Canadian government co-operation" by specifically excluding U.S. subsidiaries from engaging in unlicensed transactions with Cuba. Subsequent Treasury and State pressures on the parent companies to adhere to these new regulations were "a powerful deterrent to the expansion of Canadian-Cuban trade." The willingness of U.S. corporations to comply with government policy was not lost on Canadian firms with export markets in the United States. Irrespective of minority or majority U.S. stock ownership, they began to terminate trade with Cuba that would threaten their American market.[81]

In mid-1963, at a White House conference attended by a number of State Department NATO officers, President Kennedy expressed visible apprehension "lest Cuba become an economic showcase."[82] The White House-directed effort to prevent it extended beyond pressures on individual governments to include opposing specialized economic assistance from international agencies such as the United Nations Special Fund.

The Special Fund was established in 1959 to finance preparatory and pre-investment projects in Third World countries that would maximize follow-up technical and development assistance. The principle governing its economic assistance grants was the absence of political considerations. During Castro's visit to the

United Nations in September 1960, he initiated a request for Fund financing of a proposed agricultural diversification project in Santiago de Las Vegas. In May 1961, the Governing Council of the Fund approved a five-year $1,157,000 grant, which the U.S. government vehemently opposed on the grounds that the Castro regime had subordinated economic rationality to politics and, therefore, was an unsuitable applicant. The argument failed to make much headway within the Governing Council; most members considered the American stance to be itself rooted in politics and, additionally, none wished to create a precedent by voting separately on any one project.[83] Nonetheless, from its initial consideration at Governing Council meeting in May 1960 until the final decision to proceed with the project in February 1963, Washington engaged in sustained diplomatic efforts, both "behind the scenes and in public," to block any Fund grant to Havana.[84] These efforts were instrumental in delaying the Governing Council's decision to proceed for almost three years. United States congressional hostility toward the Council spurred the Senate Foreign Relations Committee to inaugurate subcommittee hearings on the Fund's activities. Senator Frank Church, a liberal democrat on the subcommittee, spoke for all his colleagues when he said of the Cuba grant that "it is a very regrettable thing for the United Nations that this project has been approved at this time."[85]

Yet, the tradition of nonpolitical decisionmaking within the Fund had almost always worked, as even Secretary of State Rusk acknowledged in April 1962, to the benefit of the United States. Another senior State Department official subsequently provided Congress with data showing that "even on the narrowest of political calculations the free world has got more out of the Special Fund than it has put in, while the reverse is true of the Communist bloc." All but 6 of 288 Special Fund projects were located in capitalist-bloc countries, accounting for 97 percent of total allocations.[86]

Making the transportation blockade global

In secret congressional testimony in December 1961, almost ten months before the missile crisis, Secretary of State Dean Rusk spoke to the issue of Western-bloc participation in the shipping blockade of Cuba. He termed any decision by the NATO countries not to align their policies with OAS decisions unacceptable "from our point of view."[87] Nonetheless, between January 1 and

August 31, 1962, over three-quarters of Cuba's imports were carried in 433 merchant vessels (making 572 trips) owned and operated by noncommunist shipping companies. Sixty-one percent of these ships and 60 percent of the total trips to Cuban ports came from four NATO countries:

	Ships	Trips
Greece	97 (22%)	125 (22%)
England	78 (18)	110 (19)
West Germany	46 (11)	50 (9)
Norway	42 (10)	55 (10)
TOTAL	263 (61%)	240 (60%)

In addition, Communist-bloc and capitalist-bloc vessels under charter to the socialist world each made approximately 260 trips during the same eight-month period, while Western oil tankers were shipping around 56 percent of Soviet petroleum exports to Cuba.[88] Washington's inability to "discourage" chartering arrangements resulted from the depressed state of the allied shipping industry at the time and the highly profitable terms offered Western shipowners by the Soviet Union.[89]

Addressing this question in September 1962, President Kennedy expressed great disappointment over the failure of America's European allies to lower the number of capitalist-owned ships participating in the Cuba trade.[90] Later that month, the White House launched a major diplomatic offensive to limit the activities of alliance partners in this area, mainly against the "big four" NATO shippers (see Table). The most immediate gains were registered in Turkey and West Germany. The Ankara government was the first to stop all cargo movements to Cuba in nationally owned or registered vessels, following discussions between the American Ambassador and senior Turkish officials.[91]

The issue was also a major item in talks between White House official McGeorge Bundy and West German Foreign Minister Gerhard Schroeder that same September. Bonn expressed open support for the U.S. position but, at first, pleaded the absence of legal measures available for use against domestic shipping companies. In private, officials described the shippers as resistant to appeals for voluntary restrictions. On the other hand, Hans Puehl, a spokesman for the German Shipping Association, minimized the economic importance of Cuban trade to German shippers and maintained their willingness to discontinue it "so long as the ban is not just on Germans but affects our competitors as well." He also contended that tighter controls could be applied under the country's special "Algerian Law," which prohibited German-owned vessels from hauling military cargoes to any port without a special license.[92]

After Bundy's visit, the German government handily discovered a legal solution: a requirement that shippers obtain a special license for the transportation of any commodity between socialist-bloc countries and Cuba. Through this measure, Bonn declared, "shipments of undesirable and objectionable cargoes . . . will be practically eliminated."[93] The special-license decree did not prohibit the chartering of ships for the Cuba trade, yet, it put German shipowners on notice that they "must expect an inordinate amount of complications and controls" if they persisted.[94]

Although the British formally opposed a shipping boycott, at Washington's urging they made private requests to 800 shipowners to refrain from transporting strategic items to Cuba – the appeal relayed by Transportation Minister Ernest Marples through the General Council of British Shipping.[95] British ships already had ceased the transport of military materials to Cuba in August 1960.[96] The Norwegian government viewed Cuba as an "American problem" and parried the efforts of Secretary of State Rusk and others to argue the necessity of Cuba's isolation.[97] Foreign Minister Halvard Lange said his government lacked legal jurisdiction over Norwegian shipping with long-term charters to the socialist bloc that engaged in trade with Cuba, but he did note that these vessels, "so far as we know," were not transporting military goods or highly strategic items.[98] Washington was somewhat more successful in the case of Greek ships calling at Cuban ports, for the Greek government issued a series of "categorical recommendations" to shipowners in October 1962 to halt the chartering of vessels for the hauling of military equipment to Cuba.[99]

Despite some individual successes, the Kennedy White House remained displeased with the allied responses and with the NATO Council's "indecisive response" to State Department requests for shipping controls on the movement of Soviet cargoes to Cuba.[100] Furthermore, the administration had been forced to defer any formal request for support from the Coordinating Committee on Trade with Communist Countries (CONCOM) because of the certain objections by the British, who had revealed themselves as strong advocates of trade liberalization. At the end of September, 1962, 60 ships from NATO countries were engaged in trade with

Cuba, and a much larger number were assumed to be transporting Cuba-bound cargoes from third countries.[101] Finally, U.S. policymakers were confronted with the problem of "flag-of-convenience" ships, mostly under Liberian or Panamanian colors, plying the Cuba trade routes, even though Secretary Rusk noted in September 1962 congressional testimony that "there is no American-owned ship under Liberian or Panamanian flag engaged in that trade."[102]

These continued significant breaches of the shipping embargo called for a more aggressive American strategy. On October 2, 1962, the State Department confidentially telegrammed all Latin American diplomatic posts outlining proposed new measures to tighten the global blockade. The following day, NATO was informed of the contemplated actions. They included closing U.S. ports to all ships of any country if even one of its flagships was discovered carrying arms to Cuba; declaring shipowners engaged in Cuba trade ineligible to carry U.S. foreign-aid cargoes (approximately half of which was traditionally carried in foreign ships); ordering all U.S. flagships and U.S.-owned vessels operating under foreign registry to get out of the Cuba trade; and designating American ports off-limits to any ship "that on the same continuous voyage was used or is being used in [Soviet] Bloc-Cuba trade."[103] The U.S. Maritime Commission was also directed by the White House to establish a "blacklist" of ships still active in the Cuba trade by using data from the CIA and Naval Intelligence.[104]

On October 3, Under-Secretary of State for Economic Affairs George Ball testified before a House Select Committee on Export Control inquiring into the subject of allied shipping with Cuba. He informed the Committee that West Germany, Belgium, Turkey, and Italy had taken "positive actions" to limit the availability of shipping in the Cuba trade; that Canada and France had no ships currently involved in such trade; and that ongoing discussions were taking place with the more recalcitrant NATO allies, including England, Greece, Norway, and Denmark. He noted the U.S. success in at least getting a number of these governments to initiate "quiet consultations with the shipowners" to discourage trade with Cuba.[105]

Even the Norwegian government had asked local shippers to include a clause in all new charters that would prohibit the transshipment of weapons or other strategic materials. Before Ball's presentation, it was the Norwegian Ship Owners' Association that responded to American pressures by directing its members "to make sure their vessels are not used in carrying cargoes to and from Cuba." According to the Association, "very few" Norwegian ships had called at Cuban ports in recent months and those that did carried only civilian cargoes under contracts signed earlier.[106]

With due regard for a balance between the Cuba policy and the requirements of amicable relations with individual NATO countries, Ball assayed that the U.S. government had, to this point, "done as much as is productive to bring about the isolation of the Cuban economy by the cooperation of our allies." He cited the British government's informal initiatives with local shipowners as indication of small, but important, gains.[107] Whitehall was also prepared to cooperate with Washington "in a search for a formula to reduce the volume of strategic cargoes reaching Cuba in British ships." This apparently included the possible placement of Cuba on the CONCOM list of countries to which NATO members were prohibited from selling a long list of strategic materials.[108]

The AFL-CIO and the American shipowning industry also took up the cudgel. As officials of the American Maritime Association and the Maritime Trades Department testified before the House Select Committee on Export Control,[109] the membership of the International Longshoreman's Association (ILA), who manned ports along the U.S. Atlantic and Gulf coasts, voted overwhelmingly in favor of recommendations proposed on October 8 to place a black ban on all ships participating in the Cuba trade and on companies with vessels engaged not only in this trade, but also in any trade with the Soviet Union. Their subsequent boycott contributed significantly to the decline in the number of capitalist ships docking at Cuban ports.[110] Meanwhile, in pursuit of a voluntary ban by "Free World" operators, the American Merchant Marine Institute requested an emergency meeting of the International Chamber of Shipping (ICS) in London to consider their own official embargo. Although a majority were known to oppose such action and ultimately refused to support a voluntary embargo on allied shipping to Cuba, the Americans did gain a partial victory when the ICS' Standing Committee agreed to convene a meeting of its members to discuss the issue.[111]

Within the international private shipping community, there was a growing tendency to comply with Washington's embargo objective. Although the Council of the British Chamber of Shipping's membership insisted they would brook no restrictions on trade with Cuba short of a government directive, Japan's major shipping lines apparently decided to greatly reduce their Cuban links. In

Norway, one of the country's largest steamship companies swiftly accommodated its Shipowners Association request of October 1 that members curtail their Cuba operations. In West Germany, the largest private shipowner, Rudolph A. Oetker, whose company operated 67 vessels on global routes, declared his intention to cooperate with American policy and ordered his ships to bypass Cuban ports of call.[112] Finally, U.S. grain shippers were believed to be demanding a clause in charter agreements stipulating that vessels had not called at Cuban ports within 90 days.[113]

Allied governments also contributed to the momentum. The Liberian government ordered all ships flying its flag to obtain written permission before entering Cuban ports. The order affected an enormous number of ships – nearly 900, of which 45 percent were partially American-owned.[114] The governments of Norway, Denmark, and the Netherlands "informally cautioned" their shipowners not to act in a fashion that might "disturb" bilateral relations.[115] Norwegian officials stated that local owners "now wish to head the appeal from their society, and desire to pull their ships out of the Cuban trade as soon as the present charters expire."[116]

With the lifting of the American naval quarantine of Cuba on November 20, 1962, following the Missile Crisis resolution, vessels from England, Greece, Lebanon, Spain, Norway, Italy, and Holland reappeared in Cuban ports, leading the State Department to order Embassy discussions "at the appropriate high level" with each foreign ministry.[117] But the primacy of sustaining larger relationships with these allies dictated a strategy of "constructive consultation" whereby the countries' officials were encouraged "to do what they [could], both formally and informally, so that their shipping [would] not be in the Cuban trade."[118] Secretary of State Rusk informed a closed congressional hearing on Cuba in late January 1963 that the administration was reticent to enact formal measures to force compliance "because that could create some very sharp issues with friendly governments who at the moment lack the legal resources to move promptly to comply. But we have been working with them behind the scenes and they with their ship owners to reduce their shipping in the Cuba trade."[119] In April, Secretary Rusk reported to the President that recent American efforts had achieved a number of promising gains: The governments of Liberia, Turkey, Honduras, and Panama had officially barred their ships from Cuba trade; West Germany had issued a decree prohibiting ships under its registry from participating in trade between the Soviet bloc and Cuba; the Greek government had ordered Greek ships not under charter to the Soviet bloc to desist from carrying cargoes to Cuba; the Lebanese government had promised to revise its shipping laws to accommodate American policy objectives. But the British remained an obstacle. "Repeated approaches to the United Kingdom have not been productive," Rusk told Kennedy. The primary reason was Whitehall's insistence that it had no legal basis for pulling its ships out of the Cuba trade. The Secretary of State recommended a new round of diplomatic approaches not only toward the United Kingdom but toward Italy, Spain, and Norway as well.[120]

On February 5, 1963, the Executive Committee of the National Security Council met to consider U.S. policy regarding shipments financed by the State, Defense, and Agriculture Departments, the General Services Administration, and the Agency for International Development on foreign-flag ships engaged in Cuban trade. The White House approved its recommendation that all foreign merchant vessels calling at Cuban ports on or after January 1, 1963, be denied American government-financed cargoes. Exceptions would be made only in cases where offending shipowners could give "satisfactory assurance that no ships under their control will, henceforth, be employed in the Cuba trade so long as it remains the policy of the United States Government to discourage such trade."[121] This new executive order was a "scaled down version" of the proposed regulations transmitted to Latin American embassies on October 2, 1962. The substantial decline in Western-owned ships participating in the Cuba trade since that time had rendered these measures "less necessary as well as less desirable."[122]

The multiple efforts to force the withdrawal of allied shipping from Cuban trade during 1962 were quite successful. In the first quarter of 1963, only 59 "Free World" ships called at the Caribbean island, compared to 352 for the same period in 1962.[123] Comparing the twelve-month periods, the decline is just as striking: the number of capitalist vessels participating in Cuba's international commerce fell by over 60 percent from 932 in 1962 to 359 in 1963. One of the more surprising accommodations came from Spain, whose flagships made only nine calls at Cuban ports in 1963, compared to 93 in 1962. Between 1962 and 1963, the number of noncommunist flags in the Cuba trade fell from 22 to 14.[124] Only the continued involvement of a large number of Greek ships, which Secretary Rusk described as "the most difficult problem," tempered Washington's satisfaction over its gains.[125] In July 1963, an Agency for International Development official faced hostile questioning from a congressional subcommittee unhappy over the persistence of Greek-owned vessels in the Cuba trade. He responded by pointing out that the U.S. had been pressuring Athens for some time and had "found the Greek Government quite cooperative" on this issue. The latter's attempts to deal with the problem on "an informal basis," and then by decree, had not proved successful partly because many of the ships "were under charter prior to the time that the whole question came up" and Athens had not seen fit to present firm ultimatums to these vessels' owners.[126] In late September 1963, after constant prodding by Washington, the Greek regime finally issued another decree stating that all ships flying the Greek flag must cease carrying cargo to or from Cuba.[127]

Although Western airline links with Cuba were accorded less attention than shipping links, for there remained few connections between Cuba and nonsocialist countries, Washington still sought a total rupture. In mid-1963, the State Department initiated a series of exchanges with England, Canada, Mexico, and Spain to create an "unrelenting squeeze."[128]

Whitehall refused to ban flights from Cuba to the West Indian island of Grand Cayman, but agreed to increase the monitoring of transients. Ottawa refused to halt its air linkages, but acceded to searching Cuban planes making fuel stopovers in Canada, en route between Havana and Prague. Mexico reportedly "quietly agreed to postpone indefinitely the granting of landing rights" for Cuban National Airline's Soviet-built planes, but it resisted State Department pressures to cancel Mexican National Airline's decision to resume weekly cargo flights to Havana and "do something" about Cuban flights to Mexico City.[129] Spain continued to question the effectiveness of U.S. economic sanctions against Cuba and erected no new travel bans. In fact, Iberia National Airlines increased its twice-monthly flights to Havana during the latter part of 1963. In November, the State Department mounted a high-powered diplomatic offensive to forestall the possible resumption of Cuban National Airline flights to Spain. Secretary of State Rusk exhorted the Madrid Embassy to make Washington's position "manifestly clear" to the Franco regime.[130]

The Johnson administration: continuity in policymaking

The growing immersion of U.S. resources in the Indochina war beginning in 1964 lessened the American government's "intensity of feeling [over Cuba] at the upper levels"[131] and allowed the Castro leadership some breathing space. American liberals and conservatives alike, and even the Cuban political high command, interpreted this development as a kind of policy shift in Washington. Yet the most striking feature of White House policy toward Cuba in the transition from Kennedy to Johnson is its continuity, combined with its focus on a nonmilitary solution to the conflict with the Castro government.

President Johnson's response to the "water crisis" of February 1964 evoked his determination to remain aggressive toward the Castro government. On February 6, Cuba terminated the water supply to the U.S. naval base at Guantánamo in reprisal for the seizure by U.S. Coast Guard authorities in Florida of four Cuban fishing vessels and their crew, who were accused of illegally operating in U.S. waters. Without a shred of evidence, American officials implied that the fishermen had entered the area deliberately, to provoke a crisis.[132] President Johnson described the water cut-off as "reckless and irresponsible," a move by a Cuban government that "remains a constant threat to the peace of this hemisphere."[133] Most policymakers interpreted the water cut-off as an attempt to capitalize on a dispute between the United States and Panama over the sovereignty of the Canal Zone by focusing world attention on the American military base in Cuba, which raised similar issues of territorial integrity and foreign control.[134] The fabrication of a crisis by the Johnson White House, which occasioned two top-level emergency meetings attended by senior civilian and military officials, allowed Johnson to accommodate Republican party demands for a "tough" response, but also undercut the Party's threat to make Cuba a major issue in the 1964 presidential elections.[135] Within days, however, administration officials began to concede that the Cuban vessels had not deliberately entered restricted waters, and they urged Florida authorities to end the affair.[136]

On quieter fronts, the U.S. government conjured two forms of retaliation against Havana for the Guantánamo base "water crisis." First, all Cuban nationals who worked at the naval base (approximately 2,500) would be discharged unless they agreed to become permanent residents of the base or spend all their U.S.

dollar earnings there. Either if their jobs were terminated or if all their earnings were spent on the base, the result would be a $5 million hard-currency (and foreign exchange) loss to the Cuban economy. Second, the United States accelerated plans to make the base independent of both Cuban manpower and Cuban water supplies.[137] On February 11, in line with recommendations from a special Naval survey group just returned from Guantánamo, the Department of Defense announced the first job dismissals.[138]

In the diplomatic community, there was widespread belief that Washington had completely misunderstood Cuba's intent, which was not geared to immediate confrontation over Guantánamo, but was part of a larger strategy to gain sovereignty over the U.S. base on Cuban soil. "The Castro strategy, diplomats said, appeared to be aimed at freeing Cuba from all remaining ties with the Guantánamo base to give her a better case for arguing that the treaty [allowing for the American presence] is illegal."[139] Because they insisted on viewing the problem through a Cold War prism, U.S. policymakers exaggerated the importance of such factors as job and dollar losses to the Cuban economy, for this was a time of record high world-market sugar prices. The prism also deflected comprehension of the rationale behind Cuba's action. The termination of all – even of the most limited – financial benefits enjoyed by Cuba under the Guantánamo treaty would make Havana's case for abrogating that treaty immeasurably stronger and more convincing in international forums.[140]

Soon after entering office, Johnson ordered a complete review of all public and clandestine operations against Cuba to assess their effectiveness in bolstering international opposition to Castro and strengthening the regional isolation policy.[141] At an early White House meeting, according to an involved State Department official, the President also "indicated his desire to press ahead with the [global] isolation policy." Between late 1963 and 1967, this official recalled, the President and all his senior foreign policymakers exhibited a sustained commitment to "maintaining a very firm anti-Castro policy" as long as it was "within the bounds of acceptable risk." Enforcing the economic blockade soon became "the heart and backbone of the whole Cuban policy."[142] This emphasis was evident in the new administration's determination to eliminate any loopholes in the embargo.

In February 1964, reports began reaching the Departments of State and Commerce of approaches by a Cuban trade mission to

Canadian subsidiaries of American multinationals (Swift Corporation and International Packers) to purchase a large quantity of lard – a staple in the Cuban diet that was scarce because of the U.S. blockade. Reports on the size of the transactions varied from $2 million to $15 million. The Department of Agriculture's lard specialist informed the White House that the commodity was used almost exclusively for food purposes and only rarely for the manufacture of such nonstrategic items as soap and industrial acids: "Cuba can be expected to use 100% of any lard it gets for edible purposes." Nonetheless, following a hastily organized meeting between President Johnson, Secretary of State Rusk, and Secretary of Defense McNamara, the Department of Commerce added lard to the list of export commodities requiring a special license.[143]

The Johnson administration's response to the water crisis and the lard episode were symptomatic of Washington's continuing resolve to confront the Castro regime at every opportunity. In early May, both Johnson and McNamara declared the U.S. intention to wage relentless economic warfare against the Castro regime as well as aerial reconnaissance flights over the island.[144]

Extending the global transportation blockade   Under Johnson, the shipping embargo received immediate attention and was pursued at least as rigorously as earlier. In December 1963, less than a month after his taking office, the regulations on allied shipping engaged in Cuba trade were revised. According to the new rules, vessels would be removed from the Maritime Association's "blacklist" if the offending shipowners agreed to take all their other vessels similarly involved out of the Cuba trade as charters expired. In addition, they could not allow any of their ships not then engaged in this trade to sign new charters for this purpose. If shipowners failed to behave, their entire fleets, including vessels that had never entered Cuban ports, would be blacklisted.[145] This revision was a reminder to transgressing capitalist governments that "Nothing had changed Washington's determination to press ahead with policies to weaken the Castro regime. President Johnson is known to regard the isolation of Cuba and the fight against Communist subversion in the Caribbean area as 'urgent business' for his Administration."[146] In January 1964, the State Department informed its Madrid Embassy that, while it welcomed recent actions by Liberian, Panamanian, Italian, and West German governments to "restrict or prevent their shipping from calling

[at] Cuba," administration policy would attempt to further "reduce free-world shipping calling at Cuba."[147]

Assistant Secretary George Ball singled out the Italian government for its "excellent cooperation" on this issue.[148] In late May, the American Embassy at the Hague also commended the Dutch government for its "effective cooperation" with the shipping embargo.[149]

The Moroccan government, a sore point of U.S. efforts in North Africa because of its large sugar purchases, became disposed to do Washington's bidding. At a meeting with U.S. Ambassador Ferguson in late February or early March, Moroccan Foreign Minister Guedira agreed to calculate quickly the "time it would take for Morocco to make other shipping arrangements for its trade with Cuba." The meeting seemed to resolve all aspects of Moroccan-Cuban relations to the satisfaction of the American envoy, but the shipping issue was taken up again in a meeting between State Department officials and the Moroccan Ambassador to the United States. Ambassador Ali Bengelloun expressed concern over increased shipping costs for Cuban sugar brought in by foreign vessels, on top of the already substantial expenditure of scarce hard-currency reserves for the annual purchase of some 250,000 tons. Sugared tea, he informed the meeting, was a staple of his country's largely peasant population. The senior Moroccan diplomat was mollified by being told that, once his country's vessels stopped transporting Cuban sugar, they would become eligible to carry U.S. government-financed cargoes.[150]

In sharp contrast to these countries' efforts at accommodation, British and Lebanese shipowners remained obstacles. In the absence of government directives, trips by British vessels to Cuban ports increased from 133 in 1963 to 180 in 1964. In Beirut the American Embassy attributed the flouting of the embargo by Lebanese shippers to three factors: Washington did not have the lever of economic sanctions because Lebanon no longer received U.S. foreign aid; the government had "no direct contact with or control over the owners of Lebanese flag-of-convenience vessels"; and, in any event, these ships hardly ever entered Lebanese ports. The Embassy document, noting that the owners of 30 of the 41 involved vessels resided in London, another 8 in Athens, and only one in Beirut, suggested that the strategy to remove these "flag-of-convenience" ships from the Cuba trade might be to concentrate pressures on the owners "at their home offices." Without that, there was "little prospect" that the amended shipping regulation of December 1963 would bring "significant results." Combined with a focus on the owners, Embassy officials suggested that future diplomatic representations should concentrate on getting the Lebanese to legislate "control over the vessels which fly [their] flag."[151]

The failure to arrest the increase in Lebanese flag ships engaged in the Cuba trade (they accounted for 28 percent of all noncommunist vessels calling at Cuban ports during the first four months of 1964) raised concern in the Department of State, where officials had been subjecting other governments to "heavy pressure[s]" to comply with U.S. foreign-aid provisions by withdrawing their ships from the Cuba trade. These governments, it was feared, might use the Lebanese example to renege on their promises. Such a turn of events would "create pressure here for more restrictive unilateral measures to eliminate free world participation in Cuban trade."[152] By year's end, despite mounting American diplomatic pressures, the number of trips by Lebanese vessels to Cuba had reached 91, an increase of 27 over 1963.

Although the number of trips to Cuba by noncommunist ships increased marginally from 359 in 1963 to 383 in 1964, the 271 trips made by British and Lebanese flag vessels alone accounted for more than two-thirds of the 1964 total. Another main offender during the Kennedy period, Greece, proved far more ready to bow to Washington's pressures. Vessels registered under its flag made only 27 trips in 1964, compared to 99 trips in 1963. With the exception of Italy (20 trips) and Spain (17 trips), the vessels of no other capitalist country made more than 10 trips to Cuba during this twelve-month period. Accommodation with the Johnson administration's objective was now widespread, with significant opposition confined only to England and Lebanon.[153]

The White House continued to exert worldwide diplomatic and other pressures, as well as to make occasional direct approaches to private shipowners in pursuit of the transportation blockade. By January 1965, 709 allied ships, including 329 Spanish vessels, had been committed by their owners to the boycott.[154] Following the slight rise from 359 in 1963 to 383 in 1964, the number of trips to Cuba by capitalist flag ships declined to 275 in 1965, 214 in 1966, 204 in 1967, and 195 in 1968–the last figure in striking contrast to the 932 trips made during 1962, the final year of the "insider" strategy. The number of trips by British vessels declined from 180 in 1964 to 62 in 1968, while the combined treks of

Greek and Lebanese ships to Cuban ports fell from 163 in 1963 to a mere 23 in 1968.[155]

Airline contact with Cuba was still on policymakers' minds when Johnson entered the White House, even though flights from nonsocialist countries to Cuba had declined from 20 flights weekly at the time of the October 1962 missile crisis to a single weekly flight by Spain's Iberia Airlines, an unscheduled weekly mail flight from Mexico, and weekly cargo service from Montreal. In December 1963, however, Under Secretary of State George Ball told the Madrid Embassy to remonstrate with the Franco government over the "frequency [of] non-scheduled flights" to Havana and its reported intention to allow Cubana Airlines to begin biweekly flights between Havana and Madrid.[156] Early 1964 confidential State Department documents praised England, France, Holland, Canada, Mexico, Jamaica, Trinidad, Brazil, and Ireland for their cooperation in controlling airline traffic with Cuba by restricting unscheduled flights, increasing airport surveillance, monitoring passengers and baggage, and other measures. Initiatives taken by the Conservative government of British Prime Minister Alex Douglas-Home to discourage Cuban plans landing in England and its Caribbean dependencies were particularly welcome.[157] Determined to end what few airline links remained between Cuba and the Western World, American officials pursued discussions with Mexico and Canada while debating how best to approach what Washington considered the more serious "Spanish-Cuban air bilateral."[158]

Extending the global economic blockade   Just after his accession to the White House in late November 1963, President Johnson moved on a number of fronts to consolidate Cuba's worldwide economic isolation. In preparation for a December meeting with the new West German Chancellor, Ludwig Erhard, Johnson received a memorandum from National Security Affairs advisor McGeorge Bundy suggesting that Bonn's "further cooperation in [the] reduction of Western German exports [e.g., telecommunications equipment, mining machinery, diesel engines] to Cuba" should be sought. To press home the point, Bundy suggested that the President "emphasize [the] political importance of [the] Cuban question in the U.S. and the value of U.S.-German solidarity in isolating Castro."[159] Erhard agreed to accommodate Washington's concern.[160] In May, Bundy noted that the West German head of state had "promise[d] to hold German trade with Castro at the lowest level that is legally possible and to bar export guarantees of any sort from the government."[161] By contrast, renewed pressure on the Norwegians to embargo its relatively minor trade with Cuba was less successful, with Foreign Minister Lange stating that his government was "in principle" opposed to economic embargoes "because (A) such embargoes have a way of 'striking back' and (B) GON [Government of Norway] economy [is] particularly vulnerable and necessarily based on principles of free trade and free shipping."[162]

In late January 1964, the State Department wrote to embassies in a number of European countries whose collaboration was considered vital. The secret memorandum elaborated the "basic [U.S.] policy of isolating GOC [Government of Cuba] politically, economically and psychologically from [the] free world." The Johnson White House was still seeking to make the Western-bloc shipping and trade embargo as comprehensive as possible to create economic chaos, maximize the costs to the Soviet Union of keeping the Cuban economy afloat, and ultimately replace the Castro regime with one "fully compatible with [the] interests [of the] free world."[163] This statement was the prelude to "a massive diplomatic campaign . . . mounted not only against the allies but through U.S. business contacts, aimed toward businessmen in allied nations as well."[164] Concentrating on Western Europe, Canada, and Japan "when it seemed possible that they would sell goods to Cuba,"[165] Secretary of State Rusk assailed such trade as "prejudicing" efforts to halt the spread of communism in the Western Hemisphere and dismissed "the contention that trade with Cuba is comparable to ordinary trade with any Communist country."[166] In a telegram to the Paris Embassy dated February 25, 1964, Rusk also underscored what was to become a permanent Johnson concern: "[The] U.S. attaches special importance [to the] denial [of credit guarantees and insurance] facilities by NATO governments to [the] Cuban regime."[167] What irritated the administration was that the Castro government, although forced to transact most of its nonbarter trade with the capitalist bloc on a cash basis, had established a reputation during the Kennedy period as an exceedingly reliable international creditor; and, second, that the rise in world sugar prices had allowed Havana to accumulate approximately $100 million in foreign-exchange reserves, much of which it hoped to use to purchase machinery and spare parts from the export-dependent countries of Western Europe, Canada, and Japan.[168]

These issues of trade and credit guarantees were tangible expressions of a larger dispute over capitalist trade with the whole socialist bloc. The conflict circled around two American demands that were resisted by those allied regimes most dependent on foreign trade expansion for domestic prosperity: that credit extensions to finance exports to socialist countries be applied more selectively and limited to no longer than five years, and that the list of prohibited "strategic" commodities be extended to incorporate the largest possible number of items, for Western European governments had "steadily whittled down the list of items of direct military application."[169]

Under Johnson, the United States channelled the behavior of its own largely willing multinational business executives not only through export controls but also through amplified "moral suasion." Generally, U.S. multinationals were "exceedingly cooperative" in steering clear of Cuba trade. American corporations either directly rebuffed approaches by, or on behalf of, the Castro regime or reported such proposals to the State Department for guidance on how to respond. Their complicity in furthering the state's policy was manifested in other ways as well. One large U.S. company, upon hearing that one of its major European suppliers was about to trade with Cuba, told the European firm that "if they did the deal with Cuba they would be dropped as a supplier."[170] Another example of government-business cooperation involved Belgian holdings of the Sperry Rand Corporation. In 1963, Sperry Rand acquired 65 percent of the Clayson Company of Sedelgem, a Belgian farm equipment firm. In 1967, the Cubans ordered from Clayson $1.2 million worth of harvesting and threshing machines for their rice crop, but the Treasury Department, through the Cuban Assets Control Regulations, denied the U.S.-controlled company an export license – right when this sector of Belgium's industry was in the midst of a pronounced recession.[171] The parent corporation unequivocally justified its adherence to executive-branch admonitions, saying "It is corporate policy to conduct all of our international affairs in full conformity with the policy of the United States Government."[172]

From the beginning of the Johnson presidency, American policy objectives toward the Castro government were consistent, and, like predecessor administrations, were to be gained through confrontation rather than negotiation. Under Secretary of State for Economic Affairs George Ball in April 1964 reaffirmed it: "We must rely, as our major instrument, on a systematic program of economic denial."[173] Ball proceeded to expand upon the themes of the State Department's January 1964 statement, noting that the Cuban economy was still dependent on spare parts, machinery, industrial goods, fuel, food, and raw materials from the capitalist world for its immediate and long-term operations. The island's industrial installations, power plants, transportation systems, and sugar mills, Ball declared, were "all of Western origin." Taking advantage of this weakness in the Cuban economy required increasing the "considerable, although not complete, cooperation" already provided by America's allies. Although Ball conceded that socialist-bloc shipping to Cuba probably would substitute for the withdrawal of Western vessels, he emphasized Washington's belief that noncapitalist sources of industrial goods, transport equipment, and other critical materials were not readily available. Equipment breakdowns, obsolete machinery, and the scarcity of parts, all augmented by the embargo, could only exacerbate Cuba's economic problems. Ball particularly warned against the sale of locomotives: Given the perilous state of the island's railroad system, their contribution to the Cuban economy would be enormous. He reported one Cuban estimate that the number of locomotives in operating condition had declined by three-quarters between 1959 and 1963.[174] At a May 1964 news conference, President Johnson, supporting his Under Secretary of State, again emphasized the need for cooperation with the boycott.[175]

United States officials also were not reluctant to threaten closing American markets to impress some Western governments. In July 1964, the American Ambassador to Portugal was informed by the country's foreign minister that, while Portugal "had no intention [of] establishing trade ties with Cuba," it was considering a "one-shot transaction" to encourage the Castro regime to release funds owed to a Portuguese shipping firm and to resolve the country's need for additional sugar. The Ambassador's response was pointed and threatening: He "reminded" the foreign minister that Angola, one of Portugal's colonies, was heavily dependent on U.S. markets for its exports.[176]

Record sugar prices in 1963 helped the Cubans expand trade in Western Europe and elsewhere.[177] The socialist-bloc Council for Mutual Economic Assistance (COMECON) also contributed to Cuba's newly acquired trade leverage by delaying repayment of debts to increase the amount of hard currency available to purchase goods from the capitalist bloc.[178] Widely advertised reports that financial mismanagement had forced the Cuban government to suspend credit for purchases made abroad referred only to imports of secondary importance. "When Havana has needed something badly and considered it vital," a New York banker stated, "it has been able to put up the money. The foul-ups usually occur on items the Castro government considered of subsidiary interest."[179] An indication of the island's favorable standing with international capitalists in mid-1964 may be gleaned from an enumeration of some major commercial exchanges already undertaken or in the process of consummation:

Japan this year has set up two exported factories in Cuba and is selling ships and chemicals to the Castro regime after purchasing sugar from Cuba. Canada is selling Cuba wheat fertilizer, cattle, medicine, chemical products and food. France is selling locomotives, trucks, construction equipment and drugs. Spain provides food, ships, motors, chemicals and weekly flights by Iberia Airlines to Madrid. Italy has set up a fertilizer plant and is selling other chemicals.[180]

Up to late 1964, Washington preferred imposing private and informal pressures on domestic and foreign companies, especially those receiving U.S. government contracts or loans, to refrain from trading with Cuba on the grounds that their activity "could affect transactions with [the United States Government]." Secretary Rusk described the response of the accosted companies as "generally [one of] matter-of-fact acceptance." But the tremendous growth in Cuba's imports from capitalist-bloc countries during 1964 – perhaps $225 to $230 million, or 80 percent over 1963 – led Rusk to acknowledge that "diplomatic persuasion, reinforced in some cases by direct approaches to companies involved" had not worked. In view of Cuba's increased trade with the West, the Secretary of State informed the Ambassadors of the NATO and Latin American capitals that the Department was "seriously considering" requiring all companies doing business with the U.S. government to certify that neither they nor their associated firms had transshipped goods to Cuba.[181]

During 1963, the U.S. government spent $412 million on goods from nineteen industrialized capitalist countries. An additional $200 million was projected for 1964 and beyond with Rusk describing these purchases as offering the United States "limited leverage" in constricting capitalist trade with Cuba. But Rusk also viewed such trade as potentially a very powerful tool if the United States were joined in the leverage by the governments of Central

America, Venezuela, and Colombia, whose total imports from West European, Japanese, Canadian, and other "free world" companies were valued at an estimated $170 million annually.[182] Washington further sought, with limited success, to get its Latin American allies to pressure Western European firms active in their countries to stop trading with Cuba.[183]

At the Organization of American States (OAS), the Johnson administration continued to exhort member governments to do whatever they could to make the Cuba economic blockade effective. During the OAS Foreign Ministers meeting in Washington, D.C., in July 1964, Secretary Rusk defined one of the conference's major tasks as that of "urging our own governments and those of other free-world countries to take appropriate steps in the field of trade with Cuba."[184] American officials renewed this call at a subsequent foreign ministers' gathering in Washington in September 1967. In an address, Rusk called for greater capitalist-bloc cooperation "in denying to Cuba resources which help it to carry on its subversive activities" and declared that the OAS "must persuade friendly non-member countries to understand the problem confronting us and to increase their cooperation with us, especially by refraining from acts that assist the Cuban government."[185] The conference approved a U.S.-sponsored proposal to deny port facilities and government-financed cargoes to allied countries engaged in Cuba trade. Mexico, Chile, Colombia, Uruguay, and Ecuador all objected and abstained from the final vote. Although it successfully extended the shipping blacklist to the hemisphere, Washington could not round up the votes to publicize and blacklist nonregional capitalist firms trading with Cuba.[186]

The changing distribution of Cuba's trade with the capitalist world before and after Johnson took office partially reflected the success enjoyed by the United States in its efforts to constrict Cuba's trade ties with the Western Alliance. Although Cuba's trade with nonsocialist countries grew from 17.1 percent of its total trade in 1962 to 36.9 percent in 1964, by the end of 1966 (19.6 percent) it had almost returned to the levels of the early 1960s[187] In November 1966, President Johnson restated White House policy regarding capitalist economic and transportation relations with Cuba, mincing few words: "We oppose it. We have conducted and will continue a very active effort against this trade."[188]

Consensus and conflict in executive-congressional relations

Johnson's Cuba initiatives brought about sporadic conflicts with a fundamentally supportive legislative branch. More often than not, friction revolved around what tactical and strategic options to choose: Would diplomatic flexibility or congressional mandate best achieve the shared goal? Responding to a demand for more aggressive action by the legislative branch, Secretary Rusk reminded members of the House Foreign Affairs Committee in late March 1964 that "the net purpose of all the things we are doing is to insure that this regime does not survive."[189]

In general, the legislators were content to concede policy responsibility to the administration and provide bipartisan support. The most notable exception was J. William Fulbright, chairman of the Senate Foreign Relations Committee. In a speech on the Senate floor on March 25, 1964, Fulbright broke ranks over support for the economic embargo on the grounds that it had failed. "It is simply not within our power to compel our allies to cut off their trade with Cuba, unless we are prepared to take drastic action against them." In Fulbright's view, the Castro regime had reached a level of durability and military preparedness that rendered it impervious to disintegration short of direct military intervention. He also asserted that Cuba did not constitute "an insuperable obstacle to the attainment of our objectives . . . in the hemisphere."[190]

Fulbright's failure to rally to his side even Congress' foreign-policy "liberals" was testament to the absence of virtually any support for his position. "Whether or not we may have failed with our methods of blockade and boycott,'" Senator Jacob Javits countered, "we thoroughly disapprove of Castro, and this fact that we thoroughly disapprove of Castroism is essential in American policy and must be continued to be pressed home."[191] Secretary Rusk contested Fulbright's characterization of Castro as merely a "nuisance," insisting that he remained "a threat to the hemisphere."[192] Ultimately, Fulbright's critique stirred no interest in reconsidering existing policy toward Cuba, but rather revealed Congress' historic tendency to acquiesce to the power and authority of the executive branch in the realm of foreign policy.

During Johnson's presidency, three important differences of opinion existed between the two branches of government over Cuba. The first occurred in December 1963 when a congressional

amendment to Section 620 of the Foreign Assistance Act directed
the executive "against its wishes"[193] to curtail or eliminate economic and military assistance to countries that failed to take
"appropriate steps" by February 14, 1964, to withdraw their
cargo-carrying ships and airplanes from the Cuba trade. The only
exception to this legislative mandate was a presidential waiver on
"national security" grounds. The White House opposed not only
the intent of the amendment, but also the insistence on a specific
cutoff date, which was seen as limiting Washington's flexibility in
amicably resolving this issue with allied governments.[194]

On February 18, the U.S. government terminated the small
amounts of military assistance to England, Yugoslavia, and France
– a projected $100,000 each in 1964 – on the grounds that these
countries had not taken the "appropriate steps" noted above, and
announced its intention to halt aid commitments to Spain ($30
million in military assistance in 1963) and Morocco (over $20 mil-
lion in economic aid in 1963) until both detailed measures to
accommodate the Foreign Assistance Act.[195]

A second executive-legislative dispute began in May 1966 when
the House Agriculture Committee voted 16 to 3 for a $3.3 billion
"Food for Freedom" bill that included a prohibition on food aid
to any country engaged in trade with Cuba or North Vietnam.
With this, it appeared that India, Pakistan, Yugoslavia, Poland,
Morocco, and a number of Latin American countries would no
longer be eligible. Again, the administration opposed not the bill's
intent, but its limitations on executive use of food aid as a policy
lever, and pressured for modifications.[196] The outcome was a bill
that closely resembled the original. In November, President Johnson reluctantly signed into law a two-year, $5 billion expansion of
the "Food for Peace" program, despite his concern that some provisions would "create major difficulties for our foreign policy."
One was a ban on all food shipments to any country engaged in
selling or shipping strategic or nonstrategic goods to Cuba, with a
proviso that the President could, in specific situations, waive the
ban on transactions involving medical supplies and nonstrategic
items. The White House remained "particularly troubled" by the
essence of the provision; the State Department declared that it
would sharply limit the President's capacity to use the "Food for
Peace" program as "a bargaining tool" in dealing with Third
World countries and "as a device to woo Communist nations."[197]
This concern became a reality almost immediately over the issue
of India's jute sales to Cuba.

Between April 1965 and February 1966, Havana purchased almost $4 million worth of jute for making sugar bags. According to U.S. Embassy officials in New Delhi, following the passage of the 1966 "Food for Peace" Act the executive branch accorded jute a nonstrategic status.[198] In January 1967, however, presidential advisor and Under Secretary of State for Political Affairs Eugene V. Rostow, visiting India to discuss the new Act, conferred with a negotiating subcommittee of the Indian Cabinet and found an "appreciation of the U.S. point of view [on Cuba] by the Indian side."[199]

At the time, India was on the verge of a second consecutive drought and the accompanying threat of large-scale famine in the states of Bihar and Uttar Pradesh. The New Delhi government hoped that the delivery of eleven million tons of American grain over the next year would help. Against this background, it is not unreasonable to suggest that the Rostow Mission reinforced subtle, but direct, connections between food aid and U.S. global objectives. The Indian government agreed not to expand or vary its existing commodity trade with Cuba. On February 2, 1967, President Johnson announced a two million ton allocation of American grain, valued at $150 million, for shipment to India and requested congressional approval for another three million ton shipment ($190 million) to be made available through the U.S. Commodity Credit Corporation on the understanding that it would be matched by allied countries.[200]

A third source of mild friction between Congress and the Executive derived from the Greek government's failure, in the eyes of many legislators, to sufficiently curtail local shipowners' Cuba trade. The earlier Greek-government decree banning trade with Cuba, issued at Washington's behest, apparently had failed to persuade a number of Greek shipowners to comply. Despite assorted interpretations to explain this state of affairs, there was a consensus between the Congress and the White House on the need for Athens to take a stricter line. Executive-branch officials cautioned the Greeks that under recently passed foreign-aid legislation all military and economic assistance could be terminated.[201]

In November 1966, the Greek government moved to enforce the existing ban. The Merchant Marine Ministry directed all Greek overseas consular and port authorities to investigate locally owned vessels still calling at Cuban ports, despite a 1963 decree expressly prohibiting them from carrying cargoes to and from the Caribbean island.[202] Defiant shipowners were threatened with legal sanctions: up to six months' imprisonment, substantial monetary fines, or the revocation of the ship's master's license for up to two years. In January 1967, Athens announced stepped-up sanctions against Greek-owned flagships violating the ban. "The Government has decided to take all necessary measures provided by Greek legislation," the *New York Times* reported, "to impose severe penal, economic and other sanctions on all offenders."[203]

Intercapitalist competition: cooperation and cleavage with U.S. policy

The Johnson administration's economic war against Cuba allocated considerable resources to limiting Havana's trade relations with its major capitalist customers: England, Spain, France, Japan, and Canada. "For about two years," recalled a State Department official who played a prominent role, "we were able to prevent [Cuba] from obtaining major items of equipment they needed by our very persistent pressures. Scarcely a day went by when we weren't sending a telegram to Embassies around the world. These pressures were on a very high level, our Ambassadors talking to Cabinet ministers."[204] Secretary of State Rusk was at the forefront of these efforts, aggressively lobbying the Ambassadors of Western Europe, Japan, and Canada over their countries' trade with Cuba.[205] But in the face of allies' refusals to terminate all commercial ties, Washington tried to constrain the breadth of such trade and influence its conduct, especially by discouraging state-guaranteed credits to facilitate economic transactions between national enterprises and the revolutionary regime. "Our feeling on this," Acting Secretary of State for Inter-American Affairs Robert Sayre told a House Subcommittee, "is that if you could persuade the Europeans to cut off all of their credits to Cuba it would have a substantial effect on the Cuban economy. It is not the trade as such if they have to pay cash for it. What we have really vigorously objected to on the part of the European countries is that they have granted credits to Cuba. . . . We feel sales for credit help the Cuban economy and they ought not to go on. We are doing everything we can [to] get these countries to stop it."[206] Throughout Johnson's presidency, American policymakers differentiated between cash sales that drained scarce Cuban hard currency reserves and credit-based arrangements, which were viewed as the equivalent of "strategic assets."

According to one State Department official involved in applying the blockade strategy, the issue of a country's "lack of creditworthiness" (an approach applied later to others) originated with this U.S. effort to make Western governments deny credit guarantees to their corporations' trading with Cuba. America's allies were bombarded by U.S.-government materials describing Cuba's supposed uncreditworthiness and encouraged to use this argument with companies requesting credits. "It was," this official observed, "a political argument to justify an economic act, or an economic non-act."[207]

Between the British Leyland bus deal in early 1964 and a $35 million long-term French government-guaranteed credit sale of heavy equipment in the summer of 1966, American efforts over credit guarantees were rewarded with virtually maximum success. The decline in trade between Havana and the nonsocialist world between 1964 and 1966 – from 36.9 percent of total Cuban trade to 19.6 percent – reflected Washington's success in confining most capitalist trade with Cuba to barter or cash sales.[208]

The following discussion of American efforts to constrict, if not terminate, English, Spanish, French, Japanese, and Canadian economic relations with Cuba indicates the intensity of the Johnson White House's pursuit of the economic isolation objective, as well as the degree of cooperation and cleavage with this policy among leading members of the Western alliance.

Canada   By the mid-1960s, American capital and commerce had assumed a dominant position in the Canadian economy. In 1964, almost one-third of U.S. direct investment abroad was located in Canada, amounting to 80 percent of all foreign investment in the country. These investments, with almost $13 billion in branch plants and subsidiaries, were concentrated in the strategic technological durables, manufacturing, and resource industries. Over 60 percent of Canada's total trade was with the United States.[209] The American market's importance to Canadian exports grew steadily over the decade, accounting for 56 percent of total exports in 1963 and 65 percent in 1968.[210] Meanwhile, the country's world export trade tripled from $5.3 billion in 1960 to $16.5 billion in 1970.[211] These developments – the rising dependence on export trade and on the U.S. market, in particular – at one level meant that Ottawa was vulnerable to pressures emanating from Washington. This state of affairs was almost certainly a factor in the decisions of successive Canadian administrations to tread quite carefully with Canada's Cuba connection.

Like its conservative predecessor, the liberal Pearson government (1963–1968) adhered rigorously to the agreement with Washington not to re-export U.S. goods to Cuba, but it also refused to curb trade with the Castro government in nonstrategic and nonmilitary items. One of the first major economic deals between Canada and the Soviet Union after Pearson's election involved Ottawa's economic relations with Havana. In September 1963, the Soviet Union concluded a large grain agreement with the Canadian Wheat Board for the purchase of one million tons of wheat and 750,000 tons of flour – about one-quarter of the total to be shipped directly to Cuba.[212] Despite the participation of a number of U.S. multinational subsidiaries in this transaction, Washington's response was muted, at least publicly. Few steps were taken beyond an informal protest at the Seventh Meeting of the Canadian-United States Interparliamentary Group held in Washington, D.C., in January 1964.[213] In late 1964 the sale was renegotiated, providing for the purchase of 860,000 tons each of wheat and flour during 1965–1966. The proposed Cuban allocation this time was considerably larger, and the U.S. government decided that the arrangement had "over-reached acceptable bounds."[214] It therefore invoked the Cuban Assets Control Regulations to prohibit U.S. milling subsidiaries in Canada from processing any part of the shipment for delivery to Cuba.[215]

Although Ottawa did not prevent the export of complex electrification equipment and other capital goods to Cuba during 1963 and 1964, it did try to balance Canada's profitable trade opportunities with Washington's objectives. The Johnson administration, in specific, limited circumstances, was prepared to overlook Canadian exports to Havana that included U.S. parts, where the latter formed a minimal percentage of the overall order. This concession was a relatively inconsequential gesture toward Canadian nationalism and its government's increasing sensitivity to United States' dominance of its economy. In 1966, to take a representative example, the Cuban trade commissioner in Canada ordered five refrigerator trucks built on a chassis manufactured in Canada by an American multinational subsidiary. The chassis contained 55 percent U.S.-origin parts, but these constituted only 18 percent of the trucks' total value. The Pearson government declared the trucks "Canadian products" and authorized their

sale without consulting Washington. American authorities
adhered to the general understanding regarding this category of
product when informed of the proposed sale by the parent
company.[216]

In return for these rather minor concessions, the Canadians
carefully controlled their trade exchanges with Havana. Ottawa
ensured that Canada would not become a "pass-through" for
American products destined for the Caribbean island and refused
to provide artificial encouragement to Canadian-Cuban trade
(e.g., export credits). Beyond that, the Pearson government followed a general policy of economic and diplomatic relations-as-
usual, and opposed any embargo on the sale of locally produced
commodities that did not appear on the NATO list of strategic
items. This stance reflected, in part, the Canadians growing
dependence on export expansion to sustain their economy. The
actual value of Canadian exports to Cuba during the Johnson presidency took on a sawtooth pattern – $57 million in 1964, $49 million in 1965, $57.4 million in 1966, $39.4 million in 1967, $42
million in 1968.[217]

Japan   The emergence of Japan as a competitor was linked to
the growth of a technology applied to heavy-industry and consumer exports in such areas as shipbuilding, radios, and television,
iron and steel, and automobiles. Between 1955 and 1970, Japan's
heavy-industry and chemical exports rose from 38.0 percent to
72.4 percent of the country's total exports.[218] In the decade after
1960, Japan's share of the world export market increased from 3.2
percent to 6.2 percent; the value of its exports rose almost fivefold
from $4.1 billion to $19.3 billion.[219] The largest growth was in the
American market, which absorbed only 19.5 percent of Japanese
exports in 1953, but climbed to 29.9 percent in 1963, 31.8 percent in 1968.[220] In fact, Japan's first postwar trade surplus, in
1965, resulted largely from its favorable trade balance with the
United States.[221]

Japan's economic expansion had two effects on American capital
and commerce. Although its increasingly sophisticated export-oriented economy offered a major challenge to some American producers, Japan's growth simultaneously opened new opportunities
for important sectors of U.S. industry, because the areas of greatest Japanese domestic expansion were those most dependent on
American tools and raw materials. Between 1958 and 1967, the

value of Japanese imports from U.S. and Canadian sources increased from $1.7 billion to $3.9 billion.[222]

Japanese-Cuban trade worked its way around this backdrop of increasing capitalist competition and the enormous new market for U.S. exporters – a market that American policymakers did not wish to jeopardize with conflicts over Cuba. Japan's debates about economic issues with Washington did not materialize as an independent foreign policy. Tokyo, cognizant of its military dependence on the United States, placed a premium on capitalist solidarity and good relations with the Johnson administration.

Toward the end of 1963, the Japanese International Trade Promotion Association sent a representative to Cuba and invited a Cuban technical study mission to Japan. Around this time, Japanese interests were competing unsuccessfully for a Cuban multimillion dollar bus contract, eventually awarded to the British Leyland Motor Corporation in January 1964. By mid-1964, the State Department was extremely "concerned" over the expansion of Japanese-Cuban trade; Tokyo Embassy officials were directed to renew diplomatic pressures. And yet, economic counsellor Arthur Z. Gardner was informed by the Director of the Economic Affairs Bureau in the Japanese Ministry of Foreign Affairs, Yoshihiro Nakayama, that foreign trade was the preserve of private capitalists and that, short of "administrative guidance," the government was powerless. Nakayama also defended the need to achieve a more balanced commercial relationship with Cuba, following a two-year period (1962–1963) during which Japan purchased Cuban exports worth $58.7 million, while Cuba imported Japanese goods valued at only $13.4 million.[223]

The primary source of friction was Tokyo's role as the largest capitalist buyer of Cuban sugar, with imports rising from 161,000 tons in 1963, to 415,000 tons in 1965, to 542,000 tons in 1967.[224] These purchases came about essentially because of Cuban sugar's low cost when supplies were scarce and did not involve opposition to U.S. policy. But Washington's concern was "to discourage [any] long-term [Japanese] commitment" to Cuban sugar purchases and, to this end, it sought alternative sugar sources for the Japanese.[225] Reliable substitute producers, however, were difficult to find.[226]

Given the importance of harmonious relations with Japan, American pressures over this issue were almost exclusively diplomatic. This low-profile stance was encouraged by specific Japanese concessions that exposed a concern not to force the conflict.[227] One State Department official described such actions as Japan's agreement to forbid its ships from stopping at Cuban ports and limit nonstrategic exports to the island as an "important inhibition" on Cuban-Japanese trade.[228] At the same time, the Japanese Minister for International Trade reiterated his country's intention to maintain traditional commercial relations with Havana and decried American efforts to apply pressure through third-party, Latin American states having trade ties with Tokyo.[229]

The total value of bilateral trade increased from $25.7 million in 1963 to $87.9 million in 1964, and Japan emerged as Cuba's third leading trading partner, surpassed only by the Soviet Union and China. The decline in the value of Cuban-Japanese trade between 1965 and 1968 to approximately $33 million was partly a result of Tokyo's desire to cooperate with Washington, but more the outcome of Havana's growing balance-of-payments difficulties.[230]

France   During the late 1950s and early 1960s, the deGaulle government sought an independent foreign policy both to challenge U.S. ambitions in Europe and to achieve "great power" status for France.[231] These objectives and an aggressive policy to strengthen France's competitive position in world markets in the early 1960s contrasted with its economic relations with Cuba, which followed a more ambiguous line.

Between 1959 and 1964, the French government refused to provide credit guarantees to local exporters involved in trade with Cuba – a stance Washington found commendable. France's policy on credit guarantees apparently foreclosed the Berliet Company's chance for the large Cuban bus contract awarded to British Leyland in January 1964.[232] Secretary Rusk also acknowledged that the de Gaulle regime had applied "informal pressures . . . on French ship owners to withdraw from Cuba trade," though he noted that it was not particularly effective. The Paris Embassy was directed to keep up the pressure "to obtain pledges from French ship owners with vessels in Cuba trade that all their ships would be withdrawn as charters expire or otherwise kept out of Cuban trade."[233]

By early 1964, the heavy-equipment sector of French industry had entered a recession, forcing Paris to consider promoting exports of nonstrategic industrial items to both socialist and capitalist countries. In February, the government broke with earlier policy and provided the Berliet Company with credit guarantees to bid successfully on a large deal with the Castro regime – a $10 million sale of 300 heavy trucks and tractors. The Cubans agreed to pay 20 percent in cash and 80 percent over a three-year period; the French agreed to guarantee all or part of the balance in the event of a Cuban default.[234] French officials attributed the change to "precedents established by other Western powers."[235]

In May, the French government and the engineering firm of Brissoneau et Lotz aroused the ire of U.S. policymakers with a $4-million contract to sell 20 diesel locomotives to Cuba, plus an option for 10 more. The success of this deal was linked to the availability of state credit guarantees.[236] Washington expressed "serious concern" over what it called a major strategic breach in the global economic blockade because of Cuba's limited number of functioning locomotives (from less than 600 in 1958 to below 200 in 1963),[237] but Paris called the locomotives nonstrategic, justifying the sale as an important boost to a vital, currently depressed economic sector. The *Hispanic American Report* thought the deal was approved to save the company from collapse.[238] Possibly as a gesture to Washington, the three-year credit term was shorter than usual for sales of this magnitude.[239] The French government was also careful to emphasize the selective nature of this transaction, informing American officials that it did not forecast a trend but was "the last deal which will be made with the Cubans for some time."[240] Accordingly, the French refused to provide credit guarantees on Cuban orders during the latter half of 1964 for a fertilizer plant, a yeast factory, locomotives, and earth-moving equipment.[241]

In mid-1964, the Gaullist regime opposed an effort by influential segments of the local capitalist class, especially the capital-goods industries, to eliminate the five-year limit on government-guaranteed loans to socialist countries, which included Cuba.[242]

Between 1964 and 1966, French exports to Cuba remained relatively low. Their value declined from $20.9 million in 1964 to $13.5 million in 1965, rising a bit to $14.6 million in 1966. Over about this same period, Paris' cooperation with Washington on export credits was almost total. Although French exports to Cuba grew during 1967 ($54.7 million) and 1968 ($55.8 million), due largely to sales of machinery, trucks, tractors, and fertilizer, de Gaulle's government deferred to U.S. legislation that banned France's importation of products containing materials obtained from nationalized properties in Cuba.[243] The principal substance at issue was Cuban nickel, which the French incorporated in a variety of products from steel to nuts and bolts.

Spain   Links between Franco's Spain and socialist Cuba presented American officials with a most frustrating problem. By the early 1960s, Spain's postwar industrialization had reached a point where exports were more important to economic growth than agricultural production.[244] But Spain remained a political and economic pariah in Europe, excluded from the Common Market and in search of alternative trade outlets.[245] Although manufactured products grew from 31 percent to 50 percent of the country's total exports between 1961 and 1967, Spain's exports to Europe declined by 13 percent during the 1960s, of which 8 percent was accounted for by the Common Market nations.[246] Considering both Spain's increasing dependence on exports and its exclusion from natural nearby markets, non-European possibilities, particularly in Latin America, took on ever-increasing importance.

Beginning in December 1963, the Johnson administration applied "strong diplomatic pressure" to force cooperation with the Cuba blockade policy.[247] Washington officials defined Spain's trade ties with the island as "a serious breach."[248] The State Department cautioned Franco that failure to halt expanding commerce with Cuba could imperil U.S. economic assistance. The threat alluded to the recent, five-year extension of the treaty providing for American air and naval bases in Spain. In partial exchange for this renewal of the bilateral military treaty, the U.S. committed $100 million in Export-Import loans for long-term development projects in Spain.[249]

In a highly critical January 1964 dispatch to its Embassy in Madrid, the State Department described Spain as "stand[ing] out among free-world countries in that, according to present data, all indices of economic ties with Cuba, except shipping, moved up [between 1962 and 1963]."[250] Spain's decision to negotiate multiyear Cuban sugar purchases, occasioned primarily by the decline in world sugar production, once again raised anger in the United States over another ally making long-term commitments to buy Cuban sugar – commitments beyond the period of a likely global shortage.[251] Informed of a projected $50 million shipbuilding agreement between Spain and Cuba, Washington, further aggravated, sent CIA Director John McCone in late January "to talk

Gen[eral] Francisco Franco out of trading with Cuba."[252] These diplomatic and economic pressures apparently made some headway by the end of February, when the Spanish government reportedly informed American officials that it was prepared to offer cooperation "but need[ed] time to figure out how."[253]

On December 16, 1963, in accord with congressional wishes, President Johnson signed an amendment to the Foreign Assistance Act of 1963 that legally bound the White House to halt military and economic aid to countries failing to take "appropriate steps" by February 14, 1964, to shut off transportation links with Cuba. Despite Franco's professed willingness to comply, mid-February found five Spanish-owned or registered vessels still under charter to the Cuban regime and Iberia Airlines providing the only scheduled air service between Cuba and Europe.[254]

By the February deadline, direct U.S. economic aid to Spain, with the exception of surplus agricultural commodities and Export-Import Bank loans not formally covered by the December 1963 amendment, had virtually ceased. American military assistance to Spain was not interrupted during bilateral military-aid negotiations.[255] The White House tilted toward no reprisals on the grounds that the large complex of air and sea bases and a new Polaris missile submarine facility at Rota on Spain's south coast constituted vital national security interests, compared with which the Cuba problem was a secondary issue.[256] In the course of negotiations, the Spanish government announced that it already had shipped 18 of 150 trucks it had decided to sell to Cuba.[257] Still, U.S. officials characterized the Spanish position as "reasonable," especially since Madrid was reported to have "agreed to cooperate in any move that the Administration . . . might find suitable in mollifying Congress."[258]

Although Washington's threatened economic retaliations always were balanced by the importance of military agreements, the Spanish government seemed determined to have both its trade with Cuba and American aid. This stance was writ large at a special cabinet meeting in February 1964 presided over by General Franco when a decision was taken to maintain Spain's "firm commitments" to Cuba and interpret any U.S. aid curtailment as tantamount to a breach of that 1963 military agreement.[259] In the long run, military and political relationships took precedence over frictions generated by Cuba.

The Franco regime consistently sought to rationalize the Cuba connection on practical, economic grounds, but it also was prepared to make concessions to guarantee U.S. economic assistance and not force relations with Washington to a breaking point. To accommodate U.S. foreign-aid requirements, Franco agreed to stop transporting commercial cargo on Iberia Airlines passenger flights to Havana. Madrid also decided that a number of Spanish vessels engaged in hauling cargo to Cuba would not have their charters renewed upon expiration.[260] On March 4, 1964, the State Department described these measures as "appropriate" to the meaning of the December 1963 amendment to the Foreign Assistance Act, and Spain's eligibility for continued U.S. military assistance remained unaffected.[261] Within days of the State Department announcement, the Spanish Naval Minister, Admiral Nieto Antunez, in response to Venezuela's threats to sever commercial ties with Madrid if immediate curbs were not placed on Spanish-Cuban trade, declared that locally owned ships would not call at Cuban ports after November 1964.[262] Beginning in 1965, almost all Spanish goods destined for Cuba were carried by British, Italian, Greek, and Cuban ships. Through 1968, no Spanish-owned or registered vessels docked at any Cuban port.[263]

American officials in Washington and Madrid continued to question the aviation connections between Spain and Cuba, which the Franco government justified on the grounds of cultural affinities and the need to maintain contact with the 200,000 to 300,000 Spanish nationals living in Cuba. The Johnson administration dismissed these arguments, contending that the flights persisted because they were highly profitable. But what was most aggravating from the American viewpoint was that the airline link facilitated a steady outflow of individuals considered to be potential Castro opponents.[264]

Despite selective accommodations to the U.S. blockade, total Cuban-Spanish trade reached $97 million in 1964, a more than threefold increase over 1963. Obviously, Franco was not about to allow U.S. diplomatic urgings or ideological differences with Havana to obstruct expanding economic ties with the Caribbean island.[265] The bulk of Spanish exports were agricultural machinery, electrical equipment, light machinery, foodstuffs, consumer goods, and ships, Although nonmilitary and, at least technically, nonstrategic in character, their importance to the functioning of the Cuban economy occasioned Washington's repeated displeasure. One special target of State Department hostility was the April 1964 agreement for Havana to purchase forty-two Spanish-built vessels.[266]

Negotiations in early 1965 over the annual extension of the Spanish-Cuban commercial agreement foreshadowed a decline in the level of bilateral trade because of the projected growth of local sugar production and because Spanish shipbuilders were not as concerned as earlier with obtaining Cuban contracts. Although bilateral trade fell by around $27 million between 1964 and 1965, the following year reversed this trend. In 1966, the total value of trade between Madrid and Havana exceeded $116 million, with Cuba accounting for 36 percent of Spain's exports to Latin America.[267] Under a 1966 agreement, Spain agreed to purchase 580,000 tons of Cuban sugar over a three-year period in exchange for increased Cuban imports of ships, buses, and other vehicles.[268] No large-scale decline in Cuban sugar imports took place; there was only a slight fall from 174,000 tons in 1965 to 159,000 tons in 1967.[269] A substantial decline in the volume and value of Spanish exports to Cuba during 1967–1968 was less the result of a late-blooming Franco capitulation to Washington than of Cuba's balance-of-payments problems.[270]

England   America's closest European ally was singled out as a major offender, especially because of large, government-supported sales to Havana. It became a target of the Washington blockade planners. In part, British trade with Cuba and other socialist countries during the 1960s was a response to a long-term decline in the nation's competitive position in the world market.

In the postwar era, England's trade position underwent a dramatic change. Its share of global manufactured exports fell from 25.4 percent at midcentury to 16.5 percent in 1960 to 13.9 percent in 1965 to 10.8 percent in 1970, with attendant chronic balance-of-payments deficits.[271] A major reason was the disintegration of the imperial preferences system under the weight of American and Japanese export pressures. Between 1961 and 1966, United Kingdom exports to the old Commonwealth countries fell from 35.5 percent to 25.9 percent of total exports.[272]

Following its decision not to seek membership in the European Economic Community (EEC) in 1958, the British government helped initiate a rival European Free Trade Association. Only moderate export gains resulted, and in July 1961, Whitehall, supported by export-oriented capitalists, decided to apply for Common Market membership.[273] Its application was rejected largely because the French suspected that England would be a "stalking horse" for U.S. interests. Although British exports to the EEC increased marginally as a percentage of total exports during the first half of the 1960s, exclusion from membership limited its access to these dynamic markets and the possibility of solving its balance-of-payments crisis.[274] As "export-propelled" growth gained adherents, the government sought to recoup some export losses through expanded trade with the socialist bloc.[275]

In late January 1964, Under Secretary of State George Ball sent a memorandum to the London Embassy about "our continuing concern" over British commercial relations with Cuba. In particular, Washington wanted its European ally to reconsider anticipated sales of items such as transport and electric power equipment likely to provide the basis for an upsurge in the economy and to "avoid long-term commitments, which tend [to] guarantee Cuban [foreign] exchange receipts, in order [to] permit purchases [from] free-world sources when shortages [in world sugar production] eases." The memo directed Embassy officials to make the Conservative government of Alex Douglas-Home aware of the depth of "U.S. sensitivity [to the] Cuban problem" and the "U.S. determination [to] maintain pressure on [the] GOC [Government of Cuba]."[276]

This renewal of high-level diplomatic activity over England's Cuba connections coincided with the large Cuban bus contract awarded in January 1964 to the British Leyland Motor Corporation.[277] Leyland undertook to supply the Cubans with 450 buses for an estimated $11.2 million and at least $1 million worth of spare parts and to allow Havana an option on 1,000 more between 1965 and 1968 at an approximate cost of $20 million. It also agreed to deliver the buses and spare parts and to establish offices and repair shops in Cuba.[278] The terms included a five-year credit extension guaranteed by the British government's Export Credits Guarantee Department (ECGD).

Although the Conservative government voluntarily added Cuba to NATO's list of socialist countries to which the export of strategic goods was banned, it did not restructure its diplomacy and trade with Havana. In contrast to the American position, which British officials regarded as misguided and ineffective, Whitehall preferred to view the Castro regime as "a grey area" and, like Japan, desired to expand its exports to rectify an existing trade imbalance.[279] Besides that, the Leyland transaction represented the company's largest contract in two years.[280] The chairman of the Leyland Corporation, Sir William Black, responded to Washington's criticism by bringing up America's wheat sales to the Soviet Union. "If America has a surplus of wheat," he declared, "we have a surplus of buses."[281]

United States officials described the bus contract as one that "certainly does not help our efforts to isolate the Cuban regime."[282] Since the estimated number of buses operating in Havana had declined from 1,600 in 1961 to 800 in 1963, this sale was viewed as yet another major breach of the embargo.[283] A *London Times* correspondent wrote that the Johnson administration was unhappy with the agreement "because it had recently been pleased . . . that the transport system in Cuba had been running into difficulties."[284] Short of risking a serious rupture, however, the U.S. government could do little.[285] Still, the British, according to one involved American official, did make a minor concession: The state-guaranteed loan was based on less favorable credit arrangements than originally had been contemplated.[286] The U.S. Congress strongly condemned the Leyland deal, with liberal senators such as Stephen M. Young joining conservatives in terming the arrangement "despicable."[287]

In early February, the State Department initiated unofficial contacts with Whitehall over further bus sales and government-guaranteed credits to Cuba.[288] Some senior administration officials, including Secretary of State Dean Rusk and White House aide McGeorge Bundy, raised the possibility of a domestic consumer boycott of goods produced by British companies engaged in trade with Cuba. The Leyland Corporation, for one, had annual American earnings through the sale of Triumph sports cars and other vehicles of around $42 million.[289]

England was one of the allied countries most immediately affected by the December 1963 amendment to the Foreign Assistance Act that mandated a cutoff of military and economic assistance to countries whose ships still engaged in trade with Cuba as of February 14, 1964. In the period leading up to the February deadline, U.S. officials speculated that the British government would simply make "informal approaches" that were unlikely to constitute "appropriate steps." What the State Department really wanted was that the Douglas-Home government secure formal pledges from offending British shipowners not to participate in the Cuba trade or to withdraw current charters when they expired.[290]

On the eve of the U.S. decision to terminate a projected $100,000 military-aid grant to England, President Johnson and Prime Minister Douglas-Home concluded a two-day conference in Washington, D.C. As preparation, the State Department provided extensive materials on United Kingdom-Cuba economic relations centering on American opposition to the bus deal, the need for greater British government efforts to discourage local shipping from engaging in Cuba trade, rigid enforcement of a policy denying all critical commodities to Cuba, the withdrawal of credit guarantees to British traders doing business with Havana, and a belief that the behavior of Washington's closest ally in this matter would "strongly influence" other Western countries' actions. Memos from Secretary Rusk and other Department officials advised Johnson to ask Douglas-Home to hold up the delivery of the 400 buses purchased by the Cubans and reject government credit guarantees for additional Cuban bus deals, and to accompany these suggestions with the threat "of possible countermoves against [British] firms [with American operations] trading with Cuba." Douglas-Home was to be educated: British cooperation would facilitate movement on other disagreements between the two countries through its effect on "public and Congressional opinion," whereas failing to appreciate U.S. concerns "could create problems in our economic relations."[291]

The Prime Minister countered on both political and commercial grounds: British trade excluded strategic items; it did not involve loans or aid for general purposes; and the government's insuring corporations against potential nonpayment was a practice followed by Washington in similar analogous situations.

Although the meeting produced a consensus on almost all major issues, it ended with nothing less than "complete disagreement on the issue of British trade with Cuba."[292] On his return to Whitehall, Douglas-Home expressed skepticism over whether economic sanctions would produce Washington's goal: "We have held a consistent view about this, and I hold it very strongly, that nobody like Castro is brought down by economic sanctions."[293]

Nonetheless, soon after the meeting with Johnson, the British government modified its position on Cuba trade. It informally discouraged local merchant shipping from transporting the Leyland buses to Cuba, forcing the corporation to negotiate an arrangement with East German vessel owners. During a House of Commons debate on the subject, the Prime Minister was asked:"how is it that with 20 million tons of merchant shipping we are unable to get a single ship to carry a valuable export order to Cuba and we have to go to Communist Germany to obtain these facilities?"[294] Douglas-Home's response centered on the December 1963 amendment to the U.S. Foreign Assistance Act, suggesting that Whitehall may indeed have "use[d] its influence" to get ships owned by British nationals out of the Cuba trade.

Another key shift in British policy took place in the spring of 1964 when the government "gave us [Washington] the signal that they might be able to do something about credits and there weren't any credits from the spring of 1964 to late 1966 from Britain."[295]

A third instance of Whitehall's accommodation occurred in April and involved a British manufacturer, Steel and Company, which was reported to be negotiating the sale of $1.4 million worth of heavy cranes powered by a diesel engine built in Scotland under license from Cummins Engine of Columbus, Indiana. Steel and Company had purchased 12 engines from Cummins in 1963, but Cummins announced that such sales would stop, permanently, if the Cuban deal was consummated. At State Department request, the British Board of Trade investigated the transaction on the grounds that the Johnson administration "was within its rights if it wanted to stop the delivery of the cranes, since the cranes might be on the NATO embargo list."[296] While the White House was prepared to press its overall objective with the British, there was resistance to go to extremes: "Cuba is not that important to the United States," a State Department official observed. "We would not have the CIA go out and destroy the crane factory in Great Britain to prevent Cuba from getting the cranes."[297]

Amid all these twists and turns, the British government's determination to maintain trade relations with Cuba made Washington itch. In a secret April 1964 session of the NATO Council in Paris, Under Secretary Ball denounced Britain in a blunt, aggressive speech. "Is it . . . the intention of the members," he asked, "that a single nation should be able to frustrate a serious policy affecting the defense of the free world interests in a vital area of the world?"[298] President Johnson echoed him in a private meeting later that month with British Foreign Secretary R. A. Butler.[299] Britain's official position, enunciated by Butler during his American visit in April, was that trade with Cuba was on a "purely commercial basis" and was the responsibility of the Export Credits Guarantee Department (ECGD). Butler conceded that the ECGD could not approve Cuban trade transactions without consulting the British Foreign Office and the Bank of England. But there was no intention on the part of the Conservative government to terminate such trade, especially in view of the country's persistent balance-of-payments deficit.[300]

The U.S. government sought vigorously to mobilize suppport for its position on British trade with Cuba and other socialist countries at the NATO Council. The question was raised repeatedly during the first half of 1964, culminating in a final Council vote of 15 to 1 in opposition to British actions.[301] Washington apparently was so convinced that this was the key to holding the line on Cuban trade with Western Europe, Japan, and elsewhere in the capitalist world that one American official interpolated British policy as a threat to the very unity of the NATO alliance.[302]

The precipating factor in this heightened U.S. agitation was a new round of negotiations between Leyland Corporation and the Castro regime over a further 500 buses and strong indications that the Douglas-Home government again was prepared to extend credit guarantees. American officials complained about Cuba as a poor credit risk; some asserted that Whitehall had "changed the export credit guarantee classification . . . to make the bus sale seem a more commercial transaction [while] originally there had been an element of government subsidy"[303] and some raised the old saw that British actions would unleash a "domino" effect among countries up to then largely cooperative with Washington.[304]

In early May 1964, the Cubans exercised an option for 500 more buses. In London, Leyland's chairman, Sir William Black, announced that the British Board of Trade had agreed to underwrite the sale. Meanwhile, the Douglas-Home government apparently "assured" Washington that future sales to Cuba would be kept at a level below previous years' and limited in other, unspecified ways.[305] In another "soothing gesture," it decided to consider limiting credit guarantees.[306]

On May 12, the *London Times* reported that the British, in "a fraternal half-measure believed to be acceptable to the [Johnson] Administration," had agreed to discourage trade with Cuba. Such action that might be taken, however, would not be enforced by legislative or judicial fiat, nor was it to be interpreted as a "departure from the traditional British position of untrammelled trade in non-strategic goods."[307] In the midst of this evolving competitive-collaborative response, Secretary Rusk remarked that the Anglo-American conflict over Cuba was "tactical and minor in character," with one country defining the problem as essentially "a question of trade policy" and the other seeing "a security threat to the Western Hemisphere."[308]

The application of direct and indirect American pressures on individual British firms with substantial U.S. markets to forego sales to Cuba did produce selective gains. In early 1965, the British Aircraft Corporation refused to sell VC10 jet airliners to Havana because "it did not want to endanger its position in the far more important U.S. market."[309] In August 1966, the State Department openly pressured a British shipping company, the Blue Funnel Line, to halt temporarily the delivery of tractor parts from the United States to a local firm after the ship in question had docked at a British port. The parts were destined for Pakistan but the company acceded to the American request that they not be transshipped for fear, according to Willis Armstrong, U.S. Embassy Minister for Economic Affairs, that the export agent might route them on to Cuba. On the shipment's release, Armstrong stated, "The shipping line respected our wishes. . . . They do business in the United States and they recognize we have a measure of jurisdiction."[310]

Outside the Leyland bus deal, only one major government-backed exchange occurred between a British company and the Castro regime during the Johnson presidency – a multimillion-dollar contract with the Simon-Carves engineering firm for a fertilizer complex intended as a centerpiece of the Cubans' agricultural program. At the time of initial Cuban enquiries in late 1966, there was considerable reticence on the part of most large Western European engineering enterprises to bid on the contract for fear of offending Washington.[311] The possibility raised in some quarters that no local banking institution would underwrite the sale was dispelled by the Export Credits Guarantee Department (ECGD), which noted that the Castro government had been "meticulous" in meeting its obligations in earlier trade deals, including the Leyland transactions.[312] The State Department initiated discussions with Whitehall officials "as soon as plans for the deal became known," but to no avail.[313]

In January 1967, the ECGD announced a five-year "normal insurance cover" for the construction of a $39-million fertilizer plant by the Simon-Carves Company;[314] the British Board of Trade agreed to guarantee 80 percent of the plant's value for five years after completion.[315] These decisions generated a new round of American diplomatic pressures. In preparation for his meeting with Prime Minister Harold Wilson in February 1967, senior White House official Walt W. Rostow received extensive background materials from the State Department about the Cuba trade issue. Rostow was advised to make it clear to the British leader "that public and Congressional opposition to such [government-guaranteed credit] deals is intense" and that further sales of this nature, especially involving buses, would make it increasingly difficult for Washington to support British policy in Rhodesia.[316] By early 1968, when construction began on what had become a $100-million fertilizer plant that would double Cuba's output of nitrogen fertilizer, export credits covering $45 million in equipment for construction had been granted by the British government.[317] These guarantees, according to the London-based *Latin America*, were "determined exclusively by consideration of Cuba's creditworthiness."[318] It must be added that, even with the Leyland and Simon-Carves sales, the annual value of British-Cuban trade during the Johnson years hovered at a relatively modest level.[319]

Covert politics and the global economic blockade

Once the decision was made to wage global economic warfare against Cuba, the State Department took charge of the program. Coincidentally, by the end of 1963, a number of executive-branch personnel changes had enhanced its authority in the area of foreign economic policy.[320] Although the Treasury and Commerce Departments performed important roles, they were secondary actors compared to the State Department, which directed the overall effort, and to the CIA, which engaged in economic intelligence collection, organized sabotage operations against the Cuban economy, monitored Western shipping and exports to the Carribbean island, and drew on established relationships with Western intelligence services to reinforce U.S. diplomatic representations to their governments about the blockade.[321] The West German, Dutch, and British CIA stations, according to a CIA field officer in Western Europe at the time, allocated personnel and resources to this effort "way out of proporation" to what they could be reasonably expected to achieve.[322] The Agency also maintained close liaisons with police organizations in allied countries. A Spanish official recalled a cooperative mid-1960s relationship, saying, "Madrid was a center of operations against Castro. There was one plane a week from Havana, and there was ship traffic. I don't know the degree of collaboration between CIA and Spanish police, but it was big."[323]

Under both Kennedy and Johnson, covert operations against Cuba were essential to U.S. policy and they took imaginative forms. In perhaps the most spectacular and crude example of clandestine meddling, the CIA organized a scheme to obstruct the Leyland bus shipment to Cuba on East German vessels. In October 1964, a Japanese cargo ship, the *Yamashiro Maru*, acting on Agency orders, rammed one of those East German freighters, the *Magdeberg*, as it left port moving down the Thames River. The buses lashed to the deck of the *Magdeberg* received "a damaging drenching." The Japanese knew exactly what they were doing because British intelligence had informed Washington of ships' schedules, partly through a wiretap on Cuban government offices in London.[324]

There is also evidence to suggest that the CIA sought to strike at the heart of Cuban economic life by ruining the country's sugar exports. On August 22, 1962, in San Juan, Puerto Rico, to take one verified instance, the *S.S. Streatham Hill*, a British freighter under charter to the Soviet Union, anchored for repairs, en route to a Soviet port with 80,000 bags of Cuban sugar. To make the repairs, 14,000 bags had to be unloaded and, in accordance with the U.S. embargo, placed under bond in a customs shed. During the ship's stopover, CIA operatives "entered the customs shed and contaminated the off-loaded sugar with a harmless but unpalatable substance."[325] This was not an isolated event, as an Agency official who helped orchestrate the sabotage activities pointed out. "There was lots of sugar being sent from Cuba, and we were putting a log of contaminants in it."[326] Similarly, in 1966, in Vera Cruz, Mexico, CIA employees sabotaged a $45,000 mechanical sugar-cane harvester in a warehouse waiting to be shipped to Cuba.[327]

As the Leyland bus adventure testifies, among the most sustained targets of CIA economic warfare were capitalist-bloc exports to Cuba, which were subject to not very "subtle sabotage." An Agency official offered some revealing, detailed insights. He described the addition of "invisible, untraceable chemicals" to lubricating fluids purchased by Cuba for its diesel engines, chemicals that made engine parts "wear out faster then [Cuba] could get replacements." In another instance, the CIA Station to Frankfurt convinced a West German manufacturer of ball bearings to make those bearings destined for Cuba "off center," for asymmetrical bearings readily chew up themselves and their races and can severely damage machines. It was not unusual for such accommodating businessmen to receive "several hundred thousand dollars or more" in payment. The official also recalled that, when a particular manufacturer was resistant to CIA blandishments "we would just put the science fiction crap in ourselves when the shipment was en route."[328]

Conclusion

Although the achievements of U.S. global economic warfare during the Kennedy and Johnson presidencies varied, they were nonetheless substantial. Early in the blockade (1962–1964), diplomatic and legal pressures to gain capitalist cooperation in the effort to dissolve the Cuban Revolution produced a number of partial, but important successes: a virtually complete ban on the export of strategic military goods to Cuba; an overall decline in industrial, machine, and spare-parts exports from the same sources; minimal airline links between Cuba and the nonsocialist world; and a visible contraction in the number of capitalist-owned vessels engaged in Cuban trade.

On the other hand, most countries were not prepared to terminate completely normal commercial relationships, and a few, such as England and Greece, accounted for a substantial number of flagships docking at the island's ports. While some allied governments, notably West Germany's and Turkey's, readily collaborated with U.S. objectives, there was uniform concern among all Cuba's capitalist trading partners not to flout the embargo and precipitate a conflict with the imperial power. Nonetheless, the question of extraterritorial applications of U.S. laws or regulations to subsidiaries of American multinationals in Western countries concerned all affected governments, whatever their degree of support for U.S. economic policy toward Cuba.

An internal 1964 State Department study of East–West trade described the embargo issue as "most troublesome" for Canada, France, and the United Kingdom and concluded on the following note: "All of the cooperating countries [e.g., West Germany, Japan, France, Denmark, Norway], plus the European neutrals and Spain, are increasingly reluctant to prevent exports or re-exports to Cuba when the goods are not strategic and the government has no legal authority to control the trade."[329]

During Johnson's tenure, from 1964 to 1968, there was a steady decline from 383 to 195 in the number of trips to Cuba by capitalist vessels. Meanwhile, between 1964 and 1966, Cuba's trade with the West, as a percentage of its total trade, declined by almost half – indicative of Washington's successes in insisting on barter or cash sales. Through most of the decade, large government-guaranteed credit sales occurred only sporadically and selectively and in no instance reflected an entrenched position by the government in question. Credits generally were extended to major corporations undergoing periods of recession and, without these economic downturns, there is every likelihood that cooperation with the blockade would have been stronger.

At the height of the global blockade efforts in the mid-1960s, an involved State Department official recalled, the Cubans were paying well above normal prices for major equipment imports from Western Europe partly because suppliers were jittery over dealing with Havana, fearing U.S. retaliation. Johnson administration efforts were also successful in limiting Cuba's capacity to "shop around" among various Western suppliers for heavy industry and other items its government wished to purchase – often confining the options to a single company. Moreover, whenever Washington learned of pending large-scale sales of "critical" goods such as machine tools or transportation items, it was able to bring "very considerable pressure to bear" to halt negotiations between the Castro regime and the capitalist-bloc firm. Finally, American pressures prevented a number of credit-based deals involving allied governments from being carried through. When these pressures failed to prevent Western exporters to Cuba from gaining access to government financial backing, Washington was still "very successful in preventing the Cubans from getting optimal [credit] deals."[330]

Although there was considerable "browbeating [of] the Europeans into seeing it our way,"[331] both the Kennedy and Johnson administrations exhibited a strongly pragmatic attitude. Ultimately, Washington was not prepared "to put on the screws and initiate a confrontation with [important allies] over Cuba" to a point where long-term political and military relationships were endangered.[332] As a State Department official put it, "there is a limit to which we will jeopardize relations with friendly countries by getting unity with them over something like this."[333]

The "big five" capitalist traders with Cuba all had export-oriented economies and were guided largely by commercial considerations. England and France refused to "identify with the export of revolution," according to a State Department international economic specialist, and their trade was also determined by the fact that Cuba "pays its bills" and all the deals "are well-managed and profitable."[334] In the case of Spain, U.S. policymakers were forced to weigh the additional factor of periodic renegotiations of their bilateral military agreement. "There were so many close relationships between Spain and the United States that they could rattle our cage as we rattled theirs," observed a Cuba desk officer in State. "It was a nice bargaining point."[335]

Where some allies attributed primary importance to their U.S. relationship and were substantially influenced by Washington's decisions, there was considerable convergence with White House policy toward Cuba. Otherwise, where an expanding foreign trade was vital to domestic growth, maximizing trade opportunities tended to take precedence. That arrangement loomed large in the case of Spain, whose available alternatives for trade-expansion were minimal because it was excluded from the European Economic Community. Although the distinction between more collaborative and more competitive allies is useful, it doesn't quite reveal the complexities of capitalist responses at particular moments or in specific areas of activity. Seen historically, in long terms, conflicts over the blockade merely underscored emerging intercapitalist competition and the changing nature of U.S. global dominance. But the disagreements were substantially outbalanced by overall cooperation with American policy. "By and large during this period," a State Department official asserted, "things came up pretty much our way in terms of denying shipping, the sale of goods and financial credits."[336]

The analysis presented in this chapter is support for the contention that, despite the growth of intercapitalist economic competition during the 1960s, such strains were not much reflected at the political level. The evidence presented suggests that noneconomic conflict between the United States and its senior capitalist allies was limited, dictated by considerations other than hostility to American policy, and it tended to submerge and reemerge over discrete issues. Yet, the socialist government of Cuba was able to exploit these rivalries to counter Washington's policy only to a small extent.

6. The United States against Cuba 1968–1980: intransigent policymaking and its consequences

The global and regional context

In the first two decades after World War II when the United States was the dominant capitalist economic and military power, Republican and Democratic administrations promoted an essentially bipartisan foreign policy that enjoyed widespread domestic political support. They could count on an effective and unified military apparatus and a high degree of cooperation from allies in Western Europe, Japan, Canada, and the Third World. During the late 1960s and 1970s, however, the problem for American policymakers was how to resolve challenges emanating from all these sources, including challenges resulting from America's engagement in Indochina.

The enormous cost of the Vietnam involvement combined with growing economic losses to Western Europe and Japan weakened the hegemonic position of the United States in the capitalist world economy. Between 1967 and 1974, for example, West German and Japanese direct investment abroad grew at an average annual rate almost triple that of American multinationals.[1] Moreover, trade competition from the same countries during the 1960s and 1970s lowered the U.S. portion of markets in Western Europe and Latin America and led to both an absolute and a relative decline in the percentage of global manufactured exports of American origin.[2] Within the military sphere, Washington had to accept the reality of Soviet nuclear and conventional arms parity and cope with the decline in institutional solidarity and esprit de corps inside the U.S. armed forces. Domestically, Vietnam meant that administrations could no longer automatically count on unified public support for foreign-policy initiatives, thereby weakening the U.S. capacity to militarily intervene in the affairs of other countries. Finally, Washington had to deal with the problem of fragmentation and declining consensus on political, economic, and military issues within the Western Alliance.

During the 1970s, the United States also was confronted by major social and political upheavals throughout the Third World. These developments created serious problems for American policymakers, especially where nationalist and revolutionary movements overthrew regimes closely allied to Washington and were, in certain cases, important "spokes" in the U.S. global network.

The Nixon, Ford, and Carter administrations attempted to resolve these crises or contain developments in two ways: First, through resort to a policy of global detente, which was seen as a way of preserving superpowers' spheres of influence; and, second, by a renewed emphasis on the importance of "morality" in the making of U.S. foreign policy.

From the beginning, detente was bedeviled by "ambiguity over the area that it was meant to cover, and unrealistic expectations of its scope."[3] Differing Soviet and American interpretations over precisely what detente entailed were crucial factors leading to its breakdown. Nixon and Kissinger linked detente and arms control agreements, above all alse, to Soviet global "restraint." In particular, they viewed it as a means of reducing Soviet influence in the Third World. On the other hand, Brezhnev and the Soviet leadership "never saw East-West detente as a binding commitment to Third World restraint."[4] Existing outside of the traditional Soviet and American spheres of influence, Third World countries were seen by Moscow as legitimate areas of superpower competition for influence and support.

Although the United States opposed Soviet economic or military assistance to political movements or even established governments in the Third World, it did not interpret detente as placing constraints on Western intervention in these regions to support antigovernment forces or prop up client regimes with economic or military assistance (e.g., the United States in Latin America and Asia, France in its former African colonies). Ford administration policy toward Angola and Carter White House behavior toward Ethiopia attested to the persistence of an interpretation of detente based partly on the notion that the Third World was off-limits to the Soviet Union.

Early in Carter's presidency, human rights became a priority in America's relations with the Third World. Although initially opposed by Pentagon officials who feared an adverse impact on interhemispheric military relations, by State Department officials who favored "quiet diplomacy," and by agencies seeking to protect their bureaucratic turf, forceful White House backing gave the human rights proponents a good deal of clout.[5] The State Department's Bureau of Human Rights and Humanitarian Affairs helped support legislation during 1977 and 1978 linking human rights to foreign aid; military assistance was terminated to El Salvador, Nicaragua, and Guatemala because of human rights violations; U.S. representatives in the multilateral development banks either abstained or voted against loan requests by autocratic military regimes in Chile, Argentina, and Uruguay.

The human rights doctrine did not seek to change fundamentally the ties between the United States and these transgressor allies. Diplomatic and legislative measures were not designed to challenge the origins or legitimacy of repressive regimes, but rather to force them to liberalize. Ultimately human rights considerations played a marginal, if any, role in relations with repressive regimes considered pivotal to American interests. Even during the doctrine's ascendence, military assistance flowed to dictatorial Governments in Iran, South Korea, Argentina, and Chile – notwithstanding reams of evidence of their repressive rule.[6] Where military cutbacks were made, they tended to be of limited duration, over discrete issues, and not indicative of any substantive change in bilateral relations.

Washington's economic assistance policy was similarly selective and contradictory. Following State Department Human Rights Bureau testimony about Argentine security forces' "systematic torture" and "summary executions," the Export-Import Bank rejected a $280 million loan to Argentina's military junta in late 1978. Soon after, the decision was reversed, apparently at President Carter's personal order.[7] The Carter White House supported 53 of 66 loan requests to the multilateral development banks by the Philippines' Marcos government,[8] despite irrefutable evidence of its human-rights abuses: "[The Philippines is] important to the security interests of the United States. That's it in a nutshell."[9]

By late 1978, the human rights advocates had begun to lose influence. The change coincided with the rise to prominence of National Security Council advisor Zbnigniew Brzezinski and allied forces within the government advocating a more aggressive and interventionist U.S. global policy to counteract revolutionary upheavals in the Third World. The overthrow of the Shah in Iran in early 1979 was the most important single event accelerating the shift from detente to interventionism. It also sounded the death-knell for Brzezinski's "regional influentials" doctrine unveiled to Cabinet members in May 1978.[10] One Pentagon official summarized: America can no longer depend on "local power to provide stability" in the Third World. "We've got to be there ourselves."[11] The Carter administration's growing emphasis on military power was reinforced by the demise of the Somoza regime, a longstanding American ally, in Nicaragua in July 1979 at the hands of a movement led by Sandinista guerrillas. U.S. Secretary of State Cyrus Vance tried to mobilize Organization of American States support for a hemispheric military force to intervene in Nicaragua and set up an anti-Sandinista government, but he failed.

With January 1980 came the Carter Doctrine: The United States would unilaterally intervene if its access to Persian Gulf oil was threatened.[12] Carter and Brzezinski then exploited the Doctrine's ambiguities to extend it to anywhere "vital interests" were threatened by Moscow or its "surrogates." The shift from detente to interventionism had not changed one of the central objectives of U.S. policy – to contain Soviet "adventurism" in the Third World.[13]

During 1979 and 1980, the economic and military pipeline flowed freely to the previously criticized regimes in Central and South America and other regions of the Third World.[14] Washington sought expanded military facilities in the Indian Ocean, the Middle East, and the Horn of Africa; entered into new strategic military alliances; accelerated the build-up of the Rapid Deployment Force; subordinated criticism of dictators by opposing nationalist and socialist revolutions; and began to define all Third World conflicts as extensions of East-West confrontation. With the advent of the Reagan administration, all these trends deepened and were pursued with extraordinary vigor: Human rights were not even a marginal consideration in policymaking; negotiation gave way to political and military confrontation; force became the preferred means of reasserting American global dominance.[15]

Clearly, the human rights policy was a luxury, a transitional phase. The public's anti-interventionist mood, a byproduct of Vietnam, opposed new military ventures for a while, but was too weak to sustain itself by creating a new set of structures. Lacking a firm institutional base, the public mood was overwhelmed by an effective propaganda campaign that equated Third World revolution with Soviet aggression.

In Latin America, the late 1960s and early 1970s brought rising nationalist movements, especially in the Andean countries. They were the outcome of the Alliance for Progress' failure to satisfy popular expectations of social and economic change, the continent's chronic balance-of-payments crisis, the steadily increasing external debt of most countries, and Washington's refusal to promote trade policies that benefited North and South equally. Against this background, new social forces emerged – socialist and nationalist, working-class and petty-bourgeois – willing to challenge the United States and pursue common goals. The new nationalists' principal urge was to extricate the area from its profound dependence on the hegemonic regional power and, at the same time, discover their own means for rapid economic growth. These developments confronted the United States with two problems: how to contain the nationalist upsurge and secure the region for foreign capital expansion.[16]

With Indochina and domestic resistance to expansionist policies, noninterventionism became the word during this period, along with at least formal accommodation to the notion of a plurality of governing ideologies. In October 1969, President Nixon articulated the new tolerance: "On the diplomatic level, we must deal realistically with governments in the inter-American system as they are."[17] But this "low profile" was not equivalent to a shift in White House objectives. All that changed were the modes of expression through which they were translated.

To counter regimes seeking increased autonomy, expropriating foreign-owned properties, and threatening American capital operations, imperial policymakers employed three tactics: financial and credit manipulation via bilateral, private, and international financial agencies; the build-up of allied regimes' military capabilities and contacts with U.S. military groups; and covert actions and subversion to facilitate the disintegration of hostile regimes.[18]

At the center of the regional movement was Allende's Chile (1970–1973), which nationalized U.S. properties and advanced a socialist development strategy intended to transform the Chilean economy and society on the basis of a mobilized working class. The movement's focal point was regional economic integration – the Andean Pact – involving Chile, Peru, Bolivia, Ecuador, and Colombia. Its centerpiece was an investment code designed to control the role of foreign multinationals in area economies. Despite formidable problems, the project took hold, based on the fortuitous appearance of nationalist regimes having similar goals. But the critical problem facing the regional compact was whether each regime could sustain its nationalist posture by creating a solid class base in state power.[19]

This new nationalist cycle coincided with an increase in inter-capitalist economic competition and a growing socialist-bloc commercial presence in Latin America, both leading to American losses, especially in the area of trade. Although the hemisphere's dependence on the United States for goods and markets slipped in the early 1960s, it declined dramatically during the early 1970s. Through the 1960s, U.S. exports hovered at around 40 percent of the continent's total imports; between 1970 and 1975, this figure fell from 37.2 percent to 30.6 percent. Latin America's exports to the United States as a percentage of total exports underwent a decline from about 40 percent in 1960 to 35.5 percent in 1975.[20] In 1973, Western Europe absorbed over 30 percent of the region's exports and provided about 30 percent of the region's total imports.[21]

Latin America's more diversified trade ties and the United States' declining position are strikingly illustrated in the cases of Brazil and Argentina. Although U.S. exports to Brazil increased from $676 million in 1970 to more than $1.3 billion in 1975, the combined value of West German, Japanese, and Netherlands exports to Brazil rose from $568 million to almost $2.5 billion. Meanwhile, Brazilian exports to the United States increased from $918 million in 1970 to approximately $3.4 billion in 1975, but were topped by the combined value of Brazil's exports to Japan, West Germany, the Netherlands, Italy, Sweden, Switzerland, and the U.K., which climbed from $915 million to just under $4 billion. To Argentina, U.S. exports increased from $420 million to $624 million between 1970 and 1975, while Japan's went up almost sixfold from $85 million to around $494 million and West Germany's more than doubled from $186 million to $424 million. Western European markets also assumed an increasingly important position in Argentina's trade. That country's exports to the United States increased from $159 million to $197 million between 1970 and 1975, while its exports to West Germany, Italy, and the Netherlands alone had a combined value of $651 million in 1975 compared to $560 million in 1970. The declining value of the U.S. market to Latin American exports extended to other regional countries, including Chile, where the value of its exports to the U.S. actually fell from $177 million in 1970 to $147 million in 1975. In contrast, West Germany and Japan rose in importance, accounting for Chilean exports valued at $294 million in 1970 and $426 million in 1975.[22]

From the imperial state's vantage point, regional modifications in trade and industrialization were tolerable. But the regime changes that instigated the regionalist strategy also brought, in some cases, a shift toward autonomy from the United States, which was far less tolerable. For those regimes that combined a regionalist strategy with internal structural changes and an independent foreign policy, the United States devised strategies (mediated through local institutional and class forces) to undermine them. The dependence of these "open" and "permeable" regimes on external financing for immediate and long-term economic operations (the legacy of the prenationalist period) and the parallel accumulation of large-scale foreign debts to U.S. public and private agencies and to U.S.-influenced international financial institutions further increased their vulnerability to outside pressures. The downfalls of Torres in Bolivia, Allende in Chile, Velasco in Peru, and Rodríguez in Ecuador were the result of challenges from interlocked external and internal opponents. As a by-product, the regional pact was severely undermined.

The disintegration of these nationalist processes was rooted also in the postwar diversification of American multinational capital beyond the traditional agro-mining centers of production into the industrial, service, and banking sectors of Latin America. Such permeated economies demanded political environments that would sustain and service the needs of the foreign multinationals. The political forms most appropriate to capitalist development "from above and outside" were labor-repressive, military-dominated regimes. The rise of permanent military or quasi-totalitarian dictatorships in Chile, Argentina, Peru, Uruguay, and Bolivia directly contributed to the reconstitution of U.S. hegemony and renewed high levels of multinational capital flows in the region. During the nationalist experiments (1969–1972), new U.S. direct investment in Latin America increased at an annual average rate of only $500,000; the period of disintegration or rightward shift of these popularly based regimes (1972–1976) saw this figure rise to $2 billion; while the period of dictatorial regimes promoting "free market" economic models and strict constraints on working-class organization (1976–1980) coincided with a dramatic rise in the *yearly* level of new U.S. multinational capital investment to $3.5 billion.[23]

The convergence of a disparate group of nationalist regimes in the late 1960s and early 1970s reflected their similar economic and political purposes. But also, each regime was based on a rather fragile state structure. The demise of these structures, through the working out of their conflicts and contradictions, through outside pressure, or both – paved the way for a revival of bilateralism by which the links between periphery and core were strengthened at the expense of regional ties. This shift in White House policy carried over into the Carter period. "In Latin America," wrote NSC advisor Brzezinski in early 1978, "we are no longer tied to a regional approach. We shall strengthen bilateral ties with the nations of Latin America while cooperating more fully with them in their global concerns."[24]

This overview of the currents in imperial state global and regional policy provides the context for comprehending many of the events to be described in this chapter: the breakdown of Cuba's regional political and economic isolation; the dissolution of the global economic blockade and state/class responses to this phenomenon; the failure of liberal efforts, centered in the legislative branch, to normalize bilateral relations; and shifts and changes in policy within and between administrations; and the unbroken thread of White House opposition toward Cuban foreign policy in the Third World.

The contours of Nixon-Ford-Kissinger policy toward Cuba

In 1967, President Johnson and Secretary of State Rusk directed Milton Barall, a senior State Department official, to prepare a confidential report on U.S. policy in the Caribbean. One of its conclusions was that the economic blockade of Cuba be maintained "until the Castro Government drops its Communist orientation."[25] Early during the next administration, a high-level policy review of U.S.-Cuban relations was made, at which time President Nixon remarked to an aide, "There'll be no change toward that bastard while I'm President."[26] The sentiments were echoed by his National Security Council advisor, Henry Kissinger, whose recommendations, according to a White House foreign-policy staff official, "went unerringly to the maintenance of Cuba's isolation."[27] Nixon and Kissinger also favored renewed covert operations, despite CIA Director Richard Helms' view that the risks involved in pursuing this line of action outweighed any likely gains.[28] Accompanying this predilection for "doubl[ing] our [CIA] operations against Cuba"[29] was a determination to "keep as much of our isolation policy intact as possible."[30] Speculations regarding any change in existing policy were buried in a secret February 1970 State Department telegram to American embassies in Western Europe and Latin America.[31] The Deputy Assistant Secretary of State for Inter-American Affairs, Robert Hurwitch, reaffirmed the fundamental tenants of Nixon White House policy during congressional testimony in mid-July, saying, "The Cuban Government has not abandoned or renounced its policies of engaging in subversion in the hemisphere. With respect to Cuba's military ties with the Soviet Union, we found even less reason to alter our policy toward Cuba."[32]

Two developments during the late 1960s and early 1970s, however, immensely complicated the Nixon-Kissinger effort to maintain Cuba's hemispheric isolation: the rise of ideologically diverse regimes pursuing various forms of economic nationalism and willing to take independent foreign-policy positions and an accelerated growth in trade and investment relations between Latin America and the rest of the capitalist world, principally Western Europe and Japan. This latter development contrasted sharply with the absence of serious capitalist-bloc economic competition with the United States during the 1950s and early 1960s. Also, the appearance of a cluster of popularly supported civilian regimes followed hard on the Kennedy-Johnson period when the region was dominated by dictatorial military governments enjoying close relations with Washington.

Although the anti-Castro diplomatic offensive in the first half of 1970 seemed a success, Washington was careful not to criticize publicly the two-year, $11 million trade agreement concluded between Cuba and the Christian Democratic Chilean government of Eduardo Frei. This pact reflected growing Latin American support for normal relations with Havana, for it was consummated amid a presidential campaign closely fought between antisocialist forces and an anticapitalist coalition under Salvador Allende.[33] White House concern over a possible left-wing victory in Chile was expressed in its September 1970 effort to revive fears of Soviet military involvement in Cuba as part of a broader regional strategy to influence the election.[34] But the socialists won, and Allende's decision to reestablish diplomatic relations with Cuba was extrapolated by Nixon as "a challenge to the inter-American system."[35]

The 1970 Chilean election coincided with OAS Secretary General Galo Plaza's discussions in Mexico City on the Cuba issue with representatives of a number of regional governments, all of which supported, to degrees, moves toward normalization. Yet the Nixon administration remained opposed. The State Department cabled its Latin American embassies to pressure allied governments to "hold the line."[36] In April 1971, President Nixon again dismissed negotiations with Cuba and linked any reexamination of U.S. policy to substantive, if vaguely defined, Cuban foreign-policy concessions – principally in the area of what Washington viewed as Havana's still active role in "exporting revolution" throughout Latin America.[37]

At the OAS again, December 1971 brought a series of meetings about a Peruvian proposal that members end all sanctions against Cuba. Chile, Ecuador, Jamaica, and El Salvador reportedly favored it, but the lack of a two-thirds majority forced termination of the debate.[38] Such regional efforts routinely found little favor in Washington.[39] In April 1972, Secretary of State William Rogers told an OAS General Assembly meeting that the United States could not support Peru's call for an end to Cuba's regional ostracism because the Castro regime still posed a "threat to the peace and security of Latin America and the Caribbean area."[40] Rogers' statement coincided with a White House directive to the Joint Chiefs of Staff and the Caribbean commands "to police the area 'by force if necessary'" to protect merchant ships of allied countries from harassment by Cuban naval vessels.[41] A month later, in May 1972, the OAS Permanent Council cautiously crept forward, deciding 14 to 1, with 8 abstentions, no more than to reexamine the organization's diplomatic and economic embargo of Cuba. In this instance, Washington's abstention exposed a desire to minimize its isolation on the issue, with the American delegate, Ambassador Joseph J. Jova, terming any effort to revoke the sanctions "politically unwise and juridically unsound."[42]

Growing Latin American support for reconsidering Cuba's pariah status arose not only because of a rising nationalist current in domestic and foreign policy, but must also be seen in the context of Havana's decision to institute "new policies" to meet "new conditions" in Latin America.[43] This shift was linked to the end of the guerrilla operations following Che Guevara's death in Bolivia in 1967 and the emergence of nationalist regional governments that expropriated foreign-owned properties and were prepared to pursue policies at odds with Washington. Given the divergent ideological outlooks of the political rulers of Chile, Peru, Ecuador, Venezuela, and Argentina, Havana's new regionalist strategy to break its bonds of isolation emphasized the external orientations, rather than the social bases, of these regimes. "Many forms of cooperation," Castro declared, "can be developed with countries that follow an independent foreign policy, that defend their national interests against Yankee imperialism."[44]

American officials conceded that Cuba had reduced its "subversive activities" in Latin America during the early 1970s, yet they preferred to interpret this phenomenon as a matter of more refined techniques and greater selectivity in the choice of allies, rather than as a policy switch.[45] "There will be no change," retorted President Nixon in November 1972, "no change whatever, in our policy toward Cuba unless and until – and I do not anticipate this will happen – Castro changes his policy toward Latin America and the United States."[46] Even the U.S.-Cuban hijacking agreement of February 1973 failed to generate enthusiasm to reexamine the isolation policy, for Secretary of State Rogers sharply distinguished one little accord from an overall relationship, locating the onus for any American shift squarely on changes in "the policies and attitudes of the Cuban Government. . . . We don't notice any change in the policies and attitude, and therefore our position remains the same.'[47] In March 1973, Assistant Secretary of State Hurwitch castigated those hemispheric governments such as Chile and Peru that had decided to flout OAS agreements and unilaterally move toward renewing relations with Cuba.[48] Nixon again hoisted the battering ram in his foreign-policy report to Congress in May, expounding on the Castro government's threat to regional stability and its Soviet military ties.[49]

Between 1973 and 1975, Cuba's political and economic isolation within Latin America began to crumble. A number of countries renewed diplomatic relations and even such previously hostile opponents as Venezuela and Colombia moved toward normalization, with Venezuelan Foreign Minister Aristides Calvani Silva invoking the OAS doctrine of "ideological pluralism" to justify official and unofficial exchanges with Cuba since 1973.[50] In May 1974, the outgoing Colombian government, in a surprising turnabout, formally requested a consultation among OAS foreign ministers to consider ending Cuba's exile; the request was generally interpreted as reflecting the thoughts of incoming President Alfonso López Michelsen.[51]

Cuba negotiated major financial and commercial agreements with Mexico and Argentina. In 1973, the Peronist regime in Buenos Aires extended a $1.2 billion line of credit; in mid-1974, Argentine businessmen signed agreements worth $100 million at a large Argentine trade fair held in Havana.[52] The Echevarria government extended a $20 million revolving credit line in early 1975, with the possibility of an increase to $80 million over two years to finance purchases of Mexican machinery, equipment, and raw materials; a few months later, economic cooperation agreements covering agricultural, industrial, extractive, and tourist sectors of the Cuban economy amounting to around $1.2 billion were signed in Havana.[53] During this period, the Cuban government also was highly visible in a number of subregional economic organizations, especially in Central America and the Caribbean. These included the Latin American Energy Organization established in October 1973, the Organization of Sugar Export Countries formed in 1974, the Caribbean Multinational Shipping Company of which Havana was a founding member in May 1975, and the Sistema Económico Latinoamericano (SELA) begun in October 1975 to promote economic cooperation among hemispheric countries. In May 1975, Cuba joined the Caribbean Committee for Development and Cooperation, an offspring of the United Nations Economic Commission for Latin America. Finally, it was also accorded observer status in CARICOM, the common market of the Caribbean's English-speaking countries.[54]

President Ford's installation in August 1974 did not disturb the hardline Cuba policy. The following month, the White House agreed to support an OAS review of the 1964 sanctions against the Castro government, intimating that it would abide by the majority decision.[55] Foreign ministers of the OAS gathered in November for the review and, in closed discussions, the U.S. delegation announced its intention to abstain on the vote, an action that predetermined the outcome. The final vote fell two short of the necessary two-thirds majority required to lift sanctions, as Guatemala, Brazil, Nicaragua, Bolivia, and Haiti followed Washington's lead. The Costa Rican Foreign Minister Gonzalo Facio angrily denounced the American role as one of "negative neutrality."[56]

At the same time, the bilateral relationship again had become the subject of discussions in Washington and Havana. Some U.S. officials believed that recent Cuban signals inviting a dialogue should be accorded study.[57] The assumption that conflicts in the region were in some fashion controlled by Havana was still in vogue during the Ford presidency and, therefore, any successful negotiation with the Castro government regarding its hemispheric policy could lay the basis for a strengthening of American interests in the area. A review of Cuba policy by Washington led to a series of secret "exploratory" meetings begun in November 1974 and continuing through much of 1975 attended by Assistant Secretary of State for Inter-American Affairs William D. Rogers and the executive assistant to Secretary of State Kissinger, Lawrence Eagleburger, to clarify major points of conflict and how to resolve them.[58]

Amid these developments, a provoking, agitated response to the specter of growing U.S. regional isolation over Cuba was delivered by Secretary Kissinger in March 1975. He downplayed White House concerns over Cuban behavior in Latin America and now linked any significant change in American policy "above all to [changes in] Cuba's external policies and military relationships with countries outside the hemisphere."[59] State Department officials drew a distinction between "regional considerations," which prompted Kissinger's speech, basically the administration's desire to accommodate Latin opposition to continued sanctions, and the totally separate issue of U.S.-Cuban bilateral relations: "The thing that's changed is U.S. policy in the OAS. U.S. bilateral policy has not changed."[60] Kissinger's pronouncement was intended to deflect attention from the growing rift with a majority of hemispheric countries who felt that the Cuba sanctions had outlived their usefulness and who no longer viewed Havana as a promoter of revolutionary movements against established governments. One appeasing U.S. gesture came at a July meeting of the OAS in San Jose, Costa Rica. The American delegation voted with fifteen others to terminate mandatory trade and other sanctions and allow each individual country to determine its own strategy in dealing with the Castro government.[61] Any progress on bilateral relations, however, still rested on "a change in attitude of Castro."[62] Assistant Secretary Rogers pointed out that "our policy and attitude toward Cuba are going to depend essentially on Cuba's foreign policy."[63]

As Kissinger's reference to Cuba's "relationships with countries outside the hemisphere" announced, one ironclad Ford administration condition for extending detente to Cuba was that Castro refrain from aligning with any political force or regime opposed by Washington or by American-supported movements and governments in the Third World. The Cubans, on the other hand, interpreted detente as not offering direct support to national liberation movements in the hemisphere or any significant aid to similar movements in other parts of the Third World. Castro differentiated between movements out of political power and the maintenance of independent diplomatic and political relationships with ideologically diverse *governing* regimes that might request Cuban economic or military assistance. Cuba's military involvement in Africa during the mid-1970s, principally its backing of the established, internationally recognized, socialist government of Aghostino Neto in Angola, grew out of precisely this distinction between movements and regimes.

American policy toward southern Africa during the 1960s and early 1970s favored white-minority regimes and Portuguese colonial rule.[64] Portugal's disintegrating hold on its empire's remnants created a situation in Angola in which three forces contended: the Popular Movement for the Liberation of Angola (MPLA) under the leadership of Aghostino Neto; the National Front for the Liberation of Angola (FNLA) headed by Holden Roberto; and Joseph Savimbi's National Union for the Total Independence of Angola (UNITA). Although the socialist MPLA was recognized by most African and West European governments as the legitimate successor to Portuguese rule, the U.S. executive branch's interagency "40 Committee" responsible for authorizing clandestine operation funds approved a $300,000 program of covert support for the FNLA in January 1975. That April, the CIA proposed a hundredfold expanded covert fund for both FNLA and UNITA forces in the form of an "Action Plan" including $32 million in arms assistance and the participation of CIA advisors and mercenary forces. Approval of the "Action Plan" in July by the "40 Committee" and President Ford coincided with an escalation of the struggle against the MPLA by the Portuguese military and secret police, the FNLA, and South African troops, who entered Angolan territory in early August and rapidly established a training base for anti-MPLA forces.[65]

During this period of mounting external and internal pressures against the MPLA, the Cuban presence on the side of the Neto

government was confined to 230 military instructors. In response
to an MPLA request, however, Castro dispatched several hundred
more military advisors. Bolstered thereby, and with Soviet arms
assistance, the MPLA reasserted its military superiority during
September and early October 1975, creating the likelihood that
it would continue to control the capital, Luanda, when the Portuguese were to withdraw formally from Angola on November 11,
1975. Yet South Africa launched a major invasion in late October
using 5,000 troops, which profoundly transformed things and
greatly jeopardized the MPLA's hold on Luanda. This was why
the Cubans agreed to Neto's urgent request for their military
involvement. Between November 1975 and March 1976, from
18,000 to 36,000 Cuban troops arrived to guarantee the MPLA's
survival and consolidate its hold on power, an action that determined the struggle's outcome. By mid-December, the South Africans' drive on the capital had been stopped. In February 1976,
the MPLA-Cuban forces also concluded successful military operations against UNITA and FNLA.[66]

Conservatives and liberals alike in the executive branch and in
Congress interpreted Cuba's actions in Angola not as an outgrowth of normal diplomatic and political relations between legitimate regimes, but as part of Havana's determination to sustain an
antagonistic relationship with Washington. In late November
1975, a meeting took place between Assistant Secretary of State
Rogers and a Cuban envoy, at which Rogers articulated the Ford
administration's opposition to Cuba's military support of the
MPLA government. Following a decision to break off the secret
U.S.-Cuba discussions that had begun a year earlier, the White
House continued its covert action program, which it hoped would
change the government in Luanda.

On December 21, 1975, President Ford declared that any possibility of improved bilateral relations had been vitiated by Cuba's
African venture. Shortly thereafter, Secretary Kissinger privately
concluded that the Castro government was "exporting revolution" on its own initiative, although he publicly blamed responsibility for the Cuban military presence in Angola on the Soviet
Union. His public stance was more useful for, while officials ceded
they lacked "virtually any leverage with respect to Cuba," American-Soviet detente was a basis for "considerable diplomatic leverage."[67] The White House described Castro as "an international
outlaw"[68] and even raised the possibility of direct U.S. military
involvement if Cuba widened its military role in southern Africa.[69]

In congressional testimony, Kissinger maintained that the decision to institute a formal National Security Council review on the question of military action against Cuba was simply part of normal contingency planning and represented no more than "a general precautionary review" of the Cuba problem.[70]

Cuba's foreign policy, specifically its active support of national and social revolution throughout the Third World, anchored the U.S.'s refusal to consider renewing bilateral negotiations. "There is no possibility of continuing any discussions with Cuba about the normalization of relations," announced Kissinger in April 1976, "as long as Cuban military forces are stationed in Africa, and as long as Cuba continues attacks on America, on American policy in Puerto Rico and elsewhere."[71]

The Carter administration: change with continuity

The Carter administration, inheriting an executive branch whose authority had deteriorated through America's involvement in Indochina and its role in the overthrow of the democratically elected Allende government in Chile,[72] sought ways to temper the decades-old interventionist attitude by which actual or potential challenges to particular capitalist states were perceived as threats to the whole capitalist order. Still, Carter's view of detente as encompassing the Third World coincided with Nixon's and Ford's. In a March 1978 memo to the White House, National Security Council advisor Zbigniew Brzezinski referred explicitly to this interpretation of detente in discussing Soviet involvement in the Horn of Africa: "The Soviets must be made to realize that detente, to be enduring, has to be both comprehensive and reciprocal. If the Soviets are allowed to feel they can use military force in one part of the world – and yet maintain cooperative relations in other areas – then they have no incentive to exercise any restraint."[73] Once the Carter White House realized that Third World revolution could not be contained through detente (a snag it attributed to the Soviet's lack of cooperation), the stage was set for a shift in the overall direction of American foreign policy. The assessment of Soviet behavior also became the pretext for reverting to a policy of hostility toward Cuba, which U.S. policymakers still characterized as Moscow's surrogate.

Early Carter proposals and rhetoric regarding Cuba were concrete expressions of the new anti-interventionist, anti-Cold War image the administration wanted to project. The Director of the

Office of Cuban Affairs in the State Department, Wayne S. Smith, contrasted the new policy with the "inflexible" and "anachronistic" approach of the Nixon-Ford era,[74] and an NSC official described the Carter White House in its first months as seeking "to move very quickly" to improve relations with Cuba.[75] The lines of diplomatic communication were reopened, paving the way for what one State Department Cuba specialist described as a series of "very carefully calibrated" measures to thaw bilateral ties.[76] These included the cancellation of U.S. reconnaissance flights over Cuba, discussions on terrorism, the lifting of travel restrictions on U.S. citizens visiting Cuba and the use of American dollars there, the conclusion of a fishing-rights and maritime-boundaries agreement, the exchange of middle-level diplomats, and the establishment of "special interest sections" in Washington and Havana. The NSC also ended the blacklisting of foreign ships engaged in Cuba trade, restoring their eligibility to carry U.S.-government-generated cargoes such as foreign aid and agricultural commodities.[77]

Still, the new U.S. approach did not extend to any softening in Washington's historic opposition to revolutionary Cuba's foreign policy in the Third World and its refusal to compensate expropriated American investors. In March 1977, Vice President Walter Mondale declared that the administration was "far short" of any decision to end the trade embargo.[78] Although not wedded to the rigid normalization-after-compensation formula, senior Carter policymakers still clung to the basic notion that solving the compensation issue was "a precondition for major trade,"[79] lest "a bad example [be set] for other countries and other [American] investments elsewhere."[80] That August, the State Department and the NSC joined forces to oppose a memorandum prepared by the President's medical advisor, Dr. Peter Bourne, who recommended that at least the embargo on foodstuffs and medical supplies be terminated. The White House's rejection of the Bourne proposal was influenced principally by Cuba's expanding military involvement in Africa.[81] And it was this latter issue, more than any other, that brought the temporary thaw in U.S.-Cuban relations to an abrupt halt. The buildup of Cuban troops in Angola, Ethiopia, and other parts of the African continent exhausted the possibilities for further normalization "on a measured and reciprocal basis."[82] Beginning in late 1977, Carter officials, in statements reminiscent of those uttered by President Ford and his Secretary of State, Henry Kissinger, began attributing this impasse largely, if not exclusively, to the absence of any "clear evidence of Cuban restraint in Africa."[83]

President Carter put his position clearly, if clumsily, in April 1977: "withdrawal of Cuban troops is a dominant factor in Angola and in other places around Africa [and] the attitude of Cuba to withdraw its unwarranted intrusion into the affairs of Africa and other nations would be a prerequisite for normalization, yes."[84] The White House decision to link diplomatic recognition of the MPLA government to the withdrawal of Cuban troops, even though Luanda still faced a serious military threat from South Africa and its UNITA ally operating from staging bases inside Angola, did create some unease within the State Department. Secretary Cyrus Vance termed this decision unrealistic and believed that its only effect was to erode U.S. leverage with the Angolan government.[85] United Nations Ambassador Andrew Young also argued for a tempered response to the Cubans in Angola, contending that they introduced "a certain stability and order" into a volatile situation.[86]

The President was unmoved, preferring to side most closely with NSC advisor Brzezinski's resolute belief that the Cubans were the source of unrest in Angola and the rest of southern Africa and that any major U.S. diplomatic initiative toward Angola or Cuba should be predicated on substantial Cuban troop withdrawals. In pushing these arguments within the foreign policy bureaucracy, Brzezinski was not above manipulating or distorting the meaning of CIA estimates of the number of Cuban military personnel in Africa. In a mid-November 1977 background briefing, for instance, he announced that the possibility of normalized relations with Havana had receded further as a result of CIA figures revealing that thousands more Cuban troops had arrived in Angola since July. These figures, however, were simply a revised CIA estimate of the number of Cuban troops in Angola in July.[87]

Although the Carter White House targeted Cuba's southern African involvement as a major obstacle to better relations between Washington and Havana, it was even more preoccupied with Cuba's military presence in Ethiopia and the Horn of Africa. Before its overthrow in February 1974, the Selassie monarchy in Ethiopia was America's most important postwar ally in the Horn of Africa. It provided the United States with access to airfields and ports and agreed to the establishment of the Kagnew Communications Station at Asmara, which became a key spoke in the American global communications network. Between 1951 and 1976, U.S. economic assistance to Ethiopia exceeded $350 million. During the same period, the feudal regime received the largest amount of U.S. military aid in black Africa: more than $270 million in loans and credits, and training programs in the United States for 3,500 military personnel.[88] The armed forces coup signalled a gradual deterioration in U.S.-Ethiopian relations. As the new economic policy – nationalization and land reform – took shape, American military assistance began to decline.

In December 1974, the Ford administration initiated a major reassessment of Ethiopia policy. Although critical of the Provisional Military Administrative Government's (the Dergue) domestic policies and its treatment of political opponents, the White House rejected any halt to economic and military assistance and adopted a "wait and see" approach. Although Washington responded tardily to a February 1975 Dergue request for $29 million in emergency military aid following a series of defeats in the war with Eritrea and a major challenge for control of the provincial capital of Asmara, total U.S. military aid increased from $28.5 million in 1974 to $57.5 million in 1975, and it reached its highest level ever in 1976 when cash sales alone amounted to more than $100 million.[89] Secretary of State Kissinger reportedly played a central role in formulating this aid policy, which was shaped by largely strategic considerations. In August 1976, an American official characterized the Ethiopian regime as "inconsistent" rather than "basically anti-United States."[90] By year's end, however, the White House had begun to view the Dergue's internal reforms, its footdragging on compensation for expropriated American properties, its human rights record, and its developing military relationship with the Soviet Union through a more hostile lens.[91] One of President Ford's last acts before leaving office was to terminate all military grants to Ethiopia, confining future military assistance only to credit sales.[92]

In February 1977, a bloody struggle for power occurred within the Dergue. The outcome was a victory for the most "radical" faction under the leadership of Mengistu Haile-Mariam. Later that month, the new Carter administration announced that U.S. military assistance to Ethiopia would be reduced because of human rights violations. In April, all arms supplies were suspended. The White House decided to substantially reduce its Military Assistance Advisory Group (MAAG) personnel in the country, and to close the Kagnew Communications Station.[93] Mengistu's response was to shut down the Kagnew base immediately, expel the MAAG team, terminate U.S. Information Agency operations in Addis Ababa, and dramatically expand Ethiopia's ties with the Soviet Union. In May, he signed a number of economic, scientific, and cultural pacts, and an estimated $400 million worth of military agreements with Moscow.[94] Beginning in early 1976, the Dergue also had begun to develop closer ties with Cuba, whose government was particularly impressed by the military regime's domestic policies.

Paralleling the growth in Soviet-Ethiopian relations was the rapid weakening of Moscow's longtime alliance with Somalia, whose government now expressed an interest in developing new links with the United States and the capitalist world. In April 1977, an enthusiastic President Carter directed Vice President Mondale to inform Secretary of State Vance and NSC advisor Brzezinski "that I want them to move in every possible way to get Somalia to be our friend."[95]

Amid this muddle of shifting alliances, Somalia reasserted its long-held claim to the Ogaden Province of Ethiopia. Following unsuccessful efforts by Cuba and the Soviet Union to mediate a settlement over it, several thousand Western Somali Liberation Front guerrillas invaded the Ogaden from bases in Somali territory. In July 1977, they were joined by approximately 40,000 regular Somali army troops.[96] The Dergue's unanticipated battlefield crisis was partly offset by increased military assistance from Cuba and the Soviet Union. In November, presuming that the United States and other Western countries would step in as arms suppliers, the Somali government severed diplomatic ties with Cuba and ordered the Soviet military mission to leave the country. The expected Western arms assistance failed to materialize, but the Somali actions eliminated the remaining obstacle to an immediate "full Soviet-Cuban commitment to Ethiopia."[97]

When the Somali-backed guerrillas entered the Ogaden in May 1977, the Castro government sent a military advisory group to Addis Ababa. The State Department cautioned that any large-scale military commitment by Havana would have serious consequences for the thaw in U.S.-Cuban relations.[98] At year's end, Western intelligence sources indicated a still limited Cuban military involvement of around 400 advisors. This changed dramatically within a matter of months. Agreeing to a request from an internationally recognized government confronting what it described as an emergency situation in the Ogaden, Castro despatched 17,000 Cuban combat troops to Ethiopia between January and April 1978.[99] As the conflict raged in the disputed province, NSC advisor Brzezinski was heard exclaiming that "the problem isn't the war, the problem is the Soviet and Cuban presence."[100]

Cuban and Soviet military commitments in Ethiopia and the Horn of Africa generated a major bureaucratic conflict between the National Security Council and the State Department. National Security Council advisor Brzezinski and Secretary Vance disagreed both over why the Cubans and Soviets were there and what course of action the United States should pursue to counter their presence. According to Brzezinski, the Cuban troops were a "Soviet-sponsored deployment,"[101] part of a calculated, global strategy to expand Moscow's influence in the resource-rich countries of the region and gain an important strategic foothold that could threaten the West's access to Middle East oil shipped from the Persian Gulf via the Horn of Africa. Cuba's perceived role as a "surrogate" for or "handmaiden" of the Soviets made it a potential threat to American "vital interests" in the Horn and other parts of Africa;[102] its troops were a direct challenge to the U.S. global position and could not be allowed to pass "cost free."[103] Brzezinski located the Cuban-Soviet involvement squarely within the context of East-West relations, he advocated an aggressive, confrontationist U.S. response that did not exclude the possibility of direct military action,[104] and he accused the State Department of taking "an excessively benign view of the Soviet and Cuban penetration of Africa and underestimating its strategic implications."[105] In a similar vein, Frank C. Carlucci, the CIA's Deputy Director, characterized the Cuban-Soviet presence in Africa as "the most determined campaign to expand foreign influence in Africa since it was carved up by the European powers in the late 19th century."[106]

Secretary of State Vance, not unsympathetic to the notion of Soviet "adventurism," contended that the Cubans and the Soviets were simply exploiting another "target of opportunity" in Ethiopia and the Horn, taking advantage of regional conflicts and local developments to expand their influence.[107] Regarding Cuba, another State Department official contested the simplistic "Soviet surrogate" interpretation offered by the NSC, suggesting that the explanation was more complex: Cuba was in Africa "because it wants to be," while simultaneously performing "as a military ally of the Soviet Union."[108] Secretary Vance warned the President against defining the Horn conflict exclusively as an issue involving the superpowers, because that would put the United States in the impossible position of seeking an objective it had virtually no chance of achieving, that is, the withdrawal of the Soviets and Cubans from Ethiopia.[109] The State Department presented the case for a measured White House response, one that did not threaten other American objectives and interests in Africa and elsewhere in the Third World.

Ultimately, the interagency debate was overtaken by a growing executive-branch consensus over what was perceived as an "open ended" Cuban military involvement in Africa or what one NSC staff member described as Cuba's "failure to exercise any kind of restraint internationally."[110] Playing free and fast with evidence or proof of its charges, the White House seemed determined to ascribe each and every instance of unrest in Africa to Havana's machinations. In May 1978, to take one example, Katangese exiles based in Angola invaded, for the second time in 14 months, the mineral-rich Zaire (formaly Katanga) province of Shaba. Despite Castro's rush to inform the head of the U.S. Interest Section, Lyle Lane, that his government categorically denied any participation in or support for the invasion, the White House and NSC insisted that there was "overwhelming"' evidence of Cuban complicity. Yet, when Office of Cuban Affairs Director Wayne Smith examined the exact same evidence, he reached a diametrically opposed conclusion: It provided no basis whatsoever for pronouncing that Cuba "encouraged or in any way supported it."[111] Another executive-branch official charged with evaluating the CIA intelligence reports on which most of the administration case was constructed later admitted that "the evidence just wasn't there to back [President Carter] up."[112] In his memoirs, Secretary of State Vance also conceded that the CIA evaluations were "ambiguous and, as it turned out, not very good."[113]

The Cuban-Soviet military presence in Ethiopia did prompt a major White House policy review, leading to an enlivened emphasis on East-West confrontation and a downgrading of the earlier Carter focus on African nationalism, economic development, and opposition to white minority rule. In May 1978, Secretary Vance told a closed congressional hearing that "strenuous efforts" were underway to counter Cuban and Soviet activities in Africa, including increased military assistance to friendly regional governments and various public and private diplomatic initiatives.[114] Not long after, a State Department official remarked that "the mood on Cuba [is] anti-improvement in the White House and the National Security Council."[115]

Although the White House expressed profound hostility toward Cuba's foreign policy, it lacked the levers to force any devolution of the Caribbean country's role in Africa and the Third World. Beyond forceful appeals by President Carter to the governments of Venezuela and Brazil, where he visited in March 1978, to pressure Cuba to withdraw militarily from Africa, the options remained strikingly limited.[116] A diplomatic offensive was begun within the nonaligned world to isolate Cuba on the grounds that it was a "surrogate" of the Soviet Union.[117] This U.S. attempt to induce the nonaligned nations "to put heavy pressure on the Cuban use of force in Africa" reached its peak at the nonaligned conference in Belgrade, Yugoslavia, in July, where a number of pro-American members unsuccessfully sought to rescind the decision to convene the next annual meeting in Havana.[118]

Meanwhile, although U.S.-Cuban relations deteriorated during 1978, there was a return to the bargaining table, initially at Castro's request, and a series of discussions that culminated in a unilateral Cuban decision allowing thousands of dual citizens and political prisoners to emigrate to the United States. But Cuba's Africa policy blocked any movement in the direction of normalized bilateral relations. Secret talks in May between NSC Deputy Assistant and Latin American specialist David Aaron and Cuban government representative José Luis Padrón were confined to the political prisoners issue. The NSC had instructed Aaron that all other questions were off limits until Havana indicated its readiness to repatriate its African-based troops. In August, the scene moved from New York and Washington, D.C., to Atlanta. For this new round of negotiations with Padrón, the NSC's Aaron was accompanied by Under Secretary of State for Political Affairs David Newsom. Although Cuba's military withdrawal from Africa still remained the NSC's *sine qua non* for any improvement in relations between the two countries, the State Department viewed the Atlanta meetings as an opportunity to discuss a broad range of foreign-policy issues, as well as a compensation formula for U.S. investors who suffered property losses during the early period of revolutionary reconstruction, and the release of political prisoners. But the hardline NSC position held sway as it refused to consider even minor concessions proposed by some administration officials (lifting the trade embargo on medical supplies, renewing commercial aid service, promoting a cultural exchange program) in return for the prisoners' release. No further movement was achieved at a follow-up meeting in Cuernavaca, Mexico.[119]

In early 1979, the senior State Department Cuba official, Wayne Smith, wrote an assessment of Cuba's African policy that intermingled critical comments with acknowledgment of Havana's positive role in improving relations between Angola and Zaire, its support for recent proposals by a number of Western governments for settling the Namibian dispute, and its backing of black majority rule based on democratic election in Rhodesia (Zimbabwe). Upon Smith's completion and presentation of the assessment, an NSC official set him straight on the prevailing administration line: "We aren't interested in your so-called balanced assessment. . . . We want to emphasize that the Soviets and the Cubans are the aggressors."[120] It would be a mistake, however, to conclude that the State Department was a hothouse of opposition to official policy. On the contrary, State remained no less publicly adamant than the White House that Washington's policy toward Cuba would be guided by the Castro government's preparedness to withdraw its troops from Angola, Ethiopia, and other parts of Africa, to make further concessions over political prisoners, and to satisfactorily resolve the long-standing problem of compensation for expropriated American property-holders.[121]

Although Carter administration hostility toward Cuban foreign policy in the Third World reflected a common thread linking all American administrations since 1959, it did not vitiate the White House disposition to at least keep talking with Havana. The State Department, in particular, attached considerable importance to maintaining some form of dialogue, and it opposed a June 1978 Senate resolution that would have severed all links.[122] Department officials argued that passage of this resolution "would damage important U.S. interests" especially by closing the U.S. Interest Section in Havana, which had played a key role in gaining the release of American citizens imprisoned in Cuba and in repatriating others and their families to the mainland.[123] According to an NSC staff member, the U.S. government desired to "preserve sufficient flexibility" to pursue a policy toward Cuba as it saw fit.[124]

Contrasted with Africa, Cuba's policy in Latin America elicited a much less hostile Carter White House response. This was largely a function of a series of regime transitions since the early 1970s that displaced economic and political nationalists with a more conservative set of state governments. Although Havana sought durable relations with nationalist regimes in the Caribbean and aligned itself with popular movements in Central America, State Department officials acknowledged that its direct political and military involvement was "almost negligible," or relatively low-keyed and prudent.[125] So, when Carter himself spoke of a "growing Cuban involvement" in the area to Congress in mid-June 1979, generally interpreted as a reference to the Nicaraguan conflict, State officials were at a loss to elaborate on the President's assertion.[126] For intelligence reports continued to describe Cuba's policy as one of caution, reflecting a desire to avoid any pretext for aggravating relations with Washington.[127] At the same time, the administration was determined not to allow Cuba to take advantage of "targets of opportunity" such as the March 1979 overthrow of Eric Gairy's corrupt and repressive regime in Grenada by the socialist New Jewel Movement under Maurice Bishop.[128]

During 1979, Brzezinski continued to advocate "more sustained U.S. pressure on Cuba and on the Soviet Union," but made "relatively little progress" until late July when the administration received what turned out to be highly misleading and imprecise intelligence reports referring to a possible Soviet military combat brigade in Cuba.[129] In mid-August, Brzezinski briefed the President on the "discovery" and sent a memorandum to Secretary of State Vance and Secretary of Defense Harold Brown "urging concerted action at putting more pressure on Cuba." Brown "beefed up" the memo while Vance "diluted" it. Afterwards, Brzezinski directed his staff to continue lobbying within the government "to develop wider bureaucratic consensus for a response to the Cuban problem."[130]

Secretary Vance expressed limited enthusiasm for the new intelligence data, writing to Florida Senator Richard Stone that there was "no evidence of any substantial increase in the Soviet military presence in Cuba over the past several years or the presence of a Soviet military force."[131] He subsequently noted that this was the first administration since the 1962 Kennedy-Khrushchev accords banning nuclear weapons or delivery systems in Cuba that interpreted the understanding to include Soviet military personnel. Neither the 1962 agreement nor the 1970 prohibition on Soviet submarine bases made any reference to the exclusion of Soviet ground forces. "Closer examination of the records," Vance writes, "revealed that earlier American administrations had known of Soviet ground units in Cuba and had not regarded them as worth concentrated intelligence surveillance."[132]

The alleged presence of a Soviet brigade in Cuba was first announced by the chairman of the Senate Foreign Relations Committee, Frank Church, in early September 1979, following a briefing by Under Secretary of State David Newsom. Church's action was shaped largely by personal political considerations. A liberal Democrat from conservative Idaho, he was one of the more vulnerable senators running for reelection in November 1980. Projecting a new hardline foreign-policy approach to undermine his electoral opponents, Church called on the White House to demand the brigade's immediate withdrawal from Cuba and proposed that the Senate defer consideration of a strategic arms treaty with the Soviets until the issue was resolved. Similarly, domestic political considerations conditioned President Carter's handling of the issue. With a presidential election just over a year away, Carter was anxious to dilute the growing perception that he was too indecisive, too conciliatory to confront the Soviet Union in the Third World.

When that same September the White House itself announced the "discovery" of the Soviet brigade, its timing was clever, for the announcement coincided with a meeting of nonaligned countries in Havana chaired by Fidel Castro. According to Vance, though, the urgent information had been in the pipeline for 17 years: "the unit in question had almost certainly been in Cuba continuously since 1962."[133] In fact, the largely NSC-orchestrated statement was so transparently fraudulent that even Washington's political establishment rejected it; the Democratic majority leader in the Senate, Robert C. Byrd, labelled the "discovery" a "pseudo-crisis."[134] According to Brzezinski, a private meeting with Byrd ultimately convinced Carter that the Soviet brigade did not constitute a threat to the United States.[135] Nonetheless, the "restrained" Vance proposed that the White House still should take a number of "measured unilateral actions" against Cuba, which were outlined by the President in a speech on October 1 that ended the "brigade crisis."[136] Carter announced that a Caribbean Contingency Joint Task Force would be established in Key West, Florida; the U.S. military presence in the region would be upgraded; maneuvers would be expanded and more highly coordinated; and economic and military assistance to Caribbean and Central American countries would be increased. These measures, together with efforts to establish a multinational Caribbean seagoing patrol force[137] and a hemispheric "peace-keeping force," reflected the growing ascendency of the Brzezinski position in the foreign-policy bureaucracy to "get tough" with Cuba.

Henceforth, policy toward Cuba was filtered almost exclusively through the prism of the East-West global confrontation. Determined to counter Cuban political and military influence not only in the Central American-Caribbean area, but also in Africa and other parts of the Third World, Carter ordered the State Department to consult closely with the Pentagon, the Central Intelligence Agency, and the Agency for International Development to coordinate their anti-Cuban efforts.[138] As part of the offensive, Washington tried to block Cuba's election to the United Nations Security Council during late 1979 by lobbying for Colombian membership. The resulting stalemate was resolved only after both Cuba and Colombia accepted a compromise to withdraw their candidacies and agree to Mexico's nomination to the Security Council. France supported the United States on this occasion, largely owing to displeasure over a declaration at the nonaligned countries' 1979 meeting in Havana that called for the decolonization of French possessions in the Caribbean.[139]

Secret meetings between low level State Department and NSC officials and Cuban government representatives continued into the late summer of 1980 with Washington still emphasizing that foreign-policy concessions from Havana were *the* price for any improvement in bilateral relations. Recalling the formative discussions around mid-1978, one U.S. official observed: "We wanted to explore if they were prepared to moderate their behavior – to pull out of Angola and limit their time in Ethiopia."[140] Approximately two years later, another American official brought the issue full circle: "They [the talks] didn't go anywhere because the Cubans were not willing to address improving their [international] behavior."[141]

The disintegration of the global economic blockade

Even though the Nixon, Ford, and Carter administrations successfully opposed consideration of any fundamental shift in U.S.-Cuban relations as long as Havana remained wedded to an internationalist foreign policy, they proved less adept at maintaining Cuba's international economic isolation. The Cuba blockade developed innumerable fissures after 1968 as capitalist regimes and Western financial institutions expanded trade and monetary relations with the Castro government. This unravelling was paralleled by, and must be viewed against the background of, a sharp rise in economic competition between the United States and the rest of the capitalist world. No longer the dominant economic power it was in the 1950s and through part of the 1960s, Washington's leverage in resolving economic conflicts among capitalist-bloc countries in a manner that it desired was weakened.

The accelerated intercapitalist competition between the United States, Western Europe, and Japan, and the existence of a Cuban state with strong institutional and political roots truncated Nixon's and Ford's efforts to pursue their sanctions. The European connection was immeasurably strengthened late in 1971 by the arrival in Havana of the first official British trade mission to visit since 1959 and the negotiation of a new four-year commercial agreement with Spain, which had been held up for months by the growing Cuban debt to Madrid and Spanish claims regarding nationalized properties owned by its citizens.[142] Moreover, the European Economic Community foreign ministers in mid-1972 agreed to extend general trade preferences to a number of Third World countries, including Cuba.

The island's trade with the nonsocialist world as a percentage of its total trade climbed from 25.3 percent in 1968, to 32.1 percent in 1972, to 41.2 percent in 1974.[143] Between 1971 and 1975, capitalist-bloc imports increased from 30 percent to 49 percent of Cuba's total imports.[144] And neither trade deficits with its Western commercial partners nor an accumulating short-term debt to Western private banks proved serious obstacles to multinational bank and state-guaranteed credits, principally because Havana remained a good risk.[145]

The expansion and scale of capitalist trade with Cuba during the first Nixon administration are indicated in the tables below.

The levels of Cuba's trade throughout the 1970s remained directly tied to the fortunes of the island's most important hard-currency export on the world market – sugar. Abnormally high world sugar prices, rising from 20.83 cents a pound in 1973 to 65.39 a pound in 1974, provided the wherewithal for a major expansion of capital-goods purchases from Western European, Japanese, and Canadian markets in the mid-1970s.[146] During 1975, the value of Cuban imports from the capitalist countries reached almost $1.8 billion, an increase of more than 70 percent over 1973.[147] Anticipating sustained high sugar prices, the Castro government's 1976–1980 economic plan predicted continued

Western vehicle imports 1968–1972

Origin	Automobiles and jeeps	Buses	Trucks	Spare parts
Italy	1,556	564	1,038	Total combined value
U.K.	512	217	646	of $36 million
France	538	–	1,460	
Japan	–	597	720	
Spain	–	83	1,123	

Source: Economist Intelligence Unit, *Quarterly Economic Review of Cuba*, No. 1, March 1975, p. 4.

Western market share of selected Cuban imports, 1972

Produce	Cif value (mn. pesos)	Identified Western share (percentage)	Principal Western supplier
Powdered milk	26.4	86	U.K.
Maize	10.2	60	Mexico
Beans	22.4	60	Chile
Animal feed	17.4	66	Peru
Raw materials for pharmaceuticals	6.4	41	Japan
Pesticides	19.3	89	Switzerland
Tires	13.6	30	–
Tinplate	9.3	29	Japan
Steel tubing	8.0	20	Japan
Turnkey plants	29.8	34	–
Machine tools	2.4	16	U.K.
Excavators and lifters	7.6	45	U.K.
Ball bearings	4.1	35	Sweden
Parts for agricultural equipment	12.4	12	Spain
Parts for construction equipment	6.8	69	France
Parts for railway rolling stock	5.3	35	Canada
Automobiles	2.2	20	Italy
Buses	2.3	99	Italy
Trucks	18.9	36	Japan
Automobile parts	31.4	25	U.K.

Source: Economist Intelligence Unit, *Quarterly Economic Review of Cuba*, No. 1, March 1975, p. 5.

large capital-goods purchases from nonsocialist market economies. But Havana was utterly unprepared for the dramatic collapse of sugar prices to 8 cents a pound in 1976, which stalled the
country's expansion and pushed the annual average growth rate
down from 12 percent during 1970–1974, to 8 percent or 9 percent in 1975, to 6 percent or 7 percent in 1976.[148] The value of
Cuba's hard currency exports declined from $1.6 billion in 1975
to $0.8 billion in 1977, inducing a leap in the trade deficit and
forcing the leadership to revise downward its import projections
from the capitalist bloc and renegotiate a number of delivery
schedules.[149] In early 1977, for example, the Japanese government was asked to postpone delivery of $150 million worth of
exports.[150]

The decline in Cuba's exports to nonsocialist countries from 33
percent of total exports in 1975 to 16 percent in 1979 and the
parallel fall in Cuba's imports from the same sources from 49 percent to 17 percent of total imports correlates directly with the
peaks and lows in the world market price for sugar. Nonetheless,
the Western countries still accounted for 25 percent to 30 percent
of Cuba's total annual average trade turnover during the latter
1970s. In 1979, Japan, Spain, and Canada together purchased
almost 50 percent of all Cuba's exports destined for the capitalist
world and provided 56 percent of Cuba's imports from the
West.[151] The value of Canada's exports to Cuba from 1975 to
1980 made it Canada's second most important Latin American
market.[152] Despite its shift to a socialist economy, Cuba remained
significantly dependent on critical items produced in capitalist
economies that were either unavailable within the socialist-bloc
trading system or of inferior quality or in periodic short supply.

Cuba's ability to gain access to the Eurocurrency market and
other sources of Western banking capital, and to negotiate a growing number of trade deals on credit terms underwritten by capitalist governments, helped create the cracks that appeared in the
trade blockade during the Nixon administration. The National
Westminster Bank in England, for instance, provided state-guaranteed loans totalling $12 million between 1969 and 1971 largely
for capital plant and equipment purchases.[153] In another, not atyp-
ical case, the Japanese approved a deferred-payment export valued at $10 million, financed by the Hino Motor Company, for the
sale of 550 buses in August 1970.[154] Between 1973 and 1975,
these spigots were turned on full force as Havana negotiated a
number of major state-guaranteed commercial credits from capi-

talist countries, credits augmented by sizable Eurocurrency loans. In August 1975, for example, the Cubans entered the Euromarket to acquire a $100 million loan floated by an international banking consortium. "No American bank could subscribe," wrote *The Economist*, "but Russian, Canadian, British, Italian, and Middle East capital lapped the loan up."[155] Similar examples of capitalist-bloc largesse were evident in the provision of long-term, multi-million dollar state credits to the Havana regime. These Western governments tended to identify with the statement of a senior Japanese official in 1975 who, following a fact-finding mission to Cuba, expressed support for making available state credits and export insurance to national companies trading with Havana because "the economic situation in Cuba is quite stable and their next five-year plan is really quite conservative."[156] They were also attracted to the notion of a centrally planned economy that ensured high rates of domestic savings and investment in capital goods.

Cuba's hard-currency crisis and associated external trade problems during the mid- and late 1970s, together with accumulated outstanding debts to Western bankers totaling approximately $1.3 billion by the end of 1976, did not significantly effect the island government's borrowing capacity in the international capitalist money markets. Moreover, the guarantees implied in Cuba's membership in the socialist-bloc state banking organization, COMECON, largely protected against the application of more stringent loan conditions. An idea of the extent of bilateral credits and private banking and Eurocurrency loans to Cuba over the six-year period 1973 to 1978 is indicated in the table on the opposite page.

Although Cuba's hard currency debt to these capitalist sources worsened during 1979 and 1980, credit extensions were still forthcoming in the form of state and private banking monies.[157] In 1979 it successfully negotiated a seven-year line of credit from a consortium of European banks headed by Crédit Lyonnais for 220 million Deutsche marks; a 100-million long-term credit in Belgium francs; and a 12.5-billion yen loan syndicated by the Bank of Tokyo and twenty-seven other lenders.[158] In 1980, the Spanish government organized a Canadian $150-million loan mainly for heavy equipment and ships, while Britain's Export Credits Guarantee Department underwrote an $11-million credit arranged by

International and bilateral financing extended to Cuba by Western countries, 1973–1978 ($ millions)

Source	Value	Date authorized	Terms
Argentina	1,200	August 1973	Long-term credits for the purchase of Argentine industrial and transportation equipment, to be repaid in eight years from time of delivery.
Eurocurrency market	30	1973	Medium-term credits.
Spain	900	December 1974	Trade credits for the purchase of Spanish ships and plants.
Canada	25	December 1974	Credits to cover 80% of purchase price of three small oil tankers for delivery in 1977–1978.
U.K.	408	December 1974	National Westminster Bank Loan.
Eurocurrency market	119	1974	Medium-term credits.
France	350	January 1975	Long-term credits for the purchase of French machinery, plants, and transportation equipment; to be repaid in 10 years.
Canada	155	March 1975	$100 million credit to be repaid in 10 years at competitive interest rates; $10 million development loan to be repaid over 30 years at 3% interest and a $3 million technical assistance grant extended in February 1975. Credits of $24 million extended in December 1974 and $18 million in April 1974 for purchases of oil tankers and rail equipment.
U.K.	580	May 1975	Medium-term credits at less than 7.5% interest for the purchase of British capital goods.
Canada	14	Fall 1975	Credits to cover sale of MLW-Worthington locomotives, etc.
Eurocurrency market	234	1975	Medium-term credit to be repaid in five years at 1.75% over LIBOR.
Eurocurrency market	134	1976	Medium-term credits to be repaid in five years at 1.75% over LIBOR.
Japan	10°	February 1978	Consortium of 24 private Japanese banks. Seven-year loan.
Eurocurrency market	100+	1977 & 1978	

°Billion yen.
Source: Business International Corporation, *Cuba At The Turning Point* (New York, July 1977), p. 79; "France Ready to Invest $350 Million in Cuba," *Journal of Commerce*, January 22, 1975, p.11; "Cuba: Seeking West European Ties," *Eastwest Markets*, February 10, 1975, p.3; "Canada Acts to Capture More of Cuban Markets," *Journal of Commerce*, March 30, 1975, p. 3; "Canada Steps Up Cuba Trade as US Stance Softens," *Business International*, March 21, 1975, p.91; "Canadians Arrange Loans for Cubans," *Journal of Commerce*, March 24, 1975, p.1; Malcolm Rutherford, "U.K. to give Cuba £250m. credit," *Financial Times*, May 21, 1975, p.1; "Cuba: British Credit," *Eastwest Markets*, June 2, 1975, p.7; Eileen Goodman, "Castro's Cuba not such a bad place," *Canadian Business*, September 1976, pp.81–86; World Bank, *Borrowing in International Capital Markets: Foreign and International Bond Issues, Publicized Eurocurrency Credits*, Second Quarter, 1978, EC-181/782, September 1978, Table 2.2, p.53; Economist Intelligence Unit, *Quarterly Economic Review of Cuba*, No.1, March 1978, p.7

Morgan Grenfell for Cuba's expected purchases of sugar equipment and spare parts.[159]

Although the U.S.-promoted blockade of Cuba was never airtight, and it deteriorated markedly during the first half of the 1970s, the Nixon and Ford administrations remained determined to enforce the economic isolation strategy to its fullest. The Department of Commerce actively pursued "diversions" of American goods to Cuba and prosecuted the offending companies. Between January 1969 and December 1971, penalties were imposed on a French manufacturer of agricultural chemicals who purchased materials from an American supplier for resale to Cuba, two French firms that participated in the illegal reexportation of American-produced chemical fertilizer from France to Cuba, and a Dutch company that purchased $120,000 worth of truck parts from a Canadian firm, in full knowledge that the parts were American, and sold them to Cuba.[160] Between July 1974 and June 1976, similar cases were prosecuted involving British, Dutch, Canadian, Mexican, and American firms. Helping the Department were U.S. manufacturers who volunteered information about suspicious orders.[161]

At a global level, the White House effort to sustain the embargo is illustrated by three examples involving Australia, France, and Bangladesh. In July 1970, on the basis of U.S. intelligence reports that Cuba was negotiating with the Australian subsidiary of Massey-Ferguson, a Canadian multinational, for twenty sugar-cane harvester combines, the Department of Commerce inquired as to whether any American parts or technical data were involved. Though there were none, the State Department expressed irritation that the "Australian provision of agricultural equipment and credits would help relieve some economic pressures on [the] Cuban regime," especially in the aftermath of the economic dislocations caused by the "10-million ton" sugar harvest. Telegramming the American Embassy in Canberra "to discuss this matter with appropriate GOA [Government of Australia] officials," the State Department also suggested that Embassy officials raise the specter of congressional retaliation over U.S. purchases of Australian trucks and sugar for shipment to Cambodia and Vietnam to forestall, if possible, consummation of the harvester deal.[162]

The economic counselor from the U.S. Embassy in Canberra held discussions with officials of the Australian Departments of Foreign Affairs and Trade and Shipping in mid-April and early

May. At the time, it was confirmed that Massey-Ferguson-Australia had in fact shipped the twenty harvesters worth around $640,000. Australian officials further noted that these were "part of [a] 'virtually' firm order for 100 units," and they saw "no reason for additional orders not to be placed if [the] harvesters [are] satisfactory in Cuban operations." The conservative Liberal Party government defined the harvesters as nonstrategic items, regarded the sale as a small-scale and normal commercial transaction by a company that had experienced major economic losses during the past year, and decided on a "hands-off" policy.[163]

In the U.S. Congress, both liberals and conservatives opposed the sale. The chairman of the House Agriculture Committee, Robert Poage, observed that some committee members wanted to retaliate by banning Australian sugar imports – at a moment when Canberra was seeking to increase its quota to a level worth nearly $40 million annually.[164] As Poage himself commented, "You can't slap your best friend in the face and expect to get away with it. The Australians couldn't have picked a worse subject . . . at a worse time."[165] J. William Fulbright, Senate Foreign Relations Committee chairman, also vented his ire, saying that while the Australian Prime Minister lavished praise on the United States and President Johnson "as the savior of the free world against communism," he did not see fit to stop Australian companies from "doing good business with Cuba."[166]

Washington expressed its unease over future possible Massey-Ferguson sales by continuing to pressure Canberra to "hold the line." In June 1971, Secretary of State Rogers personally "discussed firm U.S. policy on Cuba" with Australia's Deputy Prime Minister Anthony. Yet some six months later, information reached the State Department that another trade deal between Massey-Ferguson-Australia and Cuba was in the works. The Department immediately cabled the American Embassy to take the matter up with Canberra and restate U.S. opposition to such trade.[167]

The Nixon administration gained a more satisfactory outcome from its dispute with France over exports to the United States containing Cuban nickel. France was one of the countries most affected by the American decision to ban all purchases of foreign products that included Cuban-derived nickel, following the Castro government's expropriation of the U.S.-owned Nicaro nickel mining complex in late 1960. Although forceful, continuous American pressure on Paris had achieved some success during the 1960s, it was not until the Nixon period, when Washington and

Paris negotiated an arrangement that "effectively excluded Cuban nickel" from French goods destined for the United States, that the American ban on French imports containing nickel was lifted.[168] Influenced in part by its government's accord with the United States, Le Nickel of France, which purchased about one-third of Cuba's output at below world-market prices, decided not to renew its three-year agreement with Havana when it came due in December 1970. *Business International* suggested an additional reason for Le Nickel's shift: a concern not to endanger its joint nickel-extractive operations with two U.S. multinational corporations in New Caledonia.[169]

Bangladesh, the third renegade, was informed in mid-1974 that low-interest American government loans for the purchase of urgently needed food would depend on the immediate curtailment of gunnysack exports to Cuba. In September, Dacca capitulated and agreed to stop shipments. The White House kept its side of the bargain, confirming its intention to sign contracts to provide Bangladesh with 100,000 tons of wheat and 50,000 tons of rice to relieve a food shortage that had reached crisis proportions.[170]

In contrast to these discrete conflicts with particular countries, a broader tear in the blockade curtain materialized in late 1973, as various governments demanded that their countries' subsidiaries of U.S. multinationals accept orders from the Cuban government. Washington was drawn into these disputes because of the restrictions imposed on American trade with Cuba by the Trading with the Enemy Act. The Canadian and Argentine governments were in the forefront of raising this issue with the United States, most notably in three cases involving American automobile, locomotive, and office-furniture subsidiaries.

In September 1973, Juan Perón returned to the presidency of Argentina with an overwhelming 62 percent of the popular vote. A senior State Department official expressed the Nixon White House view of Perón as a stabilizing influence, perhaps the last alternative to a more radical state and social transformation.[171] The new president immediately reasserted the hegemony of the conservative sector of the Peronist movement, weakened the power of the Peronist left, and plotted to destroy the emerging guerrilla challenge. Neither the imposition of selective foreign-investment controls, nor Perón's decision to reestablish diplomatic and commercial relations with Cuba, support the economic-nationalist Andean Pact, and assume a leading role in hemispheric demands for the restructuring of the OAS lessened Washington's sympathy with the new Argentine government.[172]

The Peronist regime signed a six-year, $1.2 billion contract with Havana in 1973 to extend supplier credits, largely for purchases of locally produced industrial goods. The Cubans were especially interested in automobiles and trucks from Argentine subsidiaries of the Ford Motor Company, General Motors, and the Chrysler Corporation.[173] This initiated the first major "third-country" subsidiary conflict, and its resolution set the tone for future confrontations among host governments, subsidiaries of American multinationals trading with Cuba, and U.S. regulations covering such trade.

Scarcely two months after Perón was elected, General Motors and Chrysler, in accordance with the Cuban Assets Control Regulations, applied to the Treasury Department for licenses to enable their Argentine subsidiaries to trade legally with Cuba. An internal Department memorandum prepared for Assistant Secretary John M. Hennessy cautioned that a "strict application" of the letter of the law would probably lead to a confrontation of a kind that the Argentine government would prefer to avoid. The memorandum also noted that, while Treasury "has operational control of the granting of the licenses," this particular instance required a policy determination by the State Department before a decision could be made.[174]

The desire on the part of the White House, the State Department, and the National Security Council to maintain a cordial relationship with Buenos Aires was accorded the "highest importance" in discussions over how to resolve the dilemma.[175] However, participants also noted the possible multiplier effect of a positive decision, some arguing that even one breach in the embargo policy would trigger "an onslaught."[176] Others took the position that capitalist trade in automobiles was already going on and that sales by the Argentine subsidiaries would do no more than further erode a failing policy.

With the approval of the White House and the State Department in April 1974, Treasury granted an exemption to Argentina's three U.S. automobile subsidiaries, issuing licenses primarily to avoid a rupture in the evolving government-to-government relationship. Rejecting the most extreme policy option, the State Department still counseled against drawing sweeping conclusions about U.S.-Cuban ties. "I am not implying that there has been no change," declared Department spokesman John King. "I am asserting it."[177] The decision about Argentina, Secretary of State Kissinger remarked, "was not based on consideration of Cuba policy."[178] Toward the Castro regime, American policy remained one of "cool procrastination."[179]

The Canadian government on at least two occasions in 1974 interceded in behalf of U.S.-owned or controlled Canadian companies negotiating deals with Cuba. In March, it asked the State Department to waive Trading with the Enemy Act regulations to permit MLW-Worthington Ltd. of Montreal (59 percent controlled by Studebaker-Worthington, Inc., of New Jersey) to export a number of locomotives to Cuba. The Canadian-based subsidiary confirmed on March 18 that it had signed a $15-million contract to provide thirty new diesel locomotives and refurbish existing U.S.-built ones.[180] In this instance, both Washington and Ottawa sought to avert a conflict in the interest of their overall relationship. Although Prime Minister Pierre Trudeau insisted that the sale take place and indirectly threatened to withdraw federal orders and subsidies to the American-controlled company if it did not, he also "helped avert an angry clash with Washington by keeping the MLW-Worthington sale quiet and by not seeking a showdown on the significant question of American infringement of Canadian sovereignty."[181] Instead, Ottawa merely requested that the U.S. government not prosecute the three American members of the company's Board of Directors who, incidentally, had voted against the sale and then resigned to avoid conflicts with U.S. laws. *Business International* described the Nixon administration's response as similarly low-keyed and mindful of more important ties. "It appears that the U.S. government has chosen simply to ignore the transaction, rather than precipitate a confrontation with the Canadian government."[182]

In late 1974, the U.S. government became embroiled in a dispute with a Toronto-based manufacturer wholly owned by Litton Industries, Inc., of California over the proposed sale to Cuba of $500,000 worth of desks, chairs, and filing cabinets. On this occasion, Ottawa played a more active role than it had over the MLW-Worthington deal. After being informed of the Cuban request by its subsidiary, Litton initiated an "informal inquiry" with executive-branch officials in Washington.[183] Under the Trading with the Enemy Act the transaction was declared illegal, leading the parent company to stop the sale. But Canadian Foreign Minister Alastair Gillespie publicly raised the issue of national sovereignty, charging the United States with "intolerable interference" in Canadian affairs.[184] Litton's Californian executives reapproached the Treasury Department in January 1975 for an exemption, but the company's position as a large defense contractor left it vulnerable to reprisals. "Litton recognized its exposed position . . . and so didn't push."[185] The sale received approval on February 13, principally because "the Canadians [the Trudeau government] pressed"[186] and the Ford administration's concession had little effect on the bilateral relationship. Rather, it acknowledged the need to be flexible about U.S. subsidiaries trading with Cuba so as not to drift into "conflict situations" with important allies and "complicate our relations with those countries" over issues which many of them consider resolved.[187]

Despite such complications, a consensus endured in the American government opposing any fundamental dismantling of the U.S. trade embargo of Cuba or termination of increasingly ineffective efforts to limit Cuba's commerce with other capitalist countries. Secretary of Commerce Elliot Richardson conceded that the embargo returned few, if any, benefits to the United States and didn't "achieve our political objectives," but he supported retention of the policy for its "symbolic" value.[188] At the State Department, Assistant Secretary Rogers expressed the official view that "the economic importance of the embargo to Cuba is not inconsiderable," especially with Cuba's continued lack of access to American spare parts and technology. He also termed it an important negotiating weapon or "bargaining chip" for future discussions on normalizing bilateral relations.[189]

In August 1975, however, following the July OAS Foreign Minister's meeting that voted to end OAS trade prohibitions against Cuba, the Ford administration decided to modify three aspects of the U.S. trade embargo, including the ban on "third party" subsidiaries. This policy change was shaped largely by a White House desire to "remove a recurrent source of friction" between Washington and some of its most important Western allies who trade with Cuba. Henceforth, the United States agreed to issue licenses to American subsidiaries that asked to trade with the Castro regime in compliance with host-government policy, as long as the goods involved were nonstrategic and contained, at most, only a small portion of U.S. manufactured components; to provide bunkering facilities in U.S. ports for third-country ships engaged in the Cuba trade; and to end the ban on foreign aid to countries whose vessels or aircraft carried goods to and from the Caribbean island.[190] Predictably, the memorandum from Secretary of State

Kissinger to senior administration officials announcing the actions emphasized that they were taken "in conjunction with the OAS Resolution rather than our bilateral policies toward Cuba."[191]

The subsidiary-sales decision gave *de jure* status to what was already *de facto*. Exporters could now secure special licenses from the Treasury for transactions, but had to comply with a number of other requirements: no sales of strategic goods, no technology transfers, no involvement of U.S. dollar accounts, no long-term credit extensions, and strict limits on the amount of U.S. parts contained in the exports to Cuba.

The limited available evidence suggests that the Carter administration initially may have prosecuted the embargo policy less actively than its predecessors. Its shift to a more confrontationist foreign policy in 1979 and 1980, however, was accompanied by continued American concern to limit Cuba's economic relations with the capitalist world. Although without much success, Washington tried to prevent Western banks from participating in the multi-million Deutsche mark syndicated loan organized by the French bank, Crédit Lyonnais, in 1979. Officials at Crédit Lyonnais countered U.S. pressures with the argument that the transaction was purely commercial and bore no relation to official state policy.[192] Speculation also surfaced that the Carter White House was the "prime mover" in a cancellation by Singer and Friedlander, the Swiss subsidiary of a British bank, of a $30-million Swiss-franc issue sought by the Banco Nacional de Cuba in November 1979. Singer and Freidlander stopped the transaction on the verge of completion, contending that it preferred not to antagonize the Swiss banking establishment, which opposed the loan apparently on political grounds.[193]

Finally, the U.S. government, without warning, invoked 1963 legislation in November 1980 to ban the import of a number of special steels from the French Creusot-Loire Company because they contained Cuban nickel. One interpretation of this action was that it was a response to Creusot-Loire's success in negotiating a major supply contract with the Soviets – a contract that might have been awarded to the American consortium of oil multinationals, ARAMCO, if it had not pulled out of the bidding in the wake of the Afghanistan invasion.[194] But the ban on French steels fit the general pattern of growing support for direct action against Cuba that had taken hold at the highest echelons of the administration.

Executive-congressional relations and U.S. policy toward Cuba

American policy toward Cuba during the 1970s was characterized by a relatively high degree of consensus between the White House and Congress, punctuated by occasional efforts on the part of mainly liberal Senators to force a change in what they believed was an inflexible and increasingly counterproductive White House stance – both politically and economically. But these legislative opponents of executive-branch policy at no point spoke for more than a small minority of their colleagues in the House or the Senate. Their isolation persisted despite their motivation to push for consideration of a new approach so that the United States might maximize its possibilities of wresting those basic concessions from the Cubans (compensation, withdrawal of Cuban troops from Africa) over which there was virtually no disagreement within official Washington.

During the Nixon and Ford presidencies, some legislators specifically criticized Cuba's exclusion from the politics of global detente. Although sharing White House hostility to socialism in Cuba and looking forward to the island's reintegration into the capitalist world, these mostly liberal members of Congress supported a flexible, less schematic interpretation of the "spheres of influence" policy. This liberal challenge was shaped by several considerations that continued to be articulated through the decade. First, it was linked to changing perceptions of the Cuban regime. They acknowledged its durability and stability and noted that its "authority is unchallenged by legitimate rivals," regardless of the country's internal political and economic problems.[195] Second, it rested on the belief that Havana had largely dropped its support of Third World liberation movements, especially in Latin America, possibly to concentrate on the problems of building socialism in one country. Third, these legislators argued that, given Cuba's proliferating ties with hemispheric countries, present American policy was isolating the United States, not Cuba, from the region. Fourth, expanding economic ties between Havana and the capitalist bloc simply reinforced their view that the "rigid and inflexible" White House policy made little sense.[196] Finally, there were some advantages to reestablishing diplomatic relations. "A listening post in Cuba would be important to us," one Senator observed . "We would gain by an Ambassador and his staff including the usual CIA agents on the spot in Havana."[197]

The leading proponent of a new approach was Senator Edward M. Kennedy, who contrasted Cuba's pariah status with growing U.S. political, economic, and military relations with Latin American dictatorial regimes. He contended that the "outdated and unrealistic" approach to Cuba reflected "an archaic cold war strategy" that was strikingly inappropriate in a period of global detente and accommodation.[198] In Kennedy's view, the China analogy was apposite.[199] The growing irrelevance of isolation based on fears of the export of revolution and military ties with the Soviet Union, the mounting relevance of Cuba's commercial links with a number of Washington's closest allies, declining hemispheric support for the boycott, and the failure of the Cuban model to find favor in other parts of Latin America were sufficient evidence, according to Kennedy, that American policy toward the island regime was "crumbl[ing] under the weight of its own contradictions."[200] Another Senate advocate of a policy reassessment was succinct: "U.S. policy toward Cuba . . . should be based on U.S. interests rather than on residual antagonisms."[201]

Overall, however, congressional attitudes during this period identified with Nixon's Cold War rhetoric. Speaking for most of his colleagues, the influential chairman of the House Foreign Affairs Committee, Dante B. Fascell, declared that, in the absence of any Cuban movement out of the Soviet orbit and toward the restoration of parliamentary rule, no benefits to the United States could possibly accrue from any change in policy.[202] Some conservative members of Congress were even critical of the executive branch for its failure to apply the type of "economic screws" necessary to circumscribe Cuba's trade with the Western World.[203] In July 1970, the House Foreign Affairs Committee, a stronghold of opposition to any change in American policy in the absence of substantive Cuban concessions, held the first of a series of hearings, extending over the decade, focusing attention on the Cuban-Soviet connection.[204] Congressional opponents of Nixon's policy termed unrealistic the Committee's (and the executive branch's) demands that Cuba sever military relations with the Soviet Union and all links with nationalist and revolutionary movements in Latin America. The alternative to a policy of rapprochement was the likelihood of more and more diplomatic setbacks for the White House, especially in the region to its immediate south.

In January 1973, these early, isolated calls to rethink U.S. policy received the unexpected support of eleven Republican House members in a statement entitled "A Detente with Cuba." The signers contended that a dialogue with a view toward normalization would not only accommodate global and regional trends, but might also benefit American traders and multinationals. They were careful, though, to emphasize that a dialogue was only the beginning and that the "full restoration of diplomatic relations" would await the resolution of those basic issues that had shaped years of White House antagonism toward the Cuban Revolution.[205] Senator Robert C. Byrd, a conservative-moderate Democrat, added his voice to calls for a policy reassessment, posing the question, "At what point is a harsh, hardline policy toward Cuba no longer a viable one, or perhaps even a counterproductive one?"[206]

In late March 1973, the Western Hemisphere Affairs subcommittee of the Senate Foreign Relations Committee initiated hearings on what chairman Gale W. McGee described as the need for "a more realistic approach" to the Cuba problem.[207] The administration's position, argued before the subcommittee by Robert Hurwitch, Deputy Assistant Secretary of State for Inter-American Affairs, restated White House opposition to Cuba's Soviet military ties and the belief that Havana was still "a threat to the peace and security of the hemisphere." The Castro government has not "abandoned its goals of subverting other governments in the hemisphere. It has simply become more cautious, more selective, and more sophisticated in its 'export of revolution,' and has directed its resources to those areas where it estimates the opportunity for interference greatest." He dismissed as inappropriate the China analogy on the grounds that the decision to seek detente with both China and the Soviet Union was based on a rigid conception of great-power diplomacy and spheres-of-influence politics. "I think we have demonstrated our pragmatism with respect to Cuba: where there is no overriding U.S. interest, there are no grounds for seeking accommodation with an openly hostile nation."[208]

The majority subcommittee position decried the "rigid patterns" evident in White House thinking, viewed the rationale for existing policy with great skepticism, and expressed concern about the global and regional implications of maintaining unbending policies toward Cuba.[209] In a revealing exchange with Senator J. William Fulbright over Cuba's "export of revolution" in Latin America, Hurwitch conceded "that this threat has diminished" and acknowledged that even a country such as Venezuela, which had been on the receiving end of Castro's revolutionary foreign policy in the early and mid-1960s, concurred with the view that Cuba no longer represented a serious threat to its government.[210]

The most pressing issue for subcommittee liberals was the relationship between the divergent regional political and economic tendencies that had taken hold in a number of countries and Cuba's new hemispheric strategy that sought to promote a broad nationalist grouping increasingly independent of, and in opposition to, the United States. "Let us defuse the Cuban question," they concluded, "or it is going to blow up in our face."[211] Whereas the Nixon White House and its congressional allies insisted that any move to unravel elements of the embargo strategy would inevitably take on a "life of its own" leading to a complete dismantling of the isolation policy, congressional liberals preferred to stress the regional implications of doing nothing, particularly at a time when the Indochina experience placed significant limits on Washington's capacity to exercise its military option to safeguard threatened U.S. political and economic interests in the Third World.

Senator McGee outlined an alternative, long-term approach that did not differ markedly from that of the executive branch in its ultimate goal, which was to "exploit the situation" to produce a greater integration of Cuba within the capitalist world economy. He favored an incremental approach to restoring bilateral relations which, in the process, would gradually open more of the Cuban economy and society to American interests.[212] Assistant Secretary Hurwitch opposed this strategy, suggesting that it could merely hasten hemispheric realignments around a nationalist or anti-imperialist pole: "it is all one ball of wax and when you pull one string you really unravel the entire policy or you run a very serious risk of doing so . . . to my knowledge, there is nothing that you can touch with Cuba. As I say, this is all one ball of wax, and if you pull one string you have to be prepared to see your entire policy unravelled."[213] The subcommittee chairman expressed dismay at this lack of a "more realistic posture" and the apparent executive-branch intent to "batten down the hatches and ride it through another time around" at an upcoming OAS Foreign Ministers meeting.[214]

Throughout late 1973 and 1974, individual members of Congress persisted in their opposition to the State Department's "very intransigent policy position" over Cuba.[215] They repeatedly singled out State's failure to comprehend the impact of the policy on America's global and regional interests and of the counterproductive trade embargo that limited multinational corporations' access to the potentially valuable Cuban market."[216] In April 1974, the Senate Foreign Relations Committee approved, 12 to 0, a nonbinding resolution attached to a State Department authorization to end the trade embargo and restore relations with Havana.[217] Again, however, liberal unease was not equivalent to fundamental disagreement over the larger goals to be pursued in the process of normalization. The liberals differed with the White House over timing and tactics, but agreed that the Cubans would have to address such key issues as the Soviet military presence, the "export or revolution," and the question of compensation for nationalized American properties as part of the gradual end of hostilities. The near complete consensus over these issues in both branches of government was evident in the "liberal" Senators Jacob Javits' and Claiborne Pell's report to Congress on their trip to Cuba in September 1974.[218]

Following the transition from Nixon to Ford in August 1974, the advocates of normalization increasingly focused their efforts on repeal of the trade embargo, which they described as "a diplomatic and economic incongruity" that "in no way serves whatever purpose it was originally created to serve. The embargo simply has not worked."[219] Early in the Ford administration, the House International Relations (formerly Foreign Affairs) Committee chairman, Dante Fascell, apparently was instrumental in mobilizing a narrow majority of committee members to vote against an attempt to end the trade embargo through an amendment to the Foreign Assistance Act.[220] In March 1975, Senator Kennedy introduced a bill to bring about the embargo's demise, contending that the White House position had "not produced any discernable benefit for the United States."[221] In May, two House subcommittees jointly held a series of hearings on a bill to remove the restrictions on direct trade with Cuba and the prohibition on aid to nations that traded with Cuba or whose ships entered the island's ports. Congressional advocates of the bill based their position on the failure of most Western countries to support the economic blockade, Castro's preoccupation with internal economic development at the expense of an "adventurous" regional foreign policy, and the economic losses that resulted from "cutting off a major market for American manufactured goods."[222]

Study missions to Cuba during 1975 consistently emphasized the benefits of lifting the boycott. In discussions with Cuban officials, visiting congressmen became aware of the likely market for

American agricultural products, industrial goods, farm and heavy-equipment machinery, spare parts, medical supplies, foodstuffs, sugar-processing equipment, and technological expertise.[223] This led even some legislative supporters of executive-branch policy to push for limited changes, for they saw the economic benefits to their districts of lifting the embargo. In November 1975, for example, Senator J. Bennett Johnston and Representative John B. Breaux, both from the major rice-growing state of Louisiana, argued that the national interest would best be served by allowing direct Cuban purchases of American rice. Conferring with Cuban officials in Havana, Breaux concluded that rice imports would become a priority once the embargo was lifted. It's a crop "we have a heck of a surplus of." Before 1959, Cuba annually purchased 165,000 tons of American rice. Later, when U.S. growers were burdened with a surplus, the Castro government was forced to shift suppliers, purchasing 90,000 tons of Italian rice through a European subsidiary of an American multinational. Louisiana and other mainland rice centers were displaced not only by socialist suppliers, but by rival capitalist enterprises.[224]

Other legislators stressed the broader advantages of renewed two-way trade: "The knife of the embargo . . . is a needless division between the United States and many Latin American nations; it denies employment and earnings to American workers; it deprives American consumers of lower-priced Cuban sugar and other commodities."[225] But in Congress as a whole, support for terminating the economic sanctions always was confined to a few individuals; the majority remained profoundly hostile to any American initiative until, as one Senator put it, "we . . . have some concrete assurances that reciprocal concessions will be made by [Castro]."[226]

Again, what this debate revealed, besides congressional liberals' isolation, was the overriding consensus: Executive-branch concerns would have to be resolved in any future negotiations. The liberals, for instance, never gave consideration to developing a notion of U.S. economic interests outside the sphere of multinational capital. Their policy preference was based on the same corporate interest as that of the state. As one leading Senate advocate of normalization conceded, "my instinct would be to recognize Cuba since they obviously are in control of the island, but then once having established diplomatic relations, undertake to review all the conditions, compensation, expropriated property."[227]

There was also a shared opposition to Cuba's support of both revolutionary movements and anticapitalist regimes in the Third World. Havana's pursuit of a foreign policy that conflicted with U.S. regional and global interests was anathema to the legislative branch as a whole, as it was to the President, and liberal supporters of normalization were not about to contest Ford's shift to a more confrontationist pose in the latter half of 1975 – largely in response to Cuba's growing military involvement in southern Africa. Representative Jonathan B. Bingham, chairman of the House International Trade and Commerce Subcommittee and a leading proponent of change, terminated subcommittee efforts to lift the trade embargo, citing the Castro regime's "pattern of disruptive and interventionist activities in various parts of the world."[228] Quickly, the entire congressional offensive to normalize relations with Cuba ground to a halt.

Early Carter actions on Cuba revived hope that a change in the sanctions policy was a realistic possibility. Legislators supportive of dismantling the economic blockade reiterated their arguments to bolster the "new policy." Another special congressional study mission to Cuba in February 1977 described the embargo as having "long outlived its usefulness as a weapon against the Cuban Government. It serves no U.S. purpose."[229] One House leader declared that not only had it "not brought down the Castro government," but that "there is no evidence that it will."[230] Other elected officials stated that the longer it remained in force, the more difficult it would be for American multinationals to penetrate the Cuban market.[231] The embargo was also seen "to deny the United States even the slightest influence on Cuban policies and activities and to block any payment on U.S. claims."[232] Given the durability of Cuba's revolutionary government, Washington's policy, in the view of legislators pushing for a change, should have adjusted – even a partial lifting of the embargo would have provided American public and private agencies with "increased opportunity to influence Cuban policies and actions on issues of concern to us."[233] They were convinced that, otherwise, Havana would not negotiate the settlement of outstanding compensation claims, the removal of Cuban troops from Africa, the release of political prisoners, and other issues most crucial to the imperial state: "Without a lifting of the embargo, those disputes will simply continue to fester."[234] Subsequent congressional debate, however, still exposed overwhelming support for executive-branch policy in the absence of Cuban initiatives regarding concessions.

In May 1977, the Senate Foreign Relations Committee debated a proposal offered by George McGovern to permit two-way trade in medicine, agricultural supplies, and foodstuffs. One committee member called the proposal "a giveaway of many of our most valuable bargaining chips,"[235] and most opposed its intent. By a relatively close vote (10 to 7), however, the committee accepted a McGovern amendment to his original proposal to permit only the sale of U.S. goods to Cuba. Meanwhile, the House passed a foreign-aid bill that lifted restrictions against food aid to countries trading with Cuba and Vietnam, but voted decisively (288 to 119) in favor of an amendment barring aid to or trade with both socialist countries.[236] In June, a potential conflict between the House and Senate over trade with Cuba was resolved prematurely when McGovern voluntarily withdrew his committee-approved substitute proposal for limited one-way trade – probably because he knew the Senate would reject it.[237] That same day, June 16, 1977, Senator Robert Dole, with twenty cosponsors, introduced another amendment opposing diplomatic recognition and any modification of the trade embargo until the Castro regime agreed to accommodate the long-held executive-branch preconditions for a change in policy.[238]

Once again, the Senate debate revealed minimal divergence between the majority and minority positions. What disturbed liberals such as Senator Charles Percy was not the demands included in the Dole amendment, which "we would like to see achieved," but the lack of "flexibility" in the current policy and especially the White House's refusal "to try different and new approaches."[239] Senator McGovern agreed that the Dole amendment incorporated "all matters that need to be laid on the negotiating table as we move toward better relations with Cuba," but he objected to putting American officials "in a straightjacket as to what the agenda may be before we ever get to the negotiating table."[240]

In an effort to narrow the tactical disagreements, Senator Robert C. Byrd, backed by some of his more liberal colleagues, introduced yet another amendment. Byrd proposed that bilateral negotiations be conducted on a "reciprocal basis" and that they "take into account" such issues as compensation for affected U.S. investors and Cuba's military commitments in the Third World.[241] At the same time, he remained adamantly opposed to establishing diplomatic relations with Havana "until such time as the Cuban Government stops its adventurism in Africa." Still, Byrd favored at least reopening the lines of communication and, while he expressed support for the Dole amendment, he doubted that the United States could "realistically expect to achieve those objectives if we say, at the start there will be no diplomatic recognition until Cuba has done 1, 2, 3, and 4?"[242] The Byrd amendment was agreed to by a vote of 54 to 37, then was tacked on as an amendment to the original Dole amendment and passed by 91 to 1, with 8 not voting.[243]

Continued opposition to changing U.S. policy toward Cuba was confirmed strikingly in June 1978 when Senator Dewey Bartlett, on behalf of thirty colleagues, introduced a resolution requesting that the White House shut down the interest sections in Washington and Havana, deny all applications for commercial trade licenses related to the Cuban market, stop the normalization process, and link any future movement to Cuba's military withdrawal from Africa.[244] Following an acrimonious debate, the resolution was adopted by a vote of 53 to 29.[245] For the remainder of the Carter presidency, legislative debate on U.S. policy toward Cuba was virtually nonexistent.

The incapacity of proponents of changes in Cuba policy to gain broad congressional support was partly a reflection of the institution's parochialism – "Politically, there [were] no payoffs."[246] More important, it was an index of the legislature's historic tendency to defer to the executive branch in the area of foreign policy. The liberals' failure to affect even minor shifts in American policy during the 1970s, notwithstanding the proliferation of hearings, study missions, and reports critical of existing relations, is eloquent testimony to the Congress' marginal role in the making of U.S. foreign policy. They were unable to convince the House or Senate leadership or gain broad support among the members. Substantial majorities in both chambers remained welded to the hardline policy emanating from the White House and, over selective issues such as compensation for nationalized American property holders, were even prone toward more rigidity than the executive branch.

U.S. policy and American business interests

One of the major arguments used by congressional liberals in their efforts to lever a change in U.S. policy toward Cuba has been the potential economic losses suffered by American business interests. This theme was taken up by the business community itself during 1974 and 1975. Paralleling the renewed executive and legislative focus on Cuba, corporate executives began to exhibit a new-found interest in the Cuban market. Although viewed by most American multinational corporations as a relatively small export outlet compared to the enormous potential of the Soviet Union and China, it was still "not one to ignore if it can be served by U.S. plants."[247] An official of the Association of American Chambers of Commerce in Latin America put it this way: "They are a physically accessible market. Other countries are starting to trade and we want to be in there as early as possible to gain whatever share we can of the market."[248] But interested mainland companies labored against a rigorously enforced trade embargo that only facilitated the efforts of competitors in Western Europe, Japan, Canada, and elsewhere to capture the Cuban market.[249] American computer corporations, for example, competitively dominant around the world, blanched as their French counterparts secured an "important foothold" in the island economy.[250] They could not understand why Cuba was excluded from Washington's detente policy.[251]

The lost sales generated growing corporate disaffection with executive-branch policy. "Why," asked one U.S. businessman, "is it that Canada gains the profit from a deal, when my company, which itself manufactures the same product, is denied the ability to even compete."[252] A Massachusetts wood producer, seeing a market for sporting equipment and furniture in Cuba, similarly questioned why other capitalist competitors "should . . . be getting the business I could be getting?"[253] Another irritation was Cuba's access to generous lines of external credit. "The companies are aware that they [Cuba] can get credit and if there is any reason to open up Cuba this is one of the reasons."[254]

Exploratory U.S. corporate interest in Cuba's potential as a market for technology, agricultural machinery, transport and communications equipment, medical supplies, building materials, computers, agricultural and industrial chemicals, fertilizers, rice, office equipment, sugar cane processing equipment, spare parts, and a multitude of consumer items grew by leaps and bounds during the first half of 1975. The Burroughs Corporation, for one, initiated "'preliminary research' . . . to determine the nature and the extent of the Cuban market for business machines and other Burroughs products."[255] Other companies also awaited their first opportunities. "If Cuba was to open up today, we could start shipping traffic tomorrow," said the president of the Florida East Coast Railway. A Dow Chemical Corporation official declared "Dow is ready to go. . . . We could rent an office in Havana tomorrow and be shipping [agricultural chemicals] from our facility in Freeport, Texas, within 30 days." Numerous pre-1959 suppliers of air conditioners, refrigerators, soft drinks – all sorts of goods – were poised. The Carrier Corporation predicted a "rush of business" for U.S. air-conditioner spare parts once the embargo was lifted.[256] A survey conducted in late 1975 and early 1976 of senior officials of ten major American and Canadian companies representing at least thirteen corporations involved in the nickel industry revealed that seven of these companies were seriously interested "in pursuing the possibility of developing Cuban ores."[257]

Representatives of hundreds of American companies visited Havana during 1976 and 1977 for assessments and discussions with Cuban officials.[258] Returning from a Chamber of Commerce sponsored visit to Cuba in April 1977, for example, many in the delegation of 52 Minnesota businessmen were "convinced they will get sizable orders once President Carter ends the U.S. trade embargo."[259] A First National Bank of Minnesota official even was led to assert, with mixed exaggeration and accuracy, that "there is nothing you could take to Cuba now that would not be marketable."[260] The island's attractiveness was the central theme of a study prepared by one of the American multinational business community's most influential research firms in mid-1977. On the basis of extensive access to senior Cuban government officials, the study described a shift in policy that prefigured opportunities for U.S. corporations, especially in areas where they could outcompete other Western countries: technology, marketing expertise, administrative skills, capital goods, and basic foodstuffs. As a result of the Cuban leadership's changed attitude toward "economic management . . . a new foundation for extensive business relations with the Western world is being laid."[261] Despite intercapitalist competition, Cuba's small market, and its limited ability to generate hard-currency earnings by expanding traditional exports or creating new ones, a U.S. Department of Commerce analyst confessed that, from the vantage point of specific American companies, Cuba "could be an interesting and profitable market."[262] But the business executive had to wait out the sifting of legal restraints on bilateral trade as well as the restoration of certain prerevolutionary trade privileges accorded Cuba by U.S. governments.[263]

The American business community came into conflict with U.S. policy via the Nixon and Ford administrations' perceptions of what was in the best interests of this community and how its needs could be fulfilled. However, disagreements over how to proceed did not materialize as active corporate challenges to the trade embargo policy. Argentine and Canadian government demands during 1973 and 1974 that U.S. subsidiaries participate in Cuba trade failed to galvanize the multinationals to press for a change in White House policy.[264] Although influential corporate leaders such as Donald M. Kendall, Chairman of the Board and Chief Executive Office of Pepsico, Inc., advocated changes in the regulations to allow American subsidiaries to comply with host government laws,[265] these efforts never translated into a serious rift between the business community and the executive branch. The multinationals generally were prepared to abide by the timing and initiatives of the U.S. government and were not above collaborating with the Department of Commerce to thwart alleged or actual diversions of American merchandise to Cuba.

The problem of third-country subsidiaries "caught in the crossfire"[256] between host government policy and American regulations festered in 1975, pushing the Association of American Chambers of Commerce in Latin America to the opinion that failure to lift the restrictions on third-country trade with Cuba potentially could imperil the U.S. corporate stake in all of Latin America.[257] A senior analyst for *Business Latin America* was more blunt: "The companies would like to get off this hook because it isn't helping them at all in Latin America."[268] Complain as they did, Chambers officials and the business community still refused to take a clear-cut position on the embargo. An official of the Council of the Americas, whose membership accounted for over 90 percent of U.S. corporate investment in the hemisphere, noted the absence of concerted business lobbying on the issue and doubted that this would change before the government-to-government conflict had been resolved.[269]

As discussed earlier, in August 1975 Washington finally agreed to partial exemptions for overseas subsidiaries of American corporations from compliance with the Cuban Assets Control Regulations, permitting them to trade with Cuba at the request of host country governments and relieving U.S. executives of these subsidiaries of personal liability in the event of such trade. But the Ford administration was not prepared to lift the stringent controls over the use of U.S. materials in any Cuba-bound exports. Nor was it willing to give American exporters the authority to extend credit terms beyond a twelve-month period. This inability of American subsidiaries to offer long-term credits put them at a substantial competitive disadvantage, which loomed particularly large at this time when the Cuban desire to purchase heavy equipment goods from capitalist countries was at its peak. Dealing with the American government was emerging as an extremely frustrating experience for industrial and consumer-goods companies engaged in preliminary investigations of the Cuban market. "Overwhelmingly," concluded a *Business International Corporation* survey of these companies, "the major obstacle [to Cuba trade] cited by firms is the confusing attitude of the U.S. government, caused by varying positions taken by different government agencies, and the continuing difficulty and complexity of getting products approved for sale to Cuba."[270]

The American business community's interest in the Cuban market persisted, despite the community's refusal to initiate an overt challenge to executive-branch policy. Efforts to organize interested companies to work for the repeal of the trade embargo foundered on this refusal to take a confrontationist approach. As an official of one such company put it, "Trading with the Communists is an issue they [the multinational corporations] don't like to force."[271] Accordingly Assistant Secretary of State for Inter-American Affairs Harry Shlaudeman could tell a congressional committee in mid-1976, with little exaggeration, that "It has been our experience that the American business community in general understands and cooperates with our policy on trade with Cuba."[272]

Although loathe to contest government policy directly, representatives of major American high technology, agricultural machinery, heavy industry, and consumer goods corporations, together with U.S. bankers and officials of other financial enterprises, continued their on-the-spot assessments of the Cuban market into 1978 – in the event of a change in administration policy. Most vexing to many of these executives was the growing visibility of capitalist firms from other Western countries, especially in sectors of the Cuban economy where U.S. producers could compete actively and even dominate, were it not for the embargo. "It burnt me when I got to Cuba and saw French tractors, Japanese computers, Italian cars," one businessman remembers. "Meanwhile, here in the United States we have an auto industry that's in big trouble. We could be selling lots of cars to Cuba."[273]

By August 1979, however, a Commerce Department official monitoring Cuban trade noted that the number of calls regarding this question had declined from a high of approximately 25 per day in 1975 and 1976 to around a single daily inquiry. "Some U.S. companies with prospects," he remarked, "still keep open the lines of communication. But most now have the message."[274]

The compensation issue   Even though the most critical sticking point in U.S.-Cuba relations during the second half of the 1970s was Havana's foreign policy and support of revolutionary movements and governments in the Third World, American officials continued to press the compensation issue as a major impediment to normalized relations. Traditionally, outstanding compensation disputes between U.S. investors and socialist countries have been resolved through direct government-to-government negotiations, with American officials settling for the most favorable terms. But the Cuban expropriations occasioned a unique departure from this precedent: "Without waiting for a fund to be established, Congress directed the Federal Claims Settlement Commission [FCSC, an independent board] to receive and determine the claims immediately."[275]

The question of how compensation demands fit into a normalization process was a source of some disagreement within and between the executive and the legislature. Although the State Department and the National Security Council tended toward a somewhat flexible position compatible with the larger policy objectives, the Department of the Treasury and other agencies whose immediate constituencies were the private corporate and banking worlds espoused a narrower conception, viewing compensation as a precondition for normalization. Treasury was joined in its hardline approach by a powerful segment of the Congress that was determined to push for maximum recompense to affected U.S. investors.

In September 1974, the compensation issue resurfaced at Senate Finance Committee hearings on the repayment of war claims adjudicated by the FCSC against the government of Czechoslovakia. Before an openly hostile Committee, State Department officials announced that a relatively favorable settlement had been reached, under which Prague agreed to payment of 42 cents on the dollar – a figure that compared well with similar agreements reached with other East and West European governments. Unimpressed, the Committee maintained that, pending a full-value settlement, seized Czechoslovakian government assets in the United States, most-favored-nation status, and credits should be withheld. Chairman Russell B. Long did not mince words: "after we think this matter over I think we will conclude, and I know I will, that until these claims are paid, I would not let them have any favoritism, I would give them the back of my hand."[276] At the same time, the Committee went out of its way to elicit assurances from State that the final Czechoslovakian settlement would not be used as precedent in compensation negotiations with Cuba.[277] Within Congress as a whole, the only area of disagreement concerning the compensation issue was whether it should be used as a bargaining chip in normalization discussions *before* or *after* the repeal of the trade embargo. By the second half of the Carter presidency, few cracks had appeared in this consensus. A senior Senate foreign-policy staff assistant with responsibilities in the Latin America area expressed little doubt at the time that this problem would endure as "a real hurdle" to normalized relations between the two countries "in both the Senate and the House" beyond the current administration.[278]

Cuba's expropriations tangled the lines both of U.S. business support for and opposition to maintenance of the bilateral trade-sanctions policy. In October 1964, Congress authorized the FCSC to undertake "a presettlement adjudication of claims to determine the extent of American losses and to provide a tool for our Government in dealing with the Government of Cuba and in future on this important international issue."[279] The FCSC awarded claims to 5,013 individual investors totalling approximately $2.2 billion and 898 corporations totalling almost $1.6 billion, including 92 corporate and 39 individual claims in excess of $1 million each.[280] The Commission also added 6 percent interest annually to the losses, which as of 1977 would have more than doubled the total award to around $4 billion.[281] According to a senior analyst for *Business Latin America*, renewed congressional attention to the issue of normalizing relations with Cuba in the mid-1970s led some U.S. corporations whose holdings had been expropriated to initiate legal actions to reclaim their former properties. One agricultural machinery company "proceeded to start dusting off its books and prepare law suits." Not all parent firms responded in this manner. The Otis Elevator Company, which had maintained relations (through its Madrid subsidiary) with their former employees in the still functioning Havana operation, stood "ready to go in at a moment's notice."[282]

The sugar, petroleum, mineral-extractive, public utility, and other multinational corporations that suffered large losses and had negligible prospects of reentering the Cuban market were among the strongest advocates of compensation as a precondition for lifting the trade embargo. The Bangor Punta Corporation, with certified claims for sugar properties amounting to $53.3 million (plus 6 percent interest), opposed a 1975 House bill to remove the embargo on direct trade with Cuba before the settlement of compensation claims on the grounds that it would make it more difficult for the United States "to negotiate fair settlements with other countries tomorrow."[283] North American Sugar Industries, Inc., with a $97.4 million claim (plus 6 percent interest) pending against the revolutionary regime, opposed the bill for almost identical reasons.[284]

To those multinational corporations that had experienced small losses and stood to gain minimally, if at all, from expanded trade, it was the global implications of a "trade before compensation" agreement that formed the basis of their public opposition to any such resolution. Uniroyal, Inc., with a claim of $9.5 million (with 6 percent interest) and extensive worldwide operations, sought "prior full compensation." Any precedent-setting departure from this posture "would have disastrous effect on U.S. investments throughout the world."[285] This rationale for opposing the 1975 House bill found ready support within the extractive minerals industry. The President of the American Mining Corporation, speaking for the entire directorship, warned that Washington's failure to adhere to the "compensation before trade" formula "would appear to set a precedent that would permanently impair the interests of all U.S. citizens doing business abroad."[286]

To some U.S. multinationals whose properties were expropriated without compensation, the prospect of substantial sales to Cuba overrode their losses, relegating the compensation to an issue to be discussed later. One corporate proponent of this strategy was the Colgate-Palmolive Company, with certified claims totalling $14.4 million (plus 6 percent interest). Senior executives opposed making repeal of the trade embargo dependent on "prior full and complete satisfaction of our claims," proposing that the U.S. follow the tradition that a condition of the embargo's repeal would be Havana's acknowledgment of the legitimacy of compensation claims and its agreement to "develop a long-range plan for their repayment and satisfaction."[287] The Honeywell Corporation took a still more relaxed view, not surprisingly, for it hadn't bothered to submit a claim to the FCSC for its miniscule $50,000 worth of expropriated inventory. Nor was it about to rock the boat, given the priority Cuba attached to imports of U.S. technology for use in the country's nitrogen fertilizer plant, nickel processing, transportation, construction, agriculture, industry, textiles, plastics, and food operations. Honeywell's capacity to take advantage of such needs and of each change in the bilateral commercial relationship came through its subsidiaries in Japan, France, and Canada, which had been exporting to Cuba since the partial abrogation of "third-party" controls in August 1975.[288]

In areas such as technology, medical supplies, and pharmaceuticals, multinationals having had no investments in Cuba before 1959 reversed the hardline formula, arguing that "once trade relations have been re-established, the groundwork will have been laid for a solution of expropriation claims and other substantive issues."[289] The concern for this group was capitalist competitors moving into areas of the Cuban economy that normally would be dominated by American exporters. The fear of being displaced was spelled out by the President of Ampex Corporation, a global supplier of communications technology. His company was being forced to stand by, watching Japanese, French, and other Western competitors fill large orders for products "that, but for the embargo constraints, could have, and probably would have, been manufactured by Ampex Corporation."[290]

The last clearly definable category of U.S. investors includes the thousands of small entrepreneurs with claims against the Cuban government. Unable to cushion their losses through substantial tax write-offs, this group rigidly opposed trade normalization prior to a compensation resolution and vigorously lobbied its case with Congress. "For the small businessmen like myself, and the 5,000 other individuals who have claims outstanding against Cuba," wrote Lewis T. Kane, whose trucking-tractor business was nationalized, "the Congress provided our last chance for complete repayment. Unlike the large corporations who had holdings expropriated, we have not been able to absorb our losses into a worldwide financial structure."[291]

These various corporate and individual positions were voiced in concert by key business leaders and organizations such as the Joint Corporate Committee on Cuban Claims (JCCC), established under the leadership of Bangor Punta Corporation and Lone Star Industries, whose combined losses totalled approximately $75 million. The Committee's chairman, Robert W. Hutton, told the House Foreign Affairs Committee in September 1979 that political or economic initiatives prior to resolution of the compensation issue "would weaken the U.S. bargaining position with respect to settlement of claims and would establish a dangerous precedent which would have severe repercussions on U.S. investment abroad."[292] In addition, the JCCC maintained that the capacity of affected U.S. corporations to write off their Cuban losses was exaggerated. But then, as Alfred Padula points out, ten of the JCCC's thirteen largest members were sugar companies, "many of which had the majority of their assets in Cuba, and thus had no U.S.-based profits against which to write off their Cuban losses."[293] A 1984 study of Cuban expropriations of American properties concluded not only that the "short-term losses for large companies were greatly minimized by the application of [U.S.] tax benefits," but also that, in a number of cases, "expropriations actually enhanced the company's financial position." It also pointed out that Congress' decision in 1971 to liberalize U.S. tax laws relating to the smaller affected companies "greatly reduced their [Cuban] losses."[294] The JCCC stance, nonetheless, found favor with officials of the National Foreign Trade Council, among others: "The Council's position is that the embargo should not be removed until Cuba enters into a firm commitment to adequately compensate U.S. corporations and citizens for the expropriation of their properties, and that such compensation be made in an effective and realizable form."[295]

The Council of the Americas, whose membership includes almost all major U.S. corporations doing business in Latin America, took a somewhat more flexible stance. In testimony before the Senate Foreign Relations Committee in early 1975, Council President Henry Geyelin asserted that multinational businesses having regional investments were unanimous in their support for negotiations and the establishment of "some kind of modus vivendi" as long as Cuba agreed to settle the compensation problem "once the initial detente was established."[296] What all affected capitalist factions wanted, according to Geyelin, was Cuba's acknowledgment of the importance of the principle of compensation. "Most of the corporations have already written off the losses," he observed, "but even some of these feel strongly that the concept of compensation should be supported. . . . It's the principle of the thing. The amount is always negotiable."[297] At the same time, concern was expressed in some business quarters that American government policy was too rigid and "self-defeating," that it constrained opportunities for U.S. multinational penetration of the Cuban economy.[298]

For all the sound and fury that accompanied the 1970s debate over compensation, many U.S. policymakers and corporate officials were, and remain, resigned, privately, to receiving token payments in the event of a negotiated settlement leading to the reestablishment of diplomatic ties between Washington and Havana. Four factors appear to support the likelihood of token payments: Cuba's limited financial resources; the lack of any precedent in cases of U.S. claims against socialist countries for repayment of 100 cents, or close to it, on the dollar; affected large corporations, with some exceptions, have long since applied their Cuban losses as tax write-offs in the United States; and the Havana government's intention to seek large-scale reparations from the United States for losses suffered as a result of the global economic blockade, the Bay of Pigs invasion, and covert sabotage operations carried out during the 1960s and early 1970s.[299]

Conclusion

During the 1960s, the United States tried to isolate, undermine, and disintegrate the Cuban Revolution as a prelude to the island's reincorporation into the capitalist political and economic orbit. Executive-branch policymakers pursued an aggressive strategy with multiple dimensions: indirect military intervention; covert subversion and assassination projects; political and diplomatic isolation in Latin America; and the allocation of massive resources to construct an economic blockade around the Caribbean island. After 1962, the focal point of these efforts – the economic blockade strategy – depended in large part on the collaboration of other leading industrialized Western countries. During the Nixon-Ford-Kissinger era, however, the proliferation of trade and financial links between Havana and the capitalist world exacerbated existing cleavages between Washington and its allies. Also, shifts in the social and political nature of state governments in Latin America during the late 1960s and first half of the 1970s began to erode Cuba's political isolation and facilitate its partial reintegration into the inter-American system. By mid-decade, only a minority of hemispheric regimes, principally the right-wing military or quasimilitary dictatorships of Chile, Uruguay, Brazil, Nicaragua, and Paraguay, provided unqualified support for a hostile U.S. policy toward Cuba.

The Nixon and Ford administrations' refusal to extend the policy of global detente to Cuba was rooted in a commitment to "spheres-of-influence" politics and the primacy of great-power agreements. Further, Washington worried that a change in policy toward Havana might encourage other hemispheric forces seeking to assert similarly independent foreign policies. American policymakers also deemed the comparatively limited opportunities awaiting American multinationals in Cuba to be insufficient reason to shift from a posture of confrontation to that of detente and negotiation.[300]

The Nixon White House pursued a policy of unrelenting hostility toward the Cuban Revolution, continued to police the worldwide blockade where possible, and generally remained unenthusiastic about consideration of even a limited government-to-government accommodation. Despite a number of secret, exploratory discussions between representatives of the U.S. and Cuban governments during 1974 and 1975, the Ford administration's stance largely mirrored that of its predecessor. The onus was on Castro to make major concessions before Washington would even consider normalization. Foremost among such concessions was that Havana terminate its support for Third World revolutionary struggles and even for anticapitalist governing regimes defined as hostile to U.S. global and regional interests.

The Nixon-Ford era, however, also witnessed a shift in the bedrock agreement between liberals and conservatives that characterized disputes over Cuba in the 1960s – namely, that the overthrow of the Castro regime was desired by all. During the early and mid-1970s, some liberals, primarily in the legislative branch, defected from this consensus, citing a number of factors including the revolution's institutionalization and durability, and the ineffectiveness of current U.S. policy. But the consensus did not break down regarding opposition to Cuban support of Third World liberation movements and anticapitalist regimes or the large Cuban military commitment in Angola in late 1975.

Beginning in the Ford presidency, influential groups of American business executives also took issue, at least verbally, with the trade embargo, which increasingly allowed capitalist competitors to enter what had been a U.S.-dominated market. Yet, while business representatives visited Cuba in droves and even prepared to enter the market on short notice, they were unwilling or unable to mount a unified, aggressive lobbying effort to force the executive branch to change the blockade policy.

The Carter administration initially downplayed the spheres-of-influence approach to foreign policy in favor of a new, moral attitude toward world affairs. The imagery and rhetoric of Cold War politics were set aside as human rights leapt to center stage of foreign policy discussions. Some among the new group of policymakers also conceded that specific policies simply had failed or were no longer appropriate.

In 1977, the Carter White House outlined and instituted several symbolic and limited changes to thaw relations with Cuba. The initiatives required adaptations within the foreign-policy bureaucracy, tacitly acknowledged the consolidation of socialist power in Cuba, and represented an effort to accommodate changing regional attitudes and the growing disjunction between the original goals and the actual achievements of the global isolation strategy. Although limited, the innovations encouraged congressional liberals to renew their advocacy of normalization measures. Dealing, at last, with an administration that did not see Cuba as a threat to Latin America's security, these legislators challenged the Nixon-Kissinger-Ford policy – despite the opposition of a still overwhelming majority of their colleagues in the House and the Senate. But there remained overall opposition both to any kind of independent Cuban foreign policy in the Third World and to reestablishing diplomatic ties before an agreement was reached over compensation claims by nationalized U.S. property holders. These two issues reflected the commitment of official Washington as a whole, liberals and conservatives alike, to the interests and defense of American capitalism.

The unraveling of the fundamental strategic agreement of the 1960s between liberals and conservatives in favor of getting rid of Castro, beginning in the early 1970s, was not evidence of a critical confrontation within the foreign-policy bureaucracy, a confrontation that could provide the basis for a theory of politics stating that bureaucratic conflicts are strategic as well as tactical. Certainly, many liberals publicly defected from the original strategic consensus (largely in the belief that its objective was no longer attainable) during the Nixon, Ford, and Carter years, limiting agreement with their conservative colleagues to the much more superficial issue of being certain not to "give away" too much in the process of normalization. But the temporary, liberal challenge over Cuba and other foreign-policy issues at this time was based on a groundswell of anti-interventionist public opinion shaped by the Indochina experience, and it was soon undermined. Once it ebbed, the liberals could not sustain their positions in the legislature or the executive branch. No theory of politics can be derived on the basis of what was essentially a conjunctural phenomenon.

The peculiar interlude in U.S. foreign policy, extending roughly from 1974 to 1978, can be understood only in the context of the war in Vietnam and growing domestic opposition to the interventionist foreign policies of the Johnson and Nixon administrations. The American role in Indochina was the basis for an enormous popular political upsurge – a development that emerged outside of existing political structures, but resonated throughout the legislative branch and played an important role in Carter's early foreign policy.

During this interlude, parts of the consensus for an interventionist foreign policy broke down. An increasingly assertive Congress enacted such measures as the Clark Amendment (1976), which restrained Ford White House efforts to expand CIA covert activities in Angola; under Carter, human rights criteria initially were elevated to a central role in the shaping of U.S. military and economic assistance policy toward the Third World; the executive branch decided not to intervene to prevent the demise of the Pahlavi regime in Iran in late 1978, though Iran was a key American "regional influential"; and old political agendas such as normalized relations with Cuba were reopened. These and other actions grew out of or capitalized on the mass-mobilization politics of the anti-war movement. But because the new issues raised during this period were based on popular sentiment rather than established political structures (and, hence, lacked a secure political base within the foreign policy bureaucracy), they were ultimately ineffective, easily undermined, reversed, downgraded, or simply erased from the political agenda. The Carter White House shift to a policy of high-level confrontation with Cuba in late 1977 based on opposition to the latter's foreign policy in the Third World was an example. When senior administration officials resurrected the "export of revolution" rhetoric of the 1960s and early 1970s, they found few, if any, dissenters even among the liberals on Capitol Hill.

7. The U.S. imperial state: some final insights

This book has focused on the notion of the imperial state and imperialist behavior. Contrary to mechanistic economic analyses that center on flows of capital between countries and the actions of multinational corporations, the imperial-state framework places politics at the center of the discussion. What the study shows is that the activities of the imperial state polarize Third World societies, fuel national and social liberation movements, and not infrequently lead to the assumption of political and state power by nationalist regimes espousing noncapitalist paths to development. Moreover, the typical imperial-state response to the appearance of such regimes is the execution of a policy of outright confrontation expressed through military, economic, and political interventions calculated to destabilize and overthrow these antagonists of imperial policy.

Military intervention may be direct or indirect. Direct intervention involves American armed forces occupying a country to install a collaborator regime and secure U.S. corporate interests (e.g., Cuba 1906–1921, Dominican Republic 1965). Indirect intervention (much more commonplace, but no less destructive of national political institutions) involves efforts by U.S. policymakers to manipulate non-U.S. military forces to oust nationalist and anticapitalist regimes. This type of intervention may take one or a combination of approaches: internal subversion in the form of CIA inducements to local military officials to organize a coup (e.g., Brazil 1964, Chile 1973); external subversion or the financing, training, and directing of former regime collaborators based outside the country to invade and overthrow the change-oriented government (e.g., Guatemala 1954, Cuba 1961); and surrogates in third countries covertly recruited to train, supply arms to, or provide bases for counterrevolutionary forces and U.S. client regimes (e.g., Guatemala's and Nicaragua's role in the Bay of Pigs preparations and the activities of U.S. regional allies in Central America during the 1970s).

The imperial state also engages in multiple forms of economic intervention, as this study graphically reveals (e.g., trade sanctions, economic blockades, financial and credit squeezes), to create internal hardships, stimulate popular discontent, and tarnish the international appeal of the target regime. The imperial state intervenes in the so-called international banks to halt loans and other forms of economic assistance and, where necessary, pressures multinational corporations to take similar actions in the areas of trade, investment, spare parts, and technology transfers (e.g., Cuba during the 1960s and 1970s and Chile between 1970 and 1973). This form of warfare may drive the target regime into closer relations with the Soviet Union and the socialist bloc, thus lubricating propaganda efforts describing the "totalitarian" nature of the regime's political leadership.

Similarly, imperial-state political and diplomatic intervention is designed to isolate and destabilize the target regime. The CIA and other intelligence agencies intervene by channeling funds to sympathetic local political, economic, and cultural organizations in the target country (e.g., in Chile from 1970 to 1973) or even in other countries as part of a larger offensive against the target (for instance, recall the efforts to achieve Cuba's political isolation in Latin America during the 1960s). The recipients may include strategically placed political figures, union leaders, business executives, and mass media representatives. External funds often are diverted into the coffers of local elites to encourage them to disinvest so as to sabotage production, or money may be funneled to complicit labor unions willing to make exorbitant salary demands to provoke social disorder and undermine government economic planning (e.g., Brazil 1962–1964). In either case, the object is to set in motion conditions favoring the regime's demise. When such efforts are thwarted, the imperial state moves to propagandize the repressive character of its opposition and the lack of internal democratic forms as indications of the coercive nature of the regime and to encourage its international isolation (e.g., Cuba during the 1960s).

Although the imperial state uses a variety of instruments to defend corporate and other interests, the selection and effective application of interventionist policies (military, economic, political) depend on the historical context within which it operates. Over time, an imperial state may experience a decline in its power and its capacity to secure global support for any particular policy. Its interventionary capacities, as this work shows, depend significantly on the degree to which international or regional allies can be mobilized to provide political, diplomatic, and material support for a given policy. When such a policy fragments the alliance, it defeats the purpose of the imperial state, which is to extend the terrain of capital accumulation.

This book also has addressed three empirical questions that apply to our understanding of the making and execution of American foreign policy in the postwar era: the value of the bureaucratic politics approach to explaining policy outcomes; the possibilities for a hegemonic state in an increasingly interdependent capitalist world economy to impose its will in all circumstances and at all times; and the play of state-class relations in the policymaking process. What does this study tell us about these questions, and what theoretical insights can we gain from the empirical findings about this specific historical experience?

Assessing the bureaucratic politics model   This investigation of U.S. policy toward Cuba between 1952 and 1980 highlights a central thread that unites all executive-branch positions and actors: uniform opposition to nationalist and socialist revolution in Cuba. Although interagency debates were common, never did they split the focus of the U.S. government. Sustaining a capitalist state in Cuba was the paramount concern of all imperial policymakers prior to the overthrow of the Batista dictatorship in January 1959. Officials of the White House, National Security Council, State Department, Defense Department, and Central Intelligence Agency were all hostile to radical nationalist guerrillas hegemonizing the leadership of the antidictatorial movement and a post-Batista government. What limited bureaucratic debate that did occur in Washington was neutralized by the perception that these armed insurgents were a political threat to foreign investors and key state institutions.

Once the nationalists came to power and began implementing redistributive policies in Cuba, the imperial-state agencies homogenized their tactical differences into a common outlook opposing the changes that forecast Cuba's shift out of the capitalist political and economic orbit. Occasional differences remained, such as the State-Treasury debate over economic assistance to the Castro government early in 1959. Treasury wanted to withhold aid to help disintegrate Castro's social-political basis of support;

State desired to manipulate economic assistance to contain socio-economic changes. Both approaches, though, sought to maintain Cuba within the capitalist sphere. As Cuba's movement toward a socialist transformation became more manifest and the bourgeois opposition less effective, these tactical conflicts collapsed into a consensus favoring an aggressive, confrontationist policy. This new "outsider" emphasis initially centered around preparations for a military invasion by Cuban exiles, which culminated in the Bay of Pigs debacle of April 1961.

Through most of the 1960s, the Kennedy and Johnson administrations employed covert warfare, political-diplomatic pressures, and economic sanctions on a regional and global scale in determined efforts to change the government in Cuba. A senior Kennedy official recalled interagency, but not policy, conflicts: "Once the decision was made to isolate Cuba . . . all the rest, such as economic sanctions, was detail."[1]

During the Nixon-Ford era, rigid opposition to any accommodation with the Castro regime in the absence of fundamental Cuban concessions in the spheres of foreign and economic policy was punctuated by minor bureaucratic skirmishes. Treasury's highly aggressive "denial posture" and its vigorous efforts to track down U.S. companies trying to circumvent the trade embargo generated some tactical disagreements with both Commerce and State. As the Department primarily responsible for promoting exports, Commerce was more reluctant to oppose American traders seeking to do business with Havana in nonstrategic goods.[2] Treasury's major falling out with State occurred over the August 1975 decision to allow subsidiaries of U.S. multinational corporations to trade with Cuba, for the decision set State's broad economic and political concerns against Treasury's role as "a keeper of embargoes" and "a custodian of frozen assets in the U.S. and as custodian of the expropriation claims of U.S. citizens."[3] But, again, conficts of this kind had no consequences at the policy level. An involved State Department official remarked in mid-1973: "There aren't any differences about Cuba around here. I don't know any place in the government where there are *real* differences."[4]

The limited thaw in U.S.-Cuba relations that attended the early period of the Carter presidency was confined to negotiating issues of secondary concern to both countries. These tentative moves towards normalized relations and subsequent secret discussions between American and Cuban officials eventually sank into Washington's opposition to the Castro government's involvement with the forces of Third World revolution.

What this study shows about how U.S. policy is made is that the process cannot be reduced to "the product of a series of overlapping and interlocking bargaining processes [among government agencies]."[5] Although no comprehensive explanation can ignore the roles of specific agencies, individual policymakers' perceptions of reality, ideological commitments, and forceful personalities, the failure to integrate the bureaucratic struggle with a larger, more structurally rooted analysis limits our capacity to see the historic consistencies that characterize imperial-state policymaking, the common political and economic framework that shapes the universe within which bureaucratic disputes take place. All the involved bureaucratic institutions adhere to the logic of a particular economic system, not to the logic of the bureaucracy that forms a piece of that system. A worldwide "open door" for capital and commerce, the integration of societies within the capitalist political and economic orbit, and the maintenance of an American-dominated capitalist world define this system and determine its logic.

Global interdependence: limits on a hegemonic power   During the 1960s, Cuba's economic isolation from the capitalist world was an integral part of the U.S. goal to destabilize Castro's revolution. Washington made use of legislation, diplomacy, economic levers, and covert intelligence to elicit maximum compliance with a global economic blockade. However, imperial policymakers were not prepared to pressure or provoke key allies who insisted on maintaining trade ties with Cuba to a point where a serious rupture in bilateral relations might happen. Moreover, given that these countries had excessively export-based economies and that their trade with Cuba was shaped by commercial considerations only, even the U.S. government implicitly conceded that total obedience on their part was not realizable. Notwithstanding the determination of a number of important Western Alliance members to maintain economic relations with Cuba, there was, especially during the 1960s, an impressive degree of collaboration with America's global policy toward Cuba throughout the capitalist world.

The Kennedy administration was the first to mobilize large-scale resources for the purpose of implementing worldwide economic sanctions against the Cuban Revolution. In the areas of trade and transportation, Kennedy's use of legislative and diplomatic pressures registered a number of important gains, ranging from the withdrawal of many allied ships from the Cuba trade to a large decline in Japanese sugar imports from Cuba between 1961 and 1963. Even recalcitrant allies such as Canada, whose government remained skeptical of the whole enterprise, sought to minimize confrontation with Washington by withholding state credits to local exporters, embargoing the sale of strategic goods, and preventing American items being rerouted through Canada to Cuba.

During its tenure in office, the Kennedy White House also presided over the most intense period of the so-called secret war against Cuba which absorbed hundreds of millions of dollars and thousands of agents. Only with the Johnson presidency did all other aspects of Cuba policy become subordinate to the global blockade effort. Between late 1963 and 1968, economic sanctions were "the heart and backbone" of America's attempts to disintegrate the Cuban Revolution.

Under Johnson, capitalist-bloc cooperation with Washington's economic war against Cuba increased significantly. The new Democratic White House focused on Cuba's major Western trading partners, mounting a comprehensive, and quite successful, attack on the island's economic links with Canada, Japan, France, Spain, and England. Apart from a sizable contraction in shipping and commerce between Cuba and its "big five" capitalist traders, Johnson was particularly successful in dissuading these allies from directly promoting such trade through state credit guarantees to local exporters.

Canada, under the liberal Pearson government, maintained the ban on strategic exports and continued to oppose "pass through" trade to Cuba. Although not prepared to interrupt ongoing commercial relations, Ottawa still stepped cautiously around the issue, in part because its exporters were highly dependent on the U.S. market. Japan's accommodation to U.S. policy extended to strategic goods and shipping bans, although some friction persisted over still significant sugar purchases from Havana. Washington's opposition was expressed almost exclusively in diplomatic terms so as not to jeopardize the important new U.S. export market opened up by Japan's rapid postwar economic resurgence. The decline in Japan-Cuba trade after 1965 was primarily the result of Cuba's balance-of-payments difficulties.

Although France under de Gaulle made notable efforts to contest and limit U.S. power within Western Europe and the Atlantic Alliance during the 1960s, its efforts to develop an independent foreign policy were not reflected in its relations with Cuba. Before 1964, Paris provided no encouragement in the form of state-guaranteed credits to local companies interested in trading with Havana. On the few occasions when credits were offered early in 1964 to economically depressed companies selling nonstrategic items who could secure major Cuban contracts only if government backing was forthcoming, the credit terms apparently were shorter than normal for sales of comparable magnitude. By mid-year, Paris reverted to its earlier policy, denying credit guarantees for a number of proposed heavy industry sales by French firms to Cuba. The de Gaulle government also bowed to Johnson administration pressures to prohibit imports of goods containing Cuban nickel.

The Johnson White House vented a good deal of anger and frustration in its efforts to make Spain and England sever trade and transport links with Cuba. Eventually, each government took measures to avoid a major confrontation with Washington.

For both countries, the imperatives of export expansion are central to explaining their economic ties with Cuba. Franco's Spain had limited export outlets in Europe because of its political pariah status, while England sought to arrest its declining competitive position in the world market. In Spain, U.S. diplomatic pressures and the threatened termination of economic assistance were always tempered by the need to assure continued operations at a number of strategic American military bases on Spanish territory. Although determined to capture both Cuba trade and American aid, the Franco regime wanted to cooperate with the Johnson administration and did make concessions: Franco agreed to withdraw Spanish ships from Cuba trade on the expiration of their charters and to halt the transportation of commercial cargo on passenger airline flights. Spanish-Cuban trade (primarily in heavy industry goods, ships, consumer items, and sugar) tapered off significantly only during 1967 and 1968, a casualty, like Japan's trade, mainly of Cuba's balance-of-payments problems.

The British government considered the embargo wrongheaded and unlikely to achieve its objective, but it still confined its trade with Cuba to nonstrategic exports and agreed informally to discourage locally owned ships from participating in this activity. This much was not enough, and yet even U.S. diplomatic pressures, threats of economic retaliation against British firms in the American market, and efforts to mobilize support against British trade among members of the NATO Council failed to resolve the issue to Washington's satisfaction. What stung the Americans deeply was Whitehall's decision to underwrite a large sale of Leyland Corporation buses to Cuba in early 1964. But an effort to alleviate at least some U.S. concerns appeared by mid-1964: The Douglas-Home government successfully pressured British shipowners not to transport the Leyland buses to Cuba, forcing the company to negotiate with East German shippers, and Whitehall agreed to limit and also discourage future trade. Ironically, amid continuing U.S. dismay over British trade with Cuba during the Johnson years, the annual value of this trade between 1964 and 1968 remained at a modest level.

What is most striking about the extent of cooperation and cleavage with U.S. policy toward Cuba by Canada, Japan, France, Spain, and England is the degree to which these senior alliance partners accommodated Washington's desires in all areas – trade, shipping, airlines, credits – without breaking economic relations with Cuba. The Johnson White House was particularly successful in one objective: preventing Western governments from financing export deals between local traders and Cuba. In a number of cases, American pressures blocked such arrangements and, where this was not possible, Washington occasionally managed to secure rather unfavorable credit terms. The provision of even these credits was confined to specific companies (usually those experiencing recession) and in no case denoted consistent support for this type of activity on the part of any allied regime.

Despite these successes enjoyed by the Kennedy and Johnson administrations in constricting Cuba's economic links with the capitalist world during the 1960s, they failed to achieve their fundamental strategic goal: the demise of the Cuban Revolution. They failed partly because of the constraints imposed by an interdependent world, while a further obstacle was the emergence of a durable government in Cuba that was enhanced by the establishment of alternative political, military, economic, and financial relations with the socialist world.

With the advent of the Nixon presidency, gaping cracks appeared in the embargo as Cuba's access to Western markets, credit guarantees, and capital borrowings grew markedly. The fissures in the embargo must be viewed, in part, against the background of the American experience in Indochina. Although the growth of European and Japanese economic power already had forced a greater U.S. accommodation to the economic interests of other states and capitals, the relative trade and investment position of these alliance partners was further improved as a result of the U.S. commitment in Indochina, which shifted enormous resources from the imperial state's economic to its coercive apparatus. However, while neither Nixon nor Ford pursued the blockade with as much intensity as the Johnson White House, they still sought rigorously to enforce it when the opportunity arose – taking care, like Kennedy and Johnson, not to provoke serious ruptures in relations with key allies. The Ford administration's decision to terminate the ban on U.S. subsidiary trade with Cuba in August 1975 was a function of the need to defuse a potentially divisive Western Alliance issue that already had complicated Washington's relations with friendly governments in Argentina and Canada. Emphasis on the blockade was less apparent during the Carter years, although there is evidence to suggest that there were efforts to limit Cuba's access to Western banking capital in 1979 and 1980 in retaliation for Castro's foreign policy in the Third World.

Considering the Cuban experience and the degree of cleavage with U.S. policy, what conclusions flow from the effort to organize a political coalition to prosecute a global economic sanctions policy? Attempts to maximize economic sanctions against a target country potentially confront at least three obstacles. First, where sanctions have different impacts on coalition participants, the problem of defining and maintaining a common interest is magnified. Equal hardships evoke equal responses, just as unequal hardships entail unequal responses. If Cuba's expropriations equally had affected American, French, Spanish, English, Canadian, and Japanese investments, similar responses would in all likelihood have followed. But since only American enterprises were affected, Washington's incentive to organize sanctions was based exclusively on American hardships. By contrast, the major Canadian banking and insurance interests on the island, excluded from the 1960s expropriations, negotiated very favorable compensations.[6] Second, it is difficult to orchestrate sustained economic pressures when the invited countries have export-dependent economies and see a chance to occupy a new or formerly closed market or increase trade with a traditional market, especially to the benefit of declining industrial sectors. Third, it is unlikely that sanctions participants can be persuaded to terminate completely a critical import such as sugar from the target country when alternative sources are scarce or nonexistent.

The presence of any of these factors can undermine an embargo. Moreover, they suggest that economic sanctions by themselves are unlikely to bring about the intended goal, unless combined with other actions. Besides the loss of traditional markets and political allies, new nationalist governments in the Third World (e.g., Arbenz in Guatemala from 1950 to 1954, Castro in Cuba during the early 1960s, Goulart in Brazil from 1962 to 1964, Allende in Chile from 1970 to 1973) frequently confront hostile state structures linked to opposition class and external forces. Cuba's survival illustrates what regimes facing these problems must do to endure: They must ensure that the state apparatus is synchronized with the new political rulers and their development program, act decisively in international alignments, and move aggressively to reorient external economic ties and develop alternative sources of financing and new trading partners. Success in these areas will severely blunt the impact of a hostile power's efforts to promote economic warfare on a global scale.

State and class in the policy process   The state in this age of imperialism is global in character. The worldwide movement and growth of U.S. multinationals during this century cannot be explained without considering the posture of the United States as an imperial state creating and sustaining the environment for capital accumulation and expansion. In the case of Cuba, numerous studies highlight the role of American public agencies in establishing and recreating the conditions for foreign capitalists to dominate the Cuban economy between 1898 and 1958. Through six decades of unrelenting crisis, Washington repeatedly asserted the issues of importance to American business in Cuba: the need for political and economic treaties (1902–1903, 1934); the suppression of nationalist forces (1933–1934); and the last-ditch effort to maintain a state apparatus that favored foreign investment, while perhaps sacrificing a questionable head of state (1958). For more than half a century, this energetic involvement of the U.S. state in Cuba elevated the interests of American capitalists above the island's forces of political and economic nationalism.

Throughout most of the Batista period (1952–1958), foreign capital enjoyed a privileged position in Cuba. Generous concessions to entice new investment substantially outweighed problems of labor control, bureaucratic red tape and corruption, and other forms of friction between U.S. business and the Batista regime. Moreover, American enterprises experiencing difficulties could count on easy access to senior government officials either directly or through Embassy representatives. Recourse to Washington to solve problems was rarely necessary. For its part, the U.S. state looked with favor on Batista's economic policies, subordinating its dissatisfaction with outstanding compensation claims (a legacy of prior governments), labor concessions, the tax system, and excessive repression to Havana's favorable attitude toward the private sector, as well as to U.S. political and strategic interests.

Before Batista's overthrow, the appearance of a broad-based, nationalist opposition under the leadership of radical guerrillas put the question of governmental and state power onto a hot grill and prompted the United States to intervene. The failure of Batista's mid-1958 military offensive against the guerrillas dissolved the armed forces' cohesion and raised the possibility of the demise of regime and state both. Policymakers in the United States quickly dramatized the necessity of Batista's coercive institutions to the continued operation of capitalist interests on the island, for the guerrillas' possible victory presaged a major transformation of the Cuban economy, state, and society – with its attendant implications for the local and foreign business community. Thus, the Eisenhower administration mobilized its diplomatic and covert resources in a forelorn attempt to save the state structure (though not necessarily Batista) and deny political power to the social revolutionaries who were part of the antidictatorial movement.

Between 1959 and 1961, the Castro forces consolidated their hold on political and state power, pursuing a national and social revolution based on fundamental transformations of class and property relations. Initially, the U.S. business community in Cuba viewed Batista's overthrow with relief, hoping it would lead to a period of government stability and probity, but also with some trepidation over the absence of clear signals regarding the new regime's policy toward the private sector. Expectations and responses varied considerably. Large agro-mining interests with fixed investments difficult to uproot were the most pragmatic, and least skeptical, about reaching a modus vivendi with the nationalists. On the other hand, those public utility enterprises that experienced immediate economic losses were quick to exhort the U.S. state to take extreme retaliatory measures.

Among all U.S. enterprises operating in Cuba, the agrarian reform law of mid-1959, the accumulation of constraints on American business in the months that followed, and the emergence of a new state apparatus not as receptive to the problems facing foreign investors as Batista's was created growing discontent, but not yet a consensus over the most efficacious response. The picture that emerges is of a business community puzzling over what to do next. Disunity and vacillations were linked to the scale and importance of Cuba investments and widely differing perceptions of whether an accommodation could be reached with the regime. In March 1960, however, the situation had deteriorated to such a degree that many investors in Cuba were clamoring for Washington to do something – even though they had few suggestions. Some business executives favored an economic squeeze through sanctions; others believed that Castro could not possibly find substitute sources of trade and financing and would be forced to reach an accommodation with them. The clamoring was heard.

At the Eisenhower White House, as among the business community, the agrarian reform law's institution was a stimulating event. It was interpreted by policymakers already deeply concerned with what was happening in Cuba as setting a precedent that potentially threatened every cent of foreign investment. The law played a decisive role in shifting U.S. policy from one of barely concealed antipathy to one of open hostility. It was powerful evidence of the socioeconomic direction in which the regime intended to move. To Washington's consternation, as the process of change gathered momentum, buttressed by new state and societal structures that eliminated traditional collaborator groups, U.S. influence and its capacity to safeguard the enormous American economic stake on the island began to decline.

Assessing Castro's economic policies, the creation of armed popular militias, the shift to an independent foreign policy, and the growing concentration of political and state power in the hands of the guerrilla forces, the White House answered the businessmen's clamor by deciding, in early 1960, that the Castro leadership could be tolerated no longer. In March, Eisenhower gave his imprimatur to a program of economic, psychological, military, and covert warfare against the revolutionary regime. The U.S. state also revealed its intention to mobilize the fragmented, indecisive, sometimes unwilling American business community to participate in the confrontation – under Washington's direction. Despite the almost certain expropriation of their Cuba properties, the oil multinationals, for instance, were pressed into service by the Department of the Treasury in mid-1960, virtually being ordered not to refine Soviet crude oil in Cuba. The imperial state's preparedness to sacrifice a particular industry's investments as part of its larger destabilization goal clearly indicates its leadership role in originating and applying strategies on behalf of the whole class.

United States capitalists exhibited numerous instances of participation with the imperial state in making a success of the state's "outsider" strategy. According to a knowledgeable State Department official, American multinationals were "exceedingly cooperative" in prosecuting the global economic blockade of Cuba during the 1960s. "Most of the time, if a firm was approached [to trade with Cuba] they would either turn it down or call us and say 'We don't care what the regulations are, you just tell us not to do it and we won't.'"[7] American manufacturers of pharmaceuticals, replacement and spare parts, and heavy industry equipment and machinery for agro-mining and industrial complexes were among those who maintained a "close rapport" with the Departments of State and Commerce. Their cooperation also greatly facilitated state efforts to thwart illegal diversions of needed commodities from Western Europe and other capitalist countries to Cuba.[8] The multinationals not only rebuffed direct or indirect approaches by the Cuban government or reported to Washington for guidance, but they also, at State Department urging, pressured European firms with whom they dealt to stop trading with Cuba or risk being dropped as suppliers. Similarly, U.S. parent companies unhesitatingly supported government regulations affecting foreign companies in which they had a controlling interest from trading with Cuba.

As the state, before the blockade, had pressured the oil multinationals to inconvenience Cuba, so too, on occasion, it later pressured corporate compliance with its worldwide sanctions. By mid-1963 for instance, State and Treasury Department officials were leaning on the parent companies of Canadian subsidiaries to wrest "voluntary compliance" with newly promulgated regulations forbidding the subsidiaries from engaging in unlicensed trade with Havana. At the peak of the global blockade, the pressures escalated as multinationals performed as instruments of state policy, accepting state leadership and direction, enthusiastically or not.

In the mid-1970s, U.S. businesses surged with interest over reentering the Cuban market, occasioned by limited moves at the political level that raised the possibility of more normalized relations. From 1974 through 1977, hundreds of U.S. companies sent officials to evaluate the Cuban economy. Producers of agricultural machinery, communications and transport equipment, computers, rice, nickel, medical supplies, spare parts, and fertilizers were suitably impressed with the profitmaking potential and envious of already established competitors from Western Europe, Canada, and Japan. Particularly galling to many American executives was the sight of foreign firms operating where U.S. firms previously dominated. However, Washington's refusal to thaw economic relations (short of major Cuban concessions in the areas of foreign and, to a lesser extent, economic policy) remained the stumbling block.

The rift between the U.S. state and important segments of the capitalist class over trade with Cuba during the 1970s at no point widened into a chasm between the White House and the multinationals. The latter continued to abide, if reluctantly, by administration policy. At no time were they prepared to force the issue, to challenge state policy either individually or collectively. Although interest in the Cuban market persisted into the Carter period, the realization that no change in economic policy was on the White House agenda as long as Cuba gave sustenance to the forces of national and social liberation in the Third World eventually caused interest to subside. The only significant shift in the U.S. economic policy toward Cuba in the 1970s – allowing U.S. subsidiaries to trade with Cuba at the direction of host governments – was instituted to avoid serious friction with key allies. But even in this instance, the concession was qualified: The subsidiaries had to abide by stringent controls on the use of U.S. materials in Cuba-bound exports, and they were not allowed to extend long-term credits. The credit constraint put them at a substantial competitive disadvantage because, at this time, Cuban interest in purchasing heavy equipment from capitalist countries was at its peak.

The insight this study contributes to theorizing about state-class relations centers on its analysis of the state's supposedly autonomous behavior. This historically and empirically rooted investigation refutes the notion of an autonomous state acting independently of class and affirms the notion of the state representing class interest at all times. Even in instances of limited state autonomy where the state wields discretionary authority, linkages with the class constantly guided state policies. Although strategic thinking is fashioned by political leadership and may occasionally appear as a state acting with a high degree of autonomy (e.g., state-class relations in the making of Cuba policy during the early 1960s), the underlying boundaries of political decisionmaking are set by the capitalist class. Thus, the original confrontation between the imperial state and a nationalist or anticapitalist regime is invariably detonated by the issue of property relations: witness Guatemala under Arbenz, Brazil under Goulart, Peru under Velasco, Chile under Allende, and Cuba. But while the corporate world has primacy in outlining state policy, the state sculpts and executes that policy according to its own conceptions and time schedules.

When a state decision conflicts with the immediate interests of a multinational corporation or industry (e.g., when Presidents Ford and Carter refused to lift the U.S. trade embargo because they opposed Castro's anticapitalist foreign policy), it usually reflects merely a difference over how best to achieve the objective common to both: a global environment that will maximize labor, resource, and market exploitation. The state has a greater degree of flexibility in pursuit of this goal than the multinationals do, but the flexibility is itself a response to a set of collective class interests that the state has chosen to defend. Threats to the capital accumulation process in any one country may provoke conflicting corporate strategies or interests, forcing the state to exercise its discretionary power and leading to apparent disjunctions between corporations and the state regarding the most effective means for dealing with such challenges. Only in this narrow sense can we speak of the state acting autonomously. At all times, though, the U.S. state, as an imperial state, differentiates between the interests of or the perceived threat to the capital accumulation process as a whole, which is the primary concern, and the secondary demands of individual propertyholders or whole industries with specific problems.

While the multinationals are preoccupied with profitmaking in countries under nationalist or anticapitalist political rule, the state's response to these regimes is shaped by broader concerns. The nationalization of foreign-owned properties, for example, is evaluated in terms of whether the regime seeks to change the existing distribution of political power or the existing class structure. Does it represent an effort to move away from the capitalist mode of production? Satisfactory compensation for expropriated U.S. investments is an important determinant of state policy principally because it is viewed as an index of the scope of change and of the regime's preparedness to maintain economic relations with the United States. The imperial state becomes directly involved on the side of the multinational corporation in its conflict with a host government when the corporation is unable to gain an objective (e.g., compensation), but only when local class allies are too weak to offer support or when circumstances jeopardize the primary state concern: the maintenance of the capitalist mode of production.

Epilogue. The Reagan administration and Cuba: the revival of vendetta politics 1981–1986

When the Reagan administration assumed office in January 1981, it was determined to reverse the incremental decline in U.S. global power since the halcyon days of the 1950s. Carter had shifted to a more interventionist foreign policy late in his presidency, a policy triggered by the Shah of Iran's overthrow in January 1979 and codified in the so-called Carter Doctrine of January 1980, and this drift toward direct action was embellished by Reagan's new set of policymakers and emptied of remaining Carter ambiguities, such as his concern with human rights. In Central America, for instance, while the Carter White House had initiated military solutions to problems that were fundamentally socioeconomic by increasing military assistance and introducing Pentagon advisors into the region in 1979 and 1980 and reviving the red herring of Cuban-Soviet conspirators, this merely provided the foundation for an extraordinary intensification of U.S. military commitments during the Reagan presidency.

Military options have become paramount under Reagan. Emphasizing the buildup of U.S. military, strategic, and covert capabilities throughout the world, the Reagan White House has sought to reestablish American military superiority over the Soviet Union, limit its senior Western Alliance partners' (Western Europe and Japan) ability to pursue independent economic and foreign policies, and reverse established revolutionary governments in the Third World. Although Carter policy toward Third World revolutionary and nationalist regimes emphasized containment and isolation, under Reagan there has been a revival of the 1950s doctrine of "rollback" or "liberation" that goes well beyond his predecessor's approach. This White House refusal to accept or reconcile itself to the permanence of consolidated

317

regimes that are revolutionary or even nationalist has been accompanied by a vast expansion of CIA paramilitary assets and an intelligence budget that grew at a faster rate than did the defense budget between 1981 and 1985.[1]

The hallmark of Reagan's more aggressive, more offensive policy has been a renewal of "preventive intervention," given its most dramatic expression in the October 1983 U.S. military adventure in Grenada and in the planning and execution of strategies, using surrogate forces, to topple similar governments in Nicaragua, Angola, and elsewhere. Moreover, beyond the administration's targeting of particular regimes for destabilization and disintegration is its core strategic goal that no other popular nationalist or revolutionary movement will gain political power in these areas of the world. To achieve this, Washington has maximized the use of force to sustain repressive regimes, even at the cost of massive losses of civilian lives and even in the absence of support from its closest allies. Not surprisingly, as the use of force and military solutions in resolving Third World conflicts has escalated, enthusiasm among Reagan policymakers for diplomacy and political negotiations has declined.

The doctrine of the bipolar world also has been resuscitated. The whole thrust of Reagan's foreign policy rests on the assumption that Third World revolutions are products of Soviet expansionism. Indigenous factors are trivialized, as explanations for unrest anywhere reside solely in the activities of Moscow and its proxies or surrogates acting to extend Soviet power.[2] This despite the fact that virtually every major political upheaval in the Third World during the 1970s and 1980s has had deep national roots and has incorporated diverse social, political, religious, and ethnic groups espousing an array of ideological and political commitments.[3] But for Reagan to acknowledge the overwhelmingly local roots of Third World conflicts would flatly contradict his justification for the massive U.S. military buildup and the development of new weapons systems that flow directly from his efforts to slice the world into two camps, with all the conflicts and competition in these regions becoming extensions of the East-West confrontation.

The Reagan administration has attempted to recreate a U.S.-dominated world through military power and military victories that in turn justifies the military buildup – a convenient circle. For example, the multibillion-dollar U.S. military commitment to El Salvador since 1981, which is completely out of proportion to any political, economic, or strategic advantage likely to accrue to Washington, can be understood only in terms of the stake the Reaganites have in military successes that vindicate the militarization of American foreign policy.

The Reagan doctrine of global political, economic, and military confrontation challenges the notion that there are limits to American power in the 1980s.[4] The administration's effort to recreate *So no limits?* the golden age of the 1950s – an era of virtually unquestioned U.S. hegemony – through military spending and conceiving of the world as bipolar suggests that Reaganites do not perceive or accept the changes that have taken place within Western Europe, Japan, the Soviet Union, and the Third World over the past three decades: Soviet strategic, military, and nuclear parity with the United States; the emergence of increasingly independent and economically competitive states in Western Europe and Japan; proliferating trade and financial ties between the capitalist world and the socialist-bloc countries; the emergence of consolidated revolutionary and nationalist regimes in the Third World; and the appearance of regional organizations and cartels defining new sets of relationships among countries. It is within this context of a Cold War revival and the accompanying decline of diplomacy and political negotiations as instruments of policy, the exhumation of the "rollback" doctrine, and a predominantly military approach to international affairs that current U.S. policy toward Cuba should be examined. This context reveals both the continuities and the changes that have been a feature of imperial state attitudes toward the Cuban Revolution since the early 1960s.

Inventing the source: Reagan's military policies

> . . . as the men in his innermost circle knew, [President-elect Reagan] had had to be dissuaded from the private fantasy that Cuba might be liberated by force of arms.[5]

From the outset of the Reagan presidency, a consensus existed among senior policymakers on the need to get tough about Cuban foreign policy. Secretary of State Alexander Haig emerged as the administration's major proponent of military confrontation, but most of Reagan's senior civilian and military officials opposed Haig's direct approach at this time. Pentagon officials, including the Joint Chiefs of Staff, expressed a distinct lack of enthusiasm for sending American troops and naval vessels into the Caribbean-Central American region for the purposes of pressuring Cuba.

Department of Defense policymakers were reluctant to implement a plan that would necessitate a major diversion of American forces from theaters of greater strategic importance such as the Persian Gulf, where the Soviets might respond to a Cuban blockade. They also doubted whether a regional military mobilization could achieve the Haig objective vis-à-vis Cuba (stopping alleged weapons flows to El Salvador) and were still exceedingly wary (a legacy of the Indochina experience) of engaging in any military operation that lacked overwhelming congressional and public support. Such an operation might, in the process, wreck administration plans to modernize the armed forces and institute a large-scale weapons buildup. These concerns preoccupied the White House and the National Security Council.[6] At the State Department, some officials expressed skepticism that military action could achieve the desired goal and raised the possibility that, if the Cuban economy survived a U.S. naval-military quarantine, Castro might gain moral stature throughout Latin America.[7] But these strategic and tactical differences should not obscure the facts that the Reagan administration was determined to pursue a more hostile policy toward Cuba than Carter had and that a military response was never excluded. For under Reagan, the most profound shift that had taken place within the executive branch was the willingness, reminiscent of the early 1960s, to resort to direct military action.

In January 1981, social revolution appeared to be enveloping all of Central America. Not only was there an established revolutionary government in Nicaragua, but also urban-rural polyclass movements in El Salvador and Guatemala were challenging pro-American regimes. Too unimaginative to construct a meaningful approach to Third World upheavals and North-South conflicts and settling on military power as the means to impose political solutions, the Reagan White House focused on this region as the primary testing ground for its new policies. Thus, to meet threats to regional allies and reconsolidate Washington's hold on Central America, the Reagan administration devised a threefold strategy: escalate the direct American military presence while building up the military capabilities of local clients to make sure there would be no more Nicaraguas; reverse the process of change in Nicaragua and oust its government; and defeat the movements in El Salvador and Guatemala seeking to overthrow regimes loyal to the United States. Enhancing the attractiveness of this strategy among senior policymakers was a belief that America's problems in the

region could be traced largely to the activities of the Castro
government.

American fixation with Cuba's policy zeroed in on El Salvador
and provided much of the rationale for massive military assistance
to the Duarte regime. Secretary of State Alexander Haig
described the Castro government as both "the source of supply
and the catechist of the Salvadoran insurgency" and argued that
the administration should unleash the full weight of U.S. economic
and political influence "together with the reality of its military
power . . . in order to treat the problem at its source."[8] During
Reagan's first year, Cuba's role as an alleged source of arms for
Salvadoran guerrillas and its military relations with the Soviet
Union preoccupied State and Defense Department officials and
headed the agenda of a number of National Security Council
meetings.[9] However, while the administration waged a powerful
propaganda campaign to identify Cuba as a key player in the conflict in El Salvador, threatened military confrontation with the
Castro government, and began a sustained buildup of U.S. military
power in Central America, it stopped short of a decision to translate preparations for war against Cuba into action.

In February 1981, the State Department issued a White Paper
on El Salvador that said that Cuba was a major source of weapons
and training for Salvadoran guerrillas: "the insurgency in El Salvador has been progressively transformed into another case of
indirect armed aggression against a small Third World country by
Communist powers acting through Cuba."[10] Defining El Salvador's conflict as an East-West struggle, the White Paper deliberately ignored the facts: the country's deeply rooted unrest
expressed through political, social, and civil movements representing a wide range of political views and social strata, movements that had developed over a decade in opposition to repressive political rulers and their state apparatus.[11] Of course, this
White Paper replete with inaccuracies, unproven allegations, and
flimsy evidence about Cuba's supplying and directing the guerrilla movement, was intended to serve other purposes: to justify
the rapid buildup of U.S. interventionary capacity in El Salvador
and to portray that as a defense against Cuban and Soviet
involvement.[12]

The U.S. military buildup in Central America under the pretext
of defending El Salvador was also designed both to intimidate
Cuba by providing American troops with battle training in the
kind of terrain they could expect to encounter if an invasion of

Cuba was ordered and to put the Castro government on notice that this option was under serious consideration. Against this militarily threatening background, the Cubans strengthened their military capabilities. Soviet military aid increased by over 200 percent between 1980 and 1981 and has since remained at the 1981 level. "In addition, the Cubans reorganized their Armed Forces to make them more capable of deploying as small guerrilla units in the event of an invasion, and they organized a new militia of some 500,000 people to supplement the regular military."[13]

While the administration hastily conveyed the White Paper's message to Latin American ambassadors, Reagan officials still were studying more contingency plans, including military options, to put "a clear and unmistakable shot across the bow of Moscow and Havana."[14] The chief White House policy advisor, Edwin Meese, warned the Castro government that Washington "does not rule anything out" when it comes to stopping arms shipments to the Salvadoran guerrillas.[15] Under Secretary of State Walter J. Stoessel, Jr., made the same point in March 1981 testimony before the Senate Foreign Relations Committee. No political, economic, or military action against Cuba could be excluded if Cuba continued to provide material support to those fighting the Duarte regime.[16] For the moment, however, no concrete steps were taken to realize these threats of direct military confrontation.

In mid-1981, the plans became more active when the White House requested Congress to authorize a major increase in military and economic assistance for Central America and the Caribbean to counter Cuban and Soviet "subversion."[17] This followed speeches by Vice President George Bush and Secretary of State Haig describing Cuba as "the principal threat to peace in the region" and stating that the Castro government had been warned.[18] That September, Washington temporarily recalled the head of the U.S. Interest Section in Havana, Wayne Smith, for consultations. Weeks later, Secretary Haig announced that "extensive studies" had been completed on what to do about Cuban "subversion" in Central America, accused Havana of acting as "a proxy of the Soviet Union," and insisted that Cuba's military assistance to revolutionary movements in the area – particularly to the Salvadoran guerrillas – was on the increase.[19]

What evidence there is about Cuban assistance to Duarte's opponents reveals that Havana did provide moderate quantities of arms and limited training to the guerrillas just before their January 1981 military offensive, that thereafter arms transfers declined to a negligible or nonexistent level, and that all such transfers were rendered insignificant by the rapid escalation of U.S. military assistance to the Duarte regime (over $950 million in security assistance between 1981 and 1984) to prevent a Cuban-Soviet "takeover."[20] Despite Wayne Smith's assessment, the senior American diplomat in Cuba from 1979 to 1982, that there was "never . . . solid evidence of massive and substantial flows of arms from Cuba to Nicaragua and then to El Salvador,"[21] the Reagan administration persisted, making frantic assertions about weapons shipments and political and military advice to the Salvadoran guerrillas to excite fears about continuous outside control.

By late 1981, concern was rife that the Duarte government might fall unless the U.S. injected power. Following a memorandum authored primarily by State Department counselor (and later National Security Council advisor) Robert McFarlane, which argued that the United States was not doing enough to combat the Cuban threat, contingency planning to bolster the Salvadoran regime was stepped up. The Pentagon prepared military options, any of which could immediately be executed by the White House: a show of airpower, a major naval exercise, a quarantine, a comprehensive blockade as part of an act of war, or an invasion of the island by American and even Latin American forces. According to State Department officials, unnamed regional governments were sounded out regarding military operations against Cuba. Senior Reagan officials described this flurry of activity as "more than simply contingency planning, given the short deadlines for producing the plans and the general feeling that something must be done to prevent the collapse of the [Duarte] government."[22]

In early November 1981, the State Department dispatched a confidential report on supposed Cuban covert activities in Latin America to more than fifty U.S. diplomatic posts around the world. Embassy officials were told to circulate this report, which accused the Castro government of seeking to manipulate or overthrow Central American and Caribbean regimes.[23]

Then, at a critical November 16, 1981, National Security Council meeting, President Reagan approved a broad program of planning for paramilitary and political operations in Central America and the Caribbean designed to improve the U.S. military posture and put the revolutionary governments of Nicaragua and Cuba on notice that Washington was prepared to act unilaterally to eliminate sources of unrest in the region. Although senior Pentagon officials reportedly were still opposed to direct military intervention "on the grounds that costs and risks would be excessive in view of America's global military responsibilities," the Defense Department, on White House orders, drew up plans to deal with "unacceptable military action" by Cuba in Central America. The plans included, once again, the use of U.S. combat forces and other direct-pressure scenarios, such as a naval quarantine of Cuba to block domestic petroleum supplies and air attacks against Cuban military forces and installations. Paramilitary planning actions also were authorized by the National Security Council (NSC) against Cuban targets throughout the region. "In some circumstances," the NSC minutes state, the "CIA might (possibly using U.S. personnel) take unilateral paramilitary action against special Cuban targets." Furthermore, a new Caribbean military command was established to coordinate communications and intelligence operations by the United States and its allies; discussions began with the Honduran and Colombian governments over U.S. access to improved airfield facilities in Central America; and regular U.S. military exercises since this time have allowed Washington to engage in almost uninterruped shows of force in the region.[24]

In December 1981, Reagan formally authorized the covert action program presented at the November NSC meeting, approving the largest paramilitary and political action operation mounted by the CIA in almost a decade, with a first-stage operating budget of almost $20 million. The primary target was the Sandinista government in Nicaragua; secondary targets were Cubans and Cuban supply lines in Nicaragua and other parts of Central America.[25] Subsequent attacks on Cubans were not confined to military personnel, but extended to noncombatant civilians. The Sandinista government health and education programs, both staffed by substantial numbers of Cubans (approximately 500 and 2,200 respectively in 1983), suffered major human and material losses as a result of the CIA-orchestrated war against the regime: hundreds of schools either destroyed or closed down and more than 300 teachers killed and kidnapped through 1984; physicians and health care workers systematically attacked, tortured, and murdered by the so-called Contras, forcing the closure of dozens of health centers and health posts. By August 1986, 62 health facilities, including four large clinics and one hospital, had been completely or partially destroyed by the Contras.[26] Cubans involved in public works projects and in providing agricultural technical advice were also subject to the violent depredations perpetrated by these Washington-organized, financed, trained, and directed Nicaraguan exiles.

In April 1982, the NSC affirmed the goals of the December 1981 covert action program and approved a document stating, essentially, that, "Strategically, we have a vital interest in not allowing the proliferation of Cuba-model states. . . . In the short run we must work to eliminate Cuban-Soviet influence in the region."[27] The administration coupled these objectives with accusations of an increased Soviet military presence in Cuba and announced the largest ever naval exercise in the Caribbean.[28]

Since early 1982, military pressures have been employed by the White House to make Havana stop supporting regional allies and to keep the possibility of a more direct military confrontation on the front burner. During 1982 and 1983, for instance, the United States held a series of unprecedented naval and military maneuvers in the Caribbean and Central American region: in April and May 1982, American forces comprising 45,000 personnel, 60 warships, 360 combat aircraft, and 132 transport planes held simulated combat exercises in the Caribbean and the Gulf of Mexico; in February 1983, 4,600 U.S. army, naval, and air force personnel, 7,000 Panamanian National Guardsman, and 4,000 Honduran troops held exercises in Honduras and Panama; in March and April 1983, 36 American ships and 350 aircraft, augmented by seven British and Dutch vessels, together with an undisclosed number of personnel, held another simulated combat exercise, this time in the Western Atlantic and off Puerto Rico; from May 31 to June 15, 1983, 3,000 U.S. troops, including navy, air force, and ground crews, participated in Caribbean maneuvers in Puerto Rico and the Virgin Islands; between June and November 1983, 2,000 U.S. and 12,000 Latin American personnel from several countries participated in joint naval operations in the Caribbean; and between August 1983 and January 1984, 4,000 U.S. army and marine troops and 19 U.S. warships (including two aircraft carriers) with several thousand crewmen participated in maneuvers at a number of Central American locales.[29]

Pentagon and NSC officials justified these extraordinary military exercises on the grounds that Cuba might increase its involvement in Central America, especially Nicaragua. "All our indications," according to an NSC member in July 1983, "were that Cuba and the Soviet Union were preparing major military moves in Nicaragua, and so we had to move too." Whereas Defense

Department officials described the Pentagon's high profile in the area as "preemptive," other Reagan administration officials admitted that Washington lacked any hard evidence that Cuba was mobilizing to intervene militarily anywhere in Central America.[30]

In early 1984, a detailed study of Cuban and Soviet relations with Central American revolutionaries commissioned by the State Department's Bureau of Intelligence and Research not only gave no credence to these indications, but also implicitly criticized the administration for exaggerating the level of Cuban military activity. The report contrasted the claims of senior foreign policy officials that there were over 2,000 Cuban military advisors in Nicaragua with assessments by Latin American governments friendly to the United States who put the figure at approximately 1,000 and with the July 1983 statement of Cuban Vice-President Carlos Rafael Rodríguez that there were no more than several dozen Cuban military, intelligence, and security advisors in Nicaragua. The report proffered that Rodríguez' tally might well have been accurate, considering the wildly inflated U.S. claims (compared to Cuban figures ultimately accepted by Washington) on the number of Cuban military officials in Grenada when the Americans invaded in October 1983.[31] Adding credibility to Rodríguez' contention is the internationally respected *Jane's Defense Weekly*, which put the number of Cuban military and security advisors in Nicaragua at the beginning of 1984 at approximately 200 – a tenth of the total promoted by State Department and White House policymakers.[32]

The State Department report also questioned the accuracy of official statements and figures on Cuban military assistance to Central American revolutionary movements, singling out El Salvador: "the U.S. claim that all Salvadoran rebels have been trained by Cuba or Nicaragua, yet captured rebels assert that only specialists such as sappers and communication people have been trained by these nations."[33] William LeoGrande provides an even more telling assessment of the supposed veracity of Reaganite allegations about Cuba's role in El Salvador: "the intensity of the Administration's anti-Cuban rhetoric and its claims of new arms shipments from Cuba and Nicaragua bore an uncanny relation to the fortunes of the Salvadoran armed forces and the Congressional budget cycle. Whenever the floundering Salvadoran army needed new infusions of military aid, the Administration would report an increase in Cuban and Nicaraguan arms shipments to the guerrillas."[34]

Washington's attempts to blame Cuba for the massive U.S. military buildup in Central America between 1982 and 1984 is also contradicted by a major shift in Cuban regional policy since 1982 toward support for negotiated political settlements of area conflicts. The Castro government advised Nicaragua "to be flexible in negotiations with their neighbors and with the United States [and] press[ed] the FDR-FMLN to accept a negotiated solution to the Salvadoran civil war."[35] Havana also declared its support for the Contadora peace process, begun in January 1983 with the goal of achieving a region-wide settlement, as the only alternative to a more explosive possibility: direct U.S. military intervention in Central America.

The limited and apparently declining Cuban military presence in Central America between 1982 and 1984 contrasts dramatically with the parallel U.S. military buildup in the region that included, but was not confined to, large-scale joint armed forces maneuvers. During this three-year period, combined U.S. security assistance to El Salvador and Honduras totaled more than $1.2 billion; U.S. military exercises in Honduras accounted for more than $100 million, which did not include the costs involved in building airfields, radar stations, and a regional military training center that improved the fighting skills of thousands of Honduran and Salvadoran officers and troops; and the White House officially authorized $150 million for the CIA to organize, train, and direct thousands of Nicaraguan counterrevolutionary exiles seeking to overthrow the Sandinista government largely from staging bases inside Honduras – augmented by withdrawals from secret executive-branch contingency funds, the transfer of equipment to these exiles under cover of U.S. military maneuvers in Honduras, and the use of third-party surrogates (Argentina, Israel) to provide additional weaponry and training.[36] At the beginning of 1984, there were almost 15,000 U.S. military personnel in Central America[37] – more than seven times the number of Cuban military officials stationed in the region even according to estimates by senior Reagan administration policymakers. This massive U.S. commitment, completely out of proportion to the supposed Cuban threat, can be understood only in terms of the stake the White House has invested in military victories in Central America (rolling back established revolutionary regimes and destroying social revolutionary movements) to vindicate its larger, global policies. A defeat in El Salvador, for example, would call into question every assumption about the centrality of military power in confronting Third World revolutions.

During the first half of 1983, the rhetoric of U.S. policymakers was laced with threats of a readiness to bomb communication centers, airports, and oil refineries inside Cuba, reflecting the extent to which international state terrorism had become an established American foreign policy option under Reagan. Some of these threats stemmed from the late 1981 White House decision to launch a major propaganda offensive against the Castro government centered around the establishment of a radio station in Florida called Radio Martí that would beam broadcasts to the Caribbean island. In April and May 1983, Secretary of State Schultz, Assistant Secretary Enders, and other senior administration officials told congressional and broadcasting groups that if Castro tried to jam other American radio station broadcasts when Radio Martí went on the air, the U.S. government had a list of 40 retaliatory options, including the "surgical [military] removal of the offending [transmitting] antennas [in Cuba]" and a cutoff of communications between Havana and its overseas military forces.[38] Between April and July, American planes conducted numerous incursions over Cuban airspace, probably to evaluate the efficiency of the island's air defense network in the event that a "surgical" strike of some kind moved from the planning to the operational stage.[39]

The Reagan administration's penchant for deliberately inflating Cuba's role in Third World struggles was not confined to its relations with movements seeking political power. It extended to nationalist governments deemed hostile to U.S. strategic, political and economic interests. High on the list was the Maurice Bishop-led New Jewel Party government of Grenada, which was ostracized by Washington from its inception in March 1979 to its overthrow via invasion four and a half years later. The reason is not hard to find. The previously mentioned November 1981 State Department report on alleged Cuban subversion in the hemisphere included the accusation that Havana was turning Grenada into "a virtual client."[40] When George Shultz was appointed Secretary of State in the summer of 1982, he received a secret Department briefing paper saying that "Grenada is now a Cuban proxy."[41]

In October 1983, the White House authorized a direct military invasion of Grenada, supposedly to guarantee the safety of U.S. citizens and to restore order and democracy in the aftermath of the murder of Prime Minister Bishop and the disintegration of the New Jewel regime. Within hours of the marines' landing, however, President Reagan and senior administration officials shifted the primary justification, contending that the military operation was necessary to forestall a planned Cuban takeover of the island for the purpose of establishing a new base for exporting revolution to other countries.[42] In the absence of even minimal evidence for that, they proceeded to make sweeping charges of Cuban political and military influence over the Bishop government and announced the alleged discovery of a Cuban weapons and communications equipment base on the island. As the invasion continued, U.S. authorities inflated the number of Cuban personnel in Grenada from approximately 600 construction workers at the start of the invasion to 1,600 and strongly implied that most were military personnel or had extensive military training. To anchor the mirage of a thwarted Cuban "take-over," they also announced that the island's major development project at the time – the Port Salinas airport (described in a confidential 1980 World Bank memorandum as critical to the expansion of the tourist industry) – was a military enterprise and part of a broader Cuban strategy for turning Grenada into a staging area for terrorist activities.[43]

The veracity of these statements can be gauged from the fact that Democratic and even Republican members of the Senate Select Committee on Intelligence accused the White House of blatantly exaggerating the Cuban role. Based on access to intelligence information, including a briefing by two senior Reagan officials, these legislators concluded that the so-called evidence simply did not support the cluster of assertions, allegations, and claims made by the White House and the State Department about the Cuban presence in Grenada or its supposed plans for the island.[44] Subsequently, the administration backtracked on the number of Cubans on the island and their occupations. Indeed, it finally accepted, grudgingly, Cuba's own statement that there were only 748 of its nationals in Grenada, of which only 43 were military personnel and most of the rest construction workers – but not until Havana actually published the names and job descriptions of each person.[45] Regarding the Port Salinas airport, those facts that did not fit the White House scenario were ignored by American officials in their haste to target Cuba once more as the source of the problem: "No reference was made to the long gestation period of the [airport] or to the very cogent economic arguments there were for its completion." After the invasion, the British electronics company Plessey prepared a statement that identified 11 facilities any military airbase would require and noted that none of these features was in evidence at Port Salinas.[46]

The U.S. invasion of Grenada had a direct bearing on Washington's Cuba policy. First, it demonstrated that the Reagan administration was prepared to act unilaterally, with force, against a nationalist and/or revolutionary regime defined as hostile to American interests. In the process, it not only vindicated the use of force to roll back these kinds of governments but also indicated a willingness to exercise the military option again. Second, it illustrated Cuba's incapacity to offer military help to an ally under attack from the United States. By embarrassing and humiliating Cuba in this fashion, the United States sent a signal to Nicaragua that it could not expect military assistance from Havana in the event of a conflict with Washington or its Central American allies. The Castro government reluctantly acknowledged that it was not in a position to respond to any direct U.S. military thrust into other parts of the region. Finally, the Grenada invasion was part of an effort to undermine Cuban influence in Central America and the Caribbean and further isolate the Cuban government diplomatically. In this, the United States achieved, at least temporarily, a modicum of success. Cuba lost one of its closest regional supporters, and the implications of the U.S. invasion were not lost on other Cuban allies. Anxieties generated by the demonstration of American power, for instance, caused the revolutionary military junta in Surinam to force Havana to close its Embassy there.

The White House suffocates diplomacy

The Reagan critique of Carter administration policy toward the Third World was particularly harsh when it came to Carter's efforts to unfreeze U.S.-Cuban relations. Such initiatives were decried as simply encouraging Havana to pursue its "export of revolution." In the words of a State Department official, "The Carter Administration had an approach to Cuba that didn't work worth a damn."[47] The Reaganite assessment was that only a "get tough" approach would have any effect. Diplomacy aside, the Castro government was to be bludgeoned into making major concessions in the areas of foreign policy and ties to the Soviet Union if there was to be any basis for a rapprochement.

In February 1981, the head of the U.S. Interest Section in Havana, Wayne Smith, cabled the State Department that the

Cuban government was willing to hold bilateral discussions on El Salvador and other issues. Sometime in March, Smith extracted a reply from State's Director of Cuban Affairs who told him that the administration would not even give the Cuban request minimal consideration.[48] Recalled to Washington in June, Smith discovered why when asked to read a Cuba interagency task-force policy paper. "The basic assumption of the policy paper," he writes, "was that Castro could be intimidated. It therefore recommended a policy of steadily escalating tensions and uncertainties." In Smith's opinion, "Normalization was ruled out even as a distant possibility, no matter what Cuba did."[49] Back in Havana, Smith conferred with Cuban Vice Minister of Foreign Relations, Ricardo Alarcón, who conveyed his government's support for a negotiated political settlement in El Salvador.[50]

On November 23, one week after the National Security Council meeting at which the President gave the go-ahead for planning to increase the U.S. military and paramilitary presence in the Caribbean-Central American region, Secretary of State Haig traveled to Mexico City for a secret meeting with Vice President Carlos Rafael Rodríguez, who repeated Castro's willingness to place no restrictions on issues for discussion between the two countries and told him that the last thing Cuba wanted was a confrontation with the United States. But Haig haughtily demanded actions, not words. High-level diplomatic contacts were renewed in March 1982 when Haig dispatched Special Ambassador Vernon Walters, former CIA Deputy Director, to Havana for talks with Castro and other senior officials. Walters also heard Cuba's expressed readiness to begin negotiations on all matters of concern to Washington.[51]

These discussions occurred while the Cubans were insisting, publicly and privately, that they were no longer militarily involved in the conflict in El Salvador and while Wayne Smith's cables to Washington during 1981 about the Castro government's interest in improved relations and in helping to reduce tensions in Central America were being ignored. Havana wanted to discuss both bilateral issues and its foreign policy with Reagan officials. The State Department's eventual response to Smith's cables restated its contention that Cuba wanted to confer merely over a bilateral agenda (e.g., the economic embargo).[52] In later congressional testimony, Assistant Secretary of State Thomas Enders claimed that the Cubans had told Haig and Vernon Walters that its government's foreign policy, specifically in Central America and Africa, was "not negotiable."[53] When Smith again advocated diplomatic solutions, restating to the State Department that the Cubans were prepared to talk about Central America and other foreign policy issues, his superiors bluntly replied that Washington had no interest in negotiating with the Castro regime because to do so would be to "legitimate Cuba's presence in Central America."[54]

Smith's frustration over Washington's deflection of Cuban diplomatic overtures reached a new peak when other cables relating to a December 1981 conversation with Carlos Martínez Salsamendi, a senior Cuban foreign policy official, who told him that all forms of military assistance to the Salvadoran rebels had been terminated, were also not treated seriously. The State Department didn't even bother to answer these cables until March 1982, and then only to inform Smith that whether the Cuban claim was true was immaterial, that "we weren't interested in talks and weren't going to accept [terminated arms shipments] as a gesture."[55] In early 1982, the Reagan administration acted just as brusquely in dismissing a Mexican call for talks between the United States and Cuba and its offer to act as a mediator in any of the outstanding bilateral disputes.[56]

Meanwhile, Havana continued to press for negotiations with the White House to defuse what it viewed as "a very dangerous situation" in Central America that could easily deteriorate into armed conflict between the United States and Cuba.[57] In April 1982, a senior Cuban government official addressed, in more detail, these twin issues of Havana's policy toward El Salvador and negotiations with Washington. Acknowledging that diplomacy between the two countries was at a standstill, he nonetheless reasserted Cuba's readiness for a "relative accommodation." Cuba's foreign policy had become more restrained in recent months and the government was prepared to play "a positive role" in resolving Third World conflicts that were of concern to the White House. Regarding El Salvador, the Cuban official reiterated that military assistance to the guerrillas had terminated after the unsuccessful January 1981 military offensive against the Duarte regime and that his government was willing to participate in multilateral efforts to find a political solution to that conflict, even involving an international peacekeeping force, and even prior to a lifting of the U.S. economic embargo of Cuba.[58] Some days later, Carlos Rafael Rodríguez told the head of the U.S. Interest Section that Cuba supported "a peaceful solution in Central America."[59] These and similar statements made publicly and through diplomatic channels represented major concessions on Havana's part. For many years, the Castro government had made the termination of economic sanctions a *sine qua non* for foreign policy negotiations with Washington. But again, the Reagan administration was unmoved and treated the Cuban initiatives with disdain. About Central America, it "preferr[ed] to maintain the fiction that the Cubans were bent on exacerbating the regional crisis."[60]

Proposals from Cuba or other sources for improving bilateral ties met with persistent rejection in Washington where unsubstantiated allegations and assorted smokescreens substituted for diplomacy. Two Cuban proposals delivered through a Costa Rican intermediary and former government minister, Luis Burstin, during 1982 and 1983 were swiftly rebuffed, as was a March 1983 message from Castro, relayed through Republican Senator Lowell Weicker, suggesting talks on Central America and other areas of conflict. Apparently, when Weicker delivered the message to a senior State Department diplomat on his return from Havana, it was summarily rejected.[61]

Well-meaning allies were treated similarly by Washington. When Spanish Prime Minister Felipe González, who was presiding over a growing political rapprochement between Spain and Cuba, urged the White House to normalize ties with Havana during a Madrid meeting in early 1983 with Assistant Secretary Enders, the State Department response was quick and pointed. Intent on drowning any Cuban attempt at negotiations, it denounced Cuba for "flagrant intervention" in the internal affairs of other countries and ruled out any shift in the U.S. position until the Castro government adopted a "more responsible international role."[62]

Likewise, where the Reagan administration has entered into negotiations with Cuba over discrete bilateral issues, it has gone out of its way to emphasize the limited nature of such discussions and to minimize the effect of any successful outcome on basic U.S. policy. The immigration discussions in the latter half of 1984 were revealing on this point.

For more than four years, the United States had been pressing Cuba to take back a few thousand criminals and mental patients among the approximately 125,000 persons who left the island for Florida in the 1980 Mariel boatlift. Fearful of bolstering Reagan's 1984 presidential reelection campaign in any way, Havana preferred to leave negotiations until after the November election.

But in a concession to Washington, it agreed to begin talks in July 1984. Dismissing Castro's interest in an expanded agenda, Reagan officials made it clear that the meetings would be limited to immigration issues only.[63] When an agreement was signed in December 1984 to repatriate over 2,700 Cuban "undesirables" from American jails and hospitals and reopen Cuban emigration to the United States, White House spokesman Larry Speakes intoned that "it does not signal any change in U.S. policy toward Cuba. . . . We see no evidence that Cuba is prepared to change [its] behavior [in Central America or Africa]."[64] Responding in part to a Castro offer to participate in a mutual withdrawal of *all* foreign forces from Central America, National Security Council advisor Robert McFarlane, at the time of the immigration talks, characterized the Cuban proposals for ending regional hostilities as nothing more that "tactic[s] for diverting our attention away from the violence it is spreading . . . through Central America, Africa and the Caribbean."[65]

The State Department was particularly opposed to comprehensive discussions unless Havana proved willing to terminate military involvement in Angola. Yet there is a built-in stalemate involving this region that can be traced to U.S. policy and more than a little divisiveness on South Africa's part. For Reagan's policy on Cuba's departure from Angola has been linked to Namibian independence from South Africa. And Washington has made it clear to Pretoria that the Cubans must act first, must repatriate their troops from Angola before. . . . But then, as Cherri Waters writes, "the South Africans do not want to leave Namibia," anyway, so "they have simply applied continuous military pressure to ensure that the Angolans would not ask the Cubans to go."[66] Therefore, no extended U.S.-Cuban discussions. Guaranteed. Did the Reagan administration fail to foresee this stalemate? On the contrary, it suited their purpose: no negotiations with Cuba.

In early 1985, Castro again conveyed a willingness to negotiate with Washington over Central America and to exchange views on Cuba's military involvement in Angola and other parts of the African continent. He described recent diplomatic contacts between the two countries as "constructive and positive" and expressed the belief that immigration, coastguard, fishing-rights, radio-interference, and air-hijacking agreements provided a basis for improving relations. The State Department response was negative. One official cavalierly announced that the administration had "checked out" Castro's overtures and discovered they were "not serious." Another dismissed them bluntly with the comment that Castro wasn't saying "anything new" and restated the two preconditions for a more conciliatory U.S. attitude: Cuba must reduce or eliminate its "military and political alliance with the Soviet Union" and provide concrete evidence that it no longer supports Third World revolution.[67] More than these, it is Reagan's remarks that best expose the administration's opposition to "taking the diplomatic track," for between the lines of one of the President's flamboyant fantasies – about Cuba and four other governments "actively supporting the campaign of international terrorism against the United States, her allies and moderate Third World states" – we can read a tight-lipped intransigence.[68]

After six years of the Reagan presidency, the consensus among Western diplomats in Havana and Cuban foreign ministry officials is that the U.S.-Cuban relations are at their worst in over two decades. In January 1987, as if to emphasize the point, the State Department reassigned Curtis Kamman, the head of the U.S. Interest Section, to Washington with no plans to replace him. The top American diplomatic post in Cuba is vacant, indefinitely, for the first time since the Interest Section opened in 1977. On the social front, too, Cuba has been isolated, even insulted. Not once since he arrived in Washington, D.C., in January 1981, has the senior Cuban diplomat, Ramón Sánchez-Parodi, been invited to a U.S. government function.[69]

What the larger record since 1981 shows is that Cuba has repeatedly sought diplomatic routes to negotiate with the United States to resolve bilateral, regional, and global conflicts – only to be rebuffed by Washington's intransigence at almost every turn. The Castro government has shown itself prepared to modify its posture, to make concessions or compromises on issues such as immigration and foreign policy accorded the highest priority by the Reagan White House. Although Reagan officials feign support for the diplomatic option, they have consistently dismissed Cuban overtures as inconsequential, irrelevant, not serious, or lacking substance, and often demanded additional concessions as the price for any improvement in bilateral relations. In May 1983, Assistant Secretary of State Thomas Enders stumbled over the truth when he declared that the United States would resist Cuban requests for a dialogue because "this Cuban leadership takes negotiations as a sign of weakness."[70] But one must read that statement upside-down, as it were, for American policymakers since 1981 repeatedly have interpreted Cuban proposals as a sign of the Castro government's weakness and, thereby, have answered Havana's initiatives with new and more aggressive demands.

Reagan's Cuba diplomacy has featured two other qualities: seeming reasonableness and an interest in negotiations following harsh policy measures, and retaliations in response to Cuban concessions or failed negotiations. There was the April 1982 tightening of Cuban travel restrictions, after which U.S. officials quickly pointed out that the administration was ever ready for discussions. And there was the issue of Cuban migration to the United States. After the December 1984 immigration accord was signed, Reagan decided to go ahead with its propaganda station, Radio Martí.

In the spring of 1986, according to American officials, the Cuban government signalled its interest in reviving the 1984 accord, which it had suspended the day (May 20, 1985) Radio Martí began broadcasting, and no longer insisted that the station cease operations as a prerequisite for discussions. Instead, Havana linked support for renewing the accord with a recognition of its right to broadcast to the United States. Washington decided that this shift was reason enough for talks to get underway. On July 8, delegations headed by the original immigration agreement negotiators, the State Department's principal deputy legal advisor, Michael G. Kozak, and the Cuban deputy foreign minister Ricardo Alarcón, gathered in Mexico City. Two days later, the talks screeched to a halt over a Cuban proposal that it be granted permission to use clear-channel radio frequencies that could produce broadcasts heard throughout the United States. The State Department objected, declaring that the result would be widespread "disrupt[ion]" of the country's radio broadcasting industry.[71] The Reagan response to the failure of this latest Cuban effort at negotiations was quick: a new series of economic retaliations.

Ultimately, the Reagan White House attitude toward serious diplomatic negotiations with Havana reveals its larger, if unrealistic, objectives: to roll back the Cuban Revolution and break Havana's economic and military alliance with the Soviet Union. It is also based on the notion that diplomacy must be preceded by fundamental Cuban foreign policy concessions, even though they may be completely out of proportion to the likely benefits to be gained from normalized relations with Washington.

Bolstering the economic blockade

Although the Carter White House permitted no significant weak-
nening of U.S. bilateral and worldwide economic sanctions against
Cuba, the Reagan administration adopted a much more forceful,
aggressive approach toward this issue. Testifying before a U.S.
congressional committee in December 1981, Assistant Secretary
of State for Inter-American Affairs Thomas Enders declared that
the Cuban economic embargo would be tightened and enforced
more rigorously than it had been in the immediate past.[72] Planning
was also underway in the State Department to strengthen the
global blockade to further restrict Cuba's already minuscule
access to U.S. goods (largely via overseas subsidiaries of American
multinationals) and to the U.S. market (in the form of American
imports from third countries containing Cuban content).[73]

In April 1982, the few remaining bilateral economic links were
targeted for partial repeal or complete removal. The Reagan
administration revived the stringent pre-Carter ban on travel by
U.S. citizens to Cuba that had been in effect from 1963 to 1977.
Under the Trading with the Enemy Act, the Treasury Department
announced restrictions – principally on the use of American currency and credit cards to pay expenses related to Cuba travel –
that effectively put a stop to tourist and business travel to the
island. The Treasury also forced the closure of the major air link
between the United States and Cuba when it declared American
Airways Charter of Miami, which it said was controlled by Cuba,
a "designated Cuban national." This meant that the company's
assets were frozen and American nationals and companies were
barred, again under the Trading with the Enemy Act, from doing
business with it. The Department's Assistant Secretary for
Enforcement and Operations described these moves as part of
Washington's policy "of tightening the current trade and financial
embargo against Cuba" by reducing the country's access to hard-
currency earnings.[74]

In July 1986, the Reagan administration once again acted to
tighten the embargo, this time to force the Cubans both to moderate their demands for access to American airwaves and to revive
discussions of the immigration accord. The National Security
Council staff prepared a directive that included stronger enforcement measures to prevent hard currency and U.S. goods and technology circumventing existing restrictions and finding their way

to Cuba. The White House also planned action to halt what it alleged was the Castro government practice of selling exit permits allowing individuals to travel to third countries to apply for U.S. entry visas. On August 22, Reagan made the official proclamation: Efforts to identify and publicize "Cuba front" companies in third countries would be redoubled; U.S. citizens involved in organizing and promoting travel to Cuba would be monitored more rigorously; current restrictions on visits by Cuban citizens to the U.S. would be strictly implemented; and Cuban citizens were expressly prohibited from emigrating to the United States via "pass-through" nations.[75]

But the Reagan economic offensive against Cuba since 1981 has focused principally on the capitalist world economy and has centered around three major areas: sabotaging or obstructing Cuba's debt negotiations with its Western creditors; denying Havana access to capitalist sources of financing (governments, private banks, etc.); and pressuring allies not to sell merchandise to or purchase goods from the Caribbean island. The objective has been to shrink the Castro government's access to badly needed hard-currency earnings, which the White House views as the most effective means of fomenting internal economic disruption and slowdown.

Within weeks of the transition from Carter to Reagan, the State Department pressured the French government to cancel a planned March 1981 DM150 million syndicated medium-term Eurocredit loan to the Banco Nacional de Cuba made, at the behest of Paris and through the state-owned bank Crédit Lyonnais, by a group of Arab banks. The State Department was quick to register its disapproval and soon after the Giscard d'Estaing government announced it would get Crédit Lyonnais to delay the transaction by raising several technical problems. Days later, the credit was cancelled. Few Eurobankers did not attribute the switch to Washington's intervention.[76]

In the trade area, the new White House expressed particular concern over the striking rise in the value of purchases Cuba made from overseas subsidiaries of American corporations during Carter's last year – from $89.4 million in 1979 to $303.2 million in 1980. Attributing much of this increase to the proliferation of dummy corporations in Latin America and Europe, Washington moved quickly to close this embargo loophole. It drew on resources from the CIA, the FBI, and the Customs, Treasury, and Commerce Departments to expose these so-called bogus trading firms acting as "pass throughs" for U.S. machinery, spare parts, and luxury imports destined for Cuba. According to Treasury officials, more than 40 such companies were "exposed" during 1981 and the first half of 1982. The Treasury Department immediately termed all of them "designated Cuban nationals," which precluded any U.S. corporation or financial institution from doing business with them – at the risk of prosecution under the Trading with the Enemy Act. The effort probably contributed to the dramatic decline in sales by U.S. multinational subsidiaries to Havana between 1980 and 1981 from $303.2 million to $73.8 million.[77]

The Department of Commerce, through its Office of Export Enforcement, also was busy stemming the flow of American-controlled technology and commodities to Cuba from Western companies. In February 1982, for instance, it temporarily withdrew all U.S. export privileges of the Spanish-based Piher Semiconductors S.A., pending completion of an investigation of the firm's alleged role in the diversion of technological equipment that was on the NATO coordinating committee (COCOM's) list of materials that member states could not sell to socialist-bloc countries. In December 1983, the Department fined Toshiba Ampex Company Limited of Japan and denied it U.S. export privileges for 12 months following charges that it had participated in the illegal re-export of embargoed items (American television components) from Japan to Cuba. Six months later, the same penalty was imposed on two more Japanese companies – Saburo Soejima and Hiroshi Minabe – for re-exporting U.S. video recorders to Cuba without Washington's authorization.[78]

The rigorous enforcement of such economic sanctions against Cuba during 1982 and 1983 was accompanied by a persistent U.S. government campaign to make Cuba's foreign debt negotiations with its creditors as difficult as could be – if not impossible. By pressing Cuba's Western commercial bank and government lenders to demand the harshest terms for debt rescheduling, Washington hoped to adversely affect the internal performance of the island economy.

More than two decades after the 1959 revolution, the Cuban economy was as dependent on sugar as ever and, because it had to sell a significant part of its crop (that not purchased by the Soviets) in the world marketplace, it was still highly vulnerable to global price fluctuations. Between 1980 and September 1982, the price of sugar toppled from an already low 0.28 cents a pound to 0.07 cents. With a parallel fall in demand for other important exports, such as nickel, Cuba experienced a serious foreign exchange shortfall. The trade setbacks were accompanied by an increase in the country's debt repayment burden caused by rising interest rates which, in turn, increased pressure on the balance of payments. Higher interest rates alone added $119 million to Cuba's debt due at the end of 1980, increasing to $307 million in 1981 and to a projected $537 million by December 1982.[79] Simultaneously, the Cuban economy continued to suffer from the U.S. embargo. According to the Banco Nacional de Cuba, under Reagan the embargo was still costing the island millions of dollars annually in lost trade and investment. In March 1982, the cumulative impact of these externally induced economic pressures forced Havana to approach its capitalist-bloc financial creditors to reschedule $1.2 billion of its $3.5 billion foreign debt falling due before the end of 1985. The Castro government wanted its Western European, Japanese, and Canadian commercial bank and government creditors to postpone repayment (but not interest payments) for ten years with a three-year grace period.

As a debt-payer and credit risk, revolutionary Cuba had developed an enviable reputation with the international financial community. As recently as 1985, a Canadian banker said that "It's unanimously recognized among banks that in terms of risk Cuba is one of the best . . . [it] is the only country where banks have never had a repayment problem. . . . It's the only country that has never requested a single additional penny as part of its restructuring."[80] Still, the Reagan White House has been poised to take advantage of any opportunity to squeeze the Cuban economy and, when Havana first broached debt renegotiations in March 1982, the *Financial Times* reported: "According to the U.S. officials, Washington is actively discouraging Western banks from participation in any rescheduling of Cuba's debt to the West."[81] Over the next twelve months, American officials energetically stalked the trails to prevent foreign bankers (and governments) from dealing with the Cuban request. Cuban Vice President Carlos Rafael Rodríguez conceded that U.S. pressures were complicating the island's efforts to reach a successful outcome with its Western lenders.[82]

Although Cuba's creditors appeared likely to grant the regime some kind of breathing space, Washington was intent that the island would not receive, as one State Department official put it, "any special treatment."[83] In September 1982, another U.S. official declared that "There is a lot more we can do to hurt the

Cubans [in this area] . . . and we are seriously considering all the options."[84] One option was to challenge the credibility of the special Banco Nacional report on the Cuban economy prepared for all of the country's creditors prior to the debt renegotiation meetings. On October 17, 1982, thereby, the State Department sent a memorandum to U.S. embassies in Paris, Rome, Tokyo, and other lending countries accusing the Castro government of providing "false or misleading" economic data in the Banco Nacional study, the gist of the memo to be conveyed to involved local bankers.[85]

The Reagan administration even threatened direct U.S. intervention in debt negotiations to ensure that Cuba was accorded no special consideration by its Western creditors, arguing that it was entitled to because of outstanding loans made to prerevolutionary Cuban governments that Castro did not recognize. American strategy at the November 1982 Paris meeting of Cuba's creditors was outlined in a diplomatic cable to Washington: "We deliberately kept open the possibility we might participate as a creditor. This will give us added influence on the economic stabilization package and on the conditionality the creditors will require as the creditors now know that Cuba doesn't want a multinational rescheduling with the U.S. present." The specter of U.S. participation forcing each creditor to negotiate individually with Cuba – a prospect that appealed to none – permitted American officials to keep maximum pressure on the bankers and governments "to hang tough on a good economic program" that involved no concessions to Havana.[86]

Reagan efforts to cajole Western public and private financial institutions into setting harsh terms for renegotiating Cuba's medium- and long-term debts were, however, relatively unsuccessful for at least three reasons. First, the Castro government had successfully reduced the country's foreign debt by $795 million (38 percent) between 1979 and 1982, whereas Latin America's 12 biggest debtors' total obligations increased by $79 billion (75 percent) during this same period. Second, the creditors were influenced by the socialist bloc's Council for Mutual Economic Assistance (COMECON) helping with Cuba's debt problems. They noted an extraordinarily liberal $7 billion debt renegotiation in the mid-1970s – an interest-free 25 years with a 13-year grace period. Finally, the Cuban negotiators at the Paris meetings gave a commitment that the country would reduce industrial imports by 15 percent and increase exports by 10 percent between 1981 and 1985.[87]

In March 1983, approximately six months after the Paris meetings began, Japan and ten European governments agreed to reschedule 95 percent of $413 million due between September 1982 and December 1983 for repayment over eight and a half years with a three-year grace period. In April, Cuba's private-bank creditors rescheduled obligations totalling $468 million due before December 1983 under a similar agreement. The banks' steering committee, chaired by Crédit Lyonnais, also agreed to consider a Cuban request for new short-term credits based on Castro government calculations of hard-currency needs to normalize trade ties with the West.[88] Although forced to settle for slightly shorter payment periods than requested – and less than the average 10½ years repayment and five years grace allowed most Third World countries – the Cubans viewed the overall outcome of the negotiations as sufficiently favorable to "provide the relief needed to normalize our commercial and financial relations with the market economies."[89] French bankers concurred.

In December 1983, Washington attempted to sabotage another debt rescheduling agreement between Cuba and 150 Western banks to stretch out repayment of $130 million in short-term debts. One of the participating creditor institutions was the Swiss-based Trade Development Bank, which had extended a small loan to the Castro government in 1978. Subsequently, the American Express Company gained majority control of the Bank, which automatically made its activities subject to U.S. laws. According to American Express officials, the Trade Development Bank was directed by U.S. regulatory authorities not to participate in the rescheduling on the grounds that to do so would contravene the ban on new U.S. bank loans to Cuba. This obstacle was finally surmounted in January 1984 when the Swiss-based bank sold its loan to an unnamed bank not owned or controlled by American interests.[90]

Cuba's successful rescheduling of $254 million in short-term loans to Western governments at meetings of the so-called Paris Club in July 1984 was attributable, in large part, to its splendid economic performance over the previous twelve months. All major economic targets established in connection with the 1983 multilateral rescheduling agreement were reached or exceeded. The 1983 economic growth rate of 5.2 percent more than doubled creditors expectations, while the current account surplus of $237.8 million in convertible currencies was worlds beyond creditor projections of $5.8 million. Western governments participating in the July discussions were also impressed by notable increases in labor productivity and greater economies in the use of energy, raw materials, and imports. In the trade sphere, non-sugar exports increased between 1982 and 1983, total exports rose by 12 percent, while imports increased only marginally more than did total exports (by 12.4 percent) – figures interpreted by the creditor states as satisfactorily meeting commitments, especially given the constraints resulting from a downturn in the global economy.[91] Finally, the confidential Banco Nacional 1984 report on the Cuban economy presented to the creditor nations in Paris revealed that the island's total foreign debt in convertible currency had experienced a 6 percent decline since 1981, which compared more than favorably with the total Latin American foreign debt increase of nearly 30 percent during the same period.[92]

As mentioned, Western bankers' and governments' confidence in Cuba also was anchored in a belief that the Soviet commitment to the Castro government would obviate any serious threat to the island economy. The interpretation was not mistaken. In June 1984, for example, the Council for Mutual Economic Assistance (COMECON) reassured Havana that it would supply continued funding for nickel mining, nuclear energy projects, and petroleum imports, and it established a new agreement on Cuban sugar imports, which have preferential access to COMECON markets at protected prices. In October 1984, Cuba and the Soviet Union signed a new five-year cooperation agreement covering 1986–1990 that ratified the decisions reached at the June meeting. Under this agreement, there was a 50 percent increase in Soviet aid over the previous five-year pact and a commitment by Moscow to reschedule all Cuba's debt repayments to the bloc countries falling due before 1990, thereby significantly improving Cuba's ability to remain on good terms with its Western creditors.[93] The agreement also held in place an arrangement whereby the Castro government could sell surplus Soviet oil on the international market, which allowed Havana to offset the effect of plummeting world sugar prices (only 6.8 cents per ton in 1984).[94] In 1983 and 1984, oil sales produced almost double the amount of hard currency received from sugar exports; in 1985, petroleum export earnings totaled approximately $600 million and again exceeded the value of sugar exports.[95]

The terms of the July 1984 Paris Club meeting were formalized in December, at which time Cuba and its creditor commercial banks contracted to reschedule $100 million falling due in 1984 and to extend short-term credit lines for the equivalent of $490 million until September 1985. The banks allowed a nine-year repayment period with five years' grace – an improvement over 1983, but still unfavorable when compared with repayment terms obtained by Mexico (14 years), Argentina (12 years), Venezuela (12 years), and most other Latin American countries at this time.[96]

In May 1985, Banco Nacional President Raúl León Torrás began a new round of talks with creditor governments in Paris on debt refinancing and strategies for expanding Cuba's trade with the West, which had declined from approximately 40 percent of total trade in the mid-1970s to a current level below 15 percent. According to Cuban officials, the economy, which registered another year of impressive economic growth in 1985 (7.4 percent), was quite capable of export expansion, but required the cooperation of its capitalist trading partners. In mid-July, Cuba rescheduled $140 million out of $165 million in medium- and long-term debts falling due in 1985 to its Paris Club creditors (Western governments). The following September, Cuba negotiated another rescheduling, this time involving $82 million in medium-term debts owed to 110 foreign commercial banks, with the debtor receiving a six-year grace period with repayment to take place over the subsequent four years. This accord also rescheduled payment on approximately $375 million in short-term lines of credit provided by 70 Western financial institutions to the Banco Nacional de Cuba from September 1985 to September 1986.[97]

In late April 1986, an unusually poor sugar harvest, low world sugar prices, and the collapse of international petroleum prices forced Cuba to postpone negotiations on rescheduling $200 million in debts falling due to the Paris Club nations that year. The resale of surplus Soviet crude oil and refined products to Western Europe produced no more than $450 million in hard-currency earnings in 1986, compared with around $600 million in 1985. Instead of a planned trade surplus of $260 million, the Cuban government confronted a 1986 trade deficit of $200 million.[98] In early May, Havana also proposed deferring interest payments on the more than $1 billion of its debt owed to commercial banks in Western Europe, Japan, and Canada. A Banco Nacional de Cuba report presented at a meeting with creditors in Havana requested an additional $340 million in hard-currency loans to permit the regime to meet its debt obligations contracted in 1983, 1984, and 1985, without drastically affecting its earnings capacity. The report also proposed a 12-year rescheduling of debt with a six-year grace period for payments due in 1986–1987.[99]

On July 1, a critical hard-currency shortage forced Cuba to stop payment on both the principal and interest of most of its $3.5-billion debt, pending meetings with public and private creditors. In the weeks that followed, Havana reached agreement with the Paris Club governments to reschedule 95 percent of debts falling due in 1986, but the request for hundreds of millions of dollars in new loans fell largely on deaf ears. The steering committee of the commercial bank creditors, chaired by Crédit Lyonnais, also made a favorable determination regarding debt rescheduling and was more forthcoming in the area of new loans. Although they did not totally accept the Banco Nacional's proposed refinancing package that included a new repayment period of 12 years with three years' grace for the $100 million in payments falling due in 1986, the banks offered to reschedule $75 million of the amount over 10 years with six years' grace, to lend Cuba an additional $85 million, and to extend for another year $600 million in trade credit lines.[100] Continued sympathetic and relatively generous treatment by the Paris Club and the multinational bankers, given Cuba's fiscal circumstances, was in no small measure based on Cuba's estimable debt history, its determination not to default, and its desire to avoid a rupture in the flow of service payments.

Despite slumping world sugar prices, Cuba's internal economic problems, and Washington's ongoing efforts to impose an international debt squeeze on the Castro government, the latter's several successful debt reschedulings make it clear that Western bankers and governments preferred to make decisions on the basis of the Cuban economy's performance; Havana's track record as a scrupulous, highly responsible debtor; its commitment to maintaining good relations with creditors because of the need to expand trade with the West; and Soviet economic guarantees. By adhering to their own assessments, Cuba's creditors indirectly asserted that U.S. objectives were ineffective or counterproductive and could not be allowed to undermine profitable deals. Thus, the Reagan administration's major objective – to destabilize the Cuban economy by coercing and badgering the island's Western creditors to demand the toughest possible terms – was a spectacular failure.

Moreover, compared to both the rest of Latin America and Cuba's economic growth in the 1970s (an average annual 5.7 percent), the island's economic performance during the first half of the 1980s was exceptional. While all other regional economies languished between 1981 and 1983 (13 exhibited negative growth rates, the remaining seven averaged yearly increases between 0.8 percent and 3.3 percent), the Cuban economy grew by an annual average of 7.7 percent; in 1984, by 7.4 percent. In 1985, despite extraordinarily low sugar prices, Washington's efforts to block or limit Cuba's exports to the West, and natural disasters in the agricultural sector, the economy still grew by 4.8 percent. That year, investments increased over 1984 by 2.7 percent, exports grew by 4.8 percent, and sugar production by 2.3 percent. Cuba's Gross National Product growth rate for the period 1981 to 1985 was the highest in Latin America.[101]

The United Nations Economic Commission for Latin America (ECLA) has provided more telling confirmation of Cuba's economic achievements during the Reagan presidency. Based on official government statistics, ECLA calculated that while real per capita Gross Domestic Product in Latin America (excluding Cuba) fell at an average annual rate of 1.7 percent between 1980 and 1985, Cuba's constant price per capita Gross Social Product (as distinct from Gross Domestic Product) increased at an average annual rate of 6.7 percent during the same period.[102]

The lesson of Cuba's success and Reagan's failure is that, in an increasingly competitive capitalist world and in the absence of meaningful U.S. retaliatory measures available for use against Cuba's Western creditors, American government efforts to promote a foreign debt squeeze are likely to be as unsuccessful in the future as they have been in the past.

The Reagan White House also has conducted a highly aggressive campaign, spearheaded by the Treasury and Commerce Departments, to tighten global trade sanctions against Cuba. The most dramatic form it has taken has been the threat of "secondary boycotts" to pressure allied governments and their business communities not to purchase from or make large-scale investments in those sectors of the Cuban economy formerly controlled by American capital. This issue was given explicit expression in an April 1982 National Security Council policy recommendation calling for a "quantum tightening of the economic embargo of Cuba by stronger restrictions on Cuban content [in imports to the U.S.] from third countries."[103] The major targets were sugar and nickel.

In early 1982, the State Department reportedly considered boycotting all products that contained Cuban sugar. This threatened hundreds of processed foods, especially from such close allies as Canada, which exported annually approximately $1.5 billion worth of food and drinks to the United States. Canada was a significant importer of Cuban sugar ($117 million in 1980), some of which found its way into the country's American sales.

Canadian companies apparently were already skittish about expanding their activities in Cuba. The Cuban Deputy Chairman for Economic Cooperation told a Canadian parliamentary delegation in January 1982 that, during the previous year, other U.S. pressures were responsible for a Canadian firm's decision to withdraw from bidding on a $100 million power station contract, for Petrocanada's terminating offshore oil exploration discussions with Havana, and for the collapse of negotiations with Canada-wide Company to construct a citrus processing plant in Cuba.[104]

Cuban nickel exports had obsessed American governments throughout the 1960s and 1970s, leading to efforts to force Western governments to find alternative sources. The Reagan administration has pursued this policy with a vengeance, seeking to strengthen the worldwide U.S. ban on the import of goods containing Cuban nickel, limit the sale of Cuban nickel to the West, and discourage capitalist countries from investing or otherwise participating in Cuban plans to expand the island's nickel-producing capacity. The 1982 Banco Nacional de Cuba economic report presented to the country's creditors noted that at least six Western companies had suspended nickel investment discussions and, in some cases, actually had cancelled contracts because of explicit threats of retaliation by the United States. And in 1983, according to Western sources, a number of European enterprises also reneged on signed agreements to invest in the Cuban nickel industry.[105] Reagan policymakers consistently have justified the nickel blockade as a response to Cuba's "export of revolution" in Central America and other parts of the Third World. No surprises there.

Recent attempts to make allies certify that no products exported to America contain Cuban nickel have forced Western governments once again to balance the importance of limiting political conflicts with Washington against their own economic interests. Between 1981 and 1983, the Reagan administration sat on targeted countries to elicit commitments relating to Cuban nickel. Some were receptive. In March 1981, Washington lifted a November 1980 ban on the French engineering and steel firm Creusot Loire after the Giscard d'Estaing government certified that the company no longer used Cuban nickel. The following January, the U.S. Treasury Department negotiated a similar agreement with the Italians over a local steel manufacturer. Dealings with other countries, however proved more complicated.

Toward the end of 1982, U.S. officials looked into the possibility that Japan was exporting stainless-steel products to America that included Cuban nickel. Washington warned that unless Tokyo took appropriate measures, all exports with Cuban nickel components, including such products as automobiles and motorcycles, might be denied access to its highly profitable market. Japanese opposition to these U.S. threats was widespread, not the least because Cuba was the country's major trading partner in the Caribbean and a showcase for Japanese technology. Even though Japan imported only 1,200 tons of unrefined Cuban nickel (out of an annual import total of approximately 380,000 tons), the involved companies were reluctant to reject a reliable supplier. The Japanese government decided to take no action against those enterprises purchasing nickel from Cuba, but it did relay the U.S.'s threat to Japan's daily economic newspaper, *Nihon Keizai*.[106]

High-level meetings between U.S. Treasury and Japanese government officials in 1983 finally diluted the conflict. Tokyo consented to certification procedures, to take effect on August 19, 1983, that would ensure there would be no Cuban nickel in stainless steel and other products exported to the United States. That mollified Washington, while Japanese officials did not foresee the ban creating problems for their steel manufacturers and expressed the belief that producers of nickel-bearing commodities could adjust easily without interrupting their American sales. Meanwhile, Japanese firms indicated no intentions of cutting back on nickel imports from Cuba and industry sources noted the minuscule proportion of special steel exports that contained a Cuban component. The August agreement, however, did require Japanese companies using Cuban nickel to register with the government and keep records of the products used in exports to the United States.[107]

Like the Japanese, the Dutch accommodated Washington's concern in a manner that didn't really interfere with Netherlands-Cuba trade anyway, nor with prospects of expanded commerce once Havana's foreign debt and foreign exchange positions improved. Responding to American diplomatic overtures, The Hague ostensibly agreed to cooperate with the U.S. embargo of imports containing Cuban nickel. According to a Treasury announcement of September 1983, the Dutch government had informed Washington that virtually no Cuban nickel was to be found in exports destined for the United States. After further high-level bilateral negotiations, The Hague verified this in writing. But the Dutch action was little more than political pragmatism, cooperation at no cost, for while the Netherlands imported a relatively significant quantity of Cuban nickel, it produced no stainless-steel products and none of its manufactured exports contained more than 2.5 percent nickel, which was below the figure that would have made U.S. import restrictions on Cuban nickel apply.[108]

Having signed agreements with France, Italy, Japan, and the Netherlands, the Reagan administration turned to West Germany and even to the Soviet Union. Negotiations with West Germany, beginning in late 1983, produced an agreement in principle under which Bonn would not use Cuban nickel in stainless-steel exports to the United States. Around this time, Washington also placed a ban on Soviet semifinished nickel products (ingots, slabs, bars, etc.) entering the American market until Moscow could certify that they did not contain Cuban nickel. Discussions between the U.S. and West Germany continued until August 1984 when Bonn agreed, in return for an American pledge to institute no formal certification procedure, to notify the Treasury Department, annually, if local producers were using Cuban nickel or had it in their inventories. West German officials also consented to inform Treasury 60 days in advance if any large German company planned to import Cuban nickel. By the end of 1985, State and Treasury Department officials were reporting that West German imports of Cuban nickel had dropped to a negligible level.[109]

The Reagan efforts to blockade Cuban nickel exports to the West have brought largely symbolic adjustments by some countries and more substantive concessions by others. Cuban nickel sales to Western Europe did increase between 1982 and 1983, but this was due largely to European Economic Community restrictions on purchases of Soviet nickel. According to the London-based *Latin America Commodities Report*, this trend was reversed the following year as Cuban sales to Western Europe and Japan declined from 5,200 tons in 1983 to no more than 3,500 tons in 1984.[110] Overall, U.S. efforts have contributed to the White House goal of diminishing Cuba's nickel exports to the West, thus forcing the Castro government to sell a greater proportion of its nickel to the Soviet Union and limiting the amount of convertible currency available to Havana to purchase vital imports from the capitalist bloc.

Between the mid-1970s and the first half of the 1980s, the value of Cuba's trade (exports and imports) with the West experienced a dramatic fall from approximately 40 percent to less than 15 percent of total trade. In 1975, Cuba's five major Western trading partners (Japan, France, England, Spain, Canada) engaged in trade with the Caribbean island worth just under $1.8 billion; for the two-year period 1982–1983, this figure totalled less than $170 million.[111] Nonetheless, since 1981, Western Europe, Japan, and Canada have continued to view Cuba as an important or potentially important commercial partner and have remained willing to provide state credit guarantees to boost the competitive position of their exporters in the Cuban trade. The Japanese government, for example, sanctioned the country's Export-Import Bank offer of a medium-term credit line in fiscal 1982 that was expected to benefit the local transport industry, specifically in-progress negotiations between Cuba and three Japanese companies (Nissan, Hino, and Isuzu) bidding on orders for about 1,400 trucks.[112]

The constraints on Cuba's role as a market for Western goods during the Reagan presidency have been less a function of Washington's pressures (persistent as they have been) than of Cuba's hard-currency and foreign-debt problems. In particular, the sharp decline in the world market price for sugar which, according to the London-based *Quarterly Economic Review of Cuba*, accounted for most of the more than twelvefold increase in Cuba's trade deficit with the West between 1983 and 1984.[113] Foreign exchange problems and declining export prices continued to complicate Cuba's trade ties with its capitalist partners during 1985 and 1986. In December 1986, for instance, the Japanese Ministry of International Trade and Industry gave precisely these reasons for deciding to stop providing government export insurance to local companies trading with Cuba.[114]

Still, White House obstacles heaped in the way of Cuba's efforts to increase its exports to the capitalist bloc have had an effect, and Cuba's falling exports to the West, in turn, exacerbated the island's hard-currency problems in the early 1980s. Since the mid-1970s, there has been an absolute and a relative decline in the value of Cuba's exports to America's allies. In 1975, Cuba's $1 billion in exports to its five most important capitalist markets exceeded its imports from these countries by more than $200 million; in the two-year period 1982–1983, Cuban exports to these same markets accounted for just over 33 percent of the value of total trade with these countries ($58 million out of approximately $170 million).[115] In other words, during 1982–1983, Cuba became more of an importer than an exporter with these countries.

France, Spain, England, and other Western countries engaged in longstanding commerce with revolutionary Cuba continue to base their export decisions largely on pragmatic considerations. The French government of Francois Mitterand aggressively supported local exporters, including those selling in the Cuban market. Toward the end of 1981, the Banco Nacional secured a FR57.5 million medium-term trade-related syndicated loan managed by the French Societe Generale to enable Havana to purchase much needed transport equipment.[116] By 1983, the ready availability of state credits had consolidated France's position as the leading Western supplier of goods to Cuba. During the first half of that year, French exports to Cuba more than doubled compared with the same period in 1982, largely as a result of government credit coverage for Cuba's purchase of food and machinery worth $27 million. In October 1983, France agreed to another £12 million in commercial credits, which probably contributed to Renault Véhicules Industriels' successful pursuit of an £8 million contract for heavy trucks awarded it by Havana in January 1984.[117]

The growth of French trade with Cuba during the first part of the 1980s had been closely matched by Spain's expanding commercial ties with the revolutionary regime. Like the French, the Spanish state's role in this development – providing credit guarantees to win large export orders – has been prominent. In December 1983, for instance, Spanish shipyards received a contract to build eight merchant vessels for Cuba under a leasing deal worth £52 million to be financed by the government's Industrial Credit Bank. Reinforcing Madrid's decision was the fact that this was the first contract the shipyards had received that year.[118] A 1984 trade protocol signed between the two countries not only included Spain's agreement to participate in a number of large-scale heavy industry and industrial projects in Cuba, but also a commitment to increase its existing levels of credit assistance to local exporters in order to boost bilateral trade.

Curiously, Spain's socialist government under Felipe González has responded to the U.S. economic blockade of Cuba with much the same mixture of limited accommodation to maintain trade relations that characterized the fascist Franco regime in the 1960s. A potential conflict between Washington and Madrid over the Western embargo on the export of high-technology materials to socialist-bloc countries and their allies did surface, initially in June 1984, when State Department official Dennis Lamb warned the González government of possible restrictions on American high-technology sales to Spain if satisfactory steps were not taken to prevent this kind of technology from being re-exported to socialist-bloc countries, especially to Cuba.[119] Subsequently, in 1985, a local electronics company, Piher, was blacklisted by Washington for re-exporting American television components that were on the restricted list. Piher ultimately agreed to pay a fine imposed by Washington "after a U.S. embargo took the firm to the brink of collapse."[120] But Madrid did not appear unduly concerned over a possible repetition of this problem for, later that year, it agreed to sell Cuba a number of complete industrial plants. According to local bankers, the government and the business community were in consensus on one point: Political considerations such as foreign policy disputes between Spain and its Western allies should not be allowed to obstruct access to secure, stable, profitable markets. This pragmatic Spanish attitude toward trade with Cuba in the Reagan era has been shaped also by the fact "that the exports to Cuba most benefit those sectors of the Spanish economy facing most difficulties in competing with other Western nations – steel-making, shipbuilding and transport – as well as those Spain is trying to boost, such as agricultural machinery and chemicals."[121] By 1985, Cuba had become Spain's most important market in Latin America. In October, this development was cemented with the signing of a number of bilateral economic cooperation agreements, including a $62 million Spanish government-guaranteed credit to facilitate exports to Cuba.[122]

Spain's Prime Minister González paid a fence-mending visit to Cuba in November 1986, discussing with Fidel Castro a range of bilateral issues. González's objectives were twofold: to push for compensation payments of $120 million (scaled down from $270 million) still owed to 3,000 Spanish nationals whose properties were expropriated in the early 1960s, and to lobby for the release of political prisoners. Cuba's need to maintain continued access to Spanish government credits and a desire to negotiate an easing of debt repayment terms were key calculations in dictating Havana's response. Although not prepared to pay $120 million in compensation, the Cuban government acknowledged the substance of the Spanish argument and agreed to provide $40 million over a 15-year time period. Apparently, Castro also offered a private commitment to free some political prisoners. Spain's satisfaction with the outcome of the talks was instrumental in Madrid's decision to participate in additional government-to-government discussions about Cuba's pressing economic concerns. Soon after the González-Castro meeting, the Spanish-Cuban trade commission began a series of meetings to thrash out the questions of credits and debt repayment schedules.[123]

British trade with Cuba since the advent of the Reagan administration has deviated little from the approach pursued since the 1960s: a determination to maintain traditional commercial ties accompanied by discrete concessions to minimize potential political conflicts with Washington. The Thatcher government's policy on state credits to foster Cuban trade is revealing in this regard. In October 1981, the British Export Credits Guarantee Department (ECGD) agreed to underwrite a £5 million loan by the Midland Bank to the Banco Nacional de Cuba to allow British exporters to receive cash payments for Cuban purchases of capital and semicapital goods.[124] In May 1982, the British banking firm of Morgan Grenfell headed a consortium of financial institutions that put together a £19 million loan to the Banco Nacional.[125] Meanwhile, Whitehall has strictly limited the amount of state credit guarantees available in any one year and, on occasion, has imposed unusually stringent conditions governing exporters' access to this financial backing. In February 1983, for example, amid Cuba's debt renegotiations with its Western creditors, the ECGD tightened its conditions for credit coverage of export sales to Cuba. Companies were informed that protection would be afforded only to those holding irrevocable letters of credit.[126] These temporary or longer term credit restrictions announced by the Thatcher government appear to be partly a response to Cuban economic problems and partly an effort to accommodate U.S. concerns without fundamentally disrupting, or indeed opposing future expansion of, such trade.

The most pressing complaint of British traders engaged in Cuba trade or in producing commodities that might find a market there has been Whitehall's refusal to lift the upper limit on short-term credit coverage. Until late 1985, the maximum provided was two credit insurance facilities of £5 million each. This amount was repeatedly criticized as inadequate by the Confederation of British Industry, which was convinced that local exporters could substantially increase England's share of the Cuban market if state credit guarantees were increased.[127] The private Midland Bank in July 1985 provided a major boost to British exporters to Cuba by establishing a £30 million credit line over two or three years geared to companies producing medical, transport, maritime, and medium technology goods and sugar-refining equipment. Some months later, following discussion between the ECGD and Banco Nacional de Cuba officials, the ECGD decided to double its total insurance coverage for Cuba to £20 million, limited to a maximum of one year.[128] This increase, however was dwarfed by a January 1986 announcement of a unique five-year agreement between a United Kingdom private-sector trading company and a socialist-state trading agency aimed at increasing bilateral trade over the period of the contract by £350 million. The company, Goodward, backed by the Midland Bank, will purchase £40 million worth of Cuban exports annually, while Havana will import £30 million in British goods each year.[129] In June 1986, representatives of approximately 45 British companies visited the island to set up the new trade links made possible by Midland Bank's actions. Later that year, London Chamber of Commerce officials returning from a United Kingdom trade mission of 30 companies to Cuba described British business interest in the island economy as almost unprecedented. "One factor stimulating British trade interest," a *Financial Times* correspondent wrote, "is the attraction of doing business in America's back garden without having to compete with U.S. companies."[130]

Finally, however, it should be noted that in at least one case not all constraints on Cuba's ability to increase its trade with the West are a function of purely economic considerations or of U.S. policy pressures. The current impasse between Cuba and West Germany over the "Berlin Clause" clearly demonstrates how long-held Havana foreign policy positions can have economic consequences with countries other than the United States. The West German business community's interest in expanding its limited commercial relations with Cuba continues to founder on the reef of the "Berlin Clause," which recognizes West Berlin as part of West Germany. Havana's refusal to subscribe to that clause, which is attached to all of Bonn's bilateral agreements, has meant that West Germany's export insurance agency, Hermes AG, cannot finance exports to Cuba. A December 1984 Cuban economic mission led by Raúl Taladrid, the president of the State Commission on Economic Cooperation, failed to eliminate this impasse. Cuban Deputy Foreign Minister Jorge Bolaños was told in Bonn in March 1985 that the Castro government's insistence on West Berlin's "special status" perhaps was the key impediment to an increase in trade.[131] In April, the *Latin America Weekly Report* revealed that Bonn was not above taking advantage of Cuba's desire to renegotiate its DM8 million debt with West German private creditors by putting pressure on Havana to change its position on the Berlin Clause.[132] Meanwhile, sentiment appeared to be growing not only within the private sector but also among West German foreign ministry officials in favor of finding some way around the problem, for there was a widespread belief that the availability of West German state credits to finance trade with Cuba would lead to a substantial increase in the volume of such trade.[133]

Maintaining Cuba's political isolation

Since 1982, Cuba's relations with Latin America have improved considerably, despite the Reagan administration's continuing high-level efforts to maintain as much of a regional diplomatic quarantine as possible around the Caribbean island. The cracks in regional hostility toward the Castro government that have occurred since 1982 are a function of several hemispheric developments: changes in governments in democratic states; the Malvinas conflict between Argentina and England that created the possibility of a continent-wide political realignment on the basis of nationalist and anti-imperialist issues; the post-1983 collapse of authoritarian military regimes and their free-market economic models, which accelerated the redemocratization processes in such strategically important countries as Argentina and Brazil; and the trend toward a collective approach to regional problems (e.g., foreign debts), along with the perception that the United States is a critical part of those problems.

The breakdown of Cuba's political isolation began in 1982, but it was preceded by a period during which Havana suffered a number of diplomatic setbacks, particularly in Central America and the Caribbean. These developments were partly the result of governmental changes (Venezuela, Jamaica), but were also linked to an aggressive White House campaign to identify Cuba with and inflate its role in regional insurgencies against established regimes. Ties with Jamaica cooled immediately after the 1980 election when the social democratic government of Michael Manley, a consistent supporter of Cuba, was defeated by conservative forces under the leadership of Edward Seaga. Increased Costa Rican hostility toward Havana, on the other hand, was partly an effort by the Carazo government to divert popular attention from a severe domestic economic crisis. In Columbia, meanwhile, the Turbay Ayala regime accused the Castro government of supporting local guerrillas and uncritically accepted Washington's allegations of Cuban support for the insurgents in El Salvador and the need to isolate the island politically and economically from its neighbors.[134] At the same time, Havana's relations with Panama, Peru, and Venezuela also deteriorated. Seeking to accelerate these at least temporary political setbacks, U.S. Secretary of State Alexander Haig in an address to the General Assembly of the Organization of American States in December 1981 exhorted hemispheric governments to take some form of collective action against supposed threats to the peace and security of the region emanating from Cuba.[135]

During the first year of the Reagan presidency, Mexico was the only nonsocialist government in Latin America to go out of its way to emphasize fraternal ties with the Castro regime. In January 1981, President Jose López Portillo signed two major economic agreements with Havana. The first was an accord that committed Mexico's state oil monopoly, Petróleos Mexicanos (PEMEX), to assist Cuba's offshore petroleum exploration and the modernizing of its refineries. The agreements' real significance is that they provided Cuba "long wanted access to Western technology."[136] The Mexicans also agreed – only three days before a U.S. delegation arrived in Mexico City with "proof" of Havana's support of El Salvador's guerrillas – to purchase 100,000 tons of Cuban sugar.[137] Half a year later, however, Washington forced even Mexico's complicity in its anti-Cuba policy. The López Portillo government was made to bow to U.S. pressure in August 1981 and excluded Cuba from the North-South summit at Cancún scheduled for October as the price of Reagan's attendance.[138]

Other cracks in regional hostility emerged in 1982. Among the countries involved were Brazil, Argentina, Venezuela, and, to a lesser extent, Colombia. Improved Cuban-Brazilian relations during the early 1980s had their roots in a mid-1970s decision by Brazil's ruling generals to promote a more nonaligned, pragmatic foreign policy. But it was not until the end of the 1970s that ties between the two countries began to move off dead center. After a fierce internal military debate over how to deal with growing

Brazilian opposition to the military's power – either through a new wave of repression or through a limited *abertura*, or political opening – the success of the *abertura* generals was ratified with the inauguration of General João Baptista Figueiredo as president in March 1979. The new head of state reaffirmed his government's continued support for an independent foreign policy and began to extend this process to include rethinking Brazil's decade and a half of hostility toward Cuba. But on that question, he had to contend with powerful military sectors represented in the armed forces' ruling body, the National Security Council, who were antagonistic to any but the most limited changes in Cuba policy. During Figueiredo's tenure (1979–1985), they exercised an effective veto over any move in the direction of normalized diplomatic ties. As late as 1984, Brazil's National Security Council was still preoccupied with Cuban "subversion" in Latin America and receptive to Pentagon interpretations of Havana as the major source of Central American instability.[139]

Notwithstanding this powerful military stumbling block, Brazil's relations with Cuba did improve under Figueiredo. Brazilian passports were no longer stamped "Invalid" for Cuba; restrictions on cultural and sporting contests were lifted; and the ban on Brazilians and Cubans attending conferences in each other's countries was lifted. Consultation in regional organizations such as Geplacea, the association of Latin American and Caribbean sugar exporting nations, became the norm, not the exception.

Within Brazil's business community, support for improved relations with Havana also gained momentum. In mid-January 1982, a private trade mission headed by Ruy Barreto, president of Brazil's Confederation of Commercial Associations, returned from an unofficial visit to Cuba convinced that the Caribbean economy offered a potential annual market for Brazilian goods worth at least $200 million. The Cubans expressed particular interest in machinery and equipment used in the production of sugar and of fuel alcohol made from sugar cane from Brazil, a country whose technology in this area was as advanced as that of the United States. Trade mission members said they had initially received the go-ahead from Brazilian authorities but, under pressure from the military hardliners, the government was forced to disavow such statements and reassert its disinterest in normalizing diplomatic relations or legalizing the direct sale of Brazilian exports to Cuba.[140] Trade with Cuba, thus, was confined to inconvenient and complicated triangular operations involving third countries. During 1982, for instance, a Spanish-Italian-Brazilian consortium was involved in the construction of a $42 million juice-processing plant near Havana.[141]

The January 1985 election of Tancredo Neves, Brazil's first civilian president since 1964, brought renewed expectations of normalized relations with Cuba. Although Neves died before his inauguration, both his successor, José Sarney, and the parties in their Alianza Democrática coalition supported resuming ties with Havana. In June, foreign minister Olavo Setúbal stated that the government thought that the original reasons for severing ties were no longer valid and implied that the consensus in favor of reestablishing diplomatic ties awaited only a presidential decision.[142] Despite Sarney's rhetoric, he declared in August that renewed diplomatic ties with Cuba would be carried out "without enthusiasm."[143]

But pressure from the business community continued. It was given added force by the government's decision to embark on a diplomatic offensive to expand trade relations with the countries of the hemisphere, and third party trade flourished. In July, plans were announced to ship 30 million liters of alcohol to Cuba through Hungary. By 1986, Brazilian exports to Cuba via Mexico, Panama, Argentina, and Venezuela totalled between $8 million and $10 million annually. Financial institutions such as the Banco de Brasil also have been active in boosting this triangular trade through making credits available to Brazilian companies throughout Latin American trading with Cuba.[144]

At the beginning of 1986, President Sarney was still reluctant to force the issue of diplomatic relations with the Castro government, despite the emerging consensus within senior civilian and military circles in favor of such a move. The armed forces' National Security Council had dropped its hardline opposition to normalizing ties, although some generals were still reluctant to take the final step until Cuba reduced its military presence in Angola.[145] Foreign Minister Setúbal expressed his concurrence with a motion in favor of a complete restoration of diplomatic relations with Cuba approved by the Brazilian Congress' Foreign Relations Committee.[146] Only a presidential determination seemed to be missing. Sarney's footdragging may well have been related to American pressures as Reagan administration officials continued to counsel, privately and publicly, against a formal and definitive reconciliation with the revolutionaries in Havana.

In February, the government announced that diplomatic relations with Cuba would be restored toward the end of the year. Within weeks of this statement, however, Brazil's new foreign minister, Roberto de Abreu Sodré, cautioned against any foreign-policy initiative that might create friction between his country and the United States, singling out Cuba and the Central American conflict as having that potential.[147] Nonetheless, secret talks between Cuban and Brazilian officials about opening embassies and exchanging military attaches were scheduled for May 1986. The issue of military attaches portended a problem for the Sarney government in its relations with Washington after U.S. Under Secretary of Defense Fred Ikle made it plain that the White House strongly opposed the stationing of Cuban military personnel in Brazil.[148]

In July 1986, earlier than projected, Brazil and Cuba resumed diplomatic relations. But in an apparent concession to the United States, the agreement seemed to involve no provision for a Cuban military presence in the form of attaches in the hemisphere's most politically and economically influential country. Among the immediate beneficiaries of normalization were Brazilian exporters who could now trade directly with Cuba in automobiles, sugar cane processing equipment, consumer goods, computer technology, and other items that the Caribbean island needed. Brazilian sales to Cuba reached approximately $40 million in 1986, with projections for a growing market.[149] In the context of Cuba's current financial problems, however, the Brazilian government's failure to provide credit guarantees for local exporters engaged in trade with Cuba during the latter half of 1986 could, if this policy persists, become a major obstacle to export expansion.

The Malvinas conflict of April–May 1982 was a major turning point in contemporary Cuban-Argentine relations, which had been cool, if not hostile. Taking advantage of the crisis to reestablish hemispheric ties, Havana emerged as perhaps the strongest supporter of Argentina's right to sovereignty over the Malvinas. At the Havana nonaligned countries' meeting in early June 1982, Cuba took the lead in mobilizing support for Argentina in its conflict with Britain over the disputed islands. The 1983 election of Raúl Alfonsín, the first Argentine civilian president in almost a decade, also forecast strengthened ties between the two countries, especially in the economic sphere.

During the mid-1970s, Argentina was at the center of the conflict over U.S. multinational subsidiaries' trade with Cuba, and it has remained one of Cuba's most important economic partners in Latin America. In mid-1982, the two countries signed a $100 million economic cooperation agreement; in mid-1983, this trade pact was extended for another year and amplified to include a sizable credit line for Cuba's purchase of Argentine goods. Alfonsín next authorized a major expansion of economic ties in March 1984; the new agreement featured a $600 million, three-year credit line for Cuba to buy Argentine goods. This pact was expected to multiply Cuba's purchases from $120 million annually to approximately $300 million.[150] By 1985, Argentina had surpassed Mexico as the principal Latin American exporter to Cuba, a situation not possible without the government's steady flow of credits and loans. Just as Cuba's support of Argentine claims to the Malvinas partly involved an effort to break down its political isolation, so were Buenos Aires' burgeoning economic ties with Havana part of its own effort to end the political isolation the country suffered amid the generals' "dirty war" of 1976 to 1979 and its aftermath.

At the beginning of the Reagan presidency, relations between Cuba and Venezuela were icy, stemming largely from two events that took place in 1980: the acquittal by a Venezuelan military tribunal of four people charged with blowing up a Cuban airliner en route from Barbados to Havana, and the Castro government's refusal to grant safe conduct to Cubans who had taken asylum in the Venezuelan Embassy in Havana. In March 1981, President Luis Herrera Campíns vented his hostility toward Cuba in a speech before the Venezuelan Congress, calling Castro's regime "an Antillean dictatorship."[151] Again, bilateral relations began to thaw only with the Malvinas conflict, for both countries opposed the Thatcher government's Washington-supported actions. In mid-1982, influential figures within the two major political parties, Acción Democrática (AD) and the Christian Democratic Party (COPEI), including President Herrera, expressed sentiments favoring more normalized relations.[152] However, during the remainder of Herrera's term, no major diplomatic initiatives occurred, in part due to still cool personal relations between the Venezuelan president and Castro.

The 1983 election of Acción Democrática's Jaime Lusinchi as Venezuela's president improved the climate, for Lusinchi announced that his social democratic government's foreign policy would be pragmatic and independent of Washington. Accommodations would be sought with regimes of various ideological hues, especially in Central America and the Caribbean.[153] Since then, two successive foreign ministers, Isidro Morales Paul and Simón Alberto Consalvi, have both advocated Cuban participation in any negotiations to resolve outstanding conflicts in Central America and the Caribbean.[154] But the warming of relations under Lusinchi has not been accompanied by any spectacular breakthrough at the diplomatic level. Following a meeting with Cuban foreign minister Isidoro Malmierca in July 1985, Consalvi stated that the "special conditions" for a renewal of diplomatic ties were still missing.[155]

Even so, Cuban-Venezuelan economic relations improved somewhat during 1984 and 1985. For example, in mid-1984, Venezuela and the Soviet Union renewed an oil agreement that Herrera had let lapse in 1981 under which Caracas supplied Havana with its petroleum needs and Moscow did the same for Venezuela's customers in Europe.

The Colombian government of Julio César Turbay Ayala played a pivotal role in the successful 1980 American effort to sabotage Cuba's chance of gaining a vacant United Nations Security Council seat. This action initiated steadily worsening relations, which reached a low in March 1981 when Colombia severed diplomatic links. Turbay Ayala publicly attributed the split to Havana's support of Colombia's M-19 guerrilla movement. But in reality, his action was primarily a gesture toward the armed forces to defuse their pressure for a greater military role in Colombia's political affairs.[156] This hostile attitude toward Cuba began to change when Belisario Betancur was elected president in 1982 and shifts in foreign policy began to appear. Betancur applied for Colombian membership in the nonaligned movement and also moved to establish a direct line of communication with Castro. In his role as head of state of one of the Contadora Group nations, Betancur envisioned a Cuban role in efforts to negotiate a lasting peace settlement in Central America. Personal links between Castro and Betancur flourished during 1982 and 1983, creating concern in Washington that restored diplomatic relations might have been on the immediate agenda. Through diplomacy, the Reagan administration sought to forestall that possibility, which may partly explain Betancur's subsequent footdragging on restoring full relations with Cuba.[157]

Nevertheless, high-level contacts between the two governments have continued, including a 1985 visit to Havana by Colombian foreign minister Augusto Ramírez-Ocampo to discuss

Central America, and especially Nicaragua, with the Cuban head of state. The Betancur government has also been in the forefront of efforts to hasten Cuba's readmission to the Organization of American States (OAS). At the Fifteenth General Assembly meeting of the OAS in Cartagena, Colombia, in early December 1985, the host country proposed that membership in the regional body be open to all hemispheric nations, including Cuba. The head of the U.S. delegation, Secretary of State George Schultz, led the opposition to this proposal, charging that Cuban behavior had worsened since it was ousted from the OAS in January 1962. The American position prevailed.[158]

When the newly elected president of Uruguay, Julio Maria Sanguinetti, began to repeal more than a decade of military policy in April 1985 by lifting the bans on trade, maritime, and cultural relations with Cuba, he initiated another phase in the revolution's gradual rapprochement with its hemispheric neighbors – much to the consternation of the United States. Similarly, the same month, Ecuador's conservative president León Febres Cordero visited Havana and signed an agreement establishing reciprocal credit and trade facilities. Uruguay renewed full diplomatic relations with Cuba the following October and, seven months later, in May 1986, the two signed a three-year trade accord.[159] Entering 1986, there were numerous other indications of Cuba's growing acceptance within the inter-American system: Bolivia, having reestablished diplomatic relations in 1983, opened its Havana Embassy, which had been closed since 1959; Peruvian president Alan Garcia appointed, but did not immediately dispatch, a new ambassador to Cuba, signalling an end to five years of chilly bilateral ties; and Venezuelan officials commented on further improved relations beween Caracas and Havana. These political openings were serious enough to unearth another round of U.S. diplomatic pressure focused on Brazil, Peru, and Uruguay. "Sure there is concern," exclaimed the irritated Assistant Secretary of State for Inter-American Affairs Elliott Abrams. "We are not in favor of people restoring relations with Cuba."[160] Brazil received the most attention, but Sarney's decision to restore ties with Cuba in July dealt the most powerful blow to Reagan's isolation policy.

Amid these rebuffs of U.S. policy are sporadic instances of American power still able to constrain the region's economically weakest countries expressing interest in diplomatic ties with Cuba. For example, Dominican Republic president Joaquín Balaguer parried any action on a resolution passed by the country's

Chamber of Deputies in December 1986 supporting normalized relations with Havana on the grounds that "although we would love" to take such action, "we cannot break our links with Western democracy because to some extent we are a dependent country."[161]

The regional movement since 1981 has headed in the opposite direction, as Latin America revealed itself increasingly unwilling to accept Reagan's rhetoric about Cuba. Proliferating political and economic linkages have been accompanied by Cuba's growing participation in Latin American economic organizations such as Geplacea and its acceptance in May 1986 as an observer by the Latin American Integration Association. Hemispheric governments also have shown a greater preparedness to take Cuba's side in economic disputes with Washington. In an October 1986 Geplacea meeting, the entire membership walked out in support of Cuba after the U.S. delegate accused the Castro government of unfair trade practices. Afterwards, Brazil and Cuba agreed to a series of bilateral meetings to devise a common strategy to force the United States (and the European Economic Community) to end their restrictions on sugar imports from Latin America and the Caribbean.[162]

The United States lost out in another forum as well, despite intense lobbying by its United Nations Ambassador Vernon Walters and his staff and personal notes and telephone calls from President Reagan, when the U.N.'s Human Rights Commission voted in March 1987 to shelve an American motion to condemn Cuba for alleged human rights violations. Voting against the U.S. were Argentina, Nicaragua, Peru, Colombia, Mexico, and Venezuela. Brazil abstained, and only Costa Rica sided with Washington.[163]

Conclusion

The Reagan administration has waged a political, economic, and military offensive against the Cuban Revolution aimed at sustaining Cuba's political isolation within Latin America, disrupting and destabilizing the island economy, terminating the Cuba-Soviet alliance, and reinserting Cuba within the capitalist political-economic orbit. Militarily, the Reagan rollback policy has been a total failure due to Cuba's military alliance with the Soviet Union and the Castro government's exceptional military preparedness, making any possible U.S. invasion a high-cost operation. The Soviet Union's willingness to accede to Cuban requests for a substantially increased level of annual military provisions to resist White House interventionist threats is testament to the fact that Washington no longer can overwhelm designated revolutionary adversaries simply by sheer material might in a world where Soviet military power exists as a potential alternative source of arms for such Third World regimes. And, as appears to have been the case with Cuba to date, an albeit reluctant recognition of the current global military equilibrium between the two superpowers probably has served to temper the more extreme proposals for global confrontation periodically emanating from within the Reagan foreign policy apparatus.

Even though the Reagan administration has failed to thwart the Cuban Revolution, the unprecedented projection of U.S. military power in the Central America-Caribbean area has contained Havana's efforts to expand its ties and influence with neighboring states. The enormous U.S. arms buildup, especially in Honduras and El Salvador; the ongoing joint military maneuvers; the hundreds of millions of dollars in covert funding for the anti-Sandinista counterrevolutionaries based in Honduras; and the American marine invasion of Grenada all have combined, at least temporarily, to increase Cuba's isolation in this part of the hemisphere.

On the economic front, Reagan efforts to tighten the bilateral and global blockade around Cuba have made some gains, especially compared to those of the Ford-Carter period. Nonetheless, Washington's achievements in this realm were offset to some degree by its senior Alliance partners' continuing refusal to allow the U.S. to intrude in all aspects of their economic relationships with revolutionary Cuba. While the Reagan economic offensive, for instance, apparently contributed to a dramatic decline in Cuba's exports to the West, these same countries were determined to take advantage of opportunities to increase their exports to Cuba, often encouraged by the availability of government-guaranteed credits. The fall in Cuba's sales to the West did affect the Castro government's ability to accumulate the hard-currency earnings required to purchase capitalist-bloc goods vital to the effective operation of the Cuban economy. In this regard, one sector of the Cuban economy singled out for attention by U.S. policymakers was the nickel export industry. In 1982, Cuban nickel production reached a record 40,225 tons,[164] which the Castro government hoped would result in increased sales to Western Europe and Japan. At almost the same time, the Reagan adminis-

tration intensified its secondary boycott of Cuban nickel. The subsequent decline in Cuban nickel sales to the West, which forced
it to sell more to the Soviet Union, further contracted Cuba's
hard-currency reserves. The United States also successfully pressured Western companies to suspend or terminate investment
projects in the Cuban nickel industry. Evidently, in this instance,
even capitalist competition is negotiable.

Reagan's efforts to sabotage Cuba's foreign debt negotiations
with its capitalist-bloc creditors are a different story. They failed
miserably to achieve even limited objectives because of the
Cuban economy's sustained pattern of economic growth during
the 1970s and early 1980s; the Castro regime's exemplary debt
history, especially compared with the rest of the Third World; the
willingness of the Soviet bloc to provide needed large-scale economic help; and the absence of any U.S. lever that could force
Western creditor banks and government to toe the line. The result
was a short-circuiting of Washington's aggressive efforts between
1982 and 1985 to make Cuba's capitalist-bloc creditors extract
the most draconian and onerous concessions from Havana in
return for a series of debt reschedulings.

Helping explain the problems confronting the Reagan administration's Cuba policy during the first half of the 1980s are the
structural position of the West Europeans and Japanese in the capitalist world economy and the economic power of the Soviet
Union, for all three sources placed additional constraints on the
United States's capacity to pursue its objectives. To a greater
degree than applies to the United States, European and Japanese
economic growth is dependent on expanding trade. As a result,
these countries have been more supportive of a policy of global
detente than has Washington, and they have tended to view Reagan's inclination toward confrontation as jeopardizing the growth
of commercial relations with Eastern Europe while providing no
alternative. Moreover, competition among the United States,
Western Europe, and Japan over Third World markets, including
Latin America, has cut across White House efforts to polarize the
world into a rigid East-West configuration. Economic ties between
Cuba and the Soviet Union also have limited Washington's
attempts to confront the revolutionary regime and isolate it economically. As in the military sphere, the Cuban economic experience shows that U.S. pressures on Third World revolutionary
governments in the current epoch can be effectively neutralized

by these same countries turning more actively toward the socialist bloc as a source of markets, finance, and raw materials.

With the exception of a small group of politically and economically inconsequential U.S. client states in Central America and the Caribbean, Reagan efforts to sustain Cuba's political isolation within Latin America have been largely a failure. Regional nationalism, rising social movements, and governmental shifts involving such strategically important countries as Brazil and Argentina have extended existing or opened new cracks in the U.S. isolation policy. The cracks are widening despite intense Reagan White House efforts to maintain Cuba's political pariah status. Although several countries still have not established full diplomatic ties with Cuba, preferring a rather drawn-out shift toward more normalized relations, the relative decline in the U.S. leverage with its southern neighbors on this issue must be linked to Washington's inability to wield the kinds of economic pressures (e.g., providing or withholding aid) against many hemispheric countries with the same efficiency and impact as it did in the 1960s.

Relations between the Reagan administration and Cuba during the first half of the 1980s suggest that American policy has come full circle since the overthrow of the Batista dictatorship in 1959. Despite the existence of a consolidated revolutionary state and government in Cuba and an economy whose well-being is overwhelmingly linked to decisions within the socialist bloc, the Reagan White House has revived Washington's earlier commitment to a vigorous application of diplomatic and economic sanctions on regional and global scales, backed by the threat of resort to military force, hoping to roll back revolutionary gains and wrest major foreign policy concessions. The deepened preoccupation with Cuba's military ties to the Soviet Union and its support of Third World nationalist (let alone revolutionary) movements and governments since 1981 has created about Reagan's actions a sense of *deja vu:* The policies, rhetoric, and instrumentalities of the 1960s and early 1970s have been refurbished.

Appendix 1. The impact and effectiveness of the U.S. global economic blockade on Cuban development

The prerevolutionary Cuban agro-industrial economy was financed and controlled largely by U.S. capitalist entrepreneurs and almost totally integrated into the American industrial-productive complex. Hence the Cuban Revolution was highly vulnerable to external economic pressures – a state of affairs the Eisenhower, Kennedy, and Johnson administrations exploited with considerable success. Most discussions of developments in Cuba since 1959 have minimized the role of U.S. bilateral, regional, and global economic warfare in exacerbating the problems that confronted the Castro leadership in the struggle to attain its economic goals.

During the revolution's early years, the threat of external military intervention also posed a towering barrier to domestic economic planning, with concern for mere survival and security forcing the nationalist regime to divert scarce financial and physical resources for these purposes. In December 1958, the regular armed forces and reserves together totalled less than 50,000. After 1959, this figure skyrocketed to approximately 600,000 (half regulars and half reserves), annual military expenditures reached $500 million, and one estimate placed allocations for defense and internal order during 1963 in excess of 10 percent of the new state's budget.[1] Between 1959 and 1963, there was at least one general nationwide military mobilization annually, while U.S. paramilitary sabotage operations in the summer of 1961 forced the regime not only to transfer extra funds and workers to defense purposes, but also to establish "a large administrative bureaucracy and a whole industry [to] work on civil-defense installations."[2] Against this background, the bilateral and global blockade loomed far larger than it could have by itself.

367

Cuba's economic plans between 1961 and 1963 envisaged a complementary program of agricultural development and rapid industrial expansion on the basis of maintaining pre-1959 sugar production levels (and foreign-exchange earnings) and lowering the demand for food imports and industrial raw materials. Although a few attempts to explain Cuba's poor economic performance during this period have glanced at the spare-parts embargo, especially its effect on the agricultural sector,[3] Cuba's economic troubles are explained by most analysts primarily, if not exclusively, in terms of internal factors: the tensions, frictions, and disorganization inherent in any process of large-scale structural transformation; the lack of qualified administrative, technical, planning, and management personnel occasioned by the exodus of many skilled individuals; leadership, technical, and planning errors; poor formulation and implementation of the industrialization programs; the diversion of scarce resources for defense and security purposes; the subordination of administrative-technical expertise to the requirements of political security; the decline in the volume of sugar production from 6.77 million tons in 1961 to 3.83 million in 1963 which, at once, reduced the available foreign exchange for purchases abroad and increased the demand for raw-material and food imports;[4] and the accompanying balance-of-payments crisis (from a total trade surplus of $550 million during the 1950s to a deficit of more than $530 million over the four-year period from 1960 to 1963)[5] that exacerbated the country's export dependence and eventually dictated a renewed emphasis on agriculture as the engine of development.

By 1964, the beginning of the second "sugar-centered and export-oriented"[6] growth strategy, the U.S. global economic blockade was in high gear. Washington's capacity to wrest substantial allied compliance with its goal of isolating Cuba from the capitalist world failed to generate studies of the island's economic development trajectory that emphasized the crucial role of external factors. Even sympathetic observers such as Archibald Ritter preferred to explain poor post-1964 growth rates basically in terms of institutional problems, difficulties in mobilizing human resources, labor shortages, managerial deficiencies, inadequate cane-cutting machinery, and so forth.[7] More hostile analysts focused on leadership conflicts over economic policy (industry vs. agriculture, consumption vs. capital accumulation) and organizational models (decentralized vs. centralizing planning, moral vs. material incentives).[8]

But the evidence presented in this study makes it clear that external factors severely stressed Cuban economic planning during the 1960s, damaging overall production levels and significantly contributing to the foreclosure of rapid heavy industry development. The new government simply could not lay its hands on basic industrial equipment and parts from traditional (overwhelmingly U.S.) sources during the early years. "So enormous were the problems caused by the lack of spare parts, replacement equipment, and normal raw materials," writes one authority on the subject, "that it is difficult to realize or fully comprehend the actual magnitudes involved."[9] Hence the leadership's decision to revert to an emphasis on agriculture as the motor of industrialization.

A 1964 British study of agricultural mechanization in Cuba noted the devastating consequences of the spare-parts shortages for the sugar industry, especially in the area of transportation:

Caterpillar tractors not in operation due to lack of spare parts constitute 62 percent of the total, of which 37 percent were manufactured in capitalist countries and 25 percent in socialist countries. Wheel tractors paralyzed because they are not in working condition amount to 47 percent of the total, of which 31 percent came from capitalistic countries and 16 percent from socialist countries. There are more than 200 tractors inoperative in Oriente Province because of lack of tires. . . . In Camagüey, 220 Caterpillars have been laid aside due to lack of spare parts and 622 due to lack of tires.[10]

At the sugar mills, breakdowns and malfunctions of American-made machinery caused by spare-parts shortages were a constant problem throughout most of the 1960s.[11]

The shift toward dependence on the socialist countries as export markets and supply sources forced on the revolutionary leadership the formidable problem of integrating Communist-built machinery into U.S. and Western European industrial plants, a problem that amplified a decline in Cuba's economic efficiency.[12] Socialist-bloc exports could not be adapted to Cuban industrial plants; vehicles and tractors didn't function in the tropical climate; spare parts were frequently of inferior quality and more costly, and imports could not keep pace with the breakdowns of U.S. machines and parts; some critical parts and highly specialized chemicals and raw materials were not even produced by Communist countries; and in cases where spare parts, machinery, or equipment were purchased in Western Europe by the Soviet

Union for transshipment to Cuba, costs multiplied and increased the pressure on Cuba's low foreign-exchange reserves.

As intended, the global transportation blockade, specifically the shipping embargo, also disrupted economic planning. The U.S. shipping blacklist, for instance, substantially increased transport costs for those capitalist-owned vessels prepared to remain in the Cuba trade. Shipping costs, further inflated by Cuba's growing dependence on distant suppliers, were estimated to have tripled after 1959. In 1963 alone, about $50 million was diverted from other areas of the frail economy to pay for such extra charges.[13] A related problem for economic decisionmakers resulting from dependence on socialist-bloc suppliers was the difficulty of calculating the arrival time of deliveries. To cover this and related problems, the Cubans diverted more financial resources to construct repair facilities around the island and ports and warehouses of sufficient size to handle large shipments from the Soviet Union and Eastern Europe.

The cumulative impact of the blockade and the relative lack of trade complementarity between Cuba and the socialist economies can be outlined as follows:

> Economic boycott → lack of spare parts → breakdowns and malfunctions → idle machinery and work stoppages → decline in production → redirection of trade relations → availability of materials from alternative sources → less efficient, less adaptable, poorer quality imports → accelerated deterioration of existing machinery (in association with internal "cannibalization" of parts) → further production declines.

Under such conditions, effective economic planning and development projections were impossible. Parts, technological expertise, and raw materials problems undermined the possibility of mechanizing the sugar industry and diversifying the economy and acted as a powerful political constraint on the developing socialist economy. American measures thus directly and profoundly contributed to the perpetuation of the monoculture economy. Although nationalization provided the political tools to organize production in accord with the new state project, the scarcity of required goods and services occasioned by the economic blockade substantially reduced the effectiveness of the nationalized sectors' efforts to transform the economy and society.

A detailed study of Cuba's trade with the capitalist world during the 1970s prepared by the Department of Commerce summarized the impact of the blockade on Cuba's development possibilities:

. . . the continued denial of Cuban access to U.S. trade and financial markets has effectively restricted the potential for trade and investment by other Western countries and narrowly circumscribed Havana's options for economic development, forcing increased dependence on CMEA [Council for Mutual Economic Assistance, also known as COMECON]. Thus, the U.S. embargo has been and continues to be not only a major, but a crucial impediment to Cuba's efforts at diversifying and expanding its hard currency trade, the key to improved economic growth and living standards.[14]

Appendix 2. Tables

Table 1. *Trade of selected non-communist countries with Cuba, 1961–1975 ($ million)*

Country	1961	1962	1963	1964	1965	1966	1967	1968	1969	1970	1971	1972	1973	1974	1975
France															
Exports to	5.9	1.8	4.3	20.9	13.5	14.6	54.7	55.8	47.3	58.3	63.0	26.5	28.3	11.3	24.1
Imports from	1.2	2.3	4.1	3.4	11.4	10.2	15.7	14.7	14.9	15.8	6.0	11.7	12.0	81.6	105.2
England															
Exports to	13.2	7.2	5.8	27.2	42.2	22.7	24.1	29.8	31.8	49.3	61.0	41.7	42.8	46.7	14.0
Imports from	15.0	19.9	34.7	25.5	14.7	13.0	12.9	16.5	13.0	13.7	17.0	12.6	32.5	55.7	81.6
Canada															
Exports to	30.1	10.2	15.2	57.0	49.0	57.4	39.4	42.0	37.9	56.6	27.0	58.4	81.9	78.1	80.1
Imports from	5.0	2.6	12.1	3.2	4.9	5.2	5.9	4.7	7.2	9.1	11.0	11.2	16.6	149.2	217.1
Japan															
Exports to	11.8	10.6	2.8	34.4	3.5	6.5	7.4	2.4	9.8	39.2	60.0	50.7	107.2	442.1	340.3
Imports from	24.3	35.8	22.9	53.5	29.2	22.3	26.1	33.3	68.0	110.6	100.0	145.4	182.5	203.0	438.2
Spain															
Exports to	4.4	1.4	9.2	31.4	38.2	78.6	27.8	18.6	39.3	36.6	33.0	17.0	49.0	171.5	314.0
Imports from	9.2	8.6	21.7	65.6	31.1	38.2	37.8	40.5	42.4	35.1	36.0	44.0	63.0	62.1	180.0

Source: See Notes.

Table 2. Trips to Cuba by non-communist ships, 1963–1975

Flag of registry	1963	1964	1965	1966	1967	1968	1969	1970	1971	1972	1973	1974	1975[a]
Cypriot	—	1	17	27	42	68	115	199	173	86	96	147	52
British	133	180	126	101	78	62	45	53	18	10	6	6	—
Lebanese	64	91	58	25	16	16	4	1	—	1	—	3	8
Greek	99	27	23	27	29	7	—	—	1	—	—	—	—
Italian	16	20	24	11	11	10	15	13	9	6	23	25	11
Somali	—	—	—	—	2	11	7	4	6	2	1	7	—
French	8	9	9	10	10	4	2	5	2	8	17	26	7
Netherlands	—	4	2	—	—	—	—	1	—	—	—	—	—
Finnish	1	4	5	11	12	8	2	—	—	1	—	1	4
Spanish	9	17	—	—	—	—	—	2	—	—	—	—	4
Moroccan	9	13	1	1	4	8	1	—	—	—	—	—	—
Maltese	—	2	6	—	—	—	—	—	—	—	—	—	—
Norwegian	14	10	—	—	—	1	—	—	—	—	—	—	—
Others	6	5	4	1	—	—	—	—	1	—	—	18	15
Total	358	383	275	214	204	195	191	278	210	114	143	233	101

[a] January–May.

Source: U.S. Department of Commerce, Maritime Administration, List of Free World and Polish Flag Vessels Arriving in Cuba Since January 1, 1963. Report No. 128, September 23, 1975.

Table 3. *Cuba: sugar exports to selected non-communist countries (Thousand metric tons, raw sugar)*

Country	1958	1961	1963	1965	1967	1968	1969	1970	1971	1972	1973	1974	1975
Total exports	5,383	1,623	1,454	1,790	1,817	1,489	1,991	2,107	2,233	1,846	1,785	2,225	1,713
Canada	190	16	70	69	66	47	80	65	73	31	47	116	156
Egypt	0	75	78	125	114	66	69	32	43	21	5	—	14
Iraq	18	35	37	126	42	53	22	21	52	56	—	65	78
Japan	556	423	161	415	542	555	1,018	1,221	912	909	985	1,152	339
Malaysia	—	—	—	—	119	—	105	215	141	88	29	64	—
Morocco	156	157	285	182	153	86	176	106	165	88	62	41	100
Spain	69	53	103	174	159	176	182	143	82	55	104	363	327
Syria	38	75	21	62	64	64	87	98	116	98	107	41	53
United Kingdom	487	79	174	113	70	20	43	—	51	29	122	71	17

Source: U.S. Central Intelligence Agency, Intelligence Handbook, *Cuba: Foreign Trade,* A (ER) 75-69, July 1975, p. 10; U.S. Central Intelligence Agency, *The Cuban Economy: A Statistical Review, 1968–1976,* ER76-10708, December 1976, p. 12.

Notes

1. The U.S. imperial state: theory and historical setting

1 The accumulation of capital refers to the reproduction of capital (together with capitalist social relations of production) on an ever-expanding scale. Capitalism's worldwide expansion has both made possible and necessitated the growth of states that formulate their strategies and policies on a global scale. Imperial states seek to fulfill their task of appropriating the surplus on a global scale by accepting responsibility for creating, sustaining, and recreating durable political orders in which social control over labor makes possible the uninterrupted flow of capital, enlarges the market for goods and services, and facilitates the reproduction of exploitative social relations. See Samir Amin, *Accumulation on a World Scale, Volumes 1 and 2* (New York: Monthly Review Press, 1974); Paul Zarembka, "Accumulation of Capital in the Periphery," in Paul Zarembka, ed., *Research in Political Economy, Volume 2, 1979* (Greenwich: Jai Press, 1979), pp. 99–140.

2 See, for example, Ralph Miliband, *The State in Capitalist Society* (New York: Basic Books, 1969); Nicos Poulantzas, *Political Power and Social Classes* (London: New Left Books, 1973); Bob Jessop; *The Capitalist State: Marxist Theories and Methods* (London: Martin Robertson). 1982.

3 See, for instance, Colin Leys, *Underdevelopment in Kenya* (Berkeley: University of California Press, 1975).

4 This approach is found in Alan Wolfe, *The Limits of Legitimacy: Political Contradictions of Contemporary Capitalism* (New York: Free Press, 1977).

5 J. A. Hobson, *Imperialism* (Ann Arbor: University of Michigan Press, 1972).

6 V. I. Lenin, "Imperialism, The Highest Stage of Capitalism," in *Selected Works, Volume 1* (Moscow: Progress Publishers, 1979), p. 716.

7 Nikolai Bukharin, *Imperialism and World Economy* (New York: Monthly Review Press, 1973), p. 124.

8 Ibid., p. 60. The classic study of European finance capital during the era of monopoly capitalism is Herbert Feis, *Europe: The World's Banker 1870–1914* (New Haven: Yale University Press, 1930). Also see Roger Owen, "Egypt and Europe: from French Expedition to British Occupation," in Roger Owen and Bob Sutcliffe, eds., *Studies in the Theory of Imperialism* (London: Longman Group, 1972), pp. 195–209; Petr I. Liashchenko, *History of the National Economy of*

377

Russia (New York: The Macmillan Co., 1949); Theodore Von Laue, *Sergie Witte and the Industrialization of Russia* (New York: Columbia University Press, 1963); V. I. Lenin, *The Development of Capitalism in Russia* (Moscow: Foreign Languages Publishing House, 1956).

9 See, for example, Raymond Vernon, *Sovereignty at Bay: The Multinational Spread of U.S. Enterprise* (London: Penguin Books, 1973); Richard Barnet and Ronald E. Müller, *Global Reach: The Power of the Multinational Corporations* (New York: Simon and Schuster, 1974).

10 For purposes of historical analogy, see the literature on the role of the British imperial state during the nineteenth century in Latin America (e.g., in Argentina), the Middle East (e.g., in Egypt), and Africa. A stimulating discussion of the role of the twentieth-century British imperial state in promoting profitability environments for British investors in East Africa between 1921 and 1932 (railroads, preferential tariffs, public works, bureaucratic structures) is provided in E. A. Brett, *Colonialism and Underdevelopment in East Africa: The Politics of Economic Change 1919–1939* (London: Heinemann Educational Books, 1973).

11 The term multinational refers to the number of countries in which a corporation operates, not to the pattern of ownership of that corporation. The activities of the multinational corporation are shaped by a global perspective. Marketing, production, and research decisions are made in terms of available worldwide alternatives. By 1900, approximately half of the fifty largest U.S. corporations had major foreign operations. Nonetheless, the great majority of these corporations in the pre-World War I period were not multinational corporations and it is not until the post-World War II period that the worldwide proliferation of American multinationals reaches its zenith. See U.S. Department of Commerce, Bureau of International Commerce, Office of International Investment, *The Multinational Corporation: Studies on U.S. Foreign Investment, Volume 1*, March 1972, p. 3; Mira Wilkins, *The Emergence of Multinational Enterprise: American Business Abroad from the Colonial Era to 1914* (Cambridge: Harvard University Press, 1970), p. 207.

12 See Walter LaFeber, *The New Empire: An Interpretation of American Expansion 1860–1890* (Ithaca: Cornell University Press, 1967); Richard W. Van Alstyne, *The Rising American Empire* (Chicago: Quadrangle Books, 1965).

13 See Clyde W. Phelps, *The Foreign Expansion of American Banks* (New York: The Ronald Press Co., 1927), p. 112; Paul P. Abrahams, *The Foreign Expansion of American Finance and its Relationship to the Foreign Economic Policies of the United States 1907–1921* (Ph.D. dissertation, University of Wisconsin, 1967), p. 20; Robert Mayer, "The Orgins of the American Banking Empire in Latin America," *Journal of Interamerican Studies and World Affairs*, Vol. 15, No. 1, February 1973, pp. 60–76; Siegfried Stein, *The United States in International Banking* (New York: Columbia University Press, 1952).

14 See Richard M. Freeland, *The Truman Doctrine and the Origins of McCarthyism* (New York: Schocken Books, 1974), p. 17; Thomas G. Paterson, "The Quest for Peace and Prosperity: International Trade, Communism, and the Marshall Plan," in Barton Bernstein, ed., *Politics and Policies of the Truman Administration* (Chicago: Quadrangle Books, 1970), p. 87.

15 See Joyce Kolko and Gabriel Kolko, *The Limits of Power: The World and United States Foreign Policy, 1945–1955* (New York: Harper & Row, 1972); David Eakins, "Business Planners and America's Postwar Expansion," in David Horowitz, ed., *Corporations and the Cold War* (New York: Monthly Review Press, 1969), pp. 143–171.

16 Quoted in William A. Williams, *The Tragedy of American Diplomacy* (New York: Delta Books, 1972), p. 235. Discussing an American loan to England in 1946, President Truman also identified domestic economic growth with "the elimination of artificial barriers to international trade." Harry S. Truman, *Memoirs, Volume One: Years of Decision* (New York: Doubleday & Co., 1955), p. 480.

17 On the United States as a prime mover and influence within the International Monetary Fund and the World Bank, see Fred Block, *The Origins of International Economic Disorder* (Berkeley: University of California Press, 1977), pp. 74–75; Susan Strange, "IMF: Monetary Managers," in Robert Cox and Harold K. Jacobson, eds., *The Anatomy of Influence: Decision Making in International Organization* (New Haven: Yale University Press, 1977) pp. 74–75; Edward S. Mason and Robert E. Asher, *The World Bank Since Bretton Woods* (Washington, D.C.: The Brookings Institution, 1973), pp. 11–35.

18 Herbert Feis, "The Investment of American Capital Abroad," in Arnold J. Zurcher and Richmond Page, eds., *America's Place in the World Economy* (New York: New York University, Institute of Postwar Reconstruction, 1954), p. 78.

19 On eliminating the barriers to unrestricted global trade, see Richard N. Gardner, *Sterling-Dollar Diplomacy* (London: Oxford University Press, 1956); Lloyd C. Gardner, *Architects of Illusion: Men and Ideas in American Foreign Policy 1941–1949* (Chicago: Quadrangle Books, 1972), especially pp. 114, 126.

20 "A Report to the National Security Council by the Executive Secretary on 'United States Objectives and Programs for National Security'," Top Secret, NSC 68, April 14, 1950, in U.S. Department of State, *Foreign Relations of the United States* (hereafter FRUS), Vol I, 1950, p. 252.

21 Melvin P. Leffler, "The American Conception of National Security and the Beginnings of the Cold War, 1945–1948," *American Historical Review*, Vol. 89, No. 2, April 1984, p. 358.

22 Ibid., pp. 391–392.

23 See Thomas C. Blaisdell, Jr., and Eugene M. Braderman, "Economic Organization of the United States for International Economic Policy," Seymour E. Harris, ed., *Foreign Economic Policy for the United States* (Cambridge: Harvard University Press, 1948), pp. 40–41.

24 There has been a close, consistent relationship between U.S. imperial-state goals and the role of the World Bank, the International

Monetary Fund, and other multilateral development banks (MDBs) in promoting capitalist development strategies in the postcolonial Third World. The capacity of successive postwar U.S. administrations to mobilize support for their general policy goals within these institutions is strikingly revealed in the case of MDB assistance to Latin America during the 1960s and 1970s. Periods of MDB economic largesse to a number of countries coincided with the appearance of political regimes whose policies meshed with the needs of American capitalism; periods of restricted MDB aid to these same countries coincided with the rise of national-popular and democratic-socialist governments that tried to limit the role of foreign capital in their economies. See Teresa Hayter and Catharine Watson, *Aid: Rhetoric and Reality* (London: Pluto Press 1985); Cheryl Payer, *The World Bank* (New York and London: Monthly Review Press, 1982); U.S. Congress, House, Committee on Foreign Affairs, *The United States and the Multilateral Development Banks*, 93rd Congress, 2nd Session, Committee Print, Prepared by the Congressional Research Service, Library of Congress, March 1974 (Washington, D.C.: U.S. Government Printing Office, 1974); James F. Petras and Morris H. Morley, *The United States and Chile: Imperialism and the Overthrow of the Allende Government* (New York: Monthly Review Press, 1975); Ann Crittenden, "Loans From Abroad Flow to Chile's Rightist Junta," *New York Times,* January 20, 1976, pp. 1, 46; R. Peter DeWitt, *The Inter-American Development Bank and Political Influence* (New York: Praeger Publishers, 1977).

The Department of the Treasury in 1981 prepared a detailed assessment of American participation in the MDBs, concluding in part that these banks "by and large, have been most effective in contributing to the achievement of our *global economic and financial objectives* and thereby also helping us in our long term political/strategic interests." U.S. Department of the Treasury, *United States Participation in the Multilateral Development Banks in the 1980s* (Washington, D.C., February 1982), p. 4 (study's emphasis).

25 U.S. Congress, Senate, Committee on Government Operations, Subcommittee on National Security Policy, *Organizing for National Security: The National Security Council*, 86th Congress, 2nd Session, Committee Print, 1960 (Washington, D.C.: U.S. Government Printing Office, 1960), p. 1. Also see Robert Cutler, "The Development of the National Security Council," *Foreign Affairs*, Vol. 34, No. 3, April 1956, pp. 441–458.

26 U.S. Congress, Senate, Final Report of the Select Committee to Study Government Operations with respect to Intelligence Activites, *Supplementary Detailed Staff Reports on Foreign and Military Intelligence, Book IV*, 94th Congress, 2nd Session, Report No. 94–755, April 23, 1976 (Washington, D.C.: U.S. Government Printing Office, 1976), p. 15

27 Ibid., p. 29.

28 Leffler, "The American Conception of National Security and the Beginnings of the Cold War, 1945–1948," p. 379.

29 See Stephen E. Ambrose, *Rise to Globalism: American Foreign Pol-*

icy, 1938–1980 (New York: Penguin Books, 1980), pp. 121–185;
Kolko and Kolko, *The Limits of Power*, passim; U.S. Congress,
House, Committee on International Relations, *Military Assistance
Programs, Part 2*, Selected Executive Session Hearings of the Com-
mittee 1943–1950, Vol. VI, Historical Series, March 25, 26, April
11, 1947 (Washington, D.C.: U.S. Government Printing Office,
1976), pp. 303–462; U.S. Congress, Senate, Committee on Foreign
Relations, *Legislative Orgins of the Truman Doctrine*, Executive Ses-
sion, Historical Series, 81st Congress 1st Session, March 13, 28;
April 1, 2, 3, 1947 (Washington, D.C.: U.S. Government Printing
Office, 1973).

30 These figures were calculated on the basis of data from the following
sources: U.S. Agency for International Development, Office of Program and Information Analysis Services, Statistics and Reports Division, *U.S. Overseas Loans and Grants and Assistance from International Organizations: Obligations and Loan Authorizations, July 1,
1945–September 30, 1976* (Washington, D.C.: U.S. Government
Printing Office, 1977), p. 6; U.S. Department of Commerce, Bureau
of Economic Analysis, *International Transactions of the United States
During the War. 1940–1945* (Washington, D.C.: U.S. Government
Printing Office, 1984), p. 216; U.S. Department of Commerce,
Bureau of Foreign and Domestic Commerce, Office of Business Economics, *Survey of Current Business*, Vol. XXXI, No. 1, January 1951,
p. 22 and Vol. XXVI, No.8, August 1956, pp. 18–19; U.S. Depart-
ment of Commerce, Bureau of Foreign and Domestic Commerce,
Office of Business Economics, *Balance of Payments Statistical Sup-
plement* (Washington, D.C.: U.S. Government Printing Office, rev.
ed., 1962), pp. 210–215; U.S. Department of Commerce, Bureau of
Foreign and Domestic Commerce, Office of Business Economics,
Balance of Payments of the United States, 1949–1951 (Washington,
D.C.: U.S. Government Printing Office, 1972), p. 162; U.S. Depart-
ment of Commerce, Bureau of Economic Analysis, *Selected Data on
U.S. Direct Investment Abroad, 1966–1976* (Washington, D.C.: U.S.
Government Printing Office, 1977), p. 3–11.

31 In using the terms public capital to describe U.S. government funds
and private (corporate) capital to describe U.S. corporate funds, I
am of course cognizant that they are both agencies "of capital" and
that none of the funds at any time leaves the realm or circuits of
capital. I make this distinction, however, to serve a very specific purpose, viz., to provide a basis to differentiate between state and society, between class and state. Otherwise, the particular relationship
between state and (civil) society is fundamentally obscured and one,
therefore, cannot comprehend the nature of that relationship. Nor
can one understand the basis on which the state as a product of class
society and class struggle is, at the same time, not identical with that
society.

32 See, for example, Richard Barnet, *The Roots of War: Men and Institutions Behind U.S. Foreign Policy* (Baltimore; Pelican Books, 1973);
Seymour Melman, *The Permanent War Economy* (New York: Simon
and Schuster, 1974).

33 See Barnet and Müller, *Global Reach;* Vernon, *Sovereignty at Bay;* Raymond Vernon, *Storm over the Multinationals* (Cambridge: Harvard University Press, 1977); Robert L. Heilbroner, "Review Essay: None of Your Business," *New York Review of Books,* March 20, 1975, pp. 6–10; Stephen Hymer and Robert Rowthorn, "Multinational Corporations and International Oligopoly: The Non-American Challenge," in Charles P. Kindleberger, ed., *The International Corporation* (Cambridge: The M.I.T. Press, 1970), pp. 57–91.

34 Chester L. Cooper, "Some Perspectives on the Art of Decision-Making in National Security," in Keith C. Clark and Laurence J. Legere, eds., *The President and the Management of National Security* (New York: Praeger Publishers, 1969), p. 5. Also see I. M. Destler, "National Security Advice to U.S. Presidents," *World Politics,* Vol. XXIX, No. 2, January 1977, pp. 143–176; Bert A. Rockman, "America's Departments of State: Irregular and Regular Syndromes of Policy Making," *American Political Science Review,* Vol. 75, No. 4, December 1981, pp. 911–927.

35 See "Text of General Eisenhower's Foreign Policy Speech in San Francisco," *New York Times,* October 9, 1952, p. 24; Richard Moose, "The White House National-Security Staffs Since 1940," in Clark and Legere, eds., *The President and the Management of National Security,* p. 61; statement by Robert Cutler, Special Assistant to the President for National Security Affairs, 1953–1955 and 1957–1958, in U.S. Congress, Senate, Committee on Government Operations, Subcommittee on National Policy Machinery, *Organizing for National Security: The National Security Council, Part IV,* 86th Congress, 2nd Session, May 10 and 24, 1960 (Washington, D.C.: U.S. Government Printing Office, 1960), p. 581.

36 Dillion Anderson interview, Houston, Texas, June 13, 1966, *The Dulles Oral History Collection,* Princeton University Library, p. 41. On the Eisenhower NSC, also see Cutler, "The Development of the National Security Council," pp. 441–458. On the NSC under Truman, see Stanley L. Falk, "The National Security Council Under Truman, Eisenhower, and Kennedy," *Political Science Quarterly,* Vol. XXIX, No. 3, September 1964, pp. 403–417.

37 Moose, "The White House National-Security Staffs Since 1940," p. 61.

38 Personal Interview: White House Staff official, New Jersey, May 24, 1976. The respondent was a senior advisor on Latin American affairs during the Kennedy and Johnson administrations.

39 "Letter from McGeorge Bundy to Senator Henry M. Jackson," in Senator Henry M. Jackson, ed., *The National Security Council* (New York: Frederick A. Praeger, 1965), p. 276. Also see Bromley Smith interview, July 29, 1969, Oral History Interview, *Johnson Presidential Library,* p. 10. Smith was Executive Secretary of the NSC from 1961 to 1968.

40 "Letter from McGeorge Bundy to Senator Henry M. Jackson," p. 279.

41 David C. Humphrey, "Tuesday Lunch at the Johnson White House:

A Preliminary Assessment," *Diplomatic History*, Vol. 8, No. 1, Winter 1984, p. 90.

42 Presidential Press Secretary Bill Moyers, quoted in I. M. Destler, *Presidents, Bureaucrats, And Foreign Policy: The Politics of Organizational Reform* (Princeton: Princeton University Press, 1974), p. 10.

43 On the "Tuesday Cabinet," see Henry F. Graff, *The Tuesday Cabinet: Deliberation and Decision on Peace and War under Lyndon B. Johnson* (Englewood Cliffs, N.J.: Prentice-Hall, 1970); Humphrey, "Tuesday Lunch at the White House: A Preliminary Assessment," pp. 81–101; Bromley Smith interview, *Johnson Presidential Library*, pp. 22–23.

44 Richard M. Nixon, *United States Foreign Policy in the 1970s:* A Report to the Congress, February 18, 1970 (Washington, D.C.: U.S. Government Printing Office, 1970), p. 19.

45 See I. M. Destler, Leslie H. Gelb, and Anthony Lake, *Our Own Worst Enemy: The Unmaking of American Foreign Policy* (New York: Simon and Schuster, 1984), p. 205.

46 Presidential aide, quoted in Robert Semple, Jr., "Nixon to Revive Council's Power," *New York Times*, January 1, 1969, pp. 1, 10.

47 Quoted in William Beecher, "New Panel to Coordinate Defense Outlay and Policy," *New York Times*, November 29, 1969, p. 16. Also see Peter Grose, "Kissinger Gains a Key Authority in Foreign Policy," *New York Times*, February 5, 1969, pp. 1, 8; "Nixon Reorganizes Intelligence Work," *New York Times*, November 6, 1971, p. 14; John P. Leacacos, "Kissinger's Apparat," *Foreign Policy*, No. 5, Winter 1971–2, p.7.

48 Zbigniew Brzezinski, *Power and Principle: Memoirs of the National Security Advisor 1977–1981* (London: Wiedenfeld and Nicolson, 1983), p. 72. Also see Dom Bonafede, "Brzezinski–Stepping Out of His Backstage Role," *National Journal*, Vol. 9, No. 42, October 15, 1977, p. 1596.

49 Cyrus Vance, *Hard Choices: Critical Years in America's Foreign Policy* (New York: Simon and Schuster, 1983), p. 37.

50 Personal Interview: Department of State Official, Washington, D.C., July 11, 1973. The respondent was a specialist in Caribbean and Cuban affairs and held a number of important positions in these areas during the 1960s. Under Nixon, he was a senior Department Latin American official.

51 U.S. Congress, Senate, Committee on Government Operations, Subcommittee on National Security Staffing and Operations, *Administration of National Security: Basic Issues*, 88th Congress, 1st Session, Committee Print, 1963 (Washington, D.C.: U.S. Government Printing Office, 1963), p.8. Also see Philip Geyelin, "Charter a Course: U.S. Bolsters Foreign Policy Machinery but Critics Remain Uneasy," *Wall Street Journal*, May 31, 1961, pp. 1, 15.

52 Max Frankel, "Johnson Expands Powers of Rusk in Affairs Abroad," *New York Times*, March 5, 1966, p. 9.

53 Personal Interview: Department of the Treasury, Washington, D.C., November 5, 1976. The respondent was a Treasury official from

1950 to the mid-1970s, specializing in international economic affairs (including Latin America). He also served on the National Advisory Council for International Financial and Monetary Policies (NAC).

54 Through most of the 1950s, the average annual U.S. balance-of-payments deficit was approximately $1 billion, only to climb to around $3 billion to $4 billion between 1958 and the mid-1970s. Block, *The Origins of International Monetary Disorder*, p. 135. Also see Stephen D. Cohen, *The Making of United States International Economic Policy* (New York: Praeger Publishers, 1977), pp. 46–47. Numerous U.S. government, private sector and independent studies continue to document the American economy's increasing dependence on the profits of U.S. multinationals operating abroad. See, for example, Business International Corporation, *The Effects of Corporate Foreign Investment 1960–1970* (New York, 1972); Business International Corporation, *The Effects of U.S. Corporate Foreign Investment 1970–1976* (New York, 1978); Robert Gilpin, *U.S. Power and the Multinational Corporation* (New York: Basic Books, 1975), p. 149; Barnet and Müller, *Global Reach*, pp. 16–17; Ronald Müller, "Global Corporations: Their Impact on the United States and World Political Economy," in Commission on Critical Choices for Americans, Volume V, *Trade, Inflation & Ethics* (Lexington: D.C. Heath & Co., 1976), pp. 159–178; Obie G. Whichard, "Trends in the U.S. Direct Investment Position Abroad, 1950–1979," in U.S. Department of Commerce, Bureau of Economic Analysis, *Survey of Current Business*, Vol 61, No. 2, February 1981, pp. 50–51 (Table 7); Obie G. Whichard, "U.S. Direct Investment Abroad in 1980," in U.S. Department of Commerce, Bureau of Economic Analysis, *Survey of Current Business*, Vol, 61, No. 8, August 1981, p. 22 (Table 3), p. 32 (Table 12).

55 See U.S. Congress, Senate, Committee on Governmental Affairs, *U.S. Participation in the Multilateral Development Banks*, 96th Congress, 1st Session, Committee Print, April 30, 1979 (Washington, D.C.: U.S. Government Printing Office, 1979), pp. 23–25. During the mid-1970s, the power of the NAC was diminished, even though it still continued to advise the Secretary of the Treasury. The major responsibility for coordinating the loan-approval process shifted to the Office of Multilateral Development Banks (OMDB). In 1978, the Carter administration created the Development Coordinating Committee to coordinate all economic aid programs. This Committee then set up a Working Group in Multilateral Affairs (WGMA), under the chairmanship of the head of the OMDB, which began to assume the role previously delegated to the NAC. "By the early 1980s, all loan proposals were flowing from the banks' executive directors to the OMDB, which presented them to the WGMA for approval. The OMDB then notified the Secretary of the Treasury of the WGMA's position. Thus the NAC was all but eliminated from decision making on MDB loan proposals." Lars Schoultz, *Human Rights and United States Policy toward Latin America* (Princeton: Princeton University Press, 1981), pp. 273–274.

56 See Miles D. Wolpin, *Military Aid and Counterrevolution in the Third World* (Lexington: D.C. Heath & Co., 1972), pp. 11, 16, and passim; Miles D. Wolpin, "External Political Socialization as a Source of Conservative Military Behavior in the Third World," in Kenneth Fidel, ed., *Militarism in Developing Countries* (New Brunswick: Transaction Books, 1975), pp. 259–281; Michael Klare, *War Without End* (New York: Vintage Books, 1972), pp. 270–310; Jeffrey Stein, "Fort Lesley J. McNair: Grad School for Juntas," *The Nation*, May 21, 1977, pp. 621–624; Richard Gott, "Canal Zone School Builds Brotherhood of Latin Generals," *Washington Post*, April 16, 1977, p. A10.

57 See Philip Agee, *Inside the Company: CIA Diary* (Middlesex, England: Penguin Books, 1975); U.S. Congress, Senate, Select Committee on Intelligence, *Alleged Assassination Plots Involving Foreign Leaders*, 94th Congress, 1st Session, Report No. 94–465, November 20, 1975 (Washington, D.C.: U.S. Government Printing Office, 1975); U.S. Congress, Senate, Select Committee on Intelligence, *Covert Action in Chile, 1963–1973*, 94th Congress, 1st Session, Committee Print, December 18, 1975 (Washington, D.C.: U.S. Government Printing Office, 1975).

58 Lt. Gen. Howard M. Fish, U.S. Air Force, Director, Defense Security Assistance Agency, March 31, in U.S. Congress, House, Committee on International Relations, Subcommittee on International Security and Scientific Affairs, *Foreign Assistance Legislation for Fiscal Year 1978, Part 2*, 95th Congress, 1st Session, March 30, 31 and April 19, 20, 1977 (Washington, D.C.: U.S. Government Printing Office, 1977), p. 34.

59 U.S. General Accounting Office, Report to the Congress, *Assessment of Overseas Advisory Efforts of the U.S. Security Assistance Program*, ID-76-1, October 31, 1975, pp. 10, 11.

60 See Wolpin, "External Political Socialization as a Source of Conservative Military Behavior in the Third World," pp. 259–281.

61 Agee, *Inside the Company;* U.S. Congress, Senate, *Covert Action in Chile, 1963–1973;* Victor Marchetti and John D. Marks, *The CIA and the Cult of Intelligence* (New York: Alfred A. Knopf, 1974), pp. 41, 382–387; Statement by Mitchell Rogovin, Special Counsel to the Director of Central Intelligence, December 9, in U.S. Congress, House Select Committee on Intelligence, *U.S. Intelligence Agencies and Activities: Risks and Control of Foreign Intelligence, Part 5*, 94th Congress, 1st Session, November 4, 6, December 2, 3, 9, 10, 11, 12, and 17, 1975 (Washington, D.C.: U.S. Government Printing Office, 1976), p. 1730; Jerry Landauer, "CIA May Have Encouraged Firms to Pay Foreign Political Figures, Probe Shows," *Wall Street Journal*, March 1, 1977, p. 3; Rowland Evans and Robert Novak, "The CIA's Secret Subsidy to Israel," *Washington Post*, February 24, 1977, p. A21; Anthony Marro, "C.I.A. Money Flowed, But U.S. Aides Insist It Was for Intelligence," *New York Times*, March 1, 1977, p. 8. CIA covert intervention in a target country, according to former high-ranking Agency official Richard Bissell, is more likely to achieve maximum results "where a comprehensive

effort is undertaken with a number of separate operations designed to support and complement one another and to have a cumulatively significant effect." Quoted in Marchetti and Marks, *The CIA and the Cult of Intelligence*, p. 38.

62 See, for example, the statement by Robert Kovach, Office of Economic Research, Central Intelligence Agency, in U.S. Congress, House, Committee on International Relations, Subcommittee on International Trade and Commerce, *Export Licensing of Advanced Technology: A Review, Part II*, 94th Congress, 2nd Session, April 12, 1976 (Washington, D.C.: U.S. Government Printing Office, 1976), pp. 3–4.

63 See, for example, U.S. Congress, House, Committee on Foreign Affairs, Subcommittee on International Organizations and Movements, *Winning the Cold War: The U.S. Ideological Offensive, Part 1*, 88th Congress, 1st Session, March 28, 29; April 2 and 3, 1963 (Washington, D.C.: U.S. Government Printing Office, 1963).

64 See, for example, Ronald Radosh, *American Labor and United States Foreign Policy* (New York: Random House, 1969).

65 See R. Harrison Wagner, *United States Policy Toward Latin America* (Stanford: Stanford University Press, 1970), p. 91. C. Douglas Dillon, a senior State Department official under Eisenhower, dated State's emergence as a significant actor in the area of international economic policy with the departure of Treasury Secretary George M. Humphrey in 1957. See U.S. Congress, House, Committee on Foreign Affairs, Subcommittee on Foreign Economic Policy, *U.S. Foreign Economic Policy: Implications for Organization of the Executive Branch*, 92nd Congress, 2nd Session, June 20, 22; July 25, August 2 and September 19, 1972 (Washington, D.C.: U.S. Government Printing Office, 1972), p. 93.

66 General Nathan F. Twining interview, Washington, D.C., March 16, 1965, *The Dulles Oral History Collection*, Princeton University Library, p. 23.

67 General Maxwell D. Taylor interview, Washington, D.C., May 11, 1966, *The Dulles Oral History Collection*, Princeton University Library, p. 26.

68 Quoted in David H. Davis, *How the Bureaucracy Makes Foreign Policy* (Lexington: D.C. Heath & Co., 1972), p. 83. These interagency positions surfaced in the debate over U.S. policy toward the Venezuelan government of Carlos Andres Perez (1974–1978). See James Petras, Morris Morley, and Steven Smith, *The Nationalization of Venezuelan Oil* (New York: Praeger Publishers, 1977), pp. 102–104.

69 Personal Interview: Department of the Treasury official, Washington, D.C., November 5, 1976.

70 See Jessica Pernitz Einhorn, *Expropriation Politics* (Lexington: D.C. Heath Co., 1974), especially pp. 91–121; Mark L. Chadwin, "Foreign Policy Report/Nixon Administration debates new position paper on Latin America," *National Journal*, Vol. 4, No. 3, January 15, 1972, pp. 97–107; Mark L. Chadwin, "Foreign Policy Report/

Nixon's expropriation policy seeks to soothe angry Congress,"
National Journal, Vol. 4, No. 4, January 22, 1972, pp. 148–156.

71 Neil McElroy interview, Cincinnati, Ohio, May 6, 1964, *The Dulles Oral History Collection*, Princeton University Library, p. 15. According to a senior Eisenhower administration Pentagon and National Security Affairs official, Gordon Gray, there were "a lot of disagreements" with State over specific issues but these coexisted with a "pretty good" overall working relationship between the two departments. Gordon Gray interview, Washington, D.C., March 4, 1966, *The Dulles Oral History Collection*, Princeton University Library, pp. 25, 31. A 1960 congressional study concluded that the Departments of State and Defense had been "the dominant departmental voices" within the Eisenhower National Security Council. See U.S. Congress, Senate, Committee on Foreign Relations, *United States Foreign Policy, No. 9: The Formulation and Administration of United States Foreign Policy*, 86th Congress, 2nd Session, Committee Print, January 13, 1960 (Washington, D.C.: U.S. Government Printing Office, 1960), p. 46.

72 See John Child, *The Inter American Military System* (Ph.D. dissertation, The American University, 1978), pp. 119–360.

73 Ibid., pp. 496–499.

74 See Vance, *Hard Choices*, pp. 75, 84, 179–186; Brzezinski, *Power and Principle*, pp. 78–88; Terence Smith, "Brzezinski's Foreign Policy Role Appears to Have Been Bolstered," *New York Times*, April 29, 1980, p. 16; Dick Kirschten, "White House Report/Beyond the Vance-Brzezinski Clash Lurks an NSC under Fire," *National Journal*, Vol. 12, No. 20, May 17, 1980, pp. 814–818; Leslie H. Gelb, "Muskie and Brzezinski: The Struggle over Foreign Policy," *New York Times Magazine*, July 20, 1980, pp. 26–27, 32, 34–35, 38–40; Bernard Gwertzman, "Muskie Said to Want Major Shift in Management of Foreign Policy," *New York Times*, October 6, 1980, pp. 1, 13.

75 Personal Interview: National Security Council Staff member, Washington, D.C., August 21, 1978. The respondent was a specialist in Latin American affairs.

76 Quoted in Richard Burt, "Muskie Is Said to Have Established Harmonious Ties With Brzezinski," *New York Times*, July 14, 1980, p. 6.

77 See Destler, *Presidents, Bureaucrats, and Foreign Policy*, p. 60; Cohen, *The Making of United States International Economic Policy*, p. 35.

78 An imperial state requires that there be no serious challenge to capitalist political hegemony at home. One striking feature of political and social relations in the United States since 1945 has been the near absence of such domestic conflict–class or non-class. The U.S. capitalist class has rebounded from economic crises at home and abroad by passing the costs of economic recovery onto the working class without fear of significant, organized objections from that class. Two factors have facilitated this state of affairs and made nearly impossible the emergence of class politics: an accommodating, col-

laborative trade-union bureaucracy, and the strong ties between the national labor leadership and the Democratic Party which, no less than the Republican Party, has a fundamental commitment to U.S. domestic and global capitalist expansion. Even the two major political parties' legislative opposition to imperial-state policy has been usually ineffective (e.g., periodic criticism of CIA operations). In addition, those rare challenges to the imperial-state apparatus from the electorate have not been class-based (e.g., the massive popular antiwar movement of the late 1960s and early 1970s), and such crises always are *relative to a particular period and policy*. They have not ushered in great changes in the structure of U.S. institutions and economic interests.

79 Gabriel Kolko, *The Roots of American Foreign Policy* (Boston: Beacon Books, 1969), p. 7.

80 David T. Stanley, Dean E. Mann, and James W. Doig, *Men Who Govern: A Biographical Profile of Federal Political Executives* (Washington, D.C.: The Brookings Institution, 1967), pp. 34, 38. On corporate-policymaking linkages, also see ibid., pp. 31–39, 50–53, 123–134; Kolko, *The Roots of American Foreign Policy*, pp. 13–26; Peter J. Freitag, "The Cabinet and Big Business: A Study of Interlocks," *Social Problems*, Vol. 23, No. 2, December 1975, pp. 137–152; Dennis Ray, "Corporations and American Foreign Policy," *The Annals*, Vol. 403, September 1972, pp. 80–92; G. William Domhoff, *The Higher Circles* (New York: Vintage Books, 1971), pp. 111–155; Barnet, *The Roots of War*, 176–205. Both Freitag and Stanley et al. point out that Democratic cabinet appointees are as closely tied to private corporate world as their Republican counterparts are.

81 See Freitag, "The Cabinet and Big Business: A Study of Interlocks," pp. 142, 145.

82 An interesting discussion of this notion is found in Nora Hamilton, *The Limits of State Autonomy: Post-Revolutionary Mexico* (Princeton: Princeton University Press, 1982), pp. 4–15.

83 Ralph Miliband, *Class Power and State Power* (London: Verso Editions and New Left Review, 1983), p. 73.

84 For an example of the type of "relative autonomy of the state" analysis criticized here, see Ellen Kay Trimberger, *Revolution from Above: Military Bureaucrats and Development in Japan, Turkey, Egypt and Peru* (New Brunswick: Transaction Books, 1978).

85 For a study that argues in favor of the notion of state "autonomy" on the basis of discrete instances of particular conflicts between the U.S. state and individual multinationals, see Stephen D. Krasner, *Defending the National Interest* (Princeton: Princeton University Press, 1977).

86 See, for example, Petras and Morley, *The United States and Chile*, pp. 27–42.

87 The notion of "collaborating" or "mediating" classes as crucial to facilitating imperial expansion is discussed in Ronald Robinson, "Non-European Foundations of European Imperialism: Sketch for a Theory of Collaboration," in Owen and Sutcliffe, eds., *Studies in the Theory of Imperialism*, pp. 117–140.

88 See Barnet and Müller, *Global Reach*, pp. 148–184.
89 For a revealing study, see James Petras and Thomas Cook, "Dependency and the Industrial Bourgeoisie: Attitudes of Argentine Executives Toward Foreign Economic Investment and U.S. Policy," in James Petras, ed., *Latin America: From Dependence to Revolution* (New York: John Wiley & Sons, 1973), pp. 143–175.
90 A *colony* is a geographic unit that has come under the political, economic, and military domination of, typically, an imperial state. *Colonialism* refers to this process of direct military occupation and rule and to the subsequent development and organization of an administrative-economic ruling class that governs in the interests of the imperial state. The most critical sectors of the economy are usually under the control of foreign capital. A *neocolonial state* is one in which political and administrative posts have been transferred from the imperial regime to an indigenous ruling class, but where economic control (and possibly strategic military bases) is maintained by capitalists (and governments) located in one of the imperial centers. The usually monoculture economies remain highly vulnerable to external pressures in the postcolonial period. Dependence on raw material exports, technology imports, as well as unequal terms of trade/exchange and foreign capital control of the most dynamic and strategic sectors of the economy are characteristic of neocolonies.
91 Such peripheral state organizations may be viewed as jointly located within the peripheral state and the imperial state. Under conditions of direct imperial-state rule, of course, the agencies of the peripheral state are themselves the agencies of the imperial state. The state is conceptually separate from the government or regime, which are viewed as the agency of class rule, more temporary, and contained within the state.

   For discussions of the process of "state building" in Cuba between 1898 and 1902, see David F. Healy, *The United States in Cuba 1898–1902* (Madison: University of Wisconsin Press, 1963); Leonard Wood, "The Military Government of Cuba," *The Annals*, March 1903, pp. 153–182; Louis A. Pérez, Jr., *Army Politics in Cuba, 1898–1958* (Pittsburgh: University of Pittsburgh Press, 1976), pp. 3–16. The notion of "social investment" is discussed in James O'Connor, *The Fiscal Crisis of the State* (New York: St. Martin's Press, 1973), pp. 6–7, 101–102.
92 On U.S. military and nonmilitary interventions, see Pérez, *Army Politics in Cuba, 1898–1958*, pp. 21–54; Louis A. Pérez, Jr., *Intervention, Revolution, and Politics in Cuba, 1913–1921* (Pittsburgh: University of Pittsburgh Press, 1978); Charles P. Howland, *American Relations in the Caribbean* (New York: Arno Press and The New York Times, 1970), pp. 3–68; Howard C. Hill, *Roosevelt and the Caribbean* (Chicago: University of Chicago Press, 1927); Allen R. Millet, *The Politics of Intervention: The Military Occupation of Cuba 1906–1909* (Columbus: Ohio State University Press, 1968).
93 Pérez, *Army Politics in Cuba, 1898–1958*, p. 53.
94 See Robert F. Smith, *The United States and Cuba: Business and Diplomacy, 1917–1960* (New Haven: College and University Press,

1960), p. 29; John M. Hunter, "Investment as a Factor in the Economic Development of Cuba 1899–1935," *Inter-American Economic Affairs*, Vol. 5, No. 3, Winter 1951, p. 85; Leland H. Jenks, *Our Cuban Colony: A Study in Sugar* (New York: Arno Press and The New York Times, 1970), pp. 19, 21; The Cuban Economic Research Project, *A Study on Cuba* (Coral Gables: University of Miami Press, 1965), pp. 286–287.

95 Jules R. Benjamin, *The United States and Cuba: Hegemony and Dependent Development, 1880–1934* (Pittsburgh: University of Pittsburgh Press, 1977), p. 4; Fabio Grobart, "The Cuban Working Class Movement from 1925–1933," *Science & Society*, Vol. XXXIX, No. 1, Spring 1975, p. 83.

96 U.K. Department of Overseas Trade, *Economic Conditions in Cuba*, Report of His Majesty's Consul General, Havana, No. 518, April 1932 (London: His Majesty's Stationary Office, 1932), p. 34; Benjamin, *The United States and Cuba*, p. 99; Julio Le Riverend, *Economic History of Cuba* (Havana: Book Institute, 1967), pp. 234.

97 Ibid., p. 236; Grobart, "The Cuban Working Class Movement from 1925 to 1933," p. 91.

98 Taussig to Secretary of State Hull, undated, in Franklin D. Roosevelt, *The Public Papers and Addresses of Franklin D. Roosevelt, Vol. 2: Years of Crisis 1933* (New York: Random House, 1938), p. 181.

99 Commission on Cuban Affairs, *Problems of the New Cuba* (New York: Foreign Policy Association, 1935), pp. 182–183 (my emphasis).

100 Personal Representative Caffery to Acting Secretary of State, January 10, 1934, FRUS, Vol. V, 1934, pp. 95–96. For discussions of the Grau government and U.S. policy, see Benjamin, *The United States and Cuba*; Charles A. Thompson, "The Cuban Revolution: Reform and Reaction," *Foreign Policy Reports*, Vol. XI, No. 22, January 1, 1936, pp. 262–276.

101 See Irwin F. Gellman, *Roosevelt and Batista: Good Neighbor Diplomacy in Cuba, 1933–1945* (Albuquerque: University of New Mexico Press, 1973), p. 114

102 Frederick L. Springborn (Latin American Division, Department of the Treasury) to Duwayne G. Clark (Counselor for Economic Affairs, Havana Embassy), January 3, 1952, Cuba 0/00, Box 44/1, U.S. Department of the Treasury, *Declassified Freedom of Information Act* (hereafter DFOIA).

103 Memorandum by Acting Secretary of State Lovett to President Truman, December 7, 1948, FRUS, Vol. IX, 1948, p. 571.

104 Max Weber, *Economic and Society, Vol. 3* (New York: Bedminster Press, 1968), p. 974.

105 Thomas J. Heston, "Cuba, the United States, and the Sugar Act of 1948: The Failure of Economic Coercion," *Diplomatic History*, Vol. 6, No. 1, Winter 1982, p. 3.

106 Ibid., p. 4.

107 Quoted in ibid., p. 11.

108 Ibid., p. 18.

109 Department of State Policy Statement (Secret), "United States Pol-

icy Toward Cuba," January 11, 1950, FRUS, Vol. II: The United Nations; The Western Hemisphere, 1950, pp. 843–846, 852.
110 Ibid., p. 850.

2. The United States in Cuba 1952–1958: policymaking and capitalist interests

1 David Green, *The Containment of Latin America* (Chicago: Quadrangle Books, 1971), p. 255.

2 The relative isolation of Latin America from the economies of Western Europe during 1939 to 1945 and export expansion into the U.S. market during this same period, based on artificially constructed price controls, allowed for some national industrial development to occur in the region. After 1945, however, U.S. price controls were terminated and, in free market competition, raw material export prices declined, while the cost of purchasing American industrial and manufactured goods increased. This vulnerability in world commodity prices arrested the short-term trend toward national developmentalism in these largely monoculture economies and restored the most critical decisions affecting internal economic development in the region to the vagaries and goals of external decisionmakers.

3 Statement of Col. Goldwin Ordway, War Department General Staff and Delegate to the Latin American Defense Board, in U.S. Congress, House *Military Assistance Programs, Part 2*, p. 469.

4 Secretary of War Patterson to the Acting Secretary of State, March 27, 1947, FRUS, Vol. VIII, 1947, p. 108.

5 Gordon Connell-Smith, *The Inter-American System* (Oxford: Oxford University Press, 1966), p. 195.

6 In preparatory discussions leading to the establishment of the United Nations, senior American policymakers were preoccupied with ensuring that no new global organization would place limits on U.S. freedom of action in Latin America. In a May 1945 telephone conversation during which the issue was raised, Secretary of State Henry Stimson told Assistant Secretary of War John J. McCloy that the United States must remain the "policeman in this hemisphere." Quoted in Gabriel Kolko, *The Politics of War: The World and United States Foreign Policy, 1943–1945* (New York: Vintage Books, 1968), p. 472. On Washington's subsequent ability to successfully exploit ambiguities in the United Nations' Charter to uphold the OAS's primary jurisdiction in regional affairs, see Inis L. Claude, Jr., "The OAS,, The UN and the United States," *International Organization*, No. 547, March 1964, pp. 3–67; Aida Luisa Levin, *Regionalism and the United Nations in American Foreign Policy: The Peace-Keeping Experience of the Organization of American States* (Ph.D. dissertation, Columbia University, 1971), p. 287; Connell-Smith, *The Inter-American System*, pp. 189–345.

7 U.S. Congress, House, Committee on Foreign Affairs, *The Middle East, Africa, and Inter-American Affairs*, Selected Executive Session Hearings, 1951–1956, Volume XVI (Washington, D.C.: U.S. Government Printing Office, 1980), p. 389.

8 U.S. Congress, Senate, Committee on Foreign Relations, *Executive Sessions of the Senate Foreign Relations Committee, Vol. IV, 1952* (Historical Series), 82nd Congress, 2nd Session (Washington, D.C.: U.S. Government Printing Office, 1976), pp. 28–29.

9 John Dreier interview, Washington, D.C., May 24, 1965, *The Dulles Oral History Collection*, Princeton University Library, p. 10. The decision of the American labor leadership to promote, organize, and finance the development of an anticommunist trade union movement in Latin American in the late 1940s provided an additional "weapon" in pursuit of U.S. imperial-state objectives in the hemisphere. In 1948, the labor hierarchy helped establish the Inter-American Confederation of Labor (CIT) and, in 1949, played an instrumental role in the formation of a successor organization, the Inter-American Regional Organization of Workers (ORIT). This latter body became the regional affiliate of the anticommunist International Confederation of Free Trade Unions (ICFTU) and functioned, throughout the 1950s, as the major vehicle for AFL and CIO activities in Latin America. See Radosh, *American Labor and United States Foreign Policy*, pp. 371–372.

10 Paper prepared by the Policy Planning Staff, March 22, 1948, submitted by Secretary of State to Diplomatic Representatives in the American Republics, June 21, 1948, FRUS, Vol. IX, 1948, p. 198.

11 Stephen E. Ambrose, *Eisenhower: Volume Two, The President* (New York: Simon and Schuster, 1984), p. 621.

12 Personal Interview: Department of State official, Washington, D.C., March 10, 1975. The respondent was a senior American representative to OAS during the 1950s. Also see Stephen G. Rabe, "The Johnson (Eisenhower?) Doctrine for Latin America," *Diplomatic History*, Vol. 9, No. 1, Winter 1985, pp. 95–100.

13 See Ambrose, *Eisenhower: Volume Two, The President*, pp. 110–111.

14 Personal Interview: Central Intelligence Agency official, Washington, D.C., January 7, 1976. The respondent was a CIA official during the 1950s and 1960s. He was stationed at Agency headquarters in Langley, Virginia, specializing in the area of covert operations. More than half of the CIA budget during the mid-1950s was allocated for covert action projects. Testimony of E. Henry Knoche in U.S. Congress, Senate, Select Committee on Intelligence, *Nomination of E. Henry Knoche* (to be Deputy Directory of Central Intelligence), 94th Congress, 2nd Session, June 23, 1976 (Washington, D.C.: U.S. Government Printing Office, 1976), p. 14.

15 For discussions of U.S. policy toward these two nationalist regimes, see Cole Blasier, "The United States and the Revolution," in James M. Malloy and Richard S. Thorn, eds., *Beyond the Revolution: Bolivia Since 1952* (Pittsburgh: University of Pittsburgh Press, 1971), pp. 53–109; James M. Wilkie, *The Bolivian Revolution and U.S. Aid Since 1952* (University of California at Los Angeles: Latin American Center, 1969); Cole Blasier, *The Hovering Giant: U.S. Responses to Revolutionary Changes in Latin America* (Pittsburgh: University of Pittsburgh Press, 1976); Laurence Whitehead, *The United States and*

Bolivia: A Case of Neo-Colonialism (London: Haslemere Group Publications, 1969); Stephen Schlesinger and Stephen Kinzer, *Bitter Fruit* (New York: Doubleday & Co., 1982); Richard H. Immerman, *The CIA in Guatemala* (Austin: University of Texas Press, 1982); Susanne Jonas and David Tobis, eds., *Guatemala* (New York and Berkeley: North American Congress on Latin America, August 1974); Ambrose, *Eisenhower: Volume Two, The President*, pp. 192–197.

16 Personal Correspondence: Department of State official, Florida, March 29, 1975. The respondent had extensive field experience in Latin America during the 1950s. He was stationed in the Santiago de Cuba Consulate between 1958 and 1960.

17 U.S. Department of Commerce, Office of Business Economics, *U.S. Investments in the Latin American Economy* (Washington, D.C.: U.S. Government Printing Office, 1957), p. 5.

18 Memorandum by George Kennan to Secretary of State, March 29, 1950, FRUS, Vol II, 1950, p. 618.

19 Remarks by William M. C. Martin, Jr., President of the Export-Import Bank of Washington, before Committee IV of the Ninth International Conference of American States, Bogota, April 9, 1948, FRUS, Vol. IX, 1948, p. 38. On Eximbank operations in Latin America, see Hawthorne Arey, *History of Operations and Policies of Export-Import Bank of Washington* (Washington, D.C., November 15, 1963), pp. 40–58. Between July 1958 and June 1960, two-thirds of total authorized Eximbank credits went to Latin American countries. See Raymond F. Mikesell, "The Export-Import Bank in Washington," in Raymond F. Mikesell, ed., *U.S. Private and Government Investment Abroad* (Eugene: University of Oregon Books, 1962), p. 477.

20 Personal Interview: Department of State official, Washington D.C., July 11, 1973. The respondent held a number of senior positions in Washington, D.C., and Latin America during the 1960s and early 1970s. He was primarily involved with Cuba and the Caribbean region.

21 Burton Kauffman, *Trade and Aid: Eisenhower's Foreign Economic Policy 1953–1961* (Baltimore: The Johns Hopkins University Press, 1982), p. 32.

22 Ibid. p. 63.

23 Ibid., p. 162.

24 Ibid., pp. 157–161; Ambrose, *Eisenhower: Volume Two, The President*, p. 376–381. Ambrose also provides a discussion of Congressional opposition to this shift in U.S. foreign economic policy.

25 See Vernon, *Sovereignty at Bay*, p. 68.

26 Whichard, "Trends in the U.S. Direct Investment Position Abroad, 1950–1979," pp. 50–51 (Table 7).

27 U.S. Department of Commerce, *U.S. Investments in the Latin American Economy*, p. 3.

28 Ibid.

29 Military assistance pacts were signed with the following countries: Cuba (1952); Chile (1951); Colombia (1952); Peru (1952); Ecuador

(1952); Brazil (1953); Dominican Republic (1953); Uruguay (1955); Bolivia (1958). On the proliferation of military-to-military linkages, see Secretary of War Patterson to the Acting Secretary of State, March 27, 1947, FRUS, Vol. VIII, 1947, p. 108; "Draft Report by the National Security Council on the Position of the United States with Respect to the Military Aspects of the Implementation of the Inter-American Treaty of Reciprocal Assistance," submitted with Memorandum by the Secretary of Defense Johnson to the Executive Secretary of the National Security Council Souers, August 30, 1949, FRUS, Vol. I, 1950, p. 603.

30 Draft Statement of Policy prepared by NSC Planning Board, "U.S. Policy Toward Latin America," NSC 5163, Transmittal Memorandum by James S. Lay, Jr., Executive Secretary to the NSC. Eisenhower Presidential Library, White House Office, Office of the Special Assistant for National Security Affairs, Records, 1952–61, NSC Series, Policy Papers Subseries, Box 18, NSC 5613/1, *DFOIA*.

31 See Samuel L. Baily, *The United States and the Development of South America* (New York: New Viewpoints and Franklin Watts, 1976), pp. 73–74.

32 R. Richard Rubottom Jr. interview, Dallas, Texas, June 12, 1966, *The Dulles Oral History Collection*, Princeton University Library, pp. 26–27.

33 Personal Interview: Central Intelligence Agency official, Washington, D.C., January 7, 1976.

34 Daniel M. Braddock, Counselor, Havana Embassy (for the Ambassador) to Department of State, Subject: "Comments and Suggestions on OCB 'Outline Plan of Operations for Latin America,'" February 18, 1958, Dispatch No. 660, 611.37/2-1958, *DFOIA*. Also see the oft-quoted remark by the American Ambassador to Cuba, Earl T. Smith (1956–1958): "Whenever I asked President Batista for Cuba's vote to support the United States in the United Nations, he would instruct his Foreign Minister to have the Cuban delegation vote in accordance with the United States delegation and to give full support to the American delegation at the United Nations." Earl T. Smith, *The Fourth Floor* (New York: Random House, 1962), p. 55.

35 Havana Embassy to Department of State, Subject: "Revision of Operations Plan for Latin America," October 22, 1958, Dispatch No. 429, 611.37/10-2258, *DFOIA*.

36 Daniel M. Braddock, Counselor, Havana Embassy (for the Ambassador) to Department of State, Subject: "Progress Report on OCB 'Outline Plan of Operations for Latin America,'" February 19, 1958, Dispatch No. 661, 611.37/2-1958, *DFOIA*.

37 International Bank for Reconstruction and Development, *Report on Cuba 1950* (Baltimore: The John Hopkins Press, 1951), Especially pp. 138–152, 381–382.

38 American businessmen in Cuba viewed Batista "as representing a stabilizing interest" who would control and, if necessary, forcefully repress nationalist tendencies in society. Personal Interview: U.S. Businessman, New York City, New York, July 14, 1975. The respon-

dent was a senior executive in the Havana office of the multinational insurance brokerage firm of March & McLennan from 1947 to 1960.

39 R. Hart Phillips, "U.S. Businessmen in Cuba See Relief," *New York Times*, April 3, 1952, p. 21.

40 U.S. Department of Commerce, Bureau of Foreign Commerce, *Investment in Cuba: Basic Information for United States Businessmen* (Washington, D.C.: U.S. Government Printing Office, July 1956), p.19.

41 Personal Interview: U.S. Businessman, New York City, New York, June 26, 1975. The respondent was the manager of Bethlehem Steel's Cuban subsidiary from 1946 to 1955. A report by the Cuban National Bank in the mid-1950s commented: "Cuban labor is plentiful. Skilled and unskilled. Cuban laborers are easily trained. Wages, while reasonable, are lower than in the United States. We have unions as all free countries have. But we seldon have strikes of any serious nature." Banco de Cuba, *Why You Should Invest in Cuba* (Havana, 1956 or 1957), p. 13.

42 U.S. Congress, House, *The Middle East, Africa, and Inter-American Affairs*, p. 410.

43 Quoted in "Cuban Labor Code Will Be Changed," *New York Times*, April 27, 1954, p. 12.

44 Ibid.

45 James O'Connor, *The Origins of Socialism in Cuba* (Ithaca: Cornell University Press, 1970), p. 146.

46 United Nations, Economic Commission for Latin America, Department of Economic and Social Affairs, *Economic Survey of Latin America 1957* (New York: 1959), p. 182.

47 Personal Interview: Department of State official, Washington, D.C., June 2, 1975. The respondent was a senior Cuban affairs official during the latter half of the 1950s.

48 Personal Interview: U.S. Businessman, Washington, D.C., July 31, 1975. The respondent was the manager of Merrill Lynch's Havana branch from 1946 to 1960.

49 See Hugh Thomas, *Cuba or the Pursuit of Freedom* (London: Eyre & Spottiswoode, 1971), p. 911.

50 Personal Correspondence: U.S. Businessman, Florida, July 1975. The respondent was president and general manager of the U.S. Steamship Agency in Havana from the late 1940s until 1961. During the 1950s, he was also a senior officeholder in the American Chamber of Commerce in Havana.

51 The Cuban Economic Research Project, *A Study on Cuba*, p. 569.

52 See Fulgencio Batista, *The Growth and Decline of the Cuban Republic* (New York: The Devin-Adair Co., 1964), p. 569; Ed Cony and Williams Giles, "Cuban Slowdown: Revolt, Foul Weather, Yank Recession Harry Island's Investors," *Wall Street Journal*, February 3, 1958, pp. 1, 19.

53 See Robin Blackburn, "The Economics of the Cuban Revolution," in Claudio Velez, ed., *Latin America and the Caribbean: A Handbook* (London: Anthony Blond, 1969), p. 624.

54 U.S. Department of Commerce, *Investment in Cuba: Basic Information for United States Businessmen*, p. 155.
55 Personal Interview: Department of State official, Washington, D.C., July 30, 1976. The respondent was stationed in the Santiago de Cuba Consulate during the late 1950s to 1961.
56 Personal Interview: U.S. Businessman, New York City, New York, June 27, 1975. The respondent was the assistant manager and manager of Texaco Oil Company's Cuban subsidiary between 1956 and 1959.
57 U.S. Department of Commerce, *Investment in Cuba: Basic Information for United States Businessmen*, p. 159.
58 Government of Cuba, *Report on Cuba* (Washington, D.C.), Vol. 2, No. 5, November 1958, p.2.
59 See Cony and Giles, "Cuban Slowdown: Revolt, Foul Weather, Yank Recession Harry Island's Investors," pp. 1, 19. The tax exemptions offered by the Batista government are discussed in "Cuban Drive Attracts New Foreign Investments," *Journal of Commerce*, October 23, 1958, p. 11.
60 Havana Embassy to Department of State, Subject: "Revision of Operations Plan for Latin America," October 22, 1958.
61 See Leland L. Johnson, "U.S. Business Interests in Cuba and the Rise of Castro," *World Politics*, Vol. XVII, No. 3, April 1965, p. 441.
62 See U.S. Congress, Senate, Committe on Foreign Relations, Subcommittee on American Republic Affairs, *United States-Latin American Relations, Study No. 7: Soviet Bloc Latin American Activities*, 86th Congress, 2nd Session, Committee Print, February 28, 1960 (Washington, D.C.: U.S. Government Printing Office, 1960), pp. 108–109 (Table 1-g).
63 Havana Embassy to Department of State, Subject: "Revision of Operations Plan for Latin America," October 22, 1958.
64 Business International Corporation, *The Cuban Revolution.* Prepared by Siegfried Marks, Foreign Economist, Department 768-X (New York: January 1960), p. 11.
65 U.S. Department of Commerce, *Investment in Cuba: Basic Information for United States Businessmen*, pp. 21–22.
66 Personal Interview: U.S. Businessman, New York City, New York, July 9, 1975. The respondent was a high-ranking official of the Cuban Electric Company, a subsidiary of American & Foreign Power, in Havana during the 1950s.
67 Havana Embassy to Department of State, John F. Correll for the Ambassador, Subject: "Comparative Labor Expenditures," Dispatch No. 636, February 13, 1958, 837.061/2-1358, *DFOIA*.
68 Havana Embassy to Department of State, John F. Correll for the Ambassador, Subject: "Quarterly Labor Report-Fourth Quarter, 1957," Dispatch No. 618, February 10, 1958, 837.06/2-1058, *DFOIA*.
69 Ibid.
70 Havana Embassy to Department of State, E. A. Gilmore, Jr., Acting Counselor of Embassy for the Ambassador, Subject: "Labor Report-

Second Quarter, 1958," Dispatch, July 1, 1958, 837.06/7-158, *DFOIA*.

71 John Correll, Labor Attache, Havana Embassy to Leonard Price, Commerce Attache, Havana Embassy, Subject: "Labor Section for the Annual Economic Review, 1958," Dispatch No. 981, Havana Embassy to Department of State, March 6, 1959, 837.06/3-659 *DFOIA*.

72 Personal Interview: Department of State official, Washington, D.C., June 3, 1975. The respondent was stationed in the Havana Embassy during the 1950s. "What they were interested in mainly was a preservation of law and order so they could carry on their businesses. As long as it [the Batista government] was able to maintain law and order, business was willing to go along." Personal interview: Department of State official, Washington, D.C., March 13, 1975. The respondent was a senior Havana Embassy official from the late 1950s until 1961.

73 Personal Interview: U.S. Businessman, New York City, New York, June 25, 1975. The respondent was the manager of the Cuban subsidiary of Johnson & Higgins insurance brokerage company from the mid-1940s until 1960.

74 Personal Interview: U.S. Businessman, New York City, New York, June 26, 1975. The respondent was a senior executive of Bethlehem Steel's Cuban subsidiary from the mid-1940s until the mid-1950s.

75 Personal Interview: Central Intelligence Agency official, Washington, D.C., May 21, 1976. The respondent was a CIA field officer in Cuba from 1955 to 1960, and a senior official monitoring Cuban affairs in Latin America and Washington, D.C., during the 1960s.

76 Personal Interview: Department of State official, Washington, D.C., March 14, 1975. The respondent was stationed in the Havana Embassy from 1952 to 1955.

77 Personal Correspondence: Department of State official, Florida, March 29, 1975.

78 Ibid.

79 Personal Interview: U.S. Businessman, New York City, New York, June 25, 1975. The respondent was the official in charge of the Moa Bay Mining Company's project in Oriente Province during the 1950s. The Moa Bay Mining Company was a subsidiary of the U.S. Freeport Sulphur Company.

80 L. J. "Tex" Brewer, President Esso Standard Oil, S.A., quoted in "Damage to U.S. Firms Mounts as Rebels Push for Showdown Fight," *Wall Street Journal*, April 4, 1958, p. 1.

81 Quoted in "U.S. Business Men Eye Castro's Policies as Cuba Revolt Grows," *Wall Street Journal*, September 6, 1957, p. 3.

82 Personal Interview: U.S. Businessman, New York City, New York, July 14, 1975. Also see Smith, *The Fourth Floor*, pp. 161–162. The lack of precise data on the relationship between the inter– and intracorporate conflict and the policymaking process makes it impossible to measure the impact or influence of different capitalist fractions on the trajectory of decisionmaking within the executive branch. What is clear, however, is that, confronted with the very real pos-

sibility of the "break up" of the repressive apparatus of the Batista state, Washington moved with as much speed as possible to mobilize the resources at its command to fashion a strategy premised, in large part, on the immediate and long-term interests of foreign capital accumulation in Cuba.

83 Personal Interview: Department of State official, Washington, D.C., June 12, 1973. The respondent held a number of positions in Latin America, including Cuba, between 1955 and 1960. Also see *Business Week*, March 15, 1952, p. 176. Within hours of the March coup, Batista moved to reassure the Truman administration, via diplomatic note, on the question of Cuba's proimperial ties and obligations. See Dean Acheson (Drafted by E. G. Miller, ARA), Department of State, to Willard Beaulac, Havana Embassy, Telegram, March 12, 1952, Dispatch No. 4118, 737.00/3-1952, *DFOIA*. According to a member of the deposed Prío government, a U.S. army officer was in uniform at Camp Columbia, Cuban military headquarters, in the early hours of March 10 as the coup was being consummated: "He said this officer congratulated Cuban officers on the timing and efficiency of the coup which he was reported to have termed 'long overdue.'" A series of meetings had also taken place between Elliot Roosevelt and Batista during the immediate pre-coup period. See R. Hart Phillips, "U.S. Role Coup Suspected in Cuba," *New York Times*, March 18, 1952, p. 10.

84 Memorandum of Conversation, by the Ambassador in Cuba, Willard L. Beaulac (Secret), March 22, 1952, FRUS, Vol. IV: The American Republics, 1952–1954, p. 869.

85 See for example, Memorandum by the Secretary of State to the President (Secret). March 24, 1952. Subject: "Continuation of Diplomatic Relations with Cuba," in ibid., p. 871.

86 Ibid.

87 This was one of the issues, for example, raised by American officials in discussions with the Cuban economic and commercial delegation in Washington in November 1954. See "Extract from Current Economic Developments (prepared by the Bureau of Economic Affairs)," Issue No. 455, November 23, 1954 (Secret), in ibid., p. 924.

88 Alfred Padula, Jr., *The Fall of the Bourgeoisie: Cuba 1959–1961* (Ph.D. dissertation, University of New Mexico, 1974), pp. 66–68.

89 State Department Memo, Subject: "Hazardous Financial Policies of the Cuban Government," December 23, 1955, File: Cuba 0/00 General, Box 44/1, Department of the Treasury, *DFOIA*.

90 Personal Interview: Department of State official, Washington, D.C., June 12, 1973.

91 Personal Interview: Department of State official, Washington, D.C., May 19, 1976. The respondent was a senior political officer in the Havana Embassy from late 1956 to mid-1960. Gardner was a wealthy businessman, widely believed to have received his ambassadorial appointment as a "payoff" for major financial contributions to the 1952 Republican Party presidential compaign. Gardner's assessment of Batista was encapsulated in testimony before a U.S.

congressional subcommittee: "Batista had always leaned toward the United States. I don't think we ever had a better friend." U.S. Congress, Senate, Committee on the Judiciary, Subcommittee to Investigate the Administration of the Internal Security Act and other Internal Security Laws, *Communist Threat to the United States Through the Caribbean, Part 9*, 86th Congress, 2nd Session, August 27, 29, 30, 1960 (Washington, D.C.: U.S. Government Printing Office, 1960), p. 665.

92 Personal Interview: Department of State official, Washington, D.C., May 19, 1976.

93 Ibid.

94 Personal Interview: Department of State official, Washington, D.C., July 30, 1976.

95 Robert D. Murphy, *Diplomat Among Warriors* (New York: Doubleday & Anchor, 1964), p. 369. Murphy was the State Department's chief negotiator at these meetings.

96 Personal Interview: Department of State official, Washington, D.C., June 2, 1975. The respondent was a senior Cuban affairs official during the latter half of the 1950s.

97 Herbert L. Matthews, "Situation in Cuba Found Worsening: Batista Foes Gain," *New York Times*, June 16, 1957. p. 26.

98 Herbert L. Matthews, "Populace in Revolt in Santiago de Cuba," *New York Times*, June 10, 1957, p. 1.

99 Padula, *The Fall of the Bourgeoisie: Cuba 1959-1961*, p. 101.

100 See Herbert L. Matthews, "Situation in Cuba Found Worsening: Batista Foes Gain," p. 26. On the scope of the stepped-up repression by the dictatorial regime, see R. Hart Phillips, *Cuba: Island of Paradox* (New York: McDowell Obolensky, 1959), p. 316: "killings and torture were going on in every town on the island, especially in Oriente Province."

101 See Pérez, *Army Politics in Cuba, 1898-1958*, passim.

102 Klare, *War Without End*, p. 278.

103 See testimony of E. Perkins McGuire, Deputy Assistant Secretary of Defense for Mutual Assistance Programs, May 9, 1959, in U.S. Congress, Senate, Committee on Foreign Relations, *Executive Sessions of the Senate Foreign Relations Committee, Vol. VIII* (Historical Series), 84th Congress, 2nd Session, 1956 (Washington, D.C.: U.S. Government Printing Office, December 1978), p. 247.

104 Havana Embassy to Department of State, Subject: "Revision of Operations Plan for Latin America," October 22, 1958.

105 See Thomas, *Cuba or the Pursuit of Freedom*, pp. 946–947; Pérez, *Army Politics in Cuba, 1898-1958*.

106 U.S. Congress, Senate, Committee on Foreign Relations, *Study Mission in the Caribbean Area December 1957, Part 1*, Report by Senator George A. Aiken, 85th Congress, 2nd Session, Committee Print, January 20, 1958 (Washington, D.C.: U.S. Government Printing Office, 1958), pp. 4–5. In a letter dated January 14, 1958, Assistant Secretary of State William B. Macomber, Jr., restated the administration's formal position that U.S. military assistance to Cuba "may be used only in the implementation of defense plans agreed upon by

the United States and Cuba, under which Cuba participates in missions important to the defense of the Western Hemisphere." The letter was sent to one of the more vocal congressional critics, Representative Charles A. Porter, and reprinted in *Congressional Record-House*, 85th Congress, 2nd Session, Vol. 104, Part 4, March 26, 1958, p. 5497.

107 U.S. Congress, Senate, Committee on Foreign Relations, *Review of Foreign Policy 1958, Part 1*, 85th Congress, 2nd Session, 1958 (Washington, D.C.: U.S. Government Printing Office, 1958), pp. 361–362.

108 *Congressional Record-Senate*, Vol. 104, Part 3, 85th Congress, 2nd Session, March 6, 1958, p. 3564.

109 *Congressional Record-House*, Vol. 104, Part 4, 85th Congress, 2nd Session, March 20, 1958, p. 4948 and March 26, 1958, p. 5498.

110 Ibid., pp. 5496, 5498.

111 *Congressional Record-Senate*, Vol. 104, Part 8, 85th Congress, 2nd Session, June 5, 1958, p. 10268.

112 Colonel Thomas B. Hanford, Director, White House, Regional Office, Office of the Assistant Secretary of Defense for Regional Security Affairs, in U.S. Congress, Senate, Committee on Foreign Relations, *Mutual Security Act of 1958*, 85th Congress, 2nd Session, March 19, 20, 21, 24, 26, 27, 28, 31, 1958 (Washington, D.C.: U.S. Government Printing Office, 1958), p. 499.

113 Personal Interview: Department of State official, Washington, D.C., July 5, 1973. The respondent was involved with Latin American affairs, in both Washington and the region, from the 1940s to the late 1960s. He was a senior Cuban affairs official between 1966 and 1969.

114 Personal Interview: Department of State official, Washington, D.C., June 2, 1975. Secretary of State John Foster Dulles "was preoccupied with other parts of the world" according to the then U.S. Ambassador to Mexico Robert C. Hill. Robert C. Hill interview, New Hampshire, October 1972, *The Eisenhower Oral History Collection*, Columbia University Library, pp. 100–101. In late 1957, Hill contends that he undertook a series of unsuccessful attempts to get executive-branch officials to devise a coherent anti-Castro policy. He recalled a meeting with Dulles who dismissed his characterization of Castro as procommunist and heavily influenced by Moscow as "utter nonsense, and keep in mind his brother Allen Dulles was director of the CIA, so I made no headway there." Ibid.

115 Personal Interview: Department of State official, Washington, D.C., June 14, 1973. The respondent was a political and international affairs specialist stationed in Latin America and Washington during the 1960s and early 1970s. His responsibilities included Cuban affairs.

116 Personal Interview: Department of State official, Washington, D.C., June 12, 1973.

117 Personal Interview: Department of State official, Washington, D.C., June 14, 1973. The respondent was stationed in Latin America during the late 1950s, in the Santiago de Cuba Consulate in 1960,

returning to Washington as a State Department Cuba specialist during the first half of the 1960s.

118 Personal Interview: Department of State official, Washington, D.C.,
August 23, 1978. The respondent was a political officer in the
Havana Embassy between 1958 and 1961. He also served in the
Cuban Interest Section in Havana during the Carter administration.

119 See Wayne S. Smith, *The Closest of Enemies* (New York and London:
W. W. Norton & Company, 1987), p. 30.

120 Havana Embassy (Ambassador Earl T. Smith) to Department of
State, Subject: "Policy Paper on Cuba," August 8, 1958, 611.37/8-
858, *DFOIA*.

121 Personal Interview: Department of State official, Washington, D.C.,
June 2, 1975.

122 Quoted in Ambrose, *Eisenhower: Volume Two, The President,* p.
505.

123 Personal Interview: Department of State official, Washington, D.C.,
July 5, 1973.

124 Memorandum from Acting Secretary of State Christian Herter to
President Eisenhower, Subject: "Cuba," December 23, 1958,
737.00/12-2358, *DFOIA* (my emphasis). Also see Dwight D. Eisenhower, *The White House Years: Waging Peace, 1956–1961* (New
York: Doubleday & Co., 1965), p. 521.

125 R. Richard Rubottom, Jr. interview, *The Dulles Oral History Collection,* p. 62.

126 Memorandum from Acting Secretary of State Christian A. Herter to
President Eisenhower, Subject: "Cuba," December 23, 1958 (my
emphasis).

127 Quoted in Ambrose, *Eisenhower: Volume Two, The President,* p.
505.

128 Memorandum from Acting Secretary of State Christian A. Herter to
President Eisenhower, Subject: "Cuba," December 23, 1958.

129 Havana Embassy to Department of State, Subject: "Revision of
Operations Plan for Latin America," October 22, 1958. According
to one study, "the United States military mission proposed to Batista
the creation of a counter-insurgency elite corp to fight Castro. . . .
Batista refused because he feared that an elite corp could deliver a
coup against his regime." Harold R. Aaron, *The Seizure of Political
Power in Cuba, 1956–1959* (Ph.D. dissertation, Georgetown University, 1964), p. 91. This assertion was based on an interview conducted by Aaron with a U.S. military official stationed in Havana
during this period.

130 See U.S. Congress, Senate, Committee on the Judiciary, *Communist
Threat to the United States Through the Caribbean, Part 9,* p. 687.

131 U.S. Congress, Senate, Committee on the Judiciary, Subcommittee
to Investigate the Administration of the Internal Security Act and
other Internal Security Laws, *Communist Threat to the United States
Through the Caribbean, Part 10,* 86th Congress, 2nd Session, September 2 and 8, 1960 (Washington, D.C.: U.S. Government Printing
Office, 1960), p. 739. Assistant Secretary of State for Inter-American Affairs R. Richard Rubottom contends that Pawley made two

trips to Havana to see Batista. The first "was to try to talk Batista into making some immediate changes in the government that would broaden the base of it and give him some public support and then eventually step down." The second was "to get Batista to step aside completely and to appoint four or five men who would be representative of several different sectors of the Cuba public, in order to have a base of the government that would prevent having a complete Castro takeover." R. Richard Rubottom, Jr., interview, *The Dulles Oral History Collection*, p. 67. Pawley also played a key role in the successful U.S. effort to destabilize and overthrow the nationalist Arbenz government in Guatemala in 1954. He was the State Department's liaison with the Pentagon on the Guatemala "project." See Schlesinger and Kinzer, *Bitter Fruit*, p. 145.

132 See Mario Lazo, *Dagger in the Heart: American Foreign Policy Failures in Cuba* (Santa Monica: Fidelis Publishers, 1968), p. 174. In testimony before a U.S. congressional subcommittee in 1961, Pawley identified some of the individuals chosen to form an interim government: "The men we had selected and that had been approved and that I could tell Batista, were Colonel Barquín, Colonel Borbonnet, General Díaz Tamayo, Bosch of the Bacardí family." U.S. Congress, Senate, *Communist Threat to the United States Through the Caribbean, Part 10*, p. 739.

133 Personal Interview: Department of State official, Washington, D.C., May 19, 1976. According to this senior Embassy political officer, Ambassador Smith "had no idea at all" that Pawley was in Cuba until the former Ambassador visited Smith prior to returning to Washington. On Pawley's mission to Cuba, his meeting with Batista, and the latter's categorical rejection of the "unofficial" proposal, also see John Dorschner and Roberto Fabrico, *The Winds of December* (New York: Coward, McCann & Geoghegan, 1980). pp. 157–159.

134 See Smith, *The Closest of Enemies*, p. 34.

135 Thomas, *Cuba or the Pursuit of Freedom*, p. 1021.

136 See Dorschner and Fabrico, *The Winds of December*, pp. 166–167.

137 Ibid., pp. 284–285.

138 Thomas, *Cuba or the Pursuit of Freedom*, p. 1028. Also see Dorschner and Fabricio, *The Winds of December*, pp. 284–285; Ramón L. Bonachea and Marta San Martín, *The Cuban Insurrection 1952–1959* (New Brunswick: Transaction Books, 1974), p. 407.

139 Ibid., pp. 323–325.

140 Personal Interview: Central Intelligence Agency official, Washington, D.C., May 21, 1976.

141 The Deputy Director of Central Intelligence, General Charles Cabell, described the Agency's relationship with the State Department: "whatever we were doing in Cuba was at the direction of, and with the authority of, the incumbent Secretary of State." General Charles Cabell interview, Arlington, Virginia, May 22, 1965, *The Dulles Oral History Collection*, Princeton University Library, p. 17. Eisenhower's CIA Director, Allen Dulles, subsequently wrote that no covert operation during his tenure as head of the Agency (1953–1961) was undertaken "without appropriate approval at a high

political level in our government *outside the CIA.*" Allen Dulles, *The Craft of Intelligence* (New York: Harper & Row, 1963), p. 189 (author's emphasis).

142 Personal Interview: Department of State official, Washington, D.C., May 19, 1976. This Embassy official described the CIA's major responsibilities in Cuba as follows: "to assess the local political situation, to develop and maintain contacts with the government and all aspects of the opposition."

143 Personal Interview: Central Intelligence Agency official, Washington, D.C., May 21, 1976. Also see David A. Phillips, *The Night Watch* (New York: Atheneum Publishers, 1977) p. 64.

144 Personal Interview: Central Intelligence Agency official, Washington, D.C., May 21, 1976.

145 Memorandum from Acting Secretary of State Christian A. Herter to President Eisenhower, Subject: "Cuba," December 23, 1958.

146 Richard Bissell interview, Hartford, Connecticut, September 7, 1966, *The Dulles Oral History Collection*, Princeton University Library, p. 51.

147 Personal Interview: Central Intelligence Agency official, Washington, D.C., May 21, 1976.

148 Personal Interview: Department of State official, Washington, D.C., June 11, 1973. The respondent was a Cuba affairs official during 1958 to 1961 and 1965 to 1967.

149 Maurice Zeitlin, *Working Class Politics in Cuba: A Study of Political Sociology* (Ph.D. dissertation, University of California at Berkeley, 1964), p. 104.

150 See Maurice Zeitlin, *Revolutionary Politics and the Cuban Working Class* (Princeton: Princeton University Press, 1967); Charles A. Page, *The Development of Organized Labor in Cuba* (Ph.D. dissertation, University of California at Berkeley, 1952); Benjamin, *The United States and Cuba;* Commission on Cuban Affairs, *Problems of the New Cuba;* James Petras, "Toward a Theory of Twentieth Century Socialist Revolutions," in James Petras et al., *Critical Perspectives on Imperialism and Social Class in the Third World* (New York: Monthly Review Press, 1978), pp. 287–294.

151 See Zeitlin, *Revolutionary Politics and the Cuban Working Class;* Commission on Cuban Affairs, *Problems of the New Cuba;* Page, *The Development of Organized Labor in Cuba;* International Bank for Reconstruction and Development, *Report on Cuba 1950.*

152 The mid-year government military offensive against the guerrillas was halted in early August due to a combination of battlefield defeats, isolation from supply centers, lack of air cover, widespread desertions, heavy rains, and the superior "combat intelligence" of the rebel forces. The guerrilla counteroffensive encountered a regular army that "was tired and decimated by 'two years of a prolonged campaign.'" General Francisco Tabernilla, Sr., quoted in Bonachea and Martin, *The Cuban Insurrection 1952–1959*, p. 286. Also see Che Guevara, *Reminiscences of the Cuban Revolutionary War* (New York: Monthly Review Press, 1968); Thomas, *Cuba or the Pursuit of Freedom*, p. 997.

153 During a Cabinet debate in May, in the aftermath of Nixon's Latin
American trip, the Vice-President argued for a policy based on an
"abrazo" for democratic governments and a "formal handshake" for
dictatorships. He also expressed unease over the perception of the
United States as being more interested in sustaining the economic
oligarchies than in "raising the standard of living of the masses."
Secretary of State Dulles "pointed to the difficulty of dealing with
it since democracy as we know it will not be instituted by the lower
classes as they gain power–rather they will bring in more of a dictatorship of the masses." The Dulles policy status quo argument prevailed. Quoted in Walter LaFeber, *Inevitable Revolutions: The
United States in Central America* (New York: W. W. Norton & Co.,
1983). p. 137.

3. The United States in Cuba 1959–1961: national-social revolution; state transformation and the limits of imperial power

1 Quoted in *Public Papers of the Presidents of the United States: Dwight
D. Eisenhower 1959* (Washington, D.C.: U.S. Government Printing
Office, 1960), p. 751. This statement was made at a presidential
press conference on October 28, 1959.
2 Department of State (Secretary Herter) to Latin American Missions,
Telegram No. 953, January 26, 1960. Confidential. White House
Office, Office of the Staff Secretary, Records 1952–61, International
Series, Box 4, Cuba (2), *Eisenhower Presidential Library.*
3 Personal Interview: White House Staff official, Washington, D.C.,
May 20, 1976. The respondent was a senior advisor to the President
on national security and defense affairs from 1954 to 1960.
4 Ibid.
5 Personal Interview: Department of State official, Washington, D.C.,
July 11, 1973.
6 Personal Interview: Department of State official, Washington, D.C.,
June 20, 1973. The respondent was stationed in Latin America during the early 1960s and served as a Cuba analyst in the Department's Bureau of Intelligence and Research between 1965 and
1967.
7 Quoted in Marchetti and Marks, *The CIA and the Cult of Intelligence,*
p. 306.
8 Frederick B. Pike, "Can We Slow Our Loss of Latin America," *Inter-
American Economic Affairs,* Vol. XV, No. 1, Summer 1961, p. 18.
9 Personal Interview: Department of State official, Washington, D.C.,
May 19, 1976.
10 See Interview with CIA official Richard Bissell, Transcript of CBS
Reports, *The CIA's Secret War* (New York: CBS Inc., 1978), p. 6.
11 Quoted in Ambrose, *Eisenhower: Volume Two, The President,* p. 506
(Dulles' emphasis). Also see Eisenhower, *The White House Years,*
pp. 522–523.
12 Rufo López-Fresquet, *My 14 Months with Castro* (Cleveland and
New York: The Publishing Co., 1966), p. 110.

13 Interview with CIA official Richard Bissell, Transcript of CBS Reports, *The CIA's Secret War*, p. 6.
14 Richard M. Nixon, *Six Crises* (New York: Doubleday & Co., 1962), pp. 351–352; Thomas, *Cuba or the Pursuit of Freedom*, p. 1210.
15 Neil McElroy interview, 1967, *The Eisenhower Oral History Collection*, Columbia University Library, p. 88.
16 U.S. intelligence sources, quoted in Eisenhower, *The White House Years*, p. 522.
17 Personal Interview: Department of State official, Washington, D.C., June 11, 1973.
18 See Robert Scheer and Maurice Zeitlin, *Cuba: An American Tragedy* (London: Penguin Books, 1964), p. 76.
19 Havana Embassy (Daniel M. Braddock, Minister-Counselor, for the Ambassador) to Department of State, Subject: "The First Two Weeks of the Revolutionary Government," Dispatch No. 736, January 15, 1959, 737.00/1–1559, *DFOIA*.
20 Personal Interview: U.S. Congress, Senate Foreign Relations Committee, Washington, D.C., September 18, 1973. The respondent was a professional staff member and Latin American specialist with the Committee from the late 1950s to the early 1970s.
21 *Hispanic American Report*, Vol. XII, No. 1, March for January 1959, p. 25.
22 Quoted in William A. Williams, *The United States, Cuba and Castro* (New York: Monthly Review Press, 1962), p. 31. Also see Morse's comment in U.S. Congress, Senate Committee on Foreign Relations, *Executive Sessions of the Senate Foreign Relations Committee, Vol XII*, (Historical Series), 86th Congress, 2nd Session, January 18, 21, February 18, 1960 (Washington, D.C.: U.S. Government Printing Office, November 1982), p. 86. Most reliable accounts place the number of executions at between 450 and 700–by historical standards an extremely small number when compared to other twentieth-century large-scale social transformations (Mexico, Russia, China). See, for example, *Hispanic American Report*, Vol. XV, No. 5, July for May 1959, p. 412. In a revealing commentary on the trials, Ambassador Smith cabled the State Department: "Cubans do not appear to be especially preoccupied by the executions or the fairness of the trial methods used. They are disposed to assume that those executed are on the whole receiving their just deserts." Havana Embassy (Earl T. Smith) to Department of State, Subject: "Joint Week No. 2," Dispatch, No. 725, January 13, 1959, 737.00(W)/1–1359, *DFOIA*.
23 See Economist Intelligence Unit, *Quarterly Economic Review of Cuba*, No. 30, May 1960, p. 1.
24 Freeman Lincoln, "What Happened to Cuban Business?," *Fortune*, Vol. LX No. 3, September 1959, p. 269; Blackburn, "The Economics of the Cuban Revolution," p. 622.
25 See Robin Blackburn, "Prologue to the Cuban Revolution," *New Left Review*, No. 21, October 1963, p. 62. Nonpayment of rents reached "epidemic proportions" during the second half of 1959. Padula, *The Fall of the Bourgeoisie: Cuba 1959–1961*, p. 269.

26 Lincoln, "What Happened to Cuban Business?," p. 269.
27 Felipe Pazos, "The Economy," *Cambridge Opinion*, No. 32, 1963, p. 15.
28 Lincoln, "What Happened to Cuban Business?," p. 272.
29 According to newly appointed Treasury Minister Rufo López-Fresquet, Batista himself absconded with some $200 million. See R. Hart Phillips, "New Cuban Government Faces Huge Economic Problems," *New York Times*, January 25, 1959, p. E8.
30 U.S. Department of the Treasury, Background Briefing for Castro Visit, Subject: "Cuban Economic and Financial Situation," April 13, 1959, *DFOIA*.
31 Ibid. The Department of Commerce subsequently revised the initial Treasury figure for Cuba's foreign exchange reserves from $60 million to $77 million. See "Cuba," *Foreign Commerce Weekly*, Vol. 63, No. 12, March 21, 1960, p. S-13.
32 See Robert F. Smith, "Castro's Revolution: Domestic Sources and Consequences," in John Plank, ed., *Cuba and the United States: Long Range Perspectives* (Washington, D.C.: The Brookings Institution, 1967), pp. 61–62; Economist Intelligence Unit, *Quarterly Economic Review of Cuba*, Annual Supplement, May 1960, p. 8.
33 U.S. Department of the Treasury, Confidential Draft Memo from State Department to Havana Embassy, January 14, 1959, *DFOIA*.
34 Ibid.
35 Ibid.
36 Quoted in U.S. Department of the Treasury, Memo, Cuban Situation, March 19, 1959, *DFOIA*.
37 Ibid.
38 Personal Correspondence: Felipe Pazos (originally written on March 22, 1963), Washington, D.C., August 1971. Also see Teresa Casuso, *Cuba and Castro* (New York: Random House, 1961), p. 207. Casuso was the Castro government's first delegate to the United Nations.
39 Eisenhower, *The White House Years*, p. 523.
40 U.S. Department of the Treasury, Background Briefing for Castro Visit, April 13, 1959.
41 Ibid.
42 "What Castro Learned in the United States," *U.S. News & World Report*, May 4, 1959, p. 39.
43 See David Wise, "Castro Aids Lay Basis for U.S. Financial Help," *New York Herald Tribune*, April 19, 1959, p. 2; "What Castro Learned in the United States," pp. 38–39. Castro's instructions to the Cuban delegation are found in Fresquet, *My 14 Months With Castro* pp. 108, 110.
44 Personal Correspondence: Felipe Pazos (originally written on March 22, 1963), Washington, D.C., August 1971.
45 Personal Interview: Department of State official, Washington, D.C., June 11, 1973.
46 Personal Interview: U.S. Businessman, New York City, New York, July 9, 1975. Although the available information does not provide direct evidence of a causal relationship between the attitudes of the

U.S. government, the multilateral development banks, and the private banking community to condition economic assistance to Cuba on the maintenance of an externally oriented capitalist development strategy, the various actions proposed or taken by these organizations during this period suggest that the process of *coordination* between state and class is not the haphazard phenomenon that many believe it to be.

47 John Parke Young, "Can U.S.-Cuba Humpty Dumpty Be Mended," *Los Angeles Times*, December 14, 1977, Part II, p. 7. Pazos states that Minister of the Economy Boti informed him "that negotiations would be left to a future trip to the U.S. of the economic staff." Personal Correspondence: Felipe Pazos (originally written March 22, 1963), Washington, D.C., August 1971.

48 See O. Braun and L. Joy, "A Model of Economic Stagnation–A Case Study of the Argentine Economy," *The Economic Journal*, Vol. LXXVII, No. 312, December 1968, pp. 880–881.

49 Quoted in Wise, "Castro Aids Lay Basis for U.S. Financial Help," p. 2.

50 See E. M. Kenworthy, "'Austerity' Held Near for Castro," *New York Times*, April 23, 1959, p. 2. Also see E. W. Kenworthy, "Castro's 'Unofficial' Visit Raises a Flurry of Official Interest," *New York Times*, April 26, 1959, p. E7.

51 See testimony of Deputy Director of the CIA, General Charles Cabell, in U.S. Congress, Senate, Committee on the Judiciary, Subcommittee to Investigate the Administration of the Internal Security Act and Other Internal Security Laws, *Communist Threat to the United States through the Caribbean, Part III*, 86th Congress, 1st Session, November 5, 1959 (Washington, D.C.: U.S. Government Printing Office, 1960), pp. 162–164.

52 The decision to begin the process in Camagüey province was politically and symbolically important: "The cattle ranches in Camagüey were . . . the heart of counter-revolutionary Cuba, the home of conservative interests." Thomas, *Cuba or the Pursuit of Freedom*, p. 1229.

53 Personal Interview: Department of State official, Washington, D.C., May 19, 1976.

54 See Havana Embassy (Daniel M. Braddock, Minister-Counselor for the Ambassador) to Department of State, Subject: "Agrarian Reform," Dispatch No. 1353, June 3, 1959, 837.16/6–359, *DFOIA*.

55 Havana Embassy (Ambassador Bonsal) to Secretary of State, Telegram, June 4, 1959, 837.16/6–459, *DFOIA*. According to Hugh Thomas, anti-communist officials in the Ministry of Agriculture were "contemplating conspiracy" as early as March 1959. Thomas, *Cuba or the Pursuit of Freedom*, p. 1202.

56 Ibid., p. 1225. Eventually, five cabinet ministers resigned as a result of the law.

57 Havana Embassy (Ambassador Bonsal) to Secretary of State, Telegram, June 5, 1959, 837.16/6–559, *DFOIA*.

58 "U.S. Sugar Firms Puzzled by New Cuban Land Law, Hope for 'Reasonable' Solution," *Wall Street Journal*, May 20, 1959, p. 7.

59 See "Cuban Offer to Sell Sugar," *Wall Street Journal*, June 8, 1959, p. 20.

60 See "U.S. Investors Losing Confidence in Cuban Issues; Land Law Cited," *Wall Street Journal*, June 22, 1959, p. 16.

61 Department of State (Murphy, Acting) to Havana Embassy, Telegram, late May 1959, 837.16/6–159, *DFOIA*.

62 Quoted in U.S. Congress, Senate, Committee on Foreign Relations, *Events in United States-Cuban Relations: A Chronology, 1957–1963* (Washington, D.C.: U.S. Government Printing Office, 1963), p. 5.

63 Havana Embassy (Ambassador Bonsal) to Secretary of State, June 5, 1959.

64 *Department of State Bulletin*, Vol. XL. No. 1044, June 29, 1959, p. 958.

65 Memorandum of Conversation, Department of State, June 22, 1959, Subject: "General Views of the U.S. Government with regard to the Cuban Agrarian Law." Participants: Raúl Roa, Cuban Minister of State; Emilio Pando, Minister-Counselor of Cuban Embassy; Undersecretary C. Douglas Dillon; CMA-William A. Wieland, Director; CMA-Robert A. Stevenson, Officer in Charge, Cuban Affairs. 837.16/6–2259, *DFOIA*.

66 R. Richard Rubottom, ARA, to Secretary of State, June 23, 1959, Subject: "Visit of Mr. Robert Kleberg, Owner of the King Ranch." 837.16/6–2259, *DFOIA*; Memorandum of Conversation, Department of State, June 24, 1959, Subject: "Cuban Agrarian Reform." Participants: Secretary of State; Robert Kleberg; Jack Malone, Manager of Kleberg's Cuban Properties; William P. Snow, ARA. 837.16/6–2459, *DFOIA*.

67 Memorandum of Conversation, Department of State, July 15, 1959, Subject: "U.S. Relations with Cuba; Agrarian Reform." Participants: Lawrence Crosby, Chairman, U.S.-Cuban Sugar Council; R. Richard Rubottom, Assistant Secretary, ARA; Richard B. Owen, Assistant Officer in Charge, Cuban Affairs. 611.37/7–1559, *DFOIA*.

68 Ibid.

69 Padula, *The Fall of the Bourgeoisie: Cuba, 1959–1961*, p. 232; O'Connor, *The Origins of Socialism in Cuba*, pp. 95–96.

70 Personal Interview: Felipe Pazos, Washington, D.C., April 29, 1971.

71 *Hispanic American Report*, Vol. XII, No. 6, August for June 1959, p. 319.

72 See *Department of State Bulletin*, Vol. XLI, No. 1064, November 16, 1959, p. 717.

73 R. Richard Rubottom, Jr., interview, *The Dulles Oral History Collection*, p. 74. On the importance of "political choice" in determining the direction of socioeconomic change, see Ivan Vallier, "Recent Theories of Development," in *Trends in Social Science Research in Latin America* (Berkeley: Berkeley Institute of International Studies, 1965), p. 21.

74 R. Richard Rubottom, Jr., interview, *The Dulles Oral History Collection*, p. 74.

75 Memorandum for the President from Christian A. Herter, Depart-

ment of State, Subject: "Current Basic United States Policy Toward Cuba," October 31, 1959, *DFOIA*. The President requested additional information before approving the October 31 policy statement. Assistant Secretary Rubottom drafted a more detailed memorandum for Herter for transmission to the White House along with the original copy of the October 31 memorandum. Memorandum for the President from Christian A. Herter, Department of State, Subject: "Current Basic United States Policy Toward Cuba," November 1959, 611.37/11–559, *DFOIA*. These documents do much to demolish the myth of the State Department's "reasonableness" and "moderation" during this period.

76 Personal Interview: Department of State official, Washington, D.C., June 15, 1973. The respondent was an economic official in the Havana Embassy from 1956 to 1960 and a political and international economic official in Washington, D.C., during the 1960s. Also see Memorandum for the President from Christian A. Herter, Department of State, November 1959.

77 Havana Embassy (Ambassador Bonsal) to Department of State, Subject: "Suggested Operations Plan for Cuba," Dispatch No. 789, November 27, 1959, 611.37/11–2759, *DFOIA*.

78 Cal Brumley, "Whither Cuba: Some Yank Firms Quit, Others Seek Way Out as Red Influence Grows," *Wall Street Journal*, December 18, 1959, p.1. In early September, Ambassador Bonsal had warned the State Department of Guevara's rising influence: "There is a possibility, by the way that Che Guevara may be given an important role in the country's industrialization program, i.e., the channeling of public funds into industry, including basic industry such as steel. *This would be very bad*." Havana Embassy (Ambassador Bonsal) to Department of State (Assistant Secretary for Inter-American Affairs Rubottom), Letter, September 2, 1959, 611.37/9–259, *DFOIA* (Bonsal's emphasis).

79 Eisenhower, *The White House Years*, p. 525.

80 "Stringent Levies by Cuba Backed," *New York Times*, September 26, 1959, p. 7.

81 See "Cuban Land Reform Stepped Up. Foreign Exchange Reserves Fall," *Foreign Commerce Weekly*, Vol. 63, No. 5, February 1, 1960, p. 6.

82 "Cuba," *Foreign Commerce Weekly*, Vol. 63, No. 12, March 21, 1960, p. S-13; "Cuban Land Reform Stepped Up. Foreign Exchange Reserves Fall," p. 6.

83 Quoted in E. M. Kenworthy, "Cuba Seen Facing Crisis in Economy," *New York Times*, August 9, 1959, p. 16.

84 Personal Interview: U.S. Export-Import Bank official, Washington, D.C., August 6, 1976. The respondent was one of the highest ranking officials of the Bank during 1959 and 1960.

85 *Department of State Bulletin*, Vol. XLII, No. 1077, February 15, 1960, p. 238.

86 William J. Jorden, "U.S. vs. Cuba: Washington Acts," *New York Times*, July 10, 1960, p. E5.

87 See Robert S. Walters, "Soviet Economic Aid to Cuba: 1959–1964," *International Affairs*, Vol. 42, No. 1, January 1966, p. 74.

88 See James Reston, "Capital Considers a Tougher Policy on Castro Regime," *New York Times*, February 18, 1960, p. 1.

89 Ibid.

90 Ibid., pp. 1, 2.

91 Robert Tabor, *M-26: Biography of a Revolution* (New York: Lyle Stuart, 1961), p. 324. Also see Cal Brumley, "Mikoyan Visit to Cuba Viewed as Prelude to Russian Trade and Diplomatic Gains," *Wall Street Journal*, February 5, 1960, p. 6; Tad Szulc, "Cubans and Poles Sign Trade Treaty," *New York Times*, April 2, 1960, pp. 1, 8.

92 Ibid.; "European Loans Reported in Cuba," *New York Times*, December 5, 1959, p. 12.

93 At the end of 1958, the United States accounted for approximately 75 percent of Cuba's import and export trade. By the end of 1961, it accounted for only 4 percent of the island's import and export trade. By contrast, Cuba's total trade with the socialist-bloc countries rose from 2 percent in 1958 to 70 percent–75 percent by the end of 1961. See U.S. Department of Commerce, *Overseas Business Reports*, ("World Trade with Cuba, 1961–1962"), OBR-64-41, March 1964, p. 1; U.S. Department of State, *The Battle Act Report 1965*, Publication 8019, General Foreign Policy Series 210, February 1966, p. 124; Carmelo Mesa-Lago, *Availability and Reliability of Statistics in Socialist Cuba*, University of Pittsburgh, Latin American Studies, Occasional Papers No. 1, 1970, pp. 63–64.

94 "House Panel Bids U.S. End Cuba Aid," *New York Times*, April 1, 1960, p. 8.

95 V. I. Lenin, "One of the Fundamental Questions of the Revolution," September 27, 1917, in *Selected Works*, *Volume 2* (Moscow: Progress Publishers, 1970), p. 276.

96 Personal Interview: Central Intelligence Agency official, Washington, D.C., May 21, 1976.

97 Thomas, *Cuba or the Pursuit of Freedom*, p. 1221.

98 Personal Interview: Department of State official, Washington, D.C., March 11 and 12, 1975. The respondent was a political officer in the Havana Embassy from 1956 to 1961, and a senior Department Cuba official during the mid-1960s.

99 Personal Interview: Central Intelligence Agency official, Washington, D.C., May 21, 1976.

100 Personal Interview: U.S. Businessman, New York City, New York, July 14, 1975.

101 Padula, *The Fall of the Bourgeoisie: Cuba, 1959–1961*, p. 112.

102 Ibid., p. 138.

103 Ibid., pp. 112, 250.

104 Ibid.

105 Ibid., p. 422. Also see Leslie Dewart, *Cuba, Church and Crisis* (Great Britain: Sheed and Ward, 1964), pp. 158–159.

106 Personal Interview: Andrew McClellan, AFL-CIO, Washington, D.C., November 3, 1976. The respondent was an active participant in ORIT during the second half of the 1950s and remained a senior

AFL-CIO official with responsibilities in the area of hemispheric affairs throughout the 1960s and 1970s.

107 Havana Embassy to Department of State, Subject: "Progress Report on OCB 'Outline Plan of Operations for Latin America,'" Dispatch No. 661, February 19, 1958, 611.37/2–1958, *DFOIA*.

108 Havana Embassy to Department of State, Subject: "Revision of Operations Plan for Latin America," Dispatch No. 429, October 22, 1958, 611.37/10–2258. *DFOIA*.

109 See Hobart A. Spalding, Jr., *Organized Labor in Latin America: Historical Case Studies of Urban Workers in Dependent Societies* (New York: Harper Torchbooks, 1977), p. 239.

110 Serafino Romauldi, *Presidents and Peons* (New York: Funk & Wagnalls, 1967), p. 208.

111 Ibid.

112 Personal Interview: Andrew McClellan, AFL-CIO, Washington, D.C., November 3, 1976.

113 ORIT Press and Publications Department, *The Cuba Trade Union Movement Under the Regime of Dr. Castro* (Mexico City, October 1960), p. 45.

114 See J.P. Morray, *The Second Revolution in Cuba* (New York: Monthly Review Press, 1962), p. 63; Williams, *The United States, Cuba and Castro*, p. 135. Matos was arrested and imprisoned in late October 1959. López-Fresquet participated in antiregime activites beginning in September 1959 and continuing after his resignation from the cabinet in March 1960 until his exile in October 1960. See Fresquet, *My 14 Months with Castro*, p. 154.

115 Phillips *The Night Watch*, p. 80.

116 Personal Interview: Central Intelligence Agency official, Washington, D.C., May 21, 1976.

117 Philip W. Bonsal, *Cuba, Castro, and the United States* (Pittsburgh: University of Pittsburgh Press, 1972), p. 111.

118 Eisenhower, *The White House Years*, p. 225.

119 Memorandum of Conference between President Eisenhower and Christian A. Herter, recorded by White House Staff Secretary General Andrew J. Goodpaster, January 25, 1960. Secret. White House Series, Office of the Staff Secretary, Records 1952–61, International Series, Box 4, Cuba (2), *Eisenhower Presidential Library*. Also located in Papers of the President of the United States, 1953–61, Ann Whitman File, Dwight D. Eisenhower Diary Series. Box 27, Folder: "Staff Notes-January 1960 (1)," *Eisenhower Presidential Library*.

120 Memorandum of Conference, recorded by White House Staff Secretary General Andrew J. Goodpaster, January 26, 1960. Participants: President Eisenhower; Secretary of State Herter; Assistant Secretary of State for Inter-American Affairs Rubottom; Ambassador to Cuba Bonsal; Assistant to the President, General Wilton B. Parsons. Secret. White House Office, Office of the Staff Secretary, Records 1952–61, International Series, Box 4, Cuba (2), *Eisenhower Presidential Library*. Also located in Papers of the President of the United States, 1953–61, Ann Whitman File, Dwight D. Eisenhower

Diary Series, Box 27, Folder: "Staff Notes–January 1960, (1)" *Eisenhower Presidential Library.*

121 Personal Interview: National Security Staff official, Washington, D.C., May 18, 1976. The respondent was a senior advisor to President Eisenhower from 1958 to 1961.

122 Dewart, *Cuba, Church and Crisis,* pp. 58–59. In early 1959, the CIA set up a front organization in Miami to recruit pilots to fly anti-Castro missions over Cuba. See Dom Bonafede, "'Fliers Paid by Latins,'" *Miami Herald,* March 5, 1963, pp. 1A, 2A.

123 Personal Interview: National Security Staff official, Washington, D.C., May 18, 1976.

124 Ibid.

125 Quoted in U.S. Congress, Senate, *Alleged Assassination Plots Involving Foreign Leaders,* p. 93. Also see ibid., pp. 111–115.

126 See Cuban Study Group Report to The President, "Cuba: Bay of Pigs," June 13, 1961. Kennedy Presidential Library, *DFOIA.* This group, established in the aftermath of the April 1961 Bay of Pigs invasion, consisted of General Maxwell Taylor, Attorney General Robert Kennedy, Admiral Arleigh Burke, and the Director of the Central Intelligence Agency, Allen Dulles.

127 Personal Interview: National Security Staff official, Washington, D.C., May 18, 1976. At the times these decisions were being taken, the CIA was actively attempting to mobilize regime opponents for counterrevolution. "There is no firm evidence that during the spring of 1960 the Central Intelligence Agency was already delivering weapons to the guerrillas in the Escambray and Sierra Maestra mountains. But it is possible, since the evidence shows during the spring the C.I.A. was in high gear structuring the civilian apparatus of the counterrevolution." Rolando E. Bonachea, *United States Policy Toward Cuba: 1959–1961* (Ph.D. dissertation, Georgetown University, November 1975), p. 204. The author's evidence was based on materials in the private paper of Justo Carillo, former vice-president of the Cuban National Bank. Hugh Thomas writes that the best organized of the urban opposition groups, the Movimiento de Rescate Revolucionario (MRR), had "excellent connections in the U.S." Thomas, *Cuba or the Pursuit of Freedom,* p. 1275.

128 Personal Interview: Central Intelligence Agency official, Washington, D.C., January 7, 1976.

129 Quoted in Ambrose, *Eisenhower: Volume Two, The President,* p. 584. Also see Cuban Study Group Report to the President, June 13, 1961; Richard Bissell interview, Hartford, Connecticut, June 1967, *The Eisenhower Oral History Collection,* Columbia University Library, p. 30.

130 Ibid. Also see Cuban Study Group Report to the President, June 13, 1961.

131 Ibid.

132 Richard Bissell interview, *The Eisenhower Oral History Collection,* p. 30.

133 Memorandum of Meeting with the President (of November 29) by Gordon Gray, The White House, December 5, 1960. Participants:

Secretary Anderson, Secretary Gates, Mr. Dillon, Mr. Merchant, Mr. Douglas, General Parsons, General Goodpaster, Gordon Gray. Office of the Special Assistant for National Security Affairs (OSANSA), Special Assistant Series, Presidential Subseries, Box 5, Folder: "Meetings with President 1960 11 (2)," *Eisenhower Presidential Library.*

134 Richard Bissell interview, *The Eisenhower Oral History Collection,* pp. 32–33. Compounding the divisions within the exile community was the CIA's refusal to work with the more "liberal" exile elements grouped around Manuel Ray. The Agency opposed Ray's insistence on maintaining a degree of independence of CIA control as well as his reformist political program. See Karl E. Meyer & Tad Szulc, *The Cuban Invasion* (New York: Frederick A. Praeger, 1963), pp. 86–89.

135 See Ambrose, *Eisenhower: Volume Two, The President,* pp. 613–614. According to a participant in the discussions, while the administration at no point made any firm commitment to send the exile force into Cuba "it was clearly contemplated that there would or could be military action." Personal Interview: National Security Staff official, Washington, D.C., May 18, 1976.

136 Quoted in U.S. Congress, Senate, *Alleged Assassination Plots Involving Foreign Leaders,* p. 92.

137 Ibid., p. 93.

138 Ibid. Also see ibid., p. 110.

139 See Ambrose, *Eisenhower: Volume Two, The President,* pp. 556–557.

140 See U.S. Congress, Senate, *Alleged Assassination Plots Involving Foreign Leaders,* pp. 79–82.

141 Thomas Powers, *The Man Who Kept the Secrets* (New York: Pocket Books, 1981), p. 187. Also see U.S. Congress, Senate, *Alleged Assassination Plots Involving Foreign Leaders,* pp. 74–77.

142 Ibid., p. 77. In a statement to the FBI that was forwarded to Attorney General Robert Kennedy in late May 1961, Edwards declared "that none of Giancana's efforts have materialized to date and that several of the plans still are working and may eventually 'pay-off.'" Ibid., p. 127.

143 Personal Correspondence: U.S. Businessman, Florida, July 1975.

144 Personal Interview: U.S. Lawyer, New York City, New York, July 15, 1975. The respondent's law firm represented a number of American multinational corporations with subsidiaries in Cuba during the 1940s and 1950s.

145 Ibid. A senior executive of the U.S.-owned Moa Bay Mining Company described the impact of these early cabinet appointments on the level of business confidence: "Castro named absolutely top people . . . which was very reassuring to people like me who were going to New York and reporting to our Boards of Directors that as long as people like Pazos and Fresquet were in the government, there was hope." Personal Interview: U.S. Businessman, New York City, New York, June 25, 1975.

146 Quoted in Eisenhower, *The White House Years*, p. 522. Also see Lincoln, "What Happened to Cuban Business?," p. 272.
147 Personal Interview: Department of State official, Washington, D.C., May 19, 1976.
148 Personal Interview: U.S. Businessman, New York City, New York, July 9, 1975.
149 Personal Interview: U.S. Businessman, Washington, D.C., July 31, 1975.
150 Personal Interview: U.S. Businessman, New York City, New York, July 9, 1975.
151 Ibid.
152 See Leland L. Johnson "U.S. Business Interests in Cuba and the Rise of Castro," p. 444.
153 Personal Interview: U.S. Businessman, New York City, New York, June 27, 1975.
154 Bonsal, *Cuba, Castro, and the United States*, p. 93.
155 Cal Brumley, "Whither Cuba: Some Yank Firms Quit, Others Seek Out as Red Influence Grows," p. 22.
156 Quoted in "Many U.S. Companies in Cuba Show Deficit but They Hope To Stay," *Wall Street Journal*, March 8, 1960, p. 1.
157 Quoted in "Sentiment Grows in U.S. for Firmer Government Stand Against Castro," *Wall Street Journal*, April 11, 1960, p. 21.
158 U.S. Department of the Treasury, Lucius D. Clay, Chairman of Board, Continental Can Company, Inc., to Robert B. Anderson, Secretary of the Treasury, Letter, May 4, 1960, *DFOIA*.
159 Personal Interview: U.S. Businessman, New York City, New York, July 14, 1975.
160 Quoted in "Many U.S. Companies in Cuba Show Deficit but They Hope to Stay," p. 1.
161 Memorandum of Conference between President Eisenhower and Christian A. Herter, January 25, 1960.
162 Quoted in "Sentiment Grows in U.S. for Firmer Government Stand Against Castro," p. 21.
163 Personal Interview: Department of State official, Washington, D.C., March 20, 1975. The respondent was a U.S. Information Agency official in the Havana Embassy from October 1959 to September 1960.
164 "Property and Liberty: The Cuban Disaster Points Up the Link Between Them," *Barron's*, July 11, 1960, p. 1.
165 See Harvey O'Connor, *World Crisis in Oil* (New York: Monthly Review Press, 1962), pp. 7, 12, 14–15, 258.
166 Lewis Brigham, "Oil Firms Glum to Castro Threat," *Journal of Commerce*, June 13, 1960, p. 1.
167 See O'Connor, *World Crisis in Oil*, pp. 7, 12, 14–15.
168 See Robert Engler, *The Brotherhood of Oil* (Chicago: Chicago University Press, 1977), p. 107.
169 Memorandum of Conversation, Department of State, March 9, 1960, Subject: "Standard Oil Operations in Cuba." Participants: Martin Jones, Standard Oil Company of New Jersey: L. J. "Tex"

Brewer, Manager, ESSO Operations in Cuba; Ambassador Bonsal; Mr. Mallory (ARA); Mr. Torrey (CMA). 837.2553/3–960 *DFOIA.*

170 Memorandum of Conversation, Department of State, May 11, 1960, Subject: "Difficulties of the Texas Company in Cuba with regard to dollar remittances and concern at possibility it will be asked to refine Russian crude oil." Participants: S. P. Crossland, Texaco Company; Landon Derby, Texaco Company; James Pipkin, Texaco Company; ARA- R. Richard Rubottom, Jr., Assistant Secretary of State; ARA:CMA-Robert Stevenson, Cuban Affairs. 837.131/5–1160, *DFOIA.*

171 Department of State (Secretary Herter) to Havana Embassy, Telegram, June 1, 1960, 837.131/5–1160, *DFOIA.*

172 See *The Oil and Gas Journal,* Vol 58, No. 32, May 30, 1960, p. 71.

173 Quoted in James N. Wallace, "Cuba to Require U.S. Firms There to Refine Crude Oil from Russia," *Wall Street Journal,* May 24, 1960, p. 1.

174 *The Oil and Gas Journal,* May 30, 1960, p. 71.

175 Bonsal, *Cuba, Castro, and the United States,* p. 195.

176 Personal Interview: Department of State official, Washington, D.C., May 19, 1976.

177 Memorandum for the Files, Department of State, Subject: "Antitrust aspects of Cuban oil situation," June 24, 1960, 837.2553/6–2460, *DFOIA.*

178 Havana Embassy (Ambassador Bonsal) to Secretary of State, Telegram, June 2, 1960, 837.2553/6-260, *DFOIA.*

179 Bonsal, *Cuba, Castro, and the United States,* pp. 149–150. Prior to his appointment as Secretary of the Treasury in 1957, Robert Anderson was the manager of the $300 million W. T. Waggoner estate, which had extensive oil operations. He was a member of the National Petroleum Institute and a director of the American Petroleum Institute. See Bernard Nossiter, "Ex-Treasury Chief Received Oil Funds," *Washington Post,* July 16, 1960, pp. A1, A14.

180 See Havana Embassy (Ambassador Bonsal) to Secretary of State, Incoming Telegram, June 10, 1960, 837.2553/6–1060, *DFOIA;* Memorandum of Conversation, Department of State, June 21, 1960, Subject: "First Attempt by GOC [Government of Cuba] to Break Down the Refusal of the Oil Companies to Refine Russian Crude Oil." Participants: Mark Haider, Standard Oil Company of New Jersey; Cecil Morgan, Standard Oil Company of New Jersey; Mr. Mallory, Deputy Assistant Secretary, ARA; Mr. Vallon, Deputy Director, ARA:CMA; Mr. Stevenson, Cuban Affairs, CMA/C. 837.2553/6–2160, *DFOIA.*

181 James N. Wallace, "Oil Firms Ignore Castro Seizure Threat, Face Showdown in Rejecting Soviet Crude," *Wall Street Journal,* June 13, 1960, p. 24.

182 "Oilmen Balk at Castro's Demands," *Business Week,* June 11, 1960, p. 34.

183 "Castro Assails U.S. Anew," *New York Times,* June 25, 1960, p. 6.

184 See "$17M Debt to the Shell Company," *London Times,* July 1, 1960, p. 12; *The Oil and Gas Journal,* Vol. 58, No. 27, July 4, 1960,

p. 76; William J. Jorden, "U.S. Files Protest on Cuban Seizure of Oil Refineries," *New York Times*, July 6, 1960, p. 2.

185 Wallace, "Oil Firms Ignore Castro Seizure Threat, Face Showdown in Rejecting Soviet Crude," p. 24. According to Wallace, the three foreign oil companies were now asked to refine 6,480,000 barrels annually. Most American industry experts surmised that the Cubans, with Soviet support, could probably keep the refineries going and limit petroleum shortages to a manageable problem. See, for example, *The Oil and Gas Journal*, Vol. 58, No. 28, July 11, 1960, p. 58.

186 Memorandum of Conversation, Department of State, June 8, 1960, Subject: "Cuban Petroleum Situation." Participants: M. F. Braekel, Chairman of the Board of Directors, Sinclair Oil Company; Orvill Judd, Vice President, Sinclair Oil Company; ARA-R. Richard Rubottom, Assistant Secretary; CMA/C Torrey, Cuban Affairs, 837.2553/6–860, *DFOIA*. Secretary of State Herter alerted various American Embassies and Consulates in Latin America to the Department's strategy:

> Department has informed one oil company which has been approached that its rejection of Cuban offer would not repeat not be counter to U.S. policy and clearly intimated that acceptance would be opposed to U.S. interests. Department of State (Secretary Herter) to American Embassy, Havana, Caracas, Mexico City, Lima, La Paz; American Consul, Trinidad, Curacao, Aruba, Telegram, June 9, 1960, 837.2553/6–960, *DFOIA*.

187 Memorandum of Conversation, Department of State, June 21, 1960, Subject: "First Attempt GOC [government of Cuba] to Break Down the Refusal of the Oil Companies to Refine Russian Crude Oil," *DFOIA*.

188 Ibid.

189 Memorandum of Conversation, Department of State, July 2, 1960, Subject: "Cuban Intervention in American Oil Companies." Participants: James H. Pipkin, Vice-President, Texaco Oil Company; William Wieland, Director, Office of Caribbean and Mexican Affairs, ARA. 837.05111/7-260, *DFOIA*.

190 *Department of State Bulletin*, Vol. XLIII, No. 1100, July 25, 1960, pp. 141–142. Also see Havana Embassy (Daniel M. Braddock for the Ambassador) to Department of State, July 5, 1960, Subject: "British and American Embassies Protest Intervention of Oil Companies," Enclosure-Embassy Note No. 336. 837.3932/7-560, *DFOIA*.

191 *The Oil and Gas Journal*, Vol. 58, No. 28, July 11, 1960, p. 57.

192 See O'Connor, *The Origins of Socialism in Cuba*, p. 162; Edward Boorstein, *The Economic Transformation of Cuba* (New York: Monthly Review Press, 1968), p. 28. On the boycotts, see Michael Tanzer, *The Political Economy of International Oil and the Underdeveloped Countries* (Boston: Beacon Press, 1969), p. 338.

193 Quoted in Edward A. Morrow, "Jersey Standard Warns Ship Men," *New York Times*, July 9, 1960, p. 3.

194 Don O'Shea, "US Firms Act to Strand Red Oil," *Journal of Commerce*, July 11, 1960, p. 1.

195 Stanley Mantrop, "Soviet in 'Secret' Tanker Deals," *Journal of Commerce*, August 11, 1960, p. 1.

196 Quoted in Stanley Mantrop, "Cuba Trying to Acquire Tankers," *Journal of Commerce*, July 8, 1960, p. 1. Standard Oil's goal was given an assist by the action of British marine insurance underwriters in adding Cuba to the list of "excluded areas." This action was viewed as likely to increase the hull insurance rates for foreign shipowners operating in Cuban waters as of July 22, 1960. "Cuba Shipping Insurance Rate Boosted," *Journal of Commerce*, July 29, 1960, p. 24.

197 Quoted in "Soviet Expected to Find Tankers for Cuban Oil," *Journal of Commerce*, August 11, 1960, p. 1.

198 See O'Connor, *World Crisis in Oil*, p. 260.

199 See Stanley Mantrop, "Cuba Seeks Cargo Ships in Japan," *Journal of Commerce*, July 18, 1960, p. 1.

200 Eisenhower, *The White House Years*, p. 524.

201 R. Richard Rubottom, Jr., interview, *The Dulles Oral History Collection*, p. 75.

202 "Herter Warns Castro," *Wall Street Journal*, December 11, 1959, p. 28.

203 Memorandum of Conversation, Department of State, January 27, 1960, Subject: "Sugar Legislation." Participants: Speaker of the House Sam Rayburn; Congressman John W. McCormack (Democratic, Massachusetts); Thomas C. Mann, Assistant Secretary of State for Economic Affairs; William Pryce. 837.235/(no. unclear)-2760, *DFOIA*.

204 *Business Week*, February 20, 1960, p. 107. Also see testimony of Secretary of State Christian A. Herter, February 17, in U.S. Congress, House, Committee on Foreign Affairs, *Mutual Security Act of 1960, Part 1*, 86th Congress, 2nd Session, February 17, 18, 23, 24, & 29, 1960 (Washington, D.C.: U.S. Government Printing Office, 1960). p. 24.

205 E. M. Kenworthy, "U.S. Declines Brazil Offer to Seek Better Cuban Ties," *New York Times*, February 5, 1960, p. 2.

206 "Many U.S. Companies in Cuba Show Deficit but They Hope to Stay," p. 24.

207 Burt Schorr, "Sugar Paradox: U.S. Producers Fight Cut in Cuba's Quota," *Wall Street Journal*, March 9, 1960, p. 1.

208 Letter from Harold Cooley to William H. Doherty, November 16, 1959, Folder: "1959-Sugar," *Harold Cooley Papers*, #3801, Southern Historical Collection, University of North Carolina (Chapel Hill) Library.

209 Cooley Comments on President's Sugar Statement, January 28, 1960, Folder: "1960 Agric. Comm.-General," in ibid.

210 Statement by Congressman Harold D. Cooley, Chairman of the House Committee on Agriculture, April 20, 1960, Folder: "1960-Speeches," in ibid.

211 U.S. Congress, House, Committee on Agriculture, *Extension of the Sugar Act of 1948 Amended*, 86th Congress, 2nd Session, June 22,

1960 (Washington, D.C.: U.S. Government Printing Office, 1960), pp. 3–4.

212 Ibid., pp. 6, 5.

213 Memorandum of Conversation, Department of State, June 10, 1960, Subject: "Sugar Legislation," Telephone Conversation. Participants: C. Douglas Dillon, R. Richard Rubottom. 837.235/6–1060, *DFOIA*.

214 U.S. Congress, House, *Extension of the Sugar Act of 1948 Amended*, pp. 5, 11.

215 Ibid., p. 9.

216 Bonsal, *Cuba, Castro, and the United States*, p. 152.

217 True Morse interview, Colorado, October 1967, *The Eisenhower Oral History Collection*, Columbia University Library, pp. 109–110.

218 Harold Cooley, in *Congressional Record-House*, 86th Congress, 2nd Session, Vol. 106, Part II, June 30, 1960, p. 15235.

219 See *Congressional Record-House*, 86th Congress, 2nd Session, Vol. 106, Part II, June 20, 1960, pp. 15228–15232. The debate coincided with the Cuban government's intervention of Texaco's oil refinery and, according to the *Journal of Commerce*, this action had an important impact in accelerating congressional movement on the executive-branch request: "The Cuban seizure was followed by Democratic Congressional leaders responding to a hurry-up call from the Administration by putting a rush label on legislation to give the President authority to curtail Cuban sugar imports." "Cuba Grabs Texaco Plant for Rebuff on Soviet Oil," *Journal of Commerce*, June 30, 1960, p. 1.

220 Stanley Meisler, "The Politics of Sugar," *The Nation*, July 23, 1960, p. 50.

221 Don Paarlberg interview, Indiana, 1968, *The Eisenhower Oral History Collection*, Columbia University Library, pp. 48–49, 52–54. Paarlberg was President Eisenhower's advisor on agricultural issues from 1958 to 1961. Also see Memorandum for the Staff Secretary by Don Paarlberg, July 7, 1960, Subject: "Meeting with the President on Cuban Sugar," White House, Office of the Staff Secretary, International Series: Records 1952–61, International File, Box 4: Cuba (3), *Eisenhower Presidential Library*.

222 Havana Embassy (Ambassador Bonsal) to Secretary of State, Telegram, July 5, 1960, 837.235/7-560, *DFOIA*.

223 Havana Embassy (Ambassador Bonsal) to Secretary of State, Telegram, June 20, 1960, 837.00/6–2060, *DFOIA*.

224 See Don Paarlberg interview, *The Eisenhower Oral History Collection*, p. 53.

225 Havana Embassy (Ambassador Bonsal) to Department of State (Assistant Secretary of State for Inter-American Affairs Rubottom), Letter, August 2, 1960, 611.37/8-260, *DFOIA*. On September 5, Ambassador Bonsal was recalled to Washington and did not return to Havana.

226 *Department of State Bulletin*, Vol. XLIII, No. 1100, July 25, 1960, pp. 139–140. This action, Ambassador Bonsal later recalled, "carried with it the implication that the United States would buy no

more Cuban sugar as long as Castro was in power." Philip W. Bonsal, "Letter to the Editor," *New York Times*, December 29, 1970, p. 28. For figures on the sugar quota revision, see *Department of State Bulletin*, Vol XLIII, No. 1100, July 25, 1960, p. 140; *Hispanic American Report*, Vol. XIII, No. 7, September for July 1960, p. 447; *Facts on File*, Vol. XX, No. 1031, July 28–August 4, 1960, p. 265. Executive-branch officials were not unduly concerned, at least in private, regarding the availability of alternative sources of sugar supplies. A confidential Department of Agriculture report of January 1961 concluded on the following note: "Looking ahead over the next decade, the U.S. need not fear that the break in the traditional flow of Cuban sugar to the U.S. [even if it should persist] will bring a shortage of sugar available to it . . . The free world sugar supply is abundant." U.S. Department of Agriculture, Report of the Special Study Group on Sugar, Washington, D.C., January 1961, in *Harold Cooley Papers*.

227 Ambrose, *Eisenhower: Volume Two, The President*, p. 583.

228 *Department of State Bulletin*, Vol. XLIII, No. 1100, July 25, 1960, p. 171. The boom in the U.S. government Investment Guarantee Program originated with the Cuban expropriations: "U.S. businessmen–stung by the seizure of properties in Cuba by the Castro regime and the political turmoil in Africa–are beating on the doors of the Government seeking insurance for their overseas investments in Latin America and Africa. . . . U.S. firms apparently learned their lesson in Cuba, where although insurance against expropriation was available–*not one American firm applied for it.*" Hal Taylor, "ICA 'Swamped' by Rash of Bids for Insurance," *Journal of Commerce*, July 20, 1960, pp. 1, 4 (my emphasis). Also see Marina Von Neumann Whitman, *Government Risk-Sharing in Foreign Investment* (Princeton: Princeton University Press, 1965), p. 90.

229 See *Department of State Bulletin*, Vol. XLIII, No. 1105, August 29, 1960, p. 313; Michael Gutelman, "The Socialization of the Means of Production in Cuba," in Rudolfo Stavenhagen, ed. *Agrarian Problems & Peasant Movements in Latin America* (New York: Doubleday & Co., 1970), pp. 354–355; *Hispanic American Report*, Vol. XIII, No. 10, December for October 1960, pp. 695–696; Economist Intelligence Unit, *Quarterly Economic Review of Cuba*, No. 32, November 1960, pp. 1–2; "Cuba Seizes Nicaro Plant, 166 U.S. Firms," *Journal of Commerce*, October 28, 1960, p. 1.

230 Personal Interview: Department of State official, Washington, D.C., July 31, 1973. The respondent held assignments in Latin America between 1961 and 1968 and was a Department Cuba affairs official from 1968 to 1970. Jacques Levesque's insightful study of Soviet-Cuban relations after 1959 cogently argues that Moscow's initial attitude toward the Cuban Revolution was cautious, prudent, and highly pragmatic, shaped by a desire to maintain the existing global detente ("peaceful coexistence") with the United States and avoid giving Washington any pretext for military intervention to topple the Castro leadership. He also points out that Moscow was wary of a premature commitment to a regime that had not consolidated state

or political power. (See Jacques Levesque, *The USSR and The Cuban Revolution*. New York: Praeger Publishers, 1978, pp. 9–14). The U-2 incident and the cancellation of the April 1960 summit conference between Eisenhower and Khrushchev ended this phase of detente, leading to a fundamental shift in American-Soviet relations that created the conditions for a direct Soviet challenge to the United States in its "sphere of influence." The constraints and trade-offs inherent in detente were no longer operative, and it is conceivable that, in this new period of international competition, the Soviet leadership decided to support Cuba as a counterweight to American Cold War policies in Europe.

231 Personal Interview: Department of State official, Washington, D.C., June 20, 1973.

232 Personal Interview: Department of State official, Washington, D.C., July 13, 1973 and June 6, 1975. The respondent was a senior Department economic official between 1963 and 1967 and was intimately involved with the application of the global economic sanctions policy.

One instance of this aggressive imperial-state stance occurred in November 1960 when President Eisenhower ordered U.S. naval units to patrol Central American waters to guard against any "Communist-led invasion" of Nicaragua and Guatemala. The right-wing dictatorships were entrenched in both countries. The decision was taken following a meeting of the National Security Council and was rationalized on the grounds of possible Cuban attempts to export its revolution throughout the area. At the time, State Department officials conceded the absence of "hard evidence" of any Cuban involvement in insurgent attacks in Guatemala and Nicaragua in the week preceding the U.S. decision. Quoted in Feliz Belair, Jr., "U.S. Sends Navy to Bar any Attack Against Guatemala or Nicaragua," *New York Times*, November 18, 1960, pp. 1, 3.

233 Personal Interview: White House Staff official, Washington, D.C., May 20, 1976.

234 Personal Interview: Department of State official, Washington, D.C., June 11, 1973. Assistant Secretary of State for Inter-American Affairs Richard Rubottom put it this way: "we do have to protect our interests and make crystal clear that no country can do what [Cuba] is attempting to do to our private investments with impunity, because the effect of that would be very damaging elsewhere." U.S. Congress, Senate, *Executive Sessions of the Senate Foreign Relations Committee, Vol. XII*, p. 118.

235 Memorandum from Secretary of State Christian A. Herter to President Eisenhower, November 5, 1959, Subject: "Current Basic United States Policy toward Cuba," White House, Office of the Staff Secretary, International Series: Records 1952–61, Box 4, Folder: "Cuba (1)," *Eisenhower Presidential Library*.

236 Ibid.

237 Memorandum of Conversation, January 26, 1960, *Eisenhower Presidential Library*.

238 Memorandum of Conference. Participants: President Eisenhower,

Secretary of State Herter, General Goodpaster, August 30, 1960. Written by Goodpaster and dated September 7, 1960. Dwight D. Eisenhower Papers, 1953–61, Ann Whitman File, Dwight D. Eisenhower Diaries, Folder: "Staff Notes, August 1960," *Eisenhower Presidential Library.*

239 NSC Action, No. 2191: "U.S. Policy Toward Cuba." Record of Actions by the National Security Council, 436th Meeting, March 10, 1960. NSC Actions, NNMM "NSC Reference Collection." Record Group 218: Records of the United States Joint Chiefs of Staff, *National Archives of the United States.*

240 Memorandum for President from Secretary of State Christian A. Herter, March 17, 1960, Subject: "Status of Possible OAS Action on Cuba," White House, Office of the Staff Secretary, International Series: Records 1952–61, Ann Whitman File, Dulles-Herter Series, Box 10, Folder: "March 1960 (2)," *Eisenhower Presidential Library.*

241 Memorandum for President from Secretary of State Christian A. Herter, April 23, 1960, White House, Office of the Staff Secretary, International Series: Records 1952–61, Box 4: Cuba (2), Ann Whitman File, Dulles-Herter Series, Box 10, Folder: "April 1960 (1)," *Eisenhower Presidential Library.*

242 Ambrose, *Eisenhower: Volume Two, The President,* pp. 556, 582–583.

243 Organization of American States, Ministers of Foreign Affairs, *Seventh Meeting of Consultation,* San Jose, Costa Rica, 1960, DOC.1–83, Was that correct to put the – between those two numbers? Appendix F: "Memorandum from the Government of the United States to the Inter-American Peace Committee," June 21, 1960 (Washington, D.C.: Pan American Union).

244 J. Fred Rippy and Alfred Tischendorf, "The San Jose Conference of American Foreign Ministers," *Inter-American Economic Affairs,* Vol. XIV, No. 3, Winter 1960, p. 61.

245 Letter submitted to the United Nations Security Council, quoted in Thomas J. Hamilton, "Cuba Bids U.N. Act on U.S. Reprisals," *New York Times,* July 12, 1960, p. 1.

246 "The U.S. position regarding any Cuban approach to the UN Security Council should be that Cuba has obligations not only under the Rio Treaty and the OAS Chapter, but also under the UN Charter, to endeavor to settle disputes first by direct negotiations or bilateral procedures available and then through the regional agency, the OAS of which it is a member. . . . The U.S. position in the Security Council should therefore be that the Cuban complaint is a matter which must be acted upon in the first instance by the OAS." Memorandum on Possible Cuban Charges in the United Nations from R. Richard Rubottom, ARA, to Acting Secretary (through Secretary of State), July 5, 1960, Confidential, Subject: "Papers for Use in Your Talk with President Tomorrow," 737.00/7–560, *DFOIA.*

247 Quoted in Claude, "The OAS, The UN, and The United States," p. 34.

248 U.S. Ambassador to the United Nations, Henry Cabot Lodge, July

18, 1960, in United Nations, *Security Council Official Records*. Fifteenth Year, 874th Meeting, July 18, 1960 (New York), p. 27.

249 Milton Eisenhower, "United States-Latin American Relations: Report to the President," November 18, 1953, reprinted in *Department of State Bulletin*, Vol. XXXIX, No. 752, November 23, 1953, pp. 695–717.

250 Wagner, *United States Policy Toward Latin America*, pp. 98–100.

251 See Kauffman, *Trade and Aid*, pp. 164–165.

252 See Whitman, *Government Risk-Sharing in Foreign Investment*, p. 181.

253 Wagner, *United States Policy Toward Latin America*, p. 150.

254 Quoted in "U.S. Bids for Latin American Support," *Business Week*, July 16, 1960, p. 111.

255 Department of State (Secretary Herter) to all American Diplomatic Posts in other American Republics, Circular No. 175, July 28, 1960, White House, Office of the Staff Secretary, International Series: Records 1952–61, Box 4, Folder: Cuba (4), *Eisenhower Presidential Library*.

256 Organization of Americna States, Ministers of Foreign Affairs, *Seventh Meeting of Consultation*, San Jose, Costa Rica, 1960. DOC.38, Statement by Secretary of State of the United States in the General Committee of the OAS, August 24, 1960 (Washington, D.C.: Pan American Union), p. 6.

257 M. Margaret Ball, *The OAS in Transition* (Durham: Duke University Press, 1969), p. 459.

258 See *Deadline Data on World Affairs: Inter-American Relations*, p. 12.

259 See "Declaration of San Jose, 1960," Text of resolution adopted at the Seventh Meeting of Consultation of Ministers of Foreign Affairs, San Jose, Costa Rica, August 22–29, 1960, reprinted in U.S. Congress, House, Committee on Foreign Affairs, *Inter-American Relations*, 93rd Congress, 1st Session, November 1972, Committee Print (Washington, D.C.: U.S. Government Printing Office, 1973), p. 202.

260 Quoted in *The Economist*, September 3, 1960, p. 870.

261 Memorandum of Meeting with the President (of November 29) by Gordon Gray, the White House, December 5, 1960.

262 Memorandum of Conference of December 29, 1960. Participants: President Eisenhower, Undersecretary of State for Political Affairs Livingston T. Merchant, Staff Secretary to the President General Andrew Goodpaster. Secret. January 6, 1961, Papers of the President, 1953–61. Ann Whitman File, Dwight D. Eisenhower Diaries, Box 36, Folder: "Staff Notes, December 1960," *Eisenhower Presidential Library*.

263 Ibid.

264 Personal Interview: National Security Staff official, Washington, D.C., May 18, 1976.

265 Boorstein, *The Economic Transformation of Cuba*, p. 59.

266 U.S. Department of the Treasury, Memorandum for the Secretary re. Significance of Treasury Blocking Controls Against Cuba, July 6, 1960, *DFOIA*.

267 See Marguerite Higgins, "U.S. Undecided on Extent of Move to Curb Castro," *New York Herald Tribune*, July 8, 1960, p. 2.

268 Department of the Treasury, Memorandum No. 36001, June 16, 1960, *DFOIA*.

269 Department of the Treasury, Meeting at the State Department on Legal Aspects of the Cuban Problem, June 20, 1960, *DFOIA*.

270 Ibid.

271 Ibid.

272 Department of the Treasury, Memorandum, Subject: "Possible Cuban Projects," FAC No. 36215, July 1, 1969, *DFOIA*.

273 Memorandum from Eric H. Hager, Legal Advisor, Department of State to Secretary of State, Subject: "Department's Position as to the Desirability of a New Proclamation of Emergency under the Trading with the Enemy Act," July 8, 1960, *DFOIA*. The Department's opposition to the issuance of a special emergency proclamation is detailed in the following documents: R. Richard Rubottom, Jr., ARA, to Acting Secretary (through Secretary of State), Subject: "Possible Emergency Proclamation for Placing Controls on Cuban Transactions," July 8, 1960; Graham Parsons, FE, to Eric Hager, Legal Advisor, July 8, 1960, Subject: "Drafted Secret Proclamation," July 8, 1960; Charles E. Bohlen, Special Assistant to the Secretary of State, to Eric Hager, Legal Advisor, July 8, 1960; Roy D. Kohler, EUR, to Eric Hager, Legal Advisor, Subject: "Draft Secret Proclamation of National Emergency," July 9, 1960, *DFOIA*.

274 Secret Attachment, Mr. Hager's Memorandum of July 8 re. New Proclamation of Emergency Under the Trading with the Enemy Act, July 12, 1960, 737.00/7–1260, *DFOIA*.

275 Department of the Treasury, Memorandum for the Files, Subject: "Licensing Policy for Cuba," No. 36854, August 26, 1960, *DFOIA*; Department of the Treasury, Memorandum, Subject: "Licensing Problems for Cuba," October 5, 1960, *DFOIA*.

276 For the text of the embargo statement, see E.W. Kenworthy, "U.S. Puts Embargo on Goods to Cuba; Curb Ship Deals," *New York Times*, October 20, 1960, pp. 1, 8.

277 Eisenhower, *The White House Years*, p. 612.

278 "Embargo May Present Cuba with Severe Shortage of Spare Parts, Chemicals," *Wall Street Journal*, October 20, 1963, p. 3.

279 Don Paarlberg interview, *The Eisenhower Oral History Collection*, p. 53.

280 Department of the Treasury, Memorandum Re: Economic Measures Which May Be Taken by the United States Unilaterally vis-à-vis Cuba and Estimated Impact of Such Measures, July 12, 1960, *DFOIA*.

281 Department of State (Secretary Herter) to Paris Embassy, Telegram, July 12, 1960, 737.00/7–1260, *DFOIA*.

282 U.S. Congress, Senate, Committee on Foreign Relations, *Executive Sessions of the Senate Foreign Relations Committee*, Vol. XII, p. 93. Also see "U.S. Bids Britain Deny Jets to Cuba," *New York Times*, October 17, 1959, p. 1; *Hispanic American Report*, Vol. XII, No. 11, January 1960 for November 1959, p. 601; Thomas, *Cuba or the Pur-*

suit of Freedom, p. 1242; Department of State (Secretary Herter) to Paris Embassy, July 12, 1960.

283 See Herbert Matthews, *Castro: A Political Biography* (London: Penguin Books, 1969), p. 174.

284 "U.S. Asks NATO Support," *Journal of Commerce*, August 9, 1960, p. 4.

285 Ibid.

286 Department of State (Secretary Herter) to American Embassy, Paris, The Hague, July 15, 1960, 837.235/7–1260, *DFOIA*. The Netherlands imported approximately 200,000 tons of sugar annually. Of this amount, the Cuban portion rose from 83,000 in 1956/57 to 200,000 in 1959/60, ibid.

287 See Hal Taylor, "Another US Sanction Hits Cuban Sugar," *Journal of Commerce*, August 19, 1960, p. 1. Also see "Morocco Told Not to Use U.S. Cash for Cuban Sugar," *Washington Post*, August 21, 1960, p. A8.

288 See *Hispanic American Report*, Vol. XIII, No. 8, October for August 1960, pp. 522–523.

289 According to Castro, the support the Cuban government received from these Canadian firms regarding some important overseas financial transactions was a key factor in the treatment accorded them at the time of the virtual socialization of the Cuban economy. In May 1960, for example, Cuba transferred $120 million of deposits in American banks to the Royal Bank of Canada and the Bank of Nova Scotia. See Edward McWhinney, "Canadian-United States Commercial Relations and International Law: The Cuban Affair as a Case Study," in David R. Deener, ed., *Canada-United States Treaty Relations* (Durham: Duke University Press, 1963), pp. 136–138. Also see Richard A. Preston, *Canada in World Affairs, Vol. XII, 1959 to 1961* (Toronto: Oxford Unviersity Press, 1965), p. 180; Robert W. Reford, *Canada and Three Crises* (Ontario: The Canadian Institute of International Affairs, 1968), p. 158.

290 "A Blow–But Not a Knockout," *Business Week*, October 29, 1960, p. 111.

291 See Denis Stairs, "Confronting Uncle Sam: Cuba and Korea," in Stephen Clarkson, ed., *An Independent Foreign Policy For Canada?* (Toronto: McClelland and Stewart, 1968), pp. 60–61. Also see Harold Boyer, *Canada and Cuba: A Study in International Relations* (Ph.D. dissertation, Simon Fraser University, August 1972), p. 174.

292 Quoted in J. C. M. Ogelsby, "Canada and Latin America," in Peyton V. Lyon and Tareq Y. Ismael, eds., *Canada and the Third World* (Macmillan of Canada: MacLean-Hunter Press, 1976), p. 178. Also see McWhinney, "Canadian-United States Commercial Relations and International Law: The Cuban Affair as a Case Study," p. 137.

293 See Boyer, *Canada and Cuba*, p. 178.

294 See Preston, *Canada in World Affairs, Vol. XII, 1959–1961*, p. 181.

295 Statement before the House of Commons, quoted in Boyer, *Canada and Cuba*, p. 176. Diefenbaker's practical enforcement of this policy was favorably commented on in an internal White House document of December 1960; "Canada abides by the COCOM agreements

[regarding strategic military exports] and has always cooperated with the US in preventing illegal transshipment of US goods [to Cuba]." Staff Summary Supplement, December 22, 1960, Department of State, Confidential, White House Office, Staff Research Group, Records 1956–61, Box 20, State Department 861, *Eisenhower Presidential Library.*

296 Archibald R. M. Ritter, *The Economic Development of Revolutionary Cuba* (New York: Praeger Publishers, 1974), p. 98. On the impact of the spare parts, replacement parts, industrial equipment, and machinery "crunch," also see Dudley Seers, et al., *Cuba: The Economic and Social Revolution* (Chapel Hill: University of North Carolina Press, 1964), pp. 321–322. Efforts by the Castro government to purchase needed machinery and spare parts in the United States were uniformly rebuffed by individual capitalist enterprises. On September 22, 1960, for example, the *Wall Street Journal* carried a description of these abortive Cuban efforts:

> Fidel Castro's aides in Houston have been trying to buy more than $1,400,000 of U.S. industrial equipment but so far haven't been able to make a single purchase. Ferretería Caunedo, a Cuban government purchasing agency, has sent orders to more than 100 companies for such items as diesel locomotives, oil refinery parts and respiratory apparatus. Some of the orders were accompanied by deposits, others with checks for the full price. "U.S. Suppliers Refuse to Sell Cuban Agency, $1,400,000 Equipment," *Wall Street Journal*, September 22, 1960, p. 20.

297 Ritter, *The Economic Development of Revolutionary Cuba*, p. 106. Also see United Nations, Economic Commission for Latin America, Department of Economic and Social Affairs, *Economic Survey of Latin America 1963* (New York, 1965), pp. 262–263.

298 See *Hispanic American Report*, Vol. XIII, No. 12, February 1961 for December 1960, p. 876.

299 Memorandum of Meeting wtih the President (of January 3) by Gordon Gray, The White House, January 9, 1961. Present: Secretary Gates–Defense; Dulles, Bissell–CIA; Herter, Merchant, Mann, Wilauer, Dillon–State; Secretary Anderson–Treasury; General Goodpaster, Gray–White House. Office of the Special Assistant for National Security Affairs (OSANSA), Special Assistant Series, Presidential Subseries, Box 5, Folder: "Meetings with President 1960 11 (2)," *Eisenhower Presidential Library.*

300 Ambrose, *Eisenhower: Volume Two, The President*, p. 610.

301 Marguerite Higgins, "U.S. Breaks Relations with 'Dictator' Castro: 'Limit Has Been Reached,' Eisenhower Says," *New York Herald Tribune*, January 4, 1961, p. 4.

302 "U.S. to Favor New Moves Against Cuba," *Washington Post*, January 6, 1961, p. A1.

303 "U.S. Breaks Its Diplomatic Ties with Cuba and Advises Americans to Leave Island; Eisenhower Cites 'Vilification' by Castro," *New York Times*, January 4, 1961, p. 3.

304 Ibid.

305 Quoted in Fred L. Israel, ed., *The State of the Union Messages of the Presidents, Vol. III, 1905–1966* (New York: Chelsea House, Robert Hector, 1966), p. 3109.

306 The contrasting U.S. responses to the nationalization of American-owned properties by the Venezuelan government of Carlos Andres Perez (1974–1978) and the Chilean government of Salvador Allende (1970–1973) are instructive in this regard. In Venezuela, the nationalization of the U.S.-dominated petroleum and iron-ore industries occurred as part of a national-capitalist (nonsocialist) development strategy and in a way not antagonistic to basic U.S. interests located in industry, trade, and banking. Sectoral nationalization, with satisfactory compensation, took place within a private capitalist economy and was accompanied by the opening up of new areas for foreign capital accumulation in "downstream" non-oil economic sectors. Finally, the nationalization policy was implemented in a context of limited mass mobilization "from below." In Chile, the nationalization of U.S. properties was part of an anticapitalist (socialist) development strategy, not confined to any particular economic sector, unaccompanied by "adequate, effective, and swift" compensation, and reflected the interests and pressures of a politically mobilized working class. These political-economic differences explain why in one instance (Venezuela) the conflict was negotiable and in another (Chile) it became the occasion for sustained hostility. For extended discussions of these two cases, see James Petras and Morris Morley, *The United States and Chile;* James Petras, Morris Morley, and Steven Smith, *The Nationalization of Venezuelan Oil.* For studies of the mass base of the Cuban Revolution, see Zeitlin, *Revolutionary Politics and the Cuban Working Class;* Richard R. Fagen, *the Transformation of Political Culture in Cuba* (Stanford: Stanford University Press, 1969).

307 Bonsal, *Cuba, Castro, and the United States,* p. 135.

308 "U.S. Shows Its Fist to Castro," *Business Week,* July 9, 1960, p. 34.

309 U.S. Congress, Senate, *Alleged Assassination Plots Involving Foreign Leaders,* p. 93.

4. The United States against Cuba 1961–1968: politics of confrontation in Latin America

1 Quoted in *Hispanic American Report,* Vo. XVI, No. 9, November for September 1964, p. 799.

2 Chester Bowles interview, February 2, 1965, *The John F. Kennedy Oral History Collection,* Kennedy Presidential Library, p. 30.

3 The moralistic liberal ideology that informed Kennedy's Latin American policy bears striking resemblance to the policy pursued by the administration of Woodrow Wilson more than four decades earlier. See N. Gordon Levin, Jr., *Woodrow Wilson and World Politics* (Oxford: Oxford University Press, 1971). On the idealism that motivated the Alliance for Progress, see Jerome Levinson and Juan de Onís, *The Alliance That Lost Its Way* (Chicago: Quadrangle

Books, 1970), pp. 5–75; Arthur M. Schlesinger, Jr., *A Thousand Days* (Boston: Houghton Mifflin Co., 1966), pp. 186–205.

4 See James F. Petras and Robert LaPorte, Jr., *Cultivating Revolution: The United States and Agrarian Reform in Latin America* (New York: Random House, 1971), pp. 397–401.

5 In August 1961, the AFL-CIO established the American Institute for Free Latin Development (AIFLD) largely to counter the influence of the Cuban Revolution among hemispheric labor movements. Funded by the Agency for International Development (AID), AIFLD became the principal supplier of technical assistance – educational, training, and social projects – to Latin American trade union organizations. Between 1962 and 1967, Alliance for Progress appropriations for regional labor programs totalled approximately $24 million. See "Labor Policies and Programs," in U.S. Congress, Senate, Committee on Foreign Relations, Subcommittee on American Republic Affairs, *Survey of the Alliance for Progress*, Studies and Hearings, 91st Congress, 1st Session, Doc. 91–17, April 29, 1969 (Washington, D.C.: U.S. Government Printing Office, 1969), pp. 581–583.

6 On the flight of capital from the region during the 1960s, see Alfonso González, "Castro: Economic Effects on Latin America," *Journal of Inter-American Studies*, Vol. XI, No. 2, April 1969, p. 291; Organization of American States, General Secretariat, *External Financing for Latin American Development* (Baltimore: The Johns Hopkins Press, 1971), pp. 18–19.

7 "There are three possibilities in descending order or preference [said President Kennedy]: a decent democratic regime, a continuation of the Trujillo regime or a Castro regime. We ought to aim at the first, but we really can't renounce the second until we are sure that we can avoid the third." Quoted in Schlesinger, *A Thousand Days*, p. 769. This policy shift dictated organizational changes within the foreign policy bureaucracy to streamline the process in operational terms. During 1962 and 1963, a temporary Latin American Studies Group and an interagency Latin American Policy Committee were established, both under State Department leadership. The former was given the task of clarifying key issues requiring immediate attention and the latter with coordinating all agencies providing assistance to hemispheric governments coping with "threats to the public order." See Tad Szulc, "U.S. Closes Rift on Latin Policy," *New York Times*, April 29, 1962, p. 39; Statement of Edwin M. Martin, Assistant Secretary of State for Inter-American Affairs, in U.S. Congress, House, Committee on Foreign Affairs, Subcommittee on Inter-American Affairs, *Castro-Communist Subversion in the Western Hemisphere*, 88th Congress, 1st Session, February 18, 20, 21, 26, 27, 28, March 4, 5, and 6, 1963 (Washington, D.C.: U.S. Government Printing Office, 1963), pp. 18, 19.

8 See, for example, National Security Action Memorandum No. 2, February 3, 1961. From: McGeorge Bundy, Special Assistant to the President for National Security Affairs, To: Secretary of Defense. Subject: "Development of Counter-Guerrilla Forces," NNMM

"NSC Reference Collection," Record Group 218, *National Archives of the United States;* Letter, with enclosure and memorandum, from Chester Bowles, Acting Secretary of State, to President Kennedy, September 30, 1961. Subject: "Counter-Subversion Training for Latin American Police Forces," Secret, National Security Files, Meetings and Memoranda, NSAM 88, Box 331, *Kennedy Presidential Library.*

9   See Hanson W. Baldwin, "Army Will Train Latin Guerrillas," *New York Times,* May 5, 1961, pp. 1, 8.

10 "We've decided to quit rationalizing that our aid to Latins is based on defense of the Panama Canal or some massive outside invasions," declared a senior Administration official. "Internal subversion is the problem, and we're going to acknowledge it." Quoted in Louis Kraar, "U.S. Teaches Latins Antiguerrilla Tactics to Nip New Castros," *Wall Street Journal,* March 7, 1962, p. 25.

11 National Security Action Memorandum No. 124, January 18, 1962. From: McGeorge Bundy, White House, To: Secretary of State, Secretary of Defense, Attorney General, Chief/Joint Chiefs of Staff, Director of Central Intelligence, Administrator of AID, Director/ United States Information Agency, Military Representative of the President. Subject: "Establishment of the SG (C-1)," NNMM "NSC Reference Collection," Record Group 218, *National Archives of the United States.* The counterinsurgency program is discussed in William Beecher, "U.S. Effort to Counter Red Insurgency Guided by Little Known Group," *Wall Street Journal,* June 27, 1963, pp. 1, 14; William F. Barber and C. Neal Ronning, *Internal Security and Military Power* (Columbus: Ohio State University Press, 1966), pp. 97–99 and passim.

12 National Security Action Memorandum No. 177, August 7, 1962. From: McGeorge Bundy, To: Secretary of State, Secretary of Defense, Attorney General, Administrator of AID, Director of Central Intelligence. Subject: "Police Assistance Programs," NNMM "NSC Reference Collection," Record Group 218, *National Archives of the United States.*

13 Edwin Lieuwen, *Generals vs. Presidents: Neo-Militarism in Latin America* (New York: Frederick A. Praeger, 1966), p. 126.

14 See U.S. Agency for International Development, Office of Financial Management, Statistics and Reports Division, *U.S. Overseas Loans and Grants and Assistance from International Organizations, July 1, 1945–June 30, 1975* (Washington, D.C.: U.S. Government Printing Office, 1976), p. 33. On the productionist vs. distributionist strategies, see Petras and LaPorte, *Cultivating Revolution,* pp. 375–406.

15 For a discussion of Washington's attitude toward military seizures of power in Latin America during the 1960s, see James D. Cochrane, "U.S. Policy Toward Recognition of Governments and Promotion of Democracy in Latin America Since 1963," *Journal of Latin American Studies,* Vol. 4, No. 2, 1972, pp. 275–291.

16 Quoted in Tad Szulc, "U.S. May Abandon Effort to Deter Latin Dictators," *New York Times,* May 19, 1964, pp. 1, 2.

17 Thomas C. Mann, Assistant Secretary of State for Inter-American

Affairs, "The Democratic Ideal in Our Policy Toward Latin America," Address, University of Notre Dame, June 7, 1974, reprinted in *Department of State Bulletin*, Vol. L, No. 1305, June 29, 1964, p. 999.

18 Testimony of Secretary of Defense Robert McNamara in U.S. Congress, Senate, Committee on Appropriations and Committee on Armed Services, Subcommittee on Department of Defense, *Department of Defense Appropriations for Fiscal Year 1967, Part 1*, 89th Congress, 2nd Session, February 23, 1966 (Washington, D.C.: U.S. Government Printing Office, 1966), pp. 38–39. For discussions of the 1965 U.S. military intervention in the Dominican Republic, see Fred Goff and Michael Locker, "The Violence of Domination: U.S. Power and the Dominican Republic," in Irving Louis Horowitz, Josué de Castro, and John Gerassi, eds., *Latin American Radicalism* (New York: Vintage Books, 1969), pp. 292–313; Abraham Lowenthal, *The Dominican Intervention* (Cambridge: Harvard University Press, 1972); Piero Gleijeses, *The Dominican Crisis: The 1965 Constitutionalist Revolt and American Intervention* (Baltimore: The Johns Hopkins University Press, 1978).

19 Secretary of Defense Robert McNamara, in U.S. Congress, Senate, *Department of Defense Appropriations for Fiscal Year 1967, Part 1*, p. 38.

20 Secretary of Defense Robert McNamara, in U.S. Congress, House, Committee on Foreign Affairs, *Foreign Assistance Act of 1967, Part 1*, 90th Congress, 1st Session, April 4, 5, 11, 12, 13 and 14, 1967 (Washington, D.C.: U.S. Government Printing Office, 1967), p. 117.

21 U.S. Department of State, *Cuba*, Publication No. 7171, Inter-American Series 66, April 1961, p. 1.

22 Kent M. Beck, "Necessary Lies, Hidden Truths: Cuba in the 1960 Campaign," *Diplomatic History*, Vol. 8, No. 1, Winter 1984, p. 40.

23 "Senator John F. Kennedy on the Cuban Situation, Presidential Campaign of 1960," *Inter-American Economic Affairs*, Vol. XV, No. 3, Winter 1961, pp. 84, 90, 93.

24 Quoted in E.M. Kenworthy, "Latin's Progress Is Kennedy Goal," *New York Times*, January 26, 1961, p. 18. This argument was used as the basis for a White House decision to authorize the establishment of a government-financed program to facilitate the resettlement of Cuban "refugees" to the United States. See U.S. General Accounting Office, *Weaknesses in Negotiation and Administration of Contracts for Resettlement of Cuban Refugees*, Report to the Congress B-114836, March 24, 1965.

25 See *Hispanic American Report*, Vol. XIV, No. 2, April for February 1961, p. 128; *Department of State Bulletin*, Vol. XLIV, No. 1140, May 1, 1962, p. 618.

26 Richard Bissell, quoted in U.S. Congress, Senate, *Alleged Assassination Plots Involving Foreign Leaders*, p. 120.

27 See Memorandum of Meeting with the President (of November 29) by Gordon Gray, The White House, December 5, 1960. Participants: Secretary Anderson, Secretary Gates, Mr. Dillon, Mr. Mer-

chant, Mr. Douglas, General Lemnitzer, Allen Dulles, Richard Bissell, General Parsons, General Goodpaster, Gordon Gray. Office of the Special Assistant for National Security Affairs (OSANSA), Special Assistant Series, Presidential Subseries, Box 5, Folder: "Meetings with President 1960 11 (2)," *Eisenhower Presidential Library;* Memorandum of Meeting with the President (of January 3) by Gordon Gray, the White House, January 9, 1961. Participants: Secretary Gates, Allen Dulles, Richard Bissell, Secretary Herter, Secretary Merchant, Mr. Mann, Mr. Wilauer, Secretary Douglas, Secretary Anderson, General Goodpaster, Gordon Gray. Office of the Special Assistant for National Security Affairs (OSANSA), Special Assistant Series, Presidential subseries, Box 5, Folder: "Meetings with President 1960 11 (2)," *Eisenhower Presidential Library;* Ambrose, *Eisenhower: Volume Two, The President,* p. 615.

28 Cuban Study Group Report to the President, June 13, 1961.

29 Ibid.

30 Memorandum for the President from McGeorge Bundy, February 8, 1961, Papers of President Kennedy, National Security Files, Cuba, General (Folder), 1/61–4/61, Box 35, *Kennedy Presidential Library.*

31 Memorandum for the President from McGeorge Bundy, February 18, 1961, in ibid., *Kennedy Presidential Library.*

32 Cuban Study Group Report to the President, June 13, 1961. Also see the testimony of General Lyman L. Lemnitzer, Chairman, Joint Chiefs of Staff, "Briefing on the Cuban Situation," May 19, 1961, before the Senate Subcommittee on American Republic Affairs, in U.S. Congress, Senate, Committee on Foreign Relations, *Executive Sessions of the Senate Foreign Relations Committee, Vol. XIII, Part I* (Historical Series), 87th Congress, 1st Session, 1961 (Washington, D.C.: U.S. Government Printing Office, April 1984), pp. 573–607.

33 Memorandum for the President from Arthur Schlesinger, Jr., March 15, 1961, Subject: "Cuba," Papers of President Kennedy, National Security Files, Cuba, General (Folder), 1/61–1/64, Box 35, *Kennedy Presidential Library.*

34 Quoted in Schlesinger, *A Thousand Days,* p. 241. Also see Memorandum for the President from Arthur Schlesinger, Jr., March 15, 1961.

35 Memorandum of Discussion on Cuba, March 11, 1961, File: National Security Action Memorandum No. 31, National Security Files/National Security Council (hereafter NSF/NSC), Box 329, *Kennedy Presidential Library.*

36 See Cuban Study Group Report to the President, June 13, 1961. Also see Peter Wyden, *Bay of Pigs: The Untold Story* (New York: Simon and Schuster, 1979), p. 135. In the propaganda area, the CIA "developed an elaborate propaganda program to support the military action against Castro. This was based on the use of the clandestine radio SWAN, and programs of 11 CIA controlled radio stations and extensive leaflet drops." Cuban Study Group Report to the President, June 13, 1961.

37 See, for example, Thomas C. Mann interview, March 13, 1968, *The*

John F. Kennedy Oral History Collection, Kennedy Presidential Library, p. 20; Testimony of Allen W. Dulles, Director of the Central Intelligence Agency, "Briefing on the Cuban Situation," May 2, 1961, in U.S. Congress, Senate, *Executive Sessions of the Senate Foreign Relations Committee, Vol. XIII, Part 1,* p. 391; Testimony of Paul H. Nitze, Assistant Secretary of Defense (International Security Affairs), "The Cuban Situation," June 8, 1961, in U.S. Congress, Senate, Committee on Foreign Relations, *Executive Sessions of the Senate Foreign Relations Committee, Vol. XIII, Part 2* (Historical Series), 87th Congress, 1st Session, 1961 (Washington, D.C.: U.S. Government Printing Office, December 1984), p. 64: Roger Hilsman, *To Move a Nation: The Politics of Foreign Policy in the Administration of John F. Kennedy* (New York: Doubleday & Co., 1967), p. 32. "If we don't move now," the President stated in the week preceding the invasion, "Mr. Castro may become a much greater danger than he is to us today." Quoted in Theodore C. Sorenson, *Kennedy* (New York: Harper & Row, 1965), p. 296.

38 Memorandum for Secretary of State Rusk from Under Secretary of State Bowles, March 31, 1961, *Chester Bowles Collection,* Yale University Library.

39 Memorandum for the President from Arthur Schlesinger, Jr., April 5, 1961, Subject: "Cuba," Box 115, Papers of President Kennedy, President's Office Files, Cuba (Folders), President's Office Files/ Cuba/Security, 1961, *Kennedy Presidential Library.* Also see Schlesinger, *A Thousand Days,* p. 254.

40 Fulbright Memorandum, March 29, 1961, President's Office Files, Cuba, January–March 1961, Box 114, *Kennedy Presidential Library.*

41 Powers, *The Man Who Kept the Secrets,* p. 138.

42 Cuban Study Group Report to the President, June 13, 1961.

43 Ibid.

44 Ibid.

45 U.S. Congress, Senate, *Executive Sessions of the Senate Foreign Relations Committee, Vol. XIII, Part 1,* p. 412.

46 For the most complete narrative account of the events immediately preceding the invasion and the military conflict itself, see Wyden, *Bay of Pigs.* The Study draws on extensive interviewing of U.S. and Cuban governmental and nongovernmental participants.

47 Schlesinger, *A Thousand Days,* p. 256.

48 Chester Bowles interview, *The John F. Kennedy Oral History Collection,* p. 28.

49 Sorenson, *Kennedy,* p. 304.

50 Richard Bissell interview, April 25 and July 7, 1967, *The John F. Kennedy Oral History Collection,* Kennedy Presidential Library, pp. 74–75. White House official Arthur Schlesinger also recalled in his memoir of the episode that the problem of what to do with the exiles was a powerful factor shaping Kennedy's ultimate decision. See Schlesinger, *A Thousand Days,* pp. 257–258.

51 Ibid., pp. 520, 248.

52 Ibid., p. 259; Sorenson, *Kennedy,* pp. 304–305.

53 Ibid., pp. 302–303.
54 See, for example, Testimony of Secretary of State Dean Rusk, "Briefing on the Cuban Situation," May 1, 1961, in U.S. Congress, Senate, *Executive Sessions of the Senate Foreign Relations Committee, Vol. XIII, Part 1*, p. 342.
55 Cuban Study Group Report to the President, June 13, 1961.
56 Quoted in Lucien S. Vandenbroucke, "The 'Confessions' of Allen Dulles: New Evidence on the Bay of Pigs," *Diplomatic History*, Vol. 8, No. 4, Fall 1984, p. 367.
57 Robert Hurwitch interview, *The John F. Kennedy Oral History Collection*, pp. 11–12.
58 Roger Hilsman, *To Move a Nation*, p. 31.
59 Cuban Study Group Report to the President, June 13, 1961.
60 See Lucien S. Vandenbroucke, "Anatomy of a Failure: The Decision to Land at the Bay of Pigs," *Political Science Quarterly*, Vol. 99, No. 3, Fall 1984, p. 477.
61 Powers, *The Man Who Kept the Secrets*, p. 135. Also see Wyden, *Bay of Pigs*, p. 99.
62 See Powers, *The Man Who Kept the Secrets*, pp. 136–137; Wyden, *Bay of Pigs*, pp. 33–34.
63 Vandenbroucke, "Anatomy of a Failure: The Decision to Land at the Bay of Pigs," p. 471–491.
64 Personal Interview: Department of State official, Washington, D.C., March 12, 1975. The respondent was a senior inter-American affairs official between 1960 and 1964.
65 President John F. Kennedy, "The Lesson of Cuba," Address, American Society of Newspaper Editors, Washington, D.C., April 20, 1961, reprinted in *Department of State Bulletin*, Vol. XLIV, No. 1141, May 8, 1961, p. 659, 660.
66 Chester Bowles, *Promises to Keep: My Years in Public Life 1941–1969* (New York: Harper and Row, 1971), p. 331.
67 From McGeorge Bundy to Secretary of State and Secretary of Defense, April 25, 1961, Subject: "Caribbean Security Agency," File: National Security Action Memorandum No. 44, NSF/NSC, Box 329, *Kennedy Presidential Library*.
68 See E. W. Kenworthy, "U.S. Seeks to Spur Latins to Joint Action on Cuba," *New York Times*, April 27, 1961, p. 2; *Hispanic American Report*, Vol. XIV, No. 5, July for May 1961, p. 407.
69 Robert Amory interview, February 9, 1966, *The John F. Kennedy Oral History Collection*, Kennedy Presidential Library, p. 26.
70 Memorandum from Richard Goodwin to McGeorge Bundy, White House, April 26, 1961, draft, File: Cuba, General 1/61–4/64, National Security Files-Cuba, Box 35, *Kennedy Presidential Library*.
71 Personal Correspondence: Department of State official, California, March 7, 1975. The respondent was a senior inter-American affairs official during 1963 and 1964.
72 See U.S. Congress, Senate, *Alleged Assassination Plots Involving Foreign Leaders*, p. 209. The previous month, Arthur Schlesinger wrote a memorandum to the President which stated in part: "After

Cuba we simply cannot let another Latin American nation go Communist; if we should do so, the game would be up through a good deal of Latin America." Memorandum from Arthur Schlesinger, Jr., Special Assistant to the President, to President Kennedy, March 3, 1961, President's Office Files, Staff Memos, Schlesinger, 1961, Box 67B, *Kennedy Presidential Library* (Document received from Eisenhower Presidential Library).

73 Cuban Study Group Report to the President, June 13, 1961.

74 U.S. Congress, Senate, Final Report of the Select Committee to Study Government Operations with Respect to Intelligence Activities, *Foreign and Military Intelligence, Book 1*, 94th Congress, 2nd Session, Report No. 94–755, April 26, 1976 (Washington, D.C.: U.S. Government Printing Office, 1976), p. 56.

75 U.S. Congress, Senate, *Supplementary Detailed Staff Reports on Foreign and Military Intelligence, Book IV*, p. 67.

76 See testimony of David Phillips, in U.S. Congress, Senate, Select Committee to Study Governmental Operations with Respect to Intelligence Activities, *Senate Resolution 21, Covert Action, Vol. 7*, 94th Congress, 1st Session, December 4 and 5, 1975 (Washington, D.C.: U.S. Government Printing Office, 1976), p. 86.

77 See Taylor Branch and George Crile, III, "The Kennedy Vendetta: How the CIA Waged a Silent War Against Cuba," *Harpers Magazine*, August 1975, p. 49.

78 Richard Helms, quoted in U.S. Congress, Senate, *Alleged Assassination Plots Involving Foreign Leaders*, p. 149.

79 Ibid., pp. 157, 158.

80 Ibid., p. 119. The 1967 Report of the Inspector General of the CIA concluded on the following note: "We cannot overemphasize the extent to which responsible Agency officers felt themselves subject to the Kennedy Administration's severe pressure to do something about Castro and his regime." Ibid., p. 313.

81 Ibid., pp. 135–136.

82 Agee, *Inside the Company: CIA Diary*, p. 249.

83 U.S. Congress, Senate, *Senate Resolution 21, Covert Action, Vol. 7*, p. 91.

84 U.S. Congress, Senate, *Alleged Assassination Plots Involving Foreign Leaders*, p. 141.

85 U.S. Congress, Senate, *Supplementary Detailed Staff Reports on Foreign and Military Intelligence, Book IV*, p. 68.

86 Personal Interview: White House Special Assistant, New Jersey, May 24, 1976; Tom Wicker et al., "How the CIA Put Instant Air Force into Congo," *New York Times*, April 26, 1966, p. 30.

87 Agee, *Inside the Company: CIA Diary*, p. 498.

88 Personal Interview: Central Intelligence Agency official, Washington, D.C., May 21, 1976.

89 Roswell Gilpatric interview, May 27, 1970, *The John F. Kennedy Oral History Collection*, Kennedy Presidential Library, p. 41.

90 Testimony of CIA Case Officer, in U.S. Congress, Senate, *Alleged Assassination Plots Involving Foreign Leaders*, p. 86.

91 Personal Interview: Central Intelligence Agency official, Washington, D.C., May 21, 1976.

92 U.S. Congress, Senate, *Alleged Assassination Plots Involving Foreign Leaders*, p. 140.

93 Central Intelligence Agency, Office of National Estimates, Sherman Kent, Chairman, Memorandum for the Director, Subject: "The Situation and Prospects in Cuba," November 3, 1961, President's Office Files, CO., Cuba, Security 1961, *Kennedy Presidential Library*.

94 Memorandum from the President to the Secretary of State, in U.S. Congress, Senate, *Alleged Assassination Plots Involving Foreign Leaders*, p. 139.

95 Ibid., p. 141.

96 U.S. Congress, Senate, *Supplementary Detailed Staff Reports on Foreign and Military Intelligence, Book IV*, p. 68.

97 Branch and Crile, "The Kennedy Vendetta: How the CIA Waged a Silent War Against Cuba," p. 52.

98 Ibid., pp. 51–52.

99 See U.S. Congress, Senate, *Alleged Assassination Plots Involving Foreign Leaders*, p. 146.

100 Branch and Crile, "The Kennedy Vendetta: How the CIA Waged a Silent War Against Cuba," p. 62.

101 See Drew Fetherston and John Cummings, "Canadian Says U.S. Paid Him $5,000 to Infect Cuban Poultry," *Washington Post*, March 21, 1977, p. A18.

102 U.S. Congress, Senate, *Alleged Assassination Plots Involving Foreign Leaders*, pp. 142–143.

103 Quoted in Powers, *The Man Who Kept the Secrets*, p. 172.

104 See U.S. Congress, Senate, *Alleged Assassination Plots Involving Foreign leaders*, p. 337.

105 Ibid.

106 Ibid., p. 147.

107 Ibid.

108 Memorandum for McGeorge Bundy from William H. Brubeck, Executive Secretary, February 19, 1963. Prepared by Sterling J. Cottrell, Coordinator of Cuban Affairs, Subject: "Report of an Imminent Large-Scale Uprising in Cuba," Papers of President Kennedy, National Security Files, Cuba, General (Folder),, NSF/Cuba/ General, 2/63, Box 37, *Kennedy Presidential Library*.

109 U.S. Congress, Senate, *Alleged Assassination Plots Involving Foreign Leaders*, p. 173.

110 Ibid., p. 172.

111 Ibid.

112 Ibid.

113 Ibid.

114 See Dan Kurzman, "U.S. Builds Up Underground's Support in Cuba," *Washington Post*, August 13, 1963, p. A1.

115 Ibid. For the duration of the Kennedy administration, the anti-Castro exile leadership had virtually unlimited access to executive-branch officials. The State Department's Robert Hurwitch recalled:

"I would say I met with Cuban exiles virtually every day for there
was a fairly steady stream of people who would come up from
Miami. Miró Cardona had his own liaison man – two or three sometimes – stationed in Washington who called regularly and came in
regularly." Hurwitch believed that "a number of the activities of
the exiles were financed on a voluntary basis by some [American]
corporations." Robert Hurwitch interview, *The John F. Kennedy
Oral History Collection*, pp. 188–189.

116 McGeorge Bundy, A Check List of Current Actions Against Castro
Communism in Cuba, April 24, 1963, Papers of President Ken-
nedy, National Security Files, Cuba, General (Folder), NSF/Cuba/
General, 2/63, Box 38, *Kennedy Presidential Library*.

117 U.S. Congress, Senate, Select Committee to Study Governmental
Operations with respect to Intelligence Activities, *The Investigation
of the Assassination of President John F. Kennedy: Performance of the
Intelligence Agencies, Book V*, 94th Congress, 2nd Session, Report
No. 94–755, April 23, 1976 (Washington, D.C.: U.S. Government
Printing Office, 1976), p. 11. Also see Secretary of State Rusk to
President Kennedy, Letter, March 28, 1963, Subject: "Raids by
Cuba Exiles," File: Meetings, Vol. IV, Meetings 38–42, 1–25, 3/
29/63, Tab 42, NSF/NSC, Executive Committee, Box 316, *Ken-
nedy Presidential Library*.

118 Edwin M. Martin, Assistant Secretary of State for Inter-American
Affairs, in U.S. Congress, Senate, Committee on the Judiciary, Subcommittee to Investigate Problems Connected with Refugees and
Escapees, *Cuban Refugee Problems, Part 1*, 88th Congress, 1st Session, May 22 and 23, 1963, (Washington, D.C.: U.S. Government
Printing Office, 1963), p. 7. In early April, the National Security
Council had convened a meeting on Cuba at which the current status of measures being taken to control the Cuban exiles was discussed. National Security Council Record of Actions, NSC Action
2463, "U.S. Policy Toward Cuba," April 2, 1963, 510th Meeting,
The White House, National Security Files, Vice Presidential Security File, Folder: NSC (1), Box 4, *Johnson Presidential Library*. President Kennedy commented publicly on the problem at a news conference at around the same time: "We have attempted to
discourage [exile raids] . . . we don't think that they are effective;
we don't think they weaken Castro." Quoted in Harold W. Chase
and Allen H. Lerman, eds., *Kennedy and the Press: The News Conferences* (New York: Thomas Y. Crowell Co., 1965), p. 414.

119 U.S. Congress, Senate, *Alleged Assassination Plots Involving Foreign
Leaders*, p. 173.

120 See the statement of one of the "advisers" in Bradley E. Ayers, *The
War That Never Was: An Insider's Account of CIA Covert Operations
Against Cuba* (Indianapolis and New York: The Bobbs-Merrill Co.,
1976), pp. x, 15.

121 U.S. Congress, Senate, *Alleged Assassination Plots Involving Foreign
Leaders*, p. 173.

122 Branch and Crile, "The Kennedy Vendetta: How the CIA Waged a
Silent War Against Cuba," p. 62.

123 U.S. Congress, Senate, *Alleged Assassination Plots Involving Foreign Leaders*, p. 177.

124 Ibid.

125 Agee, *Inside the Company: CIA Diary*, p. 437.

126 CIA Director John McCone, quoted in U.S. Congress, Senate, *Alleged Assassination Plots Involving Foreign Leaders*, p. 154.

127 Ibid., p. 149.

128 Ibid., p. 103.

129 Ibid., p. 158.

130 George A. Smathers interview, March 31, 1964, Interview 1, Tape 2, *The John F. Kennedy Oral History Collection*, Kennedy Presidential Library,, p. 78.

131 U.S. Congress, Senate, *Alleged Assassination Plots Involving Foreign Leaders*, p. 84.

132 Ibid., pp. 85–86.

133 Ibid., p. 88.

134 Ibid., pp. 89–90.

135 See George Crile II, "The Riddle of AMLASH," *Washington Post*, May 2, 1976, p. C2; U.S. Congress, Senate, *Alleged Assassination Plots Involving Foreign Leaders*, pp. 89–90, 176.

136 Powers, *The Man Who Kept the Secrets*, p. 192. According to the U.S. Senate Select Committee on Intelligence, there was evidence to substantiate at least eight separate plots to assassinate Fidel Castro and other Cuban leaders between 1960 and 1965. See U.S. Congress, Senate, *Alleged Assassination Plots Involving Foreign Leaders*, p. 71. The Cuban government, however, placed the figure at twenty-one: one in 1960; seven in 1961; one in 1962; four in 1963; three in 1964; and five in 1965. It further contends that there was one in 1966, one in 1967 and one in 1971. Documentation supplied by Prime Minister Castro to Senator George McGovern during the latter's visit to Cuba in May 1975. A summary of the documentation was relased by the *Office of Senator McGovern*, with an accompanying statement by the Senator, on July 30, 1975.

137 Personal Correspondence: Department of State official, California, March 7, 1975.

138 Quoted in "U.S. Consulting Latins on Castro," *New York Times*, October 12, 1961, p. 4.

139 Personal Interview: Department of State official, Washington, D.C., June 18, 1973. The respondent was stationed in Latin America and Washington, D.C., during the 1960s. He was a senior Department Cuba official in the early 1970s.

140 See "Stevenson's Return Spurs Overhaul of Latin Policies," *New York Times*, June 23, 1961, pp. 1, 8.

141 *Department of State Bulletin*, Vol. XLV, No. 1151, July 17, 1961, p. 108. In a subsequent statement, Rusk declared: "We are developing our diplomacy and our discussions with other [Latin American] governments along both these lines [i.e., the refusal to abandon existing policy and the postion that Cuba is a hemispheric problem]." *Department of State Bulletin*, Vol. XLV, No. 1152, July 24, 1961, p. 149.

142 Organization of American States, *Annual Report of the Secretary General 1962* (Washington, D.C.: Pan American Union), p. 2.

143 W. W. Rostow, *The Diffusion of Power* (New York: The Macmillan Co., 1972), p. 218.

144 See Ball, *The OAS in Transition*, pp. 463–464.

145 See U.S. Congress, Senate, Committee on Foreign Relations, *Punta Del Este Conference January 1962*, Report of Senators Wayne Morse and Bourke B. Hickenlooper, 87th Congress, 2nd Session, Committee Print, March 1962 (Washington, D.C.: U.S. Government Printing Office, 1962), p. 4. Also see Schlesinger, *A Thousand Days*, pp 780–781; Juan de Onis, "Rusk Links Help to Latin Nations to Actions on Cuba," *New York Times*, January 22, 1962, pp. 1, 4.

146 Attachment to Memorandum from Richard Goodwin (Deputy Assistant Secretary) to McGeorge Bundy, February 7, 1962, National Security Files, Brazil Vol. 2, Box 12 and 13, *Kennedy Presidential Library*.

147 Lincoln Gordon, "Points Supplementary to R. N. Goodwin Draft of 1-1-62 (sic)," January 7, 1962, in ibid.

148 Address reprinted in Organization of American States, *Eighth Meeting of Consultation of Minister of Foreign Affairs*, Punta Del Este, Uruguay 1962, DOC. 35, 11.8 (Washington, D.C.: Pan American Union), p. 7.

149 Statement by Secretary of State Rusk, January 25, reprinted in *Department of State Bulletin*, Vol. XLVI, No. 1182, February 19, 1962, p. 276.

150 Personal Interview: White House Special Assistant, New Jersey, May 24, 1976. Also see Delesseps S. Morrison, *Latin American Mission* (New York: Simon and Schuster, 1965), pp. 165–197. Morrison was American Ambassador to the OAS at the time of the January 1962 conference.

151 See Organization of American States, *Eighth Meeting of Consultation of Ministers of Foreign Affairs*, p. 14. For a detailed narrative account of the Punta Del Este conference, see Moon Sool Kwon, *The Organization of American States and the Cuban Challenge: An Analysis of the Inter-American System and the Meeting of Consultation of Ministers of Foreign Affairs* (Ph.D. dissertation, Claremont Graduate School and University Center, 1970), pp. 187–235, 273–420.

152 "As for Haiti, we finally yielded to blackmail and agreed to resume our aid to the airport at Port au Prince." Schlesinger, *A Thousand Days*, p. 783. According to another study, Haiti received approximately $13 million from Washington for its vote. See Jerome Slater, *The OAS and United States Foreign Policy* (Columbus: Ohio State University Press, 1967), p. 156. On the purchase of Haiti's vote, also see *Hispanic American Report*, Vol. XV, No. 1, March for January 1962, p. 81.

153 Ann Van Wynen Thomas and A. J. Thomas, Jr., *The Organization of American States* (Dallas: Southern Methodist University Press, 1963), p. 328.

154 Review of the Cuban Situation and Policy (Talking Points), February 28, 1962. Attachment to Memorandum to the National Security

Council from McGeorge Bundy, White House, March 11, 1963,
Papers of President Kennedy, National Security Files, Meetings and
Memoranda (Folders), NSF/National Security Council Meetings,
1963, File No. 509, 3/13/63, Box 14–15; also used at Cabinet meeting 3/1/63, File: Cuba 1/1/62–10/22/62, President's Office Files,
Box 115, *Kennedy Presidential Library*. In March 1962, the Castro
government initiated a debate on the OAS sanctions in the United
Nations Security Council, seeking eventual referral of the issue of
sanctions to the International Court of Justice for an advisory judge-
ment. Washington successfully opposed a hearing before this international judicial body because of the likelihood that the Court
would find in favor of the Cuban position:

> As a judicial body, it was unlikely to derive its opinion from the
> general political principle of regional autonomy, which formed
> the real basis of the pro-OAS positon. What the United States and
> its friends required was an interpretation of the competence of the
> OAS based upon awareness of the political problems posed for
> them by communist tactics in the cold war, and disregarding the
> rules that had been formulated in 1945. They had made such an
> interpretation prevail in the Security Council but they could have
> no assurance that the Court would similarly place general political
> considerations above textual analysis of the Charter. Claude, "The
> OAS, The UN and the United States," p. 59.

155 Memorandum for the President, From McGeorge Bundy, Subject:
"Further Organization of the Government for dealing with Cuba,"
January 4, 1963. *DFOIA*; National Security Action Memorandum
No. 213, From McGeorge Bundy to the Secretary of State, Subject:
"Interdepartmental Organization for Cuban Affairs," January 8,
1963, National Security Council, *DFOIA*.

156 Memorandum for the National Security Council's Executive Committee, from Sterling J. Cottrell, Coordinator of Cuban Affairs, Subject: "United States Policy re Cuba in the Organization of American
States," Prepared for meeting of January 24, 1963, File: Meetings,
Vol. IV, Meetings 38–42, NSF/NSC, Executive Committee, Box
316, *Kennedy Presidential Library*.

157 Memorandum to Coordinating Committee of Cuban Affairs, From
John W. Ford, Subject: "Meeting of Chiefs of State at San Jose,
Costa Rica, March 18–20, 1963," Policy Planning Council, Depart-
ment of State, February 15, 1963, Draft, File: Cuba, General 2/63,
National Security Files-Cuba, Box 37, *Kennedy Presidential Library*
(Author's emphasis). Also see Tad Szulc, "Two Items Lead San Jose
Talks," *New York Times*, March 19, 1963, p. 2; Paul P. Kennedy,
"President Urges Wall of Liberty Encircling Cuba," *New York
Times*, March 19, 1963, pp. 1, 2; Paul P. Kennedy, "6 Latin Nations
and U.S. Sidestep Cuba Showdown," *New York Times*, March 20,
1963, pp. 1, 2.

These concerns apparently were instrumental in the formation of
a Subcommittee on Cuban Subversion of the Interdepartmental
Coordinating Committee on Cuban Affairs headed by Marine Corps

Major General Victor H. Krulac. The Subcommittee generated numerous "action papers on the movement of personnel, arms, funds and propaganda materials within and between regional countries, especially in the Caribbean, and studies of surveillance and the exchange of intelligence information." Memorandum for McGeorge Bundy from William H. Brubeck, Executive Secretary, May 22, 1963, Subject: "First Report of the Coordinator of Cuban Affairs," Office of the Coordinator, Bureau of Inter-American Affairs, Department of State, Folder: General, 4/63–5/63, *Kennedy Presidential Library*.

158 Memorandum to Coordinating Committee of Cuban Affairs, From John W. Ford, Subject: "Meeting of Chiefs of State at San Jose, Costa Rica, March 18–20, 1963," Policy Planning Council, Department of State, February 15, 1963, *DFOIA* (Ford's emphasis).

159 "Test of President Kennedy's News Conference on Foreign and Domestic Affairs," *New York Times*, March 22, 1963, p. 4.

160 Henry Raymont, "O.A.S., 14–1, Urges Cuba Travel Ban to Control Reds," *New York Times*, July 4, 1963, p. 1.

161 Memorandum for McGeorge Bundy from William H. Brubeck, February 19, 1963.

162 See Henry Raymont, "U.S. Disregards Plan on O.A.S. Embargo Against Cuba Trade," *New York Times*, July 5, 1963, pp. 1, 3.

163 Quoted in "U.S. Insists It Plans More Steps on Cuba," *New York Times*, July 6, 1963, p. 1.

164 See Hedrick Smith, "U.S. Freezes Cuban Assets in Move to Bar Subversion," *New York Times*, July 9, 1961, pp. 1, 10. Also see "Government Freezes Cuban Assets in U.S. in Stepped-up Effort to Isolate Castro," *Wall Street Journal*, July 9, 1963, p. 6.

165 Quoted in Benjamin Welles, "Rusk Urges O.A.S. to Block Castro," *New York Times*, September 24, 1967, p. 1.

166 *Hispanic American Report*, Vol. XVII, No. 7, September for July 1964, p. 666.

167 Organization De Los Estados Americanos, *Novena Reunión De. Consulta De Minstres De Relaciónes Exteriores*, Washington, D.C., 1964, DOC. 24, 11.9 (Washington, D.C.: Pan American Union), p. 7. Also see Kwon, *The Organization of American States and the Cuban Challenge*, pp. 236–272.

168 Personal Interview: Department of State official, Washington, D.C., July 11, 1973. The respondent was a Cuba specialist in the State Department between 1960 and 1963.

169 Memorandum of Conversation, Department of State, February 21, 1964, Subject: "Meeting between President Johnson and President Lopez Mateos," Collection: National Security Files, Country File-Latin America-Mexico, Folder: Mexico, Lopez Mateos Visit, 2/20–22/64, Box 61, *Johnson Presidential Library*.

170 Memorandum of Conversation, Department of State, November 12, 1964, Subject: "Mexican-Cuban Relations," Part II of II, Participants: President Johnson, President-elect Gustavo Diaz Ordaz, Ambassador Carillo Flores, Assistant Secretary of State Thomas C. Mann, in ibid.

171 The Final Act of the meeting is to be found in Organization of American States, General Secretariat, *Ninth Meeting of Consultation of Ministers of Foreign Affairs, Final Act,* July 21–26, 1964. OAS Official Records OE A/Ser. c/11.9 (Washington, D.C.: Pan American Union, 1964), p. 6. For discussions of the 1964 conference, see Connell-Smith, *The Inter-American System,* pp. 185–186; Slater, *The OAS and United States Foreign Policy,* pp. 169–170.

172 Personal Interview: Department of State official, Washington, D.C., July 11, 1973. The respondent was a Cuba specialist in the State Department between 1960–1963. Another official was just as blunt: "Where we found receptivity, we would press." Personal Interview: Department of State official, Washington, D.C., June 21, 1973. The respondent was a senior official in the U.S. Embassy in Bolivia between 1961 and 1964, a senior Latin American official in the State Department between 1964 and 1966, and a high-ranking American OAS representative during 1966 and 1967.

173 Personal Interview: Inter-American Development Bank official, Washington, D.C., April 27, 1971. The respondent was a Bank official during the period under discussion.

174 See U.S. Agency for International Development, *U.S. Overseas Loans and Grants and Assistance from International Organizations, July 1, 1945–June 30, 1975,* p. 182.

175 Aldo Ferrer, *The Argentine Economy* (Berkeley: University of California Press, 1967), p. 198.

176 Quoted in Joseph Novitski, "Latin's Dismantling U.S.-Sponsored Wall Around Cuba," *Washington Post,* November 3, 1974, p. A18.

177 See "Frondizi Bows to Military; Accepts O.A.S. Cuba Stand," *New York Times,* February 3, 1962, pp. 1, 2; Frank Manitzas, "Frondizi Attempts to Placate Military by Offer of Cuba Break," *Washington Post,* February 2, 1962, p. A14; Edward C. Burks, "Frondizi Assails Military and 'Hard Line' on Cuba," *New York Times,* February 4, 1962, pp. 1, 21.

178 See ibid.; *Hispanic American Report,* Vol. XV, No. 2, April for February 1962, p. 166.

179 See "Argentina to Receive $150M Loan," *London Times,* February 26, 1962, p. 8; "Argentina Gets $500,000,000 Aid," *New York Times,* July 28, 1962, p. 1.

180 See "Argentine Success in Paris," *London Times,* November 6, 1962, p. 17. Also see "Argentine Debts Agreement," *London Times,* November 3, 1962, p. 7.

181 Peter Pyne, "The Politics of Instability in Ecuador: The Overthrow of the President, 1961," *Journal of Latin American Studies,* Vol. 7, No. 1, 1975, p. 120.

182 Ibid., p. 122.

183 Ibid., pp. 116–117. Also see John Samuel Fitch, *The Military Coup d'Etat as a Political Process in Ecuadorian Politics: 1948–1966* (Baltimore: The Johns Hopkins University Press, 1977), p. 49.

184 Agee, *Inside the Company: CIA Diary,* pp. 114–115.

185 Ibid., pp. 185, 131.

186 Ibid., p. 216.

187 Fitch, *The Military Coup d'Etat as a Political Process in Ecuadorian Politics: 1948–1966*, p. 55.

188 Edwin M. Martin interview, May 19, 1966, *The John F. Kennedy Oral History Collection*, Kennedy Presidential Library, p. 49.

189 Agee, *Inside the Company: CIA Diary*, p. 130. Also see Roger Morris and Richard Mauzy, "Following the Scenario: Reflections on Five Case Histories in the Mode and Aftermath of CIA Intervention," in Robert L. Borsage and John Marks, eds., *The CIA File* (New York: Grossman Publishers, 1976), p. 32.

190 Fitch, *The Military Coup d'Etat as a Political Process in Ecuadorian Politics: 1948–1966*, p. 56.

191 Ibid., p. 57.

192 The CIA spending figure is provided by Morris and Mauzy, "Following the Scenario: Reflections on Five Case Histories in the Mode and Aftermath of CIA Intervention," p. 32. Accounts of the break in relations at the time included no mention of the role of the CIA. See, for example, Richard Eder, "Ecuador Breaks Tie with Cuba," *New York Times*, April 4, 1962, p. 3; *Hispanic American Report*, Vol. XV, No. 4, Events for April 1962, pp. 342–343.

193 Memorandum to Latin American Policy Committee from James M. Frey, Executive Secretary, May 5–6, 1964, Subject: "LAPC Agenda," National Security Council, File-Country File-Latin America, Box 1, Latin American, Vol. 1, 11/63–11/64, *Johnson Presidential Library*.

194 Latin American Policy Committee: Action Minutes, Meeting #90, July 9, 1964, Topic: "Chile-Contingency Plans in Connection with September 4 Presidential Election." Participants included representatives from the State Department, Defense Department, CIA, U.S. Information Agency, and the White House. National Security Files, Country File-Latin America, Box 2, Latin America, Vol. II, 6/64–8/64, *Johnson Presidential Library*.

195 Quoted in Laurence Stern, "U.S. Helped Beat Allende in 1964," *Washington Post*, April 6, 1973, pp. A1, A12. On U.S. economic assistance to the Frei administration, see Harvey S. Perloff, *Alliance for Progress* (Baltimore: The Johns Hopkins Press, 1969), p. 230 (Table A-3). Also see Levinson and de Onís, *The Alliance That Lost Its Way*, p. 91; Joan M. Nelson, *AID, Influence and Foreign Policy* (New York: The Macmillan Co., 1968), p. 99.

196 *Hispanic American Report*, Vol. XVII, No. 8, October for August 1964, p. 741.

197 Ibid.

198 See Miles D. Wolpin, *Cuban Foreign Policy and Chilean Politics* (Lexington: D. C. Heath and Co., 1972), p. 121.

199 Memorandum for the President from McGeorge Bundy, The White House, August 13, 1964, National Security Files, Aides Files, Box 2, McGeorge Bundy-Memos to President, Vol. 6, 7/1–9/30, 1964, *Johnson Presidential Library*.

200 Frank Bonilla, "Operational Neutralism: Brazil Challenges United States Leadership," *American Universities Field Service Reports*, East

Coast, South America Series, Vol. IX, No. I (Brazil), January 1962, p. 1.

201 Rio de Janiero Embassy (Ambassador Cabot) to Department of State (Secretary Rusk), Telegram, No. 1154, Confidential, March 6, 1961 (Section One of Two), 110.17-8E/3-661, *DFOIA.*

202 Ambassador John Moors Cabot interview, Washington, D.C., January 27, 1971, *The John F. Kennedy Oral History Collection,* Kennedy Presidential Library, pp. 4–5. In another interview, Cabot put the total amount Berle offered Quadros at $300 million. See Peter D. Bell, "Brazilian-American Relations," in Riordan Roett, ed., *Brazil in the Sixties* (Nashville: Vanderbilt University Press, 1972), p. 81. Also see Tad Szulc, "U.S. Brazil Talks Close in Discord Over Cuba Issue," *New York Times,* March 4, 1961, pp. 1, 6; John Hickey, "The Day Mr. Berle Talked with Mr. Quadros," *Inter-American Economic Affairs,* Vol. XV, No. 1, Summer 1961, pp. 58–71.

203 Department of State (Secretary Rusk) to Rio de Janeiro Embassy, Confidential, March 13, 1961, drafted by A. A. Berle, 110.17-8E/3-1461, *DFOIA.*

204 Rio de Janeiro Embassy (Ambassador Cabot) to Department of State (Secretary Rusk), Telegram, No. 1201, Confidential, March 14, 1961, 110.17-8E/3-1461, *DFOIA.*

205 Ralph A. Dungan, White House, from L. D. Battle, Executive Secretary, Subject: "Task Force on Latin America, Minutes of Meeting on March 16, 1961," Secret, March 30, 1961, 110.17-8E/3-3061, *DFOIA.*

206 Quoted in Bell, "Brazilian-American Relations," p. 82.

207 Niles Bond, Deputy Chief of Mission in U.S. Embassy, April 1959 to March 1963, & Minister Counsel General in São Paulo, January 1964 to July 1968, quoted in ibid., p. 83. In August 1979, Quadros told the Rio de Janeiro newspaper *O Globo* that his decision to resign in August 1961 was the result of tremendous pressures from Washington to enlist Brazil in a military invasion of Cuba. See *Latin America Political Report,* Vol. XIII, No. 34, August 31, 1979, p. 272.

208 Quoted in H. Jon Rosenbaum, "Brazil's Foreign Policy and Cuba," *Inter-American Economic Affairs,* Vol. XXIII, No. 3, Winter 1969, p. 33.

209 For a discussion of the Goulart period, see Peter Flynn, *Brazil: A Political Analysis* (Boulder: Westview Press, 1978), pp. 226–307.

210 See Ruth Leacock, "JFK, Business, and Brazil," *Hispanic American Historical Review,* Vol. 59, No. 4, November 1979, p. 640.

211 See Laurence Stern, "Ex-Spy to Give Detailed Account of Covert CIA Operations," *Washington Post,* July 11, 1974, p. A3; Leacock, "JFK, Business, and Brazil," pp. 640–641, 668–669; Agee, *Inside the Company: CIA Diary,* p. 254. According to Colonel Vernon Walters, the U.S. Defense Attache in the Rio de Janeiro Embassy, an official "high in the Kennedy administration" informed him just prior to the elections that President Kennedy would not be opposed to Goulart's ouster if he was succeeded by a stable, anticommunist, procapitalist regime. Quoted in Phyllis R. Parker, *Brazil and the*

Quiet Intervention, 1964 (Austin: University of Texas Press, 1979), pp. 62–63.

212 Personal Interview: Department of State official, Washington, D.C., July 31, 1973.

213 Leacock, "JFK, Business, and Brazil," p. 656.

214 Ibid., p. 657.

215 Memorandum for the National Security Executive Committee, Meeting of December 11, 1962, Subject: "U.S. Short Term Policy Toward Brazil," National Security Files, Vice-Presidential Security File, Box 4, Folder: National Security Council (1), *Johnson Presidential Library.*

216 See Leacock, "JFK, Business, and Brazil," p. 661.

217 Ibid., pp. 661–662; Ruth Leacock, "'Promoting Democracy': The United States and Brazil, 1964–1968," *Prologue* (Journal of the National Archives), Vol. 13, No. 2, Summer 1981, p. 88.

218 Leacock, "JFK, Business, and Brazil," p. 658.

219 See testimony of William A. Ellis, Director of U.S. Agency for International Development in Brazil, May 5, 1971, in U.S. Congress, Senate, Committee on Foreign Relations, Subcommittee on Western Hemisphere Affairs, *United States Policies and Programs in Brazil,* 92nd Congress, 1st Session, May 4, 5, and 11, 1971 (Washington, D.C.: U.S. Government Printing Office, 1971), p. 250. Also see the statement by Assistant Secretary of State for Inter-American Affairs Thomas C. Mann, quoted in Carlos F. Díaz-Alejandro, "Some Aspects of the Brazilian Experience with Foreign Aid," in Jagdish N. Bhagwati, et al., eds., *Trade, Balance of Payments and Growth* (New York: American Elsevier Publishing Co., 1971), p. 452.

220 Bell, "Brazilian-American Relations," p. 95.

221 U.S. Agency for International Development, Office of Financial Management, Statistics and Reports Division, *U.S. Overseas Loans and Grants and Assistance from International Organizations, July 1, 1945–June 30, 1973* (Washington, D.C., May 1974), p. 182.

222 See Thomas E. Skidmore, *Politics in Brazil 1930–1964* (Oxford: Oxford University Press, 1967), pp. 270–271.

223 Quoted in Parker, *Brazil and the Quiet Intervention, 1964,* p. 40.

224 Radosh, *American Labor and United States Foreign Policy,* p. 425. Also see the statement by William Doherty, Jr., Director of the Special Projects Department of AIFLD at the time of the coup, quoted in Robert H. Dockery, "Labor Policies and Programs," in U.S. Congress, Senate, *Survey of the Alliance for Progress,* p. 586.

225 Personal Interview: Department of State official, Washington, D.C., July 31, 1973.

226 See Tad Szulc, "U.S. May Abandon Efforts to Deter Latin Dictators," *New York Times,* March 19, 1964, pp. 1, 2.

227 See Parker, *Brazil and the Quiet Revolution, 1964,* pp. 68–70.

228 Ibid., pp. 73–74.

229 Quoted in ibid., pp. 75–76.

230 See Leacock, "'Promoting Democracy': The United States and Brazil, 1964–1968," p. 88; Flynn, *Brazil: A Political Analysis,* pp. 308–365.

231 U.S. Agency for International Development, *U.S. Overseas Loans and Grants and Assistance from International Organizations*, July 1, 1945–June 30, 1973, p. 40.

232 Leacock, "'Promoting Democracy': The United States and Brazil, 1964–1968," p. 89.

233 Personal Interview: Inter-American Development Bank official, Washington, D.C., April 27, 1971. Also see John W. Tuthill, "Operation Topsy," *Foreign Policy*, No. 8, Fall 1972, pp. 62, 64. Tuthill was U.S. Ambassador to Brazil from mid-1966 to January 1969. On the break in relations between Brazil and Cuba, see Juan de Onis, "Brazil Condemns Cuba, Severs Ties," *New York Times*, May 14, 1965, p. 15.

234 Wilkie, *The Bolivian Revolution and U.S. Aid Since 1952*, p. 48, Appendix A.

235 Juan de Onís, "Paz and U.S. Near an Open Quarrel," *New York Times*, August 9, 1964, p. 10.

236 Quoted in *Hispanic American Report*, Vol. XVII, No. 8, October for August 1964, p. 738.

237 Juan de Onís, "Paz and U.S. Near an Open Quarrel," p. 10.

238 Personal Correspondence: Department of State official, Massachusetts, July 17, 1978. The respondent was a senior official in the U.S. Embassy in La Paz during 1963 and 1964.

239 Henry Raymont, "Bolivia Breaks Ties with Cuba; Acts to Block a Leftist Protest," *New York Times*, August 22, 1964, pp. 1, 3.

240 Editorial, "Bolivia Gets in Line," *New York Times*, August 24, 1964, p. 26.

241 Quoted in Rebecca Jarvis Scott, *U.S. Foreign Assistance to Bolivia: 1952–1964* (Bachelor of Arts Honors Thesis, Radcliffe College, 1971), p. 55.

242 Walter LaFeber, "Latin American Policy," in Robert A. Divine, ed., *Exploring the Johnson Years* (Austin: University of Texas Press, 1981), p. 73.

243 Agee, *Inside the Company: CIA Diary*, p. 323.

244 Ibid., pp. 331, 339.

245 See *Hispanic American Report*, Vol. XVII, No. 9, November for September 1964, pp. 847–848.

246 "Uruguay Breaks Tie with Cuba; Mexico Only Holdout in O.A.S.," *New York Times*, September 9, 1964, p. 1. A U.S. Embassy transmission to the State Department in February 1964 noted that no Uruguayan registered ships had called at Cuban ports since October 23, 1962, and commented favorably on the fact "that Uruguay failed to insist on carrying some percentage of the recent Cuban sugar-rice deal in Uruguayan vessels." American Embassy, Montevideo (Wymberly DeR. Coerr) to Department of State, Airgram, Subject: "Shipping to Cuba: Foreign Assistance Act," February 8, 1964, No. A-452, *DFOIA*.

247 Personal Interview: Department of State official, Washington, D.C., July 13, 1973 (my emphasis). The respondent was a Central American/Caribbean analyst in the Department's Bureau of Intelligence and Research with a special interest in Cuba during 1959 to 1961.

248 See Arthur K. Smith, Jr., *Mexico and the Cuban Revolution: Foreign Policy-Making in Mexico Under President Adolfo Lopez Mateos (1958–1964)* (Ph.D. dissertation, Cornell University, September 1970), pp. 162–163.

249 Edwin M. Martin interview: *The John F. Kennedy Oral History Collection*, p. 33.

250 See Dan Kurzman, "High Mexicans See U.N. Best Weapon Against Castroism," *Washington Post*, March 4, 1964, p. A14.

251 See Tad Szulc, "Exporting the Cuban Revolution," in Plank, ed., *Cuba and the United States: Long Term Perspectives*, p. 85.

252 Gerry Robichaud, "Mexicans and CIA Team Up to Halt Castro Propaganda," *Washington Post*, September 13, 1964, p. A28.

253 Memorandum for McGeorge Bundy, White House, from William H. Brubeck, Executive Secretary, Department of State, May 27, 1963, Subject: "Movement of Personnel to and from Cuba," Papers of President Kennedy, National Security Files, Cuba, General (Folder), NSF/Cuba/General, 5/16/63–5/31/63, Box 38, *Kennedy Presidential Library*.

254 Agee, *Inside the Company: CIA Diary*, pp. 531, 266.

255 See, for example, Thomas C. Mann interview, *The John F. Kennedy Oral History Collection*, p. 33.

256 Dan Kurzman, "Relations of U.S. and Mexico Viewed as Warmer Than Ever," *Washington Post*, March 9, 1964, p. 33.

257 Memorandum of Conversation, Department of State, February 21, 1964, Subject: "Meeting between President Johnson and President Lopez Mateos."

258 Personal Interview: Central Intelligence Agency official, Washington, D.C., May 21 1976.

259 Personal Interview: Department of State official, Washington, D.C., July 13, 1973.

260 Personal Interview: Department of State official, Washington, D.C., July 2, 1973. The respondent was a senior economic affairs official in the Latin American area between 1960 and 1962, and a U.S. delegate to the OAS from 1964 to 1969.

261 Personal Interview: Department of State official, Washington, D.C., July 11, 1973.

262 Personal Interview: Department of State official, Washington, D.C., June 14, 1973.

263 Personal Interview: Department of State official, Washington, D.C., June 21, 1973.

264 "Minutes of the 'Bissell Meeting' at the Council on Foreign Relations, January 8, 1968," reprinted in Marchetti and Marks, *The CIA and the Cult of Intelligence*, p. 386. Also see Laurence Stern, "CIA: Silent Partner in Foreign Policy," *Washington Post*, September 29, 1974, p. C3.

5. The United States against Cuba 1961–1968: politics of global economic blockade

1 Personal Interview: Department of State official, Washington, D.C., July 13, 1973, and June 6, 1975.

2 See, for example, Robin Renwick, *Economic Sanctions* (Cambridge: Center for International Studies, Harvard University, 1981); Sidney Weintraub, ed., *Economic Coercion and U.S. Foreign Policy* (Boulder: Westview Press, 1982); Donald L. Losman, *International Economic Sanctions* (Albuquerque: University of New Mexico Press, 1979): Margaret P. Doxey, *Economic Sanctions and International Enforcement* (New York: Oxford University Press, 1980); Gunnar Adler-Karlsson, *Western Economic Warfare 1947–1967* (Stockholm: Almqvist & Wiksell, 1968); James Barber, "Economic Sanctions as a Policy Instrument," *International Affairs*, Vol. 55, No, 3, July 1979, pp. 367–384; James Barber and Michael Spicer, "Sanctions Against South Africa," *International Affairs*, Vol. 55, No. 3, July 1979, pp. 385–401; Johan Galtung, "On the Effects of International Economic Sanctions with Examples from the Case of Rhodesia," *World Politics*, Vol. 19, No. 3, April 1967, pp. 378–416; Anna P. Schreiber, "Economic Coercion as an Instrument of Foreign Policy," *World Politics*, Vol. 25, No. 3, April 1973, pp. 387–413.

3 Argentine exports to the Soviet Union increased fourfold between 1979 and 1980. During 1981, the Soviet market absorbed 77 percent of Argentina's crop exports. See Theodore Shabad, "Argentine-Russian Trade Is Surging as Soviet Takes 77% of Crop Exports," *New York Times*, April 18, 1982, p. 18.

4 Margaret P. Doxey, "Sanctions Revisited," *International Journal*, Vol. XXXI, No. 1, Winter 1975–76, p. 66.

5 Wilkins, *The Maturing of Multinational Enterprise: American Business Abroad from 1914 to 1970*, p. 331 (Table X11.3).

6 Vernon, *Sovereignty at Bay*, p. 68 (Table 3.2).

7 Ernest Mandel, *Europe vs. America* (New York: Monthly Review Press, 1974), p. 30.

8 Joyce Kolko, *America and the Crisis of World Capitalism* (Boston: Beacon Press, 1974), pp. 56–57.

9 Ernest Mandel, *Late Capitalism* (London: Verso Editions, 1978), pp. 335–336.

10 Kolko, *The Roots on American Foreign Policy*, p. 56.

11 Mandel, *Europe vs. America*, pp. 16, 18. In contrast to Mandel's focus on intercapitalist trade conflicts, other studies emphasize direct investment competition. See, for example, Bob Rowthorn, "Imperialism in the Seventies-Unity or Rivalry?," *New Left Review*, No. 69, September–October 1971, pp. 31–51.

12 A further challenge to U.S. global dominance was the growth of anti-capitalist nationalism in Asia, Africa, and Latin America which, at least potentially, threatened access to important export markets and to raw materials on which the American domestic economy was increasingly dependent. An indication of the importance attributed to these markets is reflected in the growth in the value of U.S. agricultural exports to the Third World, which increased from $2.9 billion in 1950 to $6.9 billion in 1966. Kolko, *The Roots of American Foreign Policy*, p. 57.

13 For detailed studies of the superpower confrontation and the Kennedy administration debate over policy options, see Herbert Din-

erstein, *The Making of a Missile Crisis: October 1962* (Baltimore & London: The Johns Hopkins University Press, 1976); Graham T. Allison, *Essence of Decision: Explaining the Cuban Missile Crisis* (Boston: Little, Brown and Co., 1971); Elie Abel, *The Missile Crisis* (New York: Bantam Books, 1966); Henry Pachter, *Collision Course: The Cuban Missile Crisis and Coexistence* (New York: Praeger Publishers, 1963).

14 See Richard J. Walton, *Cold War and Counterrevolution: The Foreign Policy of John F. Kennedy* (Baltimore: Pelican Books, 1972), pp. 107–113. A recent study concluded that the Cuban Missile Crisis had little or no effect on the outcome of the November 1962 congressional elections: "The historian cannot identify one election in 1962 decided by voter reaction to the missile crisis – not a single outcome where the Cuban issue made the difference between victory and defeat." Thomas G. Patterson and William J. Brophy, "October Missiles and November Elections: The Cuban Missile Crisis and American Politics, 1962," *Journal of American History,* Vol. 73, No. 1, June 1986, p. 118.

15 See Allison, *Essence of Decision,* p. 195; Robert F. Kennedy, *Thirteen Days: A Memoir of the Cuban Missile Crisis* (New York: Signet Books, 1969), p. 53; Barton J. Bernstein, "The Cuban Missile Crisis," in Lynn H. Miller and Ronald W. Pruessen, eds., *Reflections on the Cold War* (Philadelphia: Temple University Press, 1974), pp. 131–132.

16 Transcripts, Cuban Missile Crisis Meetings, October 16, 1962, President's Office Files, *Kennedy Presidential Library,* First meeting, 11.50 A.M. to 12.57 P.M., pp. 13, 25; second meeting 6.30 P.M. to 7.45 P.M., pp. 8, 19, 43.

17 Ibid., second meeting, pp. 9–10, 27, 44–48; first meeting, p. 27.

18 Ibid., second meeting, p. 12.

19 Thomas G. Paterson et al., *American Foreign Policy: A History/since 1900* (Lexington: D. C. Heath & Co., 1983), p. 545. Sorenson's assessment is contained in his memoir, Sorenson, *Kennedy,* p. 678.

20 Theodore Sorenson on the Missile Crisis, October 17, 1962, President's Office Files, Box 115, *Kennedy Presidential Library.*

21 See Kennedy, *Thirteen Days,* p. 34.

22 Sorenson, *Kennedy,* p. 688.

23 See Barton Bernstein, "A New Look at the Cuban Missile Crisis," *Los Angeles Times,* October 27, 1985, Part IV, p. 3.

24 See Marc Trachtenberg, "The Influence of Nuclear Weapons in the Cuban Missile Crisis," *International Security,* Vol. 10, No. 1, Summer 1985, p. 157; Kennedy, *Thirteen Days,* p. 55; Branch and Crile, "The Kennedy Vendetta: How the CIA Waged a Silent War Against Cuba," p. 62.

25 Special National Intelligence Estimate, The Military Buildup in Cuba, Number 85-3-62, *DFOIA.*

26 See Bernstein, "The Cuban Missile Crisis," pp. 121–123.

27 See Walter Pincus, "Standing at the Brink of Nuclear War," *Washington Post,* July 25, 1985, pp. A1, A10.

28 Trachtenberg, "The Influence of Nuclear Weapons in the Cuban Missile Crisis," p. 163.
29 Memorandum for the NSC Executive Committee from Harlan Cleveland, Subject: "Cuba," Draft, Secret, November 12, 1962, File: Cuba, General, 11/11/62–11/15/62, National Security Files-Cuba, Box 37, *Kennedy Presidential Library*. For a detailed analysis of the Soviet position, see Leslie Dewart, "The Cuban Crisis Revisited," *Studies on the Left*, Vol. 5, No. 2, Spring 1965, pp. 15–40.
30 See Connell-Smith, *The Inter-American System*, p. 237.
31 See Oliver M. Lee, *Initial World Reaction to U.S. Quarantine of Cuba*, Washington, D.C.: Congressional Research Service, Legislative Research Service, Foreign Affairs Division, JX1428, October 29, 1962, p. 11.
32 Statement by Edwin M. Martin, Assistant Secretary of State for Inter-American Affairs, in U.S. Congress, Senate, *Cuban Refugee Problems*, Part 1, pp. 9–10.
33 State Department statement on Current Cuban Policy, From Bromley Smith to the White House (cleared by McGeorge Bundy), June 1, 1963, File: Cuba 1/63–3/63, President's Office Files, Box 115, *Kennedy Presidential Library*.
34 Edwin M. Martin, Assistant Secretary of State for Inter-American Affairs, "Cuba, Latin America and Communism," Address before the Los Angeles World Council, Los Angeles, California, Septemer 20, 1963, reprinted in *Department of State Bulletin*, Vol. XLV, No. 1268, October 14, 1963, p. 575.
35 Memorandum for McGeorge Bundy from the White House, February 15, 1961. File: National Security Action Memorandum No. 19, NSF/NSC, Box 328, *Kennedy Presidential Library*.
36 Memorandum for the President from Dean Rusk, Subject: "Questions Arising from Senator Smather's Recommendation that Remaining Exports from Cuba to the United States be embargoed," February 24, 1961, File: Cuba-Security 1961, President's Office Files, Cuba, Box 114A, *Kennedy Presidential Library*.
37 Memorandum, Subject: "Cuba-Total Blockade," May 19, 1961, Office of the Secretary to the Treasury, Department of the Treasury, *DFOIA*.
38 Memorandum for the Members of the NSC Planning Group from Henry M. Fowler, Subject: "Suggesting Item for Discussion: Application of Severe Economic and Other Sanctions Cuba," File: Cuba, General 6/61–12/61, National Security Files-Cuba, Box 35, *Kennedy Presidential Library*.
39 U.S. Congress, House, Committee on Interstate and Foreign Commerce, *Trade with Cuba*, 87th Congress, 1st Session, August 29 and September 1, 1961 (Washington, D.C.: U.S. Government Printing Office, 1961), pp. 2, 3, 5, 26–27, 32.
40 Foreign Assets Control, Memorandum, Subject: "Proposed Embargo on Trade with Cuba," December 15, 1961, No. 40784, Department of the Treasury, *DFOIA*.
41 Ibid.
42 Foreign Assets Control, Memorandum for the Files, Subject:

"Embargo on Trade with Cuba under Foreign Assistance Act," December 15, 1961, Department of the Treasury, *DFOIA*.

43 Statement submitted in executive session by Luther Hodges, Secretary of Commerce, on "The Export Act of 1949," in U.S. Congress, House Select Committee on Export Control, *Investigation and Study of the Administration, Operations and Enforcement of the Export Control Act of 1949, and Related Acts*, 87th Congress, 1st Session, October 25, 26, and 30, and December 5, 6, 7, and 8, 1961 (Washington, D.C.: U.S. Government Printing Office, 1962), p. 17. The Kennedy administration also imposed new stringent restrictions on U.S. citizens travelling to Cuba. See E. W. Kenworthy, "Travel to Cuba Sharply Curbed Under U.S. Order," *New York Times*, January 17, 1961, p. 3.

44 See U.S. Congress, House, *Investigation and Study of the Administration, Operation, and Enforcement of the Export Control Act of 1949, and Related Acts*, p. 17.

45 Jack N. Behrman, Assistant Secretary of International Affairs, Department of Commerce, in ibid., p. 378.

46 Quoted in *Hispanic American Report*, Vol. XIV, No. 10. December for October 1961, p. 948.

47 See "Castro's Secret Supply Line," *U.S. News & World Report*, October 2, 1961, p. 58; "U.S. Penalized 18 on Cuban Supplies," *New York Times*, December 21, 1961, p. 16; "Illegal Transshipments to Cuba Uncovered," *Foreign Commerce Weekly*, Vol. 67, No. 2, January 8, 1962, p. 63.

48 "Tightening the Embargo on Cuba," *Business Week*, January 6, 1962, p. 45.

49 *Hispanic American Report*, Vol XIV, No. 6, August for June 1961, p. 501. Also see "Cuba Asks Bid on Blackstrap Molasses; Embargo Threat May Scare U.S. Dealers," *Wall Street Journal*, January 18, 1961, p. 11.

50 "Tightening the Embargo on Cuba," p. 45.

51 U.S. Congress, Senate, Committee on Foreign Relations, *Executive Sessions of the Senate Foreign Relations Committe, Vol. XIII, Part 2*, pp. 658–659.

52 "U.S. to Ask Allies: Halt Cuba Trade," *New York Herald Tribune*, February 19, 1962, p. 1. There was a relative lack of concern among policymakers over Cuba's trade with Latin America because with the exception of approximately $10 million barter trade with Chile, the rest of its trade with the region was inconsequential. See U.S. Department of Commerce *Overseas Business Reports*, March 1964, p. 2.

53 See W. Granger Blair, "U.S. Bids NATO End Trade in Strategic Goods with Cuba," *New York Times*, February 21, 1962, p. 4; "U.S. Asks Atlantic Council to Support Cuba Embargo," *London Times*, February 21, 1962, p. 9.

54 U.S. Congress, Senate, *Alleged Assassination Plots Involving Foreign Leaders*, p. 274.

55 Robert Hurwitch interview, *The John F. Kennedy Oral History Collection*, pp. 164–166.

56 Personal Interview: Department of State official, Washington, D.C., July 13, 1973 and June 6, 1975.

57 See Max Frankel, "West's Ships Major Carriers," *New York Times*, September 28, 1962, p. 5; "Our Allies Still Trade with Cuba," *New York Herald Tribune*, September 16, 1962, p. 41.

58 See "Japan's Increasing Trade With Cuba Worries U.S.," *The Japan Times*, June 28, 1964, p. 1. Also see "Japanese Act on Sugar," *Christian Science Monitor*, October 6, 1962, p. 12; Lewis Gulick, "Japan No. 1 Non-Red '62 Trader with Cuba," *Washington Post*, August 26, 1963, p. A13; Appendix II, Table 1.

59 See "Japan's Increasing Trade with Cuba Worries U.S.," p. 1; Appendix II, Table 1.

60 Quoted in A. M. Rosenthal, "Japan Will Shun Trade with Cuba," *New York Times*, September 26, 1962, p. 7.

61 Quoted in U.S. Congress, House, Select Committee on Export Control, *Investigation and Enforcement of the Export Control Act of 1949, and Related Acts, Part 3*, 87th Congress, 2nd Session, September 13 and 14, October 2 and 3, 1962 (Washington, D.C.: U.S. Government Printing Office, 1962), p. 808.

62 C. Harvey Gardner, "The Japanese in Cuba," *Caribbean Studies*, Vol. 12, No. 2, July 1972, p. 70. Also see U.S. Central Intelligence Agency, Intelligence Handbook, *Cuba: Foreign Trade*, A(ER) 75–69, July 1975, p. 10 (Table 6).

63 Boyer, *Canada and Cuba*, p. 202.

64 See "Not Paid for Goods; Cash Deals with Cuba New," *Toronto Globe and Mail*, November 1, 1962, p. 8.

65 Boyer, *Canada and Cuba*, p. 202.

66 Ibid., p. 211.

67 Address by Prime Minister John G. Diefenbaker, Kiwanis International Convention, Toronto, July 3, 1961, quoted in Canadian Department of External Affairs, Information Division, *Hemisphere and Global Problems*, No. 61/7.

68 See Peyton V. Lyon, *Canada in World Affairs, Vol. XII, 1961–1963* (Toronto: Oxford University Press, 1968), p. 413.

69 Ibid., p. 416.

70 Boyer, *Canada and Cuba*, p. 211.

71 See "Canadians Discount Their Cuban Trade," *New York Times*, February 18, 1962, p. 27; "Not Paid for Goods: Cash Deals with Cuba New," p. 8.

72 Quoted in Canadian Department of Foreign Affairs, Monthly Bulletin, *Canada*, Vol. XIV, No. 2, February 1962, p. 78. Also see "Canada Still Refuses to End Cuban Trade," *Washington Post*, February 3, 1962, p. A9.

73 See "U.S. Asks Atlantic Council to Support Cuba Embargo," p. 9; "Canada's Trade To Continue," *London Times*, February 21, 1962, p. 9.

74 Quoted in Lyon, *Canada in World Affairs, Vol. XII, 1961–1963*, p. 415.

75 See Boyer, *Canada and Cuba*, p. 225.

76 See "Bootleg U.S. Goods Taken Off Cuba Ship in Canada," *New*

York Herald Tribune, October 4, 1962, p. 10; "Cuba Ship Sails," *Toronto Globe and Mail,* October 5, 1962, p. 1.

77 "Continue Trade with Havana, Ottawa States," *Toronto Globe and Mail,* October 5, 1962, p. 1.

78 Boyer, *Canada and Cuba,* pp. 392–393.

79 See Ogelsby, "Canada and Latin America," p. 178.

80 Boyer, *Canada and Cuba,* p. 366.

81 Ibid., pp. 366–367.

82 Personal Interview: Department of State official, Washington, D.C., June 20, 1973. The respondent was a Latin American Desk Officer during the early 1960s and a senior Department OAS official between 1966 and 1972.

83 On the U.S. position, see Harlan Cleveland, Assistant Secretary of State for International Organization Affairs, in U.S. Congress, Senate, Committee on Appropriations, *Foreign Assistance and Related Agencies Appropriations for 1962,* 87th Congress, 1st Session, September 1, 1961 (Washington, D.C.: U.S. Government Printing Office, 1961) p. 488; Richard N. Gardner, Deputy Assistant Secretary of State for International Affairs, in U.S. Congress, House, Committee on Foreign Affairs, *The International Development and Security Act, Part III,* 87th Congress, 1st Session, June 26, 27, 28, 29, and July 6, 1961 (Washington, D.C.: U.S. Government Printing Office, 1961), p. 1319.

84 John G. Stroessinger, *The United Nations and the Superpowers* (New York: Random House, 1965), pp. 157, 161. Secretary of State Rusk told a House subcommittee in May 1963 that the Cuba project was opposed "at the very first meeting in the spring of 1961 and at every stage since." U.S. Congress, House, Committee on Appropriations, Subcommittee on Foreign Operations Appropriations, *Foreign Operations Appropriations for 1964, Part 2,* 88th Congress, 1st Session, May 14, 1963 (Washington, D.C.: U.S. Government Printing Office, 1963), p. 35.

85 U.S. Congress, Senate, Committee on Foreign Relations, Subcommittee on International Organization Affairs, *United Nations Special Fund,* 88th Congress, 1st Session, February 18, 1963 (Washington, D.C.: U.S. Government Printing Office, 1963), p. 21. On Congressional opposition to the Special Fund provisions for Cuba, see the comments of Representative John S. Monagan, *Congressional Record-House,* 87th Congress, 1st Session, Vol. 107, Part 7, June 7, 1961, p. 9693 and Senator Joseph M. Montoya, *Congressional Record-Senate,* 88th Congress, 1st Session, Vol. 109, Part 3, March 4, 1963, p. 3390.

86 U.S. Congress, Senate, *United Nations Special Fund,* especially pp. 22–30.

87 U.S. Congress, Senate, *Executive Sessions of the Senate Foreign Relations Committee, Vol. XIII, Part, 2,* p. 658.

88 From Study on "Free-World Shipping in the Cuban Trade," January 1 through August 31, 1962, prepared by the Maritime Administration, U.S. Department of Commerce, in U.S. Congress, House, *Investigation and Enforcement of the Export Control Act of 1949, and*

Related Acts, Part 3, p. 816. Also see Frankel, "West's Ships Major Carriers," p. 5.

89 Quoted in "Our Allies Still Trade with Cuba," *New York Herald Tribune*, September 16, 1962, p. 41. Also see Philip Geyelin, "U.S. Seeks to Bolster Ban on Cuban Trade by Persuading Allies to Impose Ship Curbs," *Wall Street Journal*, October 5, 1962, p. 3.

90 Quoted in "U.S. Fails to Curb Allies Over Cuba," *New York Times*, September 16, 1962, p. 24.

91 Sam Pope Brewer, "Shipping to Cuba Halted by Turks at Urging of U.S.," *New York Times*, September 28, 1962, pp. 1, 5.

92 See Flora Lewis, "German Shippers Would Accept Western Ban on Trade to Cuba," *Washington Post*, September 24, 1962, p. A9.

93 Quoted in "British Reluctant on Cuba Trade," *New York Herald Tribune*, September 26, 1962, p. A12.

94 "W. Germany Acting to Curb Cuba Shipping," *Washington Post*, September 27, 1962, p. B2.

95 Philip Geyelin, "U.S. Seeks to Bolster Ban on Cuban Trade by Persuading Allies to Impose Ship Curbs," p. 3; "British Reluctant on Cuba Trade," p. A12.

96 "Britain Has No Plan to Bar Cuba Shipping," *Washington Post*, September 27, 1962, p. B2.

97 Quoted in Stewart Hensley, "Rusk Reported Unable to Get Norway to Halt Ships to Cuba," *Washington Post*, September 25, 1962, p. A11.

98 Ibid.

99 Quoted in *New York Times*, October 2, 1962, p. 5. Also see "U.S. Will Bar Ships Hauling Arms to Cuba," *Journal of Commerce*, October 4, 1962, p. 1.

100 Robert H. Estebrook, "Nato Indecisive on Cuba Shipping," *Washington Post*, September 28, 1962, p. A16.

101 Ibid.

102 U.S. Congress, Senate, Committee on Foreign Relations and Committee on Armed Services, *Situation in Cuba*, 87th Congress, 2nd Session, September 17, 1962 (Washington, D.C.: U.S. Government Printing Office, 1962), p. 39.

103 Department of State, Telegram, Confidential, To All ARA Diplomatic Posts except Kingston and Port of Spain, Circular 588, October 3, 1962, 937.7300/10-362, *DFOIA*. Also see Tad Szulc, "U.S. Ports to Bar Ships That Carry Arms Aid to Cuba," *New York Times*, October 4, 1962, pp. 1, 11. The new regulations were drafted by an interagency committee chaired by the State Department's legal advisor Abraham L. Chayes.

104 See "U.S. to Bar Russian Ships Engaging in Cuba Trade," *Journal of Commerce*, October 5, 1962, pp. 1, 19; "U.S. Names Names in Fight on Cuban Trade," *Business Week*, October 6, 1962, p. 34.

105 U.S. Congress, House, *Investigation and Enforcement of the Export Control Act of 1949, and Related Acts, Part 3*, p. 809.

106 Ibid., p. 892.

107 Ibid., pp. 891, 900.

108 Seth S. King, "British Plan No Law Barring Routes to Cuba but Will Help U.S. Otherwise," *New York Times*, October 5, 1962, p. 15.

109 See testimony of Reginald A. Bourdon, Assistant Legislative Director, American Maritime Association, and Peter M. McGavin, Executive Secretary-Treasurer, Maritime Trades Department, AFL-CIO, in U.S. Congress, House, *Investigation and Enforcement of the Export Control Act of 1949, and Related Acts, Part 3*, pp. 737, 765–766.

110 See Walter Hamshar, "Dock Workers Won't Handle Red Cargoes," *New York Herald Tribune*, October 9, 1962, p. 25; Mary Hornaday, "Ship Sanctions on Cuba Supported," *Christian Science Monitor*, January 5, 1963, p. 15.

111 "U.S. Shipping Wins Round on Cuba Ban," *Journal of Commerce*, October 17, 1962, p. 1. Also see George Panitz, "Cuban Ship Ban Facing Crucial Test," *Journal of Commerce*, October 16, 1962, pp. 1, 21.

112 See George Panitz, "Shipowner Raps World Cargo Curbs," *Journal of Commece*, October 19, 1962, p. 7; "British Shipowners Oppose Bans to Cuba Trade," *New York Times*, October 12, 1962, p. 11.

113 "More Nations Weigh Cuban Trade Curbs," *Journal of Commerce*, October 9, 1962, pp. 1, 15.

114 "Liberia Acts to Curb Cuba Trade, Tightens Controls on its Ships," *Wall Street Journal*, October 18, 1962, p. 15.

115 Ibid.

116 American Embassy, Oslo, to Department of State, Airgram, Subject: "Shipping to Cuba: Prime Minister's Statement in Storting (includes Embassy translation of text of Prime Minister Gerhardsen's statement on shipping to Cuba made October 16)," October 17, 1962, No. A-201, 937.7300/10-1762, *DFOIA*.

117 Department of State, Telegram. To London, Athens, Bonn, Oslo, Madrid, Rome, The Hague, Beirut, Rabat, Paris, January 3, 1963, Confidential, 937.7300/1-1163, *DFOIA*. Also see Lewis Gulick, "Cuba Trade Perils Aid, U.S. Warns," *Washington Post*, January 12, 1963, p. A6.

118 Department of State, Telegram, January 3, 1963.

119 U.S. Congress, Senate, Committee on Foreign Relations, Briefing on Cuban Developments, January 25, 1962, Record Group 46: Records of the U.S. Senate, Committee on Foreign Relations, *National Archives of the United States*, p. 17.

120 Memorandum for the President from Dean Rusk, Subject: "Free World Shipping to Cuba," April 17, 1963, National Security Files, Vice President Security File, Box 4, Folder: National Security Council (III), *Johnson Presidential Library*.

121 McGeorge Bundy, White House, National Security Action. Memorandum No. 220, Subject: "U.S. Government Shipments by Foreign Flag Vessels in the Cuban Trade." To Secretaries of State, Defense, Agriculture, Commerce, Administrators of AID and GSA, February 5, 1963, *DFOIA*.

122 Max Frankel, "U.S. Denies Its Cargoes to Ships in Cuba Trade," *New York Times*, February 7, 1963, pp. 1, 2.

123 State Department statement on Current Cuban Policy, June 1, 1963.

124 See Department of State to Madrid Embassy, Airgram, Secret, January 24, 1964, Ref: CA-7325, *DFOIA;* U.S. Department of Commerce, Maritime Administration, *List of Free World and Polish Flag Vessels Arriving in Cuba Since January 1, 1963*, Report No.112, February 22, 1971; U.S. Department of Commerce, Maritime Administration, *List of Free World and Polish Flag Vessels Arriving in Cuba Since January 1, 1963*, Report No. 128, September 23, 1975.

125 U.S. Congress, Senate, Briefing by Secretary of State on the World Situation, January 11, 1963, Record Group 46, *National Archives of the United States*, p. 62.

126 William S. Gaud, Agency for International Development, in U.S. Congress, House, Committee on Appropriations, Subcommittee on Foreign Operations Appropriations, *Foreign Operations Appropriations for 1964, Part 4*, 88th Congress, 1st Session, July 17, 25, 29, 30; August 14, 1963 (Washington, D.C.: U.S. Government Printing Office, 1963), p. 1330.

127 See "Greeks Plan Stiff Penalties for Vessels in Cuba Trade," *New York Times*, September 17, 1963, p. 5; "Greece Bans Cuba Cargo," *New York Times*, September 25, 1963, p. 9.

128 Edwin M. Martin, Assistant Secretary of State for Inter-American Affairs, September 20, quoted in *Department of State Bulletin*, Vol. XLIX, No. 1268, October 14, 1963, p. 576.

129 Henry Raymont, "U.S. Allies Resist Strong Cuba Curb," *New York Times*, July 16, 1963, pp. 1, 12.

130 Department of State (Secretary Rusk) to Madrid Embassy, Telegram, November 14, 1963, Madrid Telegram 1733, STR 10 Cuba, XRAU 6, Cuba, *DFOIA*.

131 Personal Interview: White House Staff official, New Jersey, May 24, 1976.

132 See Tad Szulc, "U.S. Halts Flow of Funds to Cuba at Guantánamo," *New York Times*, February 8, 1964, p. 1.

133 Quoted in James Nelson Goodsell, "U.S. Acts to Blunt Castro's Maneuver," *Christian Science Monitor*, February 10, 1964, p. 1.

134 See James Nelson Goodsell, "Cuban Move Linked to Treaty Strategy," *Christian Science Monitor*, February 8, 1964, p. 1.

135 See Henry Raymont, "U.S. Presses Plan for Guantánamo,," *New York Times*, February 11, 1964, p. 14; Richard L. Strout, "Guantánamo Crisis Sparks 'Tough Line'," *Christian Science Monitor*, February 8, 1964, p. 1. Senator Barry Goldwater, nominated as the Republican candidate for president in the November 1964 election, declared that Cuba "must be sealed off" by a naval blockade. Quoted in Charles Mohr, "'Seal Off' Cuba, Goldwater Says," *New York Times*, February 9, 1964, p. 59. On the two White House "crisis" meetings, see Tad Szulc, "Cuba Cuts Water to Guantánamo; U.S. Sees a Crisis; Johnson Briefed," *New York Times*, February 7, 1964, p. 1; Tad Szulc, "Cuba and Guantánamo," *New York Times*, February 13, 1964, p. 2.

136 See Max Frankel, "U.S. Halts Flow of Funds to Cuba at Guantán-

amo; Sees End of Peril," *New York Times,* February 9, 1964, pp. 1, 27; Szulc, "Cuba and Guantánamo," p. 2.

137 See Szulc, "U.S. Halts Flow of Funds to Cuba at Guantánamo," pp. 1, 3.

138 See Raymont, "U.S. Presses Plan for Guantánamo," p. 14.

139 See Szulc, "Cuba and Guantánamo," p. 2.

140 Ibid. The materials in the folder on the "Water Crisis" at the Johnson Presidential Library yielded nothing in the way of substantive information on U.S. responses and policy deliberations. It was almost exclusively composed of chronologies of events, newspaper clippings, and the like.

141 Max Frankel, "President Asks Review on Cuba," *New York Times,* December 9, 1963, pp. 1, 2.

142 Personal Interview: Department of State official, Washington, D.C., July 13, 1973 and June 6, 1975.

143 Memorandum for McGeorge Bundy from Gordon Chase, The White House, February 29, 1964, Subject: "Lard to Cuba," National Security Files, Aides Files, Box 1, McGeorge Bundy-Memos to President, Vol. 1, 11/63–2/64, *Johnson Presidential Library;* Memorandum for the President from McGeorge Bundy, The White House, February 29, 1964; Fred Farris, "Lard to Cuba: Sudden Block by President," *New York Herald Tribune,* February 29, 1964, p. 1; "U.S. Curbing Sale of Lard to Cuba," *New York Times,* February 29, 1964, p. 6.

144 See "Johnson to Continue Pressures on Cuba," *New York Times,* May 7, 1964, pp. 1, 9. Also see Max Frankel, "U.S. Warns Castro on Firing at Planes," *New York Times,* April 21, 1964, pp. 1, 8.

145 Memorandum to Holders of NSAM 220 from McGeorge Bundy, The White House, Subject: "Amendment to NSAM 220 of February 5, 1963, Relating to United States Government Shipments by Foreign Flag Vessels in Cuban Trade," December 16, 1963, *DFOIA;* Thomas C. Mann (ARA), through Secretary of State, to Governor Harriman, Subject: "Your Meeting with Maritime Trade Union Officials to Discuss Shipping to Cuba," February 28, 1964, Confidential, *DFOIA.* Also see statement "U.S. Approves Amendment to Cuban Shipping Policy," December 16, reprinted in *Department of State Bulletin,* Vol. L, No. 1280, January 6, 1964, p. 10.

146 Henry Raymont, "U.S. Revises Rules on Shipping to Cut Trade with Cuba," *New York Times,* December 17, 1963, pp. 1, 20.

147 Department of State to Madrid Embassy, January 24, 1964.

148 Department of State (Assistant Secretary Ball) to Rome Embassy, Telegram, May 28, 1964, Confidential, No. 2745, *DFOIA.*

149 Department of State to Hague Embassy, Telegram, March 25, 1964, Secret, No. 2558, *DFOIA.*

150 Department of State, Memorandum of Conversation. Subject: "Moroccan Ships to Cuba," March 4, 1964, Confidential. Participants: Ali Bengelloun, Ambassador to Morocco; Henry J. Tasca, Deputy Assistant Secretary for African Affairs; James J. Blake, Deputy Director, Office of North African Affairs; Stephen H. McClintoc, OIC, Moroccan Affairs. STR 10-Cuba, *DFOIA.*

151 Beirut Embassy (Leslie C. Tihany, First Secretary for Ambassador)

to Department of State, Airgram, Subject: "Amendment to Cuban Shipping Policy," January 15, 1964, No. A-471, *DFOIA*.

152 Department of State (Secretary Rusk) to Beirut Embassy, Telegram, June 16, 1964, Confidential, No. 1158, *DFOIA*.

153 See U.S. Department of Commerce, *List of Free World and Polish Flag Vessels Arriving in Cuba since January 1, 1963*, Report No. 128.

154 See "Spain to Keep its Ships Out of Trade with Cuba," *Journal of Commerce*, February 17, 1965, p. 23.

155 See U.S. Department of Commerce, *List of Free World and Polish Flag Vessels Arriving in Cuba Since January 1, 1963*, Report No. 128.

156 Department of State (Assistant Secretary Ball) to Madrid Embassy, Telegram, December 17, 1963, Madrid 224, Secret AV9 Cuba-SP, *DFOIA*.

157 Department of State to Madrid Embassy, January 24, 1964; Memorandum for the President from Department of State, Visit of Prime Minister Alex Douglas-Home, February 12–13, 1964, Background paper: "Cuba, UK a Key Country," Briefing Book (Thirty Six Papers), February 5–7, 1964, Collection: National Security Files, Country File, Europe and USSR, United Kingdom, Box 213, Folder: United Kingdom, PM Home Visit Briefing Book 2/12–13/64, *Johnson Presidential Library*.

158 Department of State to Madrid Embassy, January 24, 1964.

159 Memorandum for the President from McGeorge Bundy, Subject: "Basic Talking Points for the President with (Chancellor) Erhard," December 27, 1963, Collection: National Security Files, Aides Files, Box 1, Folder: McGeorge Bundy-Memos to President, Vol. 1, 11/63–2/64 (Also in Collection: Confidential File CO, Box 8, Folder: CO 92 Germany, 1963–1964), *Johnson Presidential Library*.

160 See Rowland Evans and Robert Novak, *Lyndon B. Johnson: The Exercise of Power* (New York: New American Library, 1966), p. 389.

161 Memorandum for the President from McGeorge Bundy, May 15, 1964, Collection: National Security Files, Aides Files, Box 1, Folder: McGeorge Bundy–Memos to President, Vol. 4, 5/1–27/64, *Johnson Presidential Library*.

162 Oslo Embassy to Department of State (Secretary Rusk), Telegram, February 11, 1964, Confidential, Oslo 473, STR 10-Cuba, *DFOIA*.

163 Department of State to Madrid Embassy, January 24, 1964.

164 Philip Geyelin, *Lyndon B. Johnson and his World* (New York: Frederick A. Praeger, 1966), p. 92. Also see Max Frankel, "U.S. Is Pressing Cuban Embargo," *New York Times*, February 10, 1964, p. 2. In mid-March 1964, for example, senior State Department official Walt W. Rostow exhorted a London conference of 250 business executives to pressure or show support for European government reappraisals of their commercial relation with Cuba. See "U.S. Aide Asks Europeans to Halt Trade with Cuba," *New York Times*, March 11, 1964, p. 2.

165 "American Bid to Stop Cuba Trade," *London Times*, January 22, 1964, p. 12.

166 Quoted in Murrey Marder, "Rusks Raps U.S. Allies for Trade with Castro," *Washington Post*, January 23, 1964, p. A1.

167 Department of State (Secretary Rusk) to Paris Embassy, Telegram, February 25, 1964, Confidential, Paris 1210, STR 10-Cuba, *DFOIA*.
168 See Tad Szulc, "U.S. Faces Problem as Cuba Trade Rises Despite Quarantine," *New York Times*, January 28, 1964, p. 6. Cuba earned approximately $300 million from sugar exports in 1963. Ibid.
169 Edwin L. Dale, Jr., "Dispute Grows over Western Trade with the Communist Bloc," *New York Times*, March 1, 1964, p. E3.
170 Personal Interview: Department of State official, Washington, D.C., July 13, 1973 and June 6, 1975.
171 See Clyde H. Farnsworth, "Belgium Resents U.S. Order Barring Sale to Cuba," *New York Times*, February 7, 1968, p. 3.
172 Quoted in "Comment by Company Here," *New York Times*, February 7, 1968, p. 3.
173 Under Secretary of State George Ball, "Principles of Our Policy Toward Cuba," reprinted in *Department of State Bulletin*, Vol. L, No. 1298, May 11, 1964, pp. 741–743. An unnamed official described the statement as "definitive" in Tad Szulc, "U.S. Bars Easing of Cuba Policies," *New York Times*, April 24, 1964, p. 9. On the general policy position, also see Secretary Rusk's testimony before the U.S. Congress, Senate, Committee on Foreign Relations, *East-West Trade, Part 1*, 88th Congress, 2nd Session, March 13, 16, 23, April 8, 9, 1964 (Washington, D.C.: U.S. Government Printing Office, 1964), p. 15.
174 Under Secretary of State George Ball, "Principles of Our Policy Toward Cuba," pp. 741–743.
175 Presidential News Conference, Washington, D.C., May 6, 1964, in *Public Papers of the Presidents of the United States: Lyndon B. Johnson 1963–1964, Book 1* (Washington, D.C.: U.S. Government Printing Office, 1965), p. 620.
176 From Lisbon Embassy (Ambassador Anderson), Telegram, July 31, 1964, No. 76, Confidential, National Security Files, Countries, Portuguese Vol. 1, *Johnson Presidential Library*. On the bilateral trade level, the U.S. government applied one of the few remaining "turns of the screw" in May, following Cuban overtures to twelve American pharmaceutical companies for the purchase of medical supplies and foodstuffs at an estimated total value of between $6 million and $15 million. On referral of these requests by the companies involved to the Departments of State and Commerce, a determination was made to include all medical supplies and foodstuffs (with the exception of gift parcels) in the category of items that required Commerce export licenses. See "Cuba Seeks to Buy Drugs from U.S. Firms; State, Commerce Agencies Study Request," *Wall Street Journal*, May 14, 1964, p. 5; Dom Bonafede, "U.S. Tightens Cuban Sales in Medicine," *New York Herald Tribune*, May 15, 1964, p. 1; *Facts on File*, Vol. XXIV, No. 1229, May 14–20, 1964, p. 157.
177 See Juan de Onís, "Castro Presses the West for Expanded Trade," *New York Times*, March 1, 1964, p. E3.
178 See Economist Intelligence Unit, *Quarterly Economic Review of Cuba*, No. 46, June 1964, p. 6.

179 Quoted in "Cuba Suspends Credit on Foreign Purchases," *Journal of Commerce*, July 28, 1964, pp. 1, 2.
180 Norman Gall, "Cuba Seeking Better Ties with U.S. to Lessen Dependency on Moscow," *Washington Post*, July 17, 1964, P. A1.
181 Department of State (Secretary Rusk) to Ambassadors, Telegram, All NATO capitals, Embassies-Stockholm, Madrid, Tokyo, Paris, All ARA Diplomatic Posts, Embassies-Mexico City, Santiago, La Paz, Montevideo, August 6, 1964, Circular 259, Secret, *DFOIA*.
182 Ibid.
183 Personal Interview: Department of State official, Washington, D.C., July 13, 1973 and June 6, 1975.
184 Organization of American States, *Ninth Meeting of Consultation of Ministers of Foreign Affairs*, DOC. 24, p. 8.
185 Organization of American States, *Twelfth Meeting of Consultation of Ministers of Foreign Affairs*, Washington, D.C., 1967, DOC. 50, 11.12, (Washington, D.C.: Pan American Union, 1967), pp. 4–5. Also see Benjamin Welles, "Rusk Urges O.A.S. to Block Castro," *New York Times*, September 24, 1967, p. 1. The House Inter-American Affairs subcommittee issued a report two months prior to the meeting that included criticism of the United States' "friends and allies" still trading with Cuba. It recommended that the executive branch press member OAS governments into "taking the most forceful measures practicable toward terminating entirely all significant trade between the free world and Cuba." U.S. Congress, House, Committee on Foreign Affairs, Subcommittee on Inter-American Affairs, *Communist Activities in Latin America 1967*, 90th Congress, 1st Session, Report, July 11, 1967 (Washington, D.C.: U.S. Government Printing Office, 1967), p. 9.
186 See Benjamin Welles, "O.A.S. Ministers Adopt New Anti-Cuban Policies," *New York Times*, September 25, 1967, p. 1.
187 See U.S. Department of Commerce, Domestic and International Business Administration, Bureau of East-West Trade, *United States Commercial Relations with Cuba: A Survey* (Washington, D.C.: U.S. Government Printing Office, August 1975), p. 41 (Table 5).
188 Statement by President Johnson, November 12, 1966, reprinted in *Department of State Bulletin*, Vol. LV, No. 1432, December 5, 1966, p. 867.
189 U.S. Congress, House, Committee on Foreign Affairs, *Foreign Assistance Act of 1964*, *Part 1*, 88th Congress, 2nd Session, March 23, 1964 (Washington, D.C.: U.S. Government Printing Office, 1964), p. 19.
190 Quoted in *Congressional Record-Senate*, 88th Congress, 2nd Session, Vol. 110, Part 5, March 25, 1964, pp. 6320–6321. For the complete text of the speech, see ibid., pp. 6320–6327.
191 Ibid., p. 6237. Also see John D. Morris, "Fulbright Speech Draws Criticism," *New York Times*, March 27, 1964, p. 4.
192 Quoted in "Rusk Commends Fulbright View on Policy 'Myths'," *New York Times*, March 28, 1964, p. 1. Also see Address by President Johnson, "America as a Great Power," New York City, April 20, 1964, reprinted in *Department of State Bulletin*, Vol. L, No.

1298, May 11, 1964, p. 729; Dom Bonafede, "Policy on Cuba. Frustrate, Isolate, Expose," *New York Herald Tribune*, April 21, 1964, p. 12.

193 Vincent J. Burke, "U.S. Studies Policy on Cuban Traders," *Washington Post*, February 15, 1964, p. A13.

194 See "Shipments to Cuba Held Threat to U.S. Spanish Relations," *Washington Post*, February 13, 1964, p. A10.

195 See Tad Szulc, "U.S. Curtails Aid to Five Countries That Sell to Cuba," *New York Times*, February 19, 1964, pp. 1, 2.

196 See Felix Belair, Jr., "Administration is Fighting Curb on Food Aid to Other Countries," *New York Times*, May 23, 1966, p. 5.

197 Robert B. Semple, Jr., "President Signs Food Peace Plan but Scores Curbs," *New York Times*, November 13, 1966, pp. 1, 45.

198 See J. Anthony Lukas, "Indians to Limit Trade with Reds," *New York Times*, January 23, 1967, pp. 1, 6; Warren Unna, "Indian Politics Upset by Talks Over U.S. Aid," *Washington Post*, January 24, 1967, p. A12.

199 "India Agree to Provision of U.S. Food-for-Peace-Act," *The Economic Times* (Bombay), January 21, 1967, p. 1. According to Indian Prime Minister Indira Gandhi, New Delhi was told to halt trade with Cuba or risk termination of American food aid. See Unna, "Indian Politics Upset by Talks Over U.S. Aid," p. A12.

200 See *Facts on File*, Vol. XXVII, No. 1373, February 16–22, 1967, p. 56.

201 See U.S. Congress, Senate, Committee on Government Operations, Subcommittee on Foreign Aid Expenditures, *Coordination in Administration of Public Law 480*, 89th Congress, 2nd Session, June 2 and 30, 1966 (Washington, D.C.: U.S. Government Printing Office, 1966), pp. 164–165; "U.S. Gives Greece Warning on Cuba," *New York Times*, October 13, 1966, p. 15.

202 "Athens to Enforce Ban on Cuban Trade," *New York Times*, November 6, 1966, p. 7.

203 "Greece Plans Stern Action on Shipping-Ban Violations," *New York Times*, January 20, 1967, p. 85.

204 Personal Interview: Department of State official, Washington, D.C., July 13, 1973, and June 6, 1975.

205 Memorandum for McGeorge Bundy from Gordon Chase, The White House, September 4, 1964, Subject: "Latin America-Miscellaneous," National Security Files, Country File-Latin America, Box 2, Latin America, Vol. II, 9/64–12/64, *Johnson Presidential Library;* Memorandum for McGeorge Bundy from Gordon Chase, The White House, September 15, 1964, in ibid.

206 U.S. Congress, House, Committee on Foreign Affairs, Subcommittee on Inter-American Affairs, *Communist Activities in Latin America, 1967*, 90th Congress, 1st Session, April 25, May 4, 16, 17, 31, and June 7, 1967 (Washington, D.C.: U.S. Government Printing Office, 1967), p. 89.

207 Personal Interview: Department of State official, Washington, D.C., July 13, 1973, and June 6, 1975.

208 U.S. Department of Commerce, *United States Commercial Relations*

with Cuba: A Survey, p. 41 (Table 5). Also see Don Bohning, "'Non-Reds' Cuba Trade Receding," *Washington Post,* November 24, 1966, p. H6.

209 See Kari Levitt, *Silent Surrender: The Multinational Corporation in Canada* (New York: St. Martin's Press, 1970), pp. 61, 121–123; Ronald J. Wonnacott, "Trade Arrangements Among Industrial Countries: Effects on Canada," in Bela Balassa, ed., *Studies in Trade Liberalization* (Baltimore: The Johns Hopkins Press, 1967), pp. 51–52.

210 See Charles A. Barrett, *Canada's International Trade: Trends and Prospects,* Canadian Studies No. 39, A Report from the Conference Board of Canada, July 1976, pp. 16–17; Wonnacott, "Trade Arrangements Among Industrial Countries: Effects on Canada," pp. 51–52.

211 See Larry R. Riguaz and Sol. Sinclair, "Canadian Agriculture and the Common Market: Development and Trends, 1960–1970," in Peter Stingelin, ed., *The European Community and the Outsiders* (Ontario: Longman Canada, 1973), p. 63.

212 See Boyer, *Canada and Cuba,* p. 373.

213 Ibid., p. 375.

214 Ibid., pp. 375–376.

215 Ibid., pp. 375, 377–378. Also see David Leyton-Brown, "The Multinational Enterprise and Conflict in Canadian-American Relations," in Annette Fox, Alfred O. Hero, Jr., and Joseph S. Nye, Jr., eds., *Canada and the United States: Transnational and Transgovernmental Relations* (New York: Columbia University Press, 1976), p. 146.

216 See Jack N. Benrman, *National Interest and the Multinational Enterprise* (Englewood Cliffs, N.J.: Prentice-Hall, 1970), p. 108.

217 See Appendix II, Table 1.

218 Kiyoshi Kojima, *Japan and a New World Economic Order* (Boulder: Westview Press), 1970, p. 15.

219 See Leon Hollerman, "Foreign Trade in Japan's Economic Transition," in Isaiah Frank, ed., *The Japanese Economy in International Perspective* (Baltimore: The Johns Hopkins Press, pp. 169–170; Kiyoshi Kojima, *Japan and a New World Economic Order,* p. 12; Martha F. Loufti, *The Net Cost of Japanese Foreign Aid* (New York: Praeger Publishers, 1973), pp. 13–14.

220 Kojima, "Trade Arrangements Among Industrial Countries: Effects on Japan," p. 178. Also see Hollerman, "Foreign Trade in Japan's Economic Transition," p. 173.

221 See Kojima, *Japan and a New World Economic Order,* pp. 13, 16.

222 Mandel, *Europe vs. America,* pp. 85–86.

223 Quoted in "Japan's Increasing Trade With Cuba Worries U.S.," p. 1. On trade figures, see Appendix II, Table 1.

224 See U.S. Central Intelligence Agency, *Cuba: Foreign Trade,* p. 10.

225 Department of State (Secretary Rusk) to American Embassy, Tokyo, Telegram No. 1759, January 13, 1964, Confidential, National Security Files, Japan, Vol. 1, Cables, *Johnson Presidential Library;* American Embassy, Tokyo, to Department of State, Airgram, No. A-826,

January 22, 1964, Subject: "Japan's Trade with Cuba," Confidential, *DFOIA*.

226 Personal Interview: Department of State official, Washington, D.C., July 13, 1973 and June 6, 1975.

227 See "U.S. Sees Solution Through Negotiation," *The Japan Times*, August 20, 1964, p. 10.

228 Personal Interview: Department of State official, Washington, D.C., April 20, 1971 and June 22, 1973. The respondent was an economist specializing in Latin American affairs in the Department's Bureau of Intelligence and Research during the 1960s and early 1970s.

229 See Gardner, "The Japanese in Cuba," p. 71.

230 See Appendix II, Table 1.

231 Edward A. Kolodziej, *French International Policy Under De Gaulle and Pompidou* (Ithaca: Cornell University Press, 1974), pp. 71–82; Department of State, Bureau of Intelligence and Research, From Thomas L. Hughes to Secretary of State, Research Memorandum, REU-28, Subject: "De Gaulle's Foreign Policy: 1964," April 20, 1964, Secret, France Files, *Johnson Presidential Library*.

232 See Economist Intelligence Unit, *Quarterly Economic Review of Cuba*, No. 45, March 1964, p. 2.

233 Department of State (Secretary Rusk) to Paris Embassy, Telegram, February 5, 1964, Confidential, Paris 4004, STR 10 Cuba, *DFOIA*.

234 See Drew Middleton, "French Complete Cuba Truck Sale," *New York Times*, February 8, 1964, p. 2. Also see Economist Intelligence Unit, *Quarterly Economic Review of Cuba*, No. 46, June 1964, p. 6.

235 Quoted in Middleton, "French Complete Cuba Truck Sales," p. 2.

236 See Murrey Marder, "U.S. Muffles Ire over Sale to Cuba," *Washington Post*, May 6, 1964, p. A1.

237 Quoted in Robert R. Brunn, "U.S. Cuba Policy Stalled," *Christian Science Monitor*, May 7, 1964, p. 3. Also see Marder, "U.S. Muffles Ire over Sale to Cuba," p. A1.

238 See *Hispanic American Report*, Vol. XVII, No. 6, August for June 1964, p. 513.

239 Ibid.

240 Brunn, "U.S. Cuba Policy Stalled," p. 3.

241 See Economist Intelligence Unit, *Quarterly Economic Review of Cuba*, No. 48, November 1964, pp. 6–7.

242 Bernard D. Nossiter, "French Business Seeks End of Curb on Loans to Reds," *Washington Post*, June 25, 1964, p. A21.

243 On French exports to Cuba, see Appendix II, Table 1.

244 Between 1960 and 1975, the industry-construction and agriculture sectors experienced average annual growth rates of 8.9 percent and 3 percent respectively. See Alison Wright, *The Spanish Economy 1959–1976* (New York: Holmes & Meier Publishers, 1977), p. 30.

245 French commerce, for example, received a tremendous boost from membership in the EEC. In 1959, the EEC countries provided 26.8 percent of France's total imports and accounted for 27.2 percent of France's total exports. By 1968, these figures had reached 47.3 percent and 42.9 percent respectively. See J. J. Carre, P. Dubois, and

E. Malinvaud, *French Economic Growth* (Stanford: Stanford University Press, 1975), p. 405.

246 See William T. Salisbury, "Spain and Europe: The Economic Realities," in William T. Salisbury and James D. Therberge, eds., *Spain in the 1970s: Economics, Social Structure, Foreign Policy* (New York: Praeger Publishers, 1976), p. 37.

247 Tad Szulc, "Spain Is Cautioned by U.S. on Rise in Cuban Trade," *New York Times*, December 21, 1963, p. 1.

248 Ibid., p. 7.

249 Ibid., pp. 1, 7.

250 Department of State to Madrid Embassy, January 24, 1964.

251 Ibid.

252 "CIA Mission Seen Aimed at Cubans," *Washington Post*, January 28, 1964, p. A8. Also see National Security Files, Agency File, Box 5, 8, 9 and 10, Folder: Central Intelligence Agency Vol. 1, *Johnson Presidential Library*.

253 Donald May, "U.S. Denies It Wants Cuba Trader Boycott," *Washington Post*, February 21, 1964, p. A21.

254 See Vincent J. Burke, "U.S. Studies Policy on Cuban Traders," p. A13.

255 See Tad Szulc, "U.S. Curtails Aid to Five Countries That Sell to Cuba," *New York Times*, February 19, 1964, p. 2; "Shipment to Cuba Held Threat to U.S. Spanish Relations," p. A10.

256 See Jack Raymond, "U.S. Acts to Avoid Halt in Aid to Spain Despite Cuba Trade," *New York Times*, February 23, 1964, pp. 1, 8. During the course of the diplomatic negotiations, the U.S. Navy high command ordered the immediate movement of a number of units of the U.S. nuclear Polaris submarine squadron from Scotland to the Rota base, thus subtly reinforcing the White House stance. See Murrey Marder, "U.S. Is Seen Continuing Aid to Spain," *Washington Post, February 22, 1964, pp. A1, A11.*

257 Ibid.

258 Raymond, "U.S. Acts to Avoid Halt in Aid to Spain Despite Cuba Trade," p. 8.

259 Quoted in "Spain Warns on Aid Cutoff," *New York Times*, February 23, 1964, p. 8

260 See "Spain to Cut Back Air Cargo to Cuba," *New York Times*, March 3, 1964, p. 14; Tom Lambert, "Spain to Halt Cargoes to Cuba," *New York Herald Tribune*, March 5, 1964, p.3; "Spain Cutting Cuba Trade, U.S. Decides," *Washington Post*, March 5, 1964, p. A14.

261 See Secretary of State Dean Rusk News Conference, March 6, 1964, reprinted in *Department of State Bulletin*, Vol. L, No. 1291, March 23, 1964, p. 445.

262 See "Spanish Ships End Trade with Cuba," *London Times*, March 11, 1964, p. 9.

263 See "Spain to Keep its Ships Out of Trade with Cuba," *Journal of Commerce*, February 17, 1965, p. 23; U.S. Department of Commerce, *List of Free World and Polish Flag Vessels Arriving in Cuba Since January 1, 1963*, Report No. 128.

264 Madrid Embassy (Oscar H. Guerra, American Consul, for the

Ambassador) to Department of State, Airgram, March 25, 1964, Confidential, No. A-699, *DFOIA*. Also see "U.S. Cuba Stand Brings Angry Reaction in Spain," *Washington Post*, October 1, 1964, p. A30.

265 See Drew Middleton, "Spanish Increasing Cuban Trade Despite U.S. Pleas for Blockade," *New York Times*, September 28, 1964, p. 8; Richard Mowrer, "Spain Buys Red," *Christian Science Monitor*, March 2, 1965, p. 1; Richard Mowrer, "Madrid Tightens Ties with Cuba," *Christian Science Monitor*, October 21, 1964, p. 2; Appendix II, Table 1.

266 *Hispanic American Report*, Vol. XVII, No. 4, June for April 1964, p. 298.

267 See Appendix II, Table 1.

268 "Spain in World Trade," *Bank of London & South America Review*, Vol. 1, No. 5, May 1967, pp. 246–247. Also see Tad Szulc, "Madrid Doubles Exports to Cuba," *New York Times*, January 15, 1967, p. 24.

269 See U.S. Central Intelligence Agency, *Cuba: Foreign Trade*, p. 10.

270 See Appendix II, Table 1

271 Sidney Pollard, *The Development of the British Economy 1914–1967* (London: Edward Arnold, 1969), p. 444; M. W. Kirby, *The Decline of British Economic Power Since 1877* (London: George Allen & Unwin, 1981), p. 149 (Table 15).

272 Robert L. Pfaltzgraff, Jr., *Britain Faces Europe* (Philadelphia: University of Pennsylvania Press, 1969), p. 174; Mandel, *Europe vs. America*, p. 86.

273 Ibid., pp. 71–77.

274 Pfaltzgraff, *Britain Faces Europe*, p. 174. In terms of standard growth rate indices, Britain lagged behind every Common Market country. See Ibid., p. 67; Pollard, *The Development of the British Economy 1914–1967*, p. 435.

275 See F. T. Blackaby, "General Appraisal," in F. T. Blackaby, ed., *British Economic Policy 1960–64* (London: Cambridge University Press, 1978), pp. 619–655.

276 Department of State (Assistant Secretary Ball) to London Embassy, Telegram, January 24, 1964, No. 4526, STR 10 Cuba, *DFOIA*.

277 See "British Firm Sells Buses to Cuba," *London Times*, January 8, 1964, p. 10; "Other Western Bids Cited," *New York Times*, January 8, 1964, p. 11; "British Feel More Sadness Than Anger at Aid Cut," *Washington Post*, February 20, 1964, p. A15. Leyland competed for the contract with firms from France, West Germany, Italy, Spain, Japan, and Czechoslovakia. According to an economist specializing in Latin American affairs in the State Department's Bureau of Intelligence and Reseach, the Leyland buses were originally destined for Ceylon "but something happened to the deal. Britain had the buses, Cuba had the money." Personal Interview: Department of State official, Washington, D.C., April 20, 1971 and June 22, 1973.

278 "British Sell Buses to Cuba, Defying U.S. Trade Curb," *New York Times*, January 8, 1964, p. 1; Economist Intelligence Unit, *Quarterly Economic Review of Cuba*, No. 45, March 1964, p. 2.

279 Personal Interview: Department of State official, Washington, D.C., July 6, 1973. The respondent was a Department international relations official during the late 1950s and 1960s. Also see Appendix II, Table 1.

280 See Economist Intelligence Unit, *Quarterly Economic Review of Cuba*, No. 45, March 1964, p. 2. A State Department official recalled a conversation with a member of the British Embassy in Washington at the time: "I chided the British Counselor of the Embassy in Washington for having shipped buses to Cuba. He replied: 'Look old boy, Britain exports to live. You may have your little squabbles in Latin America but don't ask me to pass up the chance to make a few pounds.'" Personal Correspondence: Department of State official, California, March 7, 1975.

281 Quoted in "British Feel More Sadness Than Anger at Aid Cut," p. A15.

282 State Department spokesman Robert J. McCloskey, quoted in "U.S. Criticizes Deal," *New York Times*, January 8, 1968, p. 11.

283 See *Hispanic American Report*, Vol. XVII, No. 1, March for January 1964, p. 36.

284 "British Firm Sells Buses to Cuba," p. 10 Also see Clyde Farnsworth, "British Defend Bus Sale to Cuba as Nonpolitical," *New York Times*, January 9, 1964, p. 6

285 As Secretary of Commerce Luther Hodges commented: "I do not like it a bit; but I do not see what we can do about it." Quoted in *Keesings Contemporary Archives*, February 22–29, 1964, p. 19914.

286 Personal Interview: Department of State official, Washington, D.C., July 13, 1973, and June 6, 1975.

287 Quoted in Murrey Marder, "Rusk Raps U.S. Allies for Trade With Castro," *Washington Post*, January 23, 1974, p. A1.

288 See, for example, "U.S. Approaches on Further Buses for Cuba: Order for Britain Disapproved," *London Times*, February 4, 1964, p. 10.

289 See "Rusk Sees Public Boycott Facing Traders with Cuba," *New York Times*, February 6, 1964, pp. 1, 25; "Britain Defends Bus Sale," *New York Times*, February 20, 1964, p. 3. Subsequently, the State Department announced that it did not support consumer boycotts against countries trading with Cuba. See "U.S. Cool to Plan for Boycotting Cuba's Suppliers," *New York Times*, February 21, 1964, pp. 1, 2; Interview with Dean Rusk on Voice of America, February 14, 1964, reprinted in *Department of State Bulletin*, Vol. L, No. 1288, March 2, 1964, p. 332; Memorandum for the President from McGeorge Bundy, The White House, February 11, 1964, Collection: National Security Files, Aides Files, Box 1, Folder: McGeorge Bundy–Memos to President, Vol. 1, 11/63–2/64, *Johnson Presidential Library*. This memo related to British Prime Minister Douglas-Home's February 12 and 13 visit.

290 Department of State, From EUR-William Tyler, to Secretary of State, Subject: "Effect of Amendment of Foreign Assistance Act of 1963 on Aid to the United Kingdom and Dependent Territories," February 11, 1964, Confidential, STR 10-Cuba, *DFOIA*.

291 Memorandum for the President from Department of State, Visit of Prime Minister Alex Douglas-Home, February 12–13, 1964, Background Paper: "Cuba," Collection: National Security Files, Country File, Europe and USSR, United Kingdom, Box 213, Folder: United Kingdom, PM Home Visit Briefing Book 2/12–13/64, *Johnson Presidential Library;* Memorandum for the President from Secretary of State Rusk, Subject: "Your Meeting with Prime Minister Sir Alex Douglas-Home," in ibid.

292 Tad Szulc, "U.S. Curtails Aid to Five Countries That Sell to Cuba," p. 1; Carroll Kilpatric, "British Maintain Red Trade," *Washington Post,* February 14, 1964, pp. A1, A8.

293 Television interview, February 17, quoted in Francis Boyd, "Sir Alex Refuses to Rule Out March 19," *The Guardian* (U.K.), February 18, 1964, p. 5.

294 U.K. House of Commons, *Parliamentary Debates* (Hansard), 5th Session, 42nd Parliament, Vol. 690, February 24 to March 6, 1964 (London: Her Majesty's Stationery Office), p. 238.

295 Personal Interview: Department of State official, Washington, D.C., July 13, 1973, and June 6, 1975.

296 *Hispanic American Report,* Vol. XVII, No. 4, June for April 1964, p. 321. Also see Economist Intelligence Unit, *Quarterly Economic Review of Cuba,* No. 45, March 1964, p.2.

297 Personal Interview: Department of State official, Washington, D.C., June 14, 1973.

298 Quoted in Geyelin, *Lyndon B. Johnson and the World,* pp. 92–93.

299 See Murrey Marder, "LBJ Raps Cuba Trade in Talks with Butler," *Washington Post,* May 1, 1964, p. A14. Earlier the same week, both Secretary of State Rusk and Assistant Secretary of State Ball raised the Cuba trade issue with Butler. Ibid.

300 From James L. Greenfield to Secretary of State, April 29, 1964, Subject: "Butler Briefing," Collection: National Security Files, Country File, Europe & the USSR, United Kingdom, Box 210, 211 and 212, Folder: United Kingdom, Vol. XV, 12/63–9/65, *Johnson Presidential Library.* Also see Tad Szulc, "Rusk and Butler Look for Benefit from Reds' Split," *New York Times,* April 28, 1964, pp. 1, 13.

301 See Drew Middleton, "U.S.-British Clash on Red Trade Due," *New York Times,* May 8, 1964, p. 5.

302 See Robert H. Estabrook, "U.S. Bitterness at British Trade Affecting NATO," *Washington Post,* May 9, 1964, p. A6.

303 Ibid.

304 See, for example, ibid.; Middleton, "U.S.-British Clash on Red Trade Due," p. 5.

305 Flora Lewis, "British Firm to Sell Cuba More Buses," *Washington Post,* May 8, 1964, pp. A1, A16.

306 Sydney Gruson, "Britain Weighs Curb on Cuban Credit," *New York Times,* May 11, 1964, p. 10.

307 "British Concessions to U.S. on Cuba Trade," *London Times,* May 12, 1964, p. 10.

308 Quoted in Syndey Gruson, "Rusk Calls Dispute 'Minor'," *New York Times,* May 11, 1964, p. 10.

309 "U.K. Aircraft Firm Not To Sell to Cuba," *Journal of Commerce*, January 20, 1965, p. 13.
310 Quoted in "U.S. Delays British Cargo in London," *Washington Post*, August 6, 1966, p. D6.
311 See "Simon Carves Chasing £10M Cuba Order," *London Times*, January 4, 1967, p. 14.
312 £10M Deal with Cuba Expected to Go Through," *London Times*, January 4, 1967, p. 8
313 Quoted in "U.S. Opposed British Credit to Aid Cuba," *Washington Post*, January 4, 1967, p. A6.
314 Quoted in Karl E. Meyer, "British Give Cuba Credit for Plant," *Washington Post*, January 21, 1967, p. A9.
315 See "Cuba in £16M deal with Britain," *London Times*, May 20, 1967, p. 1.
316 Memorandum for Walt W. Rostow, The White House, from Department of State, Subject: "Briefing Book for Your Talks with Prime Minister Wilson," February 18, 1967, Collection: National Security Files, Country File, Europe and USSR, United Kingdom, Box 215, Folder: United Kingdom, WWR Talks with Wilson-Briefing Book, 2/67, *Johnson Presidential Library.*
317 See Juan de Onís, "British Building Big Plant in Cuba," *New York Times*, February 7, 1968, p. 3.
318 "Cuba: More Contracts?," *Latin America*, April 28, 1967, p. 4. In January 1968, the same journal noted that the last list of goods subject to the strategic embargo was published in the British *Board of Trade Journal* of August 19, 1966, and "in naming the countries to which the listed goods could not be sold, the *Journal* omitted any reference to Cuba, thus implicitly making clear that the British government acknowledges different rules for trade with Dr. Castro's government." "Cuba: Another Export Dilemma for the UK?," *Latin America*, January 19, 1968, p. 17.
319 See Appendix II, Table 1.
320 Edward Skloot, "The Decision to Send East-West Trade Legislation to Congress, 1965–1966," in *Commission on the Organization of the Government for the Conduct of Foreign Policy*, June 1975, Volume 3, Appendix H, Appendix I, Appendix J (Washington, D.C.: U.S. Government Printing Office, 1975), p. 75.
321 Personal Interview: Central Intelligence Agency official, Washington, D.C., January 7, 1976; Personal Interview: Department of the Treasury official, New York City, New York, June 26, 1975. The respondent was one of the highest ranking Treasury officials during the Kennedy administration.
322 Personal Interview: Central Intelligence Agency official, Washington, D.C., January 7, 1976.
323 Quoted in Miguel Acocoa, "Spain, in Turnabout, Keeps Watch on Rightest Latin Exiles," *Washington Post*, March 5, 1977, p. A12.
324 See Jack Anderson and Les Whitten, "CIA Accused in '64 Thames Collision," *Washington Post*, February 14, 1975, p. C31. An Agency official at the time conceded: "it is true that we were sabotaging the Leyland buses going to Cuba from England and that was pretty sen-

sitive business." Quoted in Branch and Crile, "The Kennedy Vendetta: How the CIA Waged a Silent War Against Cuba," p. 52.

325 "The Case of the Contaminated Sugar," *London Times*, April 28, 1966, p. 12; Tom Wicker, et al., "C.I.A. Operations: A Plot Scuttled," *New York Times*, April 28, 1966, pp. 1, 28.

326 Quoted in Branch and Crile, "The Kennedy Vendetta: How the C.I.A. Waged a Silent War Against Cuba," p. 52.

327 See Jonathan Kwitny, *Endless Enemies: The Making of an Unfriendly World* (New York: Congdon & Weed, 1984), pp. 243–244.

328 Quoted in Branch and Crile, "The Kennedy Vendetta: How the CIA Waged a Silent War against Cuba," p. 52. Ray S. Cline, former Deputy Director of the CIA, recalled this aspect of the "secret war" against Cuba during the 1960s: "if you sent a piece of machinery to a country which looks great – and yet the ball bearings are square instead of round so that in a few months it chews itself up, that's subtle sabotage, rather than – as distinct from sort of putting a booby trap in the machine that blows up immediately. So there were – there were a number of operations of subtle sabotage [against Cuba], some of them rather successful." Transcript of CBS Reports, *The CIA's Secret War*. During the Kennedy period, the head of Operation Mongoose, General Edward Lansdale, initiated a program to sabotage lubricating oil purchased abroad by Cuba. Shipments from a French petroleum company were doctored by CIA operatives as they passed through the port of Marseilles – without the knowledge of the French government or local authorities. See Kwitney, *Endless Enemies*, pp. 244–246.

329 Summary of Paper by Philip Tresize, Deputy Assistant Secretary of State for Economic Affairs, "Attitudes of Western Europe and Japan Towards East-West Trade" (Tab. 3), Undated (Written first half of 1965), Folder: Minutes of Meetings-Notes, Collection: National Security Files, Committee File, Special Committee on U.S. Trade Relations with East European Countries and the Soviet Union (Miller Committee), Box 24, *Johnson Presidential Library*.

330 Personal Interview: Department of State official, Washington, D.C., July 13, 1973, and June 6, 1975.

331 Personal Interview: Department of State official, Washington, D.C., March 14, 1975. The respondent was a Department international economic officer and foreign affairs specialist during the late 1960s and early 1970s.

332 Personal Correspondence: Department of State official, California, March 7, 1975.

333 Personal Interview: Department of State official, Washington, D.C., June 18, 1973. The respondent was stationed in Latin America and Washington during the 1960s. During the early 1970s, he was a senior Department Cuba official.

334 Personal Interview: Department of State official, Washington, D.C., April 20, 1971, and June 22, 1973.

335 Personal Interview: Department of State official, Washington, D.C., July 11, 1973. The respondent was a Department international relations officer on the Cuba Desk between 1961 and 1964.

336 Personal Interview: Department of State official, Washington, D.C., March 14, 1975.

6. The United States against Cuba 1968–1980: intransigent policymaking and its consequences

1 "Japan's Burgeoning Overseas Investments: Where, What They Are," *Business International*, February 18, 1977, p. 53.
2 See U.S. Central Intelligence Agency, National Foreign Assessment Center, *Handbook of Economic Statistics*, ER79-10274, August 1979, pp. 83–84 (Table 53); James Petras, "The Trilateral Commission and Latin American Economic Development," in James F. Petras et al., *Class, State and Power in the Third World* (New Jersey: Allanheld Osmun, 1981), p. 86; Robert L. Samuelson, "U.S., Japan Find Old Relationships Have Unravelled," *National Journal*, Vol. XI, No. 26, June 30, 1979, p. 1071; Hiroya Ichikawa, "Japan's Economic Relationship with Latin America," in Roger W. Fontaine and James D. Therberge, eds., *Latin America's New Internationalism* (New York: Praeger Publishers, 1976), pp. 78–85.
3 Jonathan Steele, *Soviet Power: The Kremlin's Foreign Policy–Brezhnev to Chernenko* (New York: Simon and Schuster, 1984), p. 58. Also see Raymond L. Garthoff, *Detente and Confrontation: American-Soviet Relations from Nixon to Reagan* (Washington: The Brookings Institution, 1985), pp. 24–105.
4 Ibid., p. 59.
5 See Richard E. Feinberg, *U.S. Human Rights Policy: Latin America* (Washington, D.C.: Center for International Policy, October 1980); Lars Schoultz, *Human Rights and United States Foreign Policy Toward Latin America* (Princeton: Princeton University Press, 1981), p. 294.
6 See, for example, William Branigan, "Vance Indicates Rights Issue, Iranian Arms Are Not Linked," *Washington Post*, May 14, 1977, pp. A1, A12; Lewis M. Simons, "U.S. to Skirt Rights Issue in Aid to Friends," *Washington Post*, September 11, 1977, p. A23; Karen DeYoung and Charles A. Krause, "Our Mixed Signals on Human Rights in Argentina," *Washington Post*, October 29, 1978, pp. C1, C2; James Morrell; *Achievements of the 1970s: Human Rights Law and Policy* (Washington, D.C.: Center for International Policy, November 1981). In May 1977, President Carter declared that conventional arms transfers would in future be confined to "exceptional" circumstances that contributed to U.S. security interests. But a detailed analysis of the first year of the Carter arms-transfer policy concluded that arms sales restraint was observable "mostly at the margin" and that "U.S. arms transfers continue[d] to occur on a rather routine basis." U.S. Congress, Senate, Committee on Foreign Relations, Subcommittee on Foreign Assistance, *Implications of President Carter's Conventional Arms Transfer Policy*, 95th Congress, 1st Session, Committee Print, Congressional Research Service, Library of Congress, December 1977 (Washington, D.C.: U.S. Government Printing Office, 1977), pp. 31, 46.

7 Quoted in Juan De Onís, "U.S. Reverses a Ban on Argentine Loan," *New York Times*, November 11, 1978, p. 1. For statistical data and analysis of Carter economic aid policy toward repressive and autocratic Third World governments, see Center for International Policy, *Human Rights and U.S. Foreign Assistance Programs: Fiscal Year 1978, Part 1 – Latin America* (Washington, D.C., 1978); James F. Petras and Morris H. Morley, "Economic Expansion, Political Crisis and U.S. Policy in Central America," in Marlene Dixon and Susanne Jonas, eds., *Revolution and Intervention in Central America* (San Francisco: Synthesis Publications, 1983), pp. 189–218.

8 Figures provided by U.S. Department of the Treasury, Office of Multilateral Development Banks (Prepared by Brian Crowe), December 31, 1980.

9 Quoted in "Human Rights: Getting Through a Policy Maze," *Congressional Quarterly Weekly Report*, Vol. XXXVI, No. 31, August 5, 1978, p. 2046.

10 "Memorandum for Members of the Cabinet," from Zbigniew Brzezinski, May 8, 1978, reprinted in *The Nation*, June 24, 1978, p. 749.

11 Quoted in *Wall Street Journal*, January 25, 1980, p. 3.

12 See Hedrick Smith, "The Carter Doctrine," *New York Times*, January 24, 1980, p. 1.

13 See Melvyn P. Leffler, "From the Truman Doctrine to the Carter Doctrine: Lessons and Dilemmas of the Cold War," *Diplomatic History*, Vol. 7, No. 4, Fall 1983, pp. 245–266.

14 See, for example, Lars Schoultz, "U.S. Economic Aid as an Instrument of Foreign Policy: The Case of Human Rights in Latin America," in Jack L. Nelson and Vera M. Green, eds., *International Human Rights: Contemporary Issues* (New York: Human Rights Publishing Group, 1980), p. 33; James F. Petras and Morris H. Morley, "Supporting Repression: U.S. Policy and the Demise of Human Rights in El Salvador, 1979–1981," in Ralph Miliband and John Saville, eds., *The Socialist Register 1981* (London: The Merlin Press, 1981), pp. 47–71.

15 There was a great deal of foreign-policy continuity in the transition from Carter to Reagan, despite the latter's even more determined commitment to reassert American hegemony through the vehicle of the state and a global strategy of military and political confrontation. For a discussion, see James F. Petras and Morris H. Morley, "The Cold War: Reagan Policy Toward Europe and the Third World," *Studies in Political Economy*, No. 9, Fall 1982, pp. 5–44.

16 The most immediate imperial-state strategy took the form of the Rockefeller Mission to Latin America. Its goal was to locate the principle problem areas that posed the most pressing threats to the political-economic status quo. See *The Rockefeller Report on the Americas* (Chicago: Quadrangle Books, 1969).

17 Richard M. Nixon, "Action for Progress for the Americas," October 31, 1969, reprinted in *Department of State Bulletin*, Vol. LXI, No. 1586, November 17, 1969, p. 413.

18 See, for example, Petras and Morley, *The United States and Chile; U.S. Congress, Senate, Covert Action in Chile 1963–1973;* Barbara

Stallings, "Peru and the Privatization of Financial Relations," in Richard R. Fagen, ed., *Capitalism and the State in U.S.-Latin American Relations* (Stanford: Stanford University Press, 1979), pp. 217–253.

19 For an extended discussion, see James F. Petras and Morris H. Morley, "The Rise and Fall of Regional Economic Nationalism in the Andean Region Countries, 1969–1977," *Social and Economic Studies*, Vol. 27, No. 2, June 1978, pp. 153–170.

20 Albert Fishlow, "The Mature Neighbor Policy: A Proposal for a United States Economic Policy for Latin America," in Joseph Grunwald, ed., *Latin America and World Economy* (Beverly Hills: Sage Publications, 1978), p. 38 (Table 2.1).

21 Lawrence B. Krause, "Latin American Economic Relations with Western Europe," in Fontaine and Therberge, eds., *Latin America's New Internationalism* pp. 150, 151 (Table 5.1). Latin America's trade relations with the Soviet Union also increased significantly during the early 1970s, especially in Chile, Bolivia, and Peru. See "Soviet Salesmen Find More Customers Among the Nations of Latin America," *Wall Street Journal*, March 13, 1972, p. 9.

22 James Wilkie, eds., *Statistical Abstract of Latin America, Volume 21* (University of California at Los Angeles: Latin American Center Publications, 1981), pp. 451 (Table 2728), 453 (Table 2730), 454 (Table 2731), 464 (Table 2741); "Japanese to Step Up Investment in Brazil," *Latin America Economic Report*, Vol. IV, No. 37, September 24, 1977, p. 147; "Growing Japanese Commitment in Brazil Shown in Recent Trade and Investment," *Business Latin America*, March 8, 1973, p. 75. In the investment sphere, Japan produced the major challenge to the United States as its total direct investment stake in the region rose from less than $100 million prior to 1969 to $1.9 billion by March 1974 – of which over $1 billion was located in the Brazilian economy. See Hiroya Ichikawa, "Japan's Economic Relationship with Latin America," p. 103. Also see "Brazil's Iron and Steel Surge Draws Multibillion Dollar Stakes," *Business Latin America*, October 24, 1973, pp. 337–338; "Brazil Continues to Attract Major Foreign Investment," *Business Latin America*, April 10, 1974, pp. 113–115; N. M. McKitterick, " . . . and in Brazil the U.S. Lag Is Shown," *New York Times*, May 27, 1973, p. 14.

23 See Whichard, "Trends in the U.S. Direct Investment Position Abroad, 1959–1979," pp. 50–51 (Table 7); Whichard, "U.S. Direct Investment Abroad in 1980," p. 22 (Table 3), p. 32 (Table 12).

24 "Memorandum for Members of the Cabinet," from Zbigniew Brzezinski, May 8, 1978, p. 749.

25 See Benjamin Welles, "New Policy on Caribbean Urged in Report to Nixon," *New York Times*, May 4, 1969, pp. 1, 24. This study was completed in mid-1968.

26 Quoted in Roger Morris, *Uncertain Greatness: Henry Kissinger and American Foreign Policy* (New York: Harper & Row, 1977), p. 106.

27 Ibid., p. 34.

28 Tad Szulc, *The Illusion of Peace: Foreign Policy in the Nixon Years* (New York: The Viking Press, 1978), p. 175. During early 1971,

CIA operatives collaborated with members of the anti-Castro exile movement on a project to introduce the highly contagious African swine fever virus into Cuba. An American intelligence official was given the virus in a sealed container at a U.S. Army and CIA training base (Fort Gulick) in the Panama Canal Zone with instructions to deliver the container to a group of anti-Castro exiles. Some weeks later, according to a study presented by Cuban scientists at a Mexico City conference in August 1971, an outbreak of swine fever among the island's pig population brought all production of pork (a staple foodstuff) to a halt. Cuban officials were forced to order the slaughter of 500,000 pigs to confine the disease to Havana province and prevent an epidemic. See Drew Fetherston and John Cummings, "CIA Linked to 1971 Swine Virus in Cuba," *Washington Post,* January 9, 1977, p. A2.

29   CIA program analyst on Nixon's early determination to do something about Cuba, quoted in Seymour M. Hersh, *The Price of Power: Kissinger in the Nixon White House* (New York: Summit Books, 1983), p. 251.

30   Personal Interview: Department of State official, Washington, D.C., June 20, 1973.

31   Department of State to Ambassadors, Telegram Secret. To: All Latin American (ARA) Diplomatic Posts, Info: Belgrade, Bonn, Bucharest, Budapest, London, Moscow, Paris, Prague, Rome, Sofia, Usun, Warsaw, Subject: "U.S. Policy Toward Cuba," February 17, 1970, No. 23858, *DFOIA.*

32   Quoted in U.S. Congress, House, Committee on Foreign Affairs, Subcommittee on Inter-America Affairs, *Cuba and the Caribbean,* 91st Congress, 2nd Session, July 8, 9, 10, 13, 20, 27, and 31 and August 3, 1970 (Washington, D.C.: U.S. Government Printing Office, 1970), p. 4.

33   See Henry Raymont, "U.S. Urges Latin Countries Not to Relax Boycott of Cuban Regime," *New York Times,* July 13, 1970, p. 13.

34   See Tad Szulc, "White House Charges on Cuba Puzzles U.S. Officials," *New York Times,* September 30, 1970, p. 2; testimony by Defense Intelligence Agency officials in U.S. Congress, House, Committee on Foreign Affairs, Subcommittee on Inter-American Affairs, *Soviet Naval Activities in Cuba,* 91st Congress, 2nd Session, September 30, October 13, November 19 and 24, 1970 (Washington, D.C.: U.S. Government Printing Office), p. 14.

35   Richard M. Nixon, U.S. Policy for the 1970s, *The Western Hemisphere* (excerpts from)... February 25, 1971 (Department of State Publication 8679, April 1971).

36   Department of State to Ambassadors, Telegram, Secret. To: All American Republic Diplomatic Posts (Except Santiago), Info: CINCSO/POLAD, Bonn, London, Paris, Rome, Ottawa, Santiago, Madrid, Tokyo, US Mission, USUN, New York, Subject: "Cuba's Relations with the Hemisphere," December 4, 1970, No. 202576, *DFOIA.*

37   Richard M. Nixon, Interview, April 16, 1971, reprinted in *Department of State Bulletin,* Vol. LXIV, No. 1662, May 3, 1971, p. 567.

Also see the statement of Assistant Secretary of State Robert Hurwitch in U.S. Congress, Senate, Committee on Foreign Relations,
United States Policy Toward Cuba, 92nd Congress, 1st Session, September 16, 1971 (Washington, D.C.: U.S. Government Printing
Office, 1971), pp. 3–4, 6.

38 See Barry Sklar, *U.S. Policy Toward Cuba: A Pro-Con Discussion on
the Resumption of Relations* (Washington, D.C.: Library of Congress,
Congressional Research Service, JX 1428 L. A. Cuba, 72-43F, February 9, 1972), p. 4.

39 See, for example, "U.S. Opposes Moves to Let Nations in OAS Lift
Sanctions Against Cubans," *New York Times*, December 17, 1971,
p. 10.

40 Quoted in Jesse W. Lewis, Jr., "U.S. Rejects Lifting of Cuban Boycott," *Washington Post*, April 13, 1972, p. A11.

41 Quoted in Jerry Landauer, "In A Change of Policy, U.S. Orders
Warships to Resist the Cubans," *Wall Street Journal*, April 13, 1972,
p. 1. Also see Benjamin Welles, "Nixon Gave Navy Power to Halt
Cuba's Seizure," *New York Times* April 14, 1972, pp. 1, 7.

42 Quoted in Marilyn Berger, "OAS Decides to Review Its Policy on
Cuba," *Washington Post*, June 1, 1972, p. A6.

43 Two senior Cuban Foreign Ministry officials, quoted in Dusko
Doder, "Cuba Setting New Policies Toward Hemisphere," *Washington Post*, November 21, 1971, p. A22.

44 Fidel Castro Speech, May 1, 1973, in *Granma Weekly Review*, May
13, 1973, p. 3.

45 See testimony of Major Gerald Cassell, Cuban Area Analyst,
Defense Intelligence Agency, in U.S. Congress, House, Committee
on Foreign Affairs, Subcommittee on Inter-American Affairs, *Soviet
Naval Activities in Cuba, Part 2*, 92nd Congress, 1st Session, September 28, 1971 (Washington, D.C.: U.S. Government Printing Office,
1971), p. 8; testimony of Paul Wallner, Western Area Analyst,
Defense Intelligence Agency, in U.S. Congress, House, Committee
on Foreign Affairs, Subcommittee on Inter-American Affairs, *Soviet
Activities in Cuba, Part 3*, 92nd Congress, 2nd Session, September
26, 1972 (Washington, D.C.: U.S. Government Printing Office,
1972), p. 8.

46 "President Discusses Foreign Policy Statement in Washington Star-
News Interview," November 5, 1972, reprinted in *Department of
State Bulletin*, Vol. LXVII, No. 1745, December 4, 1972, p. 653.

47 Quoted in Bernard Gwertzman, "Rogers Says U.S. Is Firm on
Cuba," *New York Times*, February 16, 1973, p. 1. Also see testi-
mony of Robert Hurwitch, Deputy Assistant Secretary of State for
Inter-American Affairs, in U.S. Congress, House, Committee on For-
eign Affairs, Subcommittee on Inter-American Affairs, *Hijacking
Accord Between the United States and Cuba*, 93rd Congress, 1st Ses-
sion, February 20, 1973 (Washington, D.C.: U.S. Government
Printing Office, 1973), p. 9.

48 See U.S. Congress, Senate, Committee on Foreign Relations, Subcommittee on Western Hemisphere Affairs, *U.S. Policy Toward*

Cuba, 93rd Congress, 1st Session, March 26 and April 18, 1973 (Washington, D.C.: U.S. Government Printing Office, 1974), p. 8.

49 "U.S. Foreign Policy for the 1970's: Shaping a Durable Peace," Report to the Congress by President Nixon, May 3, 1973, reprinted in *Department of State* Bulletin, Vol. LXVII, No. 1771, June 4, 1973, p. 778. Some months later, a senior staff official on Latin America in the National Security Council tersely summarized the current state of U.S.-Cuban relations: "There has been no perceptible change." Quoted in Laurence Stern, "Cuba 1973: The Looking Glass," *Washington Post*, August 19, 1973, p. C3. In 1974, Secretary of State Kissinger personally attempted to discourage two congressional study missions from visiting Cuba and only "reluctantly" agreed to validate the passports of Senators Jacob Javits and Claiborne Pell and Senate Foreign Relations Committee staff member Pat Holt for travel to the island. See U.S. Congress, Senate, Committee on Foreign Relations, *Cuba: A Staff Report*, by Pat Holt, Professional Staff Member, 93rd Congress 2nd Session, Committee Print, August 2, 1974 (Washington, D.C.: U.S. Government Printing Office, 1974), p. vii; Laurence Stern, "Pell, Javits Receive Passports for Cuba," *Washington Post*, September 6, 1974, p. 11.

50 See Marvine Howe, "Venezuela Opens Cuban Contacts," *New York Times*, April 22, 1973, p. 17.

51 See "Colombian Urges End of Cuban Boycott," *Washington Post*, May 25, 1974, p. A15.

52 "Cuba: Joining the Mainland," *Latin America*, August 9, 1974, pp. 241–242.

53 See "Revitalized Mexico-Cuba Trade Offers Export Opportunities," *Business Latin America*, June 22, 1975, pp. 27–28; "Mexico: Latin-Soviet Oil Trade," *Eastwest Markets*, April 7, 1975, p. 9; "Cuba and Mexico Establish New Trading Patterns," *Latin America Economic Report*, Vol. III, No. 38, August 29, 1975, p. 133. Two-way trade was reported to have reached $120 million in 1974. See Economist Intelligence Unit, *Quarterly Economic Review of Cuba*, No. 1, March 1975, p. 4.

54 See "Jamaica's Cuba Connection," *The Guardian Weekly* (U.K.), November 28, 1976, p. 6. Also see "Small New Countries in the Caribbean Are Starting to Follow Cuba's Example," *New York Times*, July 26, 1976, p. 3.

55 See "U.S. Agrees to Review of Cuba Ban," *Washington Post*, September 21, 1974, p. A4; "Ford Links a Shift on Cuba to OAS," *New York Times*, August 29, 1974, pp. 1., 20.

56 Quoted in "OAS to Continue Sanctions Against Cuba As Move To End 10-Year Embargo Fails," *Wall Street Journal*, November 13, 1974, p. 10. Also see Jonathan Kandell, "Pro-Cubans Short of Votes in O.A.S." *New York Times*, November 12, 1974, pp. 1, 2.

57 See Laurence Stern, "Quiet Moves Made on Restoring Relations with Cuba," *Washington Post*, August 24, 1974, p. A12; Bernard Gwertzman, "U.S. Reconsidering Its Policy on Cuba," *New York Times*, September 11, 1974, pp. 1, 14.

58 David Binder, "U.S. and Cubans Discussed Links in Talks in 1975,"

New York Times, March 29, 1977, pp. 1, 8. Also see interview with Secretary of State William Rogers, "Cuba, U.S., Rights and Diplomacy," *Washington Star*, April 7, 1977, p. A1, D16.

59 Secretary of State Kissinger, *The United States and Latin America: The New Opportunity*, Speech, Houston, Texas, March 1, 1975, Department of State, Bureau of Public Affairs, Office of Media Services.

60 Personal Interview: Department of State official, Washington, D.C., March 11, 1975. The respondent was a senior official in the Bureau of Inter-American Affairs between 1973 and 1975.

61 See David Binder, "Cuba Sanctions, in Force 11 Years, Lifted by OAS," *New York Times*, July 30, 1975, pp. 1, 4; "OAS Lifts Cuba Sanctions; U.S. Votes with Majority," *Washington Post*, July 30, 1975, pp. A1, A22.

62 Quoted in Dom Bonafede, "Relations with Cuba Unlikely Soon," *National Journal*, Vol. 7, No. 11, March 15, 1975, p. 403.

63 Quoted in David Binder, "Cuba Policy in U.S. Slowly Changing," *New York Times*, March 30, 1975, p. 17. President Ford made much the same point: "The policy today is the same as it has been, which is that if Cuba will reevaluate and give us some indication of a change of its policy toward the United States, then we certainly would take another look." President Ford News Conference, February 26, 1975, reprinted in *Department of State Bulletin*, Vol. LXXII, No. 1864, March 17, 1975, p. 334.

64 See Mohamad A. El-Khawas and Barry Cohen, *The Kissinger Study of Southern Africa*. National Security Study Memorandum 39. Secret (Westport: Lawrence Hill & Co., 1976).

65 See Nathaniel Davis, "The Angola Decision of 1975: A Personal Memoir," *Foreign Affairs*, Vol. 56, No. 1, Fall 1978, pp. 110, 116–117. Davis was Assistant Secretary of State for African Affairs in the spring and summer of 1975 and played a key role in the imperial-state debate over Angola policy.

66 For an excellent analysis, see William M. Leogrande, *Cuba's Policy In Africa, 1959–1980* (University of California at Berkeley: Institute of International Studies, 1980), especially pp. 17–19. Also see John Stockwell, *In Search of Enemies* (New York: W. W. Norton & Co., 1978). Stockwell was the CIA Chief of the Angola Task Force at the time. On the Cuban commitment to the MPLA, see Nelson P. Valdés, "Revolutionary Solidarity in Angola," in Cole Blasier & Carmelo Mesa-Lago, eds., *Cuba in the World* (Pittsburgh: University of Pittsburgh Press, 1979), pp. 87-117.

67 David Binder, "Kissinger Believes Cuba 'Exports' Revolution Again," *New York Times*, February 5, 1976, p. 2.

68 Quoted in Edward Walsh, "President Brands Castro an 'International Outlaw'," *Washington Post*, February 29, 1976, p. A4.

69 Murrey Marder, "U.S. Steps Up Warnings to Cubans," *Washington Post*, March 26, p. A1. Also see Bernard Gwertzman, "U.S. Will Not Bar Invasion of Cuba," *New York Times*, March 24, 1976, p. 7. Hostility to Cuba's African involvement also was framed by the continent's enormous importance as a source of strategic raw materials

and as an investment locale for and trade partner with the industrialized capitalist world (United States, Western Europe, and Japan). Kissinger articulated this concern before U.S. Congress, Senate, Committee on Foreign Relations, Subcommittee on African Affairs and Subcommittee on Arms Control, International Organizations and Security Agreements, *U.S. Policy Toward Africa*, 94th Congress, 2nd Session, March 5, 8, 15, 19; May 12, 13, 21, 26, and 27, 1976 (Washington: U.S. Government Printing Office, 1976), p. 184.

70 Quoted in Murrey Marder, "Kissinger on Cuba: No Crisis," *Washington Post*, March 27, 1976, p. A1. Also see David Binder, "U.S. Is Reviewing its Cuba Options," *New York Times*, March 26, 1976, pp. 1, 5.

71 Secretary of State Kissinger, *Press Conference*, Washington, D.C., April 22, 1976, Department of State, Bureau of Public Affairs, Office of Media Services. Also see Philip Shabecoff, "Ford Warns Cuba Over Puerto Rico," *New York Times*, July 27, 1976, p. 3. Cuba was a leading advocate of Puerto Rican independence and, much to Washington's displeasure, consistently raised Puerto Rico's status within the United Nations Colonization Committee.

72 See Petras and Morley, *The United States and Chile;* U.S. Congress, Senate, *Covert Action in Chile, 1963–1973*; Hersh, *The Price of Power*, pp. 258–296; James Petras and Morris Morley, "On The U.S. And The Overthrow of Allende," *Latin American Research Review*, Vol. XIII, No. 1, 1978, pp. 205–221.

73 Zbigniew Brzezinski, *Power and Principle: Memoirs of the National Security Adviser 1977–1981* (London: Weidenfeld and Nicolson, 1983), p. 186.

74 Quoted in Dom Bonafede, "The Latest Hitch in Normalizing Relations with the Cubans," *National Journal*, Vol. 10, No. 19, May 13, 1978, p. 763. A number of Carter administration foreign-policy officials – Sol M. Linowitz (chief Panama Canal negotiator), Michael Blumenthal (Secretary of the Treasury), Samuel Huntington (NSC Staff), Fred Bergsten (Assistant Secretary of the Treasury), Robert Pastor (senior Latin American advisor to NSC Advisor Zbigniew Brzezinski) – were members of the "Commission on United States-Latin American Relations," which restated the "liberal" case for a change in Cuba policy in its 1974–1975 report on interhemispheric relations. See Report of the Commission on United States-Latin American Relations, *The Americas in A Changing World* (New York: Quadrangle/The New York Times Book Co., 1975), pp. 27–28.

75 Personal Interview: National Security Council Staff member, Washington, D.C., August 21, 1978. The respondent was a specialist in Latin American affairs.

76 Personal Interview: Department of State official, Washington, D.C., August 16, 1978. The respondent was a senior Cuba affairs official in the Carter administration.

77 See Robert Morison, "US Drops Cuba Ship Blacklisting," *Journal of Commerce*, September 8, 1977, pp. 1, 21. The NSC decision was taken on June 10. 1977.

78 Quoted in "Vance Proposes Talks with Cuba, No Preconditions," *Washington Post*, March 5, 1977, p. A1.
79 Personal Interview: Department of State official, Washington, D.C., August 23, 1978.
80 Personal Interview: Department of State official, Washington, D.C., August 16, 1978.
81 See Jack Nelson, "Cuba Spurns U.S. Medicine Sales as Not Enough," *Los Angeles Times*, February 20, 1978, pp. 1, 7. Bourne submitted the memo to the State Department on August 17, 1977.
82 "The United States and Latin America," President Carter before the Permanent Council of the OAS, *News Release*, April 14, 1977, Department of State, Bureau of Public Affairs, Office of Media Services.
83 Statement of Wayne Smith, Director, Office of Cuban Affairs, Department of State, in U.S. Congress, House, Committee on International Relations, Subcommittee on Inter-American Affairs, *Impact of Cuban-Soviet Ties in the Western Hemisphere*, 95th Congress, 2nd Session, March 14, 15; April 5 and 12, 1978 (Washington, D.C.: U.S. Government Printing office, 1978), p. 6. Also see John M Goshko, "Expanded Cuban Presence in Africa Decried by U.S.," *Washington Post*, November 18, 1977, p. A22; Hedrick Smith, "U.S. Sees Cuba's African Buildup Blocking Efforts to Improve Ties," *New York Times*, November 17, 1977, p. 1.
84 Quoted in Austin Scott, "Cuba Called Stabilizer in Angola," *Washington Post*, April 17, 1977, p. A1. For an extended discussion, see Gerald J. Bender, "Angola, The Cubans, and American Anxieties," *Foreign Policy*, No. 31, Summer 1978, pp. 3–30.
85 Cyrus Vance, *Hard Choices: Critical Years in America's Foreign Policy* (New York: Simon and Schuster, 1983), p. 71.
86 Quoted in Scott, "Cuba Called Stabilizer in Angola," p. A1.
87 See Smith, *The Closest of Enemies*, p. 123.
88 Testimony of William E. Schaufele, Jr., Assistant Secretary of State for African Affairs, in U.S. Congress, Senate, Committee on Foreign Relations, Subcommittee on African Affairs, *Ethiopia and the Horn of Africa*, 94th Congress, 2nd Session, August 4, 5, and 6, 1976 (Washington, D.C.: U.S. Government Printing office, 1976), pp. 113–114; Fred Halliday & Maxine Molyneux, *The Ethiopian Revolution* (London: Verso Edition and New Left Books, 1981), p. 215.
89 See Marina Ottaway, *Soviet and American Influence in the Horn of Africa* (New York: Praeger Publishers, 1982), p. 101. Also see Bereket Habte Selassie, *Conflict and Intervention in the Horn of Africa* (New York: Monthly Review Press, 1980), pp. 137–138.
90 Ibid., p. 139.
91 Ethiopia signed a secret arms deal with Moscow valued at between $100 million and $200 million in December 1976. See David Ottaway and Marina Ottaway, *Afrocommunism* (New York: Africana Publishing Co., 1981), p. 174. The Dergue's economic and political reforms are discussed in Marina Ottaway and David Ottaway, *Ethiopia: Empire in Revolution* (New York: Africana Publishing Co., 1978).

92 See Don Oberdorfer, "The Superpowers and Africa's Horn," *Washington Post*, March 5, 1978, p. A10.
93 See ibid., p. A10; Steven David, "Realignment in the Horn: The Soviet Advantage," *International Security*, Vol. 4, No. 2, Fall 1979, p. 75.
94 Ottaway and Ottaway, *Afrocommunism*, p. 174.
95 Quoted in Oberdorfer, "The Superpowers and Africa's Horn," p. A10.
96 See Leogrande, *Cuba's Policy in Africa, 1959–1980*, pp. 38–39.
97 Ibid., p. 39.
98 See Murrey Marder, "U.S. Cautions Havana About Role in Africa," *Washington Post*, May 26, 1977, p. A1.
99 See Leogrande, *Cuba's Policy In Africa, 1959–1980*, p. 40. "In justifying their Angolan and Ethiopian expeditions," writes one authority on the subject, "the Soviets and their Cuban allies have drawn upon . . . widely recognized norms, particularly the right of recognized governments to secure foreign assistance in defending their borders and suppressing insurgents," Tom J. Farer, *War Clouds on the Horn of Africa: The Widening Storm* (Washington, D.C.: Carnegie Endowment for International Peace, 1979), p. 137. On Cuba's involvement in Ethiopia, also see *Cuban Studies/Estudios Cubanos*, Special Volume, Part 1 ("Cuba in Africa"), Vol. 10, No. 1, January 1980.
100 Quoted in Robert G. Kaiser and Don Oberdorfer, "Africa Turnabout: Concern over Soviets, Cubans Transforms U.S. Policy," *Washington Post*, June 4, 1978, p. A16.
101 Brzezinski, *Power and Principle*, p. 178.
102 Ibid., p. 187.
103 Brzezinski, quoted in Richard Burt, "Zbig Makes It Big," *New York Times Magazine*, July 30, 1978, p. 30.
104 See Brzezinski, *Power and Principle*, pp. 181–182; Vance, *Hard Choices*, pp. 86–87.
105 Brzezinski, *Power and Principle*, p. 143.
106 Quoted in Bonafede, "The Last Hitch in Normalizing Relations with the Cubans," p. 765. Also see John M. Goshko, "CIA Aide Blunt on Soviet Cuban Actions," *Washington Post*, April 11, 1978, p. A16. Carlucci's testimony was given during an executive session before the Senate Armed Services Subcommittee on Intelligence on April 10, 1978.
107 See Vance, *Hard Choices*, pp. 74, 84.
108 Personal Interview: Department of State official, Washington, D.C., August 23, 1978.
109 See Vance, *Hard Choices*, p. 88.
110 Personal Interview: National Security Council Staff Member, Washington, D.C., August 21, 1978.
111 Smith, *The Closest of Enemies*, p. 138.
112 Quoted in Murrey Marder, "Belgium Sees No Conclusive Proof on Cuban Zaire Role," *Washington Post*, June 1, 1978, p. A16. Also see Richard Burt, "Lesson of Shaba: Carter Risked Serious 'Credibility Gap'," *New York Times*, July 11, 1978, p. 2.

113 Vance, *Hard Choices*, p. 90.
114 Quoted in Kaiser and Oberdorfer, "Africa Turnabout: Concern over Soviets, Cubans Transforms U.S. Policy," p. A16.
115 Quoted in David Binder, "Carter Aides Urge a Gesture to Cuba," *New York Times*, November 12, 1978, p. 17.
116 See "Carter Asked Venezuela and Brazil to Press Cuba on African Activity," *New York Times*, June 12, 1978, p. D15.
117 "Transcript of President's News Conference on Domestic and Foreign Affairs," May 25, in *New York Times*, May 26, 1978, p. 10. Also see "Transcript of President's Speech on Soviet-American Relations at the U.S. Naval Academy," Annapolis, June 7, in *New York Times*, June 8, 1978, p. 22. NSC advisor Brzezinski described Cuba as a foreign-policy "surrogate" of the Soviet Union in remarks at a meeting of newspaper editors on September 7, 1979. Quoted in Martin Schram, "Talks Planned on Soviet Unit," *Washington Post*, September 8, 1979, p. A8.
118 Testimony of Secretary of State Vance, in U.S. Congress, Senate, Committee on Foreign Relations, Subcommittee on African Affairs, *U.S. Policy Toward Africa*, 95th Congress, 2nd Session, May 12, 1978 (Washington, D.C.: U.S. Government Printing Office, 1978), p. 15. Also see H. Michael Erisman, *Cuba's International Relations* (Boulder: Westview Press, 1985), pp. 80–82.
119 See Smith, *The Closest of Enemies*, pp. 145–149. Also see Binder, "Carter Aides Urge a Gesture to Cuba," p. 17.
120 Smith, *The Closest of Enemies*, pp. 141–142.
121 See Graham Hovey, "U.S. Calls Cubans in Africa Bar to Ties," *New York Times*, January 3, 1979, p. 3.
122 See Question and Answer Session by Secretary of State Vance, following an address in Atlantic City, New Jersey, June 20, 1978, *Department of State Press Release*, June 20, 1978, No. 257(A).
123 Quoted in Graham Hovey, "State Dept. Opposes Senate Move on Cuba," *New York Times*, June 30, 1978, p. 3.
124 Personal Interview: National Security Council Staff Member, Washington, D.C., August 21, 1978.
125 Statement of John A. Bushnell, Deputy Assistant Secretary of State, Bureau of Inter-American Affairs, in U.S. Congress, Committee on Foreign Affairs, Subcommittee on Inter-American Affairs, *Economic and Political Future of the Caribbean*, 96th Congress, 1st Session, July 24, 26, and September 29, 1979 (Washington, D.C.: U.S. Government Printing Office, 1979), p. 4.
126 See Daniel Southerland, "Reassessing Cuba's Role in Nicaragua," *Christian Science Monitor*, June 27, 1979, p. 3.
127 See Graham Hovey, "U.S. Study Says Cuba Plays Cautious Role in Nicaragua," *New York Times*, July 4, 1979, p. 3; "Cuba Sends Advisers to Nicaragua, but Counsels Caution," *New York Times*, July 9, 1980, p. 10.
128 Statement of John A. Bushnell, Deputy Assistant Secretary of State, Bureau of inter-American Affairs, in U.S. Congress, House, *Economic and Political Future of the Caribbean*, p. 4. The State Department instructed its Ambassador to Grenada, Frank Ortiz, to inform

Prime Minister Bishop that Washington "would view with displeasure . . . any tendency on the part of Grenada to develop closer ties with Cuba." Quoted from the Ambassador's instructions, in Karen DeYoung, "U.S. vs. Cuba on Caribbean Isle of Grenada," *Washington Post*, April 27, 1979. One NSC official responded to the governmental change in Grenada by declaring it now meant "a Cuban octopus is loose in the Caribbean." Quoted in Smith, *The Closest of Enemies*, p. 171.

129 Brzezinski, *Power and Principle*, p. 346.
130 Ibid., p. 347.
131 Vance, *Hard Choices*, p. 360.
132 Ibid., p. 362.
133 Ibid.
134 Quoted in Robert C. Byrd, "SALT and a Pseudo-Crisis," *Washington Post*, October 1, 1979, p. A21.
135 See Brzezinski, *Power and Principle*, p. 350. On the meeting between Carter and Byrd, see Jimmy Carter, *Keeping Faith: Memoirs of a President* (London: William Collins, 1982), p. 263.
136 Vance, *Hard Choices*, p. 364.
137 See John M. Goshko and George C. Wilson, "U.S. Seeking Multinational Force for Seagoing Caribbean Patrols," *Washington Post*, October 13, 1979, pp. A1, A19.
138 See Richard Burt, "Carter Said to Order Harder Line In Bid to Cut Cuban Role Abroad, " *New York Times*, October 17, 1979, p. 10; John K. Cooley, "Carter Goal: To Neturalize Castro Threat," *Christian Science Monitor*, October 24, 1979, p. 10.
139 See *Latin America Weekly Report*, Vol. XIII, No. 43, November 2, 1979, p. 1.
140 Quoted in Guillermo Martínez and Helga Silva, "Carter Aides, Cubans Met Secretly," *Miami Herald*, October 12, 1981, p. 8A. Also see "Top Carter Aides Reportedly Held Talks with Castro," *Houston Post*, July 7, 1981, p. 1.
141 Quoted in "Carter's Secret Link with Castro Revealed," *The Australian*, July 8, 1981, p. 5. Also see Juan de Onís, "U.S. and Cuba: Still Far Apart," *New York Times*, October 16, 1980, p. 11.
142 See "Spain and Cuba; Expensive Friends," *The Economist*, December 4, 1971, p. 102; "Cubans Drive Hard Bargain in Trade Pact with Spain," *London Times*, December 20, 1971, p. 5; Richard Mowrer, "Cuban-Spanish Temperature," *Christian Science Monitor*, August 6, 1971, p. 5.
143 U.S. Department of Commerce, *United States Commercial Relations With Cuba: A Survey*, p. 41 (Table 5). Also see "Cuba's Links with Nonsocialist World Expanding through Trade and Technology Deals," *Business Latin America*, April 20, 1972, pp. 121–122.
144 Business International Corporation, *Cuba At The Turning Point* (New York, July 1977), p. 80. For details on Cuba's trade with the industrialized capitalist countries, see U.S. Department of Commerce, *United States Commercial Relations with Cuba: A Survey*, pp. 16–17, 54–55, (Tables 15 and 16); U.S. Department of Commerce, Office of East-West Policy Planning, *Cuban Trade with the Industrialized*

West 1974–1979. Prepared by Lawrence Theriot and Linda Droker, Project D-76, May 1981, pp. 6, 9 (Table 2).

145 The transportation blockage pursued by Washington during the 1960s apparently achieved some permanent, long-term negative effects regarding the Castro regime's access to capitalist-owned shipping during the first half of the 1970s. See Appendix II, Table 2.

146 See World Bank, Commodities and Report Projections Division, Economic Analysis and Projections Department, Development Policy Staff, *Commodity Trade and Price Trends (1978 Edition)*, Report No. EC-166/78, August 1978, p. 51.

147 See U.S. Congress, House, Committee on International Relations, Subcommittee on International Trade and Commerce, *United States-Cuba Trade Promotion*, 94th Congress, 2nd Session, July 22, 1976 (Washington, D.C.: U.S. Government Printing Office, 1976), p. 73; Business International Corporation, *Cuba At The Turning Point*, p. 39; U.S. Central Intelligence Agency, *The Cuban Economy: A Statistical Review, 1968–1978*, ER76-10708, December 26, 1976, p. 9.

148 On growth rates, see Lawrence Theriot, "U.S. Cuba Trade: Question Mark," *Commerce America* (U.S. Department of Commerce), Vol. III, No. 9., April 24, 1978, pp. 2–5; Business International Corporation, *Cuba at the Turning Point*, p. 33; "Cuba: A Sustained Economic Recovery," *Bank of London & South America Review*, Vol. 9, May 1975, p. 253.

149 See U.S. Department of Commerce, *Cuban Trade with the Industrialized West 1974–1979*, pp. 6, 9 (Table 2); Lawrence Theriot, "U.S. Cuba Trade: Question Mark," pp. 3–4; U.S. Department of Commerce, Bureau of East-West Trade, Office of East-West Policy, *Cuban Foreign Trade; A Current Assessment.* Prepared by Lawrence Theoriot, 1978, p. 16.

150 *Latin America Economic Report*, Vol. V, No. 4, January 28, 1977, p. 13.

151 See U.S. Department of Commerce, *Cuban Trade with the Industrialized West 1974–1979*, p. 6 (Tables 4 and 8).

152 See D. R. Murray, "The Bilateral Road: Canada and Latin America in the 1980s," *International Journal*, Vol. XXXVII, No. 1, Winter 1981–82, pp. 119, 120. By 1979, Canada had passed Japan as Cuba's major capitalist supplier. See "Leap Forward for Trade with Cuba," *Latin America Regional Report: Caribbean* RC-81-06, July 17, 1981, p. 11.

153 See Susan Morgan, "Cubans Eager for More Trade with Britain," *London Times*, November 6, 1971, p. 19.

154 "Cuba to Get Japanese Buses," *Christian Science Monitor*, August 17, 1970, p. 5.

155 "Cuba Libre," *The Economist*, August 9, 1975, p. 64.

156 Quoted in Norman Pearlestine, "Japan Finds a Ready Market in Cuba," *Wall Street Journal*, October 27, 1975, p. 6.

157 On Cuba's growing debt, see Economist Intelligence Unit, *Quarterly Economic Review of Cuba*, No. 4., November 1979, p. 12; U.S.

Department of Commerce, *Cuban Trade with the Industrialized West 1974–1979*, p. 4.

158 See United Nations, Economic Commission for Latin America, *Economic Survey of Latin America, 1979* (Santiago, 1981), p. 195; Economist Intelligence Unit, *Quarterly Economic Review of Cuba*, No. 2, May 1979, p. 7 and No. 3, August 1979, p. 7.

159 Economist Intelligence Unit, *Quarterly Economic Review of Cuba*, No. 2, June 1980, p. 12.

160 See U.S. Congress, House, Committee on Banking and Currency, Subcommittee on International Trade, *Extension of the Export Administration Act of 1969*, 92nd Congress, 2nd Session, May 30, 1972 (Washington, D.C.: U.S. Government Printing Office, 1972), pp. 39, 44–45, 47.

161 See U.S. Congress, House, *United States–Cuba Trade Promotion*, p. 42.

162 Department of State to American Embassy, Canberra, Telegram, Secret. Info: American Embassy, Ottawa, Subject: "Australian Firm's Sale of Sugar Cane Harvesters to Cuba," April 9, 1971, No. 62030, *DFOIA*. Nearly 100 Russian combine harvesters were imported between 1965 and 1968, but their unadaptability to local conditions led the Cubans to seek other harvester suppliers. See "Cuba May Buy 100 Harvesters," *Sydney Morning Herald*, May 15, 1971, p. 13.

163 Canberra Embassy to Department of State, Telegram, Info: American Embassy, Ottawa, Secret, Subject: "Australian Sugar Cane Harvester for Cuba," May 7, 1971, Canberra 2691, *DFOIA*. Also see "Our Sale to Cuba Worries America," *Melbourne Age*, May 13, 1971, p. 1; "Govt. Denies U.S. Complaint," *Sydney Morning Herald*, May 13, 1971, p. 1; "U.S. Dissatisfied with Cuba Sale," *Sydney Morning Herald*, May 14, 1971, p. 2. Massey-Ferguson-Australia suffered losses totalling just under $3 million in 1970 and almost $1 million for the three-month period from November 1970 to January 1971. See "Our Sale to Cuba Worries America," p. 1.

164 See Roy Macartney, "Harvester Sale May Upset Our U.S. Exports," *Melbourne Age*, May 17, 1971, p. 8.

165 Quoted in Derryn Hinch, "Threat to Sugar Exports," *Sydney Morning Herald*, May 15, 1971, p. 13.

166 U.S. Congress, Senate, Committee on Foreign Relations, *Legislative Proposals Relating to the War in Southeast Asia*, 92nd Congress, 1st Session, April 20, 21, 22, and 28; May 3, 11, 12, 13, 25, 26, and 27, 1971 (Washington, D.C.: U.S. Government Printing Office, 1971), p. 394.

167 Department of State to Canberra Embassy, Telegram, Secret, Subject: "Australian Cane Harvesters for Cuba," December 17, 1971, No. 229379, *DFOIA*. A leading U.S. multinational business journal reported in April 1976 that the Cuban government was "importing hundreds of combines from Massey-Ferguson's Australian subsidiary. . . ." "Cuban Bank Report Outlines Ambitious Goals for Industrial Development," *Business Latin America*, April 14, 1976, p. 116.

168 U.S. Congress, House, Committee on International Relations, Sub-

committee on International Organizations, *The Rhodesian Sanctions Bill, Part II*, 94th Congress, 1st Session, June 19, 1975 (Washington, D.C.: U.S. Government Printing Office, 1975), p. 16.

169 "U.S. Maintains Tough Strictures on Cuba Trade," *Business International*, August 13, 1971, p. 258. Also see Economist Intelligence Unit, *Quarterly Economic Review of Cuba*, No. 4, November 1971, p. 6.

170 See Dan Morgan, "Dacca Halts Cuba Trade for Food," *Washington Post*, September 30, 1974, pp. A1, A16.

171 See David Binder, "U.S., in Shift, Views Perón As Argentina's Best Hope," *New York Times*, July 29, 1973, pp. 1, 2.

172 On the foreign investment controls, see "Milder Law on Foreign Investment Passes Argentine Congress," *Business Latin America*, November 14, 1973, pp. 361–362.

173 See "Should U.S. Affiliates Trade with Cuba? Argentina Says Yes, U.S. Says No," *Business Latin America*, December 12, 1973, pp. 393–394. Also see Lewis H. Duiguid, "U.S. Boycott of Cuba Tested," *Washington Post*, January 13, 1974, p. A29.

174 Department of the Treasury, Memorandum, From Fred D. Levy to Assistant Secretary John M. Hennessy, Subject: "Argentina Trade with Cuba," November 13, 1974, Confidential, *DFOIA*.

175 Quoted in Richard Lawrence, "Car Exports to Cuba Via Argentina Eyed," *Journal of Commerce*, April 16, 1974, p. 1. Also see Joseph Novitski, "Argentina Push Sales to Cuba," *Washington Post*, April 18, 1974, p. A2.

176 Quoted in Murrey Marder, "Embargo on Cuba Faces Challenge from Canada," *Washington Post*, February 28, 1974, p. A10.

177 Quoted in Richard Harwood, "U.S. Denies Shift on Cuba Stand," *Washington Post*, April 20, 1974, p. A1.

178 Kissinger News Conference, April 26, 1974, reprinted in *Department of State Bulletin*, Vol. LXX, No. 1821, May 20, 1974, p. 544.

179 Quoted in "Cuban Countdown," *The Economist*, May 4, 1974, p. 59.

180 See "Canada/US Rift Develops Over Cuba Trade," *Business International*, March 8, 1974, p. 75; "Locomotive Sale to Cuba Verified," *New York Times*, March 19, 1974, p. 47.

181 "A Showdown over the Ban on Cuba Trade," *Business Week*, April 3, 1974, p. 81. Also see Peyton V. Lyon and Brian W. Tomlin, *Canada as an International Actor* (Toronto: Macmillan of Canada, 1979), p. 121.

182 "U.S. Easing of Cuba Trade Embargo Is Limited," *Business Internationa*, May 10, 1974, p. 151. In the fall of 1974, the Canadian government's Export Development Corporation signed an agreement with the National Bank of Cuba to provide credits to facilitate the MLW-Worthington sale. See John D. Habron, "Canada Draws Closer to Latin America: A Cautious Involvement," in Fontaine and Therberge, eds., *Latin America's New Internationalism*, p. 129.

183 See William Borders, "U.S. Subsidiary in Canada Forced to Drop Cuba Deal," *New York Times*, December 24, 1974, p. 3.

184 Quoted in "U.S.-Canadian Conflicts on Cuba Continue to Squeeze Firms," *Business Latin America*, March 26, 1975, p. 102.

185 Personal Interview: Latin American specialist, Business International Corporation, New York City, New York, April 16, 1975. The respondent was the editor of Business Latin America.

186 Ibid.

187 Personal Interview: Department of State official, Washington, D.C., October 10, 1974. The respondent was a Department international economist between 1972 and 1975. For a discussion of the MLW-Worthington and Litton transactions, also see David Leyton-Brown, "Extraterritoriality in Canadian-American Relations," *International Journal*, Vol. XXXVI, No. 1, Winter 1980–1, pp. 190–191.

188 Quoted in "U.S. Urged to Reassess Trade, Political Goals," *Journal of Commerce*, August 18, 1976, p. 1.

189 U.S. Congress, House, Committee on International Relations, Subcommittee on International Trade and Commerce, and International Organizations, *U.S. Trade Embargo of Cuba*, 94th Congress, 1st Session, May 8, 13, 15, 20, 22, June 11, 26 and July 9, and September 23, 1975 (Washington, D.C. U.S. Government Printing Office, 1975), p. 369.

190 Ibid., pp. 361–362.

191 National Security Decision Memorandum 305, NSC, September 15, 1975, To: Secretaries of Treasury, Defense, Agriculture, Commerce, Deputy Secretary of State, The Administrator of AID, From: Henry Kissinger, Subject: "Termination of U.S. Restrictions on Third Countries Trading With Cuba." *DFOIA*.

192 See Economist Intelligence Unit, *Quarterly Economic Review of Cuba*, No. 2, May 1979, p. 7.

193 See "Swiss Gnomes Draw the Line at Cuba," *Latin America Weekly Report* WR-79-03, November 16, 1979, p. 30; Economist Intelligence Unit, *Quarterly Economic Review of Cuba*, No. 4., November 1979, p. 12.

194 See Economist Intelligence Unit, *Quarterly Economic Review of Cuba*, No. 4., November 1980, p. 8; Eileen Alt Powell, "U.S. Bans Some Creusot-Loire Products Because They Contain Nickel from Cuba," *Wall Street Journal*, November 17, 1980, p. 5.

195 Representative Paul Findley, March 9, 1977, in "Controversy in Congress over U.S. Policy Toward Cuba: Pros & Cons," *Congressional Digest*, Vol. 57, No. 2, February 1978, pp. 54–55.

196 Senator Frank Church, "U.S. Policy in the Caribbean," Address, *Congressional Record-Senate*, 91st Congress, 2nd Session, Vol. 116, Part 29, November 25, 1970, p. 38853; Senator Stephen Young, *Congressional Record-Senate*, 91st Congress, 2nd Session, Vol. 116, Part 28, November 23, 1970, p. 38462; Address by Senator Edward Kennedy, University of Montana, *Congressional Record-Senate*, 91st Congress, 2nd Session, Vol. 116, Part 9, April 20, 1970, p. 12324.

197 Senator Stephen Young, *Congressional Record-Senate*, November 23, 1970, p. 38462.

198 Address by Senator Edward M. Kennedy, Chicago Council on Foreign Relations, October 12, 1971, *Congressional Record-Senate*,

92nd Congress, 1st Session, Vol. 117, Part 30, November 2, 1971, pp. 38761–38763.

199 Opening statement by Senator Edward M. Kennedy at *Congressional Conference on U.S.-Cuba Relations,* Unofficial Transcript, April 19–20, 1972, New Senate Office Building, Washington, D.C., p. 2.

200 Ibid., p. 3. Also see Senator Edward M. Kennedy, "It Is Time to Normalize Relations with Cuba," *New York Times Magazine,* January 14, 1973, pp. 16, 19, 23.

201 Senator Harold Hughes, at *Congressional Conference on U.S.-Cuba Relations,* p. 5.

202 See U.S. Congress, House, Committee on Foreign Affairs, Subcommittee on Inter-American Affairs, *Cuba and the Caribbean,* 91st Congress, 2nd Session, July 8, 9, 10, 13, 27, 29, 31, and August 3, 1970 (Washington, D.C.: U.S. Government Printing Office, 1970), p. 32.

203 Representative H. R. Gross, in ibid., p. 117.

204 See U.S. Congress, House, Committee on Foreign Affairs, Subcommittee on Inter-American Affairs, *Soviet Naval Activities in Cuba,* 91st Congress, 2nd Session, September 30, October 13, November 19 and 24, 1970 (Washington, D.C.: U.S. Government Printing Office, 1970). Also see U.S. Congress, House, *Soviet Naval Activities in Cuba, Part 2;* U.S. Congress, House, *Soviet Activities in Cuba, Part 3;* U.S. Congress, House, Committee on Foreign Affairs, Subcommittee on Inter-American Affairs, *Soviet Activities in Cuba, Part 4 and 5,* 93rd Congress, 2nd Session, October 31, 1973, November 20 and 21, 1974 (Washington, D.C.: U.S. Government Printing Office, 1974); U.S. Congress, House, Committee on International Relations, Subcommittee on International Political and Military Affairs, *Soviet Activities in Cuba, Part VI and VII: Communist Influence in the Western Hemisphere,* 94th Congress, October 7, 1975, June 15 and September 16, 1976 (Washington, D.C.: U.S. Government Printing Office, 1976).

205 *A Detente with Cuba.* Statement prepared by 11 Republican members of the House of Representatives, January 1973, Washington, D.C.

206 Senator Robert C. Byrd, *Congressional Record-Senate,* 93rd Congress, 1st Session, Vol. 119, Part 6, March 12, 1973, pp. 7292–7293.

207 U.S. Congress, Senate, *U.S. Policy Toward Cuba,* p. 24.

208 Ibid., pp. 3, 4–5, 13.

209 Senator Gale McGee, in ibid., p. 31.

210 Ibid., p. 12.

211 Senator Gale McGee, in ibid., p. 22.

212 Ibid., p. 21.

213 Ibid., pp. 23, 28.

214 Senator Gale McGee, in ibid., p. 28.

215 Senator Gale McGee, in U.S. Congress, Senate, Committee on Foreign Relations, *Nomination of Henry A. Kissinger, Part 1,* 93rd Congress, 1st Session, September 7, 10, 11, and 14, 1973 (Washington, D.C.: U.S. Government Printing Office, 1973), p. 144.

216 Senator Robert C. Byrd, *Congressional Record-Senate*, 93rd Congress, 2nd Session, Vol. 120, Part 2, February 6, 1974, p. 234. Also see Senator Gale McGee, *Congressional Record-Senate*, 93rd Congress, 1st Session, Vol. 110, Part 23, September 11, 1973, p. 29152; Representative Michael Harrington, *Congressional Record-House*, 93rd Congress, 2nd Session, Vol. 120, No. 112, July 29, 1974, p. H7301.

217 "Senate Unit Backs Trade with Cuba," *Washington Post*, April 24, 1974, p. A1.

218 U.S. Congress, Senate, Committee on Foreign Relations, *The United States and Cuba: A Propitious Moment*, Report by Senator Jacob Javits and Senator Claiborne Pell. 93rd Congress, 2nd Session, Committee Print, October 1974 (Washington, D.C.: U.S. Government Printing Office, October 1974), p. 3. The trip took place on September 27 to 30, 1974.

219 U.S. Congress, House, Committee on International Relations, *United States Relations with Cuba*, Report of a Special Study Mission to Cuba, August 30–September 3, 1975, 94th Congress, 1st Session, Committee Print, October 31, 1975 (Washington, D.C.: U.S. Government Printing Office, 1975), p. 12.

220 See Philip Brenner and R. Roger Majak, *Congressmen As Statesmen: The Case of Cuba*. Paper prepared for delivery at the Annual Meeting of the American Political Science Association, Chicago, Illinois, September 2–5, 1976, p. 7.

221 Senator Edward M. Kennedy, *Congressional Record-Senate*, 94th Congress, 1st Session, Vol. 121, Part 4, March 4, 1975, pp. 5001–5002. Referred to the Committee on Foreign Relations.

222 Statement by Representative Michael J. Harrington, in U.S. Congress, House, *U.S. Trade Embargo of Cuba*, p. 49.

223 See, for example, U.S. Congress, House, *United States Relations with Cuba*, p. 11; U.S. Congress, House, Committee on International Relations, *United States-Cuban Perspectives–1975*, Report of a Study Visit to Cuba, September 18–October 15, 1975, 94th Congress, 2nd Session, Committee Print, May 4, 1976 (Washington, D.C.: U.S. Government Printing Office, 1976), p. 10; U.S. Congress, Senate, Committee on Foreign Relations, *Cuban Realities: May 1975*, Report by Senator George S. McGovern, 94th Congress, 1st Session, Committee Print, August 1975 (Washington, D.C.: U.S. Government Printing Office, 1975), p. 3; U.S. Congress, House, *Cuba Study Mission*, p.7.

224 U.S. Congress, Senate, Committee on Agriculture and Forestry, Subcommittee on Agricultural Production, Marketing, and Stabilization of Prices, *Rice Programs*, 94th Congress, 1st Session, November 14, 1975 (Washington, D.C.: U.S. Government Printing Office, 1975), p. 54. Also see David Binder, "Louisianans Ask Trade with Cuba," *New York Times*, November 16, 1975, p. 32.

225 U.S. Congress, Senate, *Cuban Realities: May 1975*, p. 3.

226 Senator Carl Curtis, *Congressional Record-Senate*, 94th Congress, 1st Session, Vol. 121, Part 28, November 13, 1975, pp. 36378–36379.

227 Representative Donald M. Fraser, in U.S. Congress, House, *United States-Cuba Trade Promotion*, pp. 19–20.
228 Quoted in Richard Lawrence, "Bid to Restore U.S.-Cuban Trade Fails," *Journal of Commerce*, November 24, 1975, p. 11.
229 U.S. Congress, House, Committee on International Relations, *Toward Improved United States-Cuba Relations*, Report of a Special Study Mission to Cuba, February 10–15, 1977, 95th Congress, 1st Session, Committee Print, May 23, 1977 (Washington, D.C.: U.S. Government Printing Office, 1977), p. 21.
230 Representative Jonathan B, Bingham, October 6, 1977, in "Controversy in Congress over U.S. Policy Toward Cuba: Pros & Cons," p. 58.
231 Senator George S. McGovern, May 13, 1977, in ibid., p. 54.
232 U.S. Congress, House, *Toward Improved United States-Cuban Relations*, p. 20.
233 Ibid. Also see Representative Paul Findly, March 9, 1977, in "Controversy in Congress over U.S. Policy Toward Cuba: Pros & Cons," pp. 54, 56. Senator Frank Church felt that Washington could "begin to exercise a moderating influence in Cuban affairs" if the executive branch sought to eliminate the trade embargo on a "step-by-step" basis. U.S. Congress, Senate, Committee on Foreign Relations, *Delusions and Reality: The Future of United States-Cuba Relations*, Report by Senator Frank Church on a Trip to Cuba, August 8–11, 1977, 95th Congress, 1st Session, Committee Print, October 1977 (Washington, D.C.: U.S. Government Printing Office, 1977), pp. 9–10.
234 Representative Jonathan B. Bingham, October 6, 1977, in "Controversy in Congress over U.S. Policy Toward Cuba: Pros & Cons," p. 60.
235 Senator Richard Stone, quoted in Lee Lescaze, "Senate Panel Votes to Relax Embargo Against Cuba," *Washington Post*, May 11, 1977, p. A1.
236 See "House Backs Ban on Trade with Vietnam and Cuba," *Washington Post*, May 13, 1977, p. A1.
237 See Richard Lawrence, "Cuba Trade Proposal Withdrawn," *Journal of Commerce*, June 17, 1977, pp. 1, 15.
238 *Congressional Record-Senate*, 95th Congress, 1st Session, Vol. 124, No. 104, June 16, 1977, p. S9977.
239 Ibid., p. S9980.
240 Ibid., p. S9977.
241 Ibid., p. S9983.
242 Ibid., p. S9985.
243 Ibid., pp. S9989–S9990, S9992; "Controversy in Congress over U.S. Policy Towards Cuba: Pros & Cons," p. 41.
244 95th Congress, 2nd Session, *S,CON.RES.91*, June 9 (Legislative day, May 17), 1978. Referred to the Committee on Foreign Relations.
245 The debate on the resolution is found in *Congressional Record-Senate*, 95th Congress, 2nd Session, June 28, 1978, Daily Digest, pp. S10025–S10031, June 28, 1978. A motion to table the resolution was rejected by 55 to 33 votes.

246 Personal Interview: U.S. Congress, Senate Foreign Relations Committee Staff Member, Washington, D.C., August 23, 1978.
247 Statement of Orville L. Freeman, President, Business International Corporation, in U.S. Congress, House, *United States-Cuba Trade Promotion*, p. 15.
248 Personal Interview: Senior Official of the American Chambers of Commerce in Latin America, Washington, D.C., August 6, 1975.
249 Statement of Orville L. Freeman, President, Business International Corporation, in U.S. Congress, House, *United States-Cuba Trade Promotion*, p. 5.
250 "Cuba: Lure of the Market," *Latin America*, October 20, 1972, p. 330.
251 Personal Interview: Department of Commerce official, Washington, D.C., August 2, 1976 and August 23, 1979. The respondent was a Cuba policy analyst in the Department's Bureau of East-West Trade during the 1970s. On China, Cuba, and detente policy, see Jon Nordheimer, "Cuba Just Isn't in the Same Class with China," *New York Times*, January 7, 1979, p. E2. The value of U.S. trade with China rose from $95.9 million in 1972 to $4.8 billion in 1980, to $5.5 billion in 1981. See Stuart Auerbach, "China Exerts Its Pull Once More," *Washington Post*, January 2, 1983, pp. F1, F6.
252 Quoted in U.S. Congress, House, *United States-Cuba Trade Promotion*, p. 11.
253 Quoted in David Gumpert, "Havana Hard Sell: Yankee Businessmen Get a VIP Welcome On Junkets to Cuba," *Wall Street Journal*, November 30, 1977, p. 33.
254 Personal Interview: Latin American Specialist, Business International Corporation, New York City, New York, April 16, 1975.
255 Quoted in Bill Paul, "Cuban Connection?: Chance of Resuming U.S.-Havana Trade Tie Spurs Firms' Interest," *Wall Street Journal*, July, 17, 1975, p. 1.
256 Ibid., p. 25.
257 Theodore H. Moran, "The International Political Economy of Cuban Nickel Development," *Cuban Studies/Estudios Cubanos*, Vol. 7, No. 2, July 1977, p. 149.
258 See, for example, Terrie Shaw, "U.S. Business Lines Up for Cuba Trade," *Washington Post*, January 11, 1977, p. A14; Wendy Cooper, "U.S. Business Interest in Trading With Cuba Picks Up Dramatically," *Journal of Commerce*, January 27, 1977, p. 2; "U.S. Businessmen in Cuba for Talks On Trade Outlook," *New York Times*, June 23, 1977, p. 43.
259 Robert Keatly, "U.S. Businessmen Return From Cuba; Sizeable Orders Seen Once Embargo Ends," *Wall Street Journal*, April 22, 1977, p. 10. Also see "Early-bird Businessmen Are Flying to Cuba," *Business Week*, April 18, 1977, pp. 132, 134.
260 Quoted in Jerry Flint, "Business Visiting Cuba Urge Trade," *New York Times*, April 19, 1977, pp. 51, 57.
261 Business International Corporation, *Cuba at the Turning Point*, p. i.
262 Theriot, "U.S. Cuba Trade: Question Mark," p. 3.
263 For a discussion of these questions, see U.S. Congress, House,

United States Relations with Cuba, p. 9; Theriot, "U.S. Cuba Trade: Question Mark," p. 5; "U.S.-Cuban Relations are Certain to Broaden But Timing Still Unclear," *Business Latin America,* June 8, 1977, pp. 177–178.

264   "U.S. Policy toward Cuba: Some Thoughts on a Thaw," *Business Latin America,* June 5, 1974, p. 181.

265   U.S. Congress, Senate, Committee on Banking, Housing and Urban Affairs, Subcommittee on International Finance, *The Role of the Export-Import Bank and Export Controls in U.S. International Economic Policy,* 93rd Congress, 2nd Session, April 2, 5, 10, 23, 25, and 26; and May 2, 1974 (Washington, D.C.: U.S. Government Printing Office, 1974), p. 295.

266   "Latin America in the Mid '70s': International Firms Face Crucial Issues,"*Business Latin America,* January 1, 1975, p. 3.

267   See Richard Lawrence, "Latin Trade with Cuba Could Pose Problems," *Journal of Commerce,* May 6, 1975, pp. 1, 19; Association of American Chambers of Commerce in Latin America (AACCLA), *News,* May 6, 1975.

268   Personal Interview; Latin American specialist, Business International Corporation, New York City, New York, April 16, 1975.

269   Personal Interview; Council of the Americas official, Washington, D.C., June 9, 1975. The respondent was a senior official in the Council's Washington office.

270   "Alleged U.S.-Cuban Thaw Still Looks Like Rough Weather to Firms," *Business Latin America,* September 19, 1975, p. 299. Also see Economist Intelligence Unit, *Quarterly Economic Review of Cuba,* No. 4, December 1975, p. 3; "U.S. Regulates Subsidiary Trade with Cuba," *Business Latin America,* October 22, 1975, p. 344.

271   Jerry Tripp, representative of Ampex Corporation, quoted in Richard Boudreaux, "Talks with Cuba Are Quiet," *Bucks County Courier Times,* January 18, 1976, p. D-3.

272   U.S. Congress, House, *United States-Cuba Trade Promotion,* p. 27.

273   Quoted in Maisie McAdoo, "An Embargo That Serves No Purpose," *The Nation,* December 4, 1982, p. 588.

274   Personal interview: Department of Commerce official, Washington, D.C., August 2, 1976 and August 23, 1979.

275   Stanley Friedberg, "The Measure of Damages Claims Against Cuba," *Inter-American Economic Affiars,* Vol. 23, No. 1, Summer 1969, pp. 68–69. The author was a Commissioner of the Foreign Claims Settlement Commission of the United States. On prior claims against foreign countries and the eventual dollar percentage settlements, see ibid., p. 86; Business International Corporation, *Cuba At the Turning Point,* p. 103.

276   U.S. Congress, Senate, Committee on Finance, *Czechoslovakia Claims Settlement,* (Executive Hearings), 93rd Congress, 2nd Session, September 11 and 26, 1974 (Washington, D.C.: U.S. Government Printing Office, 1974), p. 33.

277   At the end of 1981, Prague agreed to accept U.S. terms for compensation claims for American property seized during the wartime

period. Under the agreement signed by negotiators for both governments, the U.S. claimants would receive an $81.5 million settlement
or approximately 77 cents on the dollar for the $105 million in out-
standing claims and interest. This was a fourfold increase over the
Czech offer in the 1974 agreement, which Congress rejected, and
nearly $17 million more than an earlier Czech offer of $64.1 million, which the Reagan administraton rejected under congressional
pressure. See Richard Homan, "U.S., Czechoslovakia Reach New
Agreement on Return of Gold," *New York Times,* November 7,
1981, p. 22. This new agreement received congressional approval
and was enacted into law on December 29, 1981. For the preceding
congressional debate, see U.S. Congress, House, Committee on Foreign Affairs, Subcommittee on Europe and The Middle East and on
International Economic Policy and Trade, Hearings and Markup,
Final Negotiations and Settlement of Claims Against Czechoslovakia,
97th Congress, 1st Session, June 24; December 7 and 9, 1981
(Washington, D.C.: U.S. Government Printing Office, 1982).

278 Personal Interview: U.S. Congress, Senate Foreign Relations Committee Staff Member, Washington, D.C., August 23, 1978.

279 Foreign Claims Settlement Commission of the United States, *Annual
Report to the Congress for the Period January 1–December 31, 1973*
(Washington, D.C.: U.S. Government Printing Office, 1973), p. 70.

280 Ibid., pp. 412–413.

281 See John Goshko, "$1.8 Billion in U.S. Claims Hangs over Talk on
Cuba Ties," *Washington Post,* September 26, 1977, p. A3.

282 Personal Interview: Latin American specialist, Business International Corporation, New York City, New York, April 16, 1975.

283 Letter from David W. Wallace, Chairman of the Board and President, Bangor Punta Corporation, September 23, 1975, in U.S. Congress, House, *U.S. Trade Embargo of Cuba,* p. 520.

284 Letter from A. R. Rarusi, Chairman and Chief Executive Officer,
Borden, Inc., September 26, 1975, in ibid., p. 543.

285 Letter from David Beretta, Chairman and President, Uniroyal, Inc.,
September 30, 1975, in ibid., p. 548.

286 Letter from J. Allen Overton, Jr., President, American Mining Congress, October 1, 1975, in ibid., p. 547.

287 Letter from David R. Foster, Chairman of the Board and Chief Executive Officer, Colgate-Palmolive Company, September 24, 1975, in
ibid., p. 544.

288 On the Honeywell corporation, see "U.S. Business Trip to Havana
Shows Keen Interest in Trade on Both Sides," *Business Latin America,* May 4, 1977, p. 137, 139. On Cuba's interest in acquiring
American technology, see Jerry Flint, "Cubans Admit Their Economy Is in Serious Trouble," *New York Times,* April 25, 1977, pp. 1,
47.

289 Letter from Arthur H. Hausman, President and Chief Executive
Officer, Ampex Corporation, October 1, 1975, in U.S. Congress,
House, *U.S. Trade Embargo of Cuba,* p. 551.

290 Ibid.

291 Statement submitted by Lewis T. Cane, in Ibid., p. 472. Also see

"Compensation Issue Looms as Major Snag to US-Cuban Trade Prospects," *Business Latin America*, May 21, 1975, p. 161.

292 U.S. Congress, House, Committee on Foreign Affairs, Subcommittee on International Economic Policy and Trade and on Inter-American Affairs, *Outstanding Claims Against Cuba*, 96th Congress, 1st Session, September 25, 1979 (Washington, D.C.: U.S. Government Printing office, 1980), p. 6. Hutton was the Vice Chairman of Lone Star Industries, Inc. Also see "The Other Side of the Coin: Claims on Cuba," *Business Latin America*, May 4, 1977, p. 138.

293 Alfred L. Padula, "U.S. Business Squabbles over Cuba," *The Nation*, October 22, 1977, p. 391.

294 Susan Fernández, "The Sanctity of Property: American Responses to Cuban Expropriations, 1959–1984, "*Cuban Studies/Estudios Cubanos*, Vol. 14, No. 2, Summer 1984, pp. 21–34.

295 Letter from Robert M. Norris, President, National Foreign Trade Council, Inc., July 23, 1974, in U.S. Congress, House, *U.S. Trade Embargo of Cuba*, p. 482.

296 U.S. Congress, Senate, Committee on Foreign Relations, *U.S. Relations with Latin America*, 94th Congress, 1st Session, February 21, 26, 27 and 28, 1975 (Washington, D.C.: U.S. Government Printing Office, 1975), p. 114.

297 Personal Interview: Henry Geyelin, President, Council of the Americas, New York City, New York, June 25, 1975.

298 Personal Interview: Latin American specialist, Business International Corporation, New York City, New York, June 24, 1975.

299 See, for example, John Goshko, "Cuba's Money Claims Exceed Those of U.S. Trade Minister Says," *Washington Post*, October 4, 1977, p. A18.

300 In the case of China, the normalization of diplomatic and trade relations set in motion by the Nixon administration were at no point linked to the prior settlement of outstanding U.S. corporate claims against the People's Republic of China in excess of $196 million. Under the terms of a settlement finally concluded in May 1979, Peking agreed to pay the U.S. government $80.5 million (approximately 41 cents on the dollar) in compensation over a five-year period beginning in October 1979. See Natalie G. Lichtenstein, "Unfrozen Assets: The 1979 Claims Settlement Between the United States and China," in U.S. Congress, Senate, Joint Economic Committee, *China Under the Four Modernizations, Part 2: Selected Papers*, 97th Congress, 2nd Session, Joint Committee Print, December 30, 1982 (Washington, D.C.: U.S. Government Printing Office, 1982), pp. 322–325.

7. The U.S. imperial state: some final insights

1 Personal Interview: White House Special Assistant, New Jersey, May 24, 1976.

2 See, for example, "Cuban Trade and Travel: A Close-up on Washington's Position," *Business Latin America*, August 4, 1976, p. 243.

This article was partly based on interviews with U.S. government officials.

3 Personal Interview: Department of Commerce official, Washington, D.C., August 23, 1979.

4 Personal Interview: Department of State official, Washington, D.C., June 20, 1973 (my emphasis).

5 Abraham F. Lowenthal, "'Liberal', 'Radical', and 'Bureaucratic' Perspectives on U.S. Latin American Policy: The Alliance for Progress," in Julio Cotler and Richard R, Fagen, eds., *Latin America and The United States: The Changing Political Realities* (Stanford: Stanford University Press, 1974), p. 227. Also see Graham T. Allison and Morton H. Halperin, "Bureaucratic Politics: A Paradigm and Some Policy Implications," in Raymond Tanter & Richard H. Ullman eds., *Theory and Policy in International Relations* (Princeton: Princeton University Press, 1972), pp. 40–79; Destler, *Presidents, Bureaucrats, and Foreign Policy: The Politics of Organizational Reform*, pp. 56–82; Morton H. Halperin, *Bureaucratic Politics and Foreign Policy* (Washington, D.C.: The Brookings Institution, 1974), p. 28. For a case study of U.S. foreign policymaking based largely on the proposition that organizational norms are the dominant factors in shaping differing outlooks within the bureaucratic hierarchies, see Einhorn, *Expropriation Politics.*

Stimulating critiques of the bureaucratic model based on case studies of U.S. foreign policymaking drawn from the 1950s, 1960s, and 1970s are found in Robert J. Art, "Bureaucratic Politics and American Foreign Policy: A Critique," Policy Sciences, Vol. 4., No. 4, December 1973, pp. 467–490; Charles H. Lipson, "Corporate Preferences and Public Policies." *World Politics,* Vol. XXIII, No. 3, April 1976, pp. 396–421.

6 Canadian-owned assets in Cuba, principally major banking and insurance interests, were unaffected by the sweeping nationalization decrees of September–October 1960. Canadian insurance companies in Cuba underwrote $400 million of life insurance, which accounted for approximately 70 percent of all life insurance carried by the population. The Canadian companies also handled additional millions of dollars of general insurance coverage. At the time of the nationalization of all local and foreign-owned banks in Cuba (except the Canadians'), the two Canadian chartered banks operating on the island (the Royal Bank of Canada and the Bank of Nova Scotia) had combined assets minimally estimated to be worth $100 million. When, in December 1960, both banks decided to cease operations due primarily to accumulated problems associated with day-to-day operations, a satisfactory compensation agreement was negotiated with the Cuban government. Under the terms of the agreement, the Banco Nacional de Cuba assumed all the liabilities of the two financial institutions, purchased their capital assets at book value, which were paid for with American dollars, and agreed to the remission of the banks' invested capital and accumulated profits to Canada. See McWhinney, "Canadian-United States Commercial Relations and International Law: The Cuban Affair as a Case Study," pp. 136–138.

Also see B. V. Kelley, "The Royal Bank and Cuba," *Miami Herald*, October 13, 1982, p. 17A.

7 Personal Interview: Department of State official, Washington, D.C., July 13, 1973, and June 6, 1975.

8 U.S. Department of Commerce, *United States Commercial Relations with Cuba: A Survey*, p. 22.

Epilogue: The Reagan administration and Cuba: the revival of vendetta politics, 1981–1986

1 See Patrick E. Tyler and David B. Ottaway, "Casey Strengthens Role Under 'Reagan Doctrine,'" *Washington Post*, March 31, 1985, p. A14.

2 See Stanley Hoffman, *Dead Ends: American Foreign Policy in the New Cold War* (Cambridge: Ballinger Publishing Co., 1983), p. 154.

3 Soviet involvement in Third World revolutions during this period was virtually nonexistent. See Jonathan Steele, *Soviet Power: The Kremlin's Foreign Policy – Brezhnev to Chernenko* (New York: Simon & Schuster/Touchstone Books, 1984).

4 For a stimulating discussion of Reagan's foreign policy, see Fred Halliday, *The Making of the Second Cold War* (London: Verso Editions and New Left Books, 1986). Also see Petras and Morley, "The New Cold War: Reagan Policy Toward Europe and the Third World," pp. 5–44.

5 *Newsweek* (Special Issue on the 1984 Presidential Election), November/December 1984, p. 32.

6 See Alexander M. Haig, Jr., *Caveat: Realism, Reagan, and Foreign Policy* (New York: Macmillan Publishing Co., 1984), pp. 127–130; Leslie H. Gelb, "Haig Is Said to Press for Military Options for Salvador Action," *New York Times*, November 5, 1981, pp. 1, 8; Dan Oberdorfer, "More U.S. Effort Yields Less Result," *Washington Post*, March 4, 1982, p. A19.

7 See Don Oberdorfer, "Applying Pressure in Central America," *Washington Post*, November 23, 1983, p. A10.

8 Haig, *Caveat: Realism, Reagan, and Foreign Policy*, p. 122.

9 See, for example, James McCartney, "National Security Council to Meet with Reagan on Russia-to-Cuba Arms Flow," *Miami Herald*, August 13, 1981, pp. 1A, 22A.

10 U.S. Department of State, *Communist Interference in El Salvador*, Bureau of Public Affairs, Special Report No. 80, February 23, 1981, p. 1.

11 See James Dunkerly, *The Long War: Dictatorship and Revolution in El Salvador* (London: Junction Books, 1982); Tommie Sue Montgomery, *Revoution in El Salvador* (Boulder: Westview Press, 1982); Liisa North, *Bitter Grounds: Roots of Revolt in El Salvador* (Toronto: Between The Lines, 1981).

12 The most detailed, systematic critique of the White Paper is James Petras, "White Paper on the White Paper," *The Nation*, March 28, 1981, pp. 354, 367–372. Also see Robert G. Kaiser, "Further Blots

on the White Paper: Doubts About Evidence and Conclusion," in Marvin Gettleman et al., eds., *El Salvador: Central America in The New Cold War* (New York: Grove Press, 1981), pp. 254–262.

13   William M. LeoGrande, "Cuba," in Morris J. Blachman, William M. LeoGrande, and Kenneth Sharpe, eds., *Confronting Revolution: Security Through Diplomacy in Central America* (New York: Pantheon Books, 1986), p. 241. Also see Edward Cody, "Castro Building Up Cuba's Militia," *Washington Post*, July 8, 1985, p. A15.

14   Quoted in John M. Goshko, "Drawing a Hard Line Against Communism," *Washington Post*, February 22, 1981, p. A8. Also see Don Oberdorfer and John M. Goshko, "U.S. Gives Warning on Cuba-Salvador Arms Flow," *Washington Post*, February 22, 1981, pp. A1, A9.

15   Quoted in Juan de Onís, "Cuba Warned Direct U.S. Action Against It on Salvador Possible," *New York Times*, February 23, 1981, p. 1.

16   See Edward Walsh, "Wide Options Against Cuba Noted," *Washington Post*, March 19, 1981, p. A1.

17   Bernard Gwertzman, "A New Policy on Aid for Caribbean Wins Reagan's Approval," *New York Times*, June 4, 1981, pp. 1, 5.

18   Quoted in ibid., p. 5.

19   Quoted in Don Oberdorfer, "Haig Says U.S. Is Studying Ways to Put Heat on Cuba," *Washington Post*, October 30, 1981, p. A9; John M. Goshko, "Haig Voices Concern on Nicaragua," *Washington Post*, November 15, 1981, p. A1.

20   See Wayne S. Smith, "Dateline Havana: Myopic Diplomacy," *Foreign Policy*, No.48, Fall 1982, pp. 160–161; Raymond Bonner, *Weakness and Deceit: U.S. Policy and El Salvador* (New York: Times Books, 1984), pp. 264–265; William M. LeoGrande, "Cuba and Nicaragua: From the Somozas to the Sandinistas," in Barry B. Levine, ed., *The New Cuban Presence in the Caribbean* (Boulder: Westview Press, 1983), pp. 50, 51, 57. The White House-State Department rationale for the massive military involvement in El Salvador is discussed in Francis X. Clines, "Reagan Criticizes the Latin Debate," *New York Times*, April 18, 1984, p. 13.

21   Quoted in Bonner, *Weakness and Deceit: U.S. Policy and El Salvador*, p. 264.

22   Leslie H. Gelb, "Haig is Said to Press for Military Options for Salvador Actions," *New York Times*, November 5, 1981, pp. 1, 8.

23   See Don Oberdorfer, "U.S. Details 'Covert Activities' By Cubans in Latin America," *Washington Post*, December 2, 1981, p. A1.

24   See Don Oberdorfer and Patrick E. Tyler, "Reagan Backs Action Plan for Central America," *Washington Post*, February 14, 1982, pp. A1, A4; Patrick E. Tyler and Bob Woodward, "U.S. Approves Covert Plan in Nicaragua," *Washington Post*, March 10, 1982, pp. A1, A6. The quote from the NSC minutes is in Patrick E. Tyler, "U.S. Tracks Cuban Aid to Grenada," *Washington Post*, February 27, 1983, p. A1.

25   See Leslie H. Gelb, "Reagan Backing Covert Actions, Officials Assert," *New York Times*, March 14, 1982, pp. 1, 12.

26   See "War Inhibits Progress in Education and Health," *Central*

American Report, Vol.XII, No.29, August 2, 1985, pp. 228–230; "Pricing the War of Aggression," *Central America Report,* Vol.XII, No.47, December 6, 1985, pp. 369–370; LeoGrande, "Cuba," pp. 234–235; Americas Watch, *Human Rights in Nicaragua: Reagan, Rhetoric and Reality* (New York, July 1985), pp. 84–85; *Central American Historical Institute Update,* Vol.5, No.34, August 31, 1986, p. 2.

27 Quoted in "National Security Council Document on Policy in Central America and Cuba," *New York Times,* April 7, 1983, p. 16. Also see Raymond Bonner, "President Approved of Preventing 'Cuba-Model States'," *New York Times,* April 7, 1983, pp. 1, 16.

28 See Leslie H. Gelb, "U.S. Says Talks With Cuba Are Still Possible," *New York Times,* April 22, 1982, p. 11.

29 Data provided by the Department of Defense, in *New York Times,* July 31, 1983, p. 1E; Michael T. Klare, "Testing Out Haig's New War Policy," *The Nation,* June 19, 1982, pp. 735, 750–751.

30 Quoted in Alfonso Chardy, "U.S. Saw Threat by Cuba, Soviets," *Miami Herald,* July 29, 1983, p. 1A. Also see Gerald F. Seib and Walter S. Mossberg, "U.S. Latin Maneuvers Are Called Bid to Avert Soviet Military Moves," *Wall Street Journal,* July 26, 1983, pp. 1, 16.

31 U.S. Department of State, Bureau of Intelligence and Research, Office of Long-range Assessment, *Soviet Attitudes Towards Aid to and Contacts with Central American Revolutionaries,* prepared by C. G. Jacobson, June 1, 1984, pp. 13.

32 See *NACLA Report on the Americas,* Vol.XIX, No.3, May/June 1985, p. 51.

33 U.S. Department of State, *Soviet Attitutes Towards Aid to and Contacts with Central American Revolutionaries,* p. 17.

34 William M. LeoGrande, "The View from Havana: Cuba's Policy Toward Central America," p. 247.

35 Ibid., p. 26 Also see Marlise Simons, "Salvador Rebels Urged by Allies to Seek Accord," *New York Times,* August 5, 1983, pp. 1, 3.

36 See "U.S.-Nicaraguan Tension Grows as Congressional Deadline Nears," *Central America Bulletin,* Vol.IV, No.2, December 1984, p. 5; Fred Hiatt and Joanne Omang, "U.S. Buildup in Honduras Described," *Washington Post,* February 1, 1984, p. A1, A8; Robert J. McCartney, "U.S. is Dotting Honduran Countryside With Military Facilities," *Washington Post,* February 17, 1984, p. A25; Fred Hiatt, "Buildup: U.S. Has Steadily Amassed Troops, Counterrevolutionaries in Latin America," *Washington Post,* April 15, 1984, pp. A1, A28; "U.S. Hitmen: The Nicaraguan Contras," *Central America Bulletin,* Vol.IV, No.1, November 1984, pp. 11–12.

37 *NACLA Report on the Americas,* Vol.XIX, No.3, May/June 1985, p. 52.

38 Quoted in Ernest Holsendolph, "U.S. Lists 'Options' on Cuban Jamming," *New York Times,* May 7, 1983, p. 5. The administration rationale for Radio Marti is discussed in U.S. Congress, Sentate, Committee on Foreign Relations, *Radio Broadcasting To Cuba, Part 1,* 97th Congress, 2nd Session, July 1, 27, and August 9, 1982 (Wash-

ington, D.C.: U.S. Government Printing Office, 1983); U.S. Congress, Senate Committee on Foreign Relations, *Radio Broadcasting to Cuba, Part 2*, 98th Congress, 1st Session, April 27, 1983 (Washington, D.C.: U.S. Government Printing Office, 1983); U.S. Congress, House, Committee on Foreign Affairs, *Radio Broadcasting to Cuba (Radio Marti)*, 97th Congress, 2nd Session, March 3, 4 and 24, 1982 (Washington, D.C.: U.S. Government Printing Office, 1982)

39 See "A Wary Eye on Reagan's Moves," *Latin America Weekly Report* WR-83-29, July 29, 1983, p. 8.

40 Quoted in Oberdorfer, "U.S. Details 'Covert Activities' by Cubans in Latin America," p. A1.

41 Quoted in Oberdorfer, "Applying Pressure in Central America," p. A10.

42 See Hedrick Smith, "Reagan Aide Says U.S. Invasion Forestalled Cuban Arms Buildup," *New York Times*, October 27, 1981, pp. 1, 18; David Hoffman and Fred Hiatt, "Cuban Arms Cache Found, Reagan Says," *Washington Post*, October 28, 1983, pp. A1, A6, A7; Hedrick Smith, "Reagan Says Cuba Aimed to Take Grenada; Report to Nation," *New York Times*, October 28, 1983, pp. 1, 9; Don Oberdorfer, "Reagan Sought To End Cuban 'Intervention,'" *Washington Post*, November 6, 1983, pp. A1, A21.

43 Smith, "Reagan Aide Says U.S. Invasion Forestalled Cuban Arms Buildup," p. 1; Hugh O'Shaughnessy, *Grenada: Revolution, Invasion and Aftermath* (London: Sphere Books, 1984), pp. 204, 88.

44 See Philip Taubman, "Senators Suggest Administration Exaggerated Its Cuba Assessment," *New York Times*, October 30, 1982, pp. 22; Bob Woodward and Patrick E. Tyler, "CIA's" Reports Magnify Soviet-Cuban Presence," *Washington Post*, October 29, 1983, pp. A1, A10; Philip Taubman, "Invasion Intelligence," *New York Times*, November 1, 1983, pp. 1, 17.

45 See O'Shaughnessy, *Grenada: Revolution, Invasion and Aftermath*, pp. 16–17, 204; Richard Halloran, "U.S. Won't Dispute Havana on Tally," *New York Times*, October 31, 1983, pp. 1, 10; Stuart Taylor, Jr., "In Wake of Invasion, Much Official Misinformation by U.S. Comes to Light," *New York Times*, November 6, 1983, p. 20.

46 See O'Shaughnessy, *Grenada: Revolution, Invasion and Aftermath*, pp. 88–89, 205–206.

47 Quoted in Shirley Christian, "Reagan has Few Options with Cuba," *Miami Herald*, September 20, 1981, p. 17A.

48 See Smith, *The Closest of Enemies*, p. 242.

49 Ibid, p. 245.

50 See ibid., pp. 249–50.

51 See Haig, *Caveat: Realism, Reagan, and Foreign Policy*, p. 136; Smith, *The Closest of Enemies*, pp. 254, 257.

52 See Smith, "Dateline Havana: Myopic Diplomacy," pp. 161–163; Bonner, *Weakness and Deceit; U.S. Policy and El Salvador*, p. 265.

53 U.S. Congress, House, Committee on Foreign Affairs, Subcommittees on International Economic Policy and Trade and Inter-American Affairs, *Issues in United States-Cuban Relations*, 97th Congress,

2nd Session, December 14, 1982 (Washington, D.C.: U.S. Government Printing Office, 1983), p. 5. Also see ibid., p. 23.

54 Quoted in Bonner, *Weakness and Deceit: U.S. Policy and El Salvador*, p. 265.

55 Smith, *The Closest of Enemies*, pp. 255–256.

56 See ibid., p. 255.

57 Quoted in Martin Schram, "Cuba Pressing for Full-Scale Negotiations but White House says No," *Washington Post*, December 11, 1981, p. A41.

58 Quoted in Leslie H. Gelb, "'Cuban Calls for Talks with the U.S. and Accepts Part of Blame for Strains," *New York Times* April 6, 1982, p. 14; Seweryn Bialer and Alfred Stepan, "Cuban, the U.S. and the Central American Mess," *New York Review of Books*, May 27, 1982, pp. 17–21.

59 Quoted in Smith, *The Closest of Enemies*, p. 257.

60 William M. LeoGrande, "Cuba: Going to the Source," in Richard Newfarmer, ed., *From Gunboats to Diplomacy* (Baltimore and London: The Johns Hopkins University Press, 1984), p. 145. Also see Christopher Dickey, "U.S. Recalls Top Envoy From Cuba for Consultations as Relations Worsen," *Washington Post*, September 20, 1981. p. A28.

61 See Luis Burstin, "My Talks With the Cubans," *New Republic*, February 13, 1984, pp. 19–23; *Latin America Weekly Report* WR-83-14, April 15, 1983, p. 12.

62 Quoted in "U.S. Links with Cuba Ties to 'Responsible Role,'" *Miami Herald*, February 10, 1983, p. 22A. Also see Tom Burns, "Spanish Premier Said to Urge U.S. Ties with Cuba," *Washington Post*, February 9, 1982, p. A21.

63 See John M. Goshko, "U.S. and Cuba Open Official Negotiations," *Washington Post*, July 13, 1984, pp. A1, A27; Philip Taubman, "U.S.-Cuban Parley Said to Be Narrow," *New York Times*, July 14, 1984, p. 4.

64 Quoted in Joanne Omang, "U.S., Cuba End 4-Year Quarrel over Refugees," *Washington Post*, December 15, 1984, p. A1; Bernard Weinraub, "U.S. and Cuba Gain an Accord on Repatriation," *New York Times*, December 15, 1984, p. 1.

65 Quoted in Joseph B. Treaster, "What's Behind Castro's Softer Tone," *New York Times*, August 5, 1984, p. E5.

66 Cherri Waters, *Destabilizing Angola: South Africa's War and U.S. Policy* (Washington, D.C.: Washington Office on Africa Educational Fund and the Center for International Policy, December 1986), p. 4.

67 Castro and U.S. officials quoted in Joel Brinkley, "2 in Congress Urge Talks With Cuba," *New York Times*, January 31, 1985, p. 7; Leonard Downie, Jr. and Karen DeYoung, "Cuban Leader Sees Positive Signs for Ties in Second Reagan Term," *Washington Post*, February 3, 1985, pp. A1, A24. Also see "Shultz Dismisses Castro Overtures, Tells Managua to Change Behavior," *Miami Herald*, February 15, 1985, p. 22A.

68 President Reagan, *The New Network of Terrorist States*, Address,

American Bar Association, Washington, D.C., July 8, 1985, Department of State, Bureau of Public Affairs, Current Policy No.721.

69 See Julia Preston, "Cuban-U.S. Ties Termed Worst in Decades," *Washington Post*, April 19, 1987, pp. A1, A28; Joseph B. Treaster, "Downward Spiral for U.S.-Cuba Ties," *New York Times*, May 2, 1987, pp. 1, 7.

70 Quoted in Alfonso Chardy, "No Talks with Castro, U.S. Official Promises," *Miami Herald*, May 21, 1983, p. 8A.

71 State Department spokesman Bernard Kalb, quoted in John M. Goshko, "U.S.-Cuba Immigration Talks Break Down," *Washington Post*, July 11, 1986, p. A21. Also see Bernard Gwertzman, "Cuba, in Immigration Concession, Said to Drop American Radio Ban," *New York Times*, July 9, 1986, pp. 1, 6; "Talks with Havana Collapse Over Its Radio Rights in U.S.," *New York Times*, July 11, 1986, p. 3.

72 See "Enders: U.S. Tightening Embargo of Cuba," *Washington Post*, December 15, 1981, p. A6.

73 See Gelb, "Haig Is Said to Press for Military Options for Salvador Actions," pp. 1, 8.

74 Quoted in Barbara Crossette, "U.S., Linking Cuba to 'Violence,' Blocks Tourists and Business Trips," *New York Times*, April 20, 1982, p. 1. Also see John Goshko, "U.S. Acts to Tighten Cuban Embargo," *Washington Post*, April 20, 1982, p. A1; Richard J. Meislin, "Main Air Link Between U.S. and Cuba Is Stopped," *New York Times*, April 17, 1982, p. 3; "Second Step for U.S. Economic Pressure on Cuba Likely to Be Disclosed in Weeks," *Wall Street Journal*, April 21, 1982, p. 5.

75 See Robert Pear, "U.S. Said to Plan Moves to Tighten Embargo of Cuba," *New York Times*, August 11, 1986, pp. 1, 9; Lou Cannon and John M. Goshko, "Reagan to Bar Immigration of Cubans via 3rd Countries," *Washington Post*, August 12, 1986, pp. A1, A10; Gerald M. Boyd, "Reagan Acts to Tighten Trade Embargo of Cuba," *New York Times*, August 23, 1986, p. 3. The official statement is printed in "Cuba: New Migration and Embargo Measures," *Department of State Bulletin*, Vol.86, No.2116, November 1986, pp. 86–87. According to a senior Reagan administration official, Washington had identified approximately 188 companies and individuals, more than half in Panama and a large number in Mexico, as "Cuba fronts." See Boyd, "Reagan Acts to Tighten Trade Embargo of Cuba," p. 3.

76 See "Washington Attempts to Break Cuba's French Connection," *Latin America Weekly Report* WR-81-12, March 20, 1981, p. 1; Francis Chiles, "U.S. Pressure May Have Stopped Loan to Cuba," *Financial Times*, March 21, 1981, p. 26.

77 Helga Silva, "Tightening the Embargo," *Miami Herald*, September 5, 1982, pp. 1F, 4F.

78 U.S. Department of Commerce, International Trade Administration, Office of Export Administration, *Export Administration Annual Report FY 1983* (Washington, D.C., June 1984), pp. 67, 69; U.S. Department of Commerce, International Trade Administration, Office of Export Administration, *Export Administration Annual Report FY 1984* (Washington, D.C., June 1985), p. 79.

79 "Havana Pleads for a Truce," *Latin America Weekly Report* WR-82-36, September 17, 1982, p. 10; Claes Brundenius, *Revolutionary Cuba: The Challenge of Economic Growth with Equity* (Boulder: Westview Press, 1984), p. 66.

80 Quoted in Roger Lowenstein, "Cuba Is in Good Standing with Bankers Despite Castro's Talk of Canceling Debt," *Wall Street Journal*, July 30, 1985, p. 28. Also see "Bankers Confident on Debt Payments," *Latin America Weekly Report* WR-82-18, May 7, 1982, p. 4.

81 Hugh O'Shaughnessy, "U.S. Steps Up Pressure on Cuba," *Financial Times*, March 23, 1982, p. 4.

82 See "Cuban Sugar Sector Forges Ahead," *Latin America Regional Reports: Caribbean* RC-82-97, August 20, 1982, p. 8.

83 Quoted in S. Karene Witcher, "Havana's Efforts to Reschedule Its Debt Meeting Difficulties, U.S. Official Says," *Wall Street Journal*, September 13, 1982, p. 34.

84 Quoted in "Progress on Debt Rescheduling," *Latin America Regional Reports: Caribbean* RC-82-08, October 1, 1982, p. 4.

85 Quoted in Juan O. Tamayo, "Cuban Data to Creditors Termed False," *Miami Herald*, November 6, 1982, p. 21A.

86 Quoted in S. Karene Witcher, "U.K. Faults Cuba's Plan to Reschedule," *Wall Street Journal*, December 27, 1982, p. 12.

87 See "Havana's View of the Debt Talks," *Latin American Weekly Report* WR-83-18, May 13, 1983, p. 8.

88 Ibid.; Brundenius, *Revolutionary Cuba: The Challenge of Economic Growth with Equity*, p. 66. Also see Hugh O'Shaughnessy and David Marsh, "Cuba Secures Terms on Rescheduling of $1.2bn Debt to West," *Financial Times*, March 3, 1983, p. 4.

89 Quoted in "Havana's View of the Debt Talks," p. 8.

90 See Paul Lewis, "Bar to Cuba Debt Pact Reported," *New York Times*, January 9, 1984, p. D1; "Unit Sold Cuba Loan," *New York Times*, January 10 1984, p. D6; Economist Intelligence Unit, *Quarterly Economic Review of Cuba*, No.1, February 1984, p. 12.

91 "Paris Quest for Easier Debt Terms," *Latin America Weekly Report* WR-84-19, May 18, 1984, p. 3; "Sugar Cloud over July Debt Talks," *Latin America Regional Reports: Caribbean* RC-84-06, July 20, 1984, p. 2.

92 "'Fit & lean' Look for Creditors," *Latin American Regional Reports: Caribbean* RC-85-04, May 10, 1985, p. 2.

93 See "Long-term Accord with Comecon," *Latin America Weekly Report* WR-84-44, November 9, 1984. p. 10; "Cuba/Refinancing East and West," *Latin America Weekly Report* WR-84-50, December 21, 1984, p. 7; Leslie Collitt, "Cuba to Sell Surplus Soviet Oil for Hard Currency," *Financial Times*, January 8, 1986, p. 4; Terri Shaw, "Soviets Boosting Aid to Cuba by 50 Percent," *Washington Post*, April 12, 1986 p. A20; "Soviet Union Increases Aid to Cuba in Five-year Deals," *Financial Times*, April 14, 1986, p. 4; Robert Graham, "Cuba Postpones Debt Rescheduling Talks," *Financial Times*, April 21, 1986, p. 5.

94 Jean-Pierre Clerc, "Waiting for the Boom in Cuba," Le Monde Supplement of The Guardian Weekly (U.K.), February 17, 1985, p. 13.
95 See Richard Turits, "Trade, Debt, and the Cuban Economy," World Development. Vol.15, No.1, January 1987, p. 175; Colitt, "Cuba to Sell Surplus Soviet Oil for Hard Currency." p. 4; Graham, "Cuba Postpones Debt Rescheduling Talks," p. 5.
96 "Cuba/Refinancing East and West," p. 7.
97 See "Cuba Faces the Paris Club," Latin America Weekly Report WR-85-21, May 31, 1985, p. 6; "Cuba Is in Good Standing with Bankers Despite Castro's Talk of Canceling Debt," Wall Street Journal, July 30, 1985, p. 28; "Cuba Agrees to Debt Shift," New York Times, September 20, 1985, p. D11; Graham, "Cuba Postpones Debt Rescheduling Talks," p. 5.
98 See Latin America Weekly Report WR-86-16, April 25, 1986, p. 7; Graham, "Cuba Postpones Debt Rescheduling Talks," p. 5; "Creditors Doubt Deficit Size," Latin America Weekly Report WR-86-32, August 21, 1986, p. 9.
99 See "Cuba Is Proposing to Defer Interest on Its Bank Debt," Wall Street Journal, May 7, 1986, p. 34; Margarita Zimmerman, "Cuba Needs £340m New Loans," Financial Times, May 7, 1986, p. 10.
100 See "Payment Halt by Cuba Seen," New York Times, July 29, 1986, p. D9; Zimmerman, "Cuba Needs £340m New Loans," p. 10; "Smile Off the Faces of Policy-makers," Latin American Regional Reports: Caribbean RC-87-01, January 22, 1987, p. 3.
101 See United Nations, Economic Commission for Latin America and The Caribbean, Economic Survey of Latin America and The Caribbean 1983, Volume 1 (Santiago, 1985), p. 8; Claes Brundenius and Andrew Zimbalist, Recent Studies on Cuban Economic Growth: A Review, unpublished paper, September 1984, 39 pp; CEPAL News (United Nations, Economic Commission for Latin America and the Caribbean), Vol.V, No.2, September 1985, p. 1; Juan M. Del Aguila, "Political Developments in Cuba," Current History, Vol.85, No.507, January 1986, p. 13; "Castro Shuts Down Peasants' Markets," Latin America Weekly Report WR-86-21, May 30, 1986, p. 2.
102 See Andrew Zimbalist, "Cuban Industrial Growth, 1965–84," World Development, Vol.15, No.1, January 1987, p.83. The World Bank and the Wharton Econometric Forecasting Associates (under contract to the State Department) commissioned studies of Cuba's economic performance during the first half of the 1980s that challenged the official government figures. For a trenchant critique of these studies on both methodological and statistical grounds and a convincing argument for accepting the credibility of the Cuban government figures, see ibid., pp. 83–93.
103 Quoted in "National Security Council Document on Policy in Central America and Cuba", p. 16.
104 See Latin American Regional Reports: Caribbean RC-82-01, January 15, 1982, p. 4; "Canadians Urged to Invest," Latin America Weekly Report WR-82-07, February 12, 1982, p. 8.
105 See "Havana Pleads for a Truce," p. 9; "Superpowers Give Markets

a Boost," *Latin America Commodities Report* CR-84-20, October 12, 1984, p. 2.

106 See Jay Ducassi, "Cuban Nickel in Japanese Care Irks U.S.," *Miami Herald*, June 24, 1983, p. 7C; "USA Warns Japan to Stop Using Cuban Nickel," *Latin America Commodities Report* CR-84-14, July 22, 1983, p. 8; "Japan Cuts Sugar Imports from Cuba under Pressure from the US," *Latin America Commodities Report* CR-83-15, August 5, 1983, p. 1.

107 See ibid.; Economist Intelligence Unit, *Quarterly Economic Review of Cuba*, No. 3. August 1983, p. 15.

108 See Economist Intelligence Unit, *Quarterly Economic Review of Cuba*, No.4, December 1983, pp. 12–13; "Soviet Union Set to Win EEC Nickel Dumping Case," *Financial Times*, September 30, 1983, p. 7.

109 See Eduardo Lachica, "U.S. Tightens Its Embargo Against Cuba by Banning Nickel Imports from Russia." *Wall Street Journal*, November 22, 1983, p. 5; Clyde H. Farnsworth, "U.S. Bars Soviet Nickel," *New York Times*, November 22, 1983, p. D1; "Cuba Aims at Doubling Nickel Output," *Latin America Commodities Report* CR-85-13, July 5, 1985, p. 4.

110 See "Aggrieved Cuba Feels Free to Act Independently," *Latin America Commodities Report* CR-82-16, August 13, 1982, p. 3; Economist Intelligence Unit, *Quarterly Economic Review of Cuba*, No.4, December 4, 1983, p. 12; "Superpowers Give Markets a Boost," p. 2.

111 See Appendix II, Table 1; Economist Intelligence Unit, *Quarterly Economic Review of Cuba*, No.3, August 1984, Appendix 1.

112 Economist Intelligence Unit, *Quarterly Economic Review of Cuba*, No.4, November 1981, p. 10.

113 Economist Intelligence Unit, *Quarterly Economic Review of Cuba*, No.2, May 1985, p. 15.

114 See "Tokyo Stops Insurance for Exports to Cuba," *Financial Times*, December 23, 1986, p. 4.

115 See Appendix II, Table 1; Economist Intelligence Unit, *Quarterly Economic Review of Cuba*, No.3, August 1984, Appendix 1.

116 Economist Intelligence Unit, *Quarterly Economic Review of Cuba*, No.4, November 1981, p. 10.

117 See Economist Intelligence Unit, *Quarterly Economic Review of Cuba*, No.4, December 1983, p. 14; Paul Betts, "Renault Wins Deal to Supply Trucks to Cuba," *Financial Times*, January 10, 1984, p. 4.

118 David White, "Spanish Shipbuilders Win £52m Order for Cuba," *Financial Times*, December 19, 1982, p. 3.

119 See Tom Burns, "Spain Urged to Limit Resale of U.S. High-Tech Material," *Washington Post*, June 7, 1984, p. A28.

120 "Becoming Spain's Best Customer," *Latin America Weekly Report* WR-85-41, October 18, 1985, p. 3.

121 Ibid.

122 Ibid.

123 See "Spanish PM Takes Home Some Praises," *Latin America Weekly Report* WR-86-47, December 4, 1986, p. 3.

124 "ECGD Backs Deal with Cuba," *Financial Times*, October 20, 1981, p. 6; Economist Intelligence Unit, *Quarterly Economic Review of Cuba*, No.4, November 1981, p. 10.

125 Marc Webster, "Scottish Company in £22m Deal with Cuba", *Financial Times*. May 18, 1982, p. 7.

126 See *Latin America Weekly Report* WR-83-07, February 18, 1983, p. 6.

127 See, for example, Frank Gray, "Bid to Boost UK-Cuba Trade Links," *Financial Times*, May 2, 1985, p. 6.

128 Frank Gray, "Midland Bank Credit Line for Cuba Trade," *Financial Times*, July 31, 1985, p. 3; Frank Gray, "British Mission Set for Visit to Cuba, Mexico," *Financial Times*, November 1, 1985, p. 6.

129 Frank Gray, "UK and Cuba Sign £350 Trade Deal," *Financial Times*, January 31, 1986, p. 20.

130 Frank Gray, "British Business Finds Cuba a Tempting Prospect," *Financial Times*, January 6, 1987, p. 4.

131 See Economist Intelligence Unit, *Quarterly Economic Review of Cuba*, No.1, February 1985, p. 13; "No Cover for German Trade," *Latin America Weekly Report* WR-85-01, January 4, 1985, p. 1; "'Berlin Clause' Blocks Exports," *Latin America Weekly Report* WR-85-15, April 19, 1985, p. 9.

132 Ibid.

133 See "Building Bridges to West Germany." *Latin America Regional Reports: Caribbean* RC-85-04, May 10, 1985, p. 2.

134 See Christopher Dickey, "Glacial Chill Settles over Cuba's Ties with Latins," *Washington Post*, September 30, 1981, p. A22; "Colombia Takes on Caribbean Role," *Latin America Regional Reports: Caribbean* RC-82-01, January 15, 1982, p. 8.

135 See Don Oberdorfer, "Haig Asks Joint Action on Cuba," *Washington Post*, December 15, 1981, p. A20.

136 Marlise Simons, "Mexico, in Broad Energy Accord with Cuba, Will Help Search for Oil," *Washington Post*, February 8, 1981, p. A25.

137 See Alan Riding, "Mexico Stresses Ties With Cuba in an Apparent Rebuff to Reagan," *New York Times*. February 21, 1981, pp. 1, 6.

138 See "Lopez Portillo Salves Castro's Pride," *Latin America Weekly Report* WR-81-32, August 14, 1981, p. 4.

139 See "Brazil Moves to End Estrangement," *Latin America Regional Reports: Caribbean* RC-84-01, January 20, 1984, p. 3; "The Cuban Link and the Elections," *Latin America Regional Reports: Brazil* RB-84-08, September 14, 1984, p. 3.

140 See "Cuban Overture Goes Off Key," *Latin America Weekly Report* WR-82-04, January 22, 1982, p. 6; James Bruce, "Brazilians Divided over Relations with Cuba," *Journal of Commerce*. January 26, 1982, pp. A1, 5A; Jim Brooke, "Brazilian Businessmen Eye Cuban Market," *Washington Post*, February 4, 1982, p. A16; Warren Hoge, "Brazilians Favor Cuban Trade Ties." *New York Times*, February 7, 1982, p. 9.

141 Ibid.

142 See "Havana Comes Out of the Cold," *Latin America Weekly Report* WR-85-24, June 12, 1985, p. 10. Also see "Setúbal Goes for

Results," *Latin America Regional Reports: Brazil* RB-85-04, May 31, 1985, p. 6.

143 Quoted in "Sarney Turns to His Neighbors," *Latin America Weekly Report* WR-85-33, August 23, 1985, p. 8.

144 "Deal with Cuba for Alcohol," *Latin America Commodities Report* CR-85-14, July 19, 1985, pp. 6–7; "Resumption of Ties with Cuba Delayed," *Latin America Regional Reports: Brazil* RB-86-02, February 7, 1986, p. 2.

145 See "Breaking the 22-year Hiatus," *Latin America Weekly Report* WR-86-26, July 10, 1986, p. 10.

146 See "Resumption of Ties with Cuba Delayed." p. 2.

147 See "Moving Closer to the US?," *Latin America Weekly Report* WR-86-17, May 2, 1986, p. 8.

148 Ibid.

149 "Breaking the 22-year Hiatus," p. 10. Also see "New Business Leads From Brazil's New Move on Foreign Relations," *Business Latin America*, December 31, 1985, pp. 409, 411.

150 Economist Intelligence Unit, *Quarterly Economic Review of Cuba*, No.3, August 1983, p. 16; Alan Riding, "Argentina and Cuba Sign Trade Pact," *New York Times*, June 5, 1982, p. 5; Jeremy Morgan, "Argentina Grants Loan to Cuba," *Journal of Commerce*, June 11, 1984, pp. 1A, 8A; Economist Intelligence Unit, *Quarterly Economic Review of Cuba*, No.2, May 1984, p. 14.

151 Quoted in "Columbia Tightens the Noose Around Fidel Castro's Neck," *Latin America Weekly Report* WR-81-13, March 27, 1981, p. 1.

152 See "Friendly Gestures from Caracas," *Latin America Regional Reports: Caribbean* RC-82-06, July 16, 1982, p. 6.

153 See "Caribbean Priority for Venezuela," *Latin America Regional Reports: Caribbean* RC-84-01, January 20, 1984, p. 6; "Venezuelans Seek to Ease Strain With Cuba," *New York Times*, June 18, 1984, p. 10; "Improved Cuba Link One Step Closer," *Latin America Weekly Report* WR-84-27, June 18, 1984, p. 10.

154 See "Morales: Superpowers Involved in Central America," *Latin America Weekly Report* WR-84-27, July 13, 1984, p. 10; "Rapprochement Between Venezuela and Cuba Takes Big Step Forward," *Latin America Weekly Report* WR-85-21, May 31, 1985, p. 1.

155 Quoted in "Cuban-Venezuelan Rapprochement," *Latin America Regional Reports: Andean Group* RA-85-06, July 26, 1985, pp. 4–5.

156 See "Colombia Tightens the Noose Around Fidel Castro's Neck," p. 1.

157 See "Betancur Abduction Strengthens Ties Between Presidents," *Latin America Regional Reports: Andean Group* RA-83-10, December 16, 1983, p. 3. The prospect of direct U.S. military involvement in the Central American conflict at the beginning of 1983 spurred Mexico, Colombia, Venezuela, and Panama – the so called Contadora nations – to jointly outline a Document of Objectives envisioning a peace treaty that would demilitarize the region and prohibit outside intervention in any internal social struggle. The Contadora

peace process is discussed in Morris H. Morley and James F. Petras, "The Reagan Administration and Nicaragua: How Washington Constructs Its Case for Counterrevolution in Central America," in Morris H. Morley, ed., *Crisis and Confrontation: Ronald Reagan's Foreign Policy* (Totowa, NJ: Rowman and Littlefield, forthcoming).
158 See *Facts on File*, Vol. 45, No. 2352, December 1985, p. 948.
159 See "World Search for New Market," *Latin American Regional Reports: Southern Cone* RS-86-06, August 7, 1986, p. 7.
160 Quoted in Alfonso Chardy, "S. Americans Revive Relations with Cuba," *Miami Herald*, January 5, 1986, p. 24A.
161 Quoted in *Latin American Regional Reports: Caribbean* RC-86-10, December 11, 1986, p. 8.
162 See "Relations with Cuba Taking Shape," *Latin America Weekly Report* WR-86-44, November 13, 1986, p. 2.
163 See "Havana Beats Human Rights Charges," *Latin America Weekly Report* WR-87-12, March 26, 1987, p. 10; Elaine Sciolino, "Reagan's Mighty Effort to Condemn Cuba," *New York Times*, March 24, 1987, p. 28.
164 Economist Intelligence Unit, *Quarterly Economic Review of Cuba*, No.2, June 1983, p. 14.

Appendix 1: The impact and effectiveness of the U.S. global economic blockade on Cuban development

1 See Jorge I. Domínguez, "The Civic Soldier in Cuba," in Catherine McArdle Kelleher, ed., *Political-Military Systems: Comparative Perspective* (Beverly Hills: Sage Publications, 1974), pp. 215–216; Jorge I. Domínguez, "Institutionalization and Civil-Military Relations in Cuba," *Cuban Studies/Estudios Cubanos*, Vol.6, No.1, January 1976, p. 45; Carmelo Mesa-Lago, "Economic Policies and Growth," in Carmelo Mesa-Lago, ed., *Revolutionary Change in Cuba* (Pittsburgh: University of Pittsburgh Press, 1974), p. 319, Table 9; Gutelman, "The Socialization of the Means of Production in Cuba," p. 214.
2 Branch and Crile, "The Kennedy Vendetta; How the CIA Waged a Silent War Against Cuba," p. 52.
   The role of outside forces looms large for postrevolutionary Cuban political development. The growth of a centralized political structure in the early and mid-1960s cannot be understood independently of the demands of regime survival and consolidation. But international factors' influence on the evolution of political centralism remains a largely unexamined area amid the voluminous literature on the Cuban Revolution. Jorge Domínguez's *Cuba: Order and Revolution*, a most detailed study of the pre- and especially the post-1959 Cuban polity, economy, and society published in the late 1970s, is one example. Although he presents a sometimes illuminating discussion of the growth of postrevolutionary political institutions and the entrenched bureaucratic-centralist decisionmaking apparatus – which by the 1970s could no longer be justified in terms of its original raison d'être, the revolution's defense and survival – there is virtually no effort to analyze these developments in terms of their foundations in

the early 1960s. Other than some scattered, uninvestigated assertions ("How Cuba is governed is shaped by international influences;" the U.S.-Cuba conflict "required the expansion of Cuban governmental capabilities to meet the foreign threat, including the socialization of most of the economy;" U.S. hostility "brought about political centralization in Cuba"), the informing assumption of Domínguez's study is that in looking at these issues we are basically dealing with autonomous forces and developments. Yet to stay at this "intermediate" level, that is, the internal political leadership's choices, is to miss the way in which external pressures shaped these decisionmakers' actions which, in turn, distorted the development of political institutions. Even though the behavior of the political leadership may prevail at one level, such behavior cannot be evaluated without considering the outside forces and events that channeled the decisions these individuals made. No discussion of centralized political structures in postrevolutionary Cuba can be comprehensive without accounting for the international system's impact. See Jorge I. Domínguez, *Cuba: Order and Revolution*, Cambridge: Harvard University Press, 1978. The above quotations are found on pp. 237 and 148.

3 See, for example, Ritter, *The Economic Development of Revolutionary Cuba*, p. 148.

4 Ibid., p. 352.

5 See Brian H. Pollitt, "Employment Plans, Performance and Future Prospects in Cuba," in Richard Jolley et al., eds., *Third World Development* (London: Penguin Books, 1973), p. 251; United Nations, Economic Commission for Latin America, *Economic Survey of Latin America 1963*, p. 263.

6 Ritter, *The Economic Development of Revolutionary Cuba*, p. 167.

7 Ibid., p. 207.

8 Mesa-Lago, "Economic Policies and Growth," p. 281. Also see Carmelo Mesa-Lago, *Cuba in the 1970s* (Albuquerque: University of New Mexico Press, 1974), pp. 2–4, 29–60.

9 Donald L. Losman, "The Embargo of Cuba: An Economic Appraisal," *Caribbean Studies*, Vol.14, No.3, October 1974, p. 107. A revised version of this article appears in Donald L. Losman, *International Economic Sanctions* (Albuquerque: University of New Mexico Press, 1979), pp. 20–46.

10 Quoted in Losman, "The Embargo of Cuba: An Economic Appraisal," pp. 108–109.

11 Ibid., p. 109.

12 See U.S. Congress, Senate, Committee on Foreign Relations, *A Background Study on East-West Trade*, 89th Congress, 1st Session, Committee Print. Prepared by the Legislative Research Service, Library of Congress, April 1965 (Washington, D.C. U.S. Government Printing Office, 1965), p. 72.

13 See Losman, "The Embargo of Cuba: An Economic Appraisal," p. 104.

14 U.S. Department of Commerce, *Cuban Trade with the Industrialized West 1974–1979*, p. 11.

Appendix 2: Tables
Sources: Department of State, Director of Intelligence and Research, *Trade of NATO Countries with Communist Countries, 1961–1963,* Research Memorandum, REU-71, December 31, 1964, pp. 20, 24, 88, 93, 97, 100; *Trade of NATO Countries with Communist Countries, 1961–1964,* Research Memorandum, REU-1, January 12, 1966, pp. 21, 25, 90, 95, 100, 104; *Trade of NATO Countries with Communist Countries, 1963–1966,* Research Memorandum, REU-62, December 6, 1967, pp. 19, 23, 85, 89, 94, 101; *Trade of NATO Countries with Communist Countries, 1964–1967,* Research Memorandum, REU-71, December 26, 1968, pp. 13, 24, 94, 100, 106, 110; *Trade of NATO Countries with Communist Countries, 1965–1968,* Research Memorandum, REU-67, December 15, 1969, pp. 20, 25, 91, 96, 105, 108; *Trade of NATO Countries with Communist Countries, 1966–1969,* Research Study, REUS-41, December 17, 1970, pp. 21, 27, 97, 102, 107, 111; *Trade of European Non-NATO Countries and Japan with Communist Countries, 1963–1966,* Research Memorandum, REU-12, February 15, 1968, pp. 22, 25, 53, 57; *Trade of European Non-NATO Countries and Japan with Communist Countries, 1964–1967,* Research Memorandum, REU-17, March 19, 1969, pp. 24, 28, 58, 62: *Trade of European Non-NATO Countries and Japan with Communist Countries, 1964–1967,* Research Memorandum, REU-17, March 19, 1969, pp. 24, 28, 58, 62; *Trade of European Non-NATO Countries and Japan with Communist Countries, 1965–1968,* Research Study, REUS-5, April 7, 1970, pp. 21, 24, 50, 54; *Trade of European Non-NATO Countries and Japan with Communist Countries, 1966–1969,* Research Study, REUS-10, March 22, 1971, pp. 23, 27, 57, 62; *Trade Patterns of the West, 1970,* Research Study, REUS-29, July 27, 1971, pp. 5, 7, 9, 11. U.S. Department of Commerce, Bureau of International Commerce, *Overseas Business Reports* ("World Trade with Cuba, 1961– 1962"), OBR-64-41, March 1964, p. 2; U.S. Department of Commerce, Office of East-West Policy and Planning, International Trade Administration, *Cuban Trade With The Industrialized West 1974– 1979* (Prepared by Lawrence H. Theriot and Linda Droker), Project D-76, May 1981, Tables 4 and 8; Figures for 1972 and 1973 Cuban trade with the capitalist world supplied by U.S. Department of Commerce, Office of East-West Policy and Planning; U.S. Central Intelligence Agency, *The Cuban Economy: A Statistical Review, 1968–1976,* ER-10708, December 1976, pp. 8, 9, Tables 13 and 15.

Bibliography

Interviews

Unpublished
More than 100 confidential interviews (oral and written) were conducted with respondents (executive-branch policymakers, corporate officials, congressional 'influentials,' etc.) who were involved, or participated in, the events described in this book. The interviews were seen as an important untapped source of data for which no systematic, organized, written record exists. As anyone who has undertaken research of this nature in the area of U.S. foreign policy can attest (and especially where the relationship has been as delicate and controversial as that which has existed between the United States and Cuba since 1959), an agreement as to the confidentiality of the interviews was in almost all cases a *sine qua non* for gaining access to the respondents. Nonetheless, I clearly identify all other relevant information: the place and time of the interview (or written correspondence); the institution with which each particular respondent was affiliated; and the general period during which the respondent was involved with the Cuba issue. The design for the semi-structured interview questionnaire basically corresponded to that outlined in Robert Merton et al., *The Focused Interview* Glencoe, Ill.: Free Press, 1956.

Library collections
The Dulles Oral History Collection. Princeton University Library, Princeton, New Jersey.
The *Eisenhower Oral History Collection.* Columbia University Library, New York City, New York.
The *John F. Kennedy Oral History Collection.* Kennedy Presidential Library, Dorchester Point, Massachusetts.
The Johnson Oral History Collection. Johnson Presidential Library, Austin, Texas.

Manuscript collections

The Chester Bowles Collection. Yale University Library, New Haven, Connecticut.
Harold Cooley Papers. #3801, Southern History Collection, University of North Carolina at Chapel Hill.

Unpublished manuscripts

Aaron, Harold R. *The Seizure of Political Power in Cuba, 1956–1959.* Ph.D. dissertation, Georgetown University, 1964.

506

Abrahams, Paul P. *The Foreign Expansion of American Finance and its Relationship to the Foreign Economic Policies of the United States, 1907–1921*. Ph.D. dissertation, University of Wisconsin, 1967.

Bonachea, Rolando E. *United States Policy Toward Cuba: 1959–1961*. Ph.D. dissertation, Georgetown University, November 1975.

Boyer, Harold. *Canada and Cuba: A Study in International Relations*. Ph.D. dissertation, Simon Fraser University, August 1972.

Brenner, Philip, and R. Roger Majak. *Congressmen As Statesmen: The Case of Cuba*. Paper prepared for delivery at the 1976 Annual Meeting of the American Political Science Association, Chicago, Illinois, September 2–5, 1976, 29 pp.

Brundenius, Claes, and Andrew Zimbalist. *Recent Studies on Cuban Economic Growth: A Review*. September 1984. 33 pp.

Child, John. *The Inter American Military System*. Ph.D. dissertation, The American University, 1978.

Kwon, Moon Sool. *The Organization of American States and the Cuban Challenge: An Analysis of the Inter-American System and the Meeting of Consultation of Ministers of Foreign Affairs*. Ph.D. dissertation, Claremont Graduate School and University, 1970.

Levin, Luisa. *Regionalism and the United Nations in American Foreign Policy: The Peace-Keeping Experience of the Organization of American States*. Ph.D. dissertation, Columbia University, 1971.

Padula, Jr., Alfred. *The Fall of the Bourgeoisie: Cuba, 1959–1961*. Ph.D. dissertation, University of New Mexico, 1974.

Page, Charles A. *The Development of Organized Labour in Cuba*. Ph.D. dissertation, University of California at Berkeley, 1952.

Scott, Rebecca Jarvis. *U.S. Foreign Assistance to Bolivia: 1952–1964*. Bachelor of Arts Honors Thesis, Radcliffe College, 1971.

Smith, Jr., Arthur K. *Mexico and the Cuban Revolution: Foreign Policy-Making in Mexico Under President Adolfo Lopez Mateos (1958–1964)*. Ph.D. dissertation, Cornell University, September 1970.

Storrs, Keith Larry. *Brazil's Independent Foreign Policy, 1961–1964: Background, Tenents, Linkage to Domestic Politics, and Aftermath*. Ph.D. dissertation, Cornell University, January 1973.

Zeitlin, Maurice. *Working Class Politics in Cuba: A Study of Political Sociology*. Ph.D. dissertation, University of California at Berkeley, 1964.

U.S. government: archival sources

National Archives of the United States. (Washington, D.C.)
General Records of the Department of State. Record Group 59.

Records of the United States Senate, Committee on Foreign Relations. Record Group 46.

Records of the United States Joint Chiefs of Staff. Record Group 218.

Presidential libraries
The Dwight D. Eisenhower Presidential Library. Abilene, Kansas.
The Lyndon B. Johnson Presidential Library. Austin, Texas.
The John F. Kennedy Presidential Library. Dorchester Point, Massachusetts.

Freedom of Information Act Declassification Process
A large number of previously classified documents from the Department of State, the Department of the Treasury, and the National Security Council were declassified under the U.S. Freedom of Information Act for use in this study.

U.S. government: unpublished documents

Congressional Conference on U.S.-Cuba Relations. Unofficial Transcript, April 12–20, 1972. New Senate Office Building, Washington, D.C.

A Detente with Cuba. Statement prepared by 11 Republican Members of the House of Representatives, January 1973, Washington, D.C.

Summary of Documentation on Assassinations by Cuban Government Supplied to Senator George McGovern. Office of Senator George McGovern, Washington, D.C., July 30, 1975.

U.S. Department of Commerce

Maritime Administration. *List of Free World and Polish Flag Vessels Arriving in Cuba Since January 1, 1963.* Report No.112, February 22, 1971.

Maritime Administration. *List of Free World and Polish Flag Vessels Arriving in Cuba Since January 1, 1963.* Report No.128, September 23, 1975.

Office of East-West Policy and Planning, Bureau of East-West Trade, Industry and Trade Administration. *Cuban Foreign Trade: A Current Assessment.* Prepared by Lawrence H. Theriot, 1978.

Office of East-West Policy and Planning, International Trade Administration. *Cuban Trade With The Industrialized West 1974–1979.* Prepared by Lawrence H. Theriot and Linda Droker. Project D-76, May 1981.

U.S. Department of State

Director of Intelligence and Research. *Trade of NATO Countries with Communist Countries, 1961–1963.* Research Memorandum, REU-71, December 31, 1964.

Director of Intelligence and Research. *Trade of NATO Countries with Communist Countries, 1961–1964.* Research Memorandum, REU-1, January 12, 1966.

Director of Intelligence and Research. *Trade of NATO Countries with Communist Countries, 1963–1966.* Research Memorandum, REU-1, December 6, 1967.

Director of Intelligence and Research. *Trade of European Non-NATO Countries and Japan, with Communist Countries, 1963–1966.* Research Memorandum REU-1, February 15, 1968.

Director of Intelligence and Research. *Trade of NATO Countries with Communist Countries, 1964–1967.* Research Memorandum, REU-1, December 26, 1968.

Director of Intelligence and Research. *Trade of European Non-NATO Countries and Japan with Communist Countries, 1964–1967.* Research Memorandum REU-17, March 19, 1969.

Director of Intelligence and Research. *Trade of NATO Countries with Communist Countries, 1965–1968.* Research Memorandum, REU-67, December 15, 1969.

Director of Intelligence and Research. *Trade of European Non-NATO Countries and Japan with Communist Countries, 1965–1968.* Research Study, REUS-5, April 1970.

Bureau of Intelligence and Research. *Trade of NATO Countries with Communist Countries, 1966–1969.* Research Study, REUS-41, December 17, 1970.

Bureau of Intelligence and Research. *Trade of European Non-NATO Countries and Japan with Communist Countries, 1966–1969.* Research Study, REUS-10, March 22, 1971.

Bureau of Intelligence and Research. *Trade Patterns of the West, 1970.* Research Study, REUS-29, July 27, 1971.

Bureau of Intelligence and Research, Office of Long-range Assessments. *Soviet Attitudes Towards Aid To And Contacts With Central American Revolutionaries.* Prepared by C. G. Jacobsen, June 1, 1984.

Office of East-West Policy and Planning, International Trade Administration. *Figures for Cuba's Trade in 1972 and 1973 with the NATO and Non-NATO Countries and Japan.*

U.S. Department of the Treasury

Foreign Credits, by the United States Government, as of December 1, 1969. 1970.

Office of Multilateral Development Banks. *U.S. Voting Behavior in the Multilateral Development Banks during the Carter Administration.* Prepared by Brian Crowe, December 31, 1980.

U.S. government: published documents

Commission on the Organization for the Conduct of Foreign Policy. June 1975, Volume 3, Appendix H, Appendix I, Appendix J. Washington, D.C.: U.S. Government Printing Office, 1975.

"Controversy in Congress Over U.S. Policy Toward Cuba: Pros & Cons," *Congressional Digest,* Vol.57, No.2, February 1978.

Foreign Claims Settlement Commission of the United States. *Annual Report to the Congress for the Period January 1–December 31, 1973.* Washington, D.C.: U.S. Government Printing Office, 1973.

"Human Rights: Getting Through a Policy Maze," *Congressional Quarterly Weekly Report,* Vol.XXXVI, No.31, August 5, 1978, 2046–2051.

Lee, Oliver M. *Initial World Reactions to U.S. Quarantine of Cuba.* Washington, D.C.: Congressional Research Service, Legislative Research Service, Foreign Affairs Division, JX1428, October 29, 1962.

Nixon, Richard M. U.S. Policy for the 1970s. *The Western Hemisphere* (excerpts from) . . . February 25, 1971. Department of State Publication 8679, April 1971.

Peterson, Peter G. *The United States in the Changing World Economy: Volume 1, A Foreign Economic Perspective.* December 27, 1971. Washington, D.C.: U.S. Government Printing Office, 1971.

Public Papers of the Presidents of the United States: Dwight D. Eisenhower 1959. Washington, D.C.: U.S. Government Printing Office, 1960.

Public Papers of the Presidents of the United States: Lyndon B. Johnson 1963–1964, Book 1. Washington, D.C.: U.S. Government Printing Office, 1965.

Sklar, Barry. *U.S. Policy Toward Cuba: A Pro-Con Discussion on the Resumption of Relations.* Washington, D.C.: Library of Congress, Congressional Research Service, JX 1428 L.A. Cuba, 72-43F, February 9, 1972.

Theriot, Lawrence, "U.S. Cuba Trade: Question Mark," *Commerce America* (U.S. Department of Commerce), Vol. III, No.9, April 24, 1978, 2–5.

U.S. Agency for International Development

Office of Financial Management, Statistics and Reports Division. *U.S. Overseas Loans and Grants and Assistance from International Organizations: Obligations and Loan Authorizations, July 1, 1945–June 30, 1973.* Washington, D.C., May 1974.

Office of Financial Management, Statistics and Reports Division. *U.S. Overseas Loans and Grants and Assistance from International Organizations: Obligations and Loan Authorizations, July 1, 1945–June 30, 1975.* Washington, D.C., 1976.

Statistics and Reports Divison, Office of Program and Information Analysis Service. *U.S. Overseas Loans and Grants and Assistance from International Organizations: Obligations and Loan Authorizations, July 1, 1945–September 30, 1976.* Washington, D.C., 1977.

Bureau for Program and Policy Coordination, Office of Planning and Budgeting. *U.S. Overseas Loans and Grants and Assistance from International Organizations: Obligations and Loan Authorizations, July 1, 1945–September 30, 1980.* Washington, D.C., 1981.

U.S. Agency for International Development and Predecessor Agencies

Office of Program and Policy Coordination, Statistics and Reports Division. *The Economic Assistance Programs, April 3, 1948–June 30, 1968.* Washington, D.C., March 28, 1969.

U.S. Central Intelligence Agency

Intelligence Handbook. *Cuba: Foreign Trade.* A(ER)75-69, July 1975.

The Cuban Economy: A Statistical Review, 1968–1976. ER76-10708, December 1976.

National Foreign Assessment Center. *Handbook of Economic Statistics 1969*. ER70-10274. August 1979.

U.S. Congress, House

Committee on Agriculture. *Extension of the Sugar Act of 1948 as Amended*. 86th Congress, 2nd Session, June 22, 1960. Washington, D.C.: U.S. Government Printing Office, 1960.

Committee on Appropriations, Subcommittee on Foreign Operations Appropriations. *Foreign Operations Appropriations for 1964, Part 2*. 88th Congress, 1st Session, May 14, 1963. Washington, D.C.: U.S. Government Printing Office, 1963.

Committee on Appropriations, Subcommittee on Foreign Operations Appropriations. *Foreign Operations Appropriations for 1964, Part 4*. 88th Congress, 1st Session, July 17, 25, 29, 30; August 14, 1963. Washington, D.C.: U.S. Government Printing Office, 1963.

Committee on Appropriations, Subcommittee on Foreign Operations and Related Agencies. *Foreign Assistance and Related Agencies Appropriations for 1974, Part 2*. 93rd. Congress, 1st Session, 1973. Washington, D.C.: U.S. Government Printing Office, 1973.

Committee on Banking and Currency, Subcommittee on International Trade. *Extension of the Export Administration Act of 1969*. 92nd Congress, 2nd Session, May 30, 1972. Washington, D.C.: U.S. Government Printing Office, 1972.

Committee on Banking, Currency and Housing, Subcommittee on International Trade, Investment and Monetary Policy. *Oversight Hearings on the Export-Import Bank*. 94th Congress, 2nd Session, May 10 and 11, 1976. Washington, D.C.: U.S. Government Printing Office, 1976.

Committee on Banking, Finance and Urban Affairs, Subcommittee on International Development Institutions and Finance, *International Development Institutions Authorizations – 1977*, 95th Congress, 1st Session, March 22, 23, and 24, 1977. Washington, D.C.: U.S. Government Printing Office, 1977.

Committee on Foreign Affairs. *Development Assistance to Latin America*. Commitee Print, April 14, 1971. Washington, D.C.: U.S. Government Printing Office, 1971.

Committee on Foreign Affairs. *Economic and Political Future of the Caribbean*. 96th Congress, 1st Session, July 24, 26; and September 19, 1979. Washington, D.C.: U.S. Government Printing Office, 1979.

Committee on Foreign Affairs. *Foreign Assistance Act of 1964, Part 1*. 88th Congress, 2nd Session, March 23, 1964. Washington, D.C.: U.S. Government Printing Office, 1964.

Committee on Foreign Affairs. *Foreign Assistance Act of 1967, Part 1*. 90th Congress, 1st Session, April 4, 5, 11, 12, 13 and 14, 1967. Washington, D.C.: U.S. Government Printing Office, 1967.

Committee on Foreign Affairs. *Inter-American Affairs*. A Collection of Documents, Legislation, Description of Inter-American Organizations, and Other Material Pertaining to Inter-American Affairs. 93rd Congress, 1st Session, November 1973. Washington, D.C.: U.S. Government Printing Office, 1973.

Committee on Foreign Affairs. *The International Development and Security Act, Part II.* 87th Congress, 1st Session, June 26,27,28,29, and July 6, 1961. Washington, D.C.: U.S. Government Printing Office, 1961.

Committee on Foreign Affairs. *Mutual Security Act of 1955.* 84th Congress, 1st Session, May 25,26, June 8, 9, 10, 13, 14, 15, 16 & 17, 1955. Washington, D.C.: U.S. Government Printing Office, 1955.

Committee on Foreign Affairs. *Mutual Security Act of 1960, Part 1.* 86th Congress, 2nd Session, February 17, 18, 23, 24, & 29, 1960. Washington, D.C.: U.S. Government Printing Office, 1960.

Committee on Foreign Affairs. *Special Study Mission to Cuba.* Report by Representative Albert P. Moreno, 83rd Congress, 2nd Session, Committee Print, December 31, 1954. Washington, D.C.: U.S. Government Printing Office, 1955.

Committee on Foreign Affairs, *The Middle East, Africa, and Inter-American Affairs.* Selected Executive Session Hearings of the Committee, 1951–1956, Volume XVI. Washington, D.C.: U.S. Government Printing Office, 1980.

Committee on Foreign Affairs. *Radio Broadcasting To Cuba (Radio Martí),* 97th Congress, 2nd Session, March 3, 4, and 24, 1982. Washington, D.C.: U.S. Government Printing Office, 1982.

Committee on Foreign Affairs. *The United States and the Multilateral Development Banks.* 93rd Congress, 2nd Session, Committee Print, Prepared by the Congressional Research Service, Library of Congress, March 1974. Washington, D.C.: U.S. Government Printing Office, 1974.

Committee on Foreign Affairs, Subcommittee on Europe and the Middle East and on International Economic Policy and Trade, Hearings and Markup. *Final Negotiations and Settlement of Claims Against Czechoslovakia.* 97th Congress, 1st Session, June 24; December 7 and 9, 1981. Washington, D.C.: U.S. Government Printing Office, 1982.

Committee on Foreign Affairs, Subcommittee on Foreign Economic Policy. *New Realities and New Directions in United States Foreign Economic Policy.* 92nd Congress, 2nd Session, Committee Print, February 28, 1972. Washington, D.C.: U.S. Government Printing Office, 1972.

Committee on Foreign Affairs, Subcommittee on Foreign Economic Policy. *U.S. Foreign Economic Policy: Implications for Organization of the Executive Branch.* 92nd Congress, 2nd Session, June 20, 22; July 25, August 2 and September 19, 1972. Washington, D.C.: U.S. Government Printing Office, 1972.

Committee on Foreign Affairs, Subcommittee on Inter-American Affairs. *Castro-Communist Subversion in the Western Hemisphere.* 88th Congress, 1st Session, February 18, 20, 21, 26, 27, 28, March

4, 5, and 6, 1963. Washington, D.C.: U.S. Government Printing Office, 1963.

Committee on Foreign Affairs, Subcommittee on Inter-American Affairs. *Communism in Latin America.* 89th Congress, 1st Session, Report, April 14, 1965, Washington, D.C.: U.S. Government Printing Office, 1965.

Committee on Foreign Affairs, Subcommittee on Inter-American Affairs. *Communist Activities in Latin America, 1967.* 90th Congress, 1st Session, April 25, May 4, 16, 17, 31, and June 7, 1967. Washington, D.C.: U.S. Government Printing Office, 1967.

Committee on Foreign Affairs, Subcommittee on Inter-American Affairs. *Cuba and the Caribbean.* 91st Congress, 2nd Session, July 8, 9, 10, 13, 20, 27, 31, and August 3, 1970. Washington, D.C.: U.S. Government Printing Office, 1970.

Committee on Foreign Affairs, Subcommittee on Inter-American Affairs. *Hijacking Accord Between the United States and Cuba.* 93rd Congress, 1st Session, February 20, 1973. Washington, D.C.: U.S. Government Printing Office, 1973.

Committee on Foreign Affairs, Subcommittee on Inter-American Affairs. *Soviet Naval Activities in Cuba.* 91st Congress, 2nd Session, September 30, October 13, November 19 and 24, 1970. Washington, D.C.: U.S. Government Printing Office, 1970.

Committee on Foreign Affairs, Subcommittee on Inter-American Affairs. *Soviet Naval Activities in Cuba, Part 2.* 92nd Congress, 1st Session, September 28, 1971. Washington, D.C.: U.S. Government Printing Office, 1971.

Committee on Foreign Affairs, Subcommittee on Inter-American Affairs. *Soviet Activities in Cuba, Part 3.* 92nd Congress, 2nd Session, September 26, 1972. Washington, D.C.: U.S. Government Printing Office, 1972.

Committee on Foreign Affairs, Subcommittee on Inter-American Affairs. *Soviet Activities in Cuba, Part 4 and 5.* 93rd Congress, 2nd Session, October 31, 1973; November 20 and 21, 1974. Washington, D.C.: U.S. Government Printing Office, 1974.

Committee on Foreign Affairs, Subcommittees on International Economic Policy and Trade and on Inter-American Affairs. *Issues in United States-Cuban Relations.* 97th Congress, 2nd Session, December 14, 1982. Washington, D.C.: U.S. Government Printing Office, 1983.

Committee on Foreign Affairs, Subcommittees on International Economic Policy and Trade and on Inter-American Affairs. *Outstanding Claims Against Cuba.* 96th Congress, 1st Session, September 25, 1979. Washington, D.C.: U.S. Government Printing Office, 1980.

Committee on Foreign Affairs, Subcommittee on International Organizations and Movements. *Winning the Cold War: The U.S. Ideological Offensive, Part 1.* 88th Congress, 1st Session, March 28, 29, and April 2 and 3, 1963. Washington, D.C.: U.S. Government Printing Office, 1963.

Committee on International Relations. *Cuba Study Mission.* Report of Representative Steven Solarz, June 26–July 2, 1975. 94th Congress, 1st Session, Committee Print, July 15, 1975. Washington, D.C.: U.S. Government Printing Office, 1975.

Committee on International Relations. *Military Assistance Programs, Part 2.* Selected Executive Session Hearings of the Committee 1943–1950, Volume VI, Historical Series, March 25, 26, April 11, 1947. Washington, D.C.: U.S. Government Printing Office, 1976.

Committee on International Relations. *Toward Improved United States-Cuba Relations.* Report of Special Study Mission to Cuba, February 10–15, 1977. 95th Congress, 1st Session, Committee Print, May 23, 1977. Washington, D.C., U.S. Government Printing Office, 1977.

Committee on International Relations. *United States-Cuba Perspectives – 1975.* Report on a Study Visit to Cuba, September 18–October 15, 1975. 94th Congress, 2nd Session, Committee Print, May 4, 1976. Washington, D.C.: U.S. Government Printing Office, 1976.

Committee on International Relations. *United States Relations with Cuba.* Report of a Special Study Mission to Cuba, August 30–September 3, 1975. 94th Congress, 1st Session, Committee Print, October 31, 1975. Washington, D.C.: U.S. Government Printing Office, 1975.

Committee on International Relations, Subcommittee on Inter-American Affairs. *Impact of Cuban-Soviet Ties in the Western Hemisphere.* 95th Congress, 2nd Session, March 14, 15; April 5 and 15, 1978. Washington, D.C.: U.S. Government Printing Office, 1978.

Committee on International Relations, Subcommittee on Inter-American Affairs. *United States Policy Toward the Caribbean.* 95th Congress, 1st Session, June 28 and 30, 1977. Washington, D.C.: U.S. Government Printing Office, 1977.

Committee on International Relations, Subcommittee on International Economic Policy. *United States Foreign Economic Policy Objectives.* 94th Congress, 1st Session, September 26 and October 23, 1975. Washington, D.C.: U.S. Government Printing Office, 1975.

Committee on International Relations, Subcommittee on International Organizations. *The Rhodesian Sanctions Bill, Part II.* 94th Congress, 1st Session, June 19, 1975. Washington, D.C.: U.S. Government Printing Office, 1975.

Committee on International Relations, Subcommittee on International Political and Military Affairs. *Soviet Activities in Cuba, Part VI and VII: Communist Influence in the Western Hemisphere.* 94th Congress, October 7, 1975, June 15 and September 16, 1976. Washington, D.C.: U.S. Government Printing Office, 1976.

Committee on International Relations, Subcommittee on International Security and Scientific Affairs. *Foreign Assistance Legislation for Fiscal Year 1978, Part 2.* 95th Congress, 1st Session, March 30, 31, and April 19, 20, 1977. Washington, D.C.: U.S. Government Printing Office, 1977.

Committee on International Relations, Subcommittee on International Trade and Commerce. *Export Licensing of Advanced Technology: A Review, Part II.* 94th Congress, 2nd Session, April 12, 1976. Washington, D.C.: U.S. Government Printing Office, 1976.

Committee on International Relations, Subcommitee on International Trade and Commerce. *United States-Cuba Trade Promotion.* 94th Congress, 2nd Session, July 22, 1976. Washington, D.C.: U.S. Government Printing Office, 1976.

Committee on International Relations, Subcommittee on International Trade and Commerce, and International Organizations. *U.S. Trade Embargo of Cuba.* 94th Congress, 1st Session May 8, 13, 15, 20, 22, June 11, 26, July 9, and September 23, 1975. Washington, D.C.: U.S. Government Printing Office, 1975.

Committee on Interstate and Foreign Commerce. *Trade with Cuba.* 87th Congress, 1st Session, August 29 and September 1, 1961. Washington, D.C.: U.S. Government Printing Office, 1961.

Select Committee on Export Control. *Investigation and Study of the Administration, Operation, and Enforcement of the Export Control Act of 1949, and Related Acts.* 87th Congress, 1st Session, October 25, 26, and 30, and December 5, 6, 7, and 8, 1961. Washington, D.C.: U.S. Government Printing Office, 1962.

Select Committee on Export Control. *Investigation and Study of the Administration, Operation, and Enforcement of the Export Control Act of 1949, and Related Acts, Part 3.* 87th Congress, 2nd Session, September 13 and 14, and October 2 and 3, 1962. Washington, D.C.: U.S. Government Printing Office, 1962.

Select Committee on Intelligence. *U.S. Intelligence Agencies and Activities: Risks and Control of Foreign Intelligence, Part 5.* 94th Congress, 1st Session, November 4, 6, December 2, 3, 9, 10, 11, 12, and 17, 1975. Washington, D.C.: U.S. Government Printing Office, 1975.

U.S. Congress, Senate

Committee on Agriculture and Forestry, Subcommittee on Agricultural Production, Marketing, and Stabilization of Prices. *Rice Programs.* 94th Congress, 1st Session, November 14, 1975. Washington, D.C.: U.S. Government Printing Office, 1975.

Committee on Appropriations. *Foreign Assistance and Related Agencies Appropriations for 1962.* 87th Congress, 1st Session, September 1, 1961. Washington, D.C.: U.S. Government Printing Office, 1961.

Committee on Appropriations and Committee on Armed Services, Subcommittee on Department of Defense. *Department of Defense Appropriations for Fiscal Year 1967, Part 1.* 89th Congress, 2nd Session, February 23, 1966. Washington, D.C.: U.S. Government Printing Office, 1966.

Committee on Armed Services. *Military Procurement Authorization Fiscal Year 1964.* 88th Congress, 1st Session, February 19, 20, 21, 22, 26, 27, 28, March 1, 4, 5, 6, 7, 1963. Washington, D.C.: U.S. Government Printing Office, 1963.

Committee on Banking and Currency. *Nomination of Harold F. Linder.* 87th Congress, 1st Session, February 24, 1961. Washington, D.C.: U.S. Government Printing Office, 1961.

Committee on Banking, Housing and Urban Affairs, Subcommittee on International Finance. *The Role of the Export-Import Bank and Export Controls in U.S. Economic Policy.* 93rd Congress, 2nd Session, April 2, 5, 10, 23, 25, and 26; May 2, 1974. Washington, D.C.: U.S. Government Printing Office, 1974.

Committee on Finance. *Czechoslovakia Claims Settlement* (Executive Hearings). 93rd Congress, 2nd Session, September 11 and 26, 1974. Washington, D.C.: U.S. Government Printing Office, 1974.

Committee on Foreign Relations. *A Background Study on East-West Trade.* 89th Congress, 1st Session, Committee Print. Prepared by the Legislative Reference Service, Library of Congress, April 1965. Washington, D.C.: U.S. Government Printing Office, 1965.

Committee on Foreign Relations. *Bretton Woods Agreement Amendments Act of 1977.* 95th Congress, 1st Session, Report No.95-603, November 15, 1977. Washington, D.C.: U.S. Government Printing Office, 1977.

Committee on Foreign Relations. *Cuba: A Staff Report.* By Pat Holt, Professional Staff Member. 93rd Congress, 2nd Session, Committee Print, August 2, 1974. Washington, D.C.: U.S. Government Printing Office, 1974.

Committee on Foreign Relations. *Cuban Realities; May 1975.* Report of Senator George S. McGovern. 94th Congress, 1st Session, Committee Print, August 1975. Washington, D.C.: U.S. Government Printing Office, 1975.

Committee on Foreign Relations. *Delusions and Reality: The Future of United States-Cuba Relations.* Report by Senator Frank Church on a Trip to Cuba, August 8–11, 1977. 95th Congress, 1st Session, Committee Print, October 1977. Washington, D.C.: U.S. Government Printing Office, 1977.

Committee on Foreign Relations. *East-West Trade, Part 1.* 88th Congress, 2nd Session, March 13, 16, April 8, 9, 1964. Washington, D.C.: U.S. Government Printing Office, 1964.

Committee on Foreign Relations. *Events in United States-Cuban Relations: A Chronology, 1957–1963.* Prepared by the U.S. Department of State. Washington, D.C.: U.S. Government Printing Office, 1963.

Committee on Foreign Relations, *Executive Sessions of the Senate Foreign Relations Committee, Volume IV, 1952* (Historical Series). 82nd Congress, 2nd Session, Washington, D.C.: U.S. Government Printing Office, 1976.

Committee on Foreign Relations. *Executive Sessions of the Senate Foreign Relations Committee, Volume VIII* (Historical Series). 84th Congress, 2nd Session, 1956. Washington, D.C.: U.S. Government Printing Office, 1978.

Committee on Foreign Relations. *Executive Sessions of the Senate Foreign Relations Committee, Volume XII* (Historical Series). 86th Congress, 2nd Session, January 18, 21, February 18, 1960. Washington, D.C.: U.S. Government Printing Office, November 1982.

Committee on Foreign Relations. *Executive Sessions of the Senate Foreign Relations Committee, Volume XIII, Part 1* (Historical Series). 87th Congress, 1st Session, 1961. Washington, D.C.: U.S. Government Printing Office, April 1984.

Committee on Foreign Relations. *Executive Sessions of the Senate Foreign Relations Committee, Vol. XIII, Part 2* (Historical Series), 87th Congress, 1st Session, 1961. Washington, D.C.: U.S. Government Printing Office, December 1984.

Committee of Foreign Relations. *Foreign Assistance Act of 1962*, 87th Congress, 2nd Session, April 5, 9, 10, 11, 12, 13, 16, and 18, 1962. Washington, D.C.: U.S. Government Printing Office, 1962.

Committee on Foreign Relations. *Legislative Origins of the Truman Doctrine.* Executive Session, Historical Series. 81st Congress, 1st Session, March 13, and 28, and April 1, 2, and 3, 1947. Washington, D.C.: U.S. Government Printing Office, 1973.

Committee on Foreign Relations. *Legislative Proposals Relating to the War in Southeast Asia.* 92nd Congress, 1st Session, April 20, 21, 22, and 28; May 3, 11, 12, 13, 25, 26 and 27, 1971. Washington, D.C.: U.S. Government Printing Office, 1971.

Committee on Foreign Relations. *Mutual Security Act of 1958.* 85th Congress, 2nd Session, March 19, 20, 21, 24, 26, 27, 28, 31, April 1 and 2, 1958. Washington, D.C.: U.S. Government Printing Office, 1958.

Committee on Foreign Relations. *Nomination of Henry A. Kissinger, Part 1.* 93rd Congress, 1st Session, September 7, 10, 11, and 14, 1973. Washington, D.C.: U.S. Government Printing Office, 1973.

Committee on Foreign Relations. *Punta Del Este Conference January 1962.* Report of Senators Wayne Morse and Bourke B. Hickenlooper, 87th Congress, 2nd Session, Committee Print, March 1962. Washington, D.C.: U.S. Government Printing Office, 1962.

Committee on Foreign Relations. *Radio Broadcasting To Cuba, Part 1.* 97th Congress, 2nd Session, July 1, 27, and August 9, 1982. Washington, D.C.: U.S. Government Printing Office, 1983.

Committee on Foreign Relations. *Radio Broadcasting to Cuba, Part 2.* 98th Congress 2nd Session, April 27, 1983. Washington, D.C.: U.S. Government Printing Office, 1983.

Committee on Foreign Relations. *Review of Foreign Policy, 1958, Part 1.* 85th Congress, 2nd Session, February 3, 17, 18, 19, 26, and 27, March 3, 5, and 10, 1958. Washington, D.C.: U.S. Government Printing Office, 1958.

Committee on Foreign Relations. *Review of the World Situation: 1949–1950.* Executive Sessions, Historical Series. 81st Congress, 1st and 2nd Session, May 19, June 22, September 20, and October 12, 1949, and January 10, 13, 25, and 26, March 29, May 1, July 24, September 11, November 28, December 9, and 22, 1950. Washington, D.C.: U.S. Government Printing Office, 1974.

Committee on Foreign Relations. *Study Mission in the Caribbean Area December 1957, Part 1.* Report by Senator George A. Aiken. 85th Congress, 2nd Session, Committee Print, January 20, 1958. Washington, D.C.: U.S. Government Printing Office, 1985.

Committee on Foreign Relations. *The United States and Cuba: A Propitious Moment.* Report by Senator Jacob Javits and Senator Claiborne Pell. 93rd Congress, 2nd Session, Committee Print, October 1974. Washington, D.C.: U.S. Government Printing Office, 1974.

Committee on Foreign Relations. *United States Foreign Policy, No.9: The Formulation and Administration of United States Foreign Policy.* 86th Congress, 2nd Session, Committee Print, January 13, 1960. Washington, D.C.: U.S. Government Printing Office, 1960.

Committee on Foreign Relations. *United States Policy Toward Cuba.* 92nd Congress, 1st Session, September 16, 1971. Washington, D.C.: U.S. Government Printing Office, 1971.

Committee on Foreign Relations. *U.S. Relations with Latin America.* 94th Congress, 1st Session, February 21, 26, 27 and 28, 1975. Washington, D.C.: U.S. Government Printing Office, 1975.

Committee on Foreign Relations. *Vance Nomination.* 95th Congress, 1st Session, January 11, 1977. Washington, D.C.: U.S. Government Printing Office, 1977.

Committee on Foreign Relations. *Volume 1.* Executive Session, Historical Series. 80th Congress, 1st and 2nd Session, 1947–1948. Washington, D.C.: U.S. Government Printing Office, 1976.

Committee on Foreign Relations. *Volume IV.* Executive Sessions, Historical Series. 82nd Congress, 2nd Session, 1952. Washington, D.C.: U.S. Government Printing Office, 1976.

Committee on Foreign Relations, Subcommittee on African Affairs. *Ethiopia and the Horn of Africa.* 94th Congress, 2nd Session, August 4, 5, and 6, 1976. Washington, D.C.: U.S. Government Printing Office, 1976.

Committee on Foreign Relations, Subcommittee on African Affairs. *U.S. Policy Toward Africa.* 95th Congress, 2nd Session, May 12, 1978. Washington, D.C.: U.S. Government Printing Office, 1978.

Committee on Foreign Relations, Subcommittee on African Affairs and Subcommittee on Arms Control, International Organizations and Security Agreements. *U.S. Policy Toward Africa.* 94th Congress, 2nd Session, March 5, 8, 15, 19; May 12, 13, 21, 26, and 27, 1976. Washington, D.C.: U.S. Government Printing Office, 1976.

Committee on Foreign Relations, Subcommittee on American Republic Affairs. *Survey of the Alliance for Progress.* Studies and Hearings, 91st Congress, 1st Session, Doc. No.91–17, April 29, 1969. Washington, D.C.: U.S. Government Printing Office, 1969.

Committee on Foreign Relations, Subcommittee on American Republic Affairs. *United States-Latin American Relations, No.5: United States and Latin American Policies Affecting Their Economic Relations.* 86th Congress, 2nd Session, Committee Print, January 31, 1960. Washington, D.C.: U.S. Government Printing Office, 1960.

Committee on Foreign Relations, Subcommittee on American Republic Affairs. *United States-Latin American Relations, Study No. 7: Soviet Bloc Latin American Activities.* 86th Congress, 2nd Session, Committee Print, February 28, 1960. Washington, D.C.: U.S. Government Printing Office, 1960.

Committee on Foreign Relations, Subcommittee on Foreign Assistance. *Implications of President Carter's Conventional Arms Transfer Policy.* 95th Congress, 1st Session. Prepared by the Foreign Affairs and National Defense Division, Congressional Research Service, Library of Congress, Committee Print, December 1977. Washington, D.C.: U.S. Government Printing Office, 1977.

Committee on Foreign Relations, Subcommittee on Foreign Assistance. *International Financial Institutions.* 95th Congress, 1st Session, March 6 and 9, 1977. Washington, D.C.: U.S. Government Printing Office, 1977.

Committee on Foreign Relations, Subcommittee on International Organization Affairs. *United Nations Special Fund.* 88th Congress, 1st Session, February 18, 1963. Washington, D.C.: U.S. Government Printing Office, 1963.

Committee on Foreign Relations, Subcommittee on Western Hemisphere Affairs. *United States Policies and Programs in Brazil.* 92nd Congress, 1st Session, May 4, 5, and 11, 1971. Washington, D.C.: U.S. Government Printing Office, 1971.

Committee on Foreign Relations, Subcommittee on Western Hemisphere Affairs. *U.S. Policy Toward Cuba.* 93rd Congress, 1st Session, March 26 and April 18, 1973. Washington, D.C.: U.S. Government Printing Office, 1974.

Committee on Foreign Relations and Committee on Armed Services. *Situation in Cuba.* 87th Congress, 2nd Session, September 17, 1962. Washington, D.C.: U.S. Government Printing Office, 1962.

Committee on Government Operations, Subcommittee on Foreign Aid Expenditures. *Coordination in Administration of Public Law 480,* 89th Congress, 2nd Session, June 2 and 30, 1966. Washington, D.C.: U.S. Government Printing Office, 1966.

Committee on Government Operations, Subcommittee on National Policy Machinery. *Organizing for National Security: The National Security Council.* 86th Congress, 2nd Session, Committee Print, 1960. Washington, D.C.: U.S. Government Printing Office, 1960.

Committee on Government Operations, Subcommittee on National Policy Machinery. *Organizing for National Security: Selected Materials.* 86th Congress, 2nd Session, Committee Print, 1960. Washington, D.C.: U.S. Government Printing Office, 1960.

Committee on Government Operations, Subcommittee on National Policy Machinery. *Organizing for National Security: The National Security Council, Part IV.* 86th Congress, 2nd Session, May 10 and 24, 1960. Washington, D.C.: U.S. Government Printing Office, 1960.

Committee on Government Operations, Subcommittee on National Policy Machinery. *Organizing for National Security: State, Defense, and the National Security Council, Part IX.* 87th Congress, 1st Session, August 1, 7, 17 and 24, 1961. Washington, D.C.: U.S. Government Printing Office, 1961.

Committee on Government Operations, Subcommittee on National Security Staffing and Operations. *Administration on National Security: Basic Issues.* 88th Congress, 1st Session, Committee Print, 1963. Washington, D.C.: U.S. Government Printing Office, 1963.

Committee on Governmental Affairs. *U.S. Participation in the Multilateral Development Banks.* 96th Congress, 1st Session, Committee Print, April 30, 1979. Washington, D.C.: U.S. Government Printing Office, 1979.

Committee on the Judiciary, Subcommittee to Investigate the Administration of the Internal Security Act and other Internal Security Laws. *Communist Threat to the United States Through the Caribbean, Part III.* 86th Congress, 1st Session, November 5, 1959. Washington, D.C.: U.S. Government Printing Office, 1960.

Committee on the Judiciary, Subcommittee to Investigate the Administration of the Internal Security Act and other Internal Security Laws. *Communist Threat to the United States Through the Caribbean, Part 9.* 86th Congress, 2nd Session, August 27, 30, 1960. Washington, D.C.: U.S. Government Printing Office, 1960.

Committee on the Judiciary, Subcommittee to Investigate the Administration of the Internal Security Act and other Internal Security Laws. *Communist Threat to the United States Through the Caribbean, Part 10.* 86th Congress, 2nd Session, September 2 and 8, 1960. Washington, D.C.: U.S. Government Printing Office, 1960.

Committee on the Judiciary, Subcommittee to Investigate Problems Connected with Refugees and Escapees. *Cuban Refugee Problems, Part 1.* 88th Congress, 1st Session, May 22 and 23, 1963. Washington, D.C.: U.S. Government Printing Office, 1963.

Joint Economic Committee. *China Under The Four Modernizations, Part 2: Selected Papers.* 97th Congress, 2nd Session, Joint Committee Print, December 30, 1982. Washington, D.C.: U.S. Government Printing Office, 1982.

Joint Economic Committee. Special Study on Economic Change, Vol.9, *The International Economy: U.S. Role in a World Market.* 96th Congress, 2nd Session, Joint Committee Print, December 17, 1980. Washington, D.C.: U.S. Government Printing Office, 1980.

Select Committee on Intelligence. *Covert Action in Chile 1963–1973.* 94th Congress, 1st Session, Committee Print, December 18, 1975. Washington, D.C.: U.S. Government Printing Office, 1975.

Select Committee on Intelligence. *Nomination of E. Henry Knoche* (to be Deputy Director of Central Intelligence). 94th Congress, 2nd Session, June 23, 1976. Washington, D.C.: U.S. Government Printing Office, 1976.

Select Committee to Study Governmental Operations. *Alleged Assassination Plots Involving Foreign Leaders.* 94th Congress, 1st Session, Report No.94-465, November 20, 1975. Washington, D.C.: U.S. Government Printing Office, 1975.

Final Report of the Select Committee to Study Governmental Operations with respect to Intelligence Activities. *Supplementary Detailed Staff Reports on Foreign and Military Intelligence, Book IV.* 94th Congress, 2nd Session, Report 94-755, April 23, 1976. Washington, D.C.: U.S. Government Printing Office, 1976.

Select Committee to Study Governmental Operations with respect to Intelligence Activities. *The Investigation of the Assassination of President John F. Kennedy: Performance of the Intelligence Agencies, Book V.* 94th Congress, 2nd Session, Report No. 94-755, April 23, 1976. Washington, D.C.: U.S. Government Printing Office, 1976.

Select Committee to Study Governmental Operations with respect to Intelligence Activities. *Senate Resolution 21, Covert Action, Vol.7.* 94th Congress, 1st Session, December 4 and 5, 1975. Washington, D.C.: U.S. Government Printing Office, 1976.

The Special Committee to Study the Foreign Aid Program. *Foreign Aid Program: Compilation of Studies and Surveys* (Survey No. 9: 'Central America and the Caribbean Area,' by James Minotto, March 1957). 85th Congress, 1st Session, July 1957. Washington, D.C.: U.S. Government Printing Office, 1957.

U.S. Department of Commerce

Bureau of Economic Analysis. *International Transactions of The United States During the War, 1940–1945.* Washington, D.C.: U.S. Government Printing Office, 1948.

Bureau of Economic Analysis. *Selected Data on U.S. Direct Investment Abroad, 1966–1976.* Washington, D.C.: U.S. Government Printing Office, July 1977.

Bureau of Foreign Commerce. *Investment in Cuba: Basic Information for United States Businessmen.* Washington, D.C.: U.S. Government Printing Office, July 1956.

Bureau of Foreign and Domestic Commerce, Office of Business Economics. *Balance of Payments and Statistical Supplement.* Washington, D.C.: U.S. Government Printing Office, 1962, rev. ed.

Bureau of Foreign and Domestic Commerce, Office of Business Economics. *Balance of Payments of the United States, 1949–1951.* Washington, D.C.: U.S. Government Printing Office, 1972.

Bureau of International Commerce, Office of International Investment. *The Multinational Corporation: Studies on U.S. Foreign Investment Volume 1.* March 1972. Washington, D.C., 1972.

Bureau of International Commerce. *Overseas Business Reports.* ("World Trade with Cuba, 1961–1962"), OBR-64-41, March 1964.

Domestic and International Business Administration, Bureau of East-West Trade. *United States Commercial Relations with Cuba: A Sur-*

vey. August 1975. Washington, D.C.: U.S. Government Printing Office, 1975.

International Trade Administration, Office of Export Administration. *Export Administration Annual Report FY 1983.* June 1984.

International Trade Administration, Office of Export Administration. *Export Administration Annual Report FY 1984.* June 1985.

Office of Business Economics. *U.S. Investments in the Latin American Economy.* Washington, D.C.: U.S. Government Printing Office, 1957.

U.S. Department of State

The Battle Act Report 1965. Publication 8019, General Foreign Policy Series 210, February, 1966.

Communist Interference in El Salvador. Bureau of Public Affairs, Special Report No.80, February 23, 1981.

Department of State Bulletin. 1945–1980.

Foreign Relations of the United States. Published annually in one or more volumes. 1946–1954.

Press Releases.

Publications. Bureau of Public Affairs, Office of Media Services.

U.S. Department of the Treasury

Office of the General Counsel. *International and United States Agencies Financing International Operations.* 1962.

United States Participation in the Multilateral Development Banks in the 1980s. February 1982.

U.S. General Accounting Office

Assessment of Overseas Advisory Efforts of the U.S. Security Assistance Programs. Report to Congress, B-16382, October 31, 1975.

Weaknesses in Negotiations and Administration of Contracts for Resettlement of Cuban Refugees. Report to Congress, B-114836, March 24, 1965.

Books and articles

Acheson, Dean. *Present at the Creation: My Years in the State Department.* New York: W. W. Norton & Co., 1969.

Adler-Karlsson, Gunnar. *Western Economic Warfare 1974–1967.* Stockholm: Almqvist & Wiksell, 1968.

Agee, Philip. *Inside the Company: CIA Diary.* Great Britain: Penquin Books, 1975.

Allison, Graham T. *Essence of Decision: Explaining the Cuban Missile Crisis.* Boston: Little, Brown and Co. 1971.

Allison, Graham T., and Morton H. Halperin. "Bureaucratic Politics: A Paradigm and Some Policy Implications," in Raymond Tanter & Richard H. Ullman, eds., *Theory and Policy in International Relations.* Princeton: Princeton University Press, 1972, 40–79.

Ambrose, Stephen E. *Eisenhower: Volume Two, The President.* New York: Simon and Schuster, 1984.

——. *Rise to Globalism: American Foreign Policy 1938–1980.* New York: Penguin Books, 1980.

Americas Watch. *Human Rights in Nicaragua: Reagan, Rhetoric and Reality.* New York, July 1985.

Amin, Samir. *Accumulation on a World Scale.* New York: Monthly Review Press, 1974. 2 Volumes.

Arey, Hawthorne. *History of Operations and Policies of Export-Import Bank of Washington.* Washington, D.C., November 15, 1963.

Art, Robert J. "Bureaucratic Politics and American Foreign Policy: A Critique," *Policy Sciences,* Vol.4, No.4, December 1973, 467–490.

Ayers, Bradley E. *The War That Never Was: An Insider's Account of CIA Covert Operations Against Cuba.* Indianapolis and New York: The Bobbs-Merrill Co., 1976.

Baily, Samuel L. *The United States and the Development of South America.* New York: New Viewpoints and Franklin Watts, 1976.

Balassa, Bela, ed. *Studies in Trade Liberalization.* Baltimore: The Johns Hopkins Press, 1967.

Ball, M. Margaret. *The OAS in Transition.* Durham: Duke University Press, 1969.

Banco de Cuba. *Why You Should Invest in Cuba.* Havana, 1956 or 1957.

Barber, James. "Economic Sanctions as a Policy Instrument," *International Affairs,* Vol. 55, No. 3, July 1979, 367–384.

Barber, Willard F., and C. Neal Ronning. *International Security and Military Power.* Columbus: Ohio State University Press, 1966.

Barnet, Richard. *The Roots of War: Men and Institutions behind U.S. Foreign Policy.* Baltimore: Pelican Books, 1973.

Barnet, Richard, and Ronald E. Müller. *Global Reach: The Power of the Multinational Corporations.* New York: Simon and Schuster, 1974.

Barrett, Charles. *Canada's International Trade: Trends and Prospects.* Canadian Studies No.39. A Report from the Conference Board of Canada, July 1976.

Batista, Fulgencio. *The Growth and Decline of the Cuban Republic.* New York: The Devin-Adair Co., 1964.

Beck, Kent M. "Necessary Lies, Hidden Truths: Cuba in the 1960 Campaign," *Diplomatic History,* Vol.8, No.1, Winter 1984, 37–59.

Behrman, Jack N. *National Interest and the Multinational Enterprise.* Englewood Cliffs, N.J.: Prentice-Hall, 1970.

Bell, Peter D. "Brazilian-American Relations," in Riordan Roett, ed., *Brazil in the Sixties.* Nashville: Vanderbilt University Press, 1972, 77–102.

Bender, Gerald J. "Angola, The Cubans, and American Anxieties," *Foreign Policy,* No.31, Summer 1978, 3–30.

Bender, Lynn Darrell. *The Politics of Hostility: Castro's Revolution and United States Policy*. Puerto Rico: Inter American University Press, 1975.

Benjamin, Jules R. *The United States and Cuba: Hegemony and Dependent Development, 1880–1934*. Pittsburgh: University of Pittsburgh Press, 1977.

Berkowitz, Morton, P. G. Bock, and Vincent J. Fuccillo. *The Politics of American Foreign Policy: The Social Context of Decisions*. Englewood Cliffs, N.J.: Prentice-Hall, 1977.

Berle, Beatrice Bishop, and Travis Beal Jacobs, eds. *Navigating the Rapids 1918–1971: From the Papers of Adolph A. Berle*. New York: Harcourt Brace Jovanovich, 1973.

Bialer, Seweryn, and Alfred Stepan. "Cuba, the US, and the Central American Mess," *New York Review of Books*, May 27, 1982, 17–21.

Blackaby, F. T., ed. *British Economic Policy 1960–64*. London: Cambridge University Press, 1978.

Blackburn, Robin. "The Economics of the Cuban Revolution," in Claudio Velez, ed., *Latin America and the Caribbean: A Handbook*. London: Anthony Blond, 1968, 622–631.

"Prologue to the Cuban Revolution," *New Left Review*, No.21, October 1963, 52–91.

Blaisdell, Jr., Thomas C., and Eugene M. Braderman. "Economic Organization of the United States for International Economic Policy," in Seymour E. Harris, ed., *Foreign Economic Policy For the United States*. Cambridge: Harvard University Press, 1948, 37–51.

Blaisier, Cole. *The Hovering Giant: U.S. Responses to Revolutionary Changes in Latin America*. Pittsburgh: University of Pittsburgh Press, 1976.

"The United States and the Revolution," in James M. Malloy and Richard S. Thorn, eds., *Beyond the Revolution: Bolivia Since 1952*. Pittsburgh: University of Pittsburgh Press, 1971, 53–109.

Block, Fred. *The Origins of International Economic Disorder*. Berkeley: University of California Press, 1977.

Bonachea, Ramón L., and Marta San Martín. *The Cuban Insurrection 1952–1958*. New Brunswick: Transaction Books, 1974.

Bonafede, Dom. "Brzezinski-Stepping Out of His Backstage Role," *National Journal*, Vol.9, No.42, October 15, 1977, 1596–1601.

"The Last Hitch in Normalizing Relations with the Cubans," *National Journal*, Vol.10, No.19, May 13, 1978, 762–766.

"Relations with Cuba Unlikely Soon," *National Journal*, Vol. 7, No. 11, March 15, 1977, 403.

"White House Report: Peterson Unit Helps Shape Tough International Economic Policy," *National Journal*, Vol. 3, No. 46, November 13, 1971, 2238–2248.

Bonilla, Frank. "Operational Neutralism: Brazil Challenges United States Leadership," *American Universities Field Service Reports*, East

Coast, South America Series, Vol. IX, No.1 (Brazil), January 1962, 1–9.

Bonner, Raymond. *Weakness and Deceit; U.S. Policy and El Salvador.* New York: Times Books, 1984.

Bonsal, Philip W. *Cuba, Castro, and the United States.* Pittsburgh: University of Pittsburgh Press, 1972.

Boorstein, Edward. *The Economic Transformation of Cuba.* New York: Monthly Review Press, 1968.

Boudreaux, Richard. "Talks with Cuba Are Quiet," *Bucks County Courier Times* (Pennsylvania), January 18, 1976, D-3.

Bowles, Chester. *Promises to Keep: My Years in Public Life 1941–1969.* New York: Harper and Row, 1971.

Bowsher, Prentice. "CPR Department Study/The Agriculture Department," *National Journal,* Vol. 2, No. 1, January 3, 1970, 19–32.

Branch, Taylor, and George Crile III. "The Kennedy Vendetta: How the CIA Waged a Silent War against Cuba," *Harpers Magazine,* August 1975, 49–63.

Braun, O., and L. Joy. "A Model of Economic Stagnation – A Case Study of the Argentine Economy," *The Economic Journal,* Vol. LXXVII, No. 312, December 1968, 868–887.

"Brazil: Development for Whom?" *NACLA's Latin America and Empire Report,* Vol. VII, No. 4, April 1973, 1–22.

Brett, E. A. *Colonialism and Underdevelopment in East Africa: The Politics of Economic Change 1919–1939.* London: Heinemann Educational Books, 1973.

Brown, Seymon. *The Faces of Power: Constancy and Change in United States Foreign Policy from Truman to Eisenhower.* New York: Columbia University Press, 1968.

Brundenius, Claes. *Revolutionary Cuba: The Challenge of Economic Growth with Equity.* Boulder: Westview Press, 1984.

Brzezinski, Zbigniew. *Power and Principle: Memoirs of the National Security Adviser 1977–1981.* London: Wiedenfeld and Nicolson, 1983.

Bukharin, Nikolai. *Imperialism and World Economy.* New York: Monthly Review Press, 1973.

Burstin, Luis. "My Talks With The Cubans," *New Republic,* February 13, 1984, 19–23.

Business International Corporation. *Cuba At The Turning Point.* New York, July 1977.

   The Cuban Revolution. Prepared by Siegfried Marks, Foreign Economist, Department 768-X. New York, January, 1960.

   The Effects of U.S. Corporate Foreign Investment 1960–1970. Special Research Study. New York, 1972.

   The Effects of U.S. Corporate Foreign Investment 1970–1976. Special Research Study. New York, May 1978.

Campbell, John Franklin. *The Foreign Affairs Fudge Factory.* New York: Basic Books, 1971.

Canadian Department of External Affairs. Information Division. *Hemisphere and Global Problems*, No.61/7.

Canadian Department of Foreign Affairs. Monthly Bulletin. *Canada*. Vol. XIV, No. 2, February 1962.

Carre, J. J., P. Dubois, and E. Malinvaud. *French Economic Growth*. Stanford: Stanford University Press, 1975.

Carter, Jimmy. *Keeping Faith: Memoirs of a President*. London: William Collins, 1982.

Castro, Fidel. "Speech, May 1, 1973," in *Granma Weekly Review* (Cuba), May 13, 1973, 3.

Casuso, Teresa. *Cuba and Castro*. New York: Random House, 1961.

CBS Reports. *The CIA's Secret War*. Transcript. New York: CBS Inc., 1978.

Center for International Policy. *Human Rights and the U.S. Foreign Assistance Program: Fiscal Year 1978, Part 1 – Latin America*. Washington, D.C., 1978.

Central American Historical Institute Update (Georgetown University), Vol. 5, No. 34, August 31. 1986.

CEPAL News (United Nations, Economic Commission for Latin America and the Caribbean), Vol. V, No. 2, September 1985.

Chadwin, Mark L. "Foreign Policy Report/Nixon Administration Debates New Position Paper on Latin America," *National Journal*, Vol. 4, No. 3, January 15, 1972, 97–101.

  "Foreign Policy Report/Nixon's Expropriation Policy Seeks to Soothe Angry Congress," *National Journal*, Vol.4, No.4, January 22, 1972, 148–156.

Chase, Harold W., and Allen H. Lerman, eds. *Kennedy and the Press: The News Conferences*. New York: Thomas Y. Crowell Co., 1965.

Chayes, Abram. *The Cuban Missile Crisis: International Crises and the Role of Law*. New York and London: Oxford University Press, 1974.

Clark, Keith C., and Laurence J. Legere, eds. *The President and the Management of National Security*. New York: Praeger Publishers, 1969.

Claude, Jr., Inis L. "The OAS, the UN, and the United States," *International Conciliation*, No. 547, March 1964, 3–67.

Cline, Ray S. *Secrets, Spies and Scholars*. Washington, D.C.: Acropolis Books, 1976.

Cochrane, James D. "U.S. Policy Toward Recognition of Governments and Promotion of Democracy in Latin America since 1963," *Journal of Latin American Studies*, Vol. 4, No. 2, 1972, 275–291.

Cohen, Stephen D. *The Making of United States International Economic Policy*. New York: Praeger Publishers, 1977.

Commission on Cuban Affairs. *Problems of the New Cuba*. New York: Foreign Policy Associations, 1935.

Connell-Smith, Gordon. *The Inter-American System*. London: Oxford University Press, 1966.

The United States and Latin America: An Historical Analysis of Inter-American Relations. New York: Halsted Press, 1975.

Cooper, Chester L. "The CIA and Decision-Making," *Foreign Affairs*, Vol. 50, No. 2, January 1972, 223–236.

Cotler, Julio, and Richard R. Fagen, eds. *Latin America and The United States: The Changing Political Realities.* Stanford: Stanford University Press, 1974.

"Cuba: An Economy in Crisis," *Bank of London & South America Review*, Vol. 1, No. 7, July 1967, 368–371.

"Cuba: A Sustained Economic Recovery," *Bank of London & South America Review*, Vol.9, May 1975, 250–256.

The Cuban Economic Research Project. *A Study on Cuba.* Coral Gables: University of Miami Press, 1965.

Cuban Studies/Estudios Cubanos. Special Volume, Part 1 ("Cuba in Africa"), Vol.10, No.1, January 1980.

Cutler, Robert. "The Development of the National Security Council," *Foreign Affairs*, Vol. 34, No. 3, April 1956, 441–458.

David, Steven. "Realignment in the Horn: The Soviet Advantage," *International Security*, Vol.4, No.2, Fall 1979, 69–90.

Davis, David H. *How the Bureaucracy Makes Foreign Policy.* Lexington: D. C. Heath & Co., 1972.

Davis, Nathaniel. "The Angola Decision of 1975: A Personal Memoir," *Foreign Affairs*, Vol. 56, No.1, Fall 1978, 107–124.

Del Aguila, Juan M. "Political Developments in Cuba," *Current History*, Vol. 85, No. 507, January 1986, 12–15, 36–37.

Destler, I. M. "National Security Advice to U.S. Presidents," *World Politics*, Vol. XXIX, No. 2, January 1977, 143–176.

Presidents, Bureaucrats, and Foreign Policy: The Politics of Organizational Reform. Princeton: Princeton University Press, 1974.

Destler, I. M., Leslie H. Gelb, and Anthony Lake. *Our Own Worst Enemy: The Unmaking of American Foreign Policy.* New York: Simon and Schuster, 1984.

Dewart, Leslie. *Cuba, Church and Crisis.* Great Britain: Sheed and Ward, 1964.

"The Cuban Crisis Revisited," *Studies on the Left*, Vol. 5, No. 2, Spring 1965, 15–40.

Dewitt, R. Peter. *The Inter-American Development Bank and Political Influence.* New York: Praeger Publishers, 1977.

Díaz-Alejandro, Carlos F. "Some Aspects of the Brazilian Experience with Foreign Aid," in Jagdish N. Bhagwati, et al., eds., *Trade, Balance of Payments and Growth.* New York: Elsevier Publishing Co., 1971, 443–472.

Domhoff, G. William. *The Higher Circles.* New York: Vintage Books, 1971.

Domínguez, Jorge I. "The Civic Soldier in Cuba," in Catherine McArdle Kelleher, ed., *Political-Military Systems: Comparative Perspective.* Beverly Hills: Sage Publications, 1974, 209–238.

Cuba: Order and Revolution. Cambridge: Harvard University Press, 1978.

"Institutionalization and Civil-Military Relations in Cuba," *Cuban Studies/Estudios Cubanos,* Vol. 6, No.1, January 1976, 39–55.

"Taming the Cuban Shrew," *Foreign Policy,* No. 10, Spring 1973, 94–116.

Dorschner, John, and Roberto Fabricio. *The Winds of December.* New York: Coward, McCann & Geghegan, 1980.

Doxey, Margaret P. *Economic Sanctions and International Enforcement.* New York: Oxford University Press, 1980.

"Sanctions Revisited," *International Journal,* Vol. XXXI, No.1, Winter 1975–6, 53–78.

Draper, Theodore. *Castroism: Theory and Practice.* New York: Praeger, 1965.

Castro's Revolution: Myths and Realities. New York: Praeger, 1970.

DuBois, Jules. *Fidel Castro: Rebel-Liberator or Dictator?* New York: Bobbs-Merrill Co., 1959.

Dulles, Allen. *The Craft of Intelligence.* New York: Harper & Row, 1963.

Dunkerly, James. *The Long War: Dictatorship and Revolution in El Salvador.* London: Junction Books, 1982.

Eakins, David W. "Business Planners and America's Postwar Expansion," in David Horowitz, ed., *Corporations and the Cold War.* New York: Monthly Review Press, 1969, 143–171.

Einhorn, Jessica P. *Expropriation Politics,* Lexington: D. C. Heath and Co., 1974.

Eisenhower, Dwight D. *Mandate for Change 1953–1956.* New York: Doubleday & Co., 1963.

The White House Years: Waging Peace, 1956–1961. New York: Doubleday & Co., 1965.

Elder, Robert E. *The Information Machine: The United States Information Agency and American Foreign Policy.* New York: Syracuse University Press, 1968.

El-Khawas, Mohamad A., and Barry Cohen. *The Kissinger Study of Southern Africa.* National Security Study Memorandum 39 (Secret). Westport: Lawrence Hill & Co., 1976.

Engler, Robert. *The Brotherhood of Oil.* Chicago: University of Chicago Press, 1977.

The Politics of Oil. New York: The Macmillan Co., 1961.

Erisman, H. Michael. *Cuba's International Relations.* Boulder: Westview Press, 1985.

Evans, Rowland, and Robert Novak. *Lyndon B. Johnson: The Exercise of Power.* New York: New American Library, 1966.

Fagen, Richard R. *The Transformation of Political Culture in Cuba.* Stanford: Stanford University Press, 1969.

Falk, Stanley F. "The National Security Council Under Truman, Eisenhower, and Kennedy," *Political Science Quarterly,* Vol. LXXIX, No. 3, September 1964, 403–434.

Farer, Tom J. *War Clouds on the Horn of Africa: The Widening Storm.* Washington, D.C.: Carnegie Endowment for International Peace, 1979.

Feinberg, Richard E. *U.S. Human Rights Policy: Latin America.* Washington, D.C.: Center for International Policy, October 1980.

Feis, Herbert. *Europe: The World's Banker 1870–1914.* New Haven: Yale University Press, 1930.

"The Investment of American Capital Abroad," in Arnold J. Zurcher and Richmond Page, eds., *America's Place in the World Economy.* New York: New York University, Institute on Postwar Reconstruction, 1954, 73–83.

Fernández, Susan. "The Sanctity of Property: American Responses to Cuban Expropriations, 1959–1984," *Cuban Studies/Estudios Cubanos,* Vol. 14, No. 2, Summer 1984, 21–34.

Ferrer, Aldo. *The Argentine Economy.* Berkeley: University of California Press, 1967.

Fishlow, Albert. "The Mature Neighbor Policy: A Proposal for a United States Economic Policy for Latin America," in Joseph Grunwald, ed., *Latin America and World Economy.* Beverly Hills: Sage Publications, 1978, 29–71.

Fitch, John Samuel. *The Military Coup d'Etat as a Political Process in Ecuadorian Politics: 1948–1966.* Baltimore: The Johns Hopkins University Press, 1977.

Fitzsimons, Louise. *The Kennedy Doctrine.* New York: Random House, 1972.

Flynn, Peter. *Brazil: A Political Analysis.* Boulder: Westview Press, 1978.

Foner, Philip S. *The Spanish-Cuban-American War and the Birth of American Imperialism, Vol. II, 1898–1902.* New York: Monthly Review Press, 1972.

Fontaine, Roger W., and James D. Therberge, eds. *Latin America's New Internationalism.* New York: Praeger Publishers, 1976.

Ford, Gerald R. *A Time to Heal.* New York: Harper & Row, 1979.

Fowlkes, Frank V. "Economic Report/Connally Revitalizes Treasury, Assumes stewardship of Nixon's New Economic policy," *National Journal,* Vol. 3, No. 40, October 2, 1971, 1988–1997.

Frank, Richard S. "Economic Report/Schultz Takes Charge as United States Presses for Monetary Trade Reforms," *National Journal,* Vol. 5, No. 10, March 10, 1973, 353–358.

Freeland, Richard M. *The Truman Doctrine and the Origins of McCarthyism.* New York: Schocken Books, 1974.

Freidberg, Stanley. "The Measure of Damages in Claims Against Cuba," *Inter-American Economic Affairs*, Vol. 23, No. 1, Summer 1969, 67–86.

Freitag, Peter J. "The Cabinet and Big Business: A Study of Interlocks," *Social Problems*, Vol. 23, No. 2, December 1975, 137–152.

Fresquet, Rufo López. *My 14 Months with Castro*. Cleveland and New York: The Publishing Co., 1966.

Gallagher, John, and Ronald Robinson. "The Imperialism of Free Trade," *The Economic History Review*, Second Series, Vol. VI, No. 1, August 1953, 1–15.

Galtung, Johan. "On the Effects of International Economic Sanctions with Exmples Drawn from the Case of Rhodesia," *World Politics*, Vol. 19, No. 3, April 1967, 378–416.

Gardner, C. Harvey. "The Japanese in Cuba," *Caribbean Studies*, Vol. 12, No. 2, July 1972, 52–73.

Gardner, Lloyd. *Architects of Illusion: Men and Ideas in American Foreign Policy 1941–1949*. Chicago: Quadrangle Books, 1972.

Gardner, Richard N. *Sterling-Dollar Diplomacy*. London: Oxford University Press, 1956.

Garthoff, Raymond L. *Detente and Confrontation: American-Soviet Relations From Nixon to Reagan*. Washington, D.C.: The Brookings Institution, 1985.

Gellman, Irwin F. *Roosevelt and Batista: Good Neighbor Diplomacy in Cuba, 1933–1945*. Albuquerque: University of New Mexico Press, 1973.

Geyelin, Philip. *Lyndon B. Johnson and the World*. New York: Frederick A. Praeger, 1966.

Gilpin, Robert. *U.S. Power and the Multinational Corporation*. New York: Basic Books, 1975.

Gisselquist, David. *Political Economics of International Bank Lending*. New York: Praeger Publishers, 1981.

Gleijeses, Piero. *The Dominican Crisis: The 1965 Constitutionalist Revolt and American Intervention*. Baltimore: The Johns Hopkins University Press, 1978.

Goff, Fred, and Michael Locker. "The Violence of Domination: U.S. Power and the Dominican Republic," in Irving Louis Horowitz, Josué de Castro, and John Gerassi, eds., *Latin American Radicalism*. New York: Vintage Books, 1969, 292–313.

Goldenberg, Boris. *The Cuban Revolution and Latin America*. New York: Praeger Publishers, 1966.

González, Alfonso. "Castro: Economic Effects on Latin America," *Journal of Inter-American Studies*, Vol. XI, No. 2, April 1969, 386–307.

González, Edward. "Castro's Revolution, Cuban Communist Appeals, and the Soviet Response," *World Politics*, Vol. XXI, No. 1, October 1968, 39–68.

González, Edward, and Luigi R. Einaudi. "New Patterns of Leadership," in Luigi R. Einaudi, ed., *Beyond Cuba: Latin America Takes Charge of Its Future.* New York: Crane, Russate and Co., 1974, 45–57.

Goodman, Eileen. "Castro's Cuba Not Such a Bad Place," *Canadian Business,* September 1976, 81–86.

Graff, Henry F. *The Tuesday Cabinet: Deliberation and Decision on Peace and War Under Lyndon B. Johnson.* Englewood Cliffs, N.J.: Prentice-Hall, 1970.

Green, David. *The Containment of Latin America.* Chicago: Quadrangle Books. 1971.

Grobart, Fabio. "The Cuban Working Class Movement from 1925 to 1933," *Science & Society,* Vol. XXXIX, No. 1, Spring 1975, 73–103.

Guevara, Che. *Reminiscences of the Cuban Revolutionary War.* New York: Monthly Review Press, 1968.

Gutelman Michael. "The Socialization of the Means of Production in Cuba," in Rudolfo Stavenhagen, ed. *Agrarian Problems and Peasant Movements in Latin America.* New York: Doubleday & Co., 1970, 347–373.

Haig, Jr., Alexander M. *Caveat: Realism, Reagan, and Foreign Policy.* New York: Macmillan Publishing Co., 1984.

Halliday, Fred. *The Making of the Second Cold War.* London: Verso Editions and New Left Books, 1986.

Halliday, Fred, and Maxine Molyneux. *The Ethiopian Revolution.* London: Verso Edition and New Left Books, 1981.

Halperin, Morton H. *Bureaucratic Politics and Foreign Policy.* Washington, D.C.: The Brookings Institution, 1974.

Hamilton, Nora. *The Limits of State Autonomy: Post-Revolutionary Mexico.* Princeton: Princeton University Press, 1982.

Hammond, Paul Y. "The National Security Council as a Device for Interdepartmental Coordination: An Interpretation and Appraisal," *American Political Science Review,* Vol. LIV, No. 4, December 1960, 899–910.

Hayter, Teresa. *Aid as Imperialism.* Baltimore: Penguin Books, 1971.

Hayter, Teresa, and Catherine Watson. *Aid: Rhetoric and Reality.* Longon: Pluto Press, 1985.

Healy, David F. *The United States in Cuba 1898–1902.* Madison: University of Wisconsin Press, 1963.

Heilbroner, Robert L. "Review Essay: None of Your Business," *New York Review of Books,* March 20, 1975, 6–10.

Hersh, Seymour M. *The Price of Power: Kissinger in the Nixon White House.* New York: Summit Books, 1983.

Heston, Thomas J. "Cuba, the United States, and the Sugar Act of 1948: the Failure of Economic Coercion," *Diplomatic History,* Vol. 6, No. 1, Winter 1982, 1–21.

Hickey, John. "The Day Mr. Berle Talked with Mr. Quadros," *Inter-American Economic Affairs*, Vol. XV, No. 1, Summer 1961, 58–71.

Hill, Howard C. *Roosevelt and the Caribbean*. Chicago: University of Chicago Press, 1927.

Hilsman, Roger. *To Move a Nation: The Politics of Foreign Policy in the Administration of John F. Kennedy*. New York: Doubleday & Co., 1967.

The Politics of Policy Making in Defense and Foreign Affairs. New York: Harper & Row, 1971.

Hobson, J.A. *Imperialism*. Ann Arbor: University of Michigan Press, 1972.

Hoffman, Stanley. *Dead Ends: American Foreign Policy in the New Cold War*. Cambridge: Ballinger Publishing Co., 1983.

Hollerman, Leon. "Foreign Trade in Japan's Economic Transition," in Isaiah Frank, ed., *The Japanese Economy in International Perspective*. Baltimore: The Johns Hopkins University Press, 1975, 168–206.

Hoopes, Townsend. *The Devil and John Foster Dulles*. Boston: Atlantic-Little, Brown, 1973.

Howland, Charles P. *American Relations in the Caribbean*. New York: Arno Press and The New York Times, 1970.

Humphrey, David C. "Tuesday Lunch at the Johnson White House: A Preliminary Assessment," *Diplomatic History*, Vol. 8, No. 1, Winter 1984, 81–101.

Hunter, John M. "Investment as a Factor in the Economic Development of Cuba 1899–1935," *Inter-American Economic Affairs*, Vol. 5, No. 3, Winter 1951, 82–100.

Hymer, Stephen, and Robert Rowthorn. "Multinational Corporations and International Oligopoly: The Non-American Challenge," in Charles P. Kindelberger, ed., *The International Corporation*. Cambridge: The M.I.T. Press, 1970, 57–91.

Immerman, Richard H. *The CIA in Guatemala*. Austin: University of Texas Press, 1982.

International Bank for Reconstruction and Development. *Report on Cuba 1950*. Baltimore: The Johns Hopkins Press, 1951.

Israel, Fred L., ed. *The State of the Union Messages of the Presidents, Vol. III, 1905–1966*. New York: Chelsea House, Robert Hector, 1966.

Jackson, Senator Henry M., ed. *The National Security Council*. New York: Frederick A. Praeger, 1965.

Jenks, Leland H. *Our Cuban Colony: A Study in Sugar*. New York: Arno Press and The New York Times, 1970.

Jessop, Bob. *The Capitalist State: Marxist Theories and Methods*. London: Martin Robertson, 1982.

Johnson, Leland L. "U.S. Business Interests in Cuba and the Rise of Castro," *World Politics*, Vol. XVII, No. 3, April 1965, 440–459.

Jonas, Susanne, and David Tobis, eds. *Guatelmala*. New York and Berkeley: North American Congress on Latin America, 1974.

Kaiser, Robert G. "Further Blots on the White Paper: Doubts About Evidence and Conclusion," in Marvin Gettleman et al., eds. *El Salvador: Central America In The New Cold War*. New York: Grove Press, 1981, 254–262.

Kauffman, Burton. *Trade an Aid: Eisenhower's Foreign Economic Policy 1953–1961*. Baltimore: The Johns Hopkins University Press, 1982.

Kennedy, Robert F. *Thirteen Days: A Memoir of the Cuban Missile Crisis*. New York: Signet Books, 1969.

Kirby, M. W. *The Decline of British Economic Power Since 1877*. London: George Allen & Unwin, 1981.

Kirschten, Dick. "White House Report/Beyond the Vance-Brzezinski Clash Lurks an NSC under Fire," *National Journal*, Vol. 12, No. 20, May 17, 1980, 814–818.

Klare, Michael T. "Testing Out Haig's New War Policy," *The Nation*, June 19, 1982, 735, 750–751.

War Without End: American Planning for the Next Vietnams. New York: Vintage Books, 1972.

Kojima, Kiyoshi. *Japan and a New World Economic Order*. Boulder: Westview Press, 1977.

Kolodziej, Edward A. *French International Policy Under De Gaulle and Pompidou*. Ithaca: Cornell University Press, 1974.

Kolko, Gabriel. *The Politics of War: The World and United States Foreign Policy, 1943–1945*. New York: Vintage Books, 1968.

The Roots of American Foreign Policy. Boston: Beacon Books, 1969.

Kolko, Joyce. *America and the Crisis of World Capitalism*. Boston: Beacon Books, 1974.

Kolko, Joyce, and Gabriel Kolko. *The Limits of Power: The World and United States Foreign Policy, 1945–1954*. New York: Harper & Row, 1972.

Krasner, Stephen D. *Defending the National Interest*. Princeton: Princeton University Press, 1977.

Kraus, Sidney, ed. *The Great Debates*. Bloomington: Indiana University Press, 1962.

Kwitny, Jonathan. *Endless Enemies: The Making of an Unfriendly World*. New York: Congdon & Weed, 1984.

LaFeber, Walter. *Inevitable Revolutions: The United States in Central America*. New York: W. W. Norton & Co., 1983.

"Latin American Policy," in Robert A. Divine, ed., *Exploring The Johnson Years*. Austin: University of Texas Press, 1981, 63–90.

The New Empire: An Interpretation of American Expansion 1860–1890. Ithaca: Cornell University Press, 1967.

Lazo, Mario. *Dagger in the Heart: American Policy Failures in Cuba*. Santa Monica: Fidelis Publishers, 1968.

Leacacos, John P. "Kissinger's Apparat," *Foreign Policy*, No. 5, Winter 1971–72, 3–37.

Leacock, Ruth. "JFK, Business, and Brazil," *Hispanic American Historical Review*, Vol. 59, No. 4, November 1979, 636–673.

"'Promoting Democracy': The United States and Brazil, 1964–1968," *Prologue* (Journal of the National Archives), Vol. 13, No. 2, Summer 1981, 77–99.

Leffler, Melvin P. "The American Conception of National Security and the Beginnings of the Cold War, 1945–1948," *The American Historical Review*, Vol. 89, No. 2, April 1984, 346–381.

"From the Truman Doctrine to the Carter Doctrine: Lessons and Dilemmas of the Cold War," *Diplomatic History*, Vol. 7, No. 4, Fall 1983, 245–266.

Lenin, V. I. *Collected Works, Vol. 39* ("Notebooks on Imperialism"). Moscow: Foreign Languages Publishing House, 1974.

The Development of Capitalism in Russia. Moscow: Foreign Languages Publishing House, 1956.

Selected Works, Vol. 1. Moscow: Progress Publishers, 1970.

Selected Works, Vol. 2. Moscow: Progress Publishers, 1970.

LeoGrande, William M. "Cuba," in Morris J. Blachman, William M. LeoGrande, and Kennedy Sharpe, eds., *Confronting Revolution: Security Through Diplomacy in Central America.* New York: Pantheon Books, 1986, 229–255.

"Cuba and Nicaragua: From the Somozas to the Sandinistas," in Barry B. Levine, ed., *The New Cuban Presence in the Caribbean.* Boulder: Westview Press, 1983, 43–58.

"Cuba: Going to the Source," in Richard Newfarmer, ed., *From Gunboats to Diplomacy.* Baltimore and London: The Johns Hopkins University Press, 1984, 135–146.

Cuba's Policy in Africa, 1959–1980. University of California at Berkeley: Institute of International Studies, 1980.

Le Riverand, Julio. *Economic History of Cuba.* Havana: Book Institute, 1967.

Levesque, Jacques. *The USSR and the Cuban Revolution.* New York: Praeger Publishers, 1978.

Levin, Jr., N. Gordon. *Woodrow Wilson and World Politics: America's Response to War and Revolution.* New York: Oxford University Press, 1971.

Levinson, Jerome, and Juan de Onís. *The Alliance That Lost Its Way.* Chicago: Quadrangle Books, 1972.

Levitt, Kari. *Silent Surrender: The Multinational Corporation in Canada.* New York: St. Martin's Press, 1970.

Leys, Colin. *Underdevelopment in Kenya.* Berkeley: University of California Press, 1975.

Leyton-Brown, David. "Extraterritoriality in Canadian-American Relations," *International Journal*, Vol. XXXVI, No. 1, Winter 1980–1, 185–207.

"The Multinational Enterprise and Conflict in Canadian-American Relations," in Annette Fox, Alfred O. Hero, Jr., and Joseph S. Nye, Jr., eds., *Canada and the United States: Transnational and Transgovernmental Relations.* New York: Columbia University Press, 1976, 140–161.

Liashchenko, Petr I. *History of the National Economy of Russia.* New York: The Macmillan Co., 1949.

Lieberman, Sima. *The Growth of European Mixed Economies, 1945–1970.* New York: Schenkman Publishing Co./Halsted Press, 1977.

Lieuwen, Edwin. *Generals vs. Presidents: Neo-Militarism in Latin America.* New York: Praeger Publishers, 1966.

U.S. Policy in Latin America. New York: Praeger Publishers, 1965.

Lipson, Charles H. "Corporate Preferences and Public Policies," *World Politics,* Vol. XXVIII, No. 3, April 1976, 396–421.

Losman, David L. "The Embargo of Cuba: An Economic Appraisal," *Caribbean Studies,* Vol.14, No. 3, October 1974, 95–119.

International Economic Sanctions. Albuquerque: University of New Mexico Press, 1979.

Loufti, Martha F. *The Net Cost of Japanese Foreign Aid.* New York: Praeger Publishers, 1973.

Lowenthal, Abraham F. "Cuba: Time for a Change," *Foreign Policy,* No. 20, Fall 1975, 65–86.

The Dominican Intervention. Cambridge: Harvard University Press, 1972.

Lyon, Peyton V. *Canada In World Affairs, Vol. XII, 1961–1963.* Toronto: Oxford University Press, 1968.

Lyon, Peyton V., and Brian W. Tomlin. *Canada as an International Actor.* Toronto: Macmillan of Canada, 1979.

Magdoff, Harry. *The Age of Imperialism.* New York: Monthly Review Press, 1969.

Mandel, Ernest. *Europe vs. America.* New York: Monthly Review Press, 1970.

Late Capitalism. London: Verso Editions, 1978.

Marchetti, Victor, and John D. Marks. *The CIA and the Cult of Intelligence.* New York: Alfred A. Knopf, 1974.

Mason, Edward S., and Robert E. Asher. *The World Bank Since Bretton Woods.* Washington, D.C.: The Brookings Institution, 1973.

Matthews, Herbert. *Castro: A Political Biography.* London: Penguin Press, 1969.

Revolution in Cuba. New York: Charles Scribner's Sons, 1975.

Mayer, Robert. "The Origins of the American Banking Empire in Latin America," *Journal of Interamerican Studies and World Affairs,* Vol. 15, No. 1, February 1973, 60–76.

McAdoo, Maisie. "An Embargo That Serves No Purpose," *The Nation,* December 4, 1982, 586–589.

McCann, Thomas P. *An American Company: The Tragedy of United Fruit.* New York: Crown Publishers, 1976.

McGaffey, Wyatt, and Clifford R. Barnett. *Twentieth Century Cuba: The Background to the Cuban Revolution*. New York: Doubleday Anchor, 1965.

McWhinney, Edward. "Canadian-United States Commercial Relations and International Law: The Cuban Affair as a Case Study," in David R. Deener, ed., *Canada-United States Treaty Relations*. Durham: Duke University Press, 1963, 135–150.

Meisler, Stanley. "The Politics of Sugar," *The Nation*, July 23, 1960, 49–51.

Melman, Seymour. *The Permanent War Economy*. New York: Simon and Schuster, 1974.

"Memorandum for Members of the Cabinet," from Zbigniew Brzezinski, May 8, 1978, reprinted in *The Nation*, June 24, 1978, 749.

Mesa-Lago, Carmelo. *Availability and Reliability of Statistics in Socialist Cuba*. University of Pittsburgh, Latin American Studies, Occasional Papers No.1, 1970.

　　Cuba in the 1970's. Albuquerque: University of New Mexico Press, 1974.

　　ed. *Revolutionary Change in Cuba*. Pittsburgh: University of Pittsburgh Press, 1974.

Mezerik, A. G., ed. *Cuba and the United States, Vol. 1*. International Review Service, Vol. VI, No. 60, 1960.

Mikesell, Raymond F. "The Export-Import Bank of Washington," in Raymond E. Mikesell, ed., *U.S. Private and Government Investment Abroad*. Eugene: University of Oregon Books, 1962, 459–482.

Miliband, Ralph. *Class Power and State Power*. London: Verso Editions and New Left Books, 1983.

　　The State in Capitalist Society. London: Quartet Books, 1973.

Miller, Lynn H., and Ronald W. Pruessen, eds. *Reflections on the Cold War*. Philadelphia: Temple University Press, 1974.

Millett, Allen R. *The Politics of Intervention: The Military Occupation of Cuba 1906–1909*. Columbus; Ohio State University Press, 1968.

Montgomery, Tommie Sue. *Revolution in El Salvador*. Boulder: Westview Press, 1982.

Moran, Theodore H. "The International Political Economy of Cuban Nickel Development," *Cuban Studies/Estudios Cubanos*, Vol. 7, No. 2, July 1977, 145–165.

Morley, Morris H., and James F. Petras. "The Reagan Administration and Nicaragua: How Washington Constructs Its Case for Counterrevolution in Central America," in Morris H. Morley, ed., *Crisis and Confrontation on a World Scale: Ronald Reagan's Foreign Policy* (Totowa, N.J.: Rowman and Littlefield, forthcoming).

Morray, J. P. "Cuba and Communism," *Monthly Review*, Vol.13, Nos. 3 & 4, July/August 1961, 33–47.

　　The Second Revolution in Cuba. New York: Monthly Review Press, 1962.

Morrell, James. *Achievements of the 1970s: Human Rights Law and Policy.* Washington, D.C.: Center for International Policy, November 1981.

Morris, Roger. *Uncertain Greatness: Henry Kissinger and American Foreign Policy.* New York: Harper & Row, 1977.

Morris, Roger, and Richard Mauzy. "Following the Scenario: Reflections on Five Case Histories in the Mode and Aftermath of CIA Intervention," in Robert L. Borosage and John Marks, eds., *The CIA File.* New York: Grossman Publishers, 1976, 28–45.

Morrison, Delesseps S. *Latin American Mission.* New York: Simon and Schuster, 1965.

Müller, Ronald. "Global Corporations; Their Impact on the United States and World Political Economy," in Commission on Critical Choices for Americans, Volume V, *Trade, Inflation & Ethics.* Lexington: D. C. Heath & Co., 1976, 159–178.

Murphy, Robert D. *Diplomat Among Warriors.* New York: Doubleday & Co., 1964.

Murray, D. R. "The Bilateral Road: Canada and Latin America in the 1980s," *International Journal*, Vol. XXXVII, No. 1, Winter 1981–82, 108–131.

Murray, Robin. "The Internationalization of Capital and the Nation State," *New Left Review*, No.67, May–June 1971, 84–109.

NACLA's Report on the Americas (Special Issue on Brazil), Vol. XIII, No. 3, May–June 1979.

NACLA'S Report on the Americas (Special Issue on Sandinista Foreign Policy), Vol. XIX, No. 3, May/June 1985.

Nelson, Joan M. *AID, Influence and Foreign Policy.* New York: Macmillan Co., 1968.

Newsweek (Special Issue on the 1984 Presidential Election), November/December 1984.

Nixon, Richard M. *Six Crises.* New York: Doubleday & Co., 1962.

North, Liisa. *Bitter Grounds: Roots of Revolt in El Salvador.* Toronto: Behind the Lines, 1981.

O'Connor, Harvey. *World Crisis in Oil.* New York: Monthly Review Press, 1962.

O'Connor, James. *The Fiscal Crisis of the State.* New York: St. Martin's Press, 1973.

"The Meaning of Economic Imperialism," in K. T. Fann and Donald C. Hodges, eds., *Readings in U.S. Imperialism.* Boston: Porter Sargent Publisher, 1971, 23–68.

The Origins of Socialism in Cuba. Ithaca: Cornell University Press, 1970.

Ogelsby, J. C. M. "Cuba and Latin America," in Peyton V. Lyon and Tareq Y. Ismael, eds., *Canada and the Third World.* Macmillan of Canada: Maclean-Hunter Press, 1976, 162–199.

Organization of American States. General Secretary. *Annual Report of the Secretary General 1962.* Washington, D.C.: Pan American Union, 1962.

Eighth Meeting of Consultation of Ministers of Foreign Affairs. Punta Del Este, Uruguay. Washington, D.C.: Pan American Union, 1962.

General Secretariat. *External Financing for Latin American Development.* Baltimore: The Johns Hopkins Press, 1971.

Inter-American Economic and Social Council CEPCIES. *United States Economic Cooperation with Latin America.* CEPCIES Subcommittee on the United States, July 22–26, 1974, Washington, D.C. OEA/Ser.H/XIV, CEPCIES 7, July 17, 1974. Washington, D.C.: General Secretariat of the OAS, 1974.

General Secretariat. *Ninth Meeting of Consultation of Ministers of Foreign Affairs, Final Act.* July 21–26, OAS Official Records OA A/Ser. c/11.9 Washington, D.C.: Pan American Union, 1964.

Novena Reunión De Consulta De Ministres De Relaciónes Exteriores. Washington, D.C.: Pan American Union, 1964.

Seventh Meeting of Consultation of Ministers of Foreign Affairs. San Jose, Costa Rica. Washington, D.C.: Pan American Union, 1960.

Twelfth Meeting of Consultation of Ministers of Foreign Affairs. Washington, D.C.: Pan American Union, 1967.

ORIT Press and Publications Department. *The Cuban Trade Union Movement Under the Regime of Dr. Castro.* Mexico City, October 1960.

O'Shaughnessy, Hugh. *Grenada: Revolution, Invasion and Aftermath.* London: Sphere Books, 1984.

Ottaway, David, and Marina Ottaway. *Afrocommunism.* New York: Africana Publishing Co., 1981.

Ethiopia: Empire in Revolution. New York: Africana Publishing Co., 1978.

Ottaway, Marina. *Soviet and American Influence in the Horn of Africa.* New York: Praeger Publishers, 1982.

Owen, Roger and Bob Sutcliffe, eds. *Studies in the Theory of Imperialism* Great Britain: Longman Group, 1972.

Padula, Jr., Alfred. "U.S. Business Squabbles over Cuba," *The Nation,* October 22, 1977, 390–393.

Parker, Phyllis R. *Brazil and the Quiet Intervention, 1964.* Austin: University of Texas Press, 1979.

Parkinson, F. *Latin America, The Cold War, and The World Powers 1945–1973.* Beverly Hills: Sage Publications, 1974.

Paterson, Thomas G. "The Quest for Peace and Prosperity: International Trade, Communism, and the Marshall Plan," in Barton J. Bernstein, ed., *Politics and Policies of the Truman Administration.* Chicago: Quadrangle Books, 1970, 78–112.

Paterson, Thomas G., and William J. Brophy. "October Missiles and November Elections: The Cuban Missile Crisis and American Politics, 1962," *Journal of American History*, Vol. 73, No. 1, June 1986, 87–119.

Paterson, Thomas G. et al. *American Foreign Policy: A History since 1900.* Lexington: D. C. Heath & Co., 1983.

Payer, Cheryl. *The World Bank.* New York and London: Monthly Review Press, 1982.

Pazos, Felipe. "The Economy," *Cambridge Opinion*, No. 32, 1963, 13–17.

Penrose, Edith T. *The Large International Firm in Developing Countries.* Cambridge: The M.I.T. Press, 1968.

Pérez, Jr., Louis A. *Army Politics in Cuba, 1898–1958.* Pittsburgh: University of Pittsburgh Press, 1976.

Intervention, Revolution, and Politics in Cuba, 1913–1921. Pittsburgh: University of Pittsburgh Press, 1978.

Perloff, Harvey S. *Alliance for Progress.* Baltimore: The Johns Hopkins Press, 1969.

Petras, James F. "Toward a Theory of Twentieth Century Socialist Revolution," in James Petras et al., *Critical Perspectives on Imperialism and Social Classes in the Third World.* New York: Monthly Review Press, 1978, 271–314.

"The Trilateral Commission and Latin American Economic Development," in James F. Petras et al., *Class, State and Power in the Third World.* New Jersey: Allanheld Osmun, 1981, 84–95.

"The U.S.-Cuban Policy Debate," in Ronald Radosh, ed., *The New Cuba: Paradoxes and Potentials.* New York: William Morrow and Co., 1976, 177–189.

"White Paper on the White Paper," *The Nation*, March 28, 1981, 354, 367–372.

Petras, James F., and Thomas Cook. "Dependency and the Industrial Bourgeoisie: Attitudes of Argentine Executives Toward Foreign Economic Investment and U.S. Policy," in James F. Petras, ed., *Latin America: From Dependence to Revolution.* New York: John Wiley & Sons, 1973, 143–175.

Petras, James F., and Robert LaPorte, Jr. *Cultivating Revolution: The United States and Agrarian Reform in Latin America.* New York: Random House, 1971.

Petras, James F., and Morris H. Morley. "Economic Expansion, Political Crisis and U.S. Policy in Central America," in Marlene Dixon and Susanne Jonas, eds., *Revolution and Intervention in Central America.* San Francisco: Synthesis Publications, 1983, 189–218.

"The New Cold War: Reagan Policy Towards Europe and the Third World," *Studies in Political Economy* (Ottawa, Canada), No. 9, Fall 1982, 5–44.

"On The U.S. and the Overthrow of Allende," *Latin American Research Review*, Vol. XIII, No. 1, 1978, 205–221.

"The Rise and Fall of Regional Economic Nationalism in the Andean Countries 1969–1977," *Social and Economic Studies,* Vol. 27, No. 2, June 1978, 153–170.

"Supporting Repression: U.S. Policy and the Demise of Human Rights in El Salvador, 1979–1981," in Ralph Miliband and John Saville, eds., *The Socialist Register 1981.* London: The Merlin Press, 1981, 47–71.

The United States and Chile: Imperialism and the Overthrow of the Allende Government. New York: Monthly Review Press, 1975.

Petras, James F., Morris H. Morley, and Steven Smith. *The Nationalization of Venezuelan Oil.* New York: Praeger Publishers, 1977.

Petras, James F., and Robert Rhodes. "The Reconsolidation of U.S. Hegemony," *New Left Review,* No. 97, May–June 1976, 37–53.

Pfaltzgraff, Jr., Robert L. *Britain Faces Europe.* Philadelphia: University of Pennsylvania Press, 1969.

Phelps, Clyde W. *The Foreign Expansion of American Banks.* New York: The Ronald Press Co., 1927.

Phillips, David A. *The Night Watch.* New York: Atheneum Publishers, 1977.

Phillips, Mike. "Cuba's Shifting Image Lends a New Model to the Caribbean," *New Statesman,* August 18, 1978, 210–211.

Phillips, R. Hart. *Cuba: Island of Paradox.* New York: McDowell Obolensky, 1959.

The Cuban Dilemma. New York: Ivan Obolensky, 1962.

Pike, Frederick B. "Can We Slow Our Loss of Latin America," *Inter-American Economic Affairs,* Vol. XV, No. 1, Summer 1961, 3–30.

Plank, John, ed. *Cuba and the United States: Long Range Perspectives.* Washington, D.C.: The Brookings Institution, 1967.

Pollard, Sidney. *The Development of the British Economy 1914–1967.* London: Edward Arnold, 1969.

Pollitt, Brian H. "Employment Plans, Performance and Future Prospects in Cuba," in Richard Jolly et al., eds., *Third World Employment.* London: Penguin Books, 1973, 248–265.

Poulantzas, Nicos. *Political Power and Social Classes.* London: New Left Review Books, 1973.

Powers, Thomas. *The Man Who Kept the Secrets.* New York: Pocket Books, 1981.

Preston, Richard A. *Canada in World Affairs, Vol. XI, 1959–1961.* Toronto: Oxford University Press, 1965.

"Pricing the War of Aggression," *Central America Report,* Vol. XII, No. 47, December 6, 1985, 369–370.

"Property and Liberty: The Cuban Disaster Points Up Link Between Them," *Barrons,* July 11, 1960, 1.

Pyne, Peter. "The Politics of Instability in Ecuador: The Overthrow of the President, 1961," *Journal of Latin American Studies,* Vol. 7, No. 1, 1975, 109–133.

Rabe, Stephen G. "The Johnson (Eisenhower?) Doctrine for Latin America," *Diplomatic History*, Vol. 9, No. 1, Winter 1985, 95–100.

Radosh, Ronald. *American Labor and United States Foreign Policy*. New York: Random House, 1969.

"Schlesinger and Kennedy: Historian In The Service of Power," *The Nation*, August 6–13, 1977, 104–109.

Ray, Dennis M. "Corporations and American Foreign Relations," *The Annals*, Vol. 403, September 1972, 80–92.

Reford, Robert W. *Canada and Three Crises*. Ontario: The Canadian Institute of International Affairs, 1968.

Renwick, Robin. *Economic Sanctions*. Cambridge: Center for International Studies, Harvard University, 1981.

Report of the Commission on United States-Latin American Relations. *The Americas in a Changing World*. New York: Quadrangle/The New York Times Book Co., 1975.

Rigauz, Larry R., and Sol. Sinclair. "Canadian Agriculture and Common Market: Developments and Trends, 1960–1970," in Peter Stringelin, ed., *The European Community and the Outsiders*. Ontario: Longman Canada, 1973, 63–102.

Rippy, J. Fred, and Alfred Tischendorf. "The San Jose Conference of American Foreign Ministers," *Inter-American Economic Affairs*, Vol. XIV, No. 3, Winter 1960, 59–72.

Ritter, Archibald R. M. *The Economic Development of Revolutionary Cuba*. New York: Praeger Publishers, 1974.

"The Cuban Revolution: A New Orientation," *Current History*, Vol. 74, No. 434, February 1978, 53–56, 83–87.

Robinson, James A. *Congress and Foreign Policy-Making*. Homewood, Ill.: The Dorsey Press, 1962.

The Rockefeller Report on the Americas. Chicago: Quadrangle Books, 1969.

Rockman, Bert. "America's Departments of State: Irregular and Regular Syndromes of Policy Making," *American Political Science Review*, Vol. 75, No. 4, December 1981, 911–927.

Romauldi, Serafino. *Presidents and Peons*. New York: Funk & Wagnalls, 1967.

Roosevelt, Franklin D. *The Public Papers and Addresses of Franklin D. Roosevelt, Vol. 1: The Years of Crisis 1933*. New York: Random House, 1938.

Rosenau, James N. ed. *Linkage Politics: Essays on the Convergence of National and International System*. New York: Free Press, 1969.

Rosenbaum, H. Jon. "Brazil's Foreign Policy and Cuba," *Inter-American Economic Affairs*, Vol. XXIII, No. 3, Winter 1969, 25–45.

Rostow, W. W. *The Diffusion of Power*. New York: The Macmillan Co., 1972.

Rowthorn, Bob. "Imperialism in the Seventies – Unity or Rivalry?," *New Left Review*, No. 69, September–October 1971, 31–51.

Ruddle, Kenneth, and Philip Gillete, eds. *Latin American Political Statistics*. University of California at Los Angeles: Latin American Center, September 1972.

Salisbury, William T. "Spain and Europe: The Economic Realities," in William T. Salisbury and James D. Therberge, eds., *Spain in the 1970s: Economics, Social Structure, Foreign Policy*. New York: Praeger Publishers, 1976, 33–47.

Samuelson, Robert J. "U.S., Japan Find Old Relationships Have Unravelled," *National Journal*, Vol. XI, No. 26, June 30, 1979, 1068–1077.

Scheer, Robert, and Maurice Zeitlin. *Cuba: An American Tragedy*. London: Penguin Books, 1964.

Schlesinger, Jr., Arthur M. *A Thousand Days*. Boston: Houghton Mifflin Co., 1966.

Schlesinger, Stephen, and Stephen Kinzer. *Bitter Fruit*. New York: Doubleday, & Co., 1982.

Schoultz, Lars. "U.S. Economic Aid as an Instrument of Foreign Policy: The Cast of Human Rights in Latin America," in Jack L. Nelson and Vera M. Green, eds., *International Human Rights: Contemporary Issues*. New York: Human Rights Publishing Group, 1980, 317–342.

Human Rights and United States Policy Toward Latin America. Princeton: Princeton University Press, 1981.

Schreiber, Anna P. "Economic Coercion as an Instrument of Foreign Policy," *World Politics*, Vol. XXV, No. 3, April 1973, 387–413.

Seers, Dudley, et al. *Cuba: The Economic and Social Revolution*. Chapel Hill: University of North Carolina Press, 1964.

Selassie, Bereket Habte. *Conflict and Intervention in the Horn of Africa*. New York: Monthly Review Press, 1980.

"Senator John F. Kennedy on the Cuban Situation, Presidential Campaign of 1960," *Inter-American Economic Affairs*, Vol. XV, No. 3, Winter 1961, 79–85.

Serfaty, Simon. "Brzezinski: Play It Again Zbig," *Foreign Policy*, No. 32, Fall 1978, 3–21.

Shonfeld, Andrew, ed. *International Economic Relations of the Western World 1959–1971: Vol. 1, Politics and Trade*. London: Oxford University Press, 1976.

Skidmore, Thomas E. *Politics in Brazil 1930–1964*. London: Oxford University Press, 1967.

Slater, Jerome. *The OAS and United States Foreign Policy*. Columbus: Ohio State University Press, 1967.

Smith, Earl T. *The Fourth Floor*. New York: Random House, 1962.

Smith, Robert F. "Social Revolution in Latin America," *International Affairs*, Vol. 41, No. 4, October 1965, 637–649.

The United States and Cuba: Business and Diplomacy, 1917–1960. New Haven: College and University Press, 1960.

"The United States and Latin-American Revolution," *Journal of Inter-American Studies*, Vol. IV, No. 1, January 1962, 89–104.

What Happened in Cuba?: A Documentary History. New York: Twayne Publishers, 1963.

Smith, Wayne S. *The Closest of Enemies*. New York and London: W. W. Norton & Company, 1987.

"Dateline Havana: Myopic Diplomacy," *Foreign Policy*, No. 48, Fall 1982, 157–174.

Sorenson, Theodore C. *Kennedy*. New York: Harper & Row, 1965.

"Spain in World Trade," *Bank of London & South American Review*, Vol. 1, No. 5, May 1967, 243–251.

Spalding, Jr., Hobart A. *Organized Labor in Latin America: Historical Case Studies of Urban Workers in Dependent Societies*. New York: Torchbooks, 1977.

Stairs, Denis. "Confronting Uncle Sam: Cuba and Korea," in Stephen Clarkson, ed., *An Independent Foreign Policy for Canada?* Toronto: McClelland and Stewart, 1968, 57–68.

Stallings, Barbara. "Peru and the U.S. Banks: Privatization of Financial Relations," in Richard R. Fagen, ed., *Capitalism and the State in U.S.-Latin American Relations*. Stanford: Stanford University Press, 1979, 217–253.

Stanley, David T., Dean E., Mann, and Jameson W. Doig. *Men Who Govern: A Biographical Profile of Federal Political Executives*. Washington, D.C.: The Brookings Institution. 1967.

Stebbins, Richard P. *The United States in World Affairs, 1960*. New York: Harper & Brothers for the Council on Foreign Relations, 1962.

Steele, Jonathan. *Soviet Power: The Kremlin's Foreign Policy – Brezhnev to Chernenko*. New York: Simon and Schuster, 1984.

Stein, Jeffrey. "Fort Leslie J. McNair; Grad School for Juntas," *The Nation*, May 21, 1977, 621–624.

Stein, Siegfried. *The United States in International Banking*. New York: Columbia University Press, 1952.

Stockwell, John. *In Search of Enemies*. New York: W. W. Norton & Co., 1978.

Strange, Susan. "International Economics and International Relations: A Case of Mutual Neglect," *International Affairs*, Vol. XLVI, No. 2, April 1970, 304–315.

"IMF: Monetary Managers," in Robert W. Cox and Harold K. Jacobson, eds., *The Anatomy of Influence: Decision Making in International Organization*. New Haven: Yale University Press, 1977, 263–297.

Stroessinger, John G. *The United Nations and the Superpowers*. New York: Random House, 1965.

Szulc, Tad. *The Illusion of Peace: Foreign Policy in the Nixon Years*. New York: The Viking Press, 1978.

Tabor, Robert. *M-26, Biography of a Revolution.* New York: Lyle Stuart, 1961.

Tanzer, Michael. *The Political Economy of International Oil and the Underdeveloped Countries.* Boston: Beacon Press, 1969.

Thomas, Ann Van Wynen, and A. J. Thomas, Jr. *The Organization of American States.* Dallas: Southern Methodist University Press, 1963.

Thomas, Hugh. *Cuba or the Pursuit of Freedom.* London: Eyre & Spootis-woode, 1971.

Thompson, Charles A. "The Cuban Revolution: Fall of Machado," *Foreign Policy Reports,* Vol. X, No. 21, December 18, 1935, 250–260.

"The Cuban Revolution: Reform and Reaction," *Foreign Policy Reports,* Vol. XI, No. 22, Janaury 1, 1936, 262–276.

Trachtenberg, Marc. "The Influence of Nuclear Weapons in the Cuban Missile Crisis," *International Security,* Vol. 10, No. 1, Summer 1985, 137–163.

Trimberger, Ellen Kay. *Revolution From Above: Military Bureaucrats, and Development in Japan, Turkey, Egypt and Peru.* New Brunswick: Transaction Books, 1978.

Truman, Harry S. *Memoirs, Vol. One: Year of Decision.* New York: Doubleday & Co., 1955.

Turits, Richard. "Trade, Debt, and the Cuban Economy," *World Development,* Vol.15, No.1, January 1987, 163–180.

Tuthill, John W. "Operation Topsy," *Foreign Policy,* No. 8, Fall 1972, 62–85.

U.K. Department of Overseas Trade. *Economic Conditions in Cuba.* Report by His Majesty's Consul General, Havana, No. 518, April 1932. London: Her Majesty's Stationery Office, 1932.

U.K. House of Commons. *Parliamentary Debates* (Hansard). London: Her Majesty's Stationery Office, 1964.

United Nations. Economic Commission for Latin America. Department of Economic and Social Affairs. *Economic Survey of Latin America 1953.* New York, 1954.

Economic Commission for Latin America. Department of Economic and Social Affairs. *Economic Survey of Latin America 1954.* New York, 1955.

Economic Commission for Latin America. Department of Economic and Social Affairs. *Economic Survey of Latin America 1957.* New York, 1959.

Economic Commission for Latin America. Department of Economic and Social Affairs. *Economic Survey of Latin America 1963.* New York, 1965.

Economic Commission for Latin America. *Economic Survey of Latin America 1979.* Santiago, 1981.

Economic Commission for Latin America and the Caribbean. *Economic Survey of Latin America and the Caribbean 1983, Volume 1.* Santiago, 1985.

Security Council Official Records. Fifteenth Year, 1960.

"U.S. Hitmen: the Nicaraguan Contras," *Central America Bulletin,* Vol. IV, No. 1, November 1984, 11–12.

"U.S.-Nicaraguan Tension Grows as Congressional Deadline Nears," *Central America Bulletin,* Vol. IV, No. 2, December 1984, 5–6.

Valdés, Nelson P. "Revolutionary Solidarity in Angola," in Cole Blasier and Carmelo Mesa-Lago, eds., *Cuba in the World.* Pittsburgh: University of Pittsburgh Press, 1979, 87–117.

Vallier, Ivan. "Recent Theories of Development," in *Trends in Social Science Research in Latin American Studies.* Berkeley: Institute of International Studies, 1965, 7–29.

Van Alstyne, Richard W. *The Rising American Empire.* Chicago: Quadrangle Books, 1965.

Vance, Cyrus. *Hard Choices: Critical Years in America's Foreign Policy.* New York: Simon and Schuster, 1983.

Vandenbroucke, Lucien S. "Anatomy of a Failure: The Decision to Land at the Bay of Pigs," *Political Science Quarterly,* Vol. 99, No. 3, Fall 1984, 471–491.

"The 'Confessions' of Allen Dulles: New Evidence on the Bay of Pigs," *Diplomatic History,* Vol. 8, No. 4, Fall 1984, 365–375.

Vernon, Raymond. "The Multinationals: No Strings Attached," *Foreign Policy,* No. 33, Winter 1978–79, 121–134.

Sovereignty at Bay: The Multinational Spread of U.S. Enterprise. London: Pelican Books, 1973.

Storm over the Multinationals. Cambridge: Harvard University Press, 1977.

Von Laue, Theodore H. *Sergei Witte and the Industrialization of Russia.* New York: Columbia University Press, 1963.

Wagner, R. Harrison. *United States Policy Toward Latin America.* Stanford: Stanford University Press, 1970.

Walters, Robert. "Soviet Economic Aid to Cuba: 1959–1964," *International Affairs,* Vol. 42, No. 1, January 1966, 74–86.

Walton, Richard J. *Cold War and Counterrevolution: The Foreign Policy of John F. Kennedy.* Baltimore: Pelican Books, 1973.

"War Inhibits Progress in Education and Health," *Central American Report,* Vol. XII, No. 29, August 2, 1985, 228–230.

Waters, Cherri. *Destabilizing Angola: South Africa's War and U.S. Policy.* Washington, D.C.: Washington Office on Africa Educational Fund and the Center for International Policy, December 1986.

Weber, Max. *Economic and Society, Vol. 3.* New York: Bedminster Press, 1968.

Weintraub, Sidney, ed. *Economic Coercion and U.S. Foreign Policy.* Boulder: Westview Press, 1982.

Welch, Jr., Richard E. *Response to Revolution: The United States and the Cuban Revolution, 1959–1961.* Chapel Hill: University of North Carolina Press, 1985.

Whitehead, Laurence. *The United States and Bolivia: A Case of Neo-Colonialism.* London: Haslemere Group Publications, 1969.

Whitman, Marina Von Neumann. *Government Risk-Sharing in Foreign Investment.* Princeton: Princeton University Press, 1965.

Wilkie, James W. *The Bolivia Revolution and U.S. Aid Since 1952.* University of California at Los Angeles: Latin American Center, 1969.

ed. *Statistical Abstract of Latin America. Volume 17.* University of California at Los Angeles: Latin American Center Publications, 1976.

ed. *Statistical Abtract of Latin America: Volume 18.* University of California at Los Angeles: Latin American Center Publications, 1977.

ed. *Statistical Abstract of Latin America; Volume 21.* University of California at Los Angeles: Latin American Center Publications, 1981.

Wilkins, Mira. *The Emergence of Multinational Enterprises: American Business Abroad from the Colonial Era to 1914.* Cambridge: Harvard University Press, 1970.

The Maturing of Multinational Enterprise: American Business Abroad from 1914 to 1970. Cambridge: Harvard University Press, 1974.

Williams, William A. *The Roots of the Modern American Empire.* New York: Vintage Books, 1969.

The Tragedy of American Diplomacy. New York: Delta Books, 1972.

The United States, Cuba and Castro. New York: Monthly Review Press, 1962.

Wolfe, Alan. *The Limits of Legitimacy: Political Contradictions of Contemporary Capitalism.* New York: Free Press, 1977.

Wolpin, Miles D. *Cuban Foreign Policy and Chilean Politics.* Lexington: D. C. Heath & Co., 1972.

"External Political Socialization as a Source of Conservative Military Behavior in the Third World," in Kenneth Fidel, ed., *Militarism in Developing Countries.* New Brunswick: Transaction Books, 1975, 259–281.

Military Aid and Counterrevolution in the Third World. Lexington: D. C. Heath & Co., 1972.

Wood, Leonard. "The Military Government of Cuba," *The Annals,* March 1903, 153–182.

World Bank. Commodities and Export Projection Division, Economic Analysis and Projections Department, Development Policy Staff. *Borrowing in International Capital Markets: Foreign and International Bond Issues. Publicized Eurocurrency Credits.* Second Quarter, 1978. ED-181/782. September 1978.

Commodity Trade and Price Trends (1978 Edition). Report No. EC-166/78. August 1978.

"World Search for New Markets," *Latin American Regional Reports: Southern Cone* RS-86-06, August 7, 1986, p.7.

Wright, Alison. *The Spanish Economy 1959–1976.* New York: Holmes & Meier, 1977.

Wyden, Peter. *Bay of Pigs: The Untold Story.* New York: Simon and Schuster, 1979.

Zarembka, Paul. "Accumulation of Capital in the Periphery," in Paul Zarembka, ed., *Research in Political Economy, Volume 2, 1979.* Greenwich: Jai Press Inc., 1979, 99–140.

Zeitlin, Maurice. *Revolutionary Politics and the Cuban Working Class.* Princeton: Princeton University Press, 1967.

Zimbalist, Andrew. "Cuban Industrial Growth, 1965–84," *World Development*, Vol. 15, No. 1, January 1987, 83–93.

Periodicals

Business International (United States)

Business Latin America (United States)

Business Week (United States)

Deadline Data on World Affairs: Cuba, 1959–1969. Greenwich: McGraw-Hill, 1969.

Deadline Data on World Affairs: Inter-American Relations, 1959–1969. Greenwich: McGraw-Hill, 1969.

The Economist (United Kingdom)

Eastwest Markets (United States)

Facts on File (United States)

Foreign Commerce Weekly. Department of Commerce (United States)

Fortune (United States)

Hispanic American Report (United States)

Keesings Contemporary Archives (United States)

Latin America/Latin America Political Report/Latin America Weekly Report (United Kingdom)

Latin America Regional Reports: Andean Group, Brazil, Southern Cone, Caribbean (United Kingdom)

Latin America Commodities Report (United Kingdom)

Latin America Economic Report (United Kingdom)

News. Association of American Chambers of Commerce in Latin America (United States)

The Oil and Gas Journal (United States)

Quarterly Economic Review of Cuba. Economist Intelligence Unit (United Kingdom)

Report on Cuba. Government of Cuba (United States)

Survey of Current Business. Department of Commerce (United States)

U.S. Congressional Record-House of Representatives. Washington, D.C.

U.S. Congressional Record-Senate. Washington, D.C.

U.S. News & World Report (United States)

Newspapers

The Australian (Australia)

Christian Science Monitor (United States)

The Economic Times (Bombay, India)

Financial Times (United Kingdom)
The Guardian (United Kingdom)
The Guardian Weekly (United Kingdom)
Houston Post (United States)
The Japan Times (Tokyo, Japan)
Journal of Commerce (United States)
London Times (United Kingdom)
Los Angeles Times (United States)
Melbourne Age (Australia)
Miami Herald (United States)
New York Herald Tribune (Paris, France)
New York Times (United States)
Sydney Morning Herald (Australia)
Toronto Globe and Mail (Canada)
Washington Post (United States)
Wall Street Journal (United States)

Index